ROBERT ENGLER

The Politics
of Oil

A STUDY OF PRIVATE POWER
AND DEMOCRATIC DIRECTIONS

Phoenix Books

The University of Chicago Press

Library of Congress Catalog Card Number: 61–17192

THE UNIVERSITY OF CHICAGO PRESS, CHICAGO 60637

The University of Chicago Press, Ltd., London

To My Father

Preface

This book is a study of the nature of corporate power and its impact upon American political assumptions and institutions. The oil industry, which operates on the frontier of technological knowledge and economic and political organization, serves as the springboard for raising a series of questions about power, purpose, and responsibility in an industrial environment.

The original research was toward an analysis of the so-called "tidelands oil" controversy. I wanted to see what this headline issue could illustrate for students of American society. After considerable research and interviewing in Washington, I came to realize that the politics of offshore oil was a fragment of a much larger picture. The research that followed represented an attempt to obtain an overview of the political behavior of the petroleum industry and its impact upon political processes throughout the United States, as well as upon foreign policy and public opinion. The preparation of this book has given me an education about petroleum, politics, people, power, and even publishing.

The findings presented are based upon a careful examination of available documents and upon extensive travel and correspondence. Considerable time was spent in Washington, New York, North Dakota, Montana, Colorado, Oklahoma, Louisiana, Texas, and California. Many insights into the workings of the oil industry and its relation to the American political system were gained from several hundred interviews with oilmen, association officials, lobbyists, lawyers, newspaper and public relations men, government officials, members of the United States Congress and state legislatures, and citizens in the regions cited. No attempt is made here to thank these people individually by name. But I am grateful for their willingness to give so generously of their time and knowledge.

I wish to thank the William C. Whitney Foundation for grants that made possible the original travel throughout the United States and a stay in Washington. I also wish to thank the Shinner Foundation for grants during the summers of 1957 and 1958 that enabled me to complete the manuscript. And I am indebted to Helen Fuller, Benton J. Stong, and H. H. Wilson for encouragement at various stages of the research and writing. I am grateful to Richard Engler for his patience.

Portions of the materials in this book were adapted from a series of articles by the author that originally appeared in *The New Republic* magazine.

The manuscript was completed in April 1959. Certain developments and statistics since that date have been cited in the notes and occasionally in the text where they seemed pertinent to a particular theme under consideration.

Contents

1

Introduction

This is a study of the relation of power and responsibility. The illustration throughout is the private government that controls most of the petroleum resources of the world and the impact of this control upon American political life. The more impelling issue, however, is the drift and distortion of democratic society in an industrial environment.

Every human setting has a system of controls. These controls are designed to channel and uphold the particular social order to which the people and their leaders presumably are committed. These controls express attitudes and aspirations that over time have permeated the going institutions of the society. The controls are implemented by such power factors as habit, organization, status, material reward, persuasion, coercion, and formal law. Although power is frequently categorized as a corrupting and restricting force, it is inherently neither good nor bad. Power is a resource necessary for ordered action.[1] It is used to make and enforce decisions and to define behavior. As a component of every society, power can be found at all levels of organization, from the family to international relations. The controls may be employed by different groups competing to establish their particular versions of order. Or the controls may provide a relatively harmonious order. As the pattern of living becomes interdependent and complex, there is a greater need for order, and hence for the use of power. In any advanced technological setting, the hierarchy and the resulting discipline inherent in the controls over the intricate machine process inevitably spill over to embrace widening areas of life. To understand the main bent of the society, one must ask where power resides, where there are inequalities in and conflicts over power,

1

for what ends power is employed, and with what consequences.
Oil provides a unique springboard for analyzing the American
society and the problems of power that it poses. In 1959 the industry
celebrated the hundredth anniversary of "Colonel" Drake's pioneer
well at Oil Creek, Pennsylvania. Its technological and economic
achievements in transforming the American and world scene during
that span have been impressive. Petroleum has passed coal as the
most important energy resource for the United States. It supplies 45
per cent of the nation's fuel energy requirements. The closely allied
natural gas industry provides another 25 per cent.

This emergence of oil reflects the expansion of the needs, standards,
and talents of a society that has successively used crude oil as a quack
medicinal cure-all, lubricant, lighting source, fuel energy resource,
and base for a vast chemical industry. It tells the evolution of America
from farm wagon to combustion engine to synthetic fiber to jet
propulsion. It marks the transition from a simple rural society paced
by the speed and inclination of man and nature to an industrial complex where the conquests of time and space have created a dynamic
of their own, but whose institutional patterns are governed by a small
number of essentially anonymous men of power.

On a time-power scale of history, oil's reign as a basic energy could
be relatively short. Reserves are not limitless, and oil comes into its
own just prior to the dawn of the atomic age. It is but a moment in
history from 1912, when First Lord of the Admiralty Winston
Churchill was pleading for the "formidable decision" to convert the
entire British fleet from coal to oil, to 1957 when the First Lord of
the Admiralty announced the scrapping of battleships and reliance
upon the deterrent power of such nuclear weapons as guided missiles
and carrier-based atomic bombers. A similar time span may be noted
in the United States, from the setting aside of naval petroleum reserves prior to World War I to the Secretary of the Navy's statement
in 1956 that nuclear power was now conventional for all new sub-
marines and would soon be for cruisers and carriers. Less publicized
but more important has been the planning and opening of nuclear-
powered electrical generating stations in England. This does not mean
the end of oil. Released from these less efficient and less profitable
uses of crude, its value as a motor fuel, heating source, and lubricant
remains fundamental. To this must be added all the petroleum-based

industries developing in this new scientific-industrial age. Individuals, corporations, and nations search the world for new oil reserves. When these are found, they drill deeply into the earth to stake out their private claims upon energy stored up over millions of years. They are prepared to compete, fight, and, at least in the case of corporations, coalesce for this black gold. When Egypt nationalized the Suez Canal in 1956 and threatened the oil supply line of Western Europe, capitals from Moscow and Cairo to London and Washington were involved. "This is a matter of life and death," Prime Minister Anthony Eden reported to the British Parliament, giving solemn warning of the armed expedition soon to follow.

Internally, the history of oil mirrors the evolution of American capitalism from the shoestring competition of the pioneer Pennsylvania producers to the world-wide operations of the modern Jersey Standard empire, from the raw violence among early teamsters hauling wooden barrels to the electronic quiet of an automated pumping station along a steel pipeline, from the primitive stills of the first refiners to the magnificent and almost frightening spectacle of man-made fire and light in a Baton Rouge refinery at night. The free-wheeling wildcatters still survive. Their restless search for new oil and their willingness to take chances help to maintain a romantic image of rough-and-ready individualism. The wildcatters operate within the same industry as the specialized organization men who meet regularly with their committees in New York and London to direct billion-dollar enterprises and to discuss relations with nations. Oil continues in its growth as one of the gigantic industries of the country. Its effective functioning in what has become—at least for the indefinite future—a permanent war economy is a vital element of national security. In the United States this entire galaxy derives its origins from the individual right of private ownership of the oil that lies beneath the earth's surface. Upon this ethic is built one of the most complex collective systems known to modern man.

A cluster of integrated corporations controls this basic resource. They operate as political institutions, and together they take on the full nature of a government. This private government of oil moves to bring more and more of the total industrial process, from the drilling of wells to brand choices by consumers, into the realm of the predictable. At the same time it reaches beyond its economic activities to create and control a political and a social climate that will accept and encourage this economically oriented collectivization. The global interests and jurisdictions of these corporations, in turn, are part of a system of arrangements and understandings that may be called the first world government.

The men of oil have perceptive insights into the involved nature and future of an industrial social order. They operate on a frontier of scientific and technological knowledge and economic organization. Oil refineries are run by automation. Laboratories conduct nuclear and chemical research. These are backed by financial resources greater than those now available to most American states and many nations. The character of oil requires full economic coordination and planning. This need places the industry on an even more controversial frontier of political organization. Oil leaders deal with the old and the new, with small businessmen and with international cartels, with current needs and with those projected for fifty years hence. Their interests led them to follow resources and technology across property, state, and national boundaries, to negotiate with Texas politicians, Arabian sheiks, and United Nations delegates. The oil corporations participate on a level of international diplomacy charateristic of a functional world government. They do all this with a relative ease that smaller businesses and liberal democratic states have found difficult to grasp or match.

These are substantial attainments, and the economic benefits from oil have been widely spread. The private government of oil, and the new economy that it symbolizes, must also be evaluated in terms of social cost and the general impact upon the life style of the American democracy. These considerations provide the framework for this study.

The ideal of liberal democracy assumed the broadest diffusion of social power among a people confident about themselves and their destiny. At the core of this ideal was an insistence upon the worth and creative potential of the individual. It credited man with a capacity for reasoning and self-discipline. With these qualities and with access to knowledge, he could make the significant choices shaping his own future.

This view accepted change as natural and progress as inevitable. A creed of equality, with opportunity for all who would work hard, shaped the economy. Producers and consumers functioned freely in the unceasing quest for profits and goods. The motivation was self-interest. But the community was always the gainer, for the checks and balances of the market place ensured against any concentrations of economic power that could threaten the public good.

Dovetailing with these economic tenets was a political system that assumed coercion emanated primarily from the machinery of the state. Political power was to reside in the will of the people. The decision-making centers affecting private lives and public policies were to be visible and accountable to the citizenry. To preclude arbitrary or capricious rule by any class or the masses, political power was to be exercised with caution and through diffused institutions. Government was to exist for men rather than men for government.

Bountiful and unclaimed natural resources sustained this optimism. Harnessing the power of nature has made possible the development and control of tools for carving an industrial civilization out of a frontier wilderness in a remarkably short order. With 6 per cent of the world's population, the United States produces about 40 per cent of the world's industrial goods and consumes about as much.[2]

This American experience has had a profoundly revolutionary impact everywhere. The cumulative ability to understand and come to terms with nature and to extend man's mastery of things—his science and technology—has shown that hunger, disease, floods, isolation, ignorance, and the political and social institutions based upon such conditions of scarcity and disaster are not inevitable. To most of the people of the world it has become irrevocably clear that they are not getting all the goods, services, and rights they might possess. They perceive a sizable gap between a society of scarcity and of abundance, between what is and what might be. For underindustrialized regions to close this gap, cheap and plentiful high production energy is necessary. The underdeveloped countries of Asia, where nearly one-half the people of the world live, consume energy from coal, petroleum, and water power "at a rate equivalent to burning slightly over one hundred pounds of coal per person per year. This is about the amount consumed in the United States per person in two days."[3]

Shifts in energy sources and techniques—from hand and animal power to water power, from coal to oil, from oil to atomic energy, for example—prepare the groundwork for transformations in political power relationships among men, nations, and cultures. Once the futility and immorality of poverty and drudgery are demonstrated, an almost inevitable process is set in motion. This process undermines any social order based on the standard that a few shall be fat and the many lean, a few educated and the many illiterate, a few politically privileged and the many subservient. Alexis de Tocqueville's century-old prophecy that equality, fostered by all man's inventions and exercises of intellect, is the coming condition of mankind takes on renewed meaning in the light of the world-wide revolutions against feudalism, colonialism, racialism, and want.

These technological achievements also put in new perspective the problem of man's control over his fellow men and their institutions. Increased mastery over things—automobiles, hybrid corn, machine guns, dams, television, cotton pickers—carries the potential of increased control by the few over the many. Vast rational organizations—the nation-state, the military, the corporation, the labor union, the press, the university, the church—emerge. Businesses develop integrated systems, labor unions merge, and representatives of street gangs in a great city meet to work out a *modus vivendi* that will respect territorial sovereignty and eliminate rumbles. There is a polarization of power among nations.

Beyond any conscious design or planning, the machine culture forces a general systemization in wide areas of behavior. Work becomes specialized. Individuals become increasingly dependent. Coordination and control become imperative. Farming evolves into agribusiness. Labor is built into the industrial system. The distinctions between war and peace policies, military and civil considerations, blur. New social rhythms are born, and new demands of loyalty follow. "Technology," Adlai Stevenson succinctly suggested, "while adding daily to our physical ease, throws daily another loop of fine wire around our souls." [4] The new equality and the new inequality are inherent in the social revolutions taking place in feudal Asia, colonial Africa, and industrialized Russia and the United States.

The United States has become a mass society. The classic capitalist model has been replaced by an economy of giant corporations, administered prices, corporate farms, marginal small businessmen and farmers, unorganized white collar employees, and unionized yet vulnerable industrial workers. In this setting the state has been asked to assume positive responsibility for popular welfare and security. These demands accelerate the concentration of governmental power and the development of public bureaucracies. All groups seeking to achieve their public and private ends—those who want particular courses of action as well as those who resist the expansion of government into areas of private prerogative—look to the political arena. For politics is the struggle for control over the direction the society may take and over the uses of governmental apparatus. Democratic politics has promised a peaceful method for handling such conflicts and the resulting social changes. It offers legally defined, visible, and accessible channels such as public debate and voting. The choices ultimately arrived at—whether involving changes of leaders, policies, or processes—are to represent the broadest possible base of consent among the diverse citizenry.

A façade of national prosperity, the harmony of anti-communism, and the continued rituals of practical politics mask the corrosion of the democratic spirit. There are sobering inequalities in the capacities of citizens to function independently and creatively in their political and economic pursuits. Concentrated economic power over resources is being forged into political power over men and the social environment. The nature of the impersonal goliaths makes it difficult to delineate this transformation. In earlier periods of American history, men debated openly about the relation of economic and political power. They made villains of the individual giants such as Rockefeller and Carnegie, and thundered against "Wall Street" as the source of the destruction of the individual entrepreneur and the corruption of legislative halls. Formidable perimeters of defense manned by public relations specialists, lawyers, lobbyists, and vice presidents now keep corporate activities well insulated from the not too interested public. The spotlight is carefully placed on technological advances and corporate benevolence.

The scientists imply that "anything is possible" and that the first order of business is for the nation to decide in which directions it wishes to employ its collective intelligence and resources. Nevertheless, there is overwhelming evidence that the individual citizen is no longer sure either of his purpose or of his power. If there are less overt assaults upon political liberty and discussion than was true in

McCarthy's period, there is also less inclination to use these democratic tools. At a time when problems ranging from economic growth to the survival of mankind require public resolution, only surface portions of the policy struggles take place within formal political channels. Parties, the vehicles for popular participation and majority control of the government, serve less and less to focus attention upon such critical issues as economic power, foreign policy, militarism, and total destruction.

Meanwhile, the citizen appears to have lost both his sense of privacy and his identity with the community. Absorption in the acquisition of goods is made the highest national end. This pursuit is tempered by the distractions of the mass media with their accent on trivia and personalities. The public behaves as if it is unable to sustain interest in the great issues and as if it is devoid of the tools and the will required for democratic citizenship and survival. In this vacuum the modern corporation moves with purpose and plan.

The discovery of oil in North Dakota is the starting point for this study. The author wanted to see what happened to the values and institutions of a rural region when the two worlds met. The events in North Dakota offer in microcosm a portrait of the impact of oil upon the American society. Succeeding chapters explain the economics of the industry and the character of the modern oil corporation. The planning and the functioning of the industry as a private world government are traced. The study then moves to the central area of concern—how the economic power of oil becomes political and social power. There is an analysis of the range of uses of public government for the private objectives of the industry. The consequences of the strategy and tactics of oil for the American political system, foreign policy, and public opinion are explored.

The book is not intended to be a definitive study of the industry or a chronicle of the struggles over oil among the great nations. The recurring focus is upon the relationship of the new industrial system, as illustrated by oil, and the American political system. Many contemporary scholars are optimistic as to the capacity of the two systems to accommodate each other. There is less willingness to explore the terms of this accommodation. The illustration of oil suggests where effective power now lies in this relationship.

There is no claim that the industry performs as it did in 1900.

Then Standard Oil symbolized the ruthlessness inherent in corporate development. Contemporary oilmen may be more decent and enlightened than their primitive predecessors. The blunt aggressiveness identified with the pioneers in oil has been tempered by the organization of the modern corporation and the security oilmen possess from having "arrived." Contemporary capitalism is not the capitalism that existed prior to 1933. Public expectations change, corporations learn, and institutions evolve.

Nevertheless, an official history reminds us, after seven hundred pages heralding the company's evolution as a responsible institution, that "the main purpose of Standard of Indiana, or of any business, large or small, is to make money for its investors." [5] There is broadening awareness of contributions to social and economic progress, a Jersey Standard publication adds, but "it is still business, and not philanthropy, which takes oilmen abroad." [6] Oilmen are committed to profits, production, technical competence, corporate growth, personal advancement and recognition, power over men and resources, and loyalty to their organizations. None of these motivations is necessarily evil. Added together, they are not adequate for safeguarding the values of a democratic community.

The documentation that follows shows how the petroleum industry has harnessed public law, governmental machinery, and opinion to ends that directly challenge public rule. In the name of prosperity and technology, the industry has been able to destroy competition and limit abundance. In the name of national interest it has received privileges beyond those accorded to other industries. In the name of national security, oil has influenced and profited from a foreign policy that has supported the chauvinism of a few rather than generosity to the aspirations of the many in underdeveloped areas. In the name of private enterprise, it has contributed to the attenuation of vital portions of democratic life, from education to civic morality. In the name of the right of representation, it has so entrenched itself within the political processes that it becomes impossible to distinguish public from private actions. In the name of freedom, the oil industry has received substantial immunity from public accountability.

This study assumes that it is not power that modern democracy needs to fear, but rather its irresponsible use. It is not public action that necessarily threatens private initiative. It is rather the vacuums of public direction and individual commitment that invite personal helplessness, public anarchy, and private rule. It is not the absence of controls that offers genuine freedom. Freedom results rather from men's capacity to control their environment wisely and to expand the range of meaningful individual choice.

2

A Portrait in Oil

It will be exciting to be in the oil business in North Dakota where such divergent philosophies as the state and the industry have are bound to clash. The oil will finally prevail. There is nothing so soothing of passion as monthly production of royalty checks.

> —A message from Oklahoma welcoming North Dakota into the oil producing fraternity. Williston (N.D.) *Daily Herald*, April 13, 1951

It was a few days before the people of North Dakota awoke to the potentialities of the successful oil strike of April 4, 1951, on Clarence Iverson's fifteen-hundred-acre farm near Tioga in the state's portion of the Williston Basin. They had been excited and then disillusioned before.

The possibility of oil was an old story for North Dakota. Geologists had often noted that the historic geological development of the 120,000-square-mile Williston Basin, which includes portions of Canada, Montana, and South Dakota as well as western North Dakota, appeared favorable for oil. Sporadic drilling efforts had taken place ever since the turn of the century, always resulting in dry holes. In the twenties there had been several periods of claimed discoveries followed by oil hysteria. Perhaps the most dramatic of these centered around the activities of Arthur C. Townley, the founder of the Nonpartisan League, who had promoted exploration on the basis of doodlebug judgment and his own personality. "Loan me your money —but kiss it goodbye," he said, making no guarantee that oil would

11

be found. The speculator in the farmer was stronger than the skeptic, and Townley raised sizable sums.

Oilmen in Texas, Oklahoma, and elsewhere were also interested in what might be under the rolling plains. In 1938, for example, the Standard Oil Company of California drilled better than ten thousand feet into the ground not far from the site of a well abandoned in 1926 and only a few miles south of the present Beaver Lodge oil field. Some men persisted. A. M. Fruh, oil broker, independent producer, formerly a farmer and a banker and a founder of the Nonpartisan League, stuck with the vision of oil for more than twenty-five years. Much of the leasing for the Amerada Petroleum Corporation, the first and leading producer in the region, was done by Fruh and a former partner. But in 1949 a local newspaper story on the high pitch of current oil hunt fervor could conclude, "Right now the best place to get oil in this state is at a gas station."

As the pictures of Clarence Iverson Number 1 and the predictions about Williston's future spread, and the hundreds of brokers, landmen, geologists, and other oil representatives crowded the hotels and the strange license plates of Oklahoma and Texas became commonplace, black gold fever rose. "Something new has been added to a great farm state—OIL. This sample of crude direct from North Dakota's famed Williston Basin" proclaimed the label on the miniature bottles distributed by the North Dakota County Agents Association.

This was hard country, requiring a frontier toughness for survival. It was still relatively new, and pioneering days were within memory. North Dakota was not the place you generally remained in, if your quest was a fast dollar or soft living. The long winters and the constant buffeting from floods, drought, wind, dust, insects, and rust gave the tenacious Scandinavian and Russian-German farmers the right and the occasion to dream.

This was a good deal. Who could lose? An industrial society wanted oil, and the farmer sitting on top of it didn't have to do anything more than sign his name to try for the jackpot. The eagerness was not confined to the unsophisticated farmer. A frantic land play involving virtually every major company began. "When I ran across a lease held by a man in Florida, I wouldn't hesitate to charter a plane and send a man down to see him," said a Shell official. Soon nearly 70 per cent of the state's land area was under lease. Even if oil was never discovered on his land, or even if no drilling ever took place, the farmer was ahead. Interference with his farming operation was slight, and his land values were inflated. The lease money, in some areas a dollar an acre per year, and much higher with bonuses where the possibilities were better, could pay his taxes, seed bill, and other expenses.

There was some grumbling. In the days before the discovery Southern carpetbaggers rounded up leases for ten cents an acre, and those farmers who dealt with them later felt cheated. These leases subsequently ended up in the hands of the big oil companies who repurchased at a higher price from brokers with whom they had unpublicized working relationships. The resentment, however, was generally directed toward the brokers. An Amerada representative who took a 10 per cent kickback from people contracting services with his company aroused anger and was transferred after many complaints. "The arrogance of those guys burns me," a truck driver blurted out as he watched a trailer unloading new cars for the local Ford agency. Each car bore a sticker telling the world it had been "Built in Texas by Texans." The damage to roads by the heavy equipment of the oil contractors was another sore spot. (Farm equipment is notoriously harsh on the lives of roads, but farmers assume that is what they pay taxes for. The Williams County budget for highways and bridges was $290,000 in 1950 and $478,000 in 1952, "practically the entire increase being because of our new industry.") Frustrated drivers of cars piled up on the highways behind the heavy oil trucks did not always take comfort from signs placed on the rear of the tank trucks of one large fleet which did much of its hauling for Standard Oil of Indiana: "This Truck Pays $3,246.25 Yearly in Road Taxes."

Crowding of hotel and restaurant facilities was another irritant at first. Law enforcement and school facility needs increased. Perhaps more serious was the resentment of fixed-income people in the state over the jumping of rents, which they attributed to the generous expense accounts of transient oil employees rather than to Korea and the general inflationary trend. Retired railroad employees in Mandan seemed particularly upset on this score. Employers bemoaned the rise in starting wages of secretaries, waitresses, and laborers. Some merchants were irritated by the demands upon them made by the new types of middle-class customers, and privately fears were voiced as to what would happen to their quiet domination of the small towns. But the bankers, publishers, and other merchants were eager to identify themselves with progress and industrial growth. Here was a new source of wealth to provide the badly needed balance for rural North Dakota. And the new or improved bank buildings in places like Minot and Williston became visible monuments to the tangible side of their pleasure, as did the increased bank deposits. For example, deposits of the American State Bank in Williston rose from about $7.3 million in June 1951 to $12.2 million in December 1953.

Many physical changes became apparent. In the Northwest the bulky elevators set against the horizon, symbols of the rural grain economy, now had as rivals in their domination of the landscape slender oil derricks representing an industrial society's thirst for energy. Strings of tar-black tank cars moved slowly along the railroad tracks or waited at the sidings, joining the familiar grain cars in bearing raw materials out of the state. Drilling equipment, warehouses, and farm-implement depots stood side by side along the highways, and oil trucks mingled with cattle trucks in the traffic. One could find an oil crew skidding a rig across a field to a new location, where before one would have seen only the harvester crew following the crops with their machinery.

The townspeople still talk of oil—and it seems that everyone does —but not with the exaggerated tension of 1951. North Dakota has remained primarily an agricultural state. Wheat is its major crop, supplemented by barley, oats, rye, flax, and livestock. Its industries are minor and, like the bulk of the services and trade, generally related to farm products and needs. Concern over wheat rust, rainfall, and acreage allotments is far more immediate than over oil pools, well spacing, and prorationing, although the state's newspapers increasingly feature the latter as one travels west. When the Williston merchant remarks that money seems tighter, he has in mind his farmer customers, not oilmen.

There has been some sobering about oil prospects since 1951. "This won't be another boom and bust," people explain with mixed feelings. Not everyone involved with oil expects to get rich. The hazards of drilling are recognized, as is the nature of the marketing and transport difficulties. North Dakota has a population of about 640,000, which is an insufficient market for absorbing all the crude the area might produce. The oil fields are a good distance from any concentrated population centers, and the high cost of truck or rail shipment seriously lowers the price of crude at the well. (The first few years producers were getting $2.00 a barrel instead of the anticipated $2.65 or $2.90.) Pipelines make poor wildcatters, as one oilman put it, and they require sufficient production and reserves to warrant their construction. The Williston area is viewed by oil leaders as being bottled in, Canada having its own crude, Wyoming being a crude export state, and the East and West coasts having their own traditional and adequate sources. North Dakotans suspect that the major oil companies' prime interest may not be getting out the oil but rather adding to their proved reserves. Such reserves are like money in the bank to an industry that is rarely eager to produce all it can if the consequences might be the disturbances of their tight and privately governed price structure and marketing patterns.

The oil companies themselves have tried to tone down expectations to which they earlier contributed so heavily. "We have nothing to sell and we want to dampen these dreams of fortunes," explained the representative of the North Dakota Oil and Gas Association. "There will have to be considerably more evidence . . . before you and I can sit back and rest assured that North Dakota is really an oil state," a major oil-company official testified.

But if oil has not been produced freely, exploration and development continue. By the end of 1957 North Dakota had 938 wells, and that year produced nearly 14 million barrels of crude, worth $43 million. Insignificant in comparison to the national total—the state's entire 1957 output was less than two days' total for the United States —to North Dakota this enterprise has meant jobs for several thousand workers, some help for an annual per capita income considerably below the national average, and several hundred thousand dollars of increased tax revenues.

And the promise has remained. In 1955 Shell Oil Company had more than 6 million acres under lease in the Basin. Stanolind (Indiana Standard) had 4½ million acres. The Northern Pacific Railway (thanks to a fantastic land grant from the federal government in 1864), Hunt, Texas, Amerada, Union, Standard (New Jersey), Phillips, Atlantic, and Socony all had substantial holdings. At least $500 million has been invested in the region thus far. Long rated a blue-chip investment and since 1951 the major producer in North Dakota, Amerada continues to be listed on Wall Street as among the leading stock investments. A small company in oil-industry dimensions, it is the biggest nonintegrated producer in the nation.

To the genuine independent wildcatter North Dakota was just another place where oil might be struck. But the bigger outfits such as Indiana Standard were concerned that the people might create special problems. After all, North Dakota had a radical agrarian tradition. There was still a Nonpartisan League organization until 1956 when it joined forces with the Democrats. Even if the philosophy was tired or dead, the state grain elevator, flour mill, and bank remained as reminders of the political prairie fires of an earlier period. When Townley was its guiding spirit he had led farmers into the movement and into control of the state, reputedly using such class appeals as, "If you put a lawyer, a banker, and an industrialist in a barrel and roll it down hill, there'll always be a son of a bitch on top."

Dependent upon outside markets for selling their raw materials and for buying their finished goods, North Dakotans bore the deep resentment of their colonial status. They had been taken by the grain trade in Minneapolis and St. Paul as well as by the railroad barons from La Salle and Wall streets. Their extensive cooperative groups and the powerful Farmers Union all encouraged them in this hostility to outside corporate interest. "We have a big job to do," said one public relations man from a major company. "They even have a progressive income tax here, and that's socialistic. But a small minority of the people are okay."

A careful state-wide propaganda program was developed. Panels of oil speakers, planned in New York by the Oil Information Committee of the American Petroleum Institute—the public relations arm of the industry's major trade organization—visited the schools and colleges under the sponsorship of the Greater North Dakota Association and the Junior Chamber of Commerce to answer questions about oil. Pattern speeches and news releases for use throughout the state were prepared in New York by the OIC, with blank spaces where the local speaker or publicist could insert the appropriate grass-roots references. A superior film based on Clarence Iverson

Number 1 was produced on location and shown widely in order to reassure the people as to the intent and behavior of the newcomers. Some county agents helped organize film sessions. All members of the legislature were put on the API's mailing list. Advertisements were placed heralding that "North Dakota Profits from the Oil Industry" and "As Oil Profits So Does North Dakota."

The companies selected their best men for this region. Landmen were instructed as to the importance of kid-glove handling of farmers. Lawyers were cultivated throughout the state by the spreading of legal business. And of course the very presence of oil generated tremendous litigation and the expectation of more. The clergy were consulted on key problems of community relations. Great solicitude was shown for the press, and the young men assigned the title of oil editor were dined and flown around by helpful oil representatives. It became difficult for the hired scribe to be unaware of the social and business relationship developing between his editors, publishers, radio station owners, and the new oilmen. Press coverage of oil tended to consist of handouts and statistical data or, where there were hearings, factual reporting with a minimum of critical interpretation as to the broader implications for the state.

Amerada, which prided itself on not having a public relations program, was most assiduous in reaching the grass roots, especially after its defeat in an important hearing on well spacing in 1952 where it had relied on a technical presentation of its case. Its top people kept in closest contact with public officials, newsmen, and others, as did the representatives of companies such as Hunt which also disclaimed any formal public relations operations. When a Standard (Indiana) subsidiary constructed a pipeline, it was careful to explain to the community what it was doing and how farm property would be respected. Thousands of copies of a well written pamphlet, *Underand Oilway*, were distributed to schools, clubs, and citizens. The preface, called "That Rain Feeling," read:

> You know how you feel when the skies open up and let a couple of inches of good rain come pattering down. It makes you feel good inside— secure, and happy in the knowledge that the rain means the promise of good things to come. That is how you people in North Dakota have made us feel—welcome as rain. We like your warm friendliness and willingness to cooperate, and are happy to be a part of North Dakota.

When Standard felt production warranted a refinery, its top field public relations man spent a number of months studying the projected site above Mandan on the west bank of the Missouri in an attempt to predict the community problems that might arise. The company soon experienced the vagaries of Northwest rainfall. A fence had been put around the area, a normal precaution for refineries because of the dangers of heat, electric shock, and machinery to cattle, kids, and the curious. Immediately the farmers and townspeople reacted. Why the fence? What are they up to? It took special efforts, including public tours, to quiet the suspicions.

Standard, one of the largest oil companies in America, was the industry leader in this region. It sought the development of a public attitude that would regard its plants as local institutions rather than as branches of a far-flung corporate empire. Executive employees were encouraged to participate in worth-while community activities and in booster, service, and business clubs as well as in church affairs. Joining in cake sales, bazaars, and Christmas festivals by oil wives was looked upon with great favor. In addition to the general good will it promoted, one executive explained, "There is often a chance to talk about the company or oil—and something is bound to rub off."

Asked if such approaches were very successful with stubborn and sometimes suspicious North Dakota farmers, another official admitted they were still difficult at times. But, he added, his company had learned throughout the Northwest that it is more rewarding to pitch its energies and money into farm youth groups such as the 4-H clubs and Future Farmers. These kids could clearly be seen as more conservative and more sympathetic to business than their parents or their city counterparts, he continued. In all its employee literature, the company emphasized the importance of these groups and of Junior Achievement clubs. It also had regular current affairs films for schools and has contributed heavily for scholarships in liberal arts colleges throughout the Midwest. A vice president gave high school commencement addresses throughout the state.

In 1952 Amerada took the lead in creating a state-wide producers' association among the oil companies, brokers, and bankers. There had been resistance to joining either the Rocky Mountain or the Mid-Continent Oil and Gas Association, the two big regional groups, for common public relations and lobbying efforts. As one Amerada executive explained, "North Dakota has peculiar local problems, and it was considered better not to have any outside organization to arouse the suspicion of the citizenry." A member of the law firm representing most of the larger oil companies, the Great Northern Railway, the Montana Dakota Utilities Company, and the U.S. Smelting, Refining and Mining Company was temporary chairman and then became counsel. Another partner was the registered lobbyist for the North Dakota Petroleum Industries Committee, the local lobbying arm of the American Petroleum Institute. The officers of the new North Dakota Oil and Gas Association generally held interlocking positions with the larger national industry associations. On a less formal basis, the white collar oilmen established Petroleum Clubs where they met regularly for lunch and also became better acquainted with other professionals and businessmen. Their wives organized the familiar Petroleum Wives' Clubs, and news of their social and charitable work appears with growing frequency on local society pages.

All this effort was not just to win a popularity contest. Oil had a tremendous long-run investment to protect. Fearing a critical public attitude and a hostile legislature, the industry worked unceasingly for friendly legislation and sympathetic administration. Oil people recognize that wherever they go they make inviting targets for states hard pressed for new revenue sources.

They did not have long to wait in North Dakota. A legislative research subcommittee appointed to explore oil policy came up with a proposal for a gross production tax of 4¼ per cent as part of a package of recommendations. The legislature received only a summary report of the detailed analysis, the explanation being that the predominantly farmer membership could not understand or would not take the time to dig deeper.

The level of the tax precipitated an angry political battle in the state. Some felt that the tax should be much higher, with proposals ranging up to 12 per cent. More admitted uncertainty as to how one determines the ability of a corporation to pay, especially during a developmental period when the industry was pouring into the state much more than it was pumping out. Still others prophesied that if the oil companies felt threatened by taxation they would move elsewhere, especially since it was assumed they were more interested in accumulating reserves than in production. "We want industrial development . . . now," said one witness, reminding the House Finance and Taxation Committee how the state had aided the railroads in an earlier period. "But we need the people and capital and know-how for that development. . . . I think our bark is worse than our bite. . . . But we have a reputation for discouraging business."

Governor C. Norman Brunsdale, who admitted to having oil investments—"not in North Dakota . . . in Texas," he quickly explained—felt that such taxes were "punitive" and "discriminatory." The industry itself had voiced some objection to the concept but then proposed 2 to 3 per cent as the maximum. While declaring that the committee's 4¼ per cent compromise proposal was higher than they would like, a number of oilmen more privately indicated it was within reason. Some close observers believed they would have accepted 5 per cent as readily.

At every Chamber of Commerce meeting, Rotary luncheon, and public gathering the familiar theme was reiterated. "Oil will pay taxes, oil wants to pay taxes, it wants to pay its fair share but it doesn't want to be singled out and so overburdened it can't invest. It is up to you folks whether oil remains." Robert E. Wilson, chairman of the board of Indiana Standard, in an oil-day celebration speech preceded by a free barbecue paid for by his company, and with attacks on government handouts and public bureaucracy as harmful to the fiber of the nation, warned that "North Dakota must compete with other states for the oil industry's dollars. Today there is no shortage of good hunting grounds for oil." (In his 1953 stockholders' message he reported "crude oil is becoming harder to find.") Vice president C. E. Boone of Amerada repeatedly cautioned the people and their legislature to consider very carefully before they "take any action that would jeopardize what may be the promise for a very glorious future for the state of North Dakota. . . . Your problem is to provide the climate where the profit on that [investment] dollar will be equal to what other states offer." Meanwhile, Amerada built a new brick office building heavily reinforced with steel and so designed that it could be expanded to several times its present height. Across the border in Montana the oil companies hinted and threatened they would shift their operations to North Dakota.

Ultimately, the 4¼ per cent tax was adopted. It had the solid support of the Republican Organizing Committee (ROC), the very conservative faction within the Republican party whose greatest strength rested in the more prosperous Red River Valley section in the east. Oil pressures and temptations combined to swing along enough western legislators. Normally the backbone of the Nonpartisan League, the latter now were maneuvering eagerly for tax, refining, and other privileges for their new county interests. The oil industry had done its homework carefully.

Farmers in the western half of the state where the oil was first found had known depression, debt, and foreclosure. McKenzie County, for example, where there was a sizable land play and some production, was described in the thirties as the hardest-hit depression area in the country. Williams County, center of most oil activity, once had great numbers of its rural people on relief. It was such times that their representative, Usher Burdick, had in mind when in 1954 he was one of only two congressmen voting against a bill outlawing communism, explaining that basic economic distress rather than ideology was the heart of the threat:

In the dark depression days in North Dakota, when foreclosure and dispossession were rampant and whole families were being ejected out on the highways, because they were helpless; when wheat was selling for 26 cents per bushel and good steers selling for less than 2 cents per pound, and the purchasing power of the farmers had disappeared, men who were caught in this dilemma and had families to support would embrace any kind of ism that they thought might relieve them from this dire need, want and suffering. In that period the Communists had a State ticket in the field and attracted many good people to it.[1]

But many farmers were doing well in the postwar period. They were businessmen with sizable investments in livestock, machinery, and land, their farms averaging 630 acres, in Williams County 750. They tended to identify at least in part with this new oil business. There are similar elements of mystery and risk when dealing with nature in both occupations. There is also the common bond of land speculation. But there is a kind of romance to oil sorely lacking or obscured in the lives of most rural (and industrial) workers. There is also drama, movement, even envy. ("These oilmen are a wife-swapping crowd" is echoed in some quarters.) Then, too, there is a whole new language they enjoy using and being a part of, even if the understanding is not always there. Refineries do not "open"; they "go on stream." The potential economic gains for the state and themselves are also very much in mind: "The more money the oil companies have to invest, the sooner they will drill on my fields."

So when in the midst of the controversy a caravan of some three hundred descended upon Bismarck, parading through the legislative halls and urging a low tax, it was not surprising to find that many were farmers from Williams County. Historically a strong Non-partisan League area and overwhelmingly Farmers Union, the county led the state in number of wells and in production. It is noted for its extensive cooperative movement and has been labeled by some as a radical stronghold. "Those people up there want co-ops from womb to tomb," you hear said elsewhere in the state, this an apparent reference to Williston's unsuccessful experiment with a co-op burial society. (A proposal within the county Farmers Union to pool all mineral lease holdings and then divide the royalties on an acreage basis was never regarded favorably.) This grass-roots protest against a higher oil tax was organized and sponsored by the Chambers of Commerce of Williston, Dickinson, and several other towns which prided themselves on remaining "politically alert and tax-minded, helping to keep the industry in the state."

The state Farmers Union took no decisive stand. Proud of its historic role as a people's movement sensitive to agrarian discontent, the organization is generally quite vigorous on such economic issues. Its New Dealish philosophy has been pointed to as proof of its "red" tendencies by Main Street critics, and apologized for by some of its own members who find the chief attraction to be the co-op benefits. It is feared because of its great numerical strength, having about 43,000 of the state's 59,000 farmers in its ranks, as well as because of its sporadic attempts to take over the dormant Democratic party and because of its advocacy of a graduated land tax. The Farmers Union convention had discussed a severance tax, and later the board of directors decided to go along with the legislative research committee's recommendations. But the membership was obviously divided, with conflicting grass-roots delegations showing up at Bismarck.

Alec Lind, chairman of the North Dakota Farmers Union legislative committee for many years, its regular lobbyist, and a respected veteran figure in state politics, gave the organization's official position as in favor of the lower tax. Williston banker William Davidson, Sr., a power in state politics who helped line up the tax vote, credited Lind with having been more effective than any man in the state in lobbying through the 4¼ per cent tax and also a depletion allowance. Lind also served on the legislative committee of the North Dakota Oil and Gas Association. When asked whether he had any fears of oil people dominating the state, Lind's reply was: "We need industry. I have seen the grain trade cheat the farmer, I have seen the railroads dominate the legislature, but in all my years I have never seen this type of power group. They don't push, they don't demand, they don't threaten and they don't hang around the legislature unless asked." While the Farmers Union Board subsequently did support an increase, it became increasingly involved in the oil business itself. The Farmers Union Central Exchange is an integrated operation possessing sizable investments in wells, refineries, pipelines, and marketing outlets. In 1958 the Exchange received from the American Petroleum Institute a gold certificate for outstanding contributions to oil-industry public relations.

In the heat of the gross-production tax fight there was passed a depletion allowance. This law permitted the producer to deduct 27½ per cent of the gross income of a well when computing taxable income. The law assumed that part of this income represented a recovery of capital and hence should not be taxed as income. There was little serious discussion about the concept, only bickering and maneuvering as to whether the figure should be 25 or 27½ per cent. Legislators most knowing about all the technical details of the 1953 session pleaded ignorance as to the origins of this provision. It was not part of the oil and gas subcommittee's recommendations. The record shows that the ROC floor leader, Senator Clyde Duffy, had introduced the proposal with solid ROC backing. The caravan mentioned earlier urged its adoption. Some members of the NPL made support of a higher severance tax their condition for accepting this allowance. During an NPL caucus preceding the vote, a prominent legislator, whose changing stand on the severance tax provided the margin of victory, advised his colleagues that "if you want to build up and invite industry in North Dakota we must go slow at this session of the legislature. The eyes of the oil-producing states, major companies and independents are on this legislature." Depletion was adopted, with the magic figure of 27½ per cent taken over intact from federal statutes. One major oil executive explained that the industry always seeks to preserve this percentage lest any chipping away destroy some of the mystique surrounding the figure and make a breach in the dike for lower rates nationally.

The big oil companies had one further political objective. They helped frame, pressured for, and received as part of the 1953 legislative package a revision of the state's oil conservation law. The avowed purpose was to give the state the necessary power to protect the oil fields from rapacious drilling and production that would dissipate the underground gas pressures essential for driving out the petroleum and thus lose much of the oil. These, along with other measures to prevent waste, were genuine engineering considerations. Around each of them was wrapped the most sacred word for the people of the West—conservation.

To the industry, conservation also meant an orderly and predictable flow of petroleum to protect industry-set prices and investments. Drilling on as wide a spacing as possible to help keep down the number of wells, and a system of prorationing where the state set monthly production allowables for each well, were the key controls. Thus, the state-wide proration order for March 1955 read: "The reasonable market demand for oil produced in the State of North Dakota . . . is 33,599 barrels per day." Individual wells were then allocated their quotas. These quotas were considerably lower than the maximums permissible under sound physical conservation practices. All this price fixing now takes place with the sanction and police power of the state government: "The sale, purchase or acquisition, or the transporting, refining, processing, or handling in any other way of oil produced or gas produced in excess thereof is hereby prohibited and such oil and gas is thereafter contraband."

Small independent producers were not happy with these regulations. They sought a quick return on their investment. This meant getting all the oil possible out of the ground as quickly as feasible. They generally did not have alternative points of production in Texas or abroad to draw upon when market conditions were not favorable in North Dakota. Sharing this feeling were land and royalty owners who were also eager for immediate profits. To them "orderly development" meant the using of North Dakota as a kind of giant natural underground storage basin to be tapped whenever it suited the big oil companies who could operate for the long pull. And so they fought to retain spacing at 40 acres rather than the 80 or 160 sought from the Industrial Commission by Amerada and other producers. The hearings on well spacing provoked sharp controversy and led to freely made claims that decisions by the Industrial Commission and the state geologist were political rather than technical. At one such hearing the attorney for the Amerada Company was State Senator Clyde Duffy. (His leadership in the severance tax fight caused the company's vice president to declare at that time: "I am deeply indebted to Senator Duffy for carrying the load this morning. He is not on the payroll either.") On several occasions Duffy had fought the large companies, and a number of his opponents felt that no question of political morality was involved when the state ROC chairman, who had also been chairman of the Senate's oil and gas subcommittee, represented the leading producer. He was "an honorable man," and "next time he might well be against Amerada." A landowners' attorney who admitted to having rejected sizable retainers from major oil companies, proferred after he had clashed with them, agreed. "All it means is that Duffy's views on oil will carry less weight at the next session."

In North Dakota, as in other oil states, the controversies developed over oil were variations of the theme the "independent" versus the "majors," the "small man" versus the "big interests." And the public was asked to choose sides on this basis. Yet, while this dilemma may have been in harmony with a classic presentation of America's presumed choice, the realities of the North Dakota experience suggested a somewhat different problem. Involved was the formulation of a truly public policy for the use and development of a valuable natural resource. It required as a starting point something else besides a glandular orientation to the virtues of the small businessman or a "realistic" acceptance of what a growing number of liberal academicians priding themselves on their tough-mindedness now see as the new competition of bigness.

The behavior of the small landowners and producers failed to suggest any particularly notable gain for the general public because of their size. Their suspicion of "conservation" was as related to their pocketbooks as was the advocacy of "conservation" by the bigger producers. When they were cut in on the fixed market, by means of prorationing and greater discovery allowances, their outrage over such things as wide well spacing diminished noticeably, and little worry was shown over the disappearance of "free enterprise."

Genuine independents could have contributed to a more competitive spirit. But the costs of seismographic study, modern production techniques, and the nature of so much of the Williston formations made drilling prohibitive for many small producers. Independent wildcat wells were often undertaken with partial major backing, since such dry-hole financing also served as a relatively inexpensive way for a larger company to test a new area. Then, too, independent producers, like independent refiners and marketers, often existed by the good graces of the large outfits. Many in North Dakota kept in back of their heads the possibility of selling out—and hence could be expected to be on best behavior. All producers worked together in opposing the higher severance tax and in securing the depletion allowance. More easily justifiable for genuine wildcatters in initial production stages, the larger companies in the state were careful to get the little men in the forefront. When depletion was up before the legislature, Amerada asked a leading broker and independent active in the state royalty owners' association and a strong critic of the big companies to come back from his vacation in the south to lobby. The man refused on the grounds of health, but did write a letter to every member of the legislature.

The small refinery at Williston was "independent." Yet its pricing pattern when it went on stream was no different to the consumers of the region it served than that of a major company, although it was much nearer the source of supply and had been getting crude at perhaps fifty cents less a barrel than areas farther away. The refinery's stock-offering circular claimed that the proximity of the plant to the producing fields would give it advantage in the local markets. When asked if this meant lower prices, the president of the corporation offered this explanation: "If I cut my prices a little, they would all follow suit. If I cut two cents or so, Standard would cut theirs more." His supply of crude came from Standard.

Would the opening of the Standard refinery at Mandan mean cheaper oil products for North Dakota? "Well, probably not," the

Standard official answered. "You see, we are a price leader in all these states. We must live and let live. If we cut prices our competitors will cry and the Federal Trade Commission will jump on us." Besides, as another Standard executive explained in a Fourth of July speech, the people of North Dakota should realize how lucky their country is to have oil. "Some of you grumble at the price of gasoline, cheap though it is, but go to Rumania and compare."

A successful independent jobber and marketer most vigorous in his criticism of big oil's stranglehold admitted his prices were always the same as those of Standard, the largest marketer. He was as sharply antiunion as was Standard. The contractor building the Mandan refinery employed union labor. The refinery, however, following the paternalistic pattern of much of the industry, did all it could legally to convince the workers to resist the preliminary advances of the CIO's International Oil Workers Union. Good wages and working conditions were offered. "We hope we can educate them that the company will meet their needs without a union." And as one union staff member acknowledged: "We can't offer the workers anything on wages or fringe benefits. The companies can do much better." The independent jobber sharply opposed any health-insurance program among his employees. Amerada, in contrast, instituted free group-hospital and surgical-benefit insurance for all employees in 1944.

Robert E. Wilson, chairman of the board of directors of Standard, a director of the National Association of Manufacturers, on the executive committee of the board of the American Petroleum Institute, a director of the Chase National Bank and the First National Bank of Chicago (where he sat with directors of Standard of California, Continental, Gulf, and a number of gas companies), and a member of the National Petroleum Council, described the Williston development as "an up-to-date case study in the dynamic effects of free enterprise." Yet it is difficult to ignore the extent of Standard's economic power. The fifth largest oil company in the nation, it has assets of $2.8 billion and is the dominant oil company in Michigan, Wisconsin, Iowa, Indiana, Illinois, Missouri, Kansas, Minnesota, South and North Dakota—an expanse known in oil geography as Standard of Indiana territory. In the Williston Basin alone it has had some 4½ million acres under lease. Stanolind Oil and Gas (now known as Pan American Petroleum), its exploratory and producing subsidiary, is a major producer. Its output has been low in North Dakota, and it has struck many dry holes. But Standard has a close working relationship with Amerada. Stanolind Oil Purchasing Company has been the largest buyer in the region, taking some 90 per cent of the crude. The gathering lines in the field and the main crude pipelines have been operated by the Service Pipe Line Company. This is a completely owned Standard subsidiary. Its 154-mile North Dakota line carries the crude from Tioga to the state's largest refinery, Standard's 37,500-barrel plant at Mandan.

Standard kept a very close check on any attempts or even talk of competing refineries. When a group of businessmen planned a refinery for Minot, a small city on the east flank of the oil fields, they went to Amerada and Stanolind seeking a long-term assurance of crude that the banks insisted upon before backing the venture. They were told that such commitments were not made in the industry, but were promised they could buy crude. Amerada pointed out it had no contract with Stanolind, which may have been technically accurate, but did not negate the obvious mutual dependency in view of Standard's pipelines running right to Amerada's wells. Standard further explained it could not make any long-term guarantees, even if the state's allowables were raised to provide for this refinery's 2,500-barrel needs, since it was a purchaser of crude and made such purchases on a short-term basis. The promoter next went to the Hunt Company, which also refused, explaining that Standard would not like such an arrangement.

Oil has a reputation for controlling the politics of those states where it has vital interests. This has not happened in North Dakota, for it is not yet that significant a factor in the economy. But oil has achieved every one of its immediate local objectives. Its methods, however, are rarely those liberal critics anticipate. Old-time NPLers have been completely thrown off guard by their identification of corporate power with "little black bags," fraud, bullying, and even brute force.

Frequent hints about money and payoffs are encountered. Some oilmen have offered to provide substantial aid for right-wing Republican candidates, but were advised not to do so lest the stigma of being oil-backed boomerang. When asked if his ROC had received oil money, one attorney general snorted: "Why should there be? You don't give money to people with you. ROC views are sympathetic to oil. If anything, oil money would go to NPL." There has been some oil financing of candidates, coming in moderate quantities and generally from the smaller producers. Indeed, it would be surprising if this were not so. One broker even pointed out the exact room in the Patterson Hotel in Bismarck where a United States senator was offered "oil money" for his campaign. It is doubtful, however, that such behavior explains the victories of oil. And there has been little evidence of any truly unusual sums spent in campaigns since 1951. But oil has undoubtedly helped temper the older hell-raising passions within the NPL, despite the continued attacks against the "predatory interests" by United States Senator William Langer. Langer, who made the NPL his personal vehicle, consistently supported federal control of offshore oil lands, and in the crucial 1953 congressional fight was joined by his ROC colleague Senator Milton Young, who previously had favored state control.

Oilmen in North Dakota have been quick to deny they are engaged in "partisan politics." And in a sense they are right. Their techniques have been much more bipartisan, seeking to influence all political camps while playing the "grass roots" game to the hilt. They have kept in close touch with key leaders and legislators. Representatives have attended both ROC and NPL conventions, and also those of the Democratic party, now that North Dakota has emerged from its one-party shell.

There has been a good deal of lobbying and informal pressure, through company officials, their trade associations, and such allies in the power structure of the state as the bar, the bankers, the press, and civic groups. For example, working closely on oil legislation with Vice President Boone of Amerada, President Al R. Weinhandl of the First National Bank of Minot got in touch with all the state legislators from his district. The North Dakota Oil and Gas Association tried to assign one or more members of their group to be responsible for each legislator. Local Chambers of Commerce selected people who would be influential with the legislators to visit Bismarck for varying periods of time to discuss oil.

"We have good relations with the Governor," explained a major oil company representative. "But we don't camp on his doorsteps.

We work indirectly. It's better that way." For the dedication of the Mandan refinery, Standard sought out Governor Brunsdale for his suggestions for the featured speaker. The people proposed were unavailable, and so the Governor himself finally agreed to speak.

As to be expected, lobbying reports filed with the Secretary of State have not been very revealing. A number of obvious representatives of the oil associations, Amerada, the Petroleum Industries Committee, landowner associations, and also individual attorneys are listed. Purposes are vaguely defined, clients are not made clear and expenses not shown. In the interest of candor and effective lobbying regulation, those who speak for oil in the state might take a cue from a schoolboy from Cunnington. Registering himself as "interested in firecrackers," he declared that he spoke for "myself and other boys."

North Dakota has yet to challenge the assumption that the initiative and direction of public oil policy should derive so completely from the private interests of the industry. This does not imply that the burden of blame rests upon the oil companies. For if the focus is not simply the big interests versus the small, neither can it be accurately depicted as the evil and powerful corporations versus the good but helpless citizenry. Naturally the oil industry's first concern has been for its own welfare. It is not a devil for thus following the rules of the game. In many respects it is far more aware of social responsibilities than are most American industries. And in North Dakota, where other immediate prospects for industrial development are dim, its investments and efforts have brought many economic benefits. It has also given hope on two basic problems. "Maybe it will keep some of our young folks in the state," speculated a retired farmer, touching on a major sore spot. "Our schools are pretty bad, and the percentage who never finish high school is shockingly high," pointed out a PTA leader. "That oil revenue could make a difference." And it does. At one auction, for example, the Board of University and School Lands received $114,319 in bonuses and rentals from oil leases on 34,000 acres of state lands. At another it received $623,341 on 34,000 acres of school lands, with more than half the sum coming from Stanolind.

At the same time, the role of the federal government's generous depletion and depreciation allowances should not be overlooked.

Amerada, an aggressive company combining science, daring, and luck, has been called a businessman's tax dream by *Fortune* magazine because of the negligible taxes it has paid. Standard's $25 million refinery received a necessity certificate which meant that 57 per cent if its cost would be written off in five years in the interest of national defense; its pipeline was given a 25 per cent write-off. Signal's $10 million natural gas plant at Tioga was given 57 per cent under this program.

All the illustrations of pressure tactics, public relations, and politicking are incomplete without realization of the tremendous popular receptivity to the private demands of the oil industry. Obviously much of North Dakota's criticism of the importation of foreign crude oil into the United States has been generated by the vested interests of those directly in oil and by the publicity of groups like the Independent Petroleum Association of America. Yet it is impossible to divorce this economic isolationist sentiment from a deep-rooted political isolationism that predates oil in the state by many years. One can point to the huge free barbecues for as many as ten thousand people that have become annual occasions in a number of towns, with Standard, Amerada, or another corporation picking up the check. But one should also note that the "tradition" is not simply a calculated device to buy good will. At least in part it has been the eagerness of local booster groups to get oil companies to sponsor this mass freeloading.

The top oil executives have been lionized socially. Any visit into the state is greeted in a manner reminiscent of James Bryce's description of the homage accorded the railroad kings in another period of American history. Receptions are held to which are invited all the power forces and opinion makers. A sizable mythology quickly developed about Amerada's President Alfred Jacobsen, with his name, appearance, and ability to speak Danish all real assets. "He is so common, he is like one of us." "He doesn't even own a car"—this from a banker's wife. "He always buys everyone in the tavern a drink when he comes to town"; this is matched by: "He's a fine man; he never touches a drop." Jacobsen received an honorary degree from the state university. When an oilman comments favorably upon the conduct of a public hearing at which his company has been a supplicant, portions of the press blush with pride for the state. Perhaps the best summation of this whole attitude was in the advertisement for oil discovery day in Williston which announced a banquet "honoring oil dignitaries and state officials."

There have been few individuals and no groups whose primary focus has been the formulation of a long-range public policy for regulating the conservation, production, distribution, and marketing of oil. Where people have gotten worked up, it seems to have been largely in terms of "What's in it for me?" A report of one major oil company observed that the farmers take "little interest in legislation not directly concerned with their farming operations." The Farmers Union was divided on this issue. Organized labor is weak in this preponderantly rural state. Nor will the growth of the oil industry provide any mass base of added union strength and "countervailing power," for the number of people employed in oil is relatively small. A confused party system has also militated against the development of public awareness and alternative programs for oil.

"We just don't speak their language," a thoughtful Minot publisher explained in the course of defending the business community's tagging along with the oil industry. He was referring to the technical jargon. Yet the people of the state at one time did not understand the technical language of grain grading and of railroad freight rates. But they learned. In a more fundamental sense, however, he was right. Predominantly rural and Main Street, North Dakota tends to view oil with the philosophy of small business. This perspective provides as little help in understanding the giant business of oil, which is essentially national (and international), as does the county assessor's experience in evaluating farm property prepare him for determining the worth of a refinery. Failing to recognize this, they fail to recognize the need for a state policy. And because they do not attempt the latter, they are spared from learning that not even a state-wide policy will be adequate, that the nature of oil requires national policy, and that right now there is one, but it is private.

In the Oil Information Committee's film *American Frontier*, the principal figure, a skeptical schoolteacher-farmer, concludes, to the accompaniment of the New York Philharmonic orchestra: "I finally understood that oil would enrich the lives of hundreds of my neighbors. I finally knew for sure that oil was good for all of us."

Against the silence of the prairie, a retired farmer whose car had broken down on the main east-west highway cutting across the oil fields seemed less certain. He was discussing the changes in the state during his lifetime. In the background an oil derrick glistened in the midday sun. Nearby, on the edge of a pasture, a sign advised, not too helpfully for the immediate problems at hand, REPENT OR PERISH. "Do I think that the oil companies will soon dominate North Dakota? I just don't know," he mused as he tested the fan belt. "We used to talk a lot about such problems in the twenties, but now . . ." His voice trailed off. The white-faced Herefords nearby continued to graze without looking up.

3

The Private Government of Oil

To ask an oilman if he or his company is involved in politics is
equivalent to asking a businessman if his practices are unethical or
his associations dubious. The reaction is immediate—and indignant.
No industry responds more sensitively to such a suggestion than oil.
No industry sounds more eager to preserve the American mythology
of the separation of economics and politics. Yet oil is a prospering
industry that does exceedingly well in achieving all those objectives
requiring the aid or sanction of the public and its government. And
regardless of the protestations or the achievements of oil, a primary
insight into the industry shows, not the extent to which it is "in
politics," but rather that the individual oil corporations, as the characteristic institutions of modern capitalism, and the large trade associations in which they are joined, are in themselves essentially
political as well as economic institutions.

The scale of decision making involved in the corporation's internal
and external affairs has a wider consequence for the whole economy.
Choices made out of the judgment of corporate needs evoke responses
and cause social dislocations among communities and nations. It thus
becomes more and more difficult to separate private from the public aspects of its behavior. Once this is recognized, the major oil
companies increasingly include in their calculations the factor of
public opinion. Their concern is the continued acceptance of their
roles and the maintenance of a social structure that will further
this pattern of control. And so, deriving from the "natural right" of
an individual to own property, nurtured by technology, steered by
men whose organizational concern is profit and power, and blessed
by law that offers protection through the rights of charter, contract,

34

patent, due process, and property itself, the character of the modern oil corporation as a political institution takes shape. The oil corporation as a political institution has roots going back to the origins of the industry. The one-man divining-rod ventures, the stock-promotion drilling companies, the state incorporation of private refineries, the running of pipelines and the contests over their use and control, the abortive trade associations, the emergence of the Rockefeller empire, the frantic appeal of small businessmen for government to check monopoly, the famous Standard Oil dissolution decree of 1911 that split the trust into thirty-four separate companies, and the development of the industry as a carefully structured system of private government—functional, state, regional, national, and international—are each more or less distinct stages in this evolution.

Oil is one of the largest and most vital industries of the nation. Domestic crude oil production, estimated at a few thousand barrels in 1859, 500,000 in 1860 and 64 million in 1900, reached 1.4 billion in 1940 and nearly 2.6 billion in 1959. Some experts estimate a doubling of current demands by 1970. Highly profitable imports have run at a rate of 15 to 25 per cent of domestic production. There is every indication that the country's imports of crude oil will continue to exceed its exports, despite the fact that it produces about half of the world's supply. For it consumes over 9 million barrels a day, 60 per cent of the world's production. The average per capita consumption is ten times that of the rest of the world, a rough but significant index of industrial development and living-standard levels.[1]

Oil supplies the country with 45 per cent of its total fuel energy requirements, with natural gas providing another 25 per cent. In contrast, water power, which is of much greater popular political interest and is primarily used for electricity, supplies approximately 4 per cent. Oil powers the 70 million motor vehicles crowding American highways, the thousands of diesel railroad engines, ships, and airplanes, along with the countless little engines, from lawn mowers to water pumps, designed to lessen physical drudgery. Modern military efforts have been oil-based, as the British learned quite early during World War II in the struggle to maintain their sea empire, and the Nazis much later in losing their land empire when their fuel lines could not keep up with their forces. More than 60 per cent of United States shipments to Korea during the Korean War were oil and oil products. In 1958 the military spent over a billion dollars for 260 million barrels of jet fuel, aviation gas, and other petroleum products. These are not astonishing figures when one realizes that a four-engine propeller-type air liner burns a gallon of high-test gasoline every six seconds, that it takes approximately 300 gallons of jet fuel to get a B-47 jet bomber off the ground, and that a big Boeing jet uses 2,200 gallons an hour. It helps explain the Air Force's research toward nuclear-powered craft and the Navy's close watching of the atom-propelled submarine *Nautilus*, which logged 62,500 miles before changing its nuclear core. Later models have retained their cores for much longer distances. Admiral Hyman G. Rickover, who has been a pioneer in this development, calculated that a conventional submarine of equal displacement and horsepower would have burned about 2,170,000 gallons of oil. This would fill 217 tank cars and require extensive and vulnerable oil bases, storage tanks, and tankers. Nuclear propulsion makes possible higher speeds, greater cruising power, and an ability to stay under water for days. Describing comparable work on other craft, he reported that "we are right in the middle of a vast program for changing our Navy." [2] Even commercial oil supertankers will also soon be nuclear-powered.

The modern agricultural revolution is oil-based, and its growing mechanized operations use more than 16 billion gallons of crude a year. While gasoline, once a nuisance waste in the making of kerosene, is today the chief product, oil is basic to chemicals, paints, detergents, insecticides, medicines, fertilizers, synthetic rubber and fiber, asphalt, heating, lubrication, and countless other goods and processes.

Filling these needs is a domestic industry with gross assets of $60 billion. Expenditures for capital investment and exploration within the United States in the decade following World War II exceeded $46 billion. The combined outlay for 1956 and 1957 totaled $13 billion, approximately one-sixth of all capital investment by business in the United States. It is claimed that over the next decade the industry will need $75 to $100 billion in investment capital for development within the country to meet demand. To this is added another $40 billion for use in the non-Communist areas of the world. Thus far, the bulk of this expansion has been done through internal financing. The ability of the giants of the industry to generate capital out of their own earnings has given them tremendous economic power. The independence from capital markets also has special advantage in times when credit is restricted. In the period 1946 to 1955, it is estimated that the petroleum produced, including natural gas, was worth $62 billion. The combined net income of the top 33 production and refining companies for 1957 came to $3,100 million. A New York Stock Exchange study in 1954 showed that six of the fifteen "blue chip" stocks most favored by investing institutions were those of oil corporations.

Better than one-fourth of the land area of the United States is under lease for oil and gas exploration. About 50,000 wells were drilled in 1958, and over a half-million are now in operation. With gas, oil is the largest single purchaser of capital goods. For example, it took nearly 8 per cent of the national steel output in 1955. Oil is also the biggest single item in international trade, as it is in American foreign investments.[3]

It is an essential part of corporate ritual to insist that industry is competitive, presumably in the classic capitalist image, with the price mechanisms of a free market place guiding and restraining the behavior of all participants. Americans need this reassurance, judging by the cliché-ridden descriptions of their economic system so frequently voiced by the general public and by corporate spokesmen. In oil there are important areas where types of competition are visible. Certainly the picture is not quite so simple as in 1911 when antitrust action brought about the formal dissolution of the Rockefeller holding company which, with assets of under a billion dollars, handled 70 to 90 per cent of the nation's oil business.

The one-man filling station, the jobber who serves it, the giant refinery plant in Baton Rouge or Marcus Hook, the 200,000 miles of crude and products pipeline crossing the continent, the tanker fleets, the drilling contractor with a few rigs, the wildcatters gambling for oil, and the geological-geophysical team with the latest equipment are all interrelated parts of the industry. The American Petroleum Institute estimates there are about 42,000 oil businesses in addition to the 181,000 service stations. Nearly 2 million people are employed in exploration and production, transportation, refining, and marketing, the major economic divisions of the industry. At the beginning of the oil process, the individual companies hunt hard for new sources of supply. And at the consumer end, the motorist or homeowner has a choice of brands, with the companies in a given area vying for volume of sales. But it is naïve to conclude that this constitutes thoroughgoing competition; for all this activity takes place within a carefully structured framework that precludes the mutual destruction through competition of the participants.

At the top of these enterprises stand twenty corporate giants. The moderate-sized among them—Tidewater, Atlantic, Continental, Sun, Union, Sunray Mid-Continent, Pure, Ohio, Richfield, and Standard (Ohio), listed in descending order—had assets in 1959 ranging from $856 to $408 million. The remaining ten, Cities Service, Gulf, Phillips, Shell of the foreign-controlled Royal Dutch/Shell Group, Sinclair, Socony Mobil, Standard of California, Standard (Indiana), Standard (New Jersey), and The Texas Company (now called Texaco) had assets of more than a billion dollars each. There has been steady growth through expansion and mergers. Standard (Indiana) and Standard of California are rapidly approaching the $3 billion level. Texaco reported to its stockholders that "our assets passed the one-billion dollar mark in September 1947 and the billion-and-a-half dollar mark in March 1951." By the end of 1955 the company's consolidated balance sheet showed total assets of $2,115 million and by the end of 1958 they exceeded $3 billion. Socony and Gulf are also in the $3 billion class, with Gulf's assets in 1959 at $3,576 million. Gulf saw its assets of $722 million in 1946 quadruple by the end of 1956, while its crude production tripled and its net income rose from $58 million to $283 million. For the same period the net income of the extremely aggressive Phillips Petroleum Company skyrocketed from $23 million to $95 million, while its assets moved from $332 million to over $1,373 million.[4]

Each of these is dwarfed by the Standard of New Jersey colossus. Caught in the wake of a national reaction against trusts and corruption, the main heir of the original Rockefeller empire had been cut off by court decree in 1911 from the bulk of its crude supplies. Its carefully coordinated markets and transportation system were sharply reduced. But in a span of history dominated by the rise of the automobile and the airplane a new empire was forged. Today the Jersey corporation is many times the size of the original Standard Oil trust. It is, in its own words, "an organization that operates in nearly every currency, in nearly every language and under a bewildering complexity of economic, social and political circumstances." Jersey Standard produces and refines about 15 per cent of the world's supply of crude oil, thanks to the resources of such affiliates as Humble, Esso, and Carter in the United States (now absorbed into a new national Humble Oil and Refining Company), Imperial in Canada, Creole in Latin America, and a cluster of Middle East holdings. Possessing assets of $8,712 million, its subsidiaries around the globe earned $805 million after taxes in the relatively difficult economic year 1957, with profits about 14 per cent of invested capital. It earned $585 million in 1954, $709 million in 1955, and $809 million in 1956. (Jersey's assets rose to $9,895 million in 1959, but profits dropped to $630 million.) In anticipation of rising petroleum needs, Jersey embarked on a $1,100 million investment expansion during 1956. In 1957 the capital outlay was $1,380 million, bringing these investments to $8.5 billion since the close of World War II. Jersey's 146,000 employees make it the fifth largest industrial employer and it has 600,000 stockholders. Advertising expenditures are around $45 million annually.[5]

The major companies are fully integrated. This means that the corporation has coordinated control over every stage of the oil flow. In contrast, the independents, who may be big, engage in one or a few stages only. The integrated organizations must be sure of their crude supply, not just for the present but for many years ahead. This entails heavy capital investment in exploration and drilling. Rockefeller, the grand master of oil, had discovered he could dominate the world of oil by controlling the railroads, pipelines, and refineries. But an expanding economy and market for oil attracted new venture capital directly seeking reserves. The old Standard companies and the rising "non-Standard" competitors, such as Texaco and Gulf, have been forced to search intensively for crude, reaching out to overseas and even underseas sources. As further insurance, the big refiners and marketers wherever possible buy up or merge with successful producers, as did Jersey with Humble and the old Standard of New York (now Socony Mobil) with Magnolia during the period between the two world wars. When in 1955 Gulf acquired the Warren Petroleum Corporation, with assets of $164 million, it denied a government complaint that this tended to create a monopoly.

Warren had been the largest independent producer of natural gasoline and liquefied petroleum gas and the main source of supply for
independent refiners and dealers. Gulf's president described the action as fully within the spirit and letter of the antitrust laws, since
Gulf and Warren had not been competitors. "Gulf's purchase of
Warren has had just the opposite effect than that of reducing competition. It has put Warren in a position to be more strongly competitive with various large integrated oil companies which are active
in the liquefied petroleum gas and natural gasoline fields." [6]

The integrated producer controls the refining of its crude. Generally
it also refines a considerably greater volume than it produces itself.
This contributes to making smaller producers dependent upon the
refinery purchases of their presumed competitors. The giants have
their gathering and trunk pipelines, just as they have their tankers,
barges, and privileged access to railroad tank cars, which give them a
further competitive edge over the so-called independents. The prices
for crude posted in a given field rest in the hands of the dominant
oil purchaser of the area. The economic bargaining power of the independent producers frequently is inadequate to protect him from
a price squeeze that may barely allow recovery of the cost of production. Maintaining high storage stocks can also serve to control
production and prices. They may be several gathering systems in a
field, but no well is served by more than one line. Since the Hepburn
Act of 1906 pipelines have been presumed to be common carriers.
Yet of the 85 pipeline companies reporting to the Interstate Commerce Commission as common carriers, 82 are owned by one or more
oil companies, and these frequently function as plant facilities.[7] The
independent producer's oil is frequently discriminated against through
a range of practices and, in effect, flows only at the discretion of the
pipeline company. At times, pipelines take only a percentage of a
well's allowable, that is, the production for a given period authorized
by state law. This practice, known as pipeline prorationing, may serve
to favor the pipelines' own wells while acting as a private check on
the public rulings of a state's oil regulatory agency.

Some wells are completely by-passed. To ship by truck or rail is
far more expensive. The trucking lines are frequently owned by or
tied in with the pipeline companies. The producer who has no
pipeline at his well pays for trucking (in contrast to a connected

well where the purchaser pays the gathering cost) and is often told which trucks to use to deliver the oil to the lines. In Texas, independent producers have accused the Atlantic, Humble, Gulf, Magnolia, Shell, and Texaco companies, major purchasers who control the crude lines of the state, of deliberately not extending their gathering systems while stepping up their imports.[8] Thus the pipelines serve to limit the marketability of crude oil produced by nonintegrated companies, forcing them to sell at the wellhead. They also block the purchases of independent refiners located away from the fields, while giving advantage to the integrated company that may build its refineries near consumer centers.

Crude oil prices can be handled or manipulated by the giants as bookkeeping operations. Aggregate company profits are allocated to one or another division of the integrated business. When Humble, the largest domestic producer and also an important refiner, instituted a 35 cents per barrel price rise in January 1957 during the Suez oil crisis, the president of the Independent Refiners Association of America, who also ran a small refinery in Wyoming, expressed an understanding of the reasons. But he also saw this action, followed by other companies, as driving independents to the wall and furthering monopoly. The integrated company can raise the price of crude oil (paid to itself) without raising the price of gasoline. The independent, meanwhile, purchases his crude in a market largely controlled by the integrated companies and then has to sell his finished products in competition with them. Thus, "for the independent refiner . . . a change in the price of crude oil means business survival or death." [9] In contrast, President Hines H. Baker of Humble related that when in the same period he told President Rathbone of the parent Jersey Standard company, which purchases a great deal of Humble's crude through its Esso affiliate, that Humble was contemplating a raise in crude prices, "his reaction was that the price increase was past due, that as far as they were concerned, as a customer, they had no particular objection to it." [10] A forecast, prepared by Jersey's treasurer and discussed at the December 1956 meeting of the board of directors to review capital investment budgets of affiliates, indicated that the holding company had been calculating the gains from such an increase some time prior to this discussion and Humble's actions. The executives were concerned about their double responsibility of maintaining dividends while continuing to retain earnings for the large expansion judged essential, without resorting to borrowing:

It is estimated that at the present volume of business, the consolidated net earnings would rise at an annual rate of $100 million if an increase of 25 cents per barrel occurred in the price of crude, assuming that product prices also rose accordingly.[11]

Mr. Baker, who was soon to become a board member of the parent company, insisted, "I know nothing about Standard of New Jersey's business or what calculations it was making with reference to any expected income from price increases." He assured a congressional inquiry that the price rise had been inevitable, regardless of Suez. Had the increase not been passed along in refined-product prices, small refiners would have been smashed, "and I think you would have an investigation of us up here on a different angle. . . ." [12]

A refiner from Michigan who had been the first Director of the Refinery Division of the Petroleum Administration for Defense during the Korean War and was now spokesman for the Western Petroleum Refiners Association and the National Petroleum Association, representing independent refiners, readily agreed:

I don't know whether you realize it or not, but you Members of Congress and the various State legislatures, by frequent investigations, appear to be trying to scare the major oil companies about what the public may think of them if they increase the price of products that the public buys. . . . There appears to have been an extreme reluctance on the part of the major companies to pass along in the form of increased product prices, wage increases, and other increases in the cost of doing business. At this time I want to say to you that the refiner is about at the end of his rope insofar as his ability to absorb additional costs of doing business is concerned. . . . If this committee, in its enthusiasm to protect the public from what it thinks is a great wrong, has any success in its efforts to get the larger companies to absorb the increase in the price of crude oil and cut back the price of gasoline, it is about to accomplish something that no other force has been able to do—that is, put the independents out of business.

The majors, he added, were not interested in putting little people out of business. They have not drawn upon their cheap overseas reserves extensively and so have permitted independents to compete.

I . . . would like to get this point across to the committee, that we hope as a result of all these hearings that you do not come up with any suggestions or conclusions that have been suggested . . . that maybe the oil industry is making too much profit, and start whacking it down so that they will have to bring in that crude oil from over there and start using it, money that they make in Kuwait or some other place, because if they do, then we are going to get hurt and we are going to be pretty mad about that. We don't want to get hurt, and I am sure you don't want to hurt us, so don't do anything to cause them to bring in their foreign operations and put them in here. Some of the things that I think you might think sounds like a good deal could hurt us. There was a lot of conversation going on about this tax credit where those American companies have gone into Saudi Arabia, Kuwait, the Middle East, many foreign places, and they pay taxes and they get a tax credit. Now, if you figure out a way to cut that out, they are going to hurt some. And they are not going to like that very well, so they are going to have to bring their profits back up or they are going to have some new faces in their company. And by doing that they would have to bring in the oil from those countries, which is cheaper. It would hurt the independent producers, hurt the independent refiners.[13]

Meanwhile, estimates of the immediate added costs for the consumer ranged from $500 million to $1 billion. The military, which purchases well over a billion dollars of products a year and is the largest single customer, calculated that the additional cost for 1957 would be at least $85 million. As part of the Administration's economy drive some months later, a 10 to 15 per cent reduction in petroleum purchases was announced.[14]

At the marketing end of this integrated process, the constant objective of the majors is an assurance that the supply of crude and the refinery runs do not upset their command over the pricing system. Control over the bulk stations and the ability to manipulate the presumably independent jobbers help to make this possible. Retail marketing outlets often are nominally owned by the dealer, enabling the companies to avoid chain-store taxes, social security, and other responsibilities. But these stations are tied into the integrated system through techniques ranging from outright ownership, short-term leasing and licensing arrangements and exclusive-dealing requirements, to rebates, rental allowances, brand-name advertising, and nation-wide credit-card systems. The mother company sets the price at which it wholesales the gasoline. And there is considerable evidence that, in effect, it also sets the retail price. Meanwhile, the gasoline-station operator is left to assert his independence by supplying the service-conscious motorist with energetic attention and good will. Admittedly the dealer may cut his profit for competitive reasons. But he works with a very limited margin. In trying to capture or retain a share of the market, he frequently cuts his own throat. In many cases he is under the constant threat of losing the station if he does not sell the particular brands of automobile parts, tires, batteries, oil, and antifreeze the supplying company specifies and from which it profits by commission deals with the manufacturers. The integrated companies always deny this is their policy, and practices do vary among companies and regions. Socony Mobil, for example, assures its dealers that "we recognize that every Mobilgas dealer is an independent businessman free to buy and sell our products or others and free to operate his business as he deems best subject only to applicable laws and to the conditions of written contracts with us." [15] Esso also disclaims that it enters into exclusive contracts with its "dealer customers." But it does insist on standards that will not discredit the Esso name. "The Esso dealer customer is free to run his business as he sees fit," explained the general manager of marketing. "We reserve the right to do business with whom we please." [16]

Repeated testimony and appeals before congressional bodies for anticoercion legislation by small businessmen who have seen their economic freedom thwarted suggest that this relationship is less than an equal one. The pressures upon district salesmen and agencies of the distributing companies to maintain these practices are great, as are apparently the rewards. They help account for what the companies dismiss as the unfortunate, although understandable, overenthusiasm of their representatives or employees. The president of a marketing subsidiary of the Pennzoil Company, an independent refiner of Pennsylvania grade oil and grease owned in turn by the South Penn Oil Company which was capitalized at over $50 million, claimed that most gasoline dealers on the West Coast dared not purchase his products. Some dealers, a little more independent, do buy Pennzoil.

. . . . By far the majority of the service stations that sell Pennzoil do not display Pennzoil. In many instances our delivery truck cannot even deliver to their place of business. They are afraid they will be caught by the major company representative, so we deliver oil and it is written right on the order that our delivery truck carries (it) to a man's home or maybe to a small independent business alongside of him with whom he is friendly. The oil is stored in the backs of automobiles, it is stored in locked-up cabinets, in restrooms . . . where the major gasoline representative is not likely to find it.[17]

Lest one too quickly sort the heroes and the villains, a document prepared in the Antitrust Division of the Justice Department quotes a letter sent out by the parent company in the East to all its lease operators of service stations in 1948: " 'During this critical gasoline situation the Pennzoil Co. will endeavor to keep you supplied with gasoline at all times and in return will expect full cooperation in the sale of Prestolite batteries and Cooper tires. In other words we do not expect other brands of batteries and tires in our stations.' " [18]

This articulated system of all the phases of oil from wellhead to gas pump is generally acknowledged by the industry. As one prominent oil spokesman has put it:

Just as it became necessary for individuals and small business operations to integrate their resources and facilities in order to keep pace with the demands of a surging and seething economy, it was of vital importance in the public interest for oil companies to integrate their facilities into a smooth, economical and efficient over-all organization. Integration is the one essential factor that has made it possible for the oil industry to meet every demand of the American people both in peace and war.[19]

There is considerable need for a more critical examination as to the optimum size of the modern oil corporation, for asking at what point the integration process, horizontal and vertical, actually produces private efficiency and public benefits. But it is clear, as President Charles E. Spahr of Standard (Ohio) has put it, that from the perspective of corporate leadership "integration is a problem of profitability." [20]

The modern oil corporation seeks to match the logic of the separate technological processes with a comparable order within its organizational frame. While practices vary among companies, over-all decisions are made through carefully defined political processes. Functional and regional operations are divided and authority is often delegated to nominally separate companies. But lines of responsibility cut through the formal structures of the fantastically complex pyramids of subsidiaries to ensure coordination and unity. In an earlier period, personalities and promoters such as John D. Rockefeller, Harry F. Sinclair, and Henry L. Doherty symbolized the aggressive empire building. The names more recently in the headlines—H. L. Hunt, Sid W. Richardson, Clinton W. Murchison, Hugh Roy Cullen —more typically have been millionaire heads of individual, nonintegrated producing firms.

Few citizens can identify the chairman or a single member of the boards of directors, let alone know about the policies or structures of the majors, although they include six of the ten largest (in assets) industrial corporations in the United States. At the helm of the giants are organization men whose primary talents may be managerial. They fit in as part of a continuing team, and reflect the belief that differences can generally be ironed out in committee or at the club. The impersonality of the final decisions made by committees and boards tends to conceal responsibility from the public as well as from the participants themselves. Frequently actions are taken that individual members have difficulty in defending personally, but can explain as a team product. The Jersey Standard holding company prides itself on a working board of directors whose fourteen members represent the range of knowledge essential for running a world government. Together with numerous special committees it provides operating affiliates with capital, research, and general guidance distilled from the collective judgments of hundreds of experts in science, law, finance, personnel, management practices, public relations, and oil. More usual among the majors are the boards with at least partial membership from outside the company structure.

In practically all instances there is the now familiar dichotomy between ownership and control. The managements and boards are self-governing and self-perpetuating bureaucracies. The top oil executives set their own salaries. While these do not run so high as in steel, the board chairmen of the major companies draw from $175,-000 to $250,000 annually. The officers control by proxy the bulk of common stock voting. The Jersey company, for example, speaks of its striving "to exemplify . . . the progressive, democratic character of American industry." [21] At its seventy-fifth annual shareholders meeting in 1957, the fourteen directors were nominated without opposition, asked to stand, and then duly elected by the holders of 166,167,088 shares.

Ownership is generally passive, with notable exceptions such as Sun Oil which the Pew family still controls. Even where stockholding remains fairly concentrated, as for example in the Gulf company where the Mellon interests have retained extensive holdings, participation tends to be limited to profits. Any other responsibility to the stockholder is nominal. Noting that his company has nearly 40,000 stockholders, 25,000 of whom own less than 100 shares and hence are not able to keep track of or exert great influence on management, President Spahr of Standard (Ohio) has called upon his colleagues "to find the means of being sensitive to our responsibilities to stockholders. We have to have it built into us perhaps a little bit more than was the case 20 or 25 years ago." [22]

Questions and comments at stockholder meetings are generally elementary. One can also expect the inquiry as to whether Esso Extra is still the best gasoline on the market and the proposal that stockholders refrain from smoking at the meeting "as an example to our employees." Occasional objections to high prices and cartel arrangements are treated impatiently by the assembled owners and directors. At the outset of World War II, Jersey's management was sharply criticized from the floor after the disclosures of cartel arrangements with I. G. Farben. But James W. Gerard, former ambassador to Germany, probably summed up the attitude of many of his fellow stockholders in his defense of the company's officers who were resisting a resolution requiring that they would not enter such arrangements after the war.

There is an old saying that the proof of the pudding is getting it, and when we were here a year ago, the stock of this company . . . was selling at 34¾, and the last day that the Stock Exchange was open before this holiday, our stock sold at 55⅞ at the closing. That is an advance to our advantage of 20 points. That is quite an unanswerable argument as to the ability of these gentlemen to manage our interests.[23]

Policy making in oil involves weighing and harmonizing the complex factors and forces both within and outside the organization with which its professional rulers have to contend. These range from relations with individual dealers and organized labor to tax and antitrust matters with the United States and other governments, from calculations of population growth and changes in automobile engine design to expanding in a new area and predicting the economic and political consequences of a decision to raise prices. Long-range planning is central to this entire organizational effort. There is little liking and diminishing room for chance among the oil corporations. Their size and power in the economy preclude waiting for signals from the automatically governed "invisible hand" of a free market. They do not care to risk being caught by surprise, either through technological or social transformations. Dislocations at any point are viewed as potential threats to control over the entire oil process. This produces a constant drive to extend integration and also to range more widely in related industrial and political fields. To help develop what President Reese H. Taylor of Union Oil has called "integrated oil men," some corporations conduct extensive educational programs.[24] They attempt systematically to discover and develop managerial talent. To ensure continuity, Jersey's directors are responsible for training their successors, with advancement through the corporate structure taking place on a carefully programed basis.

Such planning is impossible without continuing research. Efficiency, human relations, consumer-taste and public-opinion studies are constantly in process as the oil corporations look for improved techniques of governance. One Jersey director has reported that his colleagues on the board give at least half of their working hours to problems of a human relations rather than a technical or economic nature. A study on *The Coordination of Motive, Men and Money in Industrial Research*, conducted by Standard of California, concluded that industrial research organizations, through their scientists and proper public relations, had the vital task of helping "to bring a closer balance between the politico-social aspects of human behavior and the rapid progress of science, itself." [25]

Modern oil leaders view scientific research as the first principle of organizational growth and flexibility. Robert E. Wilson, a former chemical engineering professor who served as director of research, head of the development and patent department, and ultimately chairman of the board of Standard (Indiana), explained this interest quite simply:

Why did our industry which 30 years ago employed less than 40 research workers . . . expand this activity until today it employs several thousand full-time research workers and would like to hire as many more over the next few years? I should like to be able to tell you that the oil industry's research was due to a broad, public-spirited interest in the welfare of the country. Frankness, however, compels me to let you in on a little secret. . . . The real reason why our industry has spent hundreds of millions of dollars in research and development during the past quarter century is that we thought we could make a profit by so doing.[26]

This requires substantial financing, often with no hope of immediate return. Smaller firms are less likely to afford or to display such foresight. At least $250 million in oil-company budgets is now devoted annually to research and experimentation designed to apply the findings of laboratories to production needs and changes.[27] To this should be added the sums spent by chemical companies for petroleum research and the federal government's experiments with new oil resources that will be discussed later. The twenty majors account for 90 per cent of the research funds and personnel within the industry. The Esso Research and Engineering Company operates as the central research arm of Jersey. With other Jersey research affiliates it has a budget of $62 million and employs about 3,780 people, including more than a thousand physicists, chemists, engineers, geologists, mathematicians, and other professionals. Royal Dutch/Shell, Jersey's nearest rival in size, operates a dozen laboratories in this country and Europe with a staff of over 4,000 and has facilities for fundamental research. Standard of California's research organization reports that nearly half of its 1,350 technical employees are engineers or scientists. While statistics in this area do not offer clear insights, it is not surprising that the major companies hold the bulk of oil patents and that Jersey is one of the leading corporate holders of patents in the United States.

Petroleum literature speaks a good deal about the free range of inquiry of company personnel. But it is quite clear that every effort is made to create an atmosphere where the scientist learns to appreciate and gravitate toward the needs of his employer. For a long time the major impetus for research was the desire to increase the gasoline yield from crude petroleum through improved cracking processes. Such research has become highly organized, as an account by E. D. Reeves, former executive vice president of Esso Research and Engineering, indicates:

. . . . Just before the last war, we were interested in developing a catalytic cracking process and were working on one called Fluid Catalytic Cracking. At the peak of that effort, we had about 200 people of all sorts working on the process. Some of these people were professional people and some were nonprofessional. In the group, we had physical and organic chemists; we had physicists; we had engineers of all types; we had lawyers, analysts, mechanics, operators, etc. The Research Division was working on part of it, the Process Division on another part, and the Development Division was doing the engineering and economic studies. The Baton Rouge Laboratories were running a huge pilot plant and the Esso Engineering Department engineers were designing the commercial units. In addition to that, the patent and legal people were checking to be sure that if we did develop the process we would have patent protection on it. If we have to put all of those things together and develop the process in a short period of time, it is obvious that individuals today cannot do industrial research successfully. It has to be done by groups of coordinated people.[28]

Where there is competition in the new industrial economy, it is found heavily in innovation. In the petroleum industry most of the research has remained focused upon the refining process. Refineries have become modern alchemy plants involved in the breaking down and rearranging of petroleum molecules. The industry estimates that hundreds of new uses are coming from the "magic barrel" of petroleum. The president of a major chemical firm claims that ten thousand newly synthesized petrochemical products a year, most of them not yet commercialized, are being developed. The majors are active in electronics, automation, nuclear research, and synthetics. The industry's refineries and pumping stations utilize the most advanced automatic controls in the continuing search to reduce labor costs and improve upon the human mechanism. "A refinery controlled at a central place by a group of men who have completely accurate and complete information before them at all times of the entire status of every unit in the refinery can avoid costly errors in operation and can keep the machinery interrelated in an optimum manner," the scientist Vannevar Bush has explained.[29] Investment costs per worker are high, but as chemical engineers point out, it is as easy with automatic controls to regulate operations of a 20,000-barrel-per-day catalytic cracker as it is a 5,000-barrel catalytic cracker. The major additional cost is that of the crude. This has made possible increases in refinery size and output accompanied by reduction in the number of refineries and employees. A six-man shift in an Esso refinery at Fawley can handle almost one-third of the daily oil-product needs of Great Britain.

Oil now utilizes radioactive materials in every stage of production and is the largest industrial user of atomic energy. The leading oil companies operate radiation research centers. Underground nuclear explosions for generating heat to liberate oil from shale are being studied. Several companies operate uranium mines. Kerr-McGee controls more than one-fourth of the nation's known ore reserves and has the largest uranium-ore mill.

As always, the objective of these highly developed economic and political processes is profit, and the focus of interest remains the production and sale of petroleum. But the power over these physical resources and collective properties inevitably extends the corporation's attention and impact to include great numbers of human beings whose welfare is linked to its actions. In this sense the integrated oil company properly can be considered as a private government.

It is claimed that the sheer number of oil enterprises precludes monopoly control and the degree of sovereign power suggested here. In production alone, for example, the American Petroleum Institute lists 12,000 companies. But Texas, whose 170,000 wells provide 40 per cent of the nation's crude, offers a good illustration of the reality of the presumed "checks and balances" inherent in the economic patterns of the oil industry. In this classic home of the small producer, the Humble Oil Company alone produces one-eighth of the state's oil, and the top five companies produce approximately one-third. With the next eight, they account for 50 per cent of the state's output, suggesting the marginal contribution of thousands of oil producers. Over 40 per cent of these wells produce less than ten barrels a day each, many of them yielding one, two or three. In 1946, Justice Department figures revealed that on a nation-wide basis the top twenty-one companies owned 30 per cent of the wells and produced at least 60 per cent of the oil. The pattern is even more concentrated today. The industry estimates that the productivity of about 70 per cent of all wells is extremely limited, providing not more than 20 per cent of the output.

Big oil has traditionally preferred to leave production at least partially in small hands, not out of sentiment for "free competitive enterprise," but because of the realization that here is the greatest risk. It is impossible to predict or prevent new discoveries. Nature and our legal system combine to encourage oil exploration. Petroleum is believed to be derived from organic deposits accumulated over the ages beneath the earth's surface. Potential oil-bearing geological formations are widespread throughout the country, and there is oil production in thirty-two states. The American legal system has bestowed full subsurface mineral rights upon the owner of the land. Through historic court interpretation, the "law of capture" held that all that the producer takes out from his property is his, with little responsibility to the community or to neighbors whose oil he might be taking. Although modified somewhat by more recent conservation laws, this has frequently encouraged frantic competitive drilling and tremendous waste. Nevertheless, the romantic image of bonanzas from geological structures detected by the naked eye and shrewd hunches of daredevil gamblers is fading within the United States. The Director of Reserves in the Petroleum Administration during World War II put it bluntly to senators exploring ways of encouraging oil production: "The finding of oil should henceforth be regarded as a stable industrial function to be guided by the highest technical skill and administered with efficiency and vision." [30] When wildcatters do find oil, they generally can be bought out or controlled. Some actually are agents of the major companies, quietly financed by them. Today the latter own the overwhelming percentage of the nation's proved reserves and an unknown amount of reserves on the vast undeveloped acres listed as oil lands which they have tied up for the future. Corporate reports rarely give the full picture of this wealth.

The ten leading pipeline systems within Texas control 80 per cent of the total crude mileage, with the Humble Pipe Line Company's $150 million investment holding nearly a fifth of the total. Over 90 per cent of the nation's pipeline capacity is owned or controlled by the major oil companies. A government civil action in 1941 charged that, as shippers, the oil companies were receiving substantial rebates and refunds from the pipelines "under the guise of earnings and dividends." This discriminatory practice violated the Elkins Act and mocked the regular rates filed with the Interstate Commerce Commission. After considerable behind-the-scenes political maneuvering, the triple penalty judgment of over $1.5 billion sought by the government was waived. The companies agreed to limit to 7 per cent the earnings payment from pipelines to ship-owners. Periodically there have been hints that the Justice Department has evidence of violations of the consent decree. In 1957 a full-scale investigation was announced and a series of suits, based on the charge that the companies were improperly figuring profits, were begun. In 1959 a House Judiciary Subcommittee report concluded that the consent settlement had nullified the government's antitrust policies. The majority further charged that lax Justice Department enforcement allowed some of the defendant pipeline companies to make dividend payments to their shipper-owners that were comparable to those challenged in the original suit. Nearly all the defendants were seen to have failed to comply with the requirements of the consent decree.[31]

Humble has also been the top refiner in Texas. For the nation, 33 per cent of domestic refining is done by the top four companies. Together with the next four the figure is 56 per cent. And 84 per cent of the total petroleum products output is concentrated in the first twenty of the nation's 253 refining companies.[32] Industries such as aluminum and steel have much higher concentration ratios. Yet over the years independent refiners have been forced out by the cumulative economic power of the integrated companies. The uncertainty of obtaining crude, the inability to locate in the best spots because of the pipeline situation, patent tie-ups, competitively rooted technological changes such as the constant raising of octane ratings of gasoline, and the rapid obsolescence of equipment, the growth of automation, and the financial head start of the majors and their access to long-term capital are too formidable obstacles. Today there is only one independent refiner on the Atlantic seaboard.

In the main, the major companies share economic outlooks. They appreciate the nature and utility of big organization. They are frequently linked with one another and with other oil companies through stockholder and directorship interlocks and common banking institutions where the directors of the different firms sit. For example, Sinclair and Cities Service each own about 30 per cent of Richfield. The controlling interests in Tidewater and Skelly are held by J. Paul Getty. Gulf has purchased $120 million of the convertible debentures of the Union Oil Company of California. If it exercised its option to convert this to stock, Gulf would have approximately 23 per cent control of Union. In 1959 Phillips began to purchase Union common stock in an apparent effort to gain control of the California company. Members of the boards of Standard (New Jersey), Standard (Indiana), Standard of California, Gulf and Continental have served together as directors of the Chase Manhattan Bank. The latter is closely identified with the extensive oil-stock holdings of the Rockefeller family and also plays a major role in the financial affairs of many oil companies. Attorneys and directors of organizations such as the First National City Bank of New York, the New York Trust Company, the Guaranty Trust Company of New York, and the Central Hanover Bank and Trust Company provide avenues for communication.

The giants cooperate wherever possible. Joint exploration and drilling ventures that help spread risks are common. One of these, the C.A.T.C. Offshore Group, composed of the Continental Oil, Atlantic Refining, Tidewater Oil, and Cities Service companies, has invested over $100 million in the search for oil under the Gulf of Mexico. Joint pipeline ownership exists throughout the country. Regional price leadership has been developed. If the dominant company, or "major competitor," to use the language of the industry, sets a higher price on oil products, the rest of the companies will generally follow "to meet competition." In New England and New York the leader has been Socony; in New Jersey, Maryland, Virginia, West Virginia, North Carolina, South Carolina, Tennessee, Arkansas, and Louisiana it has been Esso; in Pennsylvania and Delaware, the Atlantic Refining Company; in Ohio, Standard of Ohio; in Kentucky, Alabama, Georgia, Florida, and Mississippi the leader has been Standard (Kentucky); in Texas, The Texas Company; in the Midwest, Standard (Indiana); and the Western states are divided between Continental and Standard of California. This has not been ironclad, for there have been times when price moves have not stuck or when there have been challenges to the leadership. But the pattern has been recognizable as a basic process in the private government of oil. Long-term purchasing contracts, exchanges of gasoline to save transportation costs, joint terminal arrangements, fair-trade agreements, collusive bidding, cooperative research, patent pooling, and restrictive licensing contracts are all economic practices that the industry has institutionalized over the years.

Until 1940 the Ethyl Corporation owned by Jersey Standard and the Du Pont-controlled General Motors served to police the pricing of all gasoline companies except Sun, which had its own process, through a monopoly of an antiknock compound that it sold to refiners. Among the conditions for franchise or license was the maintenance of a two-cent differential on the sale of so-called "premium" gasoline over regular. The M. W. Kellogg Company, engaged in oil research and engineering, has served as a licensing agency linking major oil companies and preserving patents and catalytic cracking techniques.[33]

Direct financial pressures upon small organizations which seek to pursue independent policies are also a familiar part of the majors' behavior, even if the means are more sophisticated than in the age of the senior Rockefeller. Rail freight-rate discrimination, presumably relegated to the ancient past of corporate ethics, is still employed, according to the Justice Department's antitrust suits. Legal harassments in the courts over patents infringements have been another device for hampering genuine independents.

Solidifying the bargaining power of these corporations are the relationships and camaraderie in oil with other vital centers of the economy. The Union Pacific, the Northern Pacific, the Southern Pacific, the Texas and Pacific, and the Atchison, Topeka and Sante Fe railroads have valuable oil and gas operations on their extensive land holdings. The Southern Pacific is building up an important pipeline system on the West Coast. As the laboratory has drawn chemical and petroleum knowledge closer together, working agreements with chemical corporations have increased. One of the first illustrations of this was the elaborately defined agreements between Germany's I. G. Farbenindustrie and Jersey Standard. In 1955 the Monsanto Chemical Corporation merged with Lion Oil to create a new integrated petrochemical organization with assets of over $500 million. Sun Oil is partner with Olin Mathieson Chemical Corporation (chemicals, drugs, metals, firearms) in Sun-Olin Chemical Company. Texaco has a partnership with American Cyanamid Company. Oil-chemical ties are also being developed in solid fuels as the industry moves into the highly profitable area of rocket technology. Gulf owns 50 per cent of the capital stock of Callery Chemical, which works with General Motors and Thiokol Chemical in the missile and space-travel field. North American Aviation and Phillips Oil, leaders in missile frame and engine technology, are owners of Astrodyne, Inc., which is developing solid fuels.

There are partnerships with the major rubber companies in producing synthetic rubber. Oil is linked with the sulphur monopoly. Humble works closely with Freeport Sulphur in developing valuable deposits. Texaco operates with the two largest companies, Freeport Sulphur and Texas Gulf Sulphur. The latter company is controlled by Gulf. In 1958 Freeport's board chairman, who was also a director of B. F. Goodrich Rubber, joined the board of Texaco. Research projects often cut across industry lines. Socony, for example, operates a nuclear reactor with United States Rubber, Corning Glass, Continental Can, Atlas Powder, and other industrial giants. Oil machinery, precision instruments, steel pipe, and other supply and construction corporations are directly dependent upon, linked with, or owned by the major oil companies. United States Steel advertising describes the company as engaged in research and manufacturing which places it "up to its ears in every phase of the petroleum business." In oil-producing regions, the economic and social relationships interlocking oil with the other power forces of the community are even more plainly visible. The banks are generally a good starting point for tracing the lines of power that bind oil operations of the smaller entrepreneurs.

It is true that marketing rivalries among the giants are intensifying. The dissolution of 1911 actually contributed to the subsequent monopolistic pattern by assigning the split Standard companies essentially noncompetitive areas for operation. Now, however, a number of the majors are moving toward nation-wide distribution under a single brand name. Jersey Standard has invaded Indiana's territory by buying out large marketers in Wisconsin, Illinois, and Indiana. Carter, another Jersey subsidiary, has expanded into the Northwest where Standard of California has ruled. To facilitate this quest for volume, Jersey has consolidated its major domestic subsidiaries, including Esso, Humble, and Carter, into a new Humble Oil and Refining Company of Delaware. Meanwhile, the Indiana and California Standard companies have entered the rich Eastern markets with their Amoco and Chevron products.

Yet the much heralded free choice of the consumer is based largely on individual dealer preferences or immediate needs while on the road rather than on any rational discrimination among brands. Gasoline, like diesel and heating fuel, is a standardized commodity, as in fact the compulsion for ever growing promises of more power, greater power, and finally total power through new supercolossal discoveries and distinctions reveals. All the force of the mass media is harnessed to dramatize the battles of brands and secret gasoline additives. The latter derive more certain support from oil advertising agencies than from petroleum engineers, with their virtue better established in marketing than in motoring. The motorist may be dazzled by the glitter of the much heralded "four stations to an intersection" which in industry literature is cited as proof positive of the competitive nature of the market place of oil. To some critics it has reflected a competitive waste ultimately paid for by the consumers and the struggling dealers. Harold L. Ickes used to say that service stations seem to be produced in litters. This was before the age of the modern turnpike with its carefully spaced gasoline stops, an arrangement sharply criticized by much of the industry. Studies by sources friendly to the industry have shown that about 70 per cent of dealers think the major brands are more or less alike, a heresy shared by their customers in roughly the same proportion.[34] Gasoline itself is, at least for the foreseeable future, noncompetitive. The motorist has no choice of fuels; he uses gasoline or he does not drive.

The tank-wagon prices of the major suppliers in an area generally move up and down in remarkable unison. Price differences at the pump, if any, are slim, and the average motorist cannot strengthen his buying position by stocking up. The industry, in turn, assumes that total demand is relatively constant and not affected by the lowering of prices. There have been periods of price competition in the selling of crude because of heavy production. In some cases this is reflected in price wars at the tank. Once the integrated majors become involved, they go all out to destroy independents and competitors able or willing to undersell by more than one or two cents, unless it happens that they themselves are dumping "surpluses" as unbranded gasoline in competition with their own and other major dealers. There is always the fear that even a small area of price flexibility introduces chaos and makes vulnerable the administered price structure. One standard practice has involved shifting losses from one operation to another so as to beat down any competition from intruding independents or cooperative movements. At times this involves raising the price of crude while cutting that of gasoline at the majors' service stations.

In New Jersey the aggressive entry of Calso has been a major factor in precipitating one such conflict. Its quest for a share of the rich trade of this "corridor" state upset the fixed retail prices. When this happens, explained the vice president of Esso, the marketing subsidiary of Standard Oil (New Jersey), which has about 30 per cent of the New Jersey market, "the consumer has what we may consider to be an undeserved break in his price." Esso was not doing business at a loss, he added, but it was not getting the fair profit to which it felt entitled. Dealers insist, however, that they are the ones who bear the brunt of these contests. "If the law of supply and demand is to work or does work in the oil industry as it does in any other industry," asked one dealer, "why doesn't the price drop where the oversupply is, in the crude end?" As a former gasoline-station operator and long-time head of retailers' associations described the invasion, "We became a battleground. The generals on . . . [one] side were the Standard Oil Company of California and on the other side were the majors who were firmly entrenched in the New Jersey market, Esso, Sun, Tydol, Texaco and Gulf, the principal ones. They held our coats while we fought it out." "If the companies want to fight for gallonage," echoed another dealer, "let them pay the bill and not give it to us." One veteran dealer with two stations on one-year leases from Esso, after fighting cheaper-priced gasoline from competitors selling unbranded gas from branded pumps secretly subsidized by the distributor, from stations operated directly by major companies, and finally from an Esso station with a cheaper source of supply, unavailable to him, concluded that "there is no place in New Jersey for free enterprise." The state's attorney general verified this picture. "The control of the supplier over his lessee, his dealer, is so stringent that . . . the words 'independent retailer' are a misnomer in the State of New Jersey." [35]

Private governments, no less than public ones, require order. The oil companies do not want this cutthroat fighting, and many dealers prefer fair-trade price fixing. From past evidence one could prophesy that these marketing invasions and rivalries were a prelude to the establishment of a new *modus vivendi* among the giants. Esso took the lead in establishing resale-price maintenance for its gasoline. With some reluctance the other majors followed, taking advantage of a state fair-trade law. Dealers who cooperate and survive will have more stable incomes, though no more independence. To improve morale—"one of our company's most pressing problems"—Esso has set up a court system with a pyramid of appellate bodies to adjudicate dealer complaints. "Our problems should be solved by free, frank and friendly discussions—not appeals to government." [36] Other companies have initiated comparable processes. Very much in mind is the possibility of federal intervention for the regulation of marketing practices, as happened in the automobile business when dealers were feeling pressed. In the view of one retailers' representative, however, "it is impossible for any gasoline dealer anywhere in the United States to hope to profit from his ingenuity. His welfare and his future are always in the hands of his supplier." [37] Some dealers insist that black lists are maintained among the companies to keep "trouble makers" from getting leases. Meanwhile, it is estimated that as high as one-third of the nation's service-station operators go out of business each year.

The numerous regional and functional trade organizations all serve to reinforce these patterns of control. At the apex of the associational pyramid is the American Petroleum Institute. It was founded in 1919 out of a decision by major company leaders to establish on a permanent basis the useful intercorporate alliance developed during the World War I mobilization. As stated in its charter, the purposes are:

(a) To afford a means of cooperation with the government in all matters of national concern; and

(b) To foster foreign and domestic trade in American petroleum products; and

(c) To promote in general the interest of the petroleum industry in all its branches; and

(d) To promote the mutual improvement of its members and the study of the arts and sciences connected with the petroleum industry.[38]

The API serves as the meeting ground for some eight thousand individual members from most segments of the industry. Its divisions of activities—production, refining, marketing, transportation, finance and accounting, governmental and public relations (American Petroleum Industries Committee and Oil Information Committee, now merged into a Committee on Public Affairs)—parallel the structure of the integrated companies. There are special and standing committees for research and discussion in every phase of oil operation and interest, from asphalt and agriculture to safety and the United Nations. Much of the research is technical, and a list of published projects includes *The Mechanism of the Displacement of Oil from Porous Materials, Study of Near-Shore Recent Sediments and Their Environments in the Northern Gulf of Mexico* and *Fundamentals of Hydrocarbon Behavior*. But there is also a continuing concern with fundamentals of national oil policy and the behavior of governmental agencies in Washington and in state capitals.

The policies, financial contributions, and leadership are clearly dominated by the large oil companies. Statements of position generally echo their interests. Some union officials have contended that the API has been a vehicle for getting agreement on roughly uniform contracts throughout the nation during negotiations. At one time they sought to have the association banned from Texas, showing special resentment against its promotion of paternalism. The majors have employed this practice with considerable success, and it is undoubtedly a factor in the difficulties of the labor movement in this industry. Nonintegrated oilmen sometimes look upon the API as another arm of the giants, especially those with overseas reserves. Dealer and jobber representatives periodically express skepticism as to the nature of API's interest in the service-station operator, in whose name so much of oil associational and propaganda activity is advanced. For example, in commenting on the tensions in retailing, an *API Quarterly* article has said that "charges such as these—if true —would indeed be evidence of a sick industry. They would, in fact, testify to an illness spreading beyond the retail gasoline business. If the 181,000 men and women who operate service stations are willing to live their business lives in the conditions of near-servitude suggested, something in our national character would seem to have drastically changed." It reminded the dealer that generally, "with limited capital of his own, he is, in effect, given a business worth up to $50,000 or more to walk into or run. It would appear obvious that the supplier has a big stake in that dealer's success." Fortunately, however, the ways of private enterprise are still safe. The API's major members had found the answer through the new grievance machinery. In the happy language of contemporary social analysis:

It wasn't too long before suppliers began to realize that the chief source of difficulty was, quite simply, a terrible communications problem. Too often, dealer and supplier were operating on different wave lengths. Where dealers understood company policies, the majority were in agreement with them.[39]

The Institute's board of directors has over 135 oilmen, and reflects the range of membership. The much smaller executive committee comes mainly from the integrated firms. Following the practice of big business associations, in 1955 the API chose as its chairman an independent producer, Jake L. Hamon. The first such oilman to hold this office, he had previously been president of the Texas Mid-Continent Oil and Gas Association and then the general Mid-Continent Oil and Gas Association and also a director of the Independent Petroleum Association of America and of the API. The nominations committee that selected the chairman consisted of officials from leading oil companies and Mr. Hamon. In 1957, six of the nine officers, who headed the organization with the chairman, were leaders of major companies. Five of these six individuals also served as chairmen of the major divisions, with another Shell executive heading the sixth area of public relations. The remaining three officers were from the API, which employed a staff of several hundred led by a salaried president. In 1957 President H. S. M. Burns of Shell was elected chairman and in 1959 he was succeeded by M. J. Rathbone, president of Jersey Standard.

Once referred to as "the switchboard for the controlling companies" in a report to the President by Clarence Darrow on the workings of the National Recovery Administration, the API along with the major oil companies subsequently was the target of a comprehensive antitrust suit.[40] The federal government charged the API and its various committees with "promoting, supervising and enforcing policies, programs, practices and activities" of the big oil companies that were "designed to restrict the production of crude oil and petroleum products, to establish and maintain sales prices for petroleum and its products, to manipulate prices in order to restrict or eliminate competition among the independents, to deprive others of a fair opportunity to compete freely and unrestrictedly" with the big companies, and to enable the latter "to dominate, control and monopolize the petroleum industry in all its phases. . . . All of the integrated companies operate as one unit under substantially identical business policies and practices." [41]

The industry and the Institute have denied these allegations vigorously. There is evidence that some of the more obvious pricing practices of the API have been abandoned. And in a fundamental sense, the understanding of the industry's success as a private government can become distorted by looking simply for structural evidence of collusion, as important a tool as the trade association is. Increasingly the problem is more a matter of mutuality than of conspiracy.

Critics maintain, however, that most of the collusive activities enumerated in this "Mother Hubbard" suit are still pertinent. But with the outbreak of World War II, the suit disintegrated in face of the insistence of the economic and military planners—and their industry advisers—that oil cooperation toward solving the staggering supply requirements for defeating the Axis must take priority. Oil leaders made clear their feeling that such suits constituted harassment on a scale that impeded their operations. To break up or even disturb this integrated organization that was to fuel the hundreds of thousands of planes, tanks, and ships that the American industrial system was to be called upon to produce seemed like national madness. As Donald M. Nelson, the Sears, Roebuck executive who headed the defense and war-armaments program explained, they were not trying to protect industry against antitrust suits. "We had a one-track mind and over that track ran the production express which couldn't afford to be late." [42] Similar considerations helped bring about the pipeline-suit settlement.

The Mother Hubbard case was opened again after hostilities ceased, but the combination of its overwhelming nature (there were more than 350 defendants), the studied delaying tactics of the industry, and the relative indifference of responsible public officials led the Justice Department to shift its tactics. The number of defendants was cut sharply, and the original suit was divided into segments. Only fragments of the original charges have been pursued, and these have focused heavily upon the relation of service-station dealers to the majors. The most important action has been against the companies dominating the Pacific Coast area. The government's complaint has held that seven major companies there produce 50 per cent of the crude oil and are the purchasers of almost all independently produced oil. Pipelines, tankers, barges, refining and marketing capacity are almost completely in their hands. The government has sought divorcement of production, refining, and transportation from marketing ownership. In 1959—nine years after the suit was filed—a consent-decree settlement with six of the defendants enjoined them from price fixing and certain discriminatory practices. But the government abandoned its demand that the companies divest themselves of their retail outlets. In 1958 the federal government charged that Kentucky Standard and Jersey Standard had an agreement requiring the former to purchase 80 per cent of its petroleum products from Esso, while guaranteeing the territorial sovereignty of each company in its respective marketing area.[43]

There are some sharp differences and conflicts within oildom. Independent producers, jobbers, and dealers are frequently vocal in their dissatisfaction with the economic power of the giants in forcing policies on such issues as unified development of fields, imports, and prices. This dissension generally provokes fervent appeals for unity from major spokesmen. The president of the Shell Oil Company warned an American Petroleum Institute convention in 1955 that such practices invited their own destruction: "I have been given to understand that the Department of Justice gets more complaining letters and telegrams which urge action against one or another segment of the oil industry than it does in respect to all other industries put together. . . . I should be willing to bet that, of these complaints, nearly every one comes from within the industry itself." The alternative to the chaos that once characterized oil or to government regimentation was business statesmanship. Differences were to be settled away from public view by the industry itself:

Do not think for a minute that I am pleading the case of only the integrated oil companies or fearing their possible dismemberment. What I fear for is the industry as a whole. . . . The oil industry as a whole is essentially integrated. That does not mean that there is only room in the industry for integrated companies; far from it. The fact that there are some companies which have chosen to invest their capital in most or all of the phases of the oil industry does, in fact, establish a sort of framework on which the nonintegrated units can build themselves and gain support, just as roses grow on a pergola.[44]

When the chips are down, the dissenters generally do go along with the industry leaders; for while they recognize the extent to which they exist by sufferance with the majors possessing the power to destroy many of the oil businesses, through them these "independents" still see their hope of making a living and perhaps getting their share of fabulous profits in black gold. The giants, in turn, are mindful of the value of the existence of smaller businesses in dispelling charges of oligopoly and fears as to the survival of a democratic society.

John D. Rockefeller, Sr., felt that the old Standard Oil trust was a pioneer in modern economic administration. "The day of combination is here to stay. Individualism has gone, never to return." [45] With the size and economic power of the modern industry, there has since developed a domestic system reinforced by customs and rules checking what is called "the extremes of individualism." Corporations are linked by "orderly marketing practices" and a sympathetic social climate that becomes the ultimate point of integration. As one National Petroleum Council official summed up while observing a parade of complaining witnesses appearing before a congressional price-increase investigation during the summer of 1953, "These guys are fools. Price wars—that's not the big companies—that's private enterprise."

4

Toward World Government

The economics of oil, like the needs of modern industrial society, transcend national boundaries. In Western Europe crude production is scant; and although there is far less dependence on petroleum than in the United States, it ranks as the largest single import. In America the accelerating rate of consumption has accentuated the relentless search for new sources of supply. Intensive leasing, exploration and drilling efforts are carried on in Canada, Latin America, the Middle and Far East and Africa by the older industrial powers and their corporate representatives. Oil is a finite and nonreplaceable resource. But the vast reserves thus far unearthed have eased, if not eradicated, fears of any imminent end to the world's supply. In 1945, for example, global reserves were estimated at under one hundred billion barrels, while in 1959 petroleum geologists accepted 290 billion barrels as a conservative calculation of the pools of oil they considered economically recoverable. Two-thirds of this was believed to be in the Middle East. Kuwait was credited with 60 billion barrels and Saudi Arabia with 50 billion. Iran had 35 billion and Iraq had 25. Communist areas were assigned 30 billion barrels and Venezuela 18. Reserves in the United States were generally set at about 33 billion barrels.

There are variations in the estimates, and many believe that the figures are actually considerably higher than the oil companies care to indicate. Wallace E. Pratt, an internationally respected geologist who formerly worked for Jersey Standard, has concluded from his own studies and questioning within the industry that there are over 300 billion barrels of proved reserves in the non-Communist areas of the world. The major difference is explained by new data on the

Middle East, and to a lesser extent by improved techniques for recovery. This means that three-fourths of the world's known oil lies in this politically tense region. To these estimates must be added 1,250 billion barrels of oil that are generally regarded as ultimately recoverable. Of this, 250 billion barrels are within the United States. These totals do not include the abundant oil shales.

In 1959 the United States provided about 43 per cent of the non-Communist world's supply of crude oil, and Venezuela produced 16 per cent. The Middle Eastern countries produced 27 per cent, increasing from 10 per cent in 1946. During the same period production in the United States rose over 50 per cent, but its percentage of the total dropped from nearly 70 per cent to its current 43 per cent. It appears obvious that as demand increases with rising living standards, the Middle East will become the major source of supply of natural crude.[1]

Seven integrated enterprises dominate the international oil scene. Holding at least two-thirds of the world's proved reserves, they also control the bulk of world production, refining, and cracking. The major pipeline systems are in their hands. The tanker fleets are largely at their command, regardless of ownership. The Royal Dutch/Shell Group (Royal Dutch Petroleum Company and Shell Transport and Trading Company, Ltd.), which has extensive holdings in the United States, is British- and Dutch-controlled. Its assets are about $8.5 billion, making it the world's largest non-American private industrial organization. The British Petroleum Company, Ltd., formerly known as the Anglo-Iranian Oil Company, is a British organization with assets of over $2 billion. It controls over 20 per cent of world oil reserves. A majority of the shares are government-owned. This arrangement dates back to the beginning of World War I when First Lord of the Admiralty Winston Churchill insisted that the Navy must own or control its own oil supplies, while warning that "to commit the Navy irrevocably to oil was indeed 'to take arms against a sea of troubles.' "[2]

The five American giants, Standard (New Jersey), Socony Mobil, Gulf, Texas, and Standard of California, began to make their serious overseas ventures in the early twenties. Spurred on by rising domestic costs, fears on the part of government and industry officials about war shortages, and their own alarm over the prospects of complete foreign domination of new crude sources, these corporations proceeded to extend their empires wherever oil was found or marketed where they could gain an entry. In 1959 the American companies had a gross investment in overseas fixed assets estimated at $9 billion. Their contracts covered 64 per cent or more of the proved reserves of the Middle East, where they had perhaps $2 billion invested. The British and Dutch companies had 31 per cent. The Americans also control 70 per cent of production in Canada, where output has leaped from 21,000 barrels a day in 1946 to 508,000 in 1959, and production is at half-capacity because of marketing difficulties. They also account for 68 per cent of Venezuela's production.[3]

Corporate profits are heavily dependent upon this plentiful and cheaply produced foreign crude. In 1946, for example, oil from Bahrein was estimated to cost $0.25 per barrel to produce, including a $0.15 royalty to the local ruler. It was selling at $1.05 and more at the Persian Gulf. Oil from Kuwait, produced for less than $0.10 a barrel, has sold for $1.85. A study by the Secretariat of the United Nations Economic Commission for Europe in 1955 calculated that the net profit on a barrel of Saudi Arabian oil selling at $1.75 was $1.40. That year the American-owned Arabian American Oil Company netted about $272 million on its 300-million-barrel crude production operation alone, after paying a comparable sum as royalty and taxes to Ibn Saud.[4] A full profit picture would have to include the total earnings from the handling of this oil in all the stages from wellhead to consumer. About 80 per cent of the Jersey Standard corporation's crude oil production and about 75 per cent of its net income are derived from its overseas investments. (Jersey has access to reserves equal to the total proved reserves within the United States.) Creole in Venezuela is the company's greatest single source of revenue. Two-thirds of Gulf's income is derived from foreign operations.

With these discoveries of new crude supplies have come new economic challenges. The original fear of scarcity is supplanted in industry minds by the specter of uncontrolled plenty. For where the average American well produces less than 15 barrels per day, the average output in the Middle East is around 5,000 barrels. On a daily average during April 1956, the 175 flowing wells of Kuwait, a sheikdom not much larger than Connecticut, were producing one-sixth of the daily yield of the United States' 500,000 wells. **Saudi Arabia's 164 wells** provided over one million barrels a day that month. An appreciable increase of supply anywhere on this globe can disturb existing price levels, just as even a relatively small amount of independently and competitively refined oil can upset established marketing patterns. Yet new reserves must be sought constantly for future needs.

In this setting the giants have learned to appreciate their areas of mutual self-interest, just as they have recognized the costliness of much rivalry, whether for the markets of China or the fields of Mexico. Under the guidance of older European hands who had few illusions about the benefits or rationality of free competitive enterprise, the oilmen have negotiated for the establishment of codes for orderly behavior. The American members were and remain publicly indignant over a description of such arrangements as cartels. But the controls they had previously established in Venezuela and elsewhere in Latin America suggest that they were somewhat less than innocents abroad in relation to monopoly. And they were eager to get a stake in the exclusive leases and relationships in the East. From this situation there evolved the framework of the private international government of oil.

Through a series of "treaties," the international companies marked off regions as open, closed, or postponed for concessions, and developed patterns of cooperation in obtaining leases and in drilling. The most notable of these apportioned petroleum rights within a red line drawn around Iraq and the Arabian Peninsula areas of the old Turkish Empire broken up in World War I. Through this 1928 agreement Jersey and Socony joined Anglo-Persian, Royal Dutch/ Shell and Compagnie Française des Pétroles in ownership of the nonprofit Turkish Petroleum Company and control of what was then believed to be the richest Middle Eastern oil plum. Gulf, at that time partners with Jersey and Socony in the Near East Development Company and hence a tentative adherent to the agreement, turned over to Standard of California its option rights to explore in the Persian Gulf islands of Bahrein, since it was not supposed to have individual concessions in this area.[5] Monopolistic grants from feudal potentates are shared and individual operations have been converted into joint affairs, as was done, for example, by Jersey

Standard, Gulf, and Shell in Venezuela. Such treaties are favored for keeping any one company from gaining too much of an advantage in reserves while, at the same time, they serve to present a united non-competitive front to the governments involved as well as to "outside" oil interests. Widespread joint ownership of affiliates also provides meeting places for planning concerted action. When Standard of California, which was outside the "red line" pact, found oil in Bahrein and then moved to drill in Saudi Arabia, the other giants sought, over a period of years, to bring this oil within their operating control. California eventually sold a half-interest to The Texas Company in return for an equivalent portion of the latter's marketing facilities east of Suez. Standard of California and Texaco share ownership of a large cluster of subsidiaries in Europe and Asia. Together with Jersey Standard and Socony, who bought into the Saudi Arabian holdings, thus providing additional markets for the Arabian flow, they also own the Arabian American Oil Company (Aramco) and the Trans-Arabian Pipe Line Company (Tapline). Jersey, Shell, Socony, and the British Petroleum Company own the Iraq Petroleum Company and its subsidiaries. Gulf and British Petroleum are directly linked through ownership of the Kuwait Oil Company. Royal Dutch/ Shell is Gulf's largest single customer for Kuwait production. Socony and Jersey are the parents of the Near East Development Company with installations in Europe, Africa, and Asia. A "consortium" of the big seven now operates the Iranian government's facilities in a complicated manner arrived at after a three-year impasse created by ex-Premier Mossadegh's nationalization of the facilities of the long-resented Anglo-Iranian Oil Company. British Petroleum retains a 40 per cent interest. Each of the American companies has 7 per cent. Shell has 14, and Compagnie Française des Pétroles has 6. A final 5 per cent is split among eight other American companies acting through the Iricon Agency, Ltd. This latter feature was added in response to the strong protests to the American government by several smaller American companies. It served also to take the onus off an apparent government sponsorship of a cartel-like organization.

The list of such ownerships is a long one, and made complex by many interlocking ties among affiliates. After studying a map of the world of oil and the tables of organization of the companies, one gains a rough appreciation of the problems of big government, whether public or private. And one can understand the admission of Socony's board chairman who, when asked about certain affiliates in Australia, Japan, and Madagascar, replied, "There are a lot of our companies in which we own interests directly that I don't have knowledge of. . . ." [6] Generally, the negotiations for arriving at these relationships have been protracted and involved, suggesting the intricacy of oil diplomacy. But the over-all objectives and resulting patterns remain constant and clear.

Perhaps the most famous of the attempts to stabilize marketing in the oil world was the Achnacarry agreement of 1928. Here the heads of the big three of international oil—Shell, Anglo-Iranian, and Jersey—formulated the principles of a mutual security program for the acceptance of the industry:

Up to the present, each large unit has tried to take care of its own overproduction and tried to increase its sales at the expense of someone else. The effect has been destructive rather than constructive competition, resulting in much higher operating costs. [7]

Their Pool Association agreement then proposed "the acceptance by the units of their present volume of business and their proportion of any future increases in consumption." Existing facilities of all adherents to this "as is" pact were to be made available to one another at lower costs than new construction for exclusive use would require, but not lower than actual costs to the owner. The duplication of facilities was to be avoided and new ones were to be built only when there was an increase in demand. Geographic divisions of markets were to be respected and reinforced with supplies to be drawn from the nearest producing area. The agreement also sought to keep prices in a given geographic area noncompetitive. Surplus production (that is, production in excess of the estimated market demand at industry prices) was to be checked to preclude the possibility of dumping. Competitive practices that would increase costs or prices were to be avoided. Thus new reserves as well as demand were to be integrated within the existing oil system.

Presumably because of the danger of American participants running into the antitrust laws and adverse public opinion, direct American markets and trade were excluded from this written charter. Nevertheless it was anticipated that the United States oil operations would be bound to the new world government. For this agreement had a direct impact on the economic performance of the integrated industry leaders of the United States whose overseas activities were included. The domestic policies of these corporations, their joint export programs, their trade association efforts, and the industry-wide "conservation" measures were to provide the key links.

The specific instruments for implementing the Achnacarry agreement were complex; they required an administrative structure for handling information and facilitating the exchange of supplies, the pooling of transportation, and the operation of a multiple basing point system that would keep the price of crude oil uniformly low for cartel members. Meanwhile, Gulf-plus prices were to continue to govern the world market for nonmembers. This made possible a single delivered price in any given market for comparable grades of petroleum and petroleum products, regardless of geographic source, based on the published prices of the higher cost of American products, f.o.b. Gulf of Mexico ports. These prices, justified on the grounds that the United States has been the largest consumer and exporter, actually have been greater than those the majors generally pay for American oil in their contractual or integrated relationships. This artificial price pegging, coupled with the "phantom" freight frequently involved, has made for tremendous profit on the more cheaply produced Caribbean and Middle Eastern oil.

The ambition of its scope led the authors of the Federal Trade Commission staff report on *The International Petroleum Cartel* and other trained observers to conclude that Achnacarry was more a statement of broad objectives than a working blueprint for complete world control. The plans were subsequently modified and implemented by separate corporate alliances and local marketing pacts. Quotas were redefined. The "as is" agreement was broadened and tightened under the jurisdiction of separate "as is" committees in charge of supply and distribution sitting in New York and London. Intention of price changes required advance notice and discussion among participants. Competitive measures such as advertising were to be curbed, and economic sanctions were to be applied against violaters of the agreements.

Four world-wide developments during the thirties challenged the effectiveness of those plans. The discovery of fields in America and the Middle East with enormous reserves brought new participants rushing onto the oil scene. The great depression came at the same time, and the pivotal United States prices went plummeting as privately controlled pricing became difficult. The focus upon recovery and reform efforts everywhere forced public governments into more active participation in the economic arena. Help was extended to stricken industries, but with the ever present potential of investigation, public accountability, and regulation. In the United States the scarcity-oriented practices of economic "royalists" were viewed as a root factor in bringing about the depressed conditions. And finally, with the outbreak of World War II, public planning of resources became an unchallenged matter of survival as the nations involved intensified measures for assuring themselves of adequate supplies. Many of the formal cartel arrangements of the world oil government ended in the face of these demands upon national loyalty. From the perspective of the European nations, the world's production center had shifted from the Western Hemisphere to the Middle East. Under governmental pressures prices were lowered as Gulf-plus was modified and the Persian Gulf came to be recognized as a second basing point. This meant some saving for the importing countries, but the price system fundamentally remained tied to the United States standard despite the sharp percentage decline of its exports in world trade. In the United States, disclosure of Jersey Standard's restrictive patent tie-ups with Germany's I. G. Farben provoked great if short-lived public indignation, and the corporation signed a consent decree pledging itself not to become involved in price, production, or patent agreements in the future.

American oilmen have repeatedly insisted that the era of cartels, if it ever existed, has passed. In 1946 Jersey and Socony successfully challenged as restraints of trade some of the "red line" limitations they had accepted for so long. "There has been a substantial change in the attitude of the American public and Government toward restrictive agreements . . . ," explained Jersey.[8] Sensitivity to popular opinion undoubtedly was a growing business consideration in oil's postwar planning, especially in the Jersey corporation. But this particular action was less a conversion to faith in antitrust or loyalty to the teachings of public relations than in Jersey's determination to move into Saudi Arabia where oil was becoming more attractive, and to do this without its foreign associates.

The decision-making power that goes with bigness and integration remains. The tie-ups among the majors, reinforced by such practices as long-term buying contracts and world-wide patent-pooling licensing, continue. There are parallel movements of prices. Divisions of territories and functions are still respected. Legislative investigations in the United States and abroad, the Federal Trade Commission's cartel report, antitrust suits, and the United Nations study all document the continuing mechanism of monopolistic control of price and supply by the big seven.

When Iran oil was nationalized there was talk of a world shortage. This had been the largest Middle Eastern crude source and Abadan the world's largest refinery. But oildom quickly stepped up production elsewhere in the Middle East to fill the gap. Premier Mossadegh discovered that, thanks to an economic blockade by the giant oil companies and the prohibitive financial requirements of the undertaking for smaller companies or cooperatives, he could not market his oil in meaningful quantities. The issue was not resolved until the summer of 1954 when, with the aid and urging of the American and British governments, the industry and the successors to the overthrown Mossadegh negotiated an agreement for the gradual reabsorption of the Iranian flow into oil markets. This was to be done "in an orderly manner" by meeting the anticipated annual increase in world demand without upsetting the new equilibrium and current prices.

Meanwhile, in April 1953, the Attorney General of the United States replaced a criminal suit based on the cartel report and similar data with a comprehensive civil suit before a federal court. This charged the American international oil interests with continuing their restrictive practices in every aspect of the industry—from exploration to research. Their unlawful combination and conspiracy for the monopolization of products and maintenance of prices harmed American consumers. Domestic production was curtailed through their power to manipulate imports and restrict exports. Competition in foreign markets was eliminated. Even the government was subject to its powers:

Pursuant to a request for bids on crude oil on February 10, 1950 by the Armed Services Petroleum Purchasing Agency of the United States Government, defendants Jersey, Socony, Gulf, Socal and Texas, directly and through subsidiaries and jointly owned companies, submitted identical bids of $1.75 per barrel f.o.b. the Persian Gulf. Likewise, on a similar invitation for bids for crude oil dated May 29, 1950 by the Armed Services Petroleum Purchasing Agency, defendants Jersey, Socony, Texas and Socal, and Caltex, submitted identical bids of $1.75 per barrel f.o.b. Ras Tanura.[9]

As always, the American oil replies to such allegations are couched in the accepted idioms of "free enterprise" and "higher type of competition." The Texas Company, for example, told the court that the charges were "completely at variance with the whole spirit and purpose" of its enterprise. The interchanges of property and territories and the close working relations with Standard of California (Socal) and other companies had meant progress for Caltex—"the substitution of a strong integrated organization for the separate, unintegrated and comparatively weak organizations out of which it grew."

Texas, from the date of its origin in 1902, has been an aggressive and independent company acting competitively in the best interest of its stockholders (now numbering over 120,000). Any transaction between it and any other oil company has been for the sole purpose of advancing that interest and not for the purpose of creating a monopoly or restricting competition.[10]

Socony's answer was that "instead of being pursuant to a world-wide plan and agreement to monopolize and throttle commerce," its record of international cooperation had been "the very result of competition." Deriving from a need for crude supplies for its vast marketing organization that would place it "in a position to survive and compete" with the fully integrated world companies, these activities reflected the "dynamic character" of the industry.[11] In 1960, Gulf and Jersey entered into a consent judgment that prohibited future agreements to fix prices, divide markets, or allocate production with any competitors in the world market. Both companies declared that the agreement would not upset their practices.

In its original defense, the Gulf Oil Corporation simply denied the truth or knowledge of practically every allegation.[12] A Gulf statement of a somewhat different sort before a Swedish investigating committee in 1946 is more pertinent:

Hitherto, to the best of our knowledge, it has never been considered reprehensible for businessmen within a particular business to meet for discussions of mutual interests for the purpose of bringing order in the market. Insofar as the oil companies have tried to realize a somewhat uniform price level, the elimination of extra rebates, a reduction of the number of distributing points, etc., all this must be considered permissible and reasonable. . . . If in one point or another there has been achieved a regulation, it has never been unfair or uneconomical for the consumers. Considered objectively, it can never be wrong to maintain uniform prices and conditions for gasoline which for the most part is a standard product. Had the prices been set too high, or if any other criticism were to be made about the other conditions, then there would be an excuse for fault finding.[13]

And a Standard of New Jersey analysis submitted in 1955 to the Attorney General's National Committee to Study the Antitrust Laws suggested a fundamental difficulty faced by the international companies in securing oil for the American nation:

We in the United States are dedicated to a free competitive economy. In this respect, however, the United States is virtually alone among the nations of the world. At the other extreme stands state socialism which completely repudiates the free enterprise system that we wish to preserve. Between this and our system is the intermediate ground taken by many nations which encourage private enterprise but also permit and frequently insist upon cooperative action among members of industry to "rationalize" competition. In such nations quotas, price agreements, market allocations and the like are not only legal; they are regarded as necessary mechanisms to temper what are considered to be excessive and undesirable competitive pressures.

When in the Middle East or Europe, one had to follow Middle Eastern or European patterns. To impose antitrust assumptions on transactions beyond American borders was to penalize the companies involved and offend other sovereign nations:

Most Western business methods and concepts are without meaning in the Middle East. The corporation was unknown there until very recent years. Local business is conducted according to ancient Islamic law supplemented by the dictates of monarchs, like the late King Ibn Saud, who has been described as a "desert prophet, not a modern or even a medieval man but one of the last great figures of the Old Testament." In the end, it is monarchs such as he who determine the nature of the economic and political institutions of the countries. Once the method by which oil is to be produced has been elected by the monarch, it is impossible to believe that he will abandon that method because of a United States court's view that it is not compatible with a competitive economy.

Thus, regardless of action taken by our courts, the joint producing venture will doubtless remain in the Middle East. The British, the Dutch, and the French, the Iraquis, and the Saudi Arabs will see to that. We would accomplish nothing except great harm to ourselves by insisting that American companies comply with standards to which their foreign competitors are in no way obligated to adhere. This would simply straitjacket American companies in their oil operations in the Middle East and put them at a disadvantage with foreign concerns which are free to deal with Middle East countries according to the wishes of those countries. It may in the end lead to the forced withdrawal of American business interests from operations in those countries with all the damage to the interests of the United States which that would entail.

The fact that the United States cannot, through the medium of its antitrust laws, effectively deal with business conditions in the Middle East states where the ventures operate does not leave it powerless to prevent conduct prejudicial to United States interests. This country is at all times free to employ its immense political power and prestige through diplomatic channels to persuade the Middle East governments to recognize legitimate United States interests in Middle East petroleum. But persuasion through the State Department is one thing; it is quite another for the United States to institute under its laws judicial proceedings in which intimate internal affairs of the Middle East states are exposed in public litigation and made the subject of attempted control by a United States court.[14]

In a fundamental sense, then, this is the case for what one executive once referred to as the "brotherhood of oil merchants." They have developed the capital reserves to provide energy for growing technological needs. In an industry with the experience as well as the potential for competitive waste, instability, and even chaos, there has been established a functional peace among presumably sovereign corporate units that is world-wide and flexible.

They do not always agree and there is distrust. Conflicting national pulls, as between the British and American governments in the Middle East where the former has long played an active and direct role in formulating oil policy, at times keep unity tenuous within the empire of oil. At times individual companies, such as British Petroleum, feel the great need to accelerate their sale of crude. One can also exaggerate the omniscience of oil management, forgetting that much of their power derives from their sitting atop a basic energy resource that the industrial world wants and for which it has to pay tribute. They are not supermen, and their supercorporations do make miscalculations. Their price controls are not perfect. Then too, the current search for overseas reserves by aggressive "smaller" companies, acutely sensitive to present and future crude oil needs—and hence susceptible to the tougher contractual demands of producing countries—does upset the supply picture and profit margins. Since much of this oil is prevented from entering the United States, it may be offered at less than the going price set by the majors in world markets by companies pressed to recoup their investments.

The Soviet Union's stepped-up trade drive also poses a potential challenge to the world government of oil. In 1959 Russia began a seven year plan for the expansion of its petroleum industry, and it is replacing Venezuela as the world's second-ranking oil producer. The small but growing exports that Russia offers on attractive discount or barter terms are finding their way into many countries, including Italy, Sweden, Brazil, Cuba, and Japan. India, for example, which needs oil for basic economic development and is pressed for hard currency to pay for oil, has used Russian prices, along with technical and financial aid, as levers to force the international companies operating in India to reduce their prices. Producing countries, in turn, have resented such price cuts, made without their consultation, and see themselves as the losers. By chartering idle Western tankers the Soviet Union also rocks the artificial transportation pricing system. Jersey Standard, Standard of California, and several other companies warned that they would black-list tanker owners or brokers who leased to the USSR. This threat was made public after the regime of Fidel Castro had seized Texaco, Shell, and Jersey refineries subsequent to their refusal to process Russian oil, as demanded by Cuba, in place of some of the higher-priced Venezuelan crude of the private companies. The Russian oil, bartered for sugar, was shipped in European tankers. American oilmen are impressed by the Russian industry, and some have sought their government's "diplomatic representation" to advise allies against dealing with the disrupters. Meanwhile, some international oil officials feel that the wisest solution is to accept Russia's right to a share of the market and thus let business sense lead the Communists into the brotherhood of oil.

There is the precedent and machinery for private adjudication along lines of mutual advantage within the industry. The integrated companies with overseas installations have to chart a foreign policy that will enable them to utilize cheaper Eastern oil while not discouraging home production or depressing their own domestic prices. They have to be sensitive to the real pressures for high royalties coming from feudal rulers riding the nationalistic wave and from American independent producers riding the politically potent free enterprise bandwagon for high prices. If admittedly prices are artificially pegged, the London *Economist* reasoned in reviewing the United Nations Economic Commission report, the alternatives of "depressed prices, dismay and anger in the Middle East, and delay to the progress and economic benefit that oil has conferred on Western Europe" could be deplorable. "There is much that is not diabolical in the present price arrangements and they are at least the Devil that everyone knows." [15]

One might also argue that the industry leaders are generally wise enough not to set prices as high as oil's economic power might allow. Price increases were quickly instituted in 1957 during the Suez Canal closing. Again, one could also note that the industry's private government was able to redeploy its global facilities so that Europe could receive most of her oil needs. There was a good price for this service paid by consumers and their governments. But as oil men reminded their critics, that is how private enterprise works. And with justifiable pride they could underscore the conviction that in oil it does work— even if the "it" is a very different apparatus than that described in their advertisements or in the literature of capitalism. It is also significant that in the calm after the European oil lift, the British Petroleum Company raised the prices of its Persian Gulf crude. Other

Middle Eastern producers were expected to follow "to meet competition." This action in the direction of bringing Middle Eastern prices in line with those of the Western Hemisphere served to protect the gains made during Suez while toning down the demands of American producers without overseas reserves. The latter, having won their crude increase, now feared the competition of cheaper overseas crude, and were seeking more stringent import controls.

In the planning of oil leaders, United States oil was destined to serve primarily the needs of its own country, with the amount regulated in relation to increasing imports from Venezuela and other Caribbean centers which no longer are major suppliers of Europe. These prices would remain closely linked with those at the Gulf of Mexico. Europe was to receive its crude oil from the Middle East. (Discoveries in North Africa have modified this arrangement somewhat. But while transportation costs are lower, discovery costs in Algeria and Libya are considerably greater than in the Middle East.) Prices were to remain balanced within a range that kept Middle Eastern oil priced high enough so that Caribbean oil could enter Western Europe and low enough to allow Middle Eastern crude to be transported to United States Atlantic Coast markets when necessary. The producing areas of the world were to be noncompetitive with one another in terms of price. Marketing areas were to remain apportioned so that the Middle Eastern refineries owned by the giants would supply petroleum products to Eastern countries, the postwar European refineries would take care of that continent's needs, and the Western Hemisphere would get its products from North American and Caribbean refineries. Thus, while the American government was in a quandary as to how to reconcile conflicting political pressures over imports with national needs, and countries like England were struggling for the survival of their economies, if not their empires, the government of oil was moving imperfectly but with purpose to redress the grievances of its constituents and maintain the rationale of its system. Reflecting on the live-and-let-live arrangements of international oil, A. A. Berle in 1954 observed that "as an experiment in world economic government, the corporations cannot on this record be accused of failure.[16]

5

Private Planning and Public Resources

The oil industry has learned that survival on its terms depends on its ability to plan. Its history is an evolution of experimentation with techniques for creating order, whether the immediate challenge has been waste, competition, scarcity, depression, plenty, technology, war, or national boundaries.

Industry leaders understand the power and the potential of the modern state as an instrument for public control or private control. Their governing principle is that all planning for the future of petroleum and competitive resources must be private, without regulation or restriction upon the industry's normal activities. "If the dead hand of government should descend upon us," predicted the president of the Continental Oil Company in presenting to the American Petroleum Institute a report on the long-term availability of oil, "we would find our production retarded and it would be the beginning of the end of the oil industry as we know it." [1]

In oil industry councils are discussed the statehood of Alaska, mineral leasing rights in Montana, crop-utility research of the United States Department of Agriculture and nuclear development programs of the Atomic Energy Commission. The industry wishes to be the arbiter of when and where government assumes responsibility affecting oil. If any action is taken, the industry demands an active role in policy and administration.

The oil industry has under lease one-fourth of the land area of the United States. It is sensitive to the behavior of the largest landowner, the federal government, which owns more than one-fifth of the nation's total land area. Most of this public land is in the Western states, and much of this has heretofore been regarded as arid, rugged, and commercially worthless, helping to explain why it has been kept under public control. The oil industry wants to see public lands developed, that is, drilled or at least staked out, not just held by the state and federal governments. Coming on the national scene relatively late, after most of the public domain had been turned over to private hands, it has consistently argued for open access to all remaining public lands. After all, farmers had voted themselves homesteads, gold miners had often made their strikes on public property, cattlemen had boldly fenced in millions of acres of federal land, timber interests had never been too careful about fine distinctions between private and public in their cutting, and the railroads were beneficiaries of vast land subsidies.

In 1959 there were 159,000 oil and gas leases binding some 125 million acres of federal, Indian, and outer continental shelf lands. Production from these wells was valued at $829 million that year and accounted for nearly 9 per cent of the total domestic crude. Leasing on federal lands is at a fixed price of 50 cents per acre, unless the lands have proved oil deposits. Critics of this policy believe that the failure to require competitive bidding in areas where such land is surrounded by proved oil deposits loses millions of dollars of revenue for the federal government. The industry has advocated low leasing and royalty payments to the government and the liberalization of leasing provisions. The latter had been defined under the Mineral Leasing Act of 1920 in a belated effort to safeguard the remnants of the nation's lands west of the Alleghenys after a century and a half of speculation and exploitation masked by exalted references to manifest destiny and internal improvements and tempered by safety-valve theories for hard-pressed Eastern workers and homestead settlements for sturdy family farmers. Among oil's gains have been the right to larger acreage holdings by individuals, longer leases, and multipurpose leases allowing for simultaneous exploration for such minerals as uranium in which a number of oil companies have an active interest. In 1954, acreage limitations for an individual or a company were raised threefold, and the size of allowable options on land was doubled over the increased limits that had been attained after pressure in 1946. The Interior Department supported the industry's position that this would be in keeping with the risks and costs of modern exploration. The office of the Secretary expressed confidence that this remained in harmony with the intent of the original legislation seeking the orderly development of oil and gas on public lands, while in no way would this invite speculation or accelerate concentration of economic power in oil.

A Senate investigation in 1956 of actual practices disclosed that some of the large companies, as well as individuals, were circumventing the law through the use of lawyers, brokers, employees, and relatives as "dummies" for acquiring leases and options. This has been carried on to such an extent, concluded the report, that acreage limitations have become meaningless and tracts of land have been tied up over appreciable periods without genuine efforts at development. The language was more moderate, but the acts were the same as those reported some decades earlier. The Senate study also pointed out that records kept by the Bureau of Land Management were inadequate to ensure that the intent of the law was being maintained:

The detailed holdings of persons, associations, or corporations seem to be kept within the knowledge of the person, association or corporation, since the lease holder is put purely on the honor system as to whether or not they report accurately the amount of their holdings.[2]

Historically, oil operators have pushed a responsive federal government for opening Indian lands. More recently, the cause has been greater freedom for Indian tribes in the hope of then obtaining from the government's wards fee title to oil and gas under their lands. Oilmen have constantly pressured the Bureau of Land Management and the Fish and Wildlife Service of the Department of the Interior for approval of leases on the 17 million acres of natural wildlife refuges. The Eisenhower Administration was under fire from conservation and sportsmen groups because of the increased granting of such permission on the 264 refuges. Probably the most publicized of these actions was a series of leases to the Frankfort Oil Company, a subsidiary of Seagram Distilleries.[3] Charges were made that this was a reward for loyal support to the Republican party cause. Over the strong protests of the industry, the Interior Department early in 1958 announced tighter regulations on oil drilling on these lands. Abetted by indifferent, shortsighted, and corrupt state officials, oil, along with other mining and forest interests, has frequently enjoyed easy access to the lands turned over by the federal government for the support of schools and other local public functions.

The concept of setting aside some of the withdrawn public lands as naval petroleum reserves was launched in 1912 as the Navy began to switch from coal to oil. In a period when fears of shortages were rampant and the public domain was rapidly passing into private hands, it received the endorsement of Presidents Roosevelt, Taft, and Wilson. One area was established at Elk Hills, California, where reserves are estimated at one billion barrels and where there is joint minimum production with Standard of California, which owns about a third, to keep the fields in readiness for use. The other reserves are at Buena Vista, also in California, where limited production is largely under lease to private operators; at the ill-famed Teapot Dome in Wyoming, which has been shut in since 1927; at Point Barrow in northern Alaska, where over $50 million had been expended by 1953 when the Secretary of the Navy recommended the suspension of exploration; and three oil-shale areas in Colorado and Utah. In the closing hours of his Presidency, Mr. Truman set aside as naval reserves the bitterly disputed submerged lands off the continental shelf, but this was quickly rescinded by the new Administration. The Navy has estimated that from 1916 to 1953 public expenditures on these relatively modest reserves were $125 million, with $106 million recovered through income.

Oilmen have denounced these actions as inimical to private enterprise. With more insight than some of the defenders of the program, from the very beginning they feared that the precedent of naval reserves opened the door to far greater governmental activity. Some oil interests simply coveted these lands, with no pretense of political philosophy or prophecy. There was constant clamor for the reversal of this policy. Public officials soon discovered that the withdrawal of the lands was easier to proclaim than to achieve. "I have been compelled to fight almost every day of my incumbency in office to prevent the dummy entrymen and illegal operators from taking the Naval Reserves, the only hope for the Navy when the all too rapid use of American oil will leave it the only available supply," declared Josephus Daniels, Woodrow Wilson's Secretary of the Navy.[4] He reported that West Coast oilmen, using the war as an excuse, promoted a shortage scare and lined up influential citizens in politics, business, and education to plead the cause of California industry for the opening up of these reserves. In some places operators simply ignored the presidential order. The Navy found itself in constant difficulty with established private leaseholders within the naval lands who were draining the federal reserves. A long conflict with Standard Oil of California at Elk Hills led the Navy to drill offset wells to protect its oil. At several points the condemnation or purchase of the private holdings was recommended. But in 1944 the entire operation was unitized and placed under direct Navy responsibility. With the end of the war, production was cut back and Standard became restive again under the restrictions limiting the quantities it could take out from the third of the reserves it owns.

The political pressures generated by this public plum have always been great, and ugly rumors surrounded the lands throughout their history. Only after persistent inquiries by a few newsmen and congressmen, did the Harding Administration admit that it had transferred the naval reserves to the Interior Department and that leases without competitive bids had been given for the California lands to Edward L. Doheny of the Pan-American Petroleum and Transport Company and for Teapot Dome to one of Harry F. Sinclair's corporations. Each had ties to Standard of Indiana, which subsequently was to take over Pan-American. And each anticipated an eventual $100 million profit. The terms as well as the methods of these transactions represented a thorough denial of the premises of the naval reserves policy, with the Navy receiving some royalty payments but retaining very little oil. In 1927 a Supreme Court order returned the lands to the Navy after describing the arrangements as products of conspiracy, corruption, and fraud. But in the interim the American public was offered a case study of public and private immorality involving two Presidents of the United States and a number of Cabinet officers, political leaders, and leading oilmen.

Oil spokesmen have been successful in their opposition to the continuation of public explorations in the 28 million acre Alaskan reserve, a position supported by the Eisenhower Administration and many congressmen who wondered at the peacetime value of so remote and costly an undertaking. Phillips and Kerr McGee have had an operating agreement with the Department of the Interior on nearly a million acres of public lands in southeastern Alaska. Other West Coast majors and independents are also Alaska leaseholders, and an accelerated lease play has developed. Geologists believe that perhaps a fourth of the new state's 586,000 square miles may be favorable for oil, and the industry is ready to invest several hundred million dollars in the search. With the battle for statehood won and the turning over of some of the federal land to the new government, there is the hope of more sympathetic leasing terms. Oilmen have fought the Navy's exploring and drilling for oil reserves, as on San Nicolas Island off the coast of Southern California where the Navy maintains a guided-missile base. They have been wary lest such actions lead to military explorations on other lands and offshore gunnery ranges. And as shall be seen, they are especially hostile to the public development of the shale reserves that are potentially the most meaningful holding.

The industry has argued that the reserves played a very minor and expensive role in meeting military needs. "The whole concept of naval petroleum reserves is a lot of bilge water," asserts the *Oil and Gas Journal*. The Navy does not need petroleum reserves "any more than it needs iron-ore reserves to build ships, or wool-ranch reserves to make uniforms, or pulpwood reserves to sustain its paper work." Continuous peacetime development by private industry, rather than public stand-by facilities, is the way to safeguard the nation's resources, insists the National Petroleum Council in its *A National Oil Policy for the United States*.[5]

In contrast, a staunch defender like Representative Carl Vinson of Georgia, who for many years has chaired the House Naval Affairs Committee and its successor, the Armed Services Committee, points with pride to the 65,000 barrels a day produced at Elk Hills in the closing part of World War II. He has urged that it be regarded as a stockpile, and frankly fears new pretexts to open up the reserve wide:

I have no criticism of Standard for wanting the oil out of the ground. They are in the business. What I am up here for is to watch the Government's interest, and follow out what President Taft set out as a conservation program. And from that day down to this, there has been a constant raid, geological, scientific, and engineering on the reserve.[6]

Joining the oilmen have been experts, sometimes wearing the uniform of the United States Navy, who have argued that production must be maintained for conservation reasons to prevent the loss of oil. Some have concluded that it is impossible to keep reserves because private wells on the borders of the reserves, if not those within, would drain off all the oil. In his 1959 budget message, President Eisenhower accepted this and proposed that the government sell all the naval oil lands. The alternative was for the government itself to produce oil. And, Mr. Eisenhower argued, the nation must rely upon the private petroleum industry for its peace and war requirements. Representative Vinson and others, who have strenuously blocked such moves, can never forget that, however valid technically the fear of drainage, this has always been, as Senator Robert M. La Follette concluded in 1922, a "specious plea" preceding Teapot Dome, Elk Hills, and comparable giveaways.[7]

There are obvious and fundamental limitations to this naval reserves program. Military needs far exceed the petroleum requirements of World War I. And in a world that knows total war, it is difficult to make such distinctions. But the alternative here is not necessarily to abandon these holdings but rather to protect and retain public title and access to all reserves on the public domain. Tolerating the private drainage of government oil from adjoining lands reflects a distorted homage to the rights of private property. The policy of producing crude oil, selling it to the highest private bidder, and then buying back refined products at market prices, as the Navy has been required to do by law, is an awkward and inconsistent arrangement. If the idea behind naval reserves has validity, then in a fundamental sense the wider public interests should be secured through a system of controls that assures the nation of its present and future oil supply while offering a needed yardstick for gauging the efforts of the industry. But this would involve a priority of concern for public welfare and national security over private profit and predatory purposes.

Offshore Oil

No concern of the industry has been featured more consistently in the news and in political discussions than offshore oil lands. Geologists are generally agreed that the known rich land formations along the Gulf of Mexico and Pacific coast of the United States that have been major sources of oil extend seaward. The underwater plains of the continental shelf gently slope out into the Gulf for 70 to 140 miles before they attain a depth of 600 feet and then drop sharply.[8] Along the California coast these lands are much narrower and 20 miles is viewed as the operating limit for underseas exploration. Estimates of the potential supply vary, but 20 billion barrels of oil is considered a conservative figure, to which must be added great quantities of natural gas and sulphur. At current prices, a minimum of $60 billion worth of resources is involved. When one adds the estimates for possible oil-bearing lands contiguous to the coasts of Alaska, Florida, and other portions of the American continent, the oft-quoted figure of $100 billion becomes understandable.

The industry has long recognized the worth of this petroleum frontier, and there has been profitable activity along the California shore line for many years. The City of Long Beach had the greatest production of any field, with a consortium of private concerns under contract to handle the actual production. By the forties the California Company, a Standard of California subsidiary, had become the largest operator along the Gulf of Mexico. But the high cost of underwater drilling earmarked the full continental shelf for later development, when needs would be more pressing and the price market more favorable.

The urgency of World War II and the cold war, along with the acceleration of future demand that they foretold, forced government officials planning for the national interest to take an over-all inventory of resources. Offshore oil quickly became a center of attention. Naval officials, fearful for the Pacific fleet's fuel lines, spoke of setting aside offshore sources as naval reserves. The National Resources Committee, a government agency whose concern with a broader understanding and long-range planning of the economy earned it the enmity of conservative forces, raised the question as to the wisdom of the nation's ignoring of these deposits because of the historic policy of allowing subsurface mineral wealth to be privately owned and developed. With this interest there came to the fore a long-smoldering controversy over the legal title to these lands and their leasing. As was true in so many areas of oil policy, Harold L. Ickes, the Secretary of Interior under President Roosevelt, became the pivotal figure.

The prevailing practice had been that the leases for the lands along the shores were granted by the states. Under the pressure of claimants seeking federal leases off California under the Federal Mineral Leasing Act of 1920, the Department of Interior re-examined the assumption it had inherited from previous administrations and which Mr. Ickes had at first subscribed to, namely, that this was a state matter. In his diary, Ickes records that at a luncheon in 1937 the President "raised the question as to the ownership of oil found within the three mile limit. I told him that I would get an opinion from my Solicitor." [9] There is disagreement over the accuracy of this version, as over much of the details of the ensuing offshore oil struggle. But it is clear that the Secretary developed a conviction that this was a federal responsibility. Advocates of state control have constantly pointed to this turnabout as evidence of Ickes' power drive and of his susceptibility to the pressures of claim jumpers who were seeking something for nothing by filing with the federal government for these lands. There was considerable doubt as to legal title, however, and measures declaring that lands under the territorial waters of the continental United States were part of the federal domain and proposing that they be set aside as naval reserves were placed before the Congress. Stalemate developed here. To test and establish the principle, the government turned to the courts. Meanwhile, the industry braced itself against this threat to its potential reserves. It feared the loss of existing investments and leases as well as the possibility of tougher royalty terms from a federal landlord. Very much in mind also was the thought that lands federally held might be leased or drilled (perhaps by the Navy) in a manner that would ultimately upset the delicate price-supply balance basic to the industry's control of oil. Publicly, oil leaders warned against this assault upon free enterprise and states' rights and its possible extension to other areas of the economy. At the same time they tried to be as discreet as possible lest the public conclude this was an industry matter.

State officials, principally in California, Louisiana, and Texas, cognizant of the political weight of the oil producers and of the meaning of oil revenues to state government and party treasuries, plunged into the conflict. Louisiana, for example, received $24 million in rentals, bonuses, and leases from its offshore operations in 1948–1949. In Texas, oil royalties have been earmarked for schools. These states drew support from coastal and inland state officials who were led to fear federal seizure of their industries and inland waterways and loss or clouding of title to waterfront developments on lands reclaimed from the sea. Robert Moses, New York's Park Commissioner, voiced concern over Jones Beach and similar projects. New England fishing interests spoke of threats to their beds. Great Lakes state representatives envisioned a comparable fate for their properties. ". . . What of the kelp in Maine?" Eisenhower as candidate was to ask a Louisiana audience in 1952 in a slashing attack upon Washington "powermongers." (Maine received an annual income of $25.65 from the leasing of these seaweed beds eighteen miles off its coast.) "Every state has submerged lands" became the battle cry.

The drive centered upon Congress for legislation that would relinquish all federal claims before any final court ruling could be made. Numerous hearings were held, and the literature and the mythology of "tidelands" grew. "Tidelands," of course, was a misnomer, for the area under question was not and had never been the land between the low- and high-tide marks. No one was denying that the states have jurisdiction here, although one would not realize this from a reading of much of the state and oil-industry speeches. The essence of the controversy actually concerned the underwater lands seaward from the low-tide point. The "states rights" advocates claimed title to the three-mile limit, with Texas and Florida insisting on "historic boundaries" harking back prior to the time of their entry into the Union. In the case of Texas, this meant three leagues, or roughly ten and a half statute miles. As it became clear that the great potential reserves were further out, the demands grew more exaggerated, with Louisiana stretching its "historic boundaries" to thirty miles, Texas passing legislation claiming all of the continental shelf off its shores, and some officials demanding a share of royalties from all leases off their coasts, whether federal or state. It was argued that state control was in keeping with the American tradition, that it was essential that the responsibility be localized to cope with the diverse patterns of production and the need for flexible rules and prompt on-the-spot action, that private interests have been more successful in developing oil resources under state control than on the public domain, and that the nature of federal rule would discourage smaller producers in favor of the larger oil operators. "Yes, more was at stake than land or oil or sands or oysters," declared Representative Richard H. Poff of Virginia. "The sanctity of private property and the life-blood of our democracy was hanging in the balance." [10]

Defenders of federal control countered that, from the perspective of international law as well as genuine national planning, only the United States could be responsible for these lands. They warned that such demands would boomerang against American fishing interests operating off Mexico, Ecuador, Japan, and Russia in that they would encourage the latter in their claims for control beyond the generally accepted three-mile limit. They prophesied that any quit-claim action would open the door to the private grabbing and exploitation of all publicly held natural resources, including grazing, mineral, forest and park lands. In a full-page advertisement addressed to the Senate in the heat of the 1953 legislative battle, the Congress of Industrial Organizations insisted that "MORE THAN ONE TRILLION DOLLARS of wealth from the public domain" was at stake. Others saw potential threats to federal power, irrigation, and flood-control projects.

In 1945 President Truman proclaimed that the entire continental shelf was a federal responsibility, and in 1946 he vetoed a quitclaim bill, explaining that Congress was not an "appropriate forum" for deciding the essence of a case pending in the Supreme Court. A series of frequently postponed suits, at first against companies holding leases and then supplanted by suits against the states that granted the offshore leases, finally resulted in three court decisions that upheld the national claim. In the California case in 1947, the majority decreed that "the United States of America is now, and has been at all times pertinent hereto, possessed of paramount rights in, and full dominion and power over, the lands, minerals and other things underlying the Pacific Ocean lying seaward of the ordinary low-water mark on the coast of California, and outside of the inland waters, extending seaward three nautical miles. . . . The State of California has no title thereto or property interest therein." [11]

This decision notwithstanding, Texas proceeded to lease to major oil companies nearly 150,000 acres of lands on the continental shelf beyond the three-league (10.5 mile) limit. Along with Louisiana it was enjoined from continuing such action by the Supreme Court in 1950.

In the Texas case, where the state relied on its history as an independent republic prior to admission into the Union, the court insisted it had entered on an equal footing, with a relinquishment of any claim to sovereign control over the marginal sea. Once the low-water mark is passed and the international domain reached, declared Justice William O. Douglas for the majority, "property rights must then be so subordinated to political rights as in substance to coalesce and unite in the national sovereign. Today the controversy is over oil. Tomorrow it may be over some other substance or mineral or perhaps the bed of the ocean itself." In all such property cases, the "use, disposition, management and control involve national interests and national responsibilities." [12]

The court rulings served to feed rather than end the controversy. Both sides viewed themselves as fighting to preserve the Constitution with its system of separation of powers and checks and balances. The state control advocates focused on state-national relations, and the federal defenders warned that quitclaim legislation "derogates from the power of the Supreme Court in the field of Constitutional authority, and makes the legislative branch of the Government supreme." [13] A number of state-control proponents echoed the sentiment that "the doctrine laid down in these decisions finds its parallel in the writings of Marx and Lenin and the platforms and principles of the National Socialist Party, in all of which it is argued that property should be taken without compensation on the basis of 'need' for all of the people, regardless of the law of the land." [14] Leander Perez, an ardent states' righter and Dixiecrat who argued Louisiana's case in the Supreme Court and who has been known as an absolute dictator over the politics of his parish, saw it all as "a plot . . . to adopt the European or Russian ideology that the national government . . . is a government of unlimited powers. . . ." This charge prompted the *New Orleans Item* to note that it sounded as though Perez was saying anyone in favor of federal controls was in effect a Communist. "If that is true, then we must inform our readers that the United States Supreme Court is just a plain old Communist cell." [15]

The Solicitor of the Interior Department had ruled that the 1920

Mineral Leasing Act did not apply to submerged lands off the continental shelf, and the Congress compounded the confusion by refusing to authorize federal leasing of these lands. Pressures for quitclaim legislation that would in effect overrule the court mounted. President Truman subsequently vetoed another quitclaim bill as offshore oil operations remained almost at a standstill. Meanwhile, the increasingly restive major oil companies, who previously had made no secret of their preference for dealing with the states, now insisted they were not primarily interested in the federal versus state jurisdictional question. They had already invested at least a quarter of a billion dollars and they just wanted this settled so that their titles would be secure, whether guaranteed by the states or nation. But the state administrations and political figures directly involved, anticipating the eventuality of a more sympathetic president, persisted in their charges and demands. They rejected legislative compromises that allowed the states to keep the income already gained from leasing of federal lands, gave the states a share of revenues from lands beyond the three-mile limit, and made clear that inland navigable waters were not involved. This was long after the oil industry had worked out a *modus vivendi* with Mr. Truman and federal-control advocates that included an assurance that existing state leases would be respected even if transferred to federal hands.

This became a national political issue. It was featured in at least fifteen congressional hearings and high-lighted by such dramatic events as the resignation of Ickes from the Truman Cabinet in 1946 over the proposed nomination of oilman Edwin W. Pauley to be Undersecretary of the Navy, the Dixiecrat movement's bolt from the Democratic party in 1948, and Senator Wayne Morse's record-breaking twenty-two-hour filibuster in 1953. It remained unresolved until 1953 when President Eisenhower carried through an election pledge by successfully backing a Submerged Lands Act. Hailed by Republican National Chairman Leonard Hall as "the first sharp turn from the drift toward the superstate in America," it assigned the title to offshore lands within historic state boundaries to the states.[16] This legal sanction for what the pro-Eisenhower *New York Times* called "one of the greatest and surely the most unjustified give-away programs in all the history of the United States" was predicated on the assumption that the Congress had constitutional power to dispose of the federal domain.[17] Congress was thus able "to write the law for the future as the Supreme Court believed it to be in the past," and so circumvent the intent of a decision of a contemporary court.[18]

Under the Outer Continental Shelf Lands Act of the same year, leasing beyond these lines was to be under the supervision of the Secretary of the Interior. Perhaps 85 per cent of these oil resources thus remained within federal jurisdiction, a victory due in large measure to the fierce resistance put up by defenders of federal control who had managed to create some public concern by injecting the attractive political proposal of earmarking oil revenues for education. They had also forced the recognition within the new Administration—reflected in the testimony of the Secretary of State and the Attorney General, which differed with the position of the President and the Republican party—that to turn these lands over to the states was of dubious constitutionality and would almost certainly evoke a new clash over all the offshore oil. Texas and Louisiana backers were disappointed. They had won the battle and lost the war, for most of their offshore oil was beyond the line drawn by the court. California interests, with the state's trim continental shelf, were the clear gainers.

Certain boundary technicalities remained unclear, not the least of which was determining low-tide marks. The State of Louisiana, which in 1954 extended its "historic boundaries" to three leagues from a shore line so drawn as to give the state a claim for thirty miles seaward in places, has clashed sharply with the Interior Department about overlapping jurisdictional claims. Not to be outdone, Alabama in 1956 declared its historic boundaries to extend seaward twenty miles. ("Alabama goes to sea" read an oil-journal headline.) Threats followed to reopen the entire case in the courts. The State of Arkansas, acting for a nucleus of the federal-control bloc, filed a complaint in a federal district court charging that the Submerged Lands Act was "an unwarranted and invalid attempt to abdicate the sovereignty of the United States to a few of the states," a violation of the trust under which all lands beneath the marginal sea are held by the United States for the benefit of all the nation, and a deprivation of the people of their proportionate share of the resources and of the money already accruing from them.[19] Alabama and Rhode Island also sought Supreme Court permission to challenge the constitutionality of this legislation.

Late in 1957 the Solicitor General of the United States filed a brief with the Supreme Court claiming rights in all underseas lands beyond the three-mile limit in the Gulf of Mexico and the $100 million in rents and royalties from the area that were being held in escrow. This reversal of Eisenhower's position brought strong protests from Texas. The President responded, in a letter to H. J. Porter, an oilman who was also Texas Republican national committeeman, by reaffirming his support of Texas's claim to 10.5 miles from the shore. The *New York Times* reported that this undercutting was viewed in Washington as "a strictly political move that will have no effect on the Government position before the Supreme Court. . . . Justice Department officials said that the President's 'earnest hope' that Texas's three-league claim be upheld was merely a layman's expression." After examining the complicated boundary history of the states, the Supreme Court in 1960 upheld the claims of Texas and Florida to the submerged lands extending 10.5 miles from their coasts into the Gulf. Louisiana, Alabama, and Mississippi, however, were recognized as having title only 3.5 miles out. All resources beyond these boundaries on the continental shelf belonged to the federal government.[20]

Despite the legal confusion, the oil industry rushed to obtain leases after the congressional action in 1953 and to begin development as well as stake out reserves for the future. No one now was suggesting that "tidelands" oil was overrated or a political fiction. Intensive bidding for federal and state lands followed the settlement, with the heaviest interest centered off the Louisiana coast. "Offshore production looms as the richest drilling prize in the history of the oil business," exulted the *Oil and Gas Journal*.[21] At the end of 1954 the Tidewater Associated Oil Company, then a half-billion-dollar organization with some 108,000 acres of offshore leases acquired between the mouths of the Mississippi and Rio Grande rivers, reported to its stockholders: "The success of drilling offshore in the Gulf of Mexico to date substantiates the industry's opinion that this area is the largest prospective source of oil and gas reserves within the United

States." [22] President T. S. Petersen of the Standard Oil Company of California echoed the belief that the submerged part of the continental shelf was "perhaps America's greatest potential for future oil production." [23] As evidence of this belief his company had at least $175 million invested in the Gulf of Mexico. By the end of 1956 the industry had discovered over a hundred producing oil and gas fields in the gulf.

Offshore oil is a blue-chip operation. Bids are required on full tracts that may extend 1,000 to 5,000 acres each. While the prices of many tracts range from the legal minimum of $15 an acre up into the hundreds, the high bidding on key areas suggests what the companies expect to find. For example, Magnolia, a Socony Mobil subsidiary, has paid $2,209 an acre for a 1,440-acre tract. Phillips reported over 200,000 acres of holdings, with payments for these at $34 million. Humble paid the State of Louisiana more than $7 million for each of two 5,000-acre blocks. The CATC group bid $7½ million for a block 100 feet under water. Gulf Oil paid $1,200 an acre for 5,000 acres. By the middle of 1955, the Department of Interior had received more than a quarter of a billion dollars from its first three lease sales, with an expectation of garnering perhaps $6 billion eventually from leases and royalties. The equipped barges for deeper water drilling are really man-made islands, and cost several million dollars each, although such expenses are likely to drop as the rigs and techniques become more standardized and routine. Several have been capsized in storms, but the number in operation doubled in 1956. There are no small bidders. (In one case involving what was described as a "clerical error," Kerr-McGee Industries successfully bid $14.5 million for the wrong twelve tracts.) Offshore development requires a heavy investment that is justified only when holdings are sufficiently large and planned for the long pull rather than for an immediate return. It is estimated that eleven oil corporations and groups have about 75 per cent of the leases off Louisiana. Well over $1.5 billion has been invested already in the Gulf of Mexico. But there has been a very high rate of discovery with relatively few dry holes. It is anticipated that, despite discouraging production allowables set by the state, future returns will make worthwhile all the initial political and financial investment.

Synthetic Liquid Fuels

The oil industry closely watches the federal government's research in developing synthetic liquid fuels. The most notable of these experiments have involved the transformation of shale and coal into petroleum. Oil shale was in commercial production in parts of the world since the nineteenth century. In this country many oil-shale companies sprang up in the 1920's, disappearing in face of technological difficulties, inadequate finances, and plentiful natural petroleum. Meanwhile, estimates of oil shales have constantly been revised upward. In Colorado alone the United States Geological Survey now believes there are 900 billion barrels of high-grade shale oil recoverable from the rocky formations, three times the world's petroleum reserves. The most recent United States Bureau of Mines estimate places the total at 1.5 trillion barrels. There are also great quantities in neighboring Utah and Wyoming.

The Bureau of Mines has been studying technical problems associated with petroleum since its creation in 1910. Laboratory studies of shale were conducted between 1916 and 1925, and the Bureau built and operated an experimental oil-shale plant beginning in 1925. This was terminated in 1929 when funds were cut off. The shortage fears of World War II led Congress in 1944 to authorize again specific research on shale and coal. From 1944 to 1955, the Congress appropriated $88 million for this work. During that period the Bureau of Mines conducted experiments at its Rifle, Colorado, pilot plant and its Laramie, Wyoming, laboratory in the mining of shale, its conversion to crude and refining into gasoline. Considerable basic research has been completed, despite limited appropriations, and while many questions remain, there is agreement that this entire process is feasible technically. The underlying business question raised concerns what percentage of these huge reserves is recoverable at economic prices that will allow shale oil to enter the market. A 15-cent or less per gallon production cost of gasoline is now believed possible, including allowance for profit. While the industry is always reluctant to break down costs of regular crude oil production, implying this is nearly impossible, 12 cents a gallon of gasoline at the refinery was a frequently used quotation prior to the most recent crude increase. With the rise in exploration, recovery and refining costs of domestic crude, the anticipated rise in imported oil prices as world demand goes up, and the increased knowhow in shale extraction, it is expected that the present cost differential can become slight once production gets under way on a scale large enough to justify the heavy initial investments required. This gap might disappear if one were to consider the profits from chemical by-products and the favorable tax allowances the regular oil-production industry receives.

Industry spokesmen welcome the basic research knowledge gained. Even the United States Chamber of Commerce commends the Bureau "for the excellent job it has done." [24] But they want the government to get out of this field. Oilmen deplore the conducting of industrial experiments that might easily lead to full-scale operations just as they are wary of any federal research or support that ultimately could threaten their patent-based controls over petroleum. Their concern has been reinforced by subsequent proposals from cabinet and congressional figures for the federal underwriting of a large synthetic fuel industry to augment domestic supplies and make the nation less dependent on foreign sources. The big oil companies recognize that oil shale will be utilized, but insist they are the best judges as to the proper time for its introduction. Many of them have been buying up shale tracts. Claims are made that private industry has spent several hundred million dollars in synthetic research. The Union Oil Company of California, with extensive Colorado shale holdings, has had a research program, including an experimental plant. It has planned to introduce shale-derived refined products on the West Coast as the cost of its process becomes competitive with natural crude. Early in 1958 a company spokesman announced that this goal had been achieved. But "today we are concerned only about getting shale oil onto a basis competitive with Middle East oil." A few months later Union closed its pilot plant. The explanation was that world marketing conditions were unfavorable for a $300 million investment for a 50,000-barrel-a-day shale-oil plant and the necessary pipeline construction. (It should also be noted that Gulf, the largest importer, holds $120 million of Union's convertible debentures. Should Gulf exercise its option to convert these to stock, it could directly control

Union.) At one point Union suggested that the government aid in its financing as a defense measure, but it now points with pride to a $12 million investment with "not one cent . . . from the federal treasury." [25] It has also sought the raising of the depletion allowance for oil shale from 15 to 27½ per cent.

The oil industry's basic fear is of a government-encouraged synthetic-fuel program that could challenge or upset the entire industrial government of oil with its careful balance of supply and demand. It might also provide a yardstick for judging and controlling costs and profits. The Rocky Mountain congressional delegation and men like Conservation Commissioner Warwick Downing of Colorado, with visions of a great industry for their region based on the shale that they see and know is there, have generally supported the work at Rifle. Senator Eugene D. Millikan, a conservative Republican from Colorado who always made clear that he had a family financial interest in oil-shale lands, was one of the strongest advocates of this research. He reminded his Senate colleagues that he was generally "not very hot about the Government taking over that kind of work." But, he added, oil companies "are not running philanthropic institutions."

> If the private interests go ahead they will be doing it for the benefit of private interests. That is their business. I am not criticizing it. However, we set out to develop processes and methods of doing this thing which will be available to everybody, and so no one would have a monopoly as a result of the accomplishment of this plant. I am delighted that private interests are interested. I can remember when you could not get a nickel from them to do any of this work, and that was why it was done by the Government.[26]

Yet federal appropriations for research have always been contested. "The problem in recent years," explained oil-oriented Governor Allan Shivers of Texas, "has not been one of finding a substitute for a limited natural resource but rather keeping ambitious bureaus in the Federal Government from subsidizing synthetic replacements before they are needed. Economic history shows that long before the depletion of any resource a dynamic and free people have replaced it with a better substitute." [27]

At his nomination hearings in 1953, Secretary of the Interior Douglas McKay had indicated he was "very strongly for" the program. "I think we have to develop anything we can in the way of fuel these days, because we don't know when we will be at the end of our rope." [28] Nevertheless, one of the Eisenhower Administration's early moves was to prepare for the closing of the Rifle plant and its sale as surplus property to the industry. Secretary McKay now explained that the superabundance of crude supply made its continued operation doubtful. In 1954 a five-man survey team that included oil, coal, and copper corporate officials recommended that the Bureau of Mines concentrate on research improving the recovery of known crude oil reserves, which it felt was being neglected. It advised more cooperation with the American Petroleum Institute and similar industry groups:

. . . . The experimental work done solely by the Bureau on the production of oil shale and oil from shale at Rifle, Colorado, shall cease, and . . . no further work be done with the new retort (heating mechanism) unless there is a substantial contribution by industry under a cooperative agreement. If industry feels that no further experimental work is necessary, then the facilities will have served the purpose for which they were developed and constructed, and disposition should be made in accordance with established procedures.[29]

To bolster this position the Secretary of the Interior then requested the judgment of his industry advisory council, which previously had indicated its hostility to these experiments. After a poll of members the National Petroleum Council solemnly concluded it was proper and advisable to undertake this review. Under the chairmanship of B. A. Hardey, a Louisiana oil producer who had been president of the Independent Petroleum Association of America, a committee heavily dominated by executives from the major companies made a study that seconded the recommendation that the government abandon this activity:

Various companies are now engaged in experiments and development work on processes for the recovery of oil from shale, and they and others will undoubtedly continue to carry on such work to the degree warranted by present and future circumstances. In the light of this fact, the Committee feels that there is no need for further government effort along these lines.[30]

Bureau officials repeatedly assure the industry and Congress that they are cooperating with interested oil and chemical companies, citing agreements with Jersey, Socony, Standard (Indiana), Continental, Phillips, Shell, Sinclair, Tidewater, and others. They point out that part of their financing is derived from industry contributions and that the Bureau has no commercial oil-producing properties. But work has been curtailed sharply and the plant transferred to the Navy and put on a stand-by basis while technical personnel have been scattered. Meanwhile, there have been proposals that the Navy, which has done some research with its shale as part of its petroleum reserves program, take up this experimentation and contract for the private operation of a refinery. Since 1938 it has been precluded from developing or operating these shale reserves.[31]

A similar pattern has unfolded in the production of oil from coal. In 1926 Germany's goliath chemical combine, I. G. Farbenindustrie, had announced a process for making synthetic liquid fuel from coal. With this discovery there soared the dreams of autarchy for a new and greater industrial and military Reich. Germany lacked oil but was rich in coal. Yet if I. G. Farben understood that the full technical solution of this laboratory success was clearly in the national interest, it also recognized obstacles in entering this area. "The field of petroleum industry is so tremendous and is so absolutely under the command of three large concerns," explained I. G. Farben's president before a committee of the Reichstag, "that the consideration of a new production in the fight against these concerns would have been very difficult . . . and the financial needs . . . beyond any expectation." [32] The answer, concluded the German corporate directorate, was cooperation with Jersey Standard. The latter had the experience, the industrial know-how and the large-scale installations needed for further testing. If it could agree to keep its natural petroleum at pegged rather than competitive levels in Germany, this would ease the entry of the expensive synthetic fuel into the German market.

The American goliath of oil was also looking ahead. " . . . I think that this matter is the most important which has ever faced the company since the dissolution," a Jersey official wrote from Germany to President W. C. Teagle in 1926.

The Badische can make high grade motor fuel from lignite and other low quality coals in amounts up to half the weight of the coal. This means absolutely the independence of Europe on the matter of gasoline supply. Straight price competition is all that is left. . . . They can make up to 100% by weight from any liquid hydrocarbon, tar, fuel oil, or crude oil. This means that refining of oil will have as a competitive industry in America and elsewhere, catalytic conversion of the crude into motor fuel.[33]

That same year the two industrial empires began to negotiate a pact which recognized the preeminence of each organization in its major field. ". . . The I. G. are going to stay out of the oil business proper and we are going to stay out of the chemical business insofar as that has no bearing on the oil business," the head of the Standard Oil Development Company reported.[34] Two joint companies were created, to which they contributed their patents in agreed areas. Standard now had access to the hydrogenation and other oil-refining patents for its American and world use that it hoped would aid it in maintaining world domination of oil. There was an understanding that I. G. Farben would continue this work within Germany itself. As an arm of the state, it obviously was taking no chances on foreign knowledge or intervention with regard to Germany's long-run plans. In return, I. G. Farben's world-wide chemical empire specifically included the United States, and it was to receive Standard's chemical discoveries. "We were always aware of the fact that oil companies could become the most dangerous competitors to the chemical industry in general, because it was to be foreseen that from oil derivatives one could extend themselves [sic] over the entire field of synthetic production . . . ," a leading I. G. director explained during interrogation in 1945.[35]

As Nazi Germany prepared industrially for war, synthetic research in rubber, magnesium, and other materials received top priority. Its leaders were well aware that Italy's imperial aspirations and conquests would have been brought to a sharp halt had petroleum sanctions been applied by the Western powers controlling the world's oil. An I. G. report observed: ". . . It is quite out of the question that Germany will run the risk of a similar situation and for this reason also the German demand of fuel has to be covered by Germany herself before long." [36] Synthetic-fuel manufacturing was accelerated. In addition, I. G. Farben in 1938 acted for the German government to "borrow" tetraethyl lead from the Ethyl Export Corporation (owned by Jersey Standard and General Motors). The Nazis had recognized the "very friendly relationships" between the giant corporations while realizing that the German government was not likely to be successful in this quest in view of the international political climate. Earlier it had purchased from Jersey high-grade aviation fuel for stockpiling. Meanwhile, I. G. received important scientific information from Standard, including the process for producing tetraethyl lead. Du Pont, which has a controlling interest in General Motors and a major role in the production of tetraethyl, apparently warned that such an exchange might impair military security. But the sizable commitments of General Motors and Standard in Germany, where each had about half of the market in its given field, won out. Using plans from the Ethyl Gasoline Corporation, a tetraethyl plant was erected by a German corporation owned jointly by I. G. and General Motors and Jersey Standard subsidiaries.[37]

Standard's German subsidiary helped design facilities for aviation-gas refining for the Wehrmacht as late as 1939. W. S. Farish, who became president of the Jersey corporation in 1937, subsequently explained that since the United States was not at war with Germany and "commercial relations with Germany were continuing on a normal basis," the subsidiary "as a German corporation, operating in Germany . . . could not have done otherwise. . . . Refusal to assist . . . would have been unwarranted." Even if one accepts the fiction of corporate independence, this did not cover the parent Jersey company's role in the United States. ". . . I have assured Dr. Ringer [of I. G.] that we are not only willing but anxious to do everything we can to assist the Kellogg and I. G. gentlemen in preparing the process design. . . ." As further illustration of its stated position that "the company cannot constitute itself judge of the rights and wrongs of international problems," President Teagle served on the board of the American I. G. chemical company from 1929 to 1939. Holding 500,000 shares for his company, he testified before the Securities and Exchange Commission in 1938 that he did not know who owned the controlling voting stock. This arm of I. G. Farben had stock in Jersey Standard received from it as payment for the hydrogenation process and was also predecessor and then owner of General Aniline and other Farben enterprises in America.[38]

Standard, through a 50 per cent owned affiliate, the International Hydro Patents Company, granted a license to Japan for the manufacture of the chief ingredient used in 100-octane aviation gasoline and in 1939 was still exploring its earlier plans for a closer relationship or merger with the Mitsui firm. In another case of international corporate commitment, a State Department black-list threat in October 1941, based on United States Intelligence Service information, was required before Jersey finally acted to halt the supplying by a Brazilian subsidiary of Axis airlines running from Rome through Spain and Africa to Brazil and Argentina. Backed by the German and Italian governments, they served to by-pass the British blockade while transporting for propaganda and espionage efforts in the Western Hemisphere what the Chief of the American Republics Office of the Department of Commerce described as "probably the most notorious record of enemies that ever traveled on any line." [39] The Jersey corporation had refused to stop its tanker shipments, citing in justification the financial loss and possible suits. Again the question was not of national disloyalty but of business profits and contractual obligations taking precedence.

Some of these relationships were made public in 1942 through the federal government's antitrust suit against Jersey, the hearings of the Truman Committee investigating the national defense program and the Bone Committee on patents.[40] The corporation quickly sought to explain to the American people that the United States had been the real gainer in the patent exchanges, acquiring from "the best aggregation of technical talent in research in the world" basic data for producing high-octane gas, tuluol for TNT, and the buna patents. Each of these claims as to actual gains was discounted as greatly exaggerated by the Assistant Attorney General and the Truman Committee. An I. G. Farben document found in a "to be destroyed" folder by the United States forces in Germany further challenged the Jersey version:

. . . . Without lead-tetraethyl the present method of warfare would be unthinkable. The fact that since the beginning of the war we could produce lead-tetraethyl is entirely due to the circumstances that shortly before the Americans had presented us with the production plants complete with experimental knowledge. Thus the difficult work of development (one need only recall the poisonous property of lead-tetraethyl, which caused many deaths in the U.S.A.) was spared us, since we could take up the manufacture of this product together with all the experience that the Americans had gathered over long years.

It was, moreover, the first time that the Americans decided to give a license on this process in a foreign country (besides communication of unprotected secret experimental knowledge) and this only on our urgent requests to Standard Oil to fulfill our wish. Contractually we could not demand it, and we found out later that the War Department in Washington gave its permission only after long deliberation.[41]

There had been coal-oil plants in the United States turning out various oil products prior to the discovery of petroleum. Then after the patent exchanges for which it had paid $30 million in stock, Standard invested millions in developing coal-to-oil plants. But these were found too costly for the time. Again it was the impetus of World War II oil consumption that led Congress to focus on the nation's coal reserves. Coal is the world's leading fossil fuel and can serve for several thousand years. Near the close of the war the Bureau of Mines was authorized to develop these processes. Plants and laboratories were set up in Pennsylvania, West Virginia, Missouri, and Alabama, building on the technique of hydrogenation and gas synthesis the Germans were using and the Jersey corporation had acquired.

Once more the fears and pressures of big oil were to culminate in the sympathetic response of the Eisenhower Administration committed to governmental economy and business freedom. Research appropriations requests were cut and demonstration plants at Louisiana, Missouri, in which the government had invested at least $35 million, were shut down, despite the protests of coal congressmen, the United Mine Workers, and others interested in this resource. A coal-to-gas plant was sold to the Hercules Powder Company for $5 million with the explanation that "the plant was closed because it had reached a point of diminishing returns and the information to be gained by further operation would not be commensurate with the cost of operation." [42] These cuts came just as the production cost of synthetic fuel from coal was approaching that of natural crude. It is significant that National Petroleum Council estimates of cost have been far higher than those of the Bureau and of independent engineering firms. Interior officials also indicated their belief that shale-oil production research should have priority because of the more favorable cost factor. Some oil engineers, notably Lewis C. Karrick who had been prominent in the earliest coal- and shale-oil work of the Bureau of Mines, have long insisted there are cheaper ways of distilling oil from coal than the ones based on the German and Jersey Standard patents. The claim is made that the companies have not been able to get these patents on their terms and that the responsive Interior Department has therefore ignored this line of research. Meanwhile some oil companies continue their own experiments with these while also seeking to develop or obtain simpler processes in conjunction with big coal corporations.[43]

Synthetic Rubber

As the technology of modern petroleum has crossed over so completely into the chemical field, oil has developed a stake in synthetic rubber, which can be made from refinery by-products. Germany had been urgently searching for a rubber substitute even prior to World War I. This culminated in the buna processes which were to play a key role in the Nazi rearmament plans.

Jersey, subsequently interested in synthetic rubber, expected access to this knowledge by virtue of its "full marriage" to I. G. Farben. It envisioned dominating a new industry. As a consequence, synthetic development by the American rubber industry was delayed. While I. G. Farben told the Goodyear Rubber representatives in 1937 and 1938 that buna was not yet developed far enough for licensing, Jersey during the thirties implied to the American rubber and chemical companies, who finally were becoming alert to the implications of synthetic rubber, that it had the desired buna process and would work out a licensing system. For a while these companies were discouraged from going ahead, and feared restrictive licensing terms or costly patent-infringment suits if they undertook the commercial implementation of their own research. Yet in 1938, Frank A. Howard, the head of the Standard Oil Development Company, reported:

The thing that is really holding us up . . . is not the lack of a plan either from Goodyear or ourselves, but the inability of our partners to obtain the permission of their government to proceed with the development in the United States. Until they obtain this permission it is not possible for us to make any commitment at all. Our primary objective in our talk with the Goodyear and Dow people was to convince them of our good faith and our willingness to cooperate with them, in order to avoid having them proceed prematurely with an independent development which would make it impossible to bring them into any general plan later.[44]

While the Wehrmacht was safeguarding this knowledge and I. G. Farben agents in the United States were engaged in general industrial espionage, up until 1940 Standard was turning over to its partner full data, denied to American companies, about its own work on butyl. This synthetic was derived mainly from isobutylene, a relatively inexpensive and normal refinery by-product. Buna, then considered to be the superior synthetic, was less sensitive to heat, but required butadiene and styrene which were much more expensive refinery by-products.

As Howard explained:

Until we have this permission [to work out a licensing system], however, there is absolutely nothing we can do, and we must be especially careful not to make any move whatever, even on a purely informal, personal or friendly basis, without the consent of our friends. We know some of the difficulties they have, both from business complications and interrelations with the rubber and chemical trades in the United States, and from a national standpoint in Germany, but we do not know the whole situation—and since under the agreement they have full control over the exploitation of this process, the only thing we can do is to continue to press for authority to act, but in the meantime loyally preserve the restrictions they have put on us.

This course, the Jersey executive confided in another memorandum, seemed "not only the right thing to do, but the best thing" in view of "the very genuine spirit of cooperation" displayed by I. G. Farben's representatives.[45] Besides, as the president of Standard explained to a stockholders' meeting, as late as the summer of 1939— and perhaps later, since Mr. Farish refused to give any other pre-Pearl Harbor date—"I never had any idea that I. G. Farbenindustrie, as an organization, was hostile to the United States." [46] Butyl was of little value to the Germans since it was petroleum-derived, Farish insisted. This argument ignored Hitler's conquest of Austria and the historic and continued German drive east. (In March 1940, Standard accepted Farben's redefinition of German boundaries to include Austria and Czechoslovakia, thus recognizing these Nazi conquests.)

Once Germany was at war with England, Jersey Standard received the buna patent, though not the details of the all important know-how which apparently never was forthcoming from Farben. Under an agreement worked out at The Hague, several thousand other patents were turned over to Jersey as the stock of the joint company Jasco passed into Jersey's sole possession. Jasco, charged the federal government's criminal suit, was assigned all America and the British and French empires, while I. G. kept exclusive rights to these processes for the rest of the world. This was in harmony with an agreement arrived at some years earlier to the effect that "in the event the performance of these agreements or of any material provisions thereof by either party should be hereafter restrained or prevented by operation of any existing or future law, or the beneficial interest of either party be alienated to a substantial degree by operation of law or governmental authority," new negotiations should be entered "in the spirit of the present agreements." [47] Frank Howard, president of the Standard Oil Development Company and the main negotiator, reported to his chief the transfer of patents:

We did our best to work out complete plans for a modus vivendi which would operate through the term of the war, whether or not the U.S. came in. . . . All of the arrangements could not be completed, but it is hoped that enough has been done to permit closing the most important uncompleted points by cable. It is difficult to visualize as yet just how successful we shall be in maintaining our relations through this period without personal contacts.

The outbreak of war had intensified the complications of getting the Americans, British, Dutch and Germans, as Howard put it, "to lie down in the same bed " But, he reasoned, "technology has to carry on—war or no war. . . ." As Assistant Attorney General Thurman Arnold viewed it, "What these people were trying to do was to look at the war as a transitory phenomenon and at business as a kind of permanent thing: The war is bound to be over in a couple of years and let's not have it interfere any more than necessary with the commercial relationships which in the long run are bound to exist." [48]

Despite these legal precautions, the patents were seized as German property by the Alien Property Custodian. In 1944 Standard filed a suit for their recovery, but on the basis of I. G. Farben records the federal court upheld the government's action with regard to all patents Standard obtained from the time of the 1939 agreement. It found Frank A. Howard of Standard "not a credible witness" and The Hague agreement a "sham transaction" for camouflaging I. G. Farben's assets behind Jersey's friendly hands for the duration.

By 1940 the American mobilization program was well under way. The Japanese conquests had cut off reliable delivery of 95 per cent of America's normal natural rubber supply. Stockpiling and civilian rationing were limited and late. The quotas and the fears of upsetting postwar markets on the part of the British-Dutch world rubber producers' cartel (the International Rubber Regulation Committee) further hampered these efforts, despite very generous price inducements. This was the period when, in Donald M. Nelson's words, "we almost lost the war before we ever got into it." [49] After examining the rubber needs against the hesitant state of synthetic operations, the National Defense Advisory Commission, predecessor of the War Production Board, had recommended that the government back the production of 100,000 tons. But even this cautious proposal encountered obstacles and resistance. Jesse Jones, head of the Reconstruction Finance Corporation, was reluctant to see the government so deeply involved in business. With the usual ambivalence about government aid and possible competition, the rubber, oil, and chemical companies generally wanted some subsidy for commercial-scale production. This was a costly project, involving at least $100 million. They were far from in agreement as to the best techniques; the installations might quickly be found obsolete; and there was no assurance that expensive synthetic rubber could compete with natural rubber in a peacetime situation. A limited program was begun.

Jersey Standard was now offering licenses for the buna patents. It demanded royalties which, in its own words, "make the operation practical for the rubber company only so long as the product is used as a relatively high cost specialty." [50] Cross licensing and other provisions that would keep buna under its control were also required.

As late as October 1941, Jersey was taking court action to prevent independent production by Goodyear and Goodrich, who, along with Dow, Du Pont, and several other firms, had gone ahead on their experiments and, in the view of many, had learned more about synthetic rubber than had Standard. Several companies accepted terms. A patent pool on buna was formed by the major rubber companies and Standard at the request of the government. Observed the Truman Committee:

That position cannot be ascribed to lack of patriotism, and was probably due to the mere performance by the officers and directors of what they conceived to be their duty to the stockholders, but it did hamper the Government program.[51]

Meanwhile, Jersey held back licensing its butyl and in 1939 even sought to shield the process from a Navy representative studying the development of butyl. "As agreed upon," the director of Jersey's chemical laboratories wrote to a Jersey executive, "I took Mr. Werkenthin over to the 'K' Plant, when it appeared that I could not very well steer his interest away from the process. However, I am quite certain that he left with no picture of the operations other than that a considerable amount of distillation and refrigeration is involved in the handling of the light hydrocarbons, and that refinery gas rather than straight butadiene is the raw material." [52] The chemical director later became the head of the American Chemical Society, which took over the stock of Universal Oil Products, a research and licensing company controlled by some of the majors.

These oil and rubber practices culminated in federal criminal and civil conspiracy actions brought against the Jersey company, its affiliates and officers. Standard denied the charges, citing its record of cooperation with the government and industry in pushing synthetics. But it accepted the consent decree, explaining that "to obtain vindication by trying the issues in the courts would involve months of time and energy of most of its officers and many of its employees. Its war work is more important than court vindication. Nor has the company any desire to remain in a position which the Department of Justice considers in any way questionable." [53] Its officers were fined $5,000 each. The patents in question were released to the government royalty-free for the duration, with a pledge of compulsory licensing open to all for the postwar period. At the same time Standard continued its campaign to reverse the Alien Property Custodian's actions. Subsequent disclosures at the Nuremberg trials reinforced the original charges while documenting the intricate relationship between the Nazi regime and the I. G. Farben combine from the very outset of Hitler's rise to power. The indictments described the use by I. G., "the master builders of the Wehrmacht," of slaves and inmates awaiting gassing and cremation at labor concentration camps which served as adjuncts to the buna experimental and production centers.

A vast synthetic industry preparing the needed raw materials and manufacturing the rubber soon developed in the United States, with the government underwriting the risk by investing over $700 million. The giants of rubber (Firestone, Goodrich, Goodyear, and United States Rubber Company, as well as General Tire) and of chemicals (Dow, Monsanto, Carbide and Carbon, Du Pont and Koppers), together with Atlantic, Cities Service, Gulf, Phillips, Pure, Richfield, Shell, Sinclair, Standard of California, Standard (Indiana), Texas, and Jersey Standard and its affiliates were involved in operating fifty-one government-built facilities. They received management fees above all costs which were the equivalent of profits. By January 1953 these totaled $127 million. Some patent royalties were also paid.

There were rumblings from within and outside the oil industry suggesting that the men of oil were not losing sight of their postwar world. The Sun Oil Company, part owners of the Houdry Process Corporation, protested that the influence of Jersey Standard and allied interests within the government's Rubber Reserve Company had precluded a fair and impartial hearing for what was claimed as a superior Houdry process for making butadiene from petroleum.

Agricultural groups, worried about their own surpluses, persistently challenged the decision made by oilmen in government to obtain much of the butadiene, the essential hydrocarbon for buna, from petroleum rather than from alcohol. Before Pearl Harbor most industrial alcohol had come from imported blackstrap molasses, a by-product of sugar. But this supply was recognized as inadequate to meet the wartime demands for alcohol. Buttressed by the research of top chemurgists and the activities of farm congressmen, they persuasively argued that grain-derived alcohol would require far less expensive facilities which could be erected more quickly than the petroleum plants. They admitted that the considerably higher grain cost was a discouraging factor. But they pointed to this as a long-run solution for the national headache of grain surpluses while saving petroleum for higher-grade purposes. They also cited the experience of other countries converting corn, wheat, potatoes, and pulp waste into alcohol. But they did not receive the finances and the materials they were seeking.

The oil industry's early answer was that there would be adequate petroleum for butadiene. And they indicated that butadiene from alcohol was an unproved method. It was later disclosed that it was petroleum butadiene that was yet to be commercially tested, although at the time the government had appropriated about $650 million to the pool of oil, rubber, and chemical firms. President W. S. Farish of Jersey Standard denied allegations that these decisions were rooted in any selfish motives on the part of his company or the industry:

I think some people have assumed, because most of the oil refineries are using processes or designs for their butadiene plants which they obtained in part from us, that we were active partisans of a particular process and that we were trying to persuade the Government or other refiners that they should use our methods in preference to producing butadiene from alcohol or by use of other oil processes.

. . . Nothing could be further from the truth. In this business of synthetic rubber we are neither the champions for oil as a raw material nor for any particular process.

We have had to use our own best judgment and experience in preparing our own designs, and we are satisfied that we have done the best that could be done under the circumstances.

To Senator Guy Gillette, who was investigating the industrial alcohol and synthetic rubber situation for several years, "the futility, if not purposeful hampering, that has existed in some of our governmental agencies" seemed "a little short of criminal." [54]

As it turned out, alcohol was used far more than originally planned, with petroleum butadiene being utilized in the closing stages of the war when the plants were ready. But here the farm products advocates ran up against the tightly controlled industrial-alcohol industry, a portion of which was linked to oil, who feared postwar rivalry for raw materials and markets as well as the ever present bogey of "surplus" capacity. A Senate report in 1942 told that "belatedly and only after months of hearings was alcohol from agriculture products allowed to share in the program—and then only to the point—and not one step beyond—that whisky and molasses distilleries could be converted to the making of industrial alcohol from grain. Such meticulous care to avoid the possibility of post-war competition may bespeak a high degree of business shrewdness, but it likewise portrays a serious failure to appreciate the necessity of keeping America on wheels and winning the war." [55] Meanwhile, Jersey Standard and other oil companies, who have come to dominate the industrial alcohol market, have continued to pressure the Department of Agriculture against releasing surplus corn for experimental processing into industrial alcohol.

There were also parallel recommendations during the war that power alcohol be produced on a large scale. Blended with gasoline, this would serve as a satisfactory fuel while saving petroleum. But again the American Petroleum Institute and oil executives were critical of this potential competition with gasoline and tetraethyl lead.

Proposals for developing a grain-based synthetic rubber program have continued in the postwar period. There have been a number of bills in Congress calling for a federal subsidized experimental program that would use one or more of the government-built plants.[56] A major obstacle to be tackled is the relatively greater cost of grain. The oil industry publicly ridicules these efforts, along with the many suggestions made for petroleum substitutes for fuel. But, as always, it watches them carefully.

By the end of the war the new government-sponsored industry was producing under a million long tons annually. There was general agreement that the nation could never again afford to be caught without adequate rubber. The oil industry and its chemical and rubber colleagues advised that this could best be assured through private enterprise. They insisted that the government plants be sold. The Congress responded with the Rubber Act of 1948. This declared that the national security need of a "technologically advanced and rapidly expandable rubber-producing industry . . . can and will best be served by the development within the United States of a free competitive synthetic-rubber industry. . . . It is essential that Government ownership of production facilities, Government production of synthetic rubber . . . be ended and terminated whenever consistent with national security." [57]

Disposal was quickly undertaken as part of the general demobilization of $27 billion worth of declared surplus property. The Korean conflict postponed many of these sales, and government synthetic production again rose as stand-by plants were reactivated. With the cessation of hostilities the pattern of disposal was resumed, with the Eisenhower Administration viewing such action as a first step toward fulfilling the President's campaign pledges to denationalize government enterprises competing with private industry. "I am in hearty accord with the policy determination of the Congress that the security interests of the nation will best be served by the development within the United States of a free competitive synthetic rubber industry, and I believe that now is the time to undertake plant disposal." [58]

The remaining 26 plants were sold for $285 million, while one alcohol butadiene plant was leased. Trade journals were unanimous in voicing admiration for the tough price bargain government negotiators drove in receiving more than the net book value, after adjusting for depreciation. Less emphasized was the fact that these were profitable ventures, bringing the government about $166 million in profits from 1951 to 1955 in addition to an almost equal amount in depreciation. There was good promise of expanding synthetic needs, and a minority dissent by five members of the Senate Banking and Currency Committee claimed that on this basis the government could recover in profits and depreciation more money in four to five years than the proposed sales would return in ten years.[59]

The sales consolidated the patterns of control existing in rubber, petrochemicals, and oil, ensuring that the synthetic industry would develop primarily under the auspices of the corporate giants. Phillips, Shell, and Jersey Standard received about 31 per cent of the general-purpose synthetic rubber and butyl capacity; the big four rubber companies received 57 per cent. Synthetic rubber now provides two-thirds of the nation's new rubber consumption, the great bulk of this going into tires. Oil companies control about 35 per cent of synthetic capacity.

The growing working relationships between Gulf Oil and B. F. Goodrich and also between The Texas Company and the Du Pont-controlled United States Rubber Company were strengthened through the surplus purchases and subsequent expansion of Goodrich-Gulf Chemicals, Inc., and the Texas-U. S. Chemical Company. The two combines also jointly purchased the largest government butadiene plant at Port Neches, Texas, which accounted for about 30 per cent of the total petroleum butadiene capacity available. These actions have considerably furthered the integration of oil and rubber operations, both at the raw-material and fabrication stages and at the distribution end where tire sales are increasingly interwoven with the gasoline retail pattern. On the West Coast, Shell Oil bought an integrated package of butadiene, styrene, and GR-S (general purpose rubber) plants, despite some congressional opposition and competing bids for the separate facilities. Jersey Standard, which held the basic patent rights and built and operated the only two butyl plants, received these facilities. There was outside interest in their acquisition, but while Standard announced willingness to make the processes available to all on a royalty basis, there was less certainty of access to the feed stocks of isobutylene which came from nearby Standard refineries. Jersey has licensed butyl rubber patents and its research and engineering laboratories have continued their experiments with butyl. These all-synthetic tires are being used for military purposes, and in 1959 the company introduced them commercially.

The pattern of plant disposals assured the allied industries that no government plant could function as a price yardstick for natural and synthetic rubber or serve as a lever at any time the government decided production was not great enough. Public protection from the natural rubber monopoly and their prices, which invariably rise sharply at the hint of a crisis or increased demand, was also jeopardized. The sales to the existing giants substantiated the advance fears of smaller rubber users who had enjoyed the relative assurance of free and fair access when synthetic facilities were under government control. Although a majority of the firms were then or had been previously involved in antitrust suits, the Department of Justice raised no fundamental objection to the transactions which in certain respects ignored the criteria established for their sale. Some new producers have since entered the industry, but the Justice Department has noted the continuation of an almost complete lack of price competition. Through the combination of wartime necessity and an equal urgency to the presumptions of a "private enterprise" economy, the American taxpayer, having shouldered the risk and provided the capital, helped create a new billion-dollar industry for the giants of oil and rubber.

Natural Gas

If the issue of government jurisdiction over offshore oil has attracted the widest public attention, it has been the implications of federal policy concerning the production of natural gas that has aroused the deepest concern within oil circles. The role of gas is a basic consideration in the private planning of the oil industry for the country's energy patterns. The two resources derive from common geological origins, and the fear is everpresent that they might become genuinely competitive and yet share a common fate, that if anything approaching a public utility status is clearly established on an integrated basis for natural gas, it will inevitably foreshadow comparable controls over petroleum. About one-third of natural gas is produced from oil wells.

As was true with oil, one can trace back to ancient times the knowledge and limited use of combustible hydrocarbon gases and vapors that are confined under high pressure within certain rock formations. The Chinese, for example, were drilling for, piping, and burning natural gas for heat and light at least a thousand years before the birth of Christ. Some natural gas was sold for lighting in the United States beginning in 1821. Nevertheless its large-scale industrial and residential employment is of contemporary origin. While gas and the pressures it produces are key to the process of driving oil out of the ground, the natural gas itself was viewed as a waste, as the universal flaring of oil wells attested. Utilized chiefly in the immediate areas where it was found, notably the Appalachians and then the Southwest, it was available at low prices for industrial purposes and for powering oil and gas equipment in the field.

The accelerated quest for fuel and energy sources, combined with the diminishing reserves in the original Eastern fields of New York, Pennsylvania, Ohio, West Virginia, and Kentucky, and the development of modern construction techniques, led to the building of giant pipeline networks. These have spanned the nation and brought gas from the Gulf and midcontinent fields of Texas, Louisiana, Oklahoma and New Mexico to concentrated population and industrial centers in practically every region. Growing industrialization in the Southwest also enlarged the immediate market for gas which enjoyed a considerable price edge over coal and oil in providing energy for electric power generating plants and other installations. It has also been employed heavily in oil refineries and for the making of carbon black. An attractive fuel, convenient and clean for household uses and far less expensive to produce than the old manufactured gas that metropolitan utilities had so long supplied, natural gas has become a national necessity. The period 1925 to 1950 saw a fivefold increase in consumption, and by 1959 the industry was marketing over 12 trillion cubic feet of gas. While authoritative sources such as the President's Materials Policy Commission believe that "sooner or later, and probably before the end of the century, the meteoric natural gas industry will pass its peak," today it provides 25 per cent of the country's rising energy requirements.[60] This is approximately double the percentage of a decade ago. Natural gas has spiraled into the sixth largest industry of the nation, with facilities valued at $18 billion.

There are three component parts to the industry—production, transmission and distribution—in addition to a fourth concerned with such by-products as natural gasoline and petrochemicals. Distribution to the ultimate consumer is generally in the hands of long-established local utility corporations. These frequently have been linked through electric power holding companies and involved in many of the historic political conflicts over franchises and regulation that have been so characteristic a part of American municipal and state development and corruption. The natural monopoly inherent in providing gas service—for competing systems in a given area are viewed as inefficient and wasteful—has meant a public utility status under the control of local or state public service commissions.

As the urban demand for natural gas grew at the same time that many producers were in need of markets, it seemed inevitable that trunk transmission lines would be extended. But the older utilities and the oil companies that controlled the bulk of the pipelines often blocked or harassed efforts to bring in the cheaper natural gas. Through their financial and political power they used every stratagem, including pressure on banks against loans, private spying, and public bribery, to prevent competition by newer lines running from and tied in with large gas producers in the Southwest. Conscious of the power inherent in the strategic position of controlling the flow of gas from the fields—pipelines are the only effective way of transmitting gas—and confident of their immunity as interstate organizations from the jurisdiction of state regulatory bodies, the pipelines and their allies discriminated against or crushed independent producers, inflated assets, engaged in costly competitive wars and then more costly (to the consumer) territorial pacts. In all this they played off against one another the cities seeking service, frankly determined to get all the traffic would bear while keeping natural gas at rates equal to manufactured gas.[61]

Out of their unbridled arrogance and the resultant frustration of consumer-minded local public officials trying to set rates without possessing jurisdiction over the wholesale prices charged to the local utilities by the pipelines, there developed a series of congressional and Federal Trade Commission inquiries. These culminated in federal regulation of gas pipelines engaged in interstate commerce. Under the Natural Gas Act of 1938, the Congress declared that the business of transporting and selling natural gas for ultimate distribution to the public was affected with a public interest and hence federal supervision of what heretofore had been a private business was necessary. (Unlike petroleum pipelines, which are regulated by the Interstate Commerce Commission, they are not considered as common carriers legally obligated to be open to all shippers.) The Federal Power Commission was assigned responsibility for approving the construction of pipelines through the issuance of certificates of convenience and necessity and for judging the reasonableness of gas pipeline rates and corporate returns in all sales of natural gas intended for resale in interstate commerce. Today there are more than 125,000 miles of pipeline, largely in the hands of seventeen companies, that fall within this category.

While regulation of distribution and transmission has not come easily or operated without resistance and difficulty, it is in the area of production that the greatest controversy smolders. Here the oil industry is directly involved. Drilling has rarely been done primarily for gas, and most natural gas is found in the course of the quest for oil. Geologists tend to agree that natural gas by itself will be discovered in diminishing quantities and that the major supplies of this nonreplaceable resource will be found in oil fields. Gas production is heavily in the hands of or linked to oil companies who produce gas either in conjunction with oil (casing head gas) or from separate dry wells. Of the top thirty-five nontransporting producers, who in 1954 were responsible for over 70 per cent of all the natural gas sold to the interstate pipelines, twenty-two were big oil companies. Heading these were Phillips, Indiana Standard, Humble, Shell, Socony Mobil, Gulf, Cities Service, Atlantic, and Texas. Most of the nation's gas reserves are held by the major oil companies, with nineteen controlling one-half of the proved reserves. Phillips Petroleum and Jersey Standard's Humble Oil alone hold approximately a sixth.

Traditionally, the production of gas, along with oil, is under state control. Principles of conservation are presumed to be the guiding consideration. The state regulatory bodies are producer-oriented, with the latter's economic well-being a major concern. Gas prices have been rising steadily in response to the expanded demand. These have been accelerated by escalator, favored-nation, and renegotiation clauses in the pipeline contracts with producers. They call for the upward revision of rates to conform to the most recent and highest-priced contracts in the producing area. They also make possible increases in producer prices whenever the pipelines receive an increase in their resale of the gas to distributors. The industry's insistence that the price of gas is checked by its competitive relation with other fuels confirms that its immediate major objective has been to get the price of this once cheap fuel up on a par with that of petroleum. This would ensure that there is no price competition while denying to the consumer the benefits of a cheaper fuel and of the presumed virtue of a free market economy.

Proved reserves, estimated at 270 trillion cubic feet, are becoming more expensive to find. Producers like Phillips maintain that higher rates are in the public interest in that they need at least a 12 per cent return on their investments to meet replacement costs.[62] The pipeline companies, which themselves control about half of the gas wells and produce a fifth of the natural gas involved in interstate resale, are constantly in search of new fields whose reserves will justify the heavy initial investment involved in laying pipelines that cannot be moved about easily. They operate in a sellers' market, with prices set by the relatively few companies holding substantial blocks of reserves. What competition does exist takes place primarily among the pipeline buyers. There is little incentive to keep down prices paid since these frequently are bookkeeping prices paid to themselves as producers and in any case are costs that can be passed along and included within the regulated distribution utility rates. Thus the pivotal economic power in the gas industry has been shifted backward from the pipelines to the producers. A classic illustration existed in Wisconsin where the Michigan-Wisconsin Pipe Line Company, which serves all the utilities in the state, found its rates from its sole supplier, the Phillips Company, constantly moving upward in a ten-year period, with consumers, state officials, and the pipeline company almost helpless.

In the face of protests from public service commissions and utilities and out of their own experiences in administering the Natural Gas Act, the Federal Power Commission began to move actively to reexamine gas rates and their relation to the pattern of control of the industry. Sparked by Commissioner Leland Olds, a majority of the commission now concluded that natural gas regulation over pipeline and utility charges could not work without determination of what constitutes reasonable payments to the producer at the point where gas enters the trunk pipelines.[63] Such sales to pipelines were not just "incidental" to the production and gathering of gas, as frequently claimed, and therefore exempt from federal supervision. Rather were they viewed as basic to the flow of interstate commerce and hence within the purview of the original act. This law had sought to close the regulatory gap in the tripartite division of responsibility among the producing and consuming states and the federal government by assigning to the federal commission the interstate authority denied to the individual states.

On this basis the FPC determined gas prices the pipeline companies could pay to their own and subsidiary producing wells, forcing rate reductions amounting to several hundred million dollars. By court ruling in the Interstate Natural Gas Company case, its authority was extended over all sales in interstate commerce, including those made by independent producers (those not affiliated with pipelines). The Federal Power Commission then undertook a test analysis involving the rates of the Phillips Petroleum Company, the largest seller of natural gas to interstate pipelines. In 1951 a majority of the FPC, whose membership had changed again, denied to themselves this right to fix rates of a company engaged solely in the production and gathering of gas. This conclusion was challenged in court by the Wisconsin Public Service Commission and a number of county and municipality consumer bodies in Michigan, Wisconsin, and Missouri. Much of their case rested on the recognition that Phillips, far from being simply an independent producer, was also engaged in the buying of gas from other producers, processing and then sending it in its own pipelines to the Michigan-Wisconsin Pipe Line where the sale was then made. According to the chairman of the Wisconsin commission, representatives of his state received an ultimatum from a Phillips official that if they persisted in pushing this case, "the people of Wisconsin could freeze . . . they would never get another cubic foot of natural gas." [64]

The broader interpretation of their powers was reaffirmed by the decision of the United States Supreme Court in the Phillips case in 1954 which asserted that such review was the duty of the FPC. The commission, dominated by Eisenhower appointees, slowly began to take the steps indicated by the court, while making clear its overwhelming opposition to the exercise of this responsibility.

Against this setting, the political clashes have become open and sharp, paralleling at many points the offshore oil case. Gas and oil producers have resented these restrictions while anticipating demands for even more stringent federal inquiry into and control over prices at the well. The industry, with congressional representatives from the chief producing states carrying the ball, pushed legislation that clearly defined state responsibility over production and limited federal examination of the actual costs of gas by prohibiting FPC jurisdiction over independent producer sales to pipelines, in effect countering the Supreme Court. This was defended on the ground that this stage of the gas process was clearly competitive, engaging four thousand to eight thousand producers, most of whom were small and independent units not affiliated with any pipelines. Hines H. Baker, then executive vice president of the Humble Oil and Refining Company, testified:

The production and sale of oil and gas by the producer have been carried on in a free and competitive market unhampered by artificial restraint and price fixing except during the war period. Prices are controlled entirely by the natural relationships existing between supply and demand. . . . The producer of natural gas does not hold himself out to serve the public generally as does a utility, nor does he dedicate his property to a public use. He is engaged in a private, risk-taking enterprise in the same way that the producer of other commodities is engaged. There is no difference in this respect between the natural gas producing business and the business of producing corn or cotton, of mining oil or coal, or of producing the great body of goods and merchandise that enter into the American trade. . . . Furthermore, natural gas as a fuel is in competition with coal, oil, water power, and numerous other energy resources which are capable of great expansion in volume and variety of uses.[65]

Such a pattern had none of the characteristics that would justify a public utility status that in turn would serve only to limit initiative and risk capital in the private search for new gas reserves while creating an impossible bureaucratic morass. The consequences of this limitation on returns "constitute a confiscation of private property," concluded Mr. Baker. "The producer's incentive has been plowed under," and in store for the consumer was "nothing but diminished gas supplies," warned the gas company literature. Gas wells would be capped or supplies diverted to intrastate uses and the building of local industries. ". . . Thousands of miles of pipelines might ultimately have to carry orange juice or nothing," the writer David L. Cohn prophesied in a letter advertisement of the Empire Trust Company reprinted and circulated widely by the oil and gas industry. Gas is a luxury fuel, reasoned Senator J. W. Fulbright of Arkansas, who led the Senate legislative fight in 1956. For the millions of families who use gas, "it is a matter of choice. . . . They do not have to. They have an alternative . . . coal and oil. Coal is running out of our ears. Mr. Lewis is dying to sell them coal. Why do they not use coal if they do not like the price of gas? . . . It is easy to convert. . . ." Oil is available. "I can turn back to oil tomorrow if I do not like the price of gas. . . . It is not a necessity any more than a Cadillac." [66] Producer-state conservation controls, along with the effective pipeline and utility distribution machinery, could provide the necessary safeguards for gas consumers, while preserving the character of free enterprise and grass-roots democracy.

The major bills, reminiscent of offshore quitclaim legislation, were the Moore-Rizley bill in 1947, the Harris bill in 1949, the Kerr-Harris bill in 1950, and the Harris-Fulbright bill in 1956. Each met with strong resistance from a nucleus of senators, mayors, public service commissioners and, in the 1956 legislation, the local distributing utilities. The latter's championship of the consumer seemed unusual but was welcomed. Led by men like Senator Paul Douglas of Illinois and assistant corporation counsel James H. Lee of Detroit, the opponents argued the inadequacies of public utility and pipeline controls so long as producer prices were unchecked. They saw this legislation as opening the door to the destruction of gas regulation at every level, including pipeline.

In a masterfully documented speech, Mr. Douglas outlined the intent and consequences of the 1956 bill:

These pipeline companies get their gas in turn from two sets of sources, namely, first, the so-called, independent producers—approximately 79 percent or roughly four-fifths of the gas destined for interstate resale comes from this source; second, from wells which either the pipelines or their affiliates and subsidiaries own—these furnish about 21 percent or one-fifth of the total supply. Pipelines also buy a smaller quantity from other pipelines which is included in the 79 percent.

Even the big producers admit that under the present law the Federal Power Commission can control the price at which this second type of gas is charged into the system, namely, gas coming from the wells which the pipelines or their subsidiaries own.

The Kerr bill of 1949–50 did not propose to change this feature of the law but aimed to free from regulation the sales by the nontransporting producers. But the present Harris-Fulbright bill, like its grandparent, the Moore-Rizley bill, aims, however, to abolish effective regulation for both sources of gas, merely requiring the pipeline companies to charge in the gas they produce at a reasonable market price, which, if it means anything, means the prevailing price paid to the so-called nontransporting producers. Since the latter price will be unregulated under the Fulbright bill, this means that the chargeable price of the natural gas produced by the pipelines will also, in effect, be unregulated.[67]

The pattern had been unfolded the previous year in a House questioning of Jerome K. Kuykendall, Chairman of the Federal Power Commission, who favored such legislation:

Mr. Heselton: Do you believe, if Mr. Harris' bill is passed, you will have a situation where these large companies can come in and say, first, "We are not under Federal regulation," and then they can turn around and say to the State commission, "We are not under State regulation"? . . .

Mr. Kuykendall: Well, I believe it is pretty clear that these sales by producers of gas which move in interstate commerce would still be in interstate commerce and I think that it is probably true that these sales would not be covered in the Natural Gas Act and that they could not be regulated by the State authorities, except in the exercise of their powers of conservation. Two states now do control prices for that purpose; *but they put a floor under the price rather than a ceiling.* [Italics added]

There would be a gap, unless . . . competition is adequate or can be made adequate by proper application of the antitrust laws, to insure by that means that the price is fair.[68]

From the consumer's perspective, the advocates of control pointed out, the entire system is essentially monopolistic rather than competitive. The consumer has perhaps $15 billion invested in gas appliances, a factor frequently overlooked in discussions of the need to protect investments. Once he is committed to this service, he has little choice, for economically he is not likely to switch to an alternative fuel. The United Gas Improvement Company, which operates Philadelphia's municipal gas plant, testified it would cost each customer in excess of $1,000 to replace gas home heating with oil.

The distributing utilities told how field gas prices had frequently more than doubled in less than a decade, once they had been tied up to transmission lines with long-term contracts and had changed over their systems for natural gas. When asked at FPC hearings why they acceded to contracts with escalation clauses that were certain to bring price rises, transmission and distribution companies with assets of $100 million and more have explained that they felt they had no choice in their negotiations with the major producers if they wanted to be assured of a gas supply. This relationship suggests startling resemblances to that existing between the little retail gasoline station and its supplier. Utility spokesmen warned that some New England gas companies were paying prices at or approaching a breaking point where the competition from substitute fuels might be effective.

Producer representatives dismissed these as crocodile tears. "Compared to the price of other fuels and to the cost-of-living in general, natural gas has been and continues to be an outstanding bargain." [69] They argued that only the smallest part of the gas dollar goes for its production and that it is the utilities who are responsible for the high rates. But, regardless of the validity of their criticisms of utility rate regulation, this ignored the warnings of Olds and Douglas that a price increase of one cent per thousand cubic feet at the well could mean a total consumer increase of $60 million, based on 1955 sales. With prices edging up from a 10-cent average to actual and antici-pated levels of 15, 20, and even 25 cents per thousand cubic feet, prices that some industry spokesmen have made clear are justifiable, the added annual increase for consumers could be from $300 to $900 million. Under the beneficent protection of industry-sought legislation that would authorize the FPC to allow producers "the current market price," the various new and renegotiated contracts would inevitably trigger the average wellhead price upward 100 per cent or more.

It has also been pointed out that such price increases would mean a fabulous windfall totaling billions of dollars for those oil companies who control the great reserves they acquired and developed at con-siderably lower costs than would be charged to the pipelines if, as the gas industry insisted, reasonable market value prices for gas at the wellhead were to prevail. At the time of the Harris-Fulbright bill controversy, a field price rise of 5 to 10 cents per thousand cubic feet would have meant an increase of $10.5 to $21 billion in the worth of the estimated 210 trillion cubic feet of proved reserves, with Humble and Phillips alone standing to gain at least $1.5 to $3 billion. By 1957 the stake was even greater, with reserves approaching 240 trillion cubic feet in addition to offshore gas. Furthermore, as the President's Materials Policy Commission noted, "if in the future about 6 M cu. ft. of natural gas can be expected to be discovered for every barrel of oil, each 5-cent price rise of natural gas would be the equivalent, in its effect of stimulating exploration, of a 30-cent increase in the price of a barrel of oil. On the whole, the cost of finding a barrel of oil to date has probably been on the order of 30 or 40 cents in 1950 pur-chasing power, so that the possible increase of natural gas prices would be quite significant relative to that cost." [70] This is in addition to the very favorable tax allowances producers receive to encourage exploration and compensate for dry-hole expenditures. Gas men invariably exaggerate the risk for the majors in the search for gas. They rarely mention the depletion allowance and the items allowed as exploration and development cost by the FPC and Internal Revenue Service when bewailing the harm that being subject to utility regulation on a cost basis would cause in the search for new reserves. As with oil, their case here rests on the dubious assumption that the gas taken out of the ground is a capital asset and that the industry should be compensated for this loss and its replacement costs as they determine them rather than on an analysis of costs of operations and a fair profit.

Advocates of federal control have challenged the image of the small independent producer in whose name the pleas for free enterprise have been made. More than 95 per cent of the 5,500 producers not owned or affiliated with pipelines supply the pipelines with 10 per cent of their total gas purchases. In 1954, 90 per cent of all sales to pipelines were made by less than 200 gas producers; 35 accounted for over 70 per cent, and of these 22 were major oil companies. A Federal Power Commission report for 1955 indicated that the top nine producers were responsible for 36 per cent of all natural gas sales to pipelines. In order of volume, these included seven oil companies— Phillips, Stanolind (Indiana Standard), Humble, Shell, Magnolia (Socony), Texas, and Atlantic Refining. They received 34 per cent of the revenues while 95 per cent of the producers received less than 10 per cent.[71]

As proof of their sympathy for genuine small business, Leland Olds, Senator Douglas, Representative John Heselton, and others have proposed exempting from FPC control those who produce under 2 billion cubic feet a year, a provision that would cover more than 90 per cent of the gas producers and simplify regulatory problems while still maintaining under federal jurisdiction 90 per cent of the gas produced for interstate commerce. This has been rejected by the big gas and oil interests on the ground that control over some would result in control over all gas producers. It has also been argued that a principle is at stake which is not open to compromise, a position that reinforces the suspicion that the industry defense of the "small man" is a convenient if familiar subterfuge.

None of the major legislative attempts to end or limit federal controls was successful. The Moore-Rizley and Harris bills were approved by the House of Representatives, but did not get through the Senate. The Kerr bill was vetoed by President Truman, who said withdrawal from this field of regulation would not be in the public interest. The Harris-Fulbright bill suffered a similar fate at the hands of President Eisenhower. The latter's action was not taken on the ground of lack of sympathy with the basic principles. It was prompted more by an obviously unsavory situation accentuated by a disclosure by Republican Senator Francis Case of South Dakota that in the closing days of the legislative debate $2,500 had been turned over to his campaign fund by an out-of-state oil representative who had been making inquiries as to the senator's attitude on the pending natural gas bill. Expressing the sentiments of his members, President Frank M. Porter of the American Petroleum Institute declared that the industry was "deeply disappointed." He added that "in the light of the political and legislative uncertainty which that veto has created, as well as the chaos which will result in the natural gas producing industry, the initiative for any new legislation, which certainly will be needed, must now come from the President if it is to be successful." [72]

With the 1956 election out of the way, this reassurance was forthcoming. In his Budget message to the Congress, President Eisenhower indicated he still favored the basic principles of the Harris-Fulbright bill. "Legislation freeing gas producers from public utility-type regulation is essential if the incentives to find and develop new supplies of gas are to be preserved and sales of gas to interstate markets are not to be discouraged to the detriment of both consumers and producers, as well as the national interest." [73]

There was considerable soul searching within the industry concerning the black eye received during the Case incident. Some predicted that the combination of this and the oil price increase during the Suez crisis meant that it would be wisest for the industry to be silent and ask for nothing for a while. But those most concerned with gas legislation sought to repair the damage to their efforts. The call went out for industry unity. Producers, pipelines, and distributing utilities met repeatedly in search of a bill satisfactory to each segment. A compromise was worked out. Its language accepted the principle of the Phillips case ruling—but it denied the utility status of producers. The Federal Power Commission was authorized to review sales contracts made by producers, with the power to reject them if they threatened the consumer through more than a reasonable market price. Costs could not be considered as a basis for arriving at this price. Escalator clauses were limited, although by no means abolished. Producers found these gains inadequate, for the bill did accept the theory of federal control while giving up several economic rights and the possibility of state "conservation laws" guaranteeing minimum prices. But they viewed it as a step in the right direction. Limiting the escalation contracts helped win some of the big Eastern distributing utilities who in 1956 had thundered against the inequities of this legislation and the sins of the producers.

Their political standard-bearers were reluctant to get out on the front lines on this issue again, especially after the Eisenhower veto. Many of them viewed the President's action as a strategic withdrawal or desertion under fire, with the lobbying issue serving as a convenient moral posture for a political gain. Said Senator Fulbright: "I will not introduce it again. I spent a great deal of time last year on a . . . good bill . . . that the President vetoed for no relevant reason. I've put all the time into it that I'm going to put in. If it comes up, I shall no doubt vote for it—but no more than that. If the President wants a bill he can find his own sponsor for it." [74] The other former sponsor, Democratic Representative Oren Harris of Arkansas, who was chairman of the House Interstate and Foreign Commerce Committee, was more amenable. But he too indicated that the President would have to let us know "what he wants, what he will go all-out for and support, and what he will approve." [75]

A bill was offered in the House, without too much hope for its passage. Mr. Eisenhower announced his general support of its principles, as did the chairman of the Federal Power Commission. Then Administration spokesmen suggested amendments that the President indicated would safeguard the consumer, who obviously had been left out of the industry conferences. One of these called for striking out the absolute prohibition against the FPC's examining costs in determining "reasonable market prices." The other continued the power of the FPC to review escalator-clause price increases in contracts. At this point the coalition threatened to disintegrate, certain that their case was hopeless. Independent producer groups who had felt the Harris bill was inadeqate now called it "totally unacceptable." Advocates of regulation, on the other hand, labeled all these proposals, including the original bill, as sugar coating offering only the illusion of protection to the gas consumer. For "reasonable market price" was based on the myth of a free, competitive economy and in effect meant that the gas producers were free to get all that their control over the market would allow. They reminded producers that the Natural Gas Act had helped make it possible for them to sell their gas in an expanded market at prices relatively free from pipeline dictation. Their proposals to exempt the smaller producers were again brushed aside, however.

A last-minute industry plea to the President once more appeared to change the picture. In a letter to Representative Harris, the bill's co-sponsor, Mr. Eisenhower re-emphasized the importance of freeing producers. He let it be known that his amendments had been offered "as of possible desirability, but do not represent my fixed conclusions." At a press conference he added: "I didn't indicate that those amendments were of such importance that it would affect my actions." [76] With this cue, the amendments were then disposed of in the House Interstate and Foreign Commerce Committee. Hope was voiced for House passage of the bill and that by 1958 the Senate would concur. But the leadership decided that they were not likely to get adequate support, and so the measure was postponed until the next session.

If up until this point the industry was unsuccessful in Congress, it still did not have cause to despair. For despite the Supreme Court interpretation in the Phillips case that the Natural Gas Act did apply to gas sold in interstate commerce, a majority of the Federal Power Commission has repeatedly expressed the general orientation of the Eisenhower Administration by its reluctance to accept this role. It has openly supported the oil and gas interests in their quest for legislative relief, with the White House and FPC chairman Kuykendall playing an active part in getting the industry factions to coalesce. Gas companies have been filing thousands of rate-increase requests, and many are being allowed by the FPC.

In 1957 the "Memphis" decision of the Circuit Court of Appeals threw a new scare into the industry. The court held that all proposals by interstate pipelines for rate increases must have full FPC hearings, unless there was a specific contractual authorization for such boosts from all customers. The companies feared being forced to refund some $240 million for increases that had not yet been approved by the FPC. In their appeal, they pointed out that this would halt all new construction and bankrupt many of them. They had the full backing of the FPC, which warned that consumers would be hurt. The following year, by a 5 to 3 vote, the Supreme Court reversed the decision and returned to the older practice of allowing pipelines to file increases that would automatically take effect, although subject to FPC review and possible refunds. "Business reality," wrote Justice John M. Harlan for the majority, "demands that natural gas companies should not be precluded by law from increasing the prices of their products. . . ." In his dissent, Justice William O. Douglas said that the decision reduced the Natural Gas Act to a "shambles" so far as consumers are concerned, for it "turns the real regulation over to the pipeline companies." [77]

Meanwhile, net profits have risen and the industry has continued to expand, with an anticipated construction outlay of $8 billion for the period 1958–1961. It has indicated a willingness to withhold sales in interstate commerce until it receives the production regulation immunity it seeks. There is no question as to the ability of the oil and gas giants to do this for the short run, although as Leland Olds and others have noted, the consumers of producer states will suffer from higher rates. But the industry remains apprehensive and is determined to secure the necessary congressional sanction to upset the court's position as to the duty of the Federal Power Commission and the meaning of the original Natural Gas Act.

Underlying this concern is the basic belief that it is impossible technically and legally to work out costs and reasonable rates for natural gas without opening to public view the costs of oil which is produced in conjunction with the gas. In 1946 President Alfred Jacobsen of the Amerada Petroleum Corporation testified in behalf of the industry as to "the fear prevalent in many in the oil-producing industry that the Federal Power Commission will endeavor by means of a flank attack on the industry to secure direct or indirect control of oil production. . . . They have asked a lot of questions about production and production methods and production costs. It just looks very suspicious and we are afraid of it." [78]

Ernest O. Thompson, long the leading figure on the Texas Railroad Commission which regulates the industry in his state, has repeatedly supported the arguments of the industry:

One thing that we have run up against in our attempts to require that casing-head gas be collected and saved is that the oil producers have been laboring under the fear that if they hooked onto a pipe line and saved this gas and pumped it into an interstate pipe line, that they would be declared a natural gas company under the Natural Gas Act and their whole operation thereby would come under the limitation of 6½ percent earnings on their total business. . . . Their oil operations will become also subject to public utility regulation on a cost basis, giving no credit for dry holes drilled in the search for new fields; but considering only the cost of wells drilled in producing fields.[79]

This was a major contention of the various gas and oil producer associations in their unsuccessful amici curiae brief in the Phillips case.

". . . The foot is in the door looking to the jurisdiction of the Federal Power Commission over the oil industry," the president of Sun Oil told the company executives. ". . . A long step has been taken toward control of the petroleum industry" added Texaco's president. "So long as it operates in the shadow of natural gas regulation, the petroleum industry, along with other competitive industries as well, is under perhaps an even greater threat," insisted Chairman K. S. Adams of Phillips. "If the power of the federal government can reach to the wellheads of oil and gas fields in Texas or Oklahoma, it can likewise reach to the crop rows of Iowa, the dairy sheds of Minnesota, the mine faces of Illinois and wholly change the character of private enterprise as well as the character of government in this land of ours," declared Governor Allan Shivers of Texas. The Supreme Court Phillips ruling gave a toe hold to "the political and philosophic socialists who would destroy incentive by nationalizing everything in a Utopian state," concluded Walter S. Hallanan, chairman of the National Petroleum Council.[80]

Hines H. Baker of the Humble Oil Company echoed the warnings of all the oil associations:

The regulation by the Federal Power Commission of production and gathering and the price of natural gas when sold by the producer or gatherer will lead inevitably to full Federal control of oil and gas production, including conservation regulations and either ousts the States from this function or sets up a dual system of regulations with all the uncertainty, doubt, expense and bureaucratic harassment that this would involve.[81]

Proponents of federal control insist their only focus is gas and that here they recognize and would allow for the risk inherent in production which is frequently greater than that of electric and other utilities. While defending regulation as within the American tradition, they deny any ulterior intent to regulate oil, and point out that any attempt to use the Natural Gas Act for such ends "would certainly be promptly and categorically condemned by the courts." [82] But the specter that remains to haunt oilmen, beyond limitation on the sacred right to profit from natural resources, is not any assault upon abstract concepts of capitalism and states' rights. Rather is it the precedent of oil activities operating in a competitive framework and at least in part responsible to public agencies and standards. This represents a clear challenge to the private planning of the government of oil.

6

The Uses of Public Government

To accept at face value the industry's projected image of itself as self-reliant and of public government as evil is to misunderstand the nature of oil operations and philosophy. The actions of this industry are essentially realistic, not ideological. The highly developed private government of oil seeks the support of public government where-ever its own political and economic machinery is inadequate for fulfilling industry objectives and wherever its practices run counter to the legal and value systems of the American people. Nowhere is the amoral purposefulness of the oil industry and the accompanying political vacuity of America's public policy more vividly illustrated than in the areas of taxation and what is euphemistically known as "conservation." Through taxes and related subsidies the American government supports the industry in developing its productive ca-pacity. At the same time, through the whole complex conservation system the government backs the planned withholding of products.

Conservation is a genuine, if belated, concern for the nation as well as for the industry. For too long the dramatic gusher spouting black gold over the ground symbolized. the hope, greed, ignorance, and waste of oil operations. Losses by fire, water flooding, leakage, and evaporation were common. Uncontrolled production, without regard for scientifically spacing wells sufficiently far apart and such factors as proper tubing, casing, and cementing, has meant the dis-sipation of the vital underground gas and water pressures needed to bring forth the petroleum. The result has been the by-passing of much of the crude oil.

Encouraging this extravagance have been the historic court inter-pretations supporting the right of the owner of a plot of land to the

132

minerals beneath the surface. Pools of petroleum and gas were not viewed as stationary, but assumed to flow like water without regard for property lines. This underground movement was equated with the behavior of wild animals possessing the power and the tendency to escape. Under common law, a property owner had the right to all the oil he could "capture" through drilling on his land, regardless of the origins of the oil. With this rule of capture governing their activities, producers raced to sink wells within their own boundaries —often on the edge of their neighbors' property—seeking to exhaust the oil as quickly as possible lest their neighbors in the same field beat them in draining off all the oil and gas. This pattern has led more than one observer to conclude that the law forces oil production to be conducted on the principle of robbery.

Serious conservation efforts have meant the replacement of this anarchic jungle behavior by planned production. Developing maximum utilization of the underground reservoir pressures and oil recovery over a long time basis have become recognized engineering principles. Gas repressuring methods, involving the injection back into fields of dry gas that has been stripped of liquids, have been encouraged. Such efforts require coordination. Otherwise the conservation-minded producer might have the fruits of his foresight taken by others in the field. And since most fields have not been in the hands of a single operator whose economic interests conceivably might readily be served by such conservation considerations, there evolved the public regulation of private leasing and production arrangements. These laws also attempted to protect the rights of the property owners to their share of the pool beneath their land. While these developments in conservation came only after considerable controversy within the industry and in the courts, the awareness of the limits to known proved reserves and a growing reaction against the wanton despoilment of so much of the nation's physical heritage spurred popular support of such state policies.

Much less visible for public agitation but even more real in the minds of oilmen has been a somewhat different interpretation of conservation. This is economic waste. Here the ultimate conserving has to do with the investments of producing companies and the prices of refined oil. Since the earliest days of oil, it has been a basic and consistent industry objective to keep prices stable and immune from sharp drops occasioned by the increased production from new discoveries. Refiners like Rockefeller, aiming to do away with "excessive and undue competition," worked in collusion with the railroads in attempting to maintain quotas. Borrowing a technique from their avowed exploiters, some producers combined to set secret and then open production allowables. Ida M. Tarbell vividly caught the mood of the experiments with voluntary controls and planned shutdowns in the Pennsylvania oil region in 1872:

> There was nothing but public opinion to hold the producers to their pledge [to stop drilling for six months]. But public opinion in those days in the Oil Regions was fearless and active and asserted itself in the daily newspapers and in every meeting of the association. The whole body of oil men became a vigilance committee intent on keeping one another loyal to the pledge. Men who appeared at church on Sunday in silk hats, carrying gold-headed canes—there were such in the Oil Region in 1872—now stole out at night to remote localities to hunt down rumours of drilling wells. If they found them true, their dignity did not prevent their cutting the tools loose or carrying off a band wheel.[1]

But the age of concentration and integration in oil was only in its formative stage. The competitive spirit was still dominant, and the potential for new fields and new fortunes too attractive for the effective organization of oilmen along such self-denying lines. "Progress was slow," confesses the American Petroleum Institute in a recent review of conservation history, "because the petroleum industry had its share of 'rugged individualists'—many of whom had contributed much to the growth of the industry, but who wanted no abridgment of their right to produce oil when and where they pleased."[2]

After World War I the industry hunted frantically for new sources throughout the world. Once the problem shifted from that of scarcity to abundance, the imperative for dealing with flush production accelerated the trend toward state controls. From the public viewpoint this was in harmony with the general movement for conservation of natural resources and was further justified by the appeal for the protection of basic local industries. In 1915 Oklahoma passed a conservation law dealing with economic waste. Other oil states followed. On the urging of some oilmen, in 1924 President Coolidge called attention to the wastefulness of oil production on both public and private lands by creating a Federal Oil Conservation Board "to study the government's responsibilities and to enlist the full co-operation of representatives of the oil industry in the investigation. . . . The oil industry itself might be permitted to determine its own future. That future might be left to the simple workings of the law of supply and demand but for the patent fact that the oil industry's welfare is so intimately linked with the industrial prosperity and safety of the whole people, that government and business can well join forces to work out this problem of practical conservation." [3] Under the impetus of the findings of this board, which functioned actively from 1924 to 1932 with four Cabinet members and an in-dustry advisory body, the states re-examined and intensified their conservation efforts. Out of the concept of prorating for each field a percentage of its productive capacity to ensure maximum recovery, there evolved the system of prorationing. Under prorationing, state public agencies set monthly production allowables based upon what has been known as market demand. Market demand is determined after public hearings where statements (nominations) by crude oil purchasers as to the amounts they expect to buy during the next month are received and studied along with such data as the crude stock currently in storage. Once the "reasonable market demand" is estimated, individual fields and wells are then assigned their al-lowables. Where effective, this has meant "orderly marketing" charac-terized by a predictable flow of products to known markets with a minimum of "economic waste" and price fluctuation. With above-ground stockpiling of oil difficult and expensive, reason the de-fenders of this system, such support of prices encourages continued exploration and assures a dependable supply while providing the soundest incentive for physical conservation. Furthermore, this makes possible the development of productive capacity above immediate needs, as governmental defense officials have requested, and enables the industry to meet national emergency demands on short notice without adversely affecting its normal operations and profits. Con-servation thus eliminates the old bogy of "distress oil." The con-venient image is that of ten cents a barrel depression prices—a level that big oil helped to force in seeking to wipe out independents in East Texas. But the underlying fear is of competitively set prices.

The majors generally advocate state legislative and administrative rulings encouraging the widest possible well spacing. The high capital waste of unnecessary drilling has been repeatedly documented over the years. President M. J. Rathbone of Jersey Standard estimated that had the industry been able to double the spacing of the 13,000 oil wells completed in Texas in 1956, expenditures would have been reduced $360 million and there would have been an additional annual saving in operating costs of $10 million. This total saving would have been equivalent to thirty-five cents for each barrel of crude produced in Texas that year. "We should also consider that the drilling of many of these 13,000 wells in Texas did not go to increase our production, but rather resulted in further pro-rating the production from wells already drilled." [4]

The majors have also come to favor the use of state power to compel the coordinated development of a field by recalcitrant landholders, royalty owners, and producers unwilling to join voluntarily in the unitization of their operations. Under such arrangements, well placement is based on efficient production rather than on property-ownership lines. Equipment is pooled in a joint operation, with profits and dry-hole losses prorated among all the participants on the basis of such factors as individual acreage and reserves. This obviously has merit as a conservation measure. One recent study indicates that approximately 11.5 per cent of domestic production now comes from unitized projects, with sizable increases in recoverable yields. [5] Manpower, materials, and energy reserves can be saved, with some benefit ultimately accruing, presumably, to the consumer. This practice also reveals the industry's willingness to use government coercion when convenient, raising further question as to the industry's declared commitment to the virtues of an unbridled competitive economy.

But oil fields have no more respect for the sanctity of state lines than they do for property lines. The fabulous discoveries beginning in the late twenties and paralleling the great depression shook the established patterns of the industry. As noted earlier, its international leaders were searching for a formula for controlling production. Fitting the United States domestic industry into such a system posed special considerations, for this country was not directly included in the formal world-wide agreements. To compound the international companies' difficulties, the East Texas strike was largely in the hands of independent operators. This accessibility to a plentiful supply of crude opened the door to the return of the independent refiner, a situation that would undo much of the scarcity-oriented activities within the industry during its previous sixty years. Voluntary restrictions on drilling and output along with private prorationing by the pipelines were inadequate for checking rising production. State laws were limited and disparate. Direct federal controls were proposed, but rejected by much of the industry. Then too, constitutional precedents viewing petroleum production as mining, and hence essentially intrastate rather than interstate commerce, appeared to uphold the supremacy of state police power while precluding the possibility of federal regulation.

In 1928 a Committee of Nine from the national government, the Mineral Law Section of the American Bar Association, and the oil industry, was appointed by the Federal Oil Conservation Board. It recommended the furthering of voluntary integration and of voluntary output curtailment among oil producers. In the following year the American Petroleum Institute renewed earlier requests to the Federal Oil Conservation Board for approval of intercompany agreements that would dovetail with world-wide production limitations. United States output was to be maintained at the 1928 levels. Domestic producers were suspicious unless this was accompanied by import restrictions. And the entire proposal was discouraged by the Attorney General, who warned that the industry was seeking immunity from the operation of the antitrust laws, a sanction beyond the powers of the board. Meanwhile, despite the cooperative efforts of state officials through a new Oil States Advisory Committee, oil prices continued to drop below the production costs of established wells as the race for new wells continued. Not even the use of state troops in Oklahoma and Texas holding fields under martial law sufficed to check the rising production. And so in 1933 the demoralized magnates of oil, along with many smaller operators and state governors, were to descend upon Washington.

"This is not an experiment in dictatorship, it is an experiment in cooperation. . . . This is not czarism; this is industrial self-government," assured General Hugh S. Johnson in welcoming the oilmen as they privately speculated as to what manner of men these New Dealers were. The National Industrial Recovery Act with its over-all goal of revitalizing the economy and its provisions for industry-wide agreements exempt from antitrust action had just been past, and Johnson was its administrator. The representatives of the nation's oil associations were meeting in the auditorium of the United States Chamber of Commerce in Washington to discuss a proposed Code of Fair Competition for the Petroleum Industry. Most of them had met just previously in Chicago under the sponsorship of the American Petroleum Institute to prepare a united plan. There was talk about conservation and national needs. But prices, profits, and private rights clearly took precedence among oilmen worried about the chances for maintaining a social environment that had long endowed property with economic and political power. The president of the API pleaded for federal intervention to end flush and famine cycles with their accompanying price fluctuations. "First and foremost is a balancing of crude oil products with consumer demand." A Standard of California vice president won great applause for putting oil's viewpoint on the line to these new political men of power: "If you do not give us price regulation, you can make codes from now to doomsday and you will get nowhere." Another prominent oilman, the first president of the Independent Petroleum Association of America, defended the planning and price fixing inherent in the code: "The welfare of the entire nation demands that a strong hand shall control those who are operating these natural resources in which all the people have an interest." [6]

There were minority discordant notes. Some union representatives, handicapped by limited organization in the industry, felt the codes neglected labor's needs while excluding them from the proposed new administrative agencies. There were occasional warnings that the consumer would pay for all this planning. Farm cooperatives were opposed to a provision in the preliminary code that precluded the paying of rebates on petroleum purchases to members. And there was hostility from some independents who mistrusted controls in the hands of the government of oil as much as in the hands of the Government of the United States. One oilman deplored the failure to take a stand against the discriminatory practices of the pipelines owned or controlled by the major integrated companies. Like the railroads of yesterday, these supposed common carriers took rebates on every barrel of oil they shipped and drawbacks on every barrel shipped by independents, he charged. "It is the most complete monopoly that exists in the oil business today, and, therefore, it was found necessary, I presume, by the Chicago Code, to not include it within its provisions. They do not need the strong argument [*sic*] of government to perfect monopoly in pipelines. It is already perfected, and they do not want any interference with it." [7] Others were bitter at General Johnson's refusal to guarantee government-sponsored price fixing, in addition to the already gained assurances that the higher costs of smaller oilmen would be taken into consideration.

The oil code set into motion in 1933 the industrial government sought by many of the majors and independent oil interests. Its key provisions paralleled the recommendations of the API meeting, tempered by the pressures of articulate small producers. Production and consumption were to be brought into balance. State prorationing laws were now to have federal support. Interstate and foreign shipment of oil produced outside quotas formulated under the supervision of Secretary of the Interior Ickes and a Petroleum Administrative Board, who were to administer the code, were outlawed. (Oil had also won an important procedural battle in keeping the industry code separate from the rest of the NRA machinery.) A joint industry-government committee, dominated by oilmen, was created to serve as a continuing liaison in implementing the new regulations. Mr. Ickes saw this as advisory. As it turned out, the industry committee was to control the policies as well as the day-to-day workings of the entire program.

During the first months of the New Deal, Secretary Ickes reported that "I am under tremendous pressure from the oil people to put into effect a schedule of prices." [8] As the chaos and crises of depression continued, industry proposals were made to give the Petroleum Administration virtually dictatorial powers over oil. Although the majors generally opposed direct price fixing, in 1934 the president of the API was still assuring his oil brethren of the ability of the federal government to control prices and production "intelligently, fairly and courageously." At one point the head of Standard of New Jersey even proposed that the government operate the flowing East Texas field on a unitized basis.

Meanwhile, some independents remained skeptical. Their industry's private government had received through the NRA the necessary sanction to wear the mantle of public government. But neither the

policy nor the machinery was theirs. Choked by the production limitations, they regarded the code as an API device to perpetuate scarcity
and monopoly in the name of conservation and fair play. With considerable justification, they charged that local proration committees
were often dominated by the personnel of the majors and of closely
allied "independents." Industry trials, pool-buying programs, price
fixing, boycotting, and black-listing were all employed to curtail production.

The Supreme Court soon ended the NRA, viewing it as a delegation
of congressional authority to the executive branch transcending constitutional limits. It thus terminated an experiment some had hailed
as democratic captalism's answer to the challenge of planning and
others had depicted as the beginnings of corporate fascism. The oil
industry, however, was prepared. As prices rose and general economic
conditions throughout the country improved, oil leaders re-evaluated
their panic-inspired appeals to Washington. A dangerous precedent
had been created. By 1935 the head of the API was castigating the
regimentation and bureaucracy inherent in central political authority.
In contrast, he eulogized the constitutional virtues of state power.
To forestall rising interest in federal regulation and the possibility
of utility status, discussed by Ickes and attributed to the thinking of
President Roosevelt, the industry once again considered more formal
interstate cooperation that would make possible intercorporate agreements. This had previously been recommended by the old Federal
Oil Conservation Board after the rejection of the Committee of Nine
and API proposals. The NRA codes paved the way.

In 1935 the Congress authorized an Interstate Compact to Conserve Oil and Gas that formalized a working relationship among
oil-state governors that had existed prior to the NRA. Renewed periodically, the measure made possible joint consultation and action
among the member states. With promotion of "maximum ultimate
recovery" of oil and gas again the stated objective, the Compact Commission (IOCC) has been a forum, research center, and proselytizer
for better conservation methods. It has also served as an effective
meeting place for furthering the coordination of official production
and pricing controls characteristic of most oil states. These state controls have been designed to ensure that production never outruns

market demand, that is, the amount of oil the industry leaders estimate is likely to be consumed at industry-set prices.

Potential oil states are fitted into this price-support program by conservation laws based on an IOCC model. This is generally pushed for adoption by industry or Compact Commission representatives before oil becomes a public issue in the new states. Some thirty oil-producing or oil-expectant states are now linked to the Compact by treaty.[9]

All the states involved have some type of conservation law and an administrative board that supervises actual production as well as the formulation of allowables. By virtue of its control over 40 per cent of the nation's domestic supply, the Texas Railroad Commission remains the key state agency within the Interstate Oil Compact. For several years now the major oil companies have submitted estimates of their anticipated imports to this commission. Each of the states receives a monthly statement of existing petroleum stocks and a forecast of market demand for the state's oil prepared by the Bureau of Mines in the United States Department of Interior—based upon industry-furnished information—a function taken over from the former Petroleum Administration Board and then the Petroleum Administration for War. These, together with the allowables set by the state commissions, serve as industry guides. Production in excess of the prorationing orders violates state laws and is subject to confiscation, just as interstate shipment of such "hot oil" violates the Interstate Transportation of Petroleum Products Act (Connally Act). This control had been sought by the industry and the producing states to replace a section of the unconstitutional NRA. Senator Tom Connally of Texas quickly steered it through the Senate in 1935 without hearings. This law has been administered by the Federal Petroleum Board in Interior's Oil and Gas Office, and since 1958, in Geological Survey. It puts federal power behind the state agreements and serves as a weapon against the frantic and often secretive trade of determined producers frustrated by low allowables. The oil industry thus neatly avoids the twin horrors of competition and antitrust action. It obtains from the government services that support its private price fixing and that would be unlawful if provided by the API or another trade association. In a speech to petroleum men in 1954, Assistant

Secretary for Mineral Resources Felix E. Wormser depicted with pride the success of this operation: "I asked the Bureau [of Mines] to give me a total figure covering all of the forecasts made monthly from July 1935, when it started, through July 1954, and the actual crude oil production reported for the same period. I was astonished to find that the total amounted to approximately 32 billion barrels and the difference between the forecast and actual production has been less than one percent." [10] Small wonder an industry team making a survey of the Department of Interior as part of an effort to cut big government reported that "the statistical work of the Bureau with regard to oil and gas is a very important part of its contribution to industry" and that "nothing should be done to curtail this part of the Bureau's activities." [11]

This entire control system is frequently defended because it strengthens the bargaining position of independent producers by lessening competition among them and enabling them to get their fair share of the market allowables. It is also seen as cutting down on the discriminatory practices of big purchasers who otherwise might favor pools where they had their own source of gas and petroleum. The state agencies are able at least theoretically to stand up to the power of the integrated giants in cases where independent producers would remain silent out of fear of economic reprisals. Oklahoma and Kansas have had minimum wellhead price laws for natural gas sold in interstate commerce. But these have been successfully challenged in the courts by the federal government on the grounds that such control was within the jurisdiction of the Federal Power Commission. One hope of some of the interests pushing in Congress the current bills to prevent effective federal regulation of natural gas production is the granting of a go-ahead signal for state conservation agencies. In Texas, many of the smaller gas men have agitated for the extension of prorationing to gas. They have felt that if the Railroad Commission were given the authority to shut in gas fields where the preferred prices at the wellhead were too low, and presumably a threat to "conservation," they would have a powerful defense against the monopoly position that giant pipeline purchasers like the Lone Star Gas Company enjoy in some fields. Then too, this could serve as a lever to force up prices at the wellhead in face of the potential threat of Federal Power Commission price regulation. This state control measure was strongly although unsuccessfully pushed in the Texas legislature during 1955 at the very time the industry was fighting the heavy hand of government controls over gas in Washington.

At times some of the states have raised their petroleum allowables beyond purchaser nominations because of the pressures of small producers, strippers, and landowners eager to get all the oil out of the ground as quickly as feasible. Oklahoma's Corporation Commission, for example, has feared that in a declining market the integrated companies will increasingly draw selectively with their own wells getting the preference. It has tried to require purchasers to take the full allowable of lawfully produced oil set by the commission. Gulf Oil, a major importer and buyer, has challenged this attempt "to force us to buy crude oil in Oklahoma for which we have no use and do not want." [12] It has viewed the state's move as an unconstitutional restraint upon the company's freedom to buy elsewhere, including in overseas markets. A number of Western states have resisted conservation where it includes market-demand prorationing on the grounds that such limitation on production would mean gain for the more abundant states at their expense. More typically, however, the regulatory agencies seek to hold the line on production. Ernest O. Thompson, for a quarter of a century the dominant member of the Texas Railroad Commission as well as sometime chairman of the Interstate Oil Compact Commission and a national spokesman for domestic producers, has frequently made clear that a floor under prices is essential to his work and conservation and that there is more incentive for conservation in the recovery of oil bearing a good profit.[13] In the thirties he fought for a dollar a barrel, resisting the price cuts offered by the major companies and advocating the temporary shutdown of all Texas fields.

In the period prior to the Suez crisis in 1956, Texas wells were allowed to operate on an average of fifteen days a month, with some producers suffering price cuts and the integrated buyers favoring further reduction of allowables. With Nasser's seizure of the canal and the subsequent blocking of much of the Middle Eastern oil flow to Europe, positions were reversed. The Texas Railroad Commission had been sympathetic to a crude oil price increase for some time, viewing this as the best approach to satisfying restive independent producers without further upsetting the market. It now resisted big oil's pressures to step up production to fill the gap. It wanted to see the sizable gasoline and refined products stocks, which so frequently mount in the winter, cut down first. General Thompson publicly rebuked England for insisting upon crude oil instead of taking the refined:

We have already shipped her many millions of barrels of crude, but we only get criticism for not going all out at her bidding. England apparently still looks on us as a province or dominion.[14]

He feared more intensified imports by the integrated companies would be certain to follow once the Middle Eastern oil trade was restored. "The letdown would be paralyzing," he declared. Thompson also called attention to eight thousand wells in Texas unconnected to pipelines. His stance reflected the wrath of producers who have long complained that the integrated importing companies have deliberately kept down pipeline construction and are seeking to void the ratable take policy from all wells in favor of selective buying from more conveniently located and pipeline-owned wells.

Instead of increasing production, the commission successfully held out for a price rise. After stocks in storage were reduced, a 35 cent per barrel price increase was gained, with Humble setting the pace for the industry. Then, in March 1957, Texas agreed to step up its allowables to 18 days. But with crude supplies flowing again from the Arab world, by April the allowable was cut back to 15 days and in August it was at 13. (By April 1958 it was at 8 days per month.) Other states were also keeping production down. With the conservation machinery as the lever, as a result of the 1957 crude price increase, the American consumer was paying a cent more for each gallon of oil product, despite the high level of gasoline and home heating stocks. The industry, independent and integrated, had increased its revenues during the Suez crisis by at least several hundred million dollars.

Humble, Jersey Standard's producing subsidiary, defended its initiation of the price-increase wave in the face of widespread indignation in the American press, the Congress, and in Europe. It saw this action as a necessary consequence of the sharp increase in demand for domestic crude oil and the rising costs of production. "Humble has been unable to secure its requirements at former prices." The new price would bring forth the oil. President Rathbone of the Jersey company saw this as an illustration of the workings of a free enterprise economy. The increase was overdue, and "we have no apologies whatever to make for that action." [15] Significantly, Humble's president later said it did not bring forth new supplies, an admission verified by subsequent oil-supply movements. But oilmen agreed that a price rise would have come during the year, regardless of Suez, suggesting further that Nasser's blockade was a most convenient affair. Boosting American crude oil prices appeased the domestic industry while making it easier for the huge importers to raise the prices they paid to their own overseas subsidiaries for crude oil coming into the United States—thus increasing profits and shifting more of their income out of the reach of American taxes.

Although troubled by the specter of rising imports that threatened domestic producers, Commissioner Thompson repeatedly declined to offer any explanation for the price consequences:

Mr. Dingell (Rep. John D. Dingell, Michigan). . . . Returning now again to the fact that stocks of all kinds of petroleum are high in this country, would you say that would justify a price rise?

General Thompson. I know nothing about price. I don't want to go into that, because I am not an expert on it, I am advised. I do not know what goes into the making up of price.

Mr. Dingell. But generally it would be fair to say when stocks are high, gasoline and fuel prices should not rise; is that not right?

General Thompson. Well, you can say that if you wish. I do not know. (Laughter.) [16]

Some fifteen years earlier, when the nation was looking seriously for oil supplies to meet the overwhelming war demands, he had been more direct in his advice to a Senate Committee to use prices as an inducement:

If you will set the price up two bits a barrel more for crude that will get the job done, and if that first two bits didn't do it, then put on another two bits and that will accelerate the discovery and development.

Asked about the effects of such an increase on oil products and on the maintenance of wartime price controls, Thompson replied that "we cannot afford now not to try the old plan, when it is so simple and reliable." Let the Office of Price Administration "pass the increase on to the consumer. The consumer never kicks." [17]

There is a cherished image of the Interstate Oil Compact Commission as a champion of the private enterprise system and a rallying point for states' rights and grass-roots democracy. Without formal power it strives to focus and express the viewpoint of domestic producers. It is active in the fight to reduce imports, favors federal legislation exempting the production and gathering of natural gas from federal "bureaucratic" controls, and generally serves to integrate the policies of the various states. General Thompson has insisted that "in Texas we do not permit price to even be discussed at our hearings." [18] The Interstate Oil Compact Commission is equally firm in its defense that it is not a party to price fixing. But it does admit that "any limitation of production, whether to an efficient rate of recovery or to reasonable market demand may, incidentally, affect price." [19] Bureau of Mines spokesmen offer a similar defense of their role, although as Eugene Rostow observed in his trenchant legal analysis of national oil policy, "there is no such thing in business life as demand apart from price. . . . The Bureau of Mines forecasts of demand depend on the unstated premise of price stability." [20] And the American Petroleum Institute continues to proclaim that oil prices are determined "by aggressive competition within the framework of supply and demand in a freely functioning market place. They are responsive only to the demands of consumers." [21] Meanwhile, some oil refiners speak of the need for further easing of antitrust enforcement if the industry is to continue to maintain reserve capacity for mobilization needs.

Periodically there have been demands for a re-examination of the assumptions and consequences of this role of public law. Prompted by a "shortage" crisis in 1947 when Bureau of Mines forecasts were underestimating demand, a committee headed by the late Senator Kenneth Wherry, a Republican who was never noted for his hostility to business, investigated the conservation operation. They recommended that the President suspend the Connally Act prohibiting the interstate shipment of "hot oil" because of its use to create scarcity and maintain price. This advice was rejected by Mr. Truman. The Federal Trade Commission's report on *The International Pe-*

troleum Cartel had suggested the place of American conservation within the world industry and the role of the API in developing these controls. But neither the Justice nor the Interior Department was very responsive.

In 1955 the Congress attached to the joint resolution authorizing renewal of the IOCC a provision requiring the Attorney General to observe and report annually as to whether the activities of the states violate the provision in the Compact that declares it is not the purpose of the Congress to authorize the states to join in the limitation of production for considerations of price stabilization or monopolization. The Senate appropriations hearings provided a clue as to the likely outcome. Attorney General Herbert Brownell came in with a $600,000 budget for a special staff and three field offices to make a comprehensive review. He repeatedly emphasized, however, that "this is something which was imposed on us by the Congress." Senator Lyndon Johnson of Texas, who chaired the hearing, expressed outrage at an investigation that would cost perhaps six times the actual operating budget of the IOCC. "We did not think we were going to set up a new group of snoopers to invade the States and determine whether or not the States in their agreements with each other were acting properly in enforcing their own laws." [22] The probers received $100,000.

In his first report the Attorney General offered primarily a history of conservation efforts, without any conclusions as to whether the activities of the states were in violation of the antitrust laws. But the report emphasized that the problem was not simply a study of the purposes of the Compact itself, which was obviously only one cog; rather did the focus have to be the results of the entire regulatory system, both of states within the Compact and of separate areas like California, and their relation to the roles of the federal government and of the oil-production industry.[23]

State government and industry defenders challenged these suggestions as a continuing invasion of state sovereignty and a prelude to federal regulation and an ultimate public utility status for oil. Adequate funds and support were not forthcoming. The second report by the Attorney General looked into the regulatory system with notable timidity. After considerable explanation for its limited research, it concluded that "on the whole the activity of the Commission appears to have been worthwhile." It saw no element of coercion or control over the member states and it found that "the possibility of undue industry influence on committee deliberations seems rather remote." The report disputed the claim that Bureau of Mines forecasts are followed so closely as to serve as a common plan for state production quotas. And with extreme delicacy "the possibility is also suggested that the policies of the petroleum purchasers, who operate generally in all these states, may have a greater influence on approximating production to market demand than do the State regulatory agencies." [24]

It is clear that regardless of the purposes of these conservation mechanisms, their consequences are to further the private economic position of segments of the industry. Many of these measures have little to do with genuine conservation. There is also considerable evidence that even established practices to limit physical waste are often poorly administered, with the major focus being to cut every producer in on the market. Wells generally produce less than they might within the limits of sound engineering conservation standards, and the state conservation controversies tend to be over whether the pipeline purchasers or the producers are getting the best in such a situation. Similarly, most steps for the thoroughgoing conservation of petroleum resources, in terms of both production and use, are ignored by the industry as well as the nation. If the American people were serious about petroleum conservation, fundamental questions would have to be raised about a host of issues, including the extravagant marketing system, the organized pressures to consume more oil, and the very purposes for which oil is used in this country. A good starting point here would be the ridiculous horsepower race among automobile manufacturers that forces the need for heavier cars and higher octane fuel. (The lowest-priced 1958 models exceeded in horsepower the Cadillacs, Lincolns, and Chryslers of 1950. The introduction of "compact" cars, spurred by the popularity of foreign models, has changed the picture somewhat.) Refiners have been receptive to this competition, for they emerged from World War II with facilities geared to producing high-octane gasoline. A genuine conservation program would also examine the inadequate planning for public transportation in major cities that permits and encourages private driving and public congestion.

Nominally an organization of public officials, the commission is under the constant surveillance of the oil industry, which has always recognized it as an instrument for forestalling federal regulation. In past years oil companies have flown state members to the meetings, and the natural gas industry has paid for banquets. The techniques tend to be more sophisticated today, with front-line oil officials much less in attendance at the social gatherings. But oil company and association representatives participate in the periodic meetings and committee activities. And the industry's vast private airplane fleet remains one of its unobtrusive ways for serving and flattering modestly paid political and administrative personnel at all levels of public service.

Real power remains in the hands of the giant oil-purchasing companies for more substantial reasons. In addition to controlling outright a sizable percentage of the production, they have the pipelines, the refineries, and the markets which extend far beyond state and even national boundaries and police power. Viewing the world of oil as a single unit, their constant effort is to adjust domestic and international operations in light of current costs and reserves. They increasingly rely on imports, whenever conditions are favorable. This has prompted some producer groups to propose that imports be brought under prorationing through federal quotas that would be based on periodic hearings. Obviously market-demand prorationing and a tight lid on monthly allowables within individual states have become less and less effective defenses for domestic producers who are without overseas operations and who provide a declining percentage of the crude supply.

One can appreciate the awe and the outrage implicit in the report of Senator Wherry's Small Business Committee. Looking into the 1947 "shortage," they concluded that the blending of public power and private privilege had acted to bind supply and demand so tightly that a 2 per cent underestimation of demand by the Bureau of Mines caused the shortage despite price increases and abundant stocks in storage:

There is a mechanism controlling the production of crude oil to market demand (or below) that operates as smoothly and effectively as the finest watch. . . .[25]

There was an element of exaggeration in this oft-quoted observation. For, as has been suggested, there are frictions and points of imbalance within oildom. But it is clear that the controls over the flow of oil do work to attain the ends of the leaders of the industry in limiting competition, furthering price fixing, and forestalling antitrust action. The conservation machinery, by turning United States production on and off, becomes, however unwittingly, a servant of the integrated corporations. And thus, agencies of public government serve as the keystone of this modern-day empire with its fabulous Middle Eastern and Caribbean treasures. Fitting American oil activities into the larger price-supply system, they lock into place the worldwide controls of the private government of oil.

7

The Privileges of Power

The term "subsidy" is a crude one to sensitive oil ears. Yet it depicts accurately a range of financial services that the American nation renders to its largest industry. For where money is concerned, these entrepreneurs rise above their passionately (and expensively) proclaimed principles about the deadening hand of government limiting corporate wealth and its exercise. They also have a more subtle appreciation of the beneficent role a properly oriented tax power can play.

The depletion allowance offers one excellent illustration of this political realism. This tax formula was originally set up on the heels of the adoption of the income tax in 1913. It allowed those who derived income from certain extractive industries to deduct up to 5 per cent of their gross income when computing taxable income. This allowance was seen as enabling producers to recoup their capital, and was comparable to the depreciation allowance granted other industries. During World War I depletion provisions were liberalized as an incentive for oilmen to explore and drill. Very much in mind were the recognized risks of genuine wildcatting and the prevailing fear that new discoveries might not keep pace with national requirements. By 1926 the original 5 per cent rate and its underlying purposes had been expanded to take on the present-day character of this allowance.

The Internal Revenue Code permits a deduction of 27½ per cent of the gross income from oil and gas producing properties before figuring income tax, subject to a 50 per cent of net income limitation. It is premised on the assumption that oil discovered beneath privately owned ground constitutes a capital asset. Since it was not the intent of the income tax law to tax capital as income, this allowance is defended as legitimate compensation for the loss of capital value as the irreplaceable oil is removed from the ground.

Originally, the depletion had been limited to the cost of the investment, with the provision that once the cumulative allowance equaled this investment the grant was to cease. This was modified so that the capital investment, for tax purposes, came to include an estimate of the value of the oil and gas. Discovery valuation for each well was soon viewed as too complex to administer. Under the pressure of the industry, the Congress redrafted the tax laws, and depleted capital became calculated on the arbitrary basis of 27½ per cent of gross income. It was assumed that in a period of lower oil costs, profits, and corporate taxes, this percentage depletion would average out at a rate comparable to the allowance under the earlier discovery depletion. No account is taken any longer of the actual cost. Nor is any calculation made of the depletion allowance already accumulated or any estimate made of the reserves of a given property. Percentage depletion can be deducted through the full producing life of the property. Thus, the owner of wells in which $500,000 has been invested and which produce a million dollars' worth of oil each year for ten years can deduct a total of $2,750,000 from his taxable income during that period. It should also be noted that the increase in the corporate income tax rate from 13 per cent in 1926 to 52 per cent in 1959 has meant the quadrupling of the worth of the depletion allowance to oil producers.

The industry and its supporters insist that there is no special privilege involved in this arrangement since protection of capital is recognized for all businesses. To tax this way, they argue, would be to deny them the capital from their own earnings and savings that has financed so much of their expansion. The higher costs of modern and deeper drilling, as well as of financing, would become prohibitive for domestic producers who would then be forced out of business. The consumer would have to pay much higher prices, the reserve capacity built up for national protection reasons would be threatened, and the United States would be forced to depend upon unstable foreign sources.

Central in the defense of depletion has been the sturdy if somewhat shopworn figure of the small man. Independent producers and little operators working stripper wells are seen as the very first whose survival and contributions would be menaced by any reduction of what has been called "the cornerstone on which the oil industry has been built." Said Senator Mike Monroney of Oklahoma in one debate:

I think the 27½ percent depletion allowance has been very important in preventing hundreds of thousands of farmers, small land owners and royalty owners from losing their one asset, which is the oil that nature placed under their ground. Once that oil is taken out there will not be any more oil put in at the bottom of the wells. So, if we wipe this allowance off the books or reduce it, we penalize several hundreds of thousands of small land owners who receive royalties. The fact that there may be one or two examples of wealthy men who may have found ways of escaping taxation should not be used as a legitimate excuse for wiping off the books a law which has been there for 30 years and has resulted in American oil exploration reaching the highest point reached by oil exploration in any other place on the earth. . . . If the allowance did not continue no one would ever drill a well. Why risk half a million dollars in a wildcat well if one is not going to get the money back.[1]

In attacking a proposal that would cut the allowance for the large oil corporations while maintaining the 27½ per cent rate for smaller operators, Senator Russell Long of Louisiana offered a variant of the once familiar "widows and orphans" plea:

. . . I must oppose this amendment. I submit in many respects it works out to be the absolute epitome of unfairness and injustice.

This is an amendment which proposes to say: Oilman Rich can earn and receive $1 million a year and still retain the 27½ percent depletion allowance.

On the other hand, Grandma Jones, who does not have the importance or prominence of an independent oil and gas man, owns $200 worth of stock in an oil company, and she receives an income of $20 a year from that ownership. My good friend, the Senator from Illinois, under his proposal, would reduce Grandma Jones' $20 to $15, while he would permit oilman Rich to make the $1 million a year and still retain the 27½ percent depletion allowance.

I should like to be the kind of small business man oilman Rich is, whom the Senator from Illinois wishes to help. It just happens I do not have that kind of income. I wish I did.

However, on the other hand, I would like to protect Grandma Jones' little $20 dividend, which she gets on an annual basis.[2]

Former President Hines Baker of Humble Oil, Jersey Standard's biggest domestic producing affiliate, has insisted that "contrary to popular belief, oil production is not a fabulously profitable business. On the average it is only about as profitable as other businesses, and it would be far less profitable than other businesses if it were not for the tax provisions adopted by Congress in recognition of the peculiar nature of its operations." [3] Voicing the public-oriented sentiments of his industry, President Porter of the American Petroleum Institute has warned that, given "the extraordinary hazards of searching for new oil reserves . . . our ability to continue finding oil and gas reserves is now so closely related to the tax burden that repeal or reduction of the statutory depletion allowance by Congress would actually be an exercise of the power to destroy this industry through taxation." [4] Such a change, concluded a Texas banker appearing as a panelist expert before a subcommittee of the Joint Committee on the Economic Report studying federal tax policy, would be "a step in the direction of ultimate nationlization." [5]

Despite the fervor and range of these defenses, there remains considerable doubt as to the premises upon which the allowance is based and also as to the social benefits. The industry emphasizes the factor of risk, with up to eight out of nine new discovery drillings turning out to be failures. Yet only about one of five wells are of this type. In 1957, 53,000 wells were drilled. Less than 12,000 were wildcats and of these about 1,600 were producers. But of the other 41,000 development wells, over 30,000 were successful. At least 80 per cent of the wildcats are drilled by companies other than the thirty largest operators. The big companies, as noted in an earlier chapter, are generally far more cautious. Although they employ the latest scientific techniques, they still prefer to buy out successful discoveries or to share the initial costs. Thus, in a situation frequently characterized by overinvestment and excessive drilling, they receive incentive bounties for risks they do not take. Losses may be high on particular operations, but in the initial planning it is assumed these will average out among their many activities. The notion of risk seems further exaggerated in light of the blue-chip character of the stock of the major oil companies and of active smaller producers who are consistently recommended as conservative investments. Furthermore, the dry holes of the money-making producers are written off against income before

the taxable income base is arrived at, making dubious one basic justification for depletion allowance.

With oil and gas treated as capital gains for tax purposes, this
subsidy has worked out to protect profits without regard for and far
beyond investment costs. On oil company books, of course, depletion
is shown as true financial costs; only for tax purposes do they deduct
27½ per cent from the gross income to show a lower net income.
In the cases of some oil and gas companies, original investments have
been recovered many times over. A Treasury Department study for
1947 showed that oil companies with assets of more than $100 million
deducted through percentage depletion 16 times more than would
be possible under the normal depreciation methods on an original
cost basis. More recent analyses for oil and gas—which account for
some 80 per cent of all mineral depletion deductions—indicate that
the allowable may be 19 times greater than cost depletion. During
World War II the depletion allowance helped to insulate oil companies from the impact of the excess profits tax. A calculation by
economist Senator Paul Douglas of Illinois indicated that in the
period 1945–1954, 27 domestic oil companies, with a total income
before taxes of better than $3¼ billion, paid federal corporate income
taxes of $562 million. This was a 17 per cent rate. Yet during this
period other enterprises were subject to a 52 per cent rate. A study
of the 1954 published reports of 24 large oil companies indicates an
average effective tax rate of 22.6 per cent, as contrasted to 48.1 per
cent for all corporations. The result, some tax analysts estimate, has
been an annual loss to the United States Treasury of anywhere from
$750 million to $1,500 million.[6] Perhaps more important, it has meant
an erosion not just of the tax base but of the principle of equity essential to a democratic tax system.

Industry spokesmen insist that the market mechanism of supply
and demand serves to keep crude prices flexible and thus to protect
the public from any abuse of the depletion allowance. "If percentage
depletion does become excessive to the point of encouraging more
capital investment and exploration in drilling than is necessary to
meet demand, crude prices will fluctuate downward and thereby avoid
any windfall to producers."[7] This reassurance, presented in a detailed
study by the Texas Independent Producers and Royalty Owners Association, ignores the privately controlled character of oil pricing

and the contradiction of the government's subsidizing the cost of production as well as the withholding of oil. It means also that consumers and taxpayers are paying now for the acquisition of reserves—often to be capped for the future—which will strengthen the economic position of the industry and enhance its control over the market and prices.

The legislative history of the past thirty years shows clearly that this allowance has provided an incentive for a long list of mineral interests to seek and receive comparable immunity from the income tax. The National Coal Association has lobbied for an increase in coal's present 10 per cent rate. The argument offered is that coal—with reserves estimated to be sufficient for at least a thousand years—is a depressed industry beset by investment capital shortages and tax-favored competition from oil and gas. Since 1951, even sand, gravel, clam and oyster shells are provided for, although at more modest rates than oil. There is less evidence that its presumed function of providing incentive for genuine wildcatting by small domestic producers of oil has been completely successful. It undoubtedly has made money available. Thus, for example, an executive of one mid-continent firm, capitalized at $45 million, guessed that at least two-thirds of his company's 150 producing wells were made possible by depletion money. Oil-shale interests, headed by Union Oil of California, have urged moving the depletion allowance for oil shale from 15 per cent up to 27½ per cent. But this tax aid will not further a competitive situation, for the measure is most likely to be adopted at the point when the majors are ready to allow shale oil to come into the market. Certainly this oil extraction is not a small-scale venture—nor can one argue that such exploration is difficult.

But to assume that the depletion allowance affords a substantial economic assistance to the lone producer or stripper operator is like pretending that agricultural price supports fundamentally help subsistence farmers, with the important distinction that many marginal wells were once profitable. The wildcatter frequently sells out his properties during their development. He profits from favorable capital-gains tax provisions. But the percentage depletion is not too meaningful in the early stages when his expenses exceed his income from the new well. Since the earnings of stripper wells rarely are high, the limitation of the depletion allowance to 50 per cent of net income has frequently precluded these marginal producers from gaining great advantage from the 27½ per cent allowance. (A survey by the Interstate Oil Compact Commission classified 358,000 wells—out of a national total of over 500,000 wells—as strippers, with an average production of not quite 3.6 barrels a day each.) The small royalty owner does benefit. But he generally is a passive recipient of income, claiming a 27½ per cent deduction without having risked any capital investment in exploration. These allowances, then, are of greatest profit to those with large income and extensive undertakings. This situation was recognized from the earliest days of depletion. In 1926, for example, a Senate study estimated "that approximately $10,000,-000 out of the $300,000,000, or 3⅓ per cent of the annual deductions for discovery depletion (for oil and gas) has gone to the wildcatter." [8]

More significantly, Treasury studies reveal that the bulk of depletion allowances for minerals have gone to large, vertically integrated producers. For example:

. . . In 1948 60 percent of mineral depletion deductions were taken by firms whose principal business activity was manufacturing (including petroleum refining). Firms whose activities were predominantly mineral extraction had only about one-third of total depletion deductions. Classification of firms by size of total assets indicates that in 1948 two-thirds of all corporate depletion was deducted by the largest firms, those with assets of over $100,000,000. Firms with assets of $1,000,000 or more had 94 percent of total depletion. Small firms with assets of $250,000 or less had only 1.5 percent of the total.

Petroleum and natural gas accounted for over 75 per cent of all this. Producing firms received 20.1 per cent ($324 million) of this total; integrated companies, listed as refiners, had 54.1 per cent ($871 million).[9]

Some independent refiners and marketers have also pointed out that the capital reserves thus built up over the years support unfair competition by enabling the integrated producer to subsidize losses in refining and marketing. Periodically, one hears rumblings that if the majors persist in such discriminatory marketing tactics as "raiding" (direct selling to large commercial accounts), jobbers will retaliate with a public campaign against the depletion allowance. Bitter as they often are, however, jobbers are generally reluctant to antagonize their suppliers. Their loyalty has a simple premise. "I have found I have been able to make more money when my supplier was making more money."

This tax allowance has further contributed to the creation of "oil millionaires." In a survey of American's top millionaires, *Fortune* magazine found oil, either as the basis of inherited fortunes or as the root of new ones, to be the greatest single source of modern American wealth. Its list was headed by J. Paul Getty (Getty Oil, Tidewater, and so on), with assets estimated from $700 million to $1 billion. Others included Texas independent oil operators H. L. Hunt ($400 million to $700 million), Sid Richardson ($200 million to $400 million), John Mecom, Clint Murchison, James Abercrombie, R. E. Smith ($100 million to $200 million each); William Keck of Superior Oil and Jacob Blaustein of American Oil ($100 million to $200 million each), and numerous Rockefellers, Mellons (Gulf), and Pews (Sun).[10] Oil production is recommended by brokerage houses to those in upper income brackets as a fine sheltered investment for tax dollars that can then be used to build up new capital assets, which in turn can be made safe from high taxes. Most costs involved in bringing in a well can be offset against income from all sources. *Fortune* found that the strategy of wealth leads all the millionaires to seek to appreciate capital rather than increase income. "Indeed, among oil monarchs like Sid Richardson—his gross annual take: $25 million to $50 million—income can be something of a nuisance; the possibility of paying taxes on it keeps them busy pouring the cash into new wells. . . ." "When a fellow is in my income bracket, he automatically goes into the oil business," one industrialist worth $85 million confided to the *Wall Street Journal*. "This is a legal way to escape confiscation of earnings." There have been cases where incomes in the millions were taxed at the same rate as $2,000-a-year incomes. The recipients also enjoy all the regular and legal tax-avoiding devices available, including foundations, trusts, deferred salaries, vacations in company lodges and even on specially equipped tankers, and a general luxurious living through expense accounts that stretch far beyond normal business obligations. It is difficult to estimate the loss of revenue here and the erosion of respect for the purposes of progressive taxation.

There have been numerous efforts, all unsuccessful, to cut or eliminate this governmental subsidy. The Treasury Department under Presidents Roosevelt and Truman had been sharply critical, and proposed changes. In his 1950 tax message, Mr. Truman saw these provisions as bounties bearing "only a haphazard relationship" to the nation's real needs for proper incentives to encourage mineral exploration, development and conservation. "I know of no loophole in the tax laws so inequitable as the excessive depletion exemptions now enjoyed by oil and mining interests." [11] Mr. Eisenhower's Administration evaded any clear-cut expression of opinion during its first four years. Whenever prodded, Secretary of the Treasury George M. Humphrey claimed that the policy was under review, an attitude that kept critics of depletion skeptical and friends disturbed. He finally announced that this was not a tax loophole, and since the country was finding the reserves to keep pace with consumption, it seemed to be working well. No documented report accompanied this pronouncement. Up until the time of his resignation in 1957, he would not commit himself to the Senate Finance Committee as to the fitness of the rate: "I am still not prepared to tell you." His successor, Robert B. Anderson, had been president of the Texas Mid-Continent Oil and Gas Association and a strong defender of the allowance before legislative bodies. He assured the Senate Finance Committee, however, that he would approach this "as objectively as I possibly can," and would be pleased to cooperate with Congress in a review of this tax.[12]

Meanwhile, President Eisenhower was having his own difficulties. At one point after his nomination he had said, in response to a question for an opinion, that he knew nothing about the matter but that he would ask some friends in the industry for their views. At a news conference in 1957, when reporters were pressing him as to his attitude toward proposals for changes then before the Senate, he replied: "Now, the 27½ percent depletion allowance I am not prepared to say it is evil because when we find, while we do find I assume that a number of rich men take advantage of it unfairly, there must certainly be an incentive in this country if we are going to continue the exploration for oil and gas that is so important to our economy." [13] The industry remained uneasy.

Republican Senator John J. Williams of Delaware has repeatedly called for a 15 per cent rate, or even a reduction to 20 per cent. He has conservatively estimated that the latter would give the Treasury a gain in revenue of $200 million to $250 million. But he was unable to get any official Treasury reaction throughout the Eisenhower Administration's tenure—beyond the familiar statement in 1958 that the "far-reaching implications of depletion allowance" led the Department to oppose any such changes prior to "full consideration of all its possible consequences." [14]

The Senate was not interested either. Senator Paul Douglas has favored graduated rates that would continue the 27½ per cent allowance for small producers whose annual taxable incomes were under $1 million, while adjusting this downward on a sliding-scale basis to 15 per cent for those whose gross exceeds $5 million. He reasons that the larger allowance is justifiable inducement for the smaller wildcatter who does not have adequate resources to drill enough wells to average out his dry holes. But despite all the passionate declarations in behalf of the small producer by defenders of depletion, this too has been overwhelmingly defeated, leaving one of Douglas's supporters on the floor of the Senate, Republican George D. Aiken of Vermont, to reflect ruefully that "I have a feeling the little fellow is being used somewhat here today." [15]

A few critics, including Paul E. Hadlick, general counsel of the National Oil Marketers Association, have called for a limitation of depletion allowance to the amount of the original investment. Others have suggested its abolition. Replacing it, where justifiable for public ends, would be a subsidy, frankly labeled as such, or a higher consumer price, if warranted.

On the other hand, some domestic producers, perhaps on the theory that the best defense is a good offense, have insisted that the present allowance, as well as the 50 per cent limitation, is inadequate to return the capital investment of the great bulk of operators, with the exception of the overseas giants. The President's Materials Policy Commission, which in 1952 completed a comprehensive study of the nation's resources, concluded that depletion allowance should be retained but at its present rate. It viewed this as a strong and needed supplement to the incentive provided by the price structure for attracting risk capital. It saw limitations but could arrive at no alternative method of taxation. The oil industry would be quite happy to keep the present arrangement, and it does everything it can to emphasize the necessity of the precise figure as well as of the concept itself. Actually, 27½ per cent was a compromise figure arrived at in a congressional conference committee in 1926 and maintained ever since through carefully cultivated political support rather than clearcut social justification.

There is much that is not known about the economic consequences of the depletion allowance despite the ready assurances of those who profit from it. Meanwhile, oildom's public relations seeks to avoid the term "allowance," preferring the more innocent "percentage depletion." For "allowance" suggests "subsidy." And this remains an offensive concept in the lexicon of an industry dedicated to private initiative and sensitive to any suggestion of political activity or governmental interference.

Such policies as tax depreciation, overseas investment insurance, certificates of necessity, and tanker subsidies also belong in an inventory of public financial support to the oil industry. Less publicized than depletion, for example, is the fact that all costs incurred in drilling a dry hole can be deducted from a producer's gross income. All the tangible items in bringing in a well—those that have salvage value —are capitalized, and then costs can be recovered over the life of the equipment through depreciation. There are also a great range of intangible exploration and development costs involved in geological work, fuel, labor, construction, repairs, and tools that can be deducted as expenses from the profits of a producing well without affecting depletion deductions. On the average, 75 per cent of such costs of bringing in a well can be recovered through this provision for expenses. Although this too is defended in terms of the independent producer, it is obviously of little if any meaning to the very small producer who may have no other operations. As the Secretary of the Treasury testified in 1951, such provisions result in "a double deduction with respect to the same capital investment. The combined impact of percentage depletion and the privilege of deducting drilling and development costs as a current expense is to wipe out the tax liability on income running into millions of dollars." [16] A Treasury survey of 153 corporations in 1957 showed $678 million deducted for depletion, $471 million for development costs, and $200 million for

losses on abandonment. Humble, with a net income before taxes of
$193 million in 1957, paid $17 million in income taxes. Continental,
which netted $51 million, paid $4,550,000.

Although not peculiar to oil, there is also the privilege of averaging
net income through provisions that allow the carrying back and
carrying forward of losses over a period of years for tax purposes. In
effect, then, the American government bears the major share of oil-
development costs at home and, as shall be seen in the next chapter,
abroad.

Integrated oil companies have been among the leading beneficiaries
of the federal government's accelerated tax amortization program.
Initiated in World War I, revived and modified in World War II,
and intensified in the Korean and post-Korean War periods, the intended purpose has been to provide an incentive for the expansion
of private industry's productive capacity. Under the Internal Revenue
codes, companies whose plans for new or enlarged facilities meet the
war or defense goals set by the government have been issued certificates of necessity. These have permitted the depreciation for tax
purposes of a defined portion of the depreciable assets of the new
investments within a five-year period. During World War II the government issued some 40,000 certificates to approximately 4,500 taxpayers for $7.3 billion of plants. Most of them were issued by the
military, and allowed the charging off of 100 per cent of the entire
cost without any calculation for potential postwar utility. From November 1950 to June 1957, the Office of Defense Mobilization granted
accelerated tax amortizations for some 22,000 facilities capitalized
at $38 billion. Sixty per cent, or $23 billion, of this amount has been
made eligible for rapid depreciation.

Petroleum has not been the chief claimant among American industry for this special inducement—railroads, electric power, and
primary metals have received greater sums. But since the outbreak
of the Korean War $5 billion worth of expansion projects in oil and
gas have been covered by this program. Reading the ODM's bi-
monthly listings gives an insight into the meaning of these grants
for the industry. For example, in one two-week period in 1954, the
release cited: Gulf Oil Corporation, petroleum storage facilities in
New York and Pennsylvania, $486,000 and $874,800 certified, 40 per
cent allowed; The Texas Company, refining facilities in Port Arthur,

Texas, $7,250,000 and $4,150,000, with 65 per cent and 45 per cent allowed; Oil Basin Pipe Line Company, petroleum pipeline facilities in Montana, $5,286,000, 25 per cent allowed; Sun Oil Company, petroleum refining facilities at Marcus Hook, Pennsylvania, $4,400,-000 and $35,000, with 65 per cent and 45 per cent allowed; Ethyl Corporation, railroad tank cars, $452,000, with 70 per cent allowed; Kerr-McGee Oil Industries, natural gasoline processing facilities, $520,000 and $30,000, with 65 per cent and 25 per cent allowed; the Atlantic Refining Company, petroleum storage facilities in Pennsylvania, $99,000, with 40 per cent allowed. Just previously the Esso Standard Oil Company had been allowed 60 per cent and 45 per cent on petroleum refining facilities at Baltimore certified at $14,250,000 and $4,850,000, while the Union Oil Company was allowed 65 per cent and 45 per cent on refining facilities in California certified at $18,960,000 and $4,735,000. Practically every major oil company and many of the "smaller" ones have participated in these projects.

There have been many questions raised as to whether the social gains from this program have justified the costs. Sharp criticisms have been made during and after each period of its use. In 1951 a congressional report described it as "the biggest bonanza that ever came down the government pike." [17] For in a presumably temporary period of high corporate income and excess profits taxation, the privilege of writing off in five years or less an investment that more typically would be amortized over twenty years or longer, depending on the estimated normal life of the facility, makes possible the tax-free recovery of a capital outlay within a few years. Great emphasis has been made in all Office of Defense Mobilization releases that "the accelerated tax amortization certified by the agency represents investment of private capital and does not involve the investment of Government funds." When asked at a House hearing in 1951 if he considered the certificate of necessity as in effect a form of subsidy, General William H. Harrison, Administrator of the Defense Production Administration, replied:

No; I do not so construe it. My idea is the certificate of necessity was a very broad-gage approach . . . an intent on the part of the Congress to encourage the building of these facilities.

Mr. Hardy [Rep. Porter Hardy, Jr., Va.]: Subsidies, General, manifest an intent of Congress.

Mr. Harrison: Please, sir, I am not an economist and I am not a financial expert and I don't quite understand these languages. I don't know what a subsidy means. All I know is we are trying to administer the intent of Congress on that theory. I don't find the word "subsidy" in any of the records. Maybe it is there.[18]

In reality, however, this has evolved into another concealed subsidy to private enterprise, for as sometimes described, this forgiveness is a government-backed, interest-free loan. Normal taxes are paid from current income after the fast write-off period is over, providing the enterprise has been successful. But the assumption—reinforced by the organized political activities of oil and the rest of the business community—has been that tax rates would be lower then. Meanwhile, the firms involved have enjoyed the use of capital saved by the lower taxes while sharing any corporate risks with the government. It should also be noted that during World War II many plants granted certificates of necessity were then built with government loans rather than with private investment. In these instances the incentive provided by the tax privilege seemed to be to avoid private investment. Of the money for building refinery facilities during World War II, about 25 per cent came from direct government investment, with the remainder coming from private sources or government loans. During the Korean War and the continuing cold-war mobilization, governmental policy has been to avoid loans. Potentially, at least, these open the door to the participation of smaller corporations. The idea of publicly built plants was also discredited by the concentrated resistance of much of organized business.

The Senate Special Committee Investigating the National Defense Program of World War II concluded that the certificates of necessity were a source of considerable "legal profiteering." The War Production Board official responsible for issuing the certificates testified that the failure of the Army and Navy departments to give percentages of amortization, instead of the 100 per cent write-off rate they allowed in most of the cases on which they passed, cost the American government $3 billion. (It was such situations that had in an earlier period led the Nye Committee in its study of World War I to recommend the abandonment of the whole concept and the use of loans instead.) Many companies emerged from World War II with valuable new or modernized facilities, fully amortized, which they proceeded to use or sell. The provision that the full percentage of the accelerated amortizations received were to be calculated as legitimate costs not open to war contract renegotiation created a situation that led many government officials responsible for negotiation to agree that "the largest unjustifiable war profits were made as a result of the certificate of necessity program." Oil, one of the major governmental purchases, figured heavily in these transactions, the committee disclosed:

High profit war contractors profited even more when they were permitted to accelerate the rate of amortization over the period from the date of the certificate to the date of the declaration ending the war emergency. This period might be any length of time up to 5 years. When a contractor elected to do this his resulting increased annual amortization expense was credited against excessive profits that Price Adjustment Boards may have assessed against him. He would therefore have to refund a lesser amount of excessive profits and would own a fully depreciated and probably valuable facility. For example, the committee found that 20 of the largest oil companies were able to credit amortization in the amount of $59,000,000 against excessive profits determined after renegotiation to be $65,000,000. These companies had to refund only $6,000,000 and in fact paid for these facilities out of their excessive war profits. It would seem that these results redounded to the financial benefit of the high profit producer rather than the war contractors who had priced closely and made no excessive profits.[19]

The certificate of necessity program was not extended to crude oil production. There was, however, a mandatory exemption in the renegotiation statute that excluded from review contracts for crude oil and other unprocessed natural resources. Justified on the assumption that oil would be heavily depleted during the war, this gave integrated companies an extra immunity.

Crude oil, however, was under price controls during World War II. Many regional price increases were made in response to protests that the original orders had frozen inequalities and injustices, often because the public price control system accepted the industry's private pricing system. For example, some Rocky Mountain producers charged that the prewar posted prices in their areas had deliberately been kept down by the major purchasers. The industry as a whole, supported by the Petroleum Administration for War, argued for a general price increase as imperative for the necessary exploration and recovery. This was rejected as a threat to the nation's stabilization program by the Office of Price Administration. As a compromise the latter, headed by Leon Henderson, proposed instead subsidies for wildcatting and for marginal producers who might otherwise abandon their wells. Oilmen within and outside the government attacked this. The top spokesman for the Independent Petroleum Association of America likened this to the Russian experiment, and called it "a revolution in our political philosophy" with decisions made by government bureaucrats rather than by oil operators.[20] After great controversy and over the objections of oilmen, a premium price plan was put into effect in the last year of the war. This gave payments running from 20 cents to 75 cents per barrel in excess of the ceiling price to high-cost stripper wells in pools where the average production was less than 9 barrels per well. This encouragement for secondary recovery of oil was paid by the refiner to the producer, who in turn was reimbursed by the government. By the time the plan ended in early 1947, the premium payments had totaled nearly $122 million.

Rapid amortization has also been applied to ocean-going oil tankers. For example, in the midst of the oil shortage crisis in the winter of 1956–1957 after the blocking of the Suez Canal, tanker spot charter rates skyrocketed 100 to 200 per cent and more, and those under long-term contracts went up 20 to 30 per cent—as had been predicted to government officials by oilmen on the Middle East Emergency Committee. The Office of Defense Mobilization quickly issued many certificates of necessity to private tanker fleet companies and to the giant oil-importing firms, although it was recognized that these new ships would not be ready for several years. (The oil companies own half of the nation's carrying capacity, with the five big American companies holding about 80 per cent of all oil company seagoing vessels. The nonoil companies and the United States Government each have about 25 per cent, with the latter's tankers handling most military supplies. About 90 per cent of the world's oil fleet are owned by oil companies or operated for them on long-term charters. About 10 per cent are operated on the spot market.) Sun Oil received a 60 per cent allowance on $45 million worth of construction. Esso Shipping Company received 40 per cent on $67,500,000, and Socony Mobil received certificates for $19,391,200 and $8,443,000, with 40

the government's policies for what appeared to them to be surpl[us]
refinery capacity, Mr. Brown replied that such a conclusion reflecte[d]
"more on the wisdom of business than the wisdom of governmen[t]
. . . No refiner would aver that the government actually 'twisted h[is]
arm' and *made* him install basic refining capacity against his bett[er]
judgment." If they responded it was in anticipation of profit. (A
number of oilmen have also noted that the ease of keeping a moder[n]
electronic refinery going—with the crude oil the major cost—is [a]
serious temptation leading to "overproduction.")

Nevertheless, the steady rise in demand paralleling the growth o[f]
the economy and of the population continued. The unabating cold
war considerations made public officials request, again with tax inducements, an industry capacity that could anticipate crisis. A crude
oil refinery goal of 9 million barrels per day was set for January 1957.
At this point the Office of Defense Mobilization once more announced the suspension of tax concessions. But demands for new
pipelines were heard on the East and on the West coasts, with several
oil interests eager to build them. There were reminders of the transport difficulties of World War II, the havoc wrought by the German
submarine campaigns along the Atlantic shore, the costliness of rail
tank-car movements to the West Coast, and the many conflicts before the government-owned Big and Little Inch pipelines to the east
were built at a cost of $150 million. Defense officials appealed for
greater stand-by facilities at every level.

Building up "surplus" production, refineries, pipelines, and storage
for war that might never come threatens the stability of an industry
that always fears that, except when there is such stimulus as war,
the economy will generate capacity faster than markets, and hence
is founded on a system of controlled production that is judged to
work best when on the brink of planned scarcity. It had been proposed that Big and Little Inch be kept open after the war, by the
government if necessary, with continued access on an equal basis
to all shippers. But the majors' view dominated. They were closed
and then sold to the Tennessee Eastern Transmission Corporation,
which converted them to gas lines. A persistent proponent of a new
crude line from West Texas to California met resistance from the
organized interests in California who insisted there was an adequate
supply for future demands—this despite the fact that California,

per cent allowed. Within a five-month period, many independent
shippers, frequently under long-term contract to the majors, received
certificates totaling over $300 million for the building of supertankers
capable of going around the Cape of Good Hope instead of through
Suez.

In a period when mobilization and the cold war continue indefinitely, such subsidies have become semipermanent features of the
national economy. Under pressure to effect general tax relief for all
taxpayers while seeking to balance a high cold-war budget, the Eisenhower Administration became increasingly critical of tax write-offs.
Secretary of the Treasury Humphrey estimated they would cost $880
million in tax losses in 1956. The postponement of revenue receipts
caused by certificates issued between 1950 and 1956 would come to
over $4.5 billion in that decade, an amount that would have to be
made up by other taxpayers and by borrowing. Tax collections would
increase in the following period as the amortized allowances expired,
but by 1965 the losses would still be around $2.8 billion. Some of
this has been lost to the government forever. Government borrowing
has meant an interest cost estimated at $3 billion.[21]

Secretary Humphrey moved for the drastic curtailment of what
he warned was a now dangerous artificial stimulus that could lead
to inflation and government controls. He suggested the possibility
of direct subsidies openly arrived at and understood as such, if the
need developed. The program was cut back from its prior coverage
of 229 industries and limited to a few areas of national security. But
not before business interests had won a congressional repeal of the
excess profits tax and the insertion into the revenue laws of a more
liberalized depreciation method. The latter makes possible a deduction of two-thirds instead of one-half the value of new plants and
equipment during the first half of their anticipated life. Economists
have disagreed as to the ultimate cumulative cost from this erosion
of the tax base. Estimates run up to $19 billion for a fifteen-year
period.

Other questions besides financial cost have to be raised. Undoubtedly the rapid tax write-off has made certain needed capital investments attractive. There is less conclusive evidence, however, that
these new plants have always had a purely military character. Granted
that wars, by definition, are wasteful and also that any projections

as to future needs in a given area of the economy are open to interpretation. But the five-year accelerated amortization, premised on a guess as to the duration of the emergency, was designed as an incentive for the private construction of war facilities that were not expected to have any peacetime purposes. War or mobilization criteria were frequently disregarded by claimants and the government. A House Government Operations subcommittee reported "outright disregard for the safeguards from abuse" when the program was revived late in 1950. "The need for prompt action to meet the national emergency was construed as justifying a 'shovel in the barrel' approach to the certificate of necessity program as early as 10 days after it got under way." [22] This pattern has continued. In the post-Korean period, certification for accelerated depreciation exceeded the grants made throughout World War II.

The oil industry's record in World War II shows billions of dollars privately invested and publicly supported. From most accounts it was a praiseworthy achievement in providing the tremendous petroleum supplies needed. But the country had just emerged from the long depression of the thirties, and the private discussions, if not always the public statements, were of the likelihood of a return to distress after the war. "We are making, and others were making," admitted President M. J. Rathbone of Jersey Standard some years later, "the same kind of estimates, that the demand for oil which had built up during the war to very impressive levels was going to drop off very sharply because the civilian economy could not possibly use that much oil and we were looking for a terrible depression in the oil industry immediately postwar. . . . We completely misjudged the speed of the recovery. . . ." [23] The recurring fears of "surplus" oil kept the planning of industry leaders cautious, despite the politically voiced enthusiasm for expansion within the arsenal of democracy. Wherever war needs were involved, the industry first bargained for firm commitments from the government as to an assured demand and adequate profits.

There was new construction for 100-octane aviation gas, synthetic rubber, petrochemicals, and pipelines. There were considerable plant modernization and replacement to meet the many specialized war requirements. Techniques for breaking down crude were vastly improved. Catalytic cracking, which made possible the fuller use of

crude petroleum for gasoline and other desirable purposes, came into its own. But the expansion of crude refinery capacity was small, with only two completely new refineries built in the country. Most of the new or improved refinery facilities served to fill the minimum needs of an expanding economy and a growing population; they presumably would have been built regardless of the certificates of necessity program.

From 1945–1950, the nation's refinery capacity was enlarged some 30 per cent to take care of the postwar boom. Yet available supply did not keep pace with demand. With inadequate transport facilities an added factor, there were consumer shortages, notably in New England, in the winter of 1947–1948 that stirred up the general public and the Congress. This had an immediate consequence for Europe's economic recovery (and hence for American foreign policy) that was seen as threatened by a fuel shortage as its postwar dependency upon petroleum as a source of energy increased.

With the outbreak of the Korean War, responsible government officials and the Petroleum Administration for Defense called for moderately accelerated expansion rate that would bring capacity up to 8 million barrels per day to meet the anticipated mobilization needs and the growing consumer demand. To do this, industry needs and the growing consumer demand. To do this, industry spokesmen within and outside the government demanded and received fast tax write-offs. Critics deplored this as government bribes to do what they felt the oil industry would do normally. One of the most articulate defenses of these write-offs came from Bruce Brown, president of Pan-American Southern Corporation, an affiliate of Indiana Standard, and a top oil official in the government during and after World War II:

I am of the opinion that the tax amortization did what it was intended to—namely, it put the refiners back in a "pre-Korea" position—one in which they could build the basic refinery equipment that thought would be useful to them and profitable for them with the possibility of a "pay-out" approximately as good as they used to get before taxes became so severe.[24]

High refinery runs and subsequent cutbacks in the post-Korean period disturbed segments of the industry, just as price increases sparked new congressional inquiries. To those oilmen who

with petroleum productivity at its peak and demand sharply rising, was becoming an importer of fuel. The West Coast Pipeline Company, owned by some fifty independent producers concerned about shut-in oil in the Permian Basin for which they lacked transportation, received a certificate of necessity. But the refusal of refiners to commit themselves to purchase the crude made it impossible for the pipeline backers to obtain a certificate of essentiality that would open the door to a government loan or guarantee for a private loan for the $85 million they needed to supplement their own $21 million. An independent refiners' association, whose members presumably might have welcomed the possibility of additional crude, publicly joined the majors in opposition. To some who were mindful of the majors' almost complete control of the West Coast industry, it suggested that these independents privately feared being cut off from crude by the big companies if they did otherwise. All the critics of the pipeline proposal insisted that, while they thought there was no need for this crude, they had no quarrel if this was to be a completely private venture. But any government aid for the newcomer offended their dedication to private enterprise. A tabulation from the files of the Office of Defense Mobilization revealed that from 1951 to 1956 the big seven of the West Coast had received $600 million of tax-amortization certificates.[25]

At a meeting of the National Petroleum Council (NPC) in 1953, the Deputy Petroleum Administrator conveyed to the assembled oilmen the recommendation from the Petroleum Administration for Defense and the Office of Defense Mobilization for new pipeline facilities to the East Coast. He admitted this mobilization need might not be economically attractive at the moment, but held out the usual governmental financial assurances. P. C. Spencer, president of Sinclair Oil and chairman of the NPC's transportation committee, attacked the proposal, and insisted that petroleum products on the Atlantic coast were "much too adequate in many respects":

. . . As important as standby facilities may be in the petroleum industry, even more important, gentlemen, is the good health of our industry. The surpluses in our industry are an anathema, as you know. That applies to all industry, but I think we are particularly sensitive to it, or at least I feel that way about it. Surpluses not properly handled or controlled are an anathema, because they have a way of destroying price structures, they have a way of breaking down progress, and they can destroy an industry. It certainly would be a tragedy, gentlemen, to attempt to protect our national security by building up standby facilities which in the end make the industry so feeble it could not do the job in any event.

I am talking particularly here about standby pipeline facilities. It applies with equal force to standby tanker facilities, standby refining facilities, standby storage, and, if you please, standby production. It applies all through the line.

I am glad the subject came up, because I want to make a suggestion to our friends from the Government here, from the Department of the Interior and the Department of Defense. If we are going to go into this thing let us go at it in a realistic fashion. Let us have a study and investigation of this whole subject to see how it can be done without killing the goose that lays the golden egg. That is the danger. I am a rank amateur as a strategist in war or logistics, but it seems to me, perhaps somebody told me, that the greatest cushion in the world for petroleum reserves is in the elasticity of and the flexibility of civilian demand. Take it away from them, if we are going to have war. I think that is one of the many troubles with our Korean episode. We have tried to have butter and guns at the same time. We have tried to make war too comfortable and too convenient for civilians. I don't think that will ever work unless we are going to make war a profession, and I hope that never comes to pass. War should be tough. We should cut back the civilian demand. I think that is the greatest reserve cushion we have.

. . . Joe [Deputy Petroleum Administrator Joseph A. La Fortune] says he threw this out on the table as a matter of information. Perhaps somebody in the industry will be willing to pick it up and build such a line. If they were so disposed, they would find a welcome in certain defense areas in our Government. The thing I want to say is this. You might, for example, get the Government to put in some money on such a project. You might grant accelerated amortization. You might build it up with Government subsidies and what not, so that it would be economically profitable to the particular company or individuals that went into it. But at the same time through that Government subsidy, you would weaken all the rest of the industry in so doing. That is the thing we have to watch.[26]

Other oilmen joined in with reservations about the technical advisability, warnings about competition with the tanker fleets, and the specter of the general disruption of their industry. Mr. La Fortune (who was on leave from his post as vice chairman of the Warren Oil Corporation, since taken over by Gulf) replied for the government of the United States:

Gentlemen, this was given to you today to let you know that a certain amount of interest is being developed here in Washington toward the possibility of some pipeline. Our defense mobilization heads think in terms of tankers being sunk in the event of war. All these tankers that move from the gulf coast to the east coast carrying the necessary crude oil to our east-coast refineries are subject to being sunk like they were in the last World War. They are certainly not going to come to you and ask you to do this, to put in a pipeline of a million barrel capacity, or two pipelines of that capacity, if it is something that is not practical. They are putting it out to you to see whether any of you might be interested in setting up something that would be operating during peacetime, built during peacetime, and operated successfully and profitably, and have that facility available in the event of an emergency.

If you find upon study that it is not practical, you will take care of it just like you do everything else. You will forget about it. If others find that they can set up a profitable products line and operate it successfully, I see no reason why it should not be operated. It adds to our transportation facilities.

. . . I assure you that our Government is not trying to ask you to do something that is unprofitable or would be unsuccessful. They are trying to bring up something here that they think will be helpful to our country in the event of an emergency.

If it is unpractical, gentlemen, you can forget about it. If some of you find that you can operate a line from the gulf coast to the east coast profitably, I think it would be appreciated. I think the Government will cooperate with you in every way it possibly can, including the tanker situation. . . .

The matter was soon dropped. At the same government advisory meeting, the oilmen were shown an animated Technicolor film *It Never Rains Oil*. Sponsored by the leading oil associations, it presented the case for depletion allowance. According to the minutes, Deputy Petroleum Administrator La Fortune "furnished the information as to the money expended by Du Pont for having the film made in Hollywood, its fine possibility as education mediums for use in colleges, high schools, etc., availability and cost to those interested in showing the film."

Like depletion, the entire accelerated tax-amortization program contains what a congressional report by the Joint Committee on Internal Revenue Taxation has called a "built-in-bias against new or small firms with uncertain income prospects." [27] It has generally worked to favor the industrial interests with capital and current incomes big enough to take immediate advantage of tax deductions. Together with the system of war contracts and the general urgency of mobilization demands upon the economy, it has furthered the concentration of the nation's basic industries while putting other businesses in an unfair competitive position. These benefits were gained despite the solemn pledges that it was not to be used to promote monopoly and despite belated efforts to use the program to help "smaller" business.

During World War II, 80 per cent of the refinery expansion was by the twenty largest companies. Most of these plants were retained by the majors. A study by the Attorney General to gauge the effects of the program in refining since 1950 reassured that "it does not appear that issuance of these certificates has tended to promote undue concentration of economic power in the petroleum industry. Indeed it suggests that to a limited extent this program has inclined in favor of smaller concerns in the industry." Only 73 per cent of the new government-protected investments went to the twenty largest corporations. Their share of the industry's refining capacity dropped from 83.7 per cent in 1950 to 82 per cent in 1954. While admittedly not a substantial change, "at least in petroleum—[it] has not increased concentration":

Considering the emergency nature of the program and the overriding necessities of national security it is designed to serve, expansion of production is naturally sought from companies demonstrably capable of handling large-scale operations, regardless of the fact that they may be already dominant in production. In many instances, in fact, there may be no practical alternative. Nevertheless, the need to preserve the free competitive basis of our industrial economy is also urgent. That need is served only if incentive grants of any type go primarily to the smaller companies, except where immediate defense necessity otherwise requires.[28]

The comfort suggested by these figures and explanations slights the consideration that these grants have served to reinforce an existing pattern. There were practical alternatives through this entire period that might have given smaller refiners a far greater share in the wartime expansion, including the opportunity to build up the new and highly important modern catalytic cracking facilities that have so improved the majors' competitive position. Of course, to have done this would have been to challenge the entire working mechanism of the private government of oil.

There has been a political as well as an economic bias inherent in the program. Some of its consequences made vivid Harold L. Ickes's 1940 premonitions. The Secretary of the Interior, who was to play so leading a role in establishing the oil industry's participation in government, viewed with distress the building of plants at taxpayer expense and risk. President Roosevelt, he felt, was "abandoning advanced New Deal ground with a vengeance" in compromising so heavily with big business on tax amortization and excess profits taxes. ". . . It knocks the whole base from under the New Deal structure. We are running up the white flag. But if he is doing this in the expectation that he will win the support of business or wealth, he is sadly fooling himself, in my opinion." [29]

Perhaps inevitably, great political pressures were invited and brought to bear as industries and businesses vied for these lucrative privileges. Influence and prestige often became the criteria, rather than the planned growth of the economy in terms of genuine national needs. Good political tactics, increasingly built into the cost apparatus of the modern corporation, were rewarded. Oil's success in identifying all its activities with those of the national interest and in maintaining an interlocking relationship with public government helped to ensure that the exigencies of mobilization would not cause the industry to lose control of the reins. Expansion goals based on appraisals of the petroleum capacity and needs were formulated under the watchful eyes of oilmen temporarily in public service. These were then quickly implemented. Certification as to the necessity for rapid amortization has been made through the Petroleum Administration for Defense, and more recently, the Oil and Gas Division, within the Department of the Interior. These delegate agencies have been heavily staffed with industry personnel. Their responsibility has been to judge whether the applications for certificates of necessity made by individual oil companies are harmonious with the mobilization goals, set by oilmen wearing the mantle of public government.

There are many other governmental financial protections and subsidies in which the oil industry shares. These include a program by the International Cooperation Administration that guarantees foreign investments against losses due to expropriation or inability to convert foreign earnings into dollars (oil has been the single biggest buyer of this insurance), federal research and statistical services, and sympathetic local tax and zoning considerations in the construction of its plants. A student of community power could make a full-scale study just of the evolution of the struggles over the location of the Standard Oil refinery in relation to the city of Baton Rouge.

Tank fleet owners and users have always enjoyed generous public treatment, including construction subsidies, loans, and mortgage insurance. In the war and postwar periods, for example, they have operated ships leased from the government at favorable terms. Construction subsidies up to 50 per cent of cost are available, and the United States has periodically, as during Suez, urged the big oil companies to take full advantage of this to build supertankers. Government money has been available to guarantee mortgages representing up to 87.5 per cent of construction costs. But the oil companies have feared "overexpansion" of the world carrying capacity. Then too they are not willing to add to their American flag fleets, a condition for accepting such subsidies. The government offers a liberal allowance to companies trading in old tankers (they have a life expectancy of thirteen to twenty years, although many are used profitably for much longer) and building new ones. The old ones are consigned to the American reserve fleet. In 1955, for example, the Esso Shipping Company contracted with the United States Maritime Administration to trade in five 16,500-ton tankers from World War II. The $5,500,000 allowance received was then applied toward the construction in American shipyards of two large tankers costing $10 million each. For meeting Navy standards such as speed in the design of the replacements, Esso was granted an additional $2 million.

Much more attractive to oil companies than the trade-in program has been a trade-out and build program encouraging the transfer of older models to foreign countries. The requirement is that they be replaced by modern American-built ships. This has been done by the government because of the concern over the aging quality of the nation's fleet, which averages out as by far the oldest of all the major oil-transporting nations. Many World War II tankers have been disposed of in this fashion. When tankers were in demand, as during the Suez shortage, this became exceedingly profitable. At one point Esso received authorization to transfer five tankers abroad in return for building two larger ones costing over $23 million. Although they had been purchased from the government about eight years earlier for approximately $7½ million and their value after depreciation was now perhaps $4½ million, the five vessels could bring over $22 million on the foreign market. The United States also extended a million dollars to Esso for speed features incorporated into the new ships for defense purposes. Thus the oil company netted a sizable windfall on its original purchase and could rebuild its fleet with a minimum of new capital outlay.

While these inducements are utilized, the industry still prefers to construct its large tankers in the shipyards of the United Kingdom, France, Germany, Japan, and other countries where building costs may be cheaper by $100 or more per ton. (In 1957 Japan led the world in tanker tonnage construction.) Socony, for example, has estimated the cost of construction of a 16,500-deadweight-ton vessel at $5,775,000 in United States yards, as against $3,878,000 abroad; a 30,000-ton vessel at $9,600,000, as against $6,450,000; a 45,000-ton vessel at $13,500,000 as against $9,000,000.[30] There is often the chance to use currency that otherwise would be blocked, thus protecting the continuation of oil sales in these foreign markets.

The oil companies also prefer to register these tankers under the flags of Liberia, Panama, and other nations sympathetic to the tax and dollar problems of giant corporations. Earnings of American-owned foreign corporations can be taxed by the United States only when dividends are declared and returned to the United States. It is generally found expedient to reinvest these earnings abroad. Esso's Panama fleet, for example, is not subject to Panamanian income tax since its earnings are "at sea" rather than within Panama. According to a report of the Organization for European Economic Cooperation, what results is "virtual freedom from taxation," with shippers arranging their business enterprises so that "their profits are not liable to taxation in any country." [31]

About two-thirds of all the ships are now registered abroad, including most of Jersey Standard's fleet, which comprises a fourth of the oil industry's carrying capacity. Within a decade the United States' relative position has dropped from a registry of 60 per cent of the world's capacity to about 16 per cent. Liberia now has a similar percentage. Less than 5 per cent of the nation's petroleum import cargoes are now carried by United States tankers. The tankers that do operate under the American flag are engaged in intercoastal trade, mainly from the Gulf of Mexico to the East Coast, since the law requires that such cargo be carried in American bottoms. Oil companies sought waivers on this restriction during Suez.

"Flag of convenience" ships are manned with foreign crews. American maritime unions have been frustrated in their efforts to organize these ships by a Justice Department ruling to the effect that the National Labor Relations Board does not have the authority to intervene in such disputes. The State and Defense departments supported this position for "reasons of national defense." Circumventing American union scales and rules, along with taxes, results in at least a 50 per cent saving in costs. Annual operating costs of the three types of tankers cited above are estimated by Socony to be $998,600 for United States operation, compared to $511,800 for foreign-flag operation of a 16,500-ton vessel; $1,340,000 as compared to $699,000 for a 30,000-ton vessel; and $1,650,000 as compared to $890,700 for a 45,000-ton tanker. Socony primarily uses seamen from India and officers from Germany and England. (A survey of 95 foreign ships operating as subsidiaries of United States companies showed 25 American seamen out of their combined crews of more than 4,000 and 144 American officers of the 1,145 licensed personnel.) Basic wages, overtime, pensions, and fringe benefits for manning for one calendar day the 16,500-ton tanker under the United States flag were calculated in 1957 to be $1,200 for a crew of 40, as contrasted with $280 for a crew of 40 to 46 men under a foreign flag. Parent companies are then billed for the shipping of petroleum at United States Maritime Commission rates, although the actual costs to their subsidiaries are far less.

These ships are less accessible to the immediate jurisdiction of the United States Government during defense and comparable national emergency periods—including control over rates. (In 1959 United States Government war-risk insurance was offered to American-controlled ships operating under the flags of Panama, Liberia, and Honduras. Under the terms of the insurance such vessels were to be made available to the United States, upon request, in event of national emergency.) Should these ships get into trouble, however, presumably it would be American rather than Panamanian diplomatic representation and possibly naval assistance that would be expected to intervene in their behalf. Critics of the trade-out program, like Senator Warren Magnuson, chairman of the Committee on Interstate and Foreign Commerce, have also been disturbed by the lack of any modern tankers in the national defense reserve fleet and the reliance of the Military Sea Transportation Service upon chartered tankers for military needs. A good mothball fleet might give the government a potential check on shipping rates.

The American Merchant Marine Institute, the leading shipowners' association, which includes among its members the principal oil companies, has defended the overseas fleet as a "fifth arm of defense." (The domestic merchant marine is called the "fourth arm.") Without any direct government subsidy such as many other national fleets enjoy, these ships are seen as able to engage in the highly competitive international trade for the benefit of the United States while ready to serve the national interest in any crisis. "Panama and Liberia have been described as godsons of Uncle Sam. Any assertion that the authorities of these countries should, in an emergency, act against the wishes of the United States owners of the vessels and the United States Defense Department is pure fantasy." [32]

American shipyards, labor organizations, and domestic oil producers are bitter at such claims of patriotic intent. And they are skeptical as to the degree of effective control the United States can maintain over the rates, usage, and loyalty of these ships—even though they are frequently classified for mobilization purposes as part of the United States merchant fleet. Joseph Curran, president of the National Maritime Union (A.F.L.-C.I.O.), calls the "fifth arm" of defense a cloak:

> The big oil and steel companies . . . should stop trying to wrap their greed in the American flag. . . . The runaway fleet is only an extra arm by which some corporations which are doing very well indeed can pick extra profit out of the pockets of the American people and rob them of security at the same time.[33]

European maritime countries and shipping interests have also been troubled by this cheaper competition and their resulting income losses. There have been movements for tax, insurance, and other sanctions to curtail their American rivals sailing under "friendly flags." In the United Nations' sessions on codifying the law of the sea, they have advocated that if a ship is to have the privileges of international recognition there must be a genuine link between it and the flag it flies. This has been strenuously opposed by the oil and shipping interests:

Their [the traditional maritime countries] propaganda and conspiracies against United States-controlled ships under Panamanian and Liberian flags are unfriendly acts against the United States, and it should be made clear to them that they are so regarded by the United States Government, business community and public. A country like Norway is too dependent on the good-will of the United States to afford to persist in unfriendly agitation and one-sided propaganda against important United States interests. The reservoir of good-will enjoyed by Norway is great, but not inexhaustible.[34]

The oil-shipping position has been supported at the United Nations by United States representatives. In another instance, the United States Department has backed Aramco in its protests to Saudi Arabia over a contract made by the latter with Aristotle Onassis. The ambitious head of a vast independent tanker fleet had arranged to carry Arabian oil on terms that the American company viewed as a monopolistic threat to the shipping profits of its parents and to its contract with the Saudi government, with the ever present danger that this would create a precedent for other producing areas. "Our Government . . . rose in horror at such a thought," explained George Wadsworth, the United States ambassador to Saudi Arabia.[35] The situation provoked Aramco and other oil giants into an international boycott against Onassis ships and accelerated recurring United States investigations of his many activities in the States, including a series of tanker transfer deals.

There may be nothing necessarily reprehensible in this international extension of the oil corporations' quest for thrift and government protection. But it does offer further evidence that, despite all the industry's claims to be serving as an instrument of national security,

the giants of oil do not let the flag obscure their vision of their prime
and natural purpose—the quest for profits and power.

The industry prides itself on its ability to stand on its own feet.
In its literature on depletion, for example, the American Petroleum
Institute solemnly declares that the oil producer "doesn't ask for any
favoritism or special privilege." [36] From the industry's perspective,
there is never any preferential tax treatment or federal support. Where
these appear to be such, they must be understood as special situations.
The defense is always in terms of the peculiar nature of the industry
and its intimate identification with the well-being of the country.
The justification for policies of conservation and subsidization is
abundance and national security; the reality is planned scarcity and
private power.

The nation's largest industry is increasingly public in every aspect
except that of responsibility and profit. Despite the support for oil
from public law and financing, the government neither sets standards
nor demands conformance to broader public policies. The taxpayers'
chief return is the privilege of buying in markets subsidized by their
government and controlled by the industry, whether it is "cheap" oil
from the Persian Gulf or high-cost oil from the Gulf of Mexico. Few
questions are asked about this furthering of private wealth and power
and its impact upon the American society. To oilmen, such aids as
the depletion allowance are natural rights divorced from political
creation or popular control. "Any congressional tampering with this
provision of our tax law may well jeopardize the destiny of our
country," warned George R. Bryant, vice president of The Texas
Company.[37] A policy thoroughly inadequate and inconsistent for the
nation is invaluable for the industry.

This record of subsidies and tax privileges makes clear that it is
not the power of public government that oil fears. Rather is it a
positive government responsive to the welfare of the majority.

8

The Blending of Public and Private Abroad

Oil has brought to its corporate masters the greatest concentration of private wealth and economic power in history. It has also brought them into contact with governments and people in every region of the world. Inevitably, the oil corporations have had to formulate and implement policies to guide these political relationships.

The first principle of this private diplomacy aims for a favorable atmosphere for obtaining and maintaining concessions, contracts, and profits wherever oil may be found and traded. Regimes sympathetic to the industry have been backed, regardless of internal political alignments, ideological considerations and, on occasions, the formal position of the American Government. General Pérez Jiménez's brutal dictatorship in Venezuela—with nearly a billion dollars annual oil revenue—long enjoyed corporate support, as has an autocratic king in Saudi Arabia dependent upon his $300 million oil income. Oildom's much emphasized posture of strict neutrality generally develops only after its interests have reached a point of security where they no longer need to be party to the daily political higgling or where there is serious opposition to their presence and to the regime with whom they have negotiated. Yet the widespread awareness of their political involvement, their vulnerability to fresh contractual demands, and their very presence tend to make them continual targets for public attacks and for private requests for help by ambitious factions and figures—thus serving to keep oil interests entrenched, if only for defensive purposes, in the inner political life of these communities. (Parallel situations are quite common within producing

182

states in the United States.) Similarly, wherever there is internal strife in producing areas today, the first rumor remains that "oil" is backing the rebels or the government—whether the setting be Indonesia or Algeria. (Once again students of United States state politics will find similarities.)

A clue to oil's position is revealed in a salesletter from Time, Inc., pushing a 1953 issue of *Life* magazine:

. . . The late great Ibn Saud, king of Saudi Arabia, was dead. His son, now King Saud Ibn Abdul Aziz, reigned in his stead. *Life* . . . rushed *Life* Photographer David Douglas Duncan down from Arab Jerusalem to do a story on the new king. Duncan did not have a valid visa for Saudi Arabia, but he went anyway.

Luck was with him in two ways. First, as his plane touched down on the runway the front right tire blew out. That at least insured him several hours in Saudi Arabia before the wheel could be changed.

The second lucky break was that the airport telephone was functioning. Photographer Duncan was told that the phone was not working, public services having been suspended since the old king's death. But Duncan got a call through to Garry Owen, the top man in Aramco handling relations with the Saudi Arabian government. . . . Sitting with Owen at that moment was Aramco's President Robert Keyes; Chairman of the Board Fred Davies; Floyd Ohlinger, Director and Vice president; and a couple of other high officials.

Owen and Ohlinger rushed to the field where *Life*'s Duncan had been detained for lack of a visa. Airport officials were planning to put him on the first plane out of the country going in any direction.

As the Aramco officials walked in the door, they met the commanding general of the Saudi Arabian army. They introduced Duncan. Within ten minutes, Duncan had been cleared and was out of the building after a phone call to Crown Prince Faisal personally. . . .

Within a matter of minutes, King Saud was due to leave for Mecca for his first prayers as King of Saudi Arabia. In an Aramco car, Duncan was rushed straight from the airport to Crown Prince Faisal's palace. A message to the royal palace suggested to the new king that this was the time to have his first portraits made. With a tentative approval, the party drove at once to King Saud's palace and were ushered to the second floor, the heart and most private section of the palace.

. . . Duncan found a good place on a wide shaded balcony for portraiture. The new king walked out and Duncan made the *Life*-exclusive portrait of King Saud. . . . Duncan's Aramco friends and the king's secretary helped to get the relaxed, spontaneous type of portraiture *Life* wants by talking with the king while Duncan worked. Meanwhile, the palace yard was teeming with armed jeeps waiting to escort King Saud in grand style for his first official entry. . . .

From the time the wheel of Duncan's plane blew out to the time *Life*'s David Douglas Duncan had his pictures and the king started for Mecca —three hours.

The king's consideration for Duncan extended far beyond this first camera session. . . . Duncan was permitted later to follow him around the palace as he went about his royal duties. . . .

The same courtesies were extended to Duncan in relation to his expired visa. Crown Prince Faisal, as Foreign Minister, issued an order to the immigration authorities that Duncan was to be permitted to remain in the country under his sponsorship and as his guest. . . .

While Duncan was in the palace, the most powerful men of the Moslem world . . . were also present, but nobody once objected to Photographer Duncan's activities. He was the only infidel in this Wahhabi court which is the most orthodox Islamic circle in the world.[1]

But then this gesture may seem commonplace in a region where American Foreign Service officials are transported in Aramco's sizable air fleet and the 13,000 native workers are warned by the Saudi Arabian Government that a strike against Aramco would be a strike against their own government.

Out of obligation and out of foresight, the newer overseas enclaves, like some domestic oil communities, have taken on the character of miniature welfare states. Invariably the benefits have expanded beyond the enclaves. Loans have been extended to governments and all kinds of technical and financial aid in the nature of private "point four" programs made available. In Venezuela, for example, the major companies—Gulf, Shell, and Creole (Jersey), which have several billion dollars of investments—avow their determination not to repeat the errors once made in Mexico. Says Jersey:

Esso . . . has followed a policy of standing aside from purely Venezuelan affairs, while trying to fulfill in all respects its obligations as a good corporate citizen.[2]

The companies have contributed substantially to the International Basic Economy Corporation that was set up under Nelson Rockefeller's sponsorship and has sought to teach the people how to improve their economic life. Aramco's assistance program in Saudi Arabia has helped its own employees and neighboring communities deal with problems of education, health, sanitation, housing, electric power, water, and the development of agriculture, fishing, and local industry. Aramco even operates a television station for its Arabic-speaking employees. Stanvac (Standard-Vacuum Oil Company, owned by Jersey and Socony) has built a mosque for its Moslem employees in the South Sumatra oil fields.

This aid is not always welcomed with open arms. These innovations upset historic living patterns and can arouse suspicion. And so, in self-protection the modern oil company has had to pay attention to the culture within which it has moved. The efforts to "sow the petroleum" have emphasized the gross disparities in living conditions between the relatively limited number who benefit directly from the oil industry's presence and the great masses down to whom the economic gains may barely filter. For the great new oil discoveries today generally are in regions where the social systems are sharply stratified economically and politically. This has been true in Venezuela, Saudi Arabia, and most other overseas oil centers. It is said, for example, that "Saudi Arabia" receives each year nearly $300 million in oil revenues. But the 6 to 7 million inhabitants of the desert kingdom subsist on annual average incomes of perhaps $40, and 95 per cent of them are illiterate.

The companies have discovered that it is cheaper to buy than to bully. In Venezuela, for example, the fifty-fifty division of profits begun in 1943 has become a model for other areas. Nevertheless, the men of oil have set in motion or accelerated forces hostile to their presence or impatient with the degree of local benefit from industries obviously built for export markets. By 1959 the Venezuelan "model" had been breached through new tax laws that increased the government's share of production profits to 60 per cent. One growing center of discontent is among the young, trained technically by the foreign corporations, educated politically by the nationalist upsurges taking place everywhere. They frequently are frustrated by the gap between their personal potentials and the opportunities they see ahead for themselves and their homelands.

Yet not to train native workers for more skilled posts and leadership, oil companies have learned, is to inflame further these national-ist movements. Standard-Vacuum sends Indonesians to study in the United States while maintaining full teaching programs on the islands. It was a young Saudi Arabian engineer, Sheik Abdullah Tariki, educated at the University of Texas and a trainee with Texaco, who returned home to become Director of Petroleum and Mineral Affairs and a dedicated guardian of his nation's rights. "Saudi Arabia has nothing but oil. It is only money to the companies. To Saudi Arabia it is her life blood." Tariki sees the Venezuelan tax revision showing the way for the Middle East. "The oil companies screamed they were being ruined, but they're still in business in Venezuela. The industry didn't collapse. It won't collapse in the Middle East when the Arabs get more." Tariki has also been prominent in establishing an Organization of Petroleum Exporting Countries. The principals—Iraq, Iran, Kuwait, Saudi Arabia, and Venezuela—have sought to develop an international prorationing system that would stabilize markets, prevent production from exceeding demand, and prevent the international companies from playing off one producing area against the other.

One of Tariki's lessons from America concerns the worth of integration. He envisions an integrated Aramco, weaned from its parents who heretofore have performed most of the transportation, refining, and marketing functions. "I don't care how Aramco's structure has to be changed, I want an Arab company in all phases of oil operations and that's what we are going to have," warns Tariki. "What if the concession agreement does run on for years? No agreement is worth anything if the people of the country aren't satisfied with it." [3] This proposal would enable Saudi Arabia to exercise greater control and to profit from every stage of the oil business, right up to the gasoline pump, rather than primarily from the production end, as is now the case. A recent contract for offshore exploration rights in the Neutral Zone between Kuwait and Saudi Arabia, made with a Japanese oil group, has such provisions, along with a pledge by the latter to erect a refinery plant. It also carries with it a potential threat to the world pricing system. Abdullah Tariki has also received an education in the finer points of corporate bookkeeping. He has fought against certain of Aramco's discount practices in its sales to the four owner companies, thus seeking to end an Aramco technique for excluding Saudi Arabia from a full share in the profits. In May 1959 Tariki and one other representative from the Saudi Arabian Government were appointed to Aramco's board of directors. With other informed Arabs, Tariki has openly speculated about control of the pipeline networks as keys to the control of the Middle East oil flow. There is considerable talk about insisting that any future pipelines contemplated by the Western corporations be placed in Arab hands —another page from the Rockefeller textbook. Thus, modern industrialism explodes in an environment that is still in the midst of a conscious transformation from a tribal to a feudal social structure.

These challenges to corporate sovereignty have pushed oilmen further into the social and political fabric of the producing countries at the very time they have been most eager to prove their political nonpartisanship. But they feel puzzled and persecuted when references are made to their imperial roles:

Mr. Rathbone [President of Jersey Standard]. You indicated a feeling, sir, that the oil companies control the governments in these countries.

Senator O'Mahoney. Oh no; I don't say they control the government. I say they know what is going on before anybody in that country knows, and before we in Congress know.

Mr. Rathbone. We do know what is going on in these various countries because we feel that we can't possibly operate efficiently and intelligently there unless we do know. . . . I would say that rather often I have wished I did control one or two of these foreign governments.

But we do not—there is no country, you can go right around the world—we do not control the government in any one of these countries around the world. They are sovereign governments and they control us to a very great measure.[4]

All these factors strengthen the private determination of the international companies to get the oil out as quickly as possible. (One hears much less discussion among Western oilmen about conservation principles applying to the Middle East. But native geologists are becoming alert to the need to develop all the resources for the long pull, rather than just taking the cream from the most attractive producing fields.)

Oil companies are frequently viewed and view themselves as representing the United States abroad, while at the same time they function as separate and sovereign governments with their own foreign policies. In a critique of the United States cartel suit, Standard of New Jersey declared:

This increase of military, technical and economic contacts between the United States and Saudi Arabia, with their rich increment of good will, is of tremendous importance to the United States Government. The United States trifles with all this when it seeks by force of law to impose its antitrust ideology upon that country and challenges the lawfulness of the very company which, in the Arab mind, is a symbol of the United States·and which, in a large measure, is responsible for the phenomenal progress of Saudi Arabia in recent years and that country's sympathy with the United States and its objectives.[5]

Since mineral rights in most areas of the world belong to the state rather than to private property holders, the heads of the governments of oil negotiate pacts with the heads of political states, as happened recently in Iran. The major companies have their private emissaries to foreign capitals who constitute a diplomatic service. Their task is to develop good contacts and respect for the problems in developing oil resources while gathering basic data on the political and economic climate for the home office. A memorandum on the "Political and Economic Effects of Middle East Developments and the European Fuel Crisis," prepared in early 1957 by a member of Jersey Standard's government-relations staff who had been covering Europe, provides a glimpse of these concerns and activities:

In assessing the longer range effects of recent Middle East developments and the resulting European fuel crisis it is important to realize that we are also in the midst of a major political crisis. Important political changes have already occurred and others are in the making which will result in shifts in balance of power, especially in the Middle East, but also among the Western powers. We face probable changes in alliances and pacts, and a great many problems in replacing influences that may be lost. It is too early even to speculate on details of these changes, but we certainly can assume that the conditions for future operations in the Middle East will be different, as will also the climate in which we shall be doing business.

With such major adjustments on the move, or in the offing, it is natural that there should be a strong head of emotional steam which tends to distort issues and encourage extreme attitudes. So in assessing longer range effects of recent developments we need to ignore the criticisms and recriminations of the moment and to look for attitudes that are likely to influence governments and international organizations in future policy decisions and actions. We need to look to the period beyond the present emergency and to the longer future, because steps being planned or taken now will have repercussions over several years and may result in permanent changes.

The report then discusses in some detail European planning for integrated measures (1) to reduce dependence on oil through greater coal imports from the United States and through nuclear development and (2) to achieve greater security for its future petroleum supply through possible measures involving equitable distribution, United Nations operation of pipelines and the Suez Canal, and the assumption of greater responsibility for the general development of Middle Eastern countries (using oil revenues):

Having seen how quickly the flow of Middle East oil to Europe could be interrupted, and how difficult it is to obtain even partial replacements from other sources, governments and the public want assurances that will give a sense of greater security. The public looks to governments and governments in turn are looking to international organizations to get these assurances. The present drive to reduce Europe's dependence on oil will naturally subside somewhat with the end of the crisis, but the severity of long-range policies in this direction will depend on the success achieved in restoring confidence in the reliability of Middle East sources. Any plans the United Nations may have for intervention in the Middle East will certainly be formed in New York, as will also be Jersey policy regarding these plans, but the determination and urgency behind them rest again on the security issue.

Whatever can be done to increase the security of transportation means, particularly pipeline, will help this situation. Stabilizing developments such as those we hope will grow from the new Eisenhower policy will also be very important. The problem of restoring confidence in Middle East oil is one which concerns every member of the petroleum industry active in Europe.

Insofar as plans and specific actions by the different governments and international bodies are concerned, we shall need to be constantly alert, not only to activities and decisions but also to attitudes and trends of thinking. This means improving and extending our contracts with all of these different groups. Good working relations exist now with the High Authority and technical departments in Luxembourg, where initiative has already been taken in consulting with representatives of the oil industry, including our own, on points of policy. With the Energy Advisory Commission and Energy Committee now moving into the European energy picture, we shall undoubtedly see a considerable expansion of O.E.E.C. activity. Our good contacts during the past with the Oil Committee and other groups in the O.E.E.C. have already paved the way to close cooperation with these new groups. Since the days of the Price Report our knowledge of E.C.E. activities, and understanding in Geneva of oil industry problems and methods have both developed substantially, and energy problems are now discussed as matters of mutual interest. Regular contacts are maintained with economic representatives in the important U.S. Embassies throughout Europe and with national bodies in the different nations responsible for energy matters. Valuable contacts and communications have been developed with government quarters in Washington and with the U.S. Regional Office and special embassies in Europe charged with representing U.S. interests to the main supranational groups. These are based on confidence and friendly discussion of problems of common interest. Close working relations between managements and local government departments provide constructive backing for activities at the international level.

In assessing and dealing with the long-range repercussions of the present crisis it is a case of knowing what is being planned and discussed everywhere, of coordinating information, of taking initiative where we can in steering matters which directly concern us, and of working patiently and carefully to be sure that our point of view is known and considered wherever decisions are made. We must be sure that we come out of the present emergency with undiminished prestige and strength.[6]

In a world where nation states still dominate, the public government is expected to play a substantial role in furthering the private ends of these international corporate citizens. Oilmen assume that the American Government accepts as a first article of faith the proposition advanced by the National Petroleum Council that "the participation of United States nationals in the development of world oil resources is in the interest of all nations and essential to our national security." [7] The primary task of the American Government is to create a "political and financial climate both here and abroad . . . conducive to overseas investment," the chairman of Texaco has explained.[8] This message is echoed on the mimeograph machines and at the luncheon clubs by executives of all the international oil companies. American foreign policy should work toward gaining the respect of other nations for the virtues of "free enterprise" and equal access to oil development.

Oil's own diplomatic corps relies upon the support of American foreign embassies, consular offices, the State Department and, on occasions, the Presidency itself. In an earlier period, companies regularly received the fullest protection of the flag in their extensive and profitable marketing operations in China that were made difficult by the inability of the central government to control the arbitrary taxation and outright banditry of local warlords. Summing up its role, the State Department has said:

Many such cases required long and difficult work. . . . A study of the cases in which requests for aid were made and of the action taken in such cases by representatives of this government would reveal that the latter consistently did their best to render effective assistance to oil companies; that measured in terms of dollars and cents, the cumulative value of such assistance would reach a very impressive figure. . . .[9]

During the thirties, the American Embassy in Tokyo aided the Standard-Vacuum Oil Company by having the application of a 1934 Japanese law requiring oil companies to maintain a six-month stock on hand at all times postponed. This costly provision, of special attraction to the Japanese military, was thoroughly distasteful to the oil concerns. Some oil representatives fought within American Government circles against the cutting off of oil supplies to Japan as she prepared for World War II. They also resisted or ignored efforts to prevent indirect shipments by way of "neutrals" or "independent brokers," and even were reluctant to stop the refueling of Axis ships. Earlier, during the Ethiopian War when the League of Nations was testing its strength by attempting to apply sanctions against Italy, the companies won in their efforts to enjoin the State Department against placing an embargo on oil to the aggressor.

After World War I the State Department had ardently advocated the full implementation of the "open door" policy. When it appeared that the Netherlands Government was planning to turn over to Shell the German concessions in the Netherlands Indies, ignoring Standard Oil (New Jersey), which was also in the area, American diplomats argued for equal opportunity. At first they were unsuccessful. But a reciprocity clause in the newly passed Mineral Leasing Act and the knowledge that Shell was searching for crude oil in the western parts of the United States provided weapons. A State Department memorandum tells what happened next:

With a view to exerting further pressures on the Netherlands Government the American Government took steps to block the issuance of further concessions to the Royal Dutch Shell in public lands in the United States. The final result was that the New Jersey company was given additional producing concessions in the Indies which turned out to be some of the richest in the islands.[10]

The State Department also advocated the right of American oil interests to share equally in the concessions involved in the "development" of the mandated territories of the old Turkish Empire. Coveted by the Germans, these were eagerly being divided by the British, French, and Dutch, for earlier successes in Persia had made geologists alert to prospects in neighboring Iraq. "This Government has contributed to the common victory, and has a right, therefore, to insist that American nationals shall not be excluded from a reasonable share in developing the resources of territories under mandate. . . ."[11]

Once a foot in the door was secured, with Jersey and Socony becoming partners with these foreign interests in the Iraq Petroleum Company, the same oil companies lost much of their zeal for the further application of the principle in this region. Seeking government backing, they now participated in exclusive agreements that kept out competition. Thus the State Department played an important part in bringing together the international oil companies, just as it was to pave the diplomatic path with the British for entry of other American interests into Bahrein, Kuwait, and other Persian Gulf oil fields. To some these successive intercessions in behalf of oil were viewed as fulfilling the moral purposes and political needs of the natural overseas extension of nineteenth century manifest destiny. To the less reverent they earned Charles E. Hughes, Secretary of State from 1921 to 1925, the title of Secretary for Oil. And more significantly, these moves announced that the United States and its corporate citizens were now in truth world powers, with continuing economic interests on every continent.

Political and diplomatic intercession followed corporate expansion into Mexico, Venezuela, Argentina, Guatemala, Colombia, and Bolivia. When there has been pressure for greater control over the companies and when new legislation has been planned, as happened in Colombia, Venezuela, and Mexico during the twenties, the American embassies have engaged in what the State Department has described as "the closest collaboration" with the corporations and producing countries in representing and safeguarding private investments and profits.[12] Countries like Brazil and Argentina, which have sought to develop their oil resources without foreign corporate involvement, have discovered that the United States Government is hostile to extending loans and technical advice to state enterprises where American corporations are seeking entry. In Spain, the $2 billion outlay for military bases and financial aid by the United States Government since 1954, along with direct intervention with Generalissimo Franco by President Eisenhower and other American officials, have been encouraged by the major oil companies. The latter sought help in ending resistance to foreign capital and in negotiating and then protecting their $200 million investment for oil development in Spain and Spanish Sahara.

Historically, the oil companies preferred to work without any help, for government support always carried with it the potential of accountability. And so their appeals have often come in especially difficult situations. At times the gains in these cases have been short run. In Mexico, which in 1921 was the second largest oil producer and provided 25 per cent of the world's supply, the British and Americans had oil investments of at least $300 million. But the companies saw, even if they did not understand, that their position was tenuous. They were operating on a powder keg of nationalistic and social revolutionary tensions. The economic penetration of the oil companies and other foreign interests brought political intervention in its wake, and the rivalries of the British and Americans for privileges intensified the widespread corruption. The people were provided with an intolerable reminder of their exploited condition, whether by domestic feudalism, Spanish conquistadores, French and British imperialism, or the dollar diplomacy of the colossus from the North.

The political and military conflicts among Mexican factions led the oil interests to fear for the safety of their installations. American naval vessels patrolled the Gulf Coast. Their purpose, it was once explained by Philander C. Knox, who was President Taft's Secretary of State, was to keep Mexicans "in a salutary equilibrium, between a dangerous and exaggerated apprehension and a proper degree of wholesome fear." [13] During the revolutionary period the companies apparently financed armed bands. The immediate threat to the oilmen was the government's return to an old constitutional principle that viewed all subsoil rights of ownership as vested in the state. Current holdings were regarded as concessions of limited duration and condition, raising the fear within the oil group that the next step would be to make this retroactive to cancel the original land titles under which the companies were operating.

Preliminary action in this direction and in agrarian reforms led Secretary of State Frank B. Kellogg in 1925 to warn that "the Government of Mexico is now on trial before the world." [14] This prompted an unequivocal rejoinder from the Mexican president that his nation would fulfill its obligations to foreign residents but that such insulting threats to the sovereignty of Mexico placed the American Government on trial. At one point it appeared that there would be war, with the American Secretary seeing Bolshevist intrigue as a fundamental factor in Mexican behavior. Nationalistic Mexicans saw the American Embassy (standing on a site given by oilman Edward L. Doheny who pioneered in opening up Mexican oil fields) as an agent of the oil interests. But a compromise was worked out that appeared to assure retention of the early oil privileges. Nevertheless, the oil companies gradually curtailed operations, shifting energy and investments to Venezuela and other more inviting areas.

When the explosion of expropriation came in 1938, the oil-government alliance was unable to reverse the action. As during an earlier seizure of Jersey Standard property in Bolivia, it provided a difficult test of the sincerity of the United States in the Good Neighbor Policy with its emphasis on nonintervention and its determination to reverse the image of Yankee imperialism. To the chagrin of the oilmen, the United States publicly accepted Mexico's sovereign right of expropriation. It reminded its neighbor, however, of the obligation of prompt payment for the involved properties, and worked hard until Jersey Standard and the other companies received compensation. A major stumbling block at first was the companies' insistence upon including the oil still in the ground as part of their losses, rather than calculating on the basis of their investments. Some unreconstructed oilmen in the Shell and Jersey Standard organizations apparently were in no hurry for a settlement. Thoroughly misunderstanding the temper of the people, they were hoping and planning for a counterrevolution or collapse that would bring back the ousted companies.

Meanwhile, the nationalized industry in Mexico (Petróleos Mexicanos) found itself boycotted by the international companies who were determined to cut off Mexican oil from world markets. For several years Pemex was denied access to tetraethyl. The major tanker fleets avoided her ports, and drilling equipment from the United States became difficult to obtain because of the relationship between big oil and the supply companies. At least one oil company used its travel services to discourage tourists from entering "dangerous" Mexico. To support their private war, the involved interests sought to get the United States Government to adjust its import quotas to discriminate against Mexico and to reject contract bids offering Mexican oil. A proposal to cut off United States Government purchases of Mexican silver was weighed. This would have struck very hard at the economic life of the country, but it would also have boomeranged since this was essentially an American-owned enterprise and it would have involved a clash with the well established silver bloc in Congress and also with interests who exported goods to Mexico. They also pressured the United States Government to turn down requests from Mexico for capital loans, hoping that public development of oil would be discredited and that the Mexicans would be forced to seek the return of foreign private capital and management. War requirements ended much of this retaliation. Yet only after considerable internal conflict among oilmen and public officials in Washington was an Export-Import Bank loan extended and aviation gas facilities built in Mexico. These were not ready until after the war. With active support from within the State Department, the expelled companies had sought to use the need for 100-octane gasoline as a way of reentering Mexico. According to a 1943 memorandum from oilman Max Thornburg, the State Department's oil adviser, to Undersecretary of State Sumner Welles, these companies deserved "preferential rights." But they "must not return in popularly recognizable form" and "must be ostensibly Mexican. . . ." Deputy Petroleum Administrator Ralph K. Davies saw this as "a shameful hindrance in the prosecution of the war." Being "a party to any proposal that these companies reenter Mexico under cover of darkness draws fire from me not alone as a Government official but as an oil man." He and his superior, Secretary of Interior Harold L. Ickes, were also strongly critical of the State Department's employment of the Universal Oil Products Company as a consultant in the State Department's Mexican negotiations, since this process-engineering firm was conttolled by the expropriated majors. California oilman Edwin W. Pauley, who in 1946 was to be the center of a bitter political skirmish over his nomination as Undersecretary of the Navy, charged that the State Department adviser blocked a contract he was arranging for a refinery in Mexico. When Mr. Thornburg said the project was in conflict with State Department policy, explained Pauley, Thornburg "meant that no group of independent oil men could do business in Mexico, even if that business would have been of direct aid to our war program. He meant that his interests— the interests of the expropriated major oil companies by whom he was employed—came first. . . ." [15]

The expropriated American and British interests have insisted they brought prosperity and integrity in their dealings with Mexico. They have viewed themselves as the victims of political demagoguery and cupidity. Undoubtedly oil did bring progress to Mexico in the form of capital, technology, and a focused discontent. But whether one looked at the flagrant waste in production techniques, the location of the pipelines and refineries, the treatment of Mexican labor, or the general superior and manipulative attitude toward the culture, this was a foreign industry geared for export of oil and profits rather than for the advancement of the people.

To all of the oil world and the Western powers who rely upon its services, the Mexican experience remains a vivid and troubling warning. For the richest new fields of oil are in areas such as the Middle East where the multiple ingredients for the revolutionary character of our times are present and seething. This concern is compounded by the strategic location of these oil sources and the ominous proximity of the Soviet empire. How the oil leaders use their power —and the political power of their country to which they have such ready access—has the profoundest meaning for the course of international events.

These experiences only confirm the conviction of the National Petroleum Council that "the federal government . . . by diplomatic representation . . . should seek to secure the observance of agreements made between foreign governments and American nationals and to minimize the political risks involved in foreign operations." [16] No one questions the right of a nation to nationalize domestic private property in the public interest, assuming just compensation, oil leaders now assert in a burst of abstract social progressiveness. But where oil development is concerned, explained R. G. Follis, chairman of Standard Oil of California, "governments make contracts with nationals of other countries which, in essence, surrender voluntarily the right to nationalize for a definite period of time." The United States has the obligation to affirm in every way the sanctity of such solemn agreements. Their abrogation "should never go unchallenged by responsible nations, nor should any nation enjoy the fruits of such action." [17] For nothing is more sacred than a contract, the industry repeatedly reminds the State Department in demanding that it make clear to the world its intent to support the oil companies. Oil representatives have warned the State Department against accepting the United Nations' proposed Covenant of Human Rights because of a provision asserting the right of peoples to self-determination including "permanent sovereignty over their natural wealth and resources." [18] Governments may change, rulers may be deposed, and feudal social systems overturned. But the right granted by an existing state to a company to take out the oil wealth of a people should not be interfered with—even where the investment has been paid off many times over.

In this respect, Italy has been a troublesome thorn in recent years. In Italy itself, where there is now promise of oil, the United States Government has actively and openly supported American interests led by Jersey Standard and Gulf. These companies have clashed with the Italian Government and Enrico Mattei, head of ENI (Ente Nazionale Idrocarburi), the huge public oil and gas corporation, which is a direct descendant of the fascist experiment, over such issues as leasing areas, production levels, and royalties. Some Italian political groups favor complete nationalization. Others have rejected as inadequate the American oil offer of a fifty-fifty division of profits, explaining, "We're not Arabs." United States Ambassador Clare Booth Luce warned that oil and other foreign capital investments could not operate in a climate lacking in "political safety." Despite this intercession and repeated discussions by oil and diplomatic representatives, the parliament finally passed what the industry regarded as a tough oil law. Gulf withdrew from the mainland, where it had a fifty-fifty partnership with a huge Italian chemical firm, giving up at least one major oil strike. It kept its operations in Sicily, where the law is viewed as more sympathetic to private development. Other American companies, notably Cities Service, still show interest.

But the deeper stir in the oil world and the American State Department is caused by Mattei's overseas ventures. ENI has sought leases in Egypt, Morocco, Iran, and elsewhere in the Mediterranean and Middle East. In Libya the world oil companies with huge exploration investments worked hard in an attempt to keep Mattei out, prompting the latter to complain that "the Americans have done a nasty thing to Italy in Libya." In contrast to the fifty-fifty division which oilmen consider generous, Mattei promises that up to 75 per cent of the returns will accrue to the producing country, an arrangement that challenges all existing concessions and the world industry's pricing system. He has completed one such deal with Iran, despite the opposition of the consortium of oil companies and the British and American governments. More disturbing, in 1958 Standard of Indiana, in its quest for overseas crude supplies, formed a joint operating company with the Iranian Government's oil company for offshore exploration. Profits were to be split 75–25 and Iran was to receive a cash bonus, something oilmen have pointed out Italy has not been offering in its contracts.

Says Mattei:

The people of Islam are weary of being exploited by foreigners. The big oil companies must offer them more for their oil than they are getting. I not only intend to give them a more generous share of the profits but to make them my partners in the business of finding and exploiting petroleum resources.[19]

Increasing the take will not necessarily help the masses of Arab people, given the greed of corrupt ruling classes and the continuation of social systems that are so inequitable in their distribution of rights and resources. But it does scare oildom. And it can act as a catalytic agent in furthering resentment against Western influence.

With two-thirds of the world's crude reserves in the Middle East, the internationally integrated members of the industry are understandably sensitive to Arab nationalist movements. They have installations, long-term commitments, and profit expectations worth billions of dollars. They fear fresh upward demands in royalty percentages and rights, behind which lies the ever present threat of nationalization. Oil wants stability in this region—which means maintenance of the status quo for as long as possible while it races to take out the highly profitable petroleum. Its leaders have been consistent advocates of the appeasement of Middle Eastern feudal rulers.

During World War II, the Texas and California companies brought great pressure upon the American Government to use the newly established lend-lease program to meet King Ibn Saud's demands upon their California-Arabian Standard Oil Company subsidiary (later known as the Arabian American Oil Company, or Aramco) for a company loan of $6 million a year for the next five years. The war had cut off the king's revenues from the pilgrims en route to Mecca and Medina, and since the companies were not increasing production sufficiently to enable him to maintain his enlarged army, he wanted this advance on royalties. "The company took the position not expressed to the King that the international situation did not justify any substantial additional investment of their own capital." [20]

James A. Moffett, formerly senior vice president of Jersey and then chairman of the Bahrein and Caltex subsidiaries of the Texas and California companies, who was assigned as their Washington representative to arrange this, later explained that it was not so much the money that was troubling the oil directors. For this was a fabulously successful venture "when through luck on an investment of $50,000 you discover oil and on this basis you acquire a concession in Arabia for $500,000 and find yourself after an expenditure of $27,-000,000 owning a property worth billions." [21] They wanted government protection abroad, including insurance against any shifts in the regime. They also were increasingly embarrassed at home by the public spectacle of their funds making possible Ibn Saud's military and propaganda campaigns against the Jews and Palestine. Then too, The Texas Company had just previously found it wise public relations to remove Captain Torkild Rieber from its chairmanship because of his Nazi associations. A letter from Moffett to President H. D. Collier of California, written in August 1940, offered a good insight into corporate strategy and tactics. Expressing sadness over the Rieber episode, Moffett indicated that naturally he would be expected to withdraw from Caltex's board. But as far as he knew "there has been no repercussion upon our business throughout the British Empire." Public-relations efforts made it clear that "we, Caltex, are pro-English from the standpoint of the war."

This brings up a point which I want to pass on for your consideration.

You are doing a very large business with the Japanese and therefore must take as strong a pro-Japanese position as possible to maintain this business. Caltex, however, really must be anti-Japanese, because we have a large investment in China, do a large business directly with China, and practically nothing in Japan, and our main business is in the British Empire, which is having real difficulties with the Japanese and must be anti-Japanese at the present time.

Then again, we operate under foreign laws and are a foreign company and have no domestic connection except through directors who may be connected with domestic corporations.

From a straight business standpoint, it does not make any difference in your control of the activities of this company whether you or any member of the California company is a member of the Board of Directors and it seems to me that we should give this very careful consideration.[22]

But at the time of the Saudi Arabian negotiations, Moffett stressed to his friend President Roosevelt the pitiful plight of the Moslem masses, and warned that without the requested governmental assistance "this independent kingdom, and perhaps with it the entire Arab world, will be thrown into chaos." [23] As an added inducement for the President's advisers, he pledged annual delivery for the next five years of $6 million worth of petroleum to the United States armed forces at very low prices. The exact nature of this last feature of the proposal subsequently became a subject of great debate and was a contributing factor leading to a federal suit against the major overseas corporations.

At first Roosevelt and his aides found this aid inadvisable because of the terms of the lend-lease program, public opinion, and a reluctance to move in a sphere of influence that was traditionally British. But although the President regarded direct aid as "a little far afield for us" and his close adviser Harry L. Hopkins wondered "how we can call that outfit a democracy," it was subsequently arranged that the British Government would make these payments, presumably from its share of American loans.

Oilmen feared that the British Government's increasing financial role in Saudi Arabia, resulting from its dispensing of this indirect aid, might pave the way for British access to or control of these resources. They renewed their pleas for direct American lend-lease. This national loyalty of oil was re-enforced by the possibility of Saudi Arabia's becoming a sterling area favoring British companies. Presidents W. S. S. Rodgers of The Texas Company and H. D. Collier of California Standard argued their case for maintaining the American character of the enterprise before the top war agencies; meanwhile Aramco continued to operate within the State Department and its own private diplomatic channels to ensure that its role as an intermediary between the two governments was preserved and with it Aramco's advantages and prestige with the Arab ruler, who apparently was being kept in the dark about much of this. In 1943 President Roosevelt informed the Lend-Lease Administration that "I hereby find that the defense of Saudi Arabia is vital to the defense of the United States." By 1947 it was estimated that the nation—or rather, the king—had received approximately $100 million.

After World War II ended, a huge air base was built at Dhahran where Aramco has its headquarters and which is used by the oil company's planes. In addition to British objections, there had been considerable doubt voiced as to the military worth to the United States of this $43 million investment which under agreement reverted to Saudi Arabia and for which the American Government paid a high annual rental. While the United States uses it as a major military transport stopover point, some observers have insisted that Aramco has been the chief beneficiary.

In keeping with the spirit of this entire Arabian venture, Moffett brought a $6 million suit against his erstwhile corporate colleagues for compensation for securing the British-American financing of their obligations to Ibn Saud. This seems less inconsistent or outlandish when one realizes that under Treasury Department rulings bribes to foreign governments to receive contracts have been deductible as "ordinary and necessary to the taxpayer's business." [24]

The same companies, with Gulf Oil, also sought government construction of a $200 million pipeline which they would gradually pay for while the Government retained ownership. They admitted they could finance this 1,200-mile system across the Arabian Peninsula to Sidon on the Mediterranean themselves. But they preferred to have the government involved in this always explosive area so as to help in their rivalry with British-blessed oil interests and in getting the necessary approval from the Arab countries. ". . . Possibly I am a little old fashioned," pleaded James Terry Duce of Aramco, "but I think the American companies deserve the protection of the United States Government. We do our best. . . ." [25] They encountered the hostility of Jersey Standard and Socony, who had nothing to gain from this pipeline, as well as of smaller domestic producers who resented the strengthening of Middle Eastern sources. Tapline ultimately was built by private capital, with the two leading critics, Jersey and Socony, coming in as partners in all Aramco holdings just as the "Truman doctrine" declaring American interest in Greece and Turkey was launched. The United States Government played an important behind-the-scenes role in clearing the right of way. Pressure was then successfully directed to convince the Department of Commerce and other agencies to release the scarce steel, once again in face of hostility from American producers who could not see why this project should be given priority while they themselves were having difficulty in obtaining the materials for expansion to meet war needs.

The American industry had been unsuccessful in obtaining a foothold in Iran, despite attempts by a number of companies and the pleadings of the State Department after World War I and during World War II. This strategically located country had long been sought by the Germans, the Russians, and the European trading countries. But the concessions gained at the opening of the twentieth century had given England the basis for its controlling influence. When in 1951 the group headed by Premier Mohammed Mossadegh moved zealously for nationalization of the Anglo-Iranian Oil Company operations, the Americans were presented with a new opportunity as a result of actions in which they were participants and beneficiaries.

The dispute, rooted in the history of the concession, had taken on an irreconcilable character as each side stood on high principle while denouncing the other. There were strong feelings against British colonialism. The company's labor policy was viewed as precluding Iranian nationals from rising above the level of laborers. The high profits were inflammatory; with annual oil exports valued at $360 million, Iran was getting $35 million in royalties and $65 million through the company's local expenditures. Great Britain was receiving more in taxes from the profits than was Iran, a smoldering source of contention in all oil-producing countries. A seven-year national development program for the economy and welfare needs financed from oil revenues and based upon a comprehensive study by outside experts had been begun in 1949. The consultants maintained that Iran had the resources to handle this. But a selfish and corrupt ruling class and a politically inept bureaucracy helped dissipate the oil revenues. Of the 20 million population, 90 per cent were illiterate; the infant mortality rate was 500 deaths for every 1,000 live births; 70 per cent of the land was held by 2 per cent of the people, although farming was the major occupation.[26] (Oil employed only 120,000.) In this setting, Anglo-Iranian became a symbol and a scapegoat for all the difficulties and obstacles to social change.

On England's part, the much admired ability to compromise and the sensitivity for strategic retreat so frequently forced into play in the twilight of its empire were strangely absent or obscured in the concern for oil and position voiced by foreign officers and underscored by their oil-company advisers. Discounting the genuine grievances against Anglo-Iranian, forgetting the lessons of Mexico and Venezuela, and flaunting the tide of nationalism, Britain stood firmly behind the corporation. Although the country had just gone through nationalization of several of its own basic industries, the leadership found it difficult to accept such acts in Iran. As Benjamin Schwadran has noted in his fine study of great-power oil rivalries in the Middle East, "Time and time again the notion of sanctity of contract was pointed out as the real issue in the controversy." [27] Only when it was too late, did the company make the kind of fifty-fifty profit-sharing offer that conceivably might have set a basis for agreement. The giant oil companies stood together, and Anglo-Iranian warned of legal reprisals against any interest outside the world brotherhood of oil who dared to purchase the disputed Iranian oil. It is difficult to believe this exercise of raw power was made without the approval of the British Government, which holds a majority of the stock and is represented on the company's board of directors. Such resolution would have been impossible, of course, if oil supplies had not been assured, with the international companies having increased production in other countries.

The United States Government sought to mediate the dispute, ever mindful of Russia's past interests in Iran, its abortive attempt to remain in northern Iran at the close of World War II, and the reality of a 1,000-mile common northern border between the two countries. The State Department and its oil advisers were also aware of the rich oil reserves there and of the consequences of nationalization for oil regions where American interests predominated. The industry received full backing in its economic blockade of Iran throughout the struggle. This meant government sanction for the private pricing and marketing controls governing the world supply. Oilmen had an assurance of immunity from antitrust action as the Petroleum Administration for Defense worked with companies in the states to synchronize refining, storage, and shipments to compensate for the oil lost through the closedown. The chief threat to the order of oil was not so much shortages or even nationalization, but rather the possibility of oil flowing into world markets outside the control system.

Iran had been the first country to receive Point Four aid. Now the limited assistance of $1 million for the fiscal year 1951 was increased to $23 million in 1952 and in 1953. But the Western nations and companies expected that Mossadegh could not last in office. They grew tougher in their determination to break him or force a settlement on their terms. At one point the State Department apparently advised him to make arrangements with Shell if he could not allow the return of Anglo-Iranian. The premier grew increasingly intransigent as he learned more about the realities of an integrated world industry. He wanted Iran to be able to sell its oil in abundant quantities, not set by the dictates of the industry's private production plans. The large-scale purchasers he needed could not be found. Iran had the oil, but without the technicians, the markets, and the transportation it was caught by a system of power that, at least for the short run, was able to get along without these supplies.

Requests to the United States by Mossadegh for additional loans to meet budgetary needs aggravated by the complete loss of oil revenues were turned down. In the closing days of the regime, President Eisenhower made clear the position of the United States in support of Anglo-Iranian:

There is a strong feeling in the United States . . . that it would not be fair to the American taxpayers for the United States Government to extend any considerable amount of economic aid to Iran so long as Iran could have access to funds derived from the sale of its oil and oil products if a reasonable agreement were reached with regard to compensation whereby the large-scale marketing of Iranian oil would be resumed. Similarly, many American citizens would be deeply opposed to the purchase by the United States Government of Iranian oil in the absence of an oil settlement.[28]

The State Department also pointed out that it did not appreciate Dr. Mossadegh's laxity in dealing with the domestic Communist party, whose position was strengthened by the economic squeeze play engineered by the anti-communist West. While no comparable public statement was made, it is apparent that the Western public-private allies had at least equal distaste for Iran's success in the last months in dealing with Japan for the sale of oil.

There is evidence that the United States also worked behind the scenes for the overthrow of Mossadegh that came in August 1953, with the Central Intelligence Agency playing a key part. Questions about the United States' role in Iran and about the activities of this secret arm of the United States—which operates with a budget and personnel concealed from the Congress and the public—are generally shunted aside or remarks placed "off the record." [29]

When Mossadegh was being replaced, it was the American-trained and -equipped army of the Shah that supported his military successor who was pledged to come to terms with the Western private and public powers. Major General George C. Stewart, Director of the United States Office of Military Assistance of the Department of Defense, later testified that

. . . when this crisis came on and the thing was about to collapse, we violated our normal criteria and among the other things we did, we provided the army immediately on an emergency basis blankets, boots, uniforms, electric generators, and medical supplies that permitted and created an atmosphere in which they could support the Shah. . . . The guns that they had in their hands, the trucks that they rode in, the armored cars that they drove through the streets, and the radio communications that permitted their control, were all furnished through the military defense assistance program. . . . had it not been for this program, a government unfriendly to the United States probably would now be in power.[30]

The new government was immediately assured by President Eisenhower of "sympathetic consideration" for its financial needs, as had been promised by Ambassador Henderson and other American representatives before the overthrow. Eighty-five million dollars of mutual security and technical assistance program funds were sent in 1954, $76 million in 1955, and $73 million in 1956. In the first year $1.7 million of these funds went for bonuses to the Iranian army, gendarmerie, and police. Twelve million dollars was used for carrying the pay roll and other expenses of the National Iranian Oil Company, an item not on the regular Iranian budget, until an oil settlement was made that would put the national company on a self-sustaining basis. There were also sizable budget expenses for defense, and it will be recalled that Iran entered the Baghdad Pact not long after the change in governments.

Serious criticisms of the amount, the administration, and the purposes of this $250 million aid have been voiced in the United States by the Congress and the General Accounting Office.[31] But it was clear that the overriding motive was to stabilize the new government and prepare the climate for fresh negotiations with the oil industry. As discussed earlier, the terms for the oil agreement with the consortium of international oil companies provided for the gradual absorption of Iran's production into the world market. In effect then, the United States Government was subsidizing the Iranian economy to compensate for the limited oil production allowed by the private government of oil. It was also supporting a regime that, had it desired to make necessary tax reforms, introduce efficient fiscal policies and thoroughgoing social changes beginning with land reform, might well have been able to handle much of its economic responsibilities out of its oil and other income. But such measures would have threatened the privilege and power of an Iranian ruling group. And the United States was committed to keeping this friendly military dictatorship on the side of freedom, anticommunism, and oil.

Meanwhile, the United States Government served as the chief instrument for the new negotiations between the oil industry and the involved nations. Oilman Herbert Hoover, Jr., who earlier had been consultant for the Iranian Government on oil development, represented the State Department. The British company received compensation and was allowed to retain a 40 per cent interest in the new organization created to operate most of the nationalized industry for the Iranian Government. The five American international giants entered the scene with a 40 per cent interest, while Shell was given 14 per cent and Compagnie Française des Pétroles received 6 per cent. Profits were to be divided equally between the companies and Iran.

Through a decision of the National Security Council the Americans had been given the assurance that their participation in the consortium would not subject them to prosecution under the antitrust laws.[32] This protection was beyond the limits of the Defense Production Act that was slated to expire soon and that did allow temporary exceptions for the "national interest." The Justice Department advised the President that this would hold only for the consortium, not for any existing or new system of transportation and distribution.

Some American producers, especially those without overseas reserves, were suspicious of the latest pact among the giants. Several, including Ralph Davies, the former California Standard vice president whose World War II role as Deputy Petroleum Administrator under Secretary Ickes had displeased many in the industry, protested to the State Department. Davies was president of the American Independent Oil Company, a small company with holdings in the Kuwait Neutral Zone owned by a number of oil interests including

Signal, Hancock, Ashland, and Phillips. The insistent oilmen were warned that they were rocking the diplomatic boat and playing into the hands of international communism. After considerable pressure, a number of "smaller" American companies—including Tidewater, Richfield, Standard Oil (Ohio), Atlantic Refining, Pacific Western, Signal, San Jacinto, and American Independent—were allowed to share among themselves 5 per cent from the 40 per cent American allotment. This arrangement was then to serve as convenient evidence of the open nature of the Iranian settlement.

Screening of the smaller companies to determine their financial responsibility was done by the Price Waterhouse accounting firm, which also serves the major oil companies, in consultation with the American members of the consortium. The official State Department explanation for this procedure was that it did not want to assume responsibility in an area of private contract. American Independent's bid was rejected at first, but the listing of the owners and the ultimate backing of the Bank of America made it impossible to maintain this exclusion. The International Cooperative Petroleum Association, of which the Consumer Cooperative Association in the United States was a member, earlier had proposed a cooperative approach to Iran; it was now turned down for membership by the participating giant oil companies and Price Waterhouse on the technical ground that it was an international rather than an American organization. This provoked the charge that this was done because of the consortium's fear that the cooperative's access to a half of one per cent of Iran's oil could destroy the delicate marketing arrangements of the world cartel. It is interesting to note that the 60 per cent foreign, 40 per cent American ratio worked out in Iran has been the familiar division for Eastern Hemisphere markets among the world leaders since 1928.

The Iranian agreement of 1954 was signed by Vice President Howard W. Page of Standard Oil (New Jersey), representing the consortium, and Dr. Ali Amini, Iran's finance minister and chief negotiator, while President Eisenhower and Prime Minister Eden issued statements of praise for the solution. The industry was hailed for acceding to government requests for a settlement with Iran, implying this was done at a sacrifice in the greater interest of American security, for unless Iranian oil was flowing again, that country would fall under Communist domination. Herbert Hoover, Jr., insisted that "one of the greatest difficulties we had . . . was to get the companies who did participate in the Iranian consortium to do so," since this meant additional fully developed oil-producing facilities to be fitted into the world marketing picture.[33]

Oil leaders responded modestly. Vice President Page of Jersey Standard praised the consortium members for "submerging their individual interests, at a time when both crude oil production and refinery capacity are at potentials greater on the world-wide scale than present market requirements." He also pointed out that, despite the recognition of nationalization, the companies gained rights just as effective as ownership for the duration of the agreement.[34] As an official high in oil circles and involved in the pact observed during the bitter struggle within the industry over the 5 per cent finally allocated for independents, "This was most profitable patriotism."

In deference to the presumed sensitivity of the Western nations and business interests involved, as well as of Iran, Secretary of State Dulles repeatedly refused to release the key details of the agreement among the oil companies dividing Iran's production and also the favorable American tax provisions made available to the United States companies. "There is danger that the exposure of these issues could again be used by irresponsible elements contrary to the interests of the United States and its allies . . . and making them public would affect adversely the foreign relations of the United States." [35] He and representatives of the Justice Department explained this classification was made at the behest of the National Security Council, the highest government advisory body, which meets in closed sessions to help the President integrate American military, economic, and foreign policy. Thus, the government of oil shared in a decision directly involving public policy, the details of which were formally denied to the American people and most of their elected representatives.

The Iranian affair had direct bearing on another struggle in Washington. This concerned the famous report *The International Petroleum Cartel* prepared by the staff of the Federal Trade Commission. The international corporations deeply resented this research. They challenged its central allegation and fought against its release. Said Jersey to its stockholders and employees:

This company is not a party to illegal arrangements of any kind, including those which fix prices, allocate markets, or control or restrict production anywhere in the world.[36]

With some justification, oil companies have viewed this report as a perfect illustration of their treatment as a political football by ambivalent public policies. On the one hand, the government repeatedly encourages their increased operations throughout the world. It sponsors such devices as the Iranian consortium, and more recently during the Suez crisis, the committee of oilmen planning to meet the European shortages; hence, it gives tacit approval to the world price-supply control system that keeps the flow of oil from the well to the ultimate consumer under the apportioned domination of seven companies and their intricately linked affiliates and satellites. And then, most ungratefully, they feel, the same government rewards their successes in this cooperation by seeking to brand the international companies as criminal conspirators.

Oil spokesmen have felt impelled to join with other corporate interests to oppose American support in the United Nations' Economic and Social Council of draft agreements for defining restrictive business practices. These had been proposed to encourage member nations to take action against cartels and monopolies in the interest of world trade and economic development. Jersey Standard has pointed out to the Attorney General's National Committee to Study the Antitrust Laws how the joint actions of American oil companies with their billions of dollars in overseas investment, their "aggressiveness, business acumen, and willingness and capacity to take great risks have given them an interest in concessions covering over one-half of the proved reserves of the area . . ." as "they have replaced the British as the principal producers in the area":

To date the United States has not been associated with economic or political imperialism in the Eastern Hemisphere. It has established a reservoir of good will by its missionary, educational, and charitable works, all so patently unselfish in motive, and by its "good neighbor policy"— which, partially translated, has meant noninterference in the internal affairs of other governments. The resultant predilection toward the United States is reflected in the statement of the late King Ibn Saud during the negotiations of the Aramco concession "that he was glad to make an agreement with a company that would not involve itself in the complicated politics of the Middle East but would carry out its commercial mission of exploring for and developing oil fields."

Attempts by the United States to enforce its antitrust laws in such manner as to control the economic institutions within Middle East countries can only inspire the impression that the United States has abandoned the traditional policy for which it has received great credit with such fruitful results. Such action will inevitably be interpreted as a new form of economic imperialism, since the Middle East governments and peoples cannot be expected to appraise our motives except in terms of the effects of our actions upon them. The irritation generated by our attempt to extend our antitrust laws into areas where their own economic interest is paramount would be intensified by the fact that the challenge is not only to the economic interests but to the political sovereignty of the countries involved.

Once cast in such a role the United States faces grave perils. Not only would the prestige of American companies abroad be seriously damaged, but their ouster could result. Nationalism, when aroused by such an act of foreign interference takes easy refuge in the policy that industry and other economic activity should be locally handled. The result is turbulent agitation against the resident commercial enterprises of the offending nation. Russian Communist activity is struggling to fertilize the area for just this. Its tactics are designed to use the banner of nationalism in the Middle East countries in order to weaken and drive out western influence. These petroleum-producing countries, with their politically unsophisticated peoples and strong nationalistic yearnings, are logical prey for such tactics. Their nationalistic fervor, especially in this nascent period, develops momentum and intensity when large foreign petroleum companies are involved, since such companies are of course developing the principal national asset of those countries.

Jersey believes that the current attack against the oil companies has in fact already prejudiced American petroleum interests in the Middle East. The prestige and respect which the companies have so earnestly worked to establish have been damaged by the challenge to the ventures. The allegations of antitrust violations are interpreted in the Middle East as official and outright repudiation by the United States of the behavior of its own nationals in the conduct of their business in that area. What is incorrectly thought to be a profound lack of confidence by the United States Government in its own companies has created grave distrust of the companies in the countries where they do business. Deserted and repudiated by their own Government, as they appear to be in the Middle

East mind, the American companies are marked as fair game for attacks and hostile action by different nationalist, Communist, or religious factions, which would not occur if the companies were thought to have the full backing and confidence of their Government.[37]

Armed with the support of the Central Intelligence Agency, the departments of State and Defense and, for a while, President Truman, the international giants concluded that if the government released the cartel report it would preclude a favorable Iranian settlement, set off a Middle Eastern powder keg, and invite a Kremlin victory. (Several years later, comparable attacks were leveled at the United Nations report *The Price of Oil in Western Europe,* again with oil and State Department arguments warning that such data was best kept secret since it played into the hands of anti-American sentiments and that, anyway, there was nothing new in the facts.)

The Federal Trade Commission Report finally was made public in 1952. But first there was a careful editing, on the grounds of national security, of the nature of the current negotiations with Iran and of some blunter illustrations of international corporate diplomacy. One might guess, as Senator Thomas C. Hennings, Jr., of Missouri suggested when campaigning for its release, that surely "the Iranian Government, unable to sell its oil to any of the large oil companies of the West, must have concluded that an oil cartel agreement was responsible." [38] One might accept the industry charge, echoed by much of the Republican party, that its release through the Senate Small Business Committee, under the chairmanship of Senator John Sparkman of Alabama, was politically timed to give the candidate for Vice President a chance to prove his economic liberalism to Democrats unenthused about his position on civil rights. But this did not explain away either the substance of the report or the full motives of those who so strenuously operated behind the scenes, first to keep its contents classified, and then to prevent, postpone, or limit its distribution.

There was considerable documentation for what Senator Hennings called "an American powder keg," startling only to an American public uninformed about the activity of the world government of oil that "strikes at the heart of the American free-enterprise system," rather than to any Kremlin or Middle Eastern potentates, that was feared by the Anglo-American oildom. "Concerning our foreign policy I fear the report's suppression will have just as bad or even worse effect than at home," Senator Hennings had written to Secretary of State Dean Acheson. ". . . It perhaps ill behooves this nation, on the one hand, to talk of democracy and the development of backward countries and to make promises of assistance to peoples throughout the world still living under feudal conditions and, on the other hand, to refrain from disclosing information possibly indicating the efforts of large financial interests to hamper and defeat the attempts of the peoples in various parts of the world to free themselves through their own efforts from feudalism and economic imperialism."

At the same time the very companies involved in the conspiracy charges worked with the State Department and oilman Herbert Hoover, Jr. (Mr. Dulles's Special Petroleum Adviser who was subsequently appointed to the post of Undersecretary) to resolve the Iranian oil dispute, another segment of the government was continuing to act out the antitrust ritual. A major grand jury investigation into the activities of the five American members was under way, with the foreign companies excluded because of the refusal of their governments to allow the subpoenaing of records. The American companies sought to have the grand jury discharged, and they also resisted turning over their documents to the Justice Department on the grounds of jeopardy to the national interest and to their overseas concessions.

In early January of 1953, on the eve of the grand jury meeting to review the government's cartel case, and just as his Administration was leaving office, President Truman proposed to the industry the substitution of civil proceedings in place of a criminal indictment. This action in "the interest of national security" was taken "for foreign policy reasons" on the advice of the National Security Council. Again the behind-the-scenes insistence that foreign oil investments must be encouraged and protected emanated from the State and Defense departments, bolstered by the judgment of the industry which, in the words of Federal Trade Commissioner Stephen J. Spingarn, was "moving heaven and earth" to have the charges dropped. Mr. Truman's offer set as a condition for this change the turning over of basic documents that the companies were required to produce by subpoena under grand jury action. The President's letter and additional terms presented to the oil firms by the Attorney General required their pledge to hold off any motion to dismiss or amend the new suit, which would be introduced at once in skeleton form, until a period after the documents were received and the specifics of the government's case spelled out.

The oilmen knew that the Justice Department position had been undercut once more. And they knew also that within a fortnight a Republican Administration would be in office. There was no need to compromise, let alone acquiesce. After the terms were conveyed and discussed, the *New York Times* reported that "indignation was written on every face as the thirty-five attorneys for the oil companies stormed out of the Attorney General's office." Arthur H. Dean, of the law firm of Sullivan and Cromwell, which represented Standard (New Jersey) and whose senior member had been incoming Secretary of State John Foster Dulles, called the offer "outrageous blackmail." As Mr. Dean recounted the episode, the Attorney General was in an angry mood:

When I asked him if he wasn't holding a gun to our heads and demanding that we swallow his offer hook, line and sinker or not at all, he said we could take it or leave it. . . .

It seemed to us that this was cold blackmail by a high Government official, and we said so. That kind of thing happens behind the iron curtain, but I didn't think it would happen here.

When reminded at the meeting that the Attorney General said he spoke for the President of the United States, Mr. Dean's reply was: "That's right. And speaking for Standard Oil of New Jersey, I said I wanted no part of his proposition and rejected it in its entirety." [39]

During the grand jury proceedings, an arrangement had been formulated for the screening of the documents by the CIA and the State, Defense, and Justice departments that was to become the basis for deciding which materials could be used. (For example, the Federal Trade Commission report was kept classified, even after it had been released to the public.) But the companies still resisted, determined not to publicize contracts and agreements covering overseas shipments of petroleum products. "If it were not for the question of national security, we would be perfectly willing to face either a criminal or a civil suit," explained Mr. Dean. "But this is the kind of information that the Kremlin would love to get its hands on." Presumably the private government of oil was a more reliable guardian of national security than agents of the public government. This despite the requirement that the documents be classified and the government personnel involved be cleared for handling top secrets. No such surveillance was suggested for the industry.

Without revealing the source of his information or admitting to any knowledge of the meeting of the National Security Council held a few days earlier, Mr. Dean also reported that the Joint Chiefs of Staff were concerned lest the oil companies or their executives be labeled criminal conspirators, a stigma that might result in their expulsion from foreign concessions.

These have been the recurring arguments of the industry and its public defenders. Leonard Emmerglick, the former special assistant to the Attorney General who had been in charge of the case until he resigned from the Justice Department, later testified that "every objection which human ingenuity could devise was used to prevent the Government from getting these documents all during the progress of the grand jury proceedings, from the late summer of 1952 onward until April 1953, and all of that time was lost in procedural motions with the Government winning all along the line but . . . getting no documents." [40] Company attorneys had argued that this was too costly a procedure for them and that the foreign countries where many records were kept would object to their removal. When the United States Government agreed to ask only for pertinent documents within this country, beginning in 1941 rather than 1928 as originally requested, one answer from Mr. Dean to the new Republican Attorney General, Mr. Herbert Brownell, was that "the heads of at least five governments have asked us not to produce documents that are physically located in this country, some of which were originally executed abroad or at least arise out of our operations abroad." [41] Oil spokesmen also insisted that Washington was an improper place for such an investigation since fourteen of the twenty-three grand jurors were public servants. Besides, the District of Columbia Federal Grand Jury had no right to conduct this inquiry since no overt acts of conspiracy took place in the nation's capital. Throughout, they sought to have the courts quash a grand jury subpoena of their records. Some documents were received, but Justice Department lawyers have told how in this as well as in comparable cases they have been confronted by the destruction of records, their shipment out of the country to overseas headquarters, and on occasions the dumping by truckload of unorganized files on the undermanned investigators. There are also instances where they have been offered full access to any records requested.

The incoming Eisenhower Administration quickly moved for a dismissal of the grand jury inquiry and a vacating of the existing subpoenas. In its place it prepared a civil suit. The new Attorney General met many of the oil lawyers' objections about procedure and documents before filing the complaint. In turn, the corporate representatives expressed appreciation of "the broader approach" taken by the new Administration, noting that "we are undoubtedly going to work together a long time." The feeling was voiced by a Socony counsel that "it would be a tragedy if we got into a wrangling atmosphere of ordinary litigation, and that adversary position developed into a situation which impaired the broader aspects of cooperation which are bound to take place and should take place in the interests of the country, as well as of our private industries." They balked, however, at any advance agreement about the documents requested in the earlier action, insisting that the two be separated completely and that the government's continued interest in documents be handled afresh in the civil suit after the complaint was filed, rather than carried over from the grand jury action.

Mr. Dean: Let me make one thing clear. In our public relations with foreign countries, in our public relations with our own stockholders, this is a terrifically important part of our public and operating relations in certain foreign countries. We do not wish to be placed in any bargaining position with our own government. We don't want any of these ministers or any of the heads of these foreign governments to say that we were afraid to stand trial on the criminal side of the court. Speaking only for Jersey as a pure litigating matter outside the security interests of the United States, we would prefer to be tried on the criminal side of the court.

Mr. Emmerglick: That is refreshingly new.

Mr. Dean: We don't want to have any misunderstanding on that point. We don't want to be put in a position of saying to Judge Kirkland, "We are so afraid of an indictment being returned against us, we are so afraid we could not win an acquittal that we have therefore entered into a bargain with our own government." We honestly feel in the interest of the whole situation, if you have made your decision not to go before the grand jury you ought to say to Judge Kirkland and Chief Judge Laws that you have no further use for this grand jury and ask it be dismissed, period. Whatever we do with respect to the production of the documents we will work out on the civil side of the Court without any reference whatsoever to this being taken into consideration by Judge Kirkland.[42]

The civil suit instituted alleged that the five American companies violated the Sherman Antitrust and the Wilson Tariff acts by conspiring to divide and control foreign production and distribution while fixing prices and limiting competition. This is still pending. Again much effort has gone to secure the evidence, with the companies objecting at some points, and at others the Justice Department announcing it had already received 60,000 documents. But the case has been given a minimum of encouragement and an inadequate staff to make meaning out of the complex industrial diplomacy involved, as if the intent has been to allow the suit to peter out quietly. In 1960 a consent decree ended the case against Jersey and Gulf. The two international giants were forbidden to engage in a range of cartel practices. Jersey was required to terminate its joint ownership with Socony Mobil of the Standard-Vacuum Oil Company which operated in the Eastern Hemisphere, a step which the two partners had contemplated for business reasons for some time. Jersey and Gulf both announced that the settlements would not affect their future operations.

The blending of public and private responsibility was built into the postwar planning for restoration of the European economy. With petroleum the continent's major import as well as leading source of overseas income, the Marshall Plan focused heavily on oil needs and costs. Before the war, the international companies had preferred to do their refining at the point of overseas production or shipment. The European countries purchased most of their petroleum requirements as refined products, chiefly from the Western Hemisphere, and in dollar payments. Now the hard-pressed nations were intent on saving scarce dollars while expanding the petroleum base for their increasingly industrialized economies. A reassessment of the international economy of Europe led to plans for bringing Middle Eastern crude oil to European markets.

The international companies became active participants on the European and American governmental committees, formulating and pushing a program that viewed the Western nations and their petroleum demand on an integrated supranational basis. European refinery capacity, in part financed by European Cooperation Administration (ECA) funds and generally owned by the giants, was expanded to handle the crude. Care was taken not to overbuild so as to upset big-seven price control or existing marketing apportionments. The Foreign Assistance Act, which set the machinery of the Marshall Plan into operation, had called for the procurement of petroleum from sources outside the United States and it was judged technically possible to get all the oil from nondollar sources. But plans were coordinated to maintain "the historical pattern of the oil trade." The American giants were to continue to have their percentage of the European market, with this crude coming from their overseas holdings, and they were to have the largest part of the increase in refining capacity. Special arrangements were made for payments in nondollar currency for crude imports so as to ensure that American companies would not lose their share of this trade. This program also served to stimulate new capital expenditures in Europe by the American oil corporations. Investment guarantees by the European Cooperation Administration assured the convertibility into dollars of foreign profits and also loss by expropriation. (Since 1948 this insurance has covered over $200 million of contracts for a range of industries, including $32 million for refineries in Italy owned by Jersey Standard, Socony and Caltex.)[43] By the summer of 1956, 80 per cent of the supplies for Western Europe and North Africa were coming from the Persian Gulf. Most of this was crude oil in sterling payments. All of these measures made the role of the independent producer in the United States and of the independent refiner in Europe more marginal with regard to European markets, thus adding further material cause for the frequent isolationist attitudes of the former.

There were other questions about these transactions to be raised. Of the $4,606 million worth of crude oil and refined products purchased from April 1948 to December 1951 by the Marshall Plan nations, $2,124 million came from the big five American companies, with the European Cooperation Administration financing $1,202 million of this. Before the program ended in December 1952, its successor, the Mutual Security Administration, financed another half-billion. Soon after this attempt to lessen the dollar drainage was under way, the ECA concluded that Middle Eastern crude was not being sold at the lowest competitive market price, as pledged, for the prices on shipments to the United States were considerably lower than those of ECA-financed purchases. After considerable negotiations—with the companies insisting that the rising shipments to the United States from the Middle East were "temporary and marginal," and hence not a valid basis for comparison—reductions of 34 cents from the majors' uniform price of $2.22 a barrel of crude oil in the Middle East were forced. (There had been a 100 per cent increase in the price between 1945 and 1948 as the giant Middle East producers pushed up their prices to keep pace with the rising United States Gulf prices that had been freed from wartime controls.) The ECA, however, felt that "not only had the companies offered no rationalization to support the $1.88 price, but it was still considerably higher than the $1.30 price which the companies realized on shipments to the United States. . . ." [44] The Federal Trade Commission's cartel report commented that much of the decrease could not be explained within their oil pricing formula system "and appears to have been made for the sole purpose of improving the industry's public relations." [45]

A further reduction to $1.75 came about as the ECA acted to implement a regulation which forbids purchases at prices higher than regularly charged by the supplier in comparable dealings with other customers. Earlier the oil companies had been granted a temporary waiver from this requirement. This was the same price submitted in 1950 in identical bids by the five majors to the Armed Services Purchasing Agency and cited in the cartel suit. American and ECA rates were now equalized, and it appeared that the ECA policy was being respected.

But ECA officials soon suspected that the juggling of shipping-rate calculations combined with a complicated basing point system that kept prices uniform and stabilized provided a cloak for continued discrimination against European buyers. From company documents covering shipments of Middle East crude oil, the agency discovered that "all shipments to the Western Hemisphere since the date of its regulation had been billed not at $1.75 but at a uniform f.o.b. price of $1.43 per barrel." [46]

By 1951 oil from Saudi Arabia had begun to flow through the new Trans-Arabian pipeline to the Mediterranean terminus at Sidon, Lebanon. There was no reduction in transport price, for the companies made the pipeline tariff equivalent to tanker and Suez Canal charges. The ECA reminded the owners of Tapline (Jersey Standard, Socony, Texas, and Standard of California) that a sizable saving over the shorter route had been a key argument employed when government sponsorship was originally sought and when they secured an export license for the scarce steel for the private construction. The oil companies explained this price in terms of the high risk involved and the need to amortize the pipeline quickly. They also felt that since some oil was still going by tanker, they would either be forced to sell to some purchasers at higher prices or absorb the difference. Actually, Tapline was an immediate financial success and it has been estimated that the out-of-pocket cost was recovered within a year.

After further examination of company records, the MSA concluded that the prices for crude and for pipeline transportation were considerably lower for intracompany purchases destined for subsidiaries in the Americas. With the giants standing firm—in some instances refusing to have further dealings with the MSA—the MSA discontinued the financing of shipments of Middle East oil to the Marshall Plan countries. The issue was then turned over to the Justice Department, which unsuccessfully sought $50 million as payment for overcharges.[47] In 1952, the Truman Administration filed a suit for $100 million, with the defendant companies denying the charges and in turn accusing the ECA and MSA of "attempting to interfere with normal competitive prices." [48]

If there was doubt as to the zeal of the Eisenhower Administration in the pursuance of this case, there was at least hope of the recovery of some of this money. In contrast, there is no likelihood of the government's regaining millions in a related Navy overcharge controversy rooted in the complex wartime oil diplomacy centering upon Saudi Arabia. As part of the package offerings by Moffett and later Rodgers of Aramco in 1941 and 1943 to secure the protection of the flag and lend-lease, there were several much debated pledges to make petroleum available to the armed services at cost or a nominal profit. When oil was sold in 1945 to the Navy for delivery to the French Government under lend-lease, it was at prices based on $1.05 a barrel for crude oil rather than at the $0.25 to $0.40 production costs in Bahrein and Saudi Arabia or the $0.40 featured in the original proposal. This arrangement provided a needed market for oil whose possible sale had been seriously limited by cartel allotments of regional outlets. (The problem was solved on a more permanent basis when Jersey Standard and Socony-Vacuum with their greater marketing potential bought into Aramco. All Aramco oil, beyond what is marketed locally within Saudi Arabia, is sold to the four partners—whose posted prices are identical—in the same proportion as their stockholding percentages. The penalty for any partner taking less under this "off-take" agreement is the right of the others to purchase its untaken share at cost plus $0.15 per barrel.) The world-wide pricing system was maintained, for Aramco had successfully established United States Gulf prices in an area where prevailing prices in other contracts had been considerably lower. The Senate Investigation of the National Defense Program, Republican Senator Owen Brewster of Maine, chairman, calculated that the American taxpayers were overcharged some $38 million.

The Texas and Standard of California companies, who were then the sole owners of Aramco, denied that any moral or legal commitment had been violated. ". . . We gave the United States Government a marvelous break," insisted the chairman of the Texas Board of Directors. Mr. Moffett, his former colleague, declared that the United States had been "duped" by this outrageous breach of good faith.[49] As in the ECA case, there was evidence that the concentrated focus of the industry helped make possible a profitable advantage in dealing with a diffused governmental machinery where one branch was ill informed about the activities of another. The Navy negotiators did not know of, and Aramco did not inform them of, the earlier price discussions. Those who represented the government in studying and approving the contracts—who were oilmen in uniform—were less careful or dedicated than those who formally represented oil. Confronted by a "take it or leave it" proposition with "no offer of compromise or deviation," the Navy negotiators accepted Aramco's cost assumptions and took the oil at $1.05, rationalizing this acceptance in terms of military necessity. After an unraveling of the details, the Brewster committee concluded that in refusing to supply oil to the United States except on their own terms "the oil companies have shown a singular lack of good faith, an avaricious desire for enormous profits, while at the same time they constantly sought the cloak of United States protection and financial assistance to preserve their vast concessions." [50]

There had been another selling point advanced by Aramco and its parents in their quest for government support for these overseas adventures. That was the glowingly portrayed prospect, always attractive to budget-conscious legislators, of a high percentage of the profits from the overseas subsidiaries going into the United States Treasury under the tax laws. Yet the actual practices subsequently disclosed were to provide what Senator Brewster called a "liberal education" in corporate tax evasion. At the 1947 Senate hearings on the Saudi Arabian and related arrangements, it was brought out that the Bahrein Petroleum Company, Ltd., operating the concession on the Persian Gulf islands of Bahrein, which is a British protectorate, was organized in Canada with an original capital investment of $100,000. In fifteen years it had accumulated profits and surplus of over $91 million, without paying any taxes to Canada or the United States. The California-Texas Oil Company, Ltd. (Caltex), a marketing subsidiary of Bahrein which could have been American but was set up as a Bahaman corporation instead, in a ten-year period accumulated $25 million on an original capital stock of $1 million, and claimed to have paid $1 million taxes to the United States. Paying no dividends to their American parents (The Texas Company and Standard of California), the great bulk of this reserve legally remained tax exempt. Had the subsidiaries been American organized, the wartime tax rate might have taken up to 90 per cent of their earnings.

The Suez inquiries of 1957 afforded a glimpse of how the government of oil and the Government of Saudi Arabia, if not the government of the American people, had learned from the earlier disclosures. Up until 1950, Aramco, a Delaware corporation, had been paying American income taxes on its increasingly fabulous Saudi Arabian earnings. In 1949, for example, it paid $48 million. But in 1950 it paid $199,000. And in 1956 its bill was $282,000, all of this on earnings outside Saudi Arabia.

The arrangements that made possible such tax thrift were ingenious if not simple models of corporate enterprise and diplomacy. As King Saud viewed the rigged prices and spiraling profits of his American concessionaires, he understandably grew restive with his fixed royalty of $0.21 cents a barrel. According to F. A. Davies, chairman of the board of Aramco, the king knew that countries like Venezuela and Iran were gaining far more income from their oil resources. And as had happened in Venezuela and Iran, Saudi Arabians "weren't a darn bit happy" that the income taxes paid by Aramco to the United States exceeded the producing countries' total take. "They felt the United States was getting too big a percentage of the profits from the venture. . . ." For, as Mr. Davies explained, "it is very difficult for many countries to realize why the United States should participate in the profits from the development of their natural resources." But if Aramco was to raise Saudi Arabia's share by the payment of a 50 per cent royalty, the financial cost "would have made our position out there pretty bad competitivewise." Fortunately, Mr. Davies elaborated, King Saud's objections were not directed against the company's share. Rather was he seeking an increase "which would result in no additional burden on the company." [51]

Under the original sixty-year contract signed in 1933, Saudi Arabia had pledged not to levy further taxes on Aramco. With the help of an American tax consultant, a United States Treasury Department representative, and the general guidance of the oil companies' regular experts, in 1950 a decree was promulgated that set the Saudi Arabian income tax on petroleum-producing companies (Aramco was then the only such company in Saudi Arabia) at a rate which, together with royalties, gave it 50 per cent of their net profits. This was achieved without technically raising the Arabian royalty or diminishing Aramco's earnings.

This alchemy was made possible through the familiar benevolence of the United States Government. Under a 1918 tax law designed to encourage foreign investment of American capital by removing the threat of double taxation, taxes paid abroad could be written off, dollar for dollar, against American obligations. State taxes, in contrast, are regarded as business expenses and are subtracted from gross income in computing federal taxes. In 1955, when Aramco grossed $724 million, it paid $78 million in royalties and $193 million in "income tax" to Saudi Arabia. It netted $272 million, without having to pay any United States income tax. Out of the $749 million which Aramco grossed in 1956, Saudi Arabia received approximately $80 million in royalties and $200 million in "income tax" for the 360 million barrels of crude oil produced. The royalty was properly deductible from Aramco's taxable income obligations to the United States, while the $200 million "income tax" was applied as a foreign tax credit directly against the amount due as American income tax. Aramco paid no taxes on its Arabian venture while retaining $280 million as its net reward for initiative and risk. This was on a capital investment then estimated to be $471 million, nearly all of which "represents cash, accounts receivable and so forth," an admission which suggests the extent to which it is profits rather than investments that lie at the root of oil's solicitude.[52] Had the United States classified all of Saudi Arabia's 50 per cent share as a royalty, the Treasury would have gained over $100 million, considering the 52 per cent corporate tax rate that year. (Significantly, the 1950 decree allowed Aramco to deduct its payments of American income taxes in calculating its net profit. But in 1952 this provision was removed.)

In 1955 the Bureau of Internal Revenue ignored the possibility of deception by Aramco and upheld the validity of this tax credit that has meant the transfer of most of Aramco's American income taxes to Saudi Arabia. Thus, in one year alone, Standard (New Jersey) and Socony Mobil, owning 30 per cent and 10 per cent respectively of Aramco, each recovered through profits more than their original investment of $76 and $25 million which they had paid the California and Texas companies in 1947.

The depletion allowance was also a major factor in Aramco's bookkeeping feats. As discussed earlier, this allowance was developed at a time when American oil exploration was primarily domestic and there were fears of shortages. Yet this tax benefit has been applied to overseas activities as well. In Saudi Arabia, operations have been relatively inexpensive and dry holes rare, thanks to fabulous oil reservoirs near the surface with their daily production averaging in the thousands of barrels. Nevertheless, Aramco received a depletion allowance of $148 million in 1955 and $152 million in 1956. This loophole deprived the United States Treasury of $124 million for the two years.[53] Combined with the offset, it wiped out all income-tax obligations to the American Government. With some modifications, a similar pattern holds true for Gulf's 50 per cent share in the oil-rich kingdom of Kuwait, for the American members of the Iranian consortium and for the Jersey-controlled Creole Corporation, which is the dominant producer in Venezuela. The worth of these tax privileges and of the diplomatic backing of the United States becomes clearer when it is realized that three-fourths of Jersey Standard's $809 million earnings after taxes in 1956 were derived from its overseas activities.

Arabian-American Oil Company officials have expressed difficulty in understanding the suspicions and attacks in their direction. To their tax counsel, Mr. Douglas Erskine, the picture was quite simple:

What has happened to the United States tax is the Saudi Arabian Government imposed an income tax upon us, for reasons best known to themselves, but they did it. Under the United States income-tax law we are entitled to a credit for that income tax and we take the credit and the Bureau of Internal Revenue has allowed it. If that is taking money from the United States Treasury—and may I remark, Senator, that the United States Treasury loses no money if the United States tax law does not provide for its payment in the first place. The tax law does not provide for payment to the United States so nothing has been lost.

Senator Carroll. Let's see how consistent your statement is. You did pay an income tax in 1949.

Mr. Erskine. Before there was a Saudi Arabian income tax.

Senator Carroll. So, therefore, when that money isn't coming into the Treasury, we have lost that money, haven't we?

Mr. Erskine. No.

Senator Carroll. We haven't lost it?

Mr. Erskine. No. Under the circumstances prior to 1950, under the income-tax law the United States Treasury was entitled to $49 million. Under the circumstances that existed in 1950, and they were quite changed circumstances because of the new Saudi Arabian income law, the United States Treasury was not entitled to $49 million.[54]

Aramco had at first objected to this tax, Mr. Erskine explained, for it was under no legal obligation to increase the royalty or pay the income tax. As a result it "found itself faced with increasing pressures and deteriorating relations." Confronted by changing times, with the threat of nationalization always a possibility, the practical solution was to submit to Saudi Arabia's new requirements. Surely the United States Government could appreciate the national sovereignty of oil-producing companies and the private rights of corporate enterprises.

United States policy has long encouraged U.S. businesses to invest and operate abroad. The United States has had, however, to face the fact that it has neither legal nor moral right to direct any foreign country's tax policies and that the United States businessman who operates abroad is necessarily subject to foreign taxes. Without foreign tax credit American businesses operating in foreign countries would be left with less profit than that of their foreign competitors who pay only the local taxes and that of their domestic competitors who pay only the United States tax.[55]

In this situation, the oil companies insist that every deduction they have taken "complies not only with the letter of the internal revenue laws of the United States, but with the spirit. . . ." From the industry's perspective, to expect tax payments on their overseas earnings would subject them to double taxation, since Aramco-derived dividends received by the parent companies and their stockholders are subject to taxation. "Let's not get the idea that because you don't get an income tax you aren't getting anything," cautioned Aramco's board chairman.[56] But since a company like Jersey is able to take advantage of an intercorporate dividend-received credit amounting to 85 per cent of its corporate rate of 54 per cent, it actually pays 15 per cent of 54 per cent—an 8 per cent income tax on these earnings. Creole files a consolidated return with Jersey that enables the latter to escape a tax on this dividend, paying at a slightly higher corporate rate. The ultimate individual stockholder is of course liable to taxation on any dividends received, but this is no different than would be true for such income from any stock.

At another level and at a time when the issue was less freighted with emotion, oilmen have argued that the root of the difficulty lies in the American Government's high tax rates on overseas investments and also the foreign tax-credit system itself. These serve to encourage countries such as Saudi Arabia to raise their taxes to the American level. They have urged reducing the rate, as has been done in the case of Western Hemisphere corporations, as an incentive for trade. In testimony before the House Ways and Means Committee in 1953, a director of the Standard-Vacuum Oil Company, an overseas firm owned equally by Socony and Jersey and operating in some fifty countries and territories in Africa and Asia, proposed that "the United States refrain from taxing income accruing to United States business corporations from regularly established branches . . . subsidiaries and affiliated companies engaged in business outside of the United States.

This principle, that business income should be taxed only at source, is in accord with good international practice and is ideally suited to meet the present requirements of the United States. If such income is not subjected to taxation in the United States, foreign governments will be able to improve the climate for investment in their respective countries by lowering tax rates, providing for extraordinary depreciation or amortization, adopting the American principles of depletion for extractive industries and, in general, by offering to foreign investors whatever tax incentives are best suited to the local situation and most conducive to the desired result. The artificial pressure on foreign governments to add corporate income taxes or to substitute them for property and excise taxes would be eliminated, so that each country could design its tax structure and set its level of taxation without regard to effects in the United States.[57]

When asked about the American Government's sanction for Aramco's private tax diplomacy in Saudi Arabia, the company's board chairman reported a conference with George C. McGhee, Assistant Secretary of State for Near Eastern and African Affairs, who was an oilman. "They did not approve it," explained Mr. Davies. "They did not so far as I know disapprove it. They listened and expressed an appreciation of the pressure we were under." [58] The President of the United States seemed equally appreciative but vaguely informed when he was asked in the spring of 1957 about corporate-tax diversions in the Middle East. "I will have to talk to [Secretary of the Treasury] George Humphrey about this one. I have never had—this is too—" he concluded.[59] This was at the very time his Administration was seeking a $200 million authorization for the "Eisenhower doctrine," a program that would provide military and economic aid to protect American national interests in this region. Not the least of these has been the integrity of oil contracts and such partnerships as between the Arabian American Oil Company and Saudi Arabia.

The Congress had little data and less inclination to explore this situation—even when it was forced as an issue in the wake of the chain of investigations following Nasser's seizure of Suez. With the story of Aramco's tax arrangements before it, the Senate still overwhelmingly defeated proposals for a change in the depletion allowance. Most of the press ignored the entire matter. Yet there is ample evidence that all these illustrations of corporate foreign relations and domestic deception took place with the knowledge, consultation, and active intervention of responsible officials in the State and Treasury departments and in the American Embassy in Saudi Arabia. An American Treasury official was even sent to Saudi Arabia at the request of Aramco and helped on the tax manipulations. But when questions were asked in the Congress and elsewhere, the focus was placed largely on consumer costs, Treasury losses, antitrust violations, and most of all, the unfairness to domestic oil producers. A Senate staff report did properly challenge the use and circumventing of the public government of the American people for the private ends of an oil company acting in a semisovereign capacity:

. . . The question posed is whether in the U.S. 1918 foreign tax deduction provision Congress in fact intended to create a situation wherein an American corporation could negotiate with a sovereign power to the extent of rearranging tax statutes in such a manner and form as to take away all revenue from the U.S. and split the resulting profit equally between the sovereign power and the domestic corporation. . . . It illustrates the manner in which oil companies act to influence foreign governments and shape the foreign policy of the United States.[60]

But there seemed little likelihood that the problem would be pursued at this level. And a larger question, explored neither by the critics of these tax havens nor by those who profit, concerns the justification for and consequences of either the United States Government or its corporate citizens gaining so heavily and dominating so thoroughly in the development of the natural resources of underdeveloped areas.

9

Private Profits and National Security

One by-product of the tax-subsidy disclosures has been the trigger-
ing within the petroleum industry of a long-brewing conflict over
imports. The issue of imports periodically threatens to destroy the
heavily financed image of oildom as one big happy family. The
international-minded integrated companies, with vast overseas holdings from which comes the greatest part of their production, today
play an active role in furthering free or reciprocal trade policies.
National self-sufficiency in oil is seen as a fallacy and a costly
fantasy. To them, one world—the oil world—far from being an
idealist's dream or a traitor's plot, is an economic reality. Quantities
of imports allowed into the United States are to be flexible enough
to enable these companies to take the most favorable advantage
of changing world-wide production costs and market needs to sell
the most cheaply produced oil at industry-pegged prices. Building
up world trade, explained the chairman of the board of Jersey
Standard, is imperative for world economic help and American self-
preservation.

Improving the world economically is a vital job in itself. It is also an essential foundation of something far greater—international political
strength. The cooperative, mutually sustaining framework of free nations which we have set before ourselves as a political ideal can only be
built by prosperous countries. In the effort to bring about prosperity,
therefore, we shall at the same time be making great contributions to
international strength and to peace. . . . The full benefits of world trade
can never be obtained if a policy which should be truly national in purpose is unduly influenced by domestic special interest groups.[1]

230

Nonintegrated domestic producers view this sophisticated internationalism as a mask for self-interest. They see rising import percentages as the chief threat to their own prices as well as to their survival, for paralleling these shipments there has been a cutting of production allowables by regulatory commissions in Gulf and midcontinent producing states. In Texas, for example, in the summer of 1956 wells were shut in about 15 days each month, with the allowable for each oil well averaging about 18 barrels per day. Caught by rising production costs, they have found that some of the major purchasers have not always thought price increases are justified, and just prior to the Suez stoppage they were confronted with price cuts in Texas and Oklahoma. "The torrent of foreign oil . . . robs Texas of her oil market" and of nearly a million dollars a day, charged Ernest O. Thompson, chairman of the Railroad Commission responsible for regulating oil production. "Denied its place in the growing market, the domestic oil industry is producing at only three-fourths of capacity." [2] An Oklahoma producer described what he regarded as the impossibility of the nonintegrated firm's situation:

When we go before a market demand hearing in Oklahoma, the representatives of these companies who have these products in storage . . . come there and offer testimony to the extent that their crude storage tanks are full, that they have gasoline and products running out of their ears and, therefore, we must cut back and restrict our production in Oklahoma in order to give them an opportunity to work off the surplus of above-ground stored products and crude oil.

But they do not work it off, they keep it filled with the products of imported oil and with imported crude oil, and are thereby enabled to take lesser amounts of domestic crude at a higher price per barrel, and thus make room economically for the oil that they bring into the country and the products that they refine from it with a greater margin of profit than if they had to actually compete with unrestricted sale of domestic crude oil. [3]

These producers have felt that the Iranian settlement, the European refinery expansion program, and similar actions have been at their expense, making for a further cutting down of domestic purchases. They warn of the loss of incentive to produce at home if costs are to be determined by Middle East oil. "Independents have no objection—and are likely to have none—to profits, however large, by their major companies brethren," declared the Texas Independent Producers and Royalty Owners Association. "Profits make the wheels of industry go round, and are an integral part of our free enterprise economy. Their objection rather is to the combination of circumstances which enable profitable foreign operations to deny them access to the profits stimulus which would logically be theirs if imports were brought under reasonable control." [4]

To allow foreign oil to supplant rather than supplement American sources is to risk the security of the nation, they add, citing such illustrations as Nazi submarine successes, Russia's growing underwater fleet, and Nasser's Suez seizure. "No American would consider building our atomic or aircraft plants in the Middle East, under the shadow of Russia. Yet, through excessive imports, we are following that course as to oil." [5] "Although Middle Eastern oil is so abundant that it can be developed at a fraction of the cost of our own, it is far from 'cheap.' On the contrary, Middle East oil may already be the most expensive in the world market today when consideration is given to the fact that vast amounts of public funds are spent on the defense mechanism which is intended largely to protect American interest in Middle Eastern oil fields. Moreover, in these troublesome times that oil could become costly in American lives as well. . . ." [6]

The big importers—there are also small ones who complicate the picture since they can and do upset any voluntary control program —have repeatedly promised to keep imports down since the early thirties and the days of the National Industrial Recovery Act code. One pledge—never put into any formal terms—was to maintain the 1954 relationship of imports to domestic products at a level recommended by the President's Advisory Committee on Energy Supplies and Fuel Resources. (The top five importing firms were responsible for nearly 70 per cent of all crude imports in that year.) This ratio, sanctioned by the Congress and policed by the Director of Defense Mobilization, had crude at about 10 per cent of domestic production and residual fuel at about 6 per cent. Oil from Venezuela and Canada was not counted in arriving at this determination. Despite the pledge, the Director of Defense Mobilization, Arthur S. Flemming, admitted that for over a year and a half "we tried vigorously to get the companies voluntarily to take steps which would remove that threat. We did not succeed as far as the companies as a whole were concerned." [7] Meanwhile, smaller producers have become increasingly troubled as more than half of the East Coast refinery runs utilize imported crude (mostly from the Caribbean) and have been incensed by such ironic situations as the unloading of Middle Eastern oil in Texas ports. Looking ahead, some of them are alarmed by the development of the St. Lawrence Seaway that will enable tankers to bring overseas crude to the great Midwestern population centers formerly served by the midcontinent fields. While some of the majors are careful in their words not to offend the sensitive domestic producers, Gulf, the nation's largest importer, has been a consistent and outspoken critic of import restrictions. It has questioned the validity of the contention that current levels of imports have adversely affected the incentive for the search for new domestic sources of oil. One of their officials has summed up the feelings of the majors by saying that the domestic companies have been crying wolf about the dangers of imports for nearly thirty years, beginning with the Venezuelan shipments. The latter, in turn, claim the importers have been raising false alarm about supposedly dwindling domestic reserves over the same period.

Yet the giants do protect their smaller brethren, even if the motive is self-interest. If Middle Eastern oil prices were competitive and the savings passed along to the consumer, a sizable reduction in American prices would be in order, considering that the cost of producing a barrel of this crude is at the most about forty cents, without transportation, as contrasted with domestic production costs of at least $2. Of course this would hurt the major companies' own domestic operations while provoking agitation for a high tariff. Speaking as president of the Sinclair Oil Corporation and as chairman of the American Petroleum Institute, P. C. Spencer has said "we must sacrifice some higher profit margins for the sake of domestic production." He urged the nonintegrated oilmen not to turn to government. "Government doesn't get into something in a small way. There cannot long be such a thing as 'a little government control.'" [8] Fearful of independent producer support for congressional criticisms of international oil's tax subsidies, President H. S. M. Burns of the Shell Oil Company has pleaded for industry harmony. "Even the Hatfields and the McCoys . . . had enough sense to team up and present a united front when the 'revenooers' came around. . . . To you oilmen I should like . . . to say, 'Since you are so rich—why ain't you smart?' " [9]

Domestic producers have been well aware of how big oil's overseas depletion allowances have stimulated the further importation of foreign crude by helping to make this oil low cost and high profit. But their dependency on the majors and the latter's support of the depletion allowance for domestic production and of high domestic crude prices heretofore have worked to restrain any organized outburst—lest they all suffer the loss or cutting of this tax benefit. Big oil could do without it; it is questionable whether some moderate-size producers could continue. But as imports have continued to rise, the independents have become increasingly dubious about the words and behavior of their big brethren. The excise taxes put into effect in the thirties under the pressure of the Independent Petroleum Association of America (IPAA), which had been created to fight imports, have seemed to be inadequate safeguards. With the possibility of support for imports relief from a public which might be critical of giant oil's profits and power (the Suez windfall was soon to dramatize this), these nonintegrated oil groups began publicly to reexamine their industry solidarity on overseas depletion, governmental controls, and related matters. In a letter to the IPAA's membership, the organization's general counsel warned:

I would like to point out to Mr. Holman [Chairman of Jersey] and to all of the oil-importing company officials that their interpretation of "business statesmanship" is causing domestic-oil producers to lose faith in their motives. . . . Their motivations have taken on a new and foreign accent as they have become companies of the world rather than of this nation.[10]

The conclusion? ". . . If economics is to decide the domestic industry's future, it will not survive. It cannot compete with vastly cheaper foreign oil even for the home market," the Texas Independent Producers and Royalty Owners Association (TIPRO) has insisted.[11] The solution? As Warwick Downing, a highly respected and genuinely independent spokesman who served as chairman of the Colorado Oil and Gas Conservation Commission reasoned, "if the states regulate production, we think the federal government should do the same thing for the international scene—regulate imports." Judge Downing proposed that the Congress set up an agency that would receive the nominations of importers and then allow the importation only of such oil as is needed to supplement American production. Echoed TIPRO: "The security and economy of this nation, insofar as oil imports affect both, cannot safely be left to the determination of the few importing companies with a vested interest in foreign oil. The public interest makes this the responsibility of the Congress." [12]

To this end, the independents and their organizations have been vigorous opponents of American participation in reciprocal trade agreements, the International Trade Organization, the General Agreement on Tariffs and Trade (GATT) and its administrative agency, the Organization for Trade Cooperation, each of which seeks to break down restrictive trade barriers. They have insisted on retention of the depression-born Buy American Act which generally requires the government to purchase domestically produced materials, unless certain prescribed conditions justify otherwise. In 1952 the President's Materials Policy Commission concluded this "relic . . . of depression psychology . . . ignores the Nation's growing need for imported raw materials . . . works against national security in encouraging a more rapid depletion of United States resources than the market would justify. It serves no useful purpose. . . ." [13]

While somewhat troubled about the possible consequences of federal regulations, the independents have asked for the formal implementation of the "defense" amendment to the Reciprocal Trade Agreement Extension of 1955, added largely because of their pressure. This gives the President power to cut oil imports to 10 per cent of domestic demand when the quantity "impairs" national security. It is interesting to note that as of May 1956, "as many industries had applied to the Office of Defense Mobilization for relief from foreign competition on the grounds of defense essentiality as there were pending applications before the Tariff Commission for relief under the escape clause." [14] There also have been calls for a 50 per cent tariff.

Hearings on the petitions of the domestic producers were held in 1956 by the Office of Defense Mobilization. According to Director

Arthur S. Flemming, the findings left no alternative but to certify to the President that the import situation threatened national security. Then in the summer of that same year Egypt nationalized the Suez Canal Company.

All these considerations were shunted aside. Public and oil leaders had long been watchful over the status and operation of the canal which lies at the crossroads of three continents. Two-thirds of its daily tonnage has been oil, and it serves as a channel for the shipment of at least two-thirds of Europe's crude-oil needs. Now public officials feared an immediate threat to Europe's growing dependency upon crude oil—heavily from the Persian Gulf since the Marshall Plan, with continental refining output up fivefold since 1947—which would impair economic recovery and the military worth of the North Atlantic Treaty Organization. Oilmen also anticipated a further spread of this nationalistic zeal against their vulnerable pipelines and concessions, for the canal has been the most visible symbol of Western economic hegemony for Middle Eastern rulers and popular anti-imperialist sentiments. The notes of a Socony Mobil representative on a meeting of oil executives serving on the United States Government's Foreign Petroleum Supply Committee held in August 1956 suggested that the Administration was not lacking in sympathy for this industry concern:

Secretary Dulles then addressed the meeting. . . . He was quite concerned over the fact that there was no plan of action available to handle alternative means of meeting supply and distribution problems in the event we lose the Canal or pipeline facilities. He also indicated concern over possible loss of production in the Arab countries, although the main problem is the transportation through the Suez Canal and pipelines. He then stated that he recognizes the oil companies were very much interested in the nationalization issue and wanted to put forth his views and what line he expected to take at the London Conference. He indicated that the United States would not acquiesce in the rights of nationalization that would affect any other facilities in our own economic interests.

He commented that International law recognizes the right to nationalize if adequate compensation is paid, but he admits that actually adequate compensation is never really paid and nationalization in effect thereby becomes confiscation.

The line he expected to take on the problem at the London Conference, and which was written up in his communique, was to the effect that the United States felt it was "o.k." to nationalize only if *assets were not impressed with international interest*. What he meant by International interest was where a foreign government had made promises of fixed duration in the form of concessions or contracts, upon which other nations would rely on fixing their courses of action and their own economies on the basis that these certain promises would be fulfilled. Therefore, he indicated, nationalization of this kind of an asset, impressed with International interest goes far beyond compensation of shareholders alone and should call for International intervention.[15]

With transportation viewed as the immediate challenge, the individual international companies began to replan their tanker movements for costlier and longer trips around the Cape of Good Hope while stepping up shipments from the Western Hemisphere. Supertanker construction was accelerated.

Meanwhile the American Government turned to the industry, reactivating the private advisory machinery that had been called into play during the Iranian situation. Enjoying government-sanctioned immunity from antitrust prosecution, the representatives of the major importing companies sat with government representatives on a Middle East Emergency Committee to work out a voluntary program to collect information, pool tankers, reroute shipments, trade supplies, adjust pipeline schedules, and reverse pipeline flows. A prime objective was to divert Middle Eastern oil from American and Canadian ports to Europe. This arrangement fitted in with the long-run planning of the industry formulated before Suez.

In the late fall of 1956 Israel, long aroused by such factors as the Arab economic boycott, the Egyptian blockade preventing merchant ships from using the Gulf of Aqaba and the Suez Canal to reach Israel ports, the unabating fedayeen raids across its borders, and the failure of the great powers and the United Nations to end these provocations, embarked upon a preventive war. Its armies advanced across the Sinai Peninsula and cooperating British-French forces entered the Suez Canal zone. Egypt scuttled ships in the canal. The daily traffic of 1,500,000 barrels of oil was blocked. Then the Iraq Petroleum Company's pipelines to the eastern Mediterranean, with a 500,000-barrel-a-day capacity, were sabotaged in Syria. Tapline, then capable of carrying 320,000 barrels a day of Saudi Arabian oil, was not touched. But King Saud asserted his Arab loyalties by banning shipments of any of its oil to England and France.

Stories of shortages, rationing, factory closedowns, and the drainage of gold and dollar reserves in Europe filled the headlines. Cartoons featured Texas holding up Europe and the United States. At one point shipments were lower than before the plan was instituted. Yet by the spring of 1957, the crisis was viewed as ended and the oil lift was terminated in April 1957.

There was and remains considerable disagreement and uncertainty as to exactly what transpired in the intervening months. Estimates as to the extent of the European shortage had varied, but it was clear that the Western countries' primary need was for fuel oil. They preferred receiving crude oil from which their refineries could get a higher per cent of fuel oil. (American production maximizes the gasoline return from refinery runs.) This also meant an appreciable dollar saving.

The American international companies had announced their determination to step up their shipments of crude from the Gulf Coast. Here they ran up against the Texas Railroad Commission, which refused to raise the allowables appreciably, pointing to the thousands of wells not connected to pipeline and the surplus gasoline and refined stocks. Colonel Thompson called the public outcry over the oil shortage more a newspaper crisis than anything else. He told how Magnolia (Socony) and Humble (Jersey) had asked for all the oil they could get from wells near the coast, a request the Texas Commission rejected as denying the state's responsibility to allocate fairly among all the wells. Meanwhile, nonintegrated domestic producers pointed to the flow of crude from the Caribbean to the East Coast of the United States. They wanted to know why this was not going directly to Europe and why more domestic crude was not going to the Atlantic Coast. From the perspective of these producers, the importers were using the Suez affair as a convenient device for maintaining or even increasing the percentage of imports while cutting out domestic markets. The producers charged the members of the Middle East Emergency Committee with being more concerned about the greater profits from refining their own overseas crude than about cutting down their refinery runs for gasoline and thus meeting the government's announced objectives for Europe. They also reported that refiners were forcing upon overseas buyers tie-in sales of gasoline with crude oil, although Europe did not want gasoline. The Jersey Company later admitted that some refiners, including Sinclair, were making these sales demands. But Jersey denied passing along these forced purchases to its overseas subsidiaries. As for the 35-cent price increase, domestic producers said this had been long overdue. This was only a partial restoration of the price cuts made in the previous year by the major buyers and they felt they could not continue to absorb them in addition to the rising costs of production. To the producers, then, the giants of oil had manipulated the entire situation to further the national discrediting of "Texas oilmen" and to obscure the security risks involved in relying upon overseas crude supplies. "If there is any shortage," the West Central Texas Oil and Gas Association insisted before the Railroad Commission's state-wide hearing in November 1956, "it is a matter of long-range policy of the major purchasers." [16]

The spokesmen for the empire of oil denied these allegations, pointing to the rapid disappearance of the panic. That fuel-oil shipments had run perhaps 20 per cent below the original target meant discomfort rather than crisis in Europe. (A mild winter also helped.) The continued Venezuelan imports that so antagonized domestic producers were largely specialty grades of crude for which substitution was difficult, if not impossible, insisted the president of Jersey Standard. Besides, it was economically unprofitable to make fuel oil from United States Gulf crude that was best for gasoline. The entire oil-lift program that they had been responsible for was handled without shortage or rationing at home. When the full truth was known, predicted the head of the American Petroleum Institute in the midst of congressional inquiries on the oil lift, the representatives of the American people would have to "pin a rose" on the industry for its ability to do all this while maintaining competition of the highest order.[17]

The American Government's position was vague and evasive. Federal officials did have the authority under the Defense Production Act to move directly to allocate oil rather than work through an industry voluntary advisory agency. But in Mr. Flemming's words, it was judged "unwise to exercise that authority," introducing controls over one segment of an interrelated problem that would lead only to unfortunate complications forcing additional controls in other areas. This choice, further explained Assistant Secretary of the Interior Felix E. Wormser, the public official immediately responsible, was in keeping with "the customary United States policy of interfering as little as possible with the operations of our commercial enterprises." [18]

As the public criticisms of the inadequacies of the oil lift intensified, federal officials outdid one another in disclaiming either responsibility or the ability to step up production, control prices, or judge profits. The Interior Department had admitted its unhappiness over the failure to meet the fuel-oil objectives, and President Eisenhower at one point suggested that the federal government might have to act directly. But caught between the national myth of private enterprise, the constitutional shield of states' rights, and the legal fiction that allowed American tankers to sail under foreign flags, federal officials concluded that they had no power of appeal over a voluntary action of the majors or the regulatory power of the state commissions. Reducing the refinery runs of gasoline so as to make available more crude would have been in harmony with the over-all objective. But, Mr. Flemming added, "the companies themselves, of course, must make that decision." The increased importation of Venezuelan oil to East Coast ports was also disturbing, but again it was not the function of the government to appeal to the companies involved to divert this to Europe. If the importing firms would cooperate to cut down imports, explained Mr. Wormser, why then "perhaps our friends in the Gulf States would increase their production and supply that deficiency." To put pressure on the oil companies, however, would be beyond the province of the federal government and of the Middle East Emergency Committee, that is, the oil-importing companies. And it was the considered judgment of the federal agencies that it would be inappropriate to make any official or unofficial contact with the Texas and other state commissions to request an increase in allowables.

> Mr. Wormser. . . . We have left it to their own individual decision. . . . We recognize that they have certain responsibilities, just as we have, and we are hoping that they are supplied with all the information possible to make a decision, and we have felt that—well, it's just not our business to interfere with their own activities.

The Chairman [House Committee on Interstate and Foreign Commerce]. Even though there is a national crisis affecting our national security, as you have said?

Mr. Wormser. Yes, sir.

The Chairman. A national crisis affecting our national security and you do not feel it is your responsibility, or your Department's or the Government's responsibility to suggest . . . that there be just a slight increase to meet that crisis?

Mr. Wormser. I am not sure that it would have been welcome, to have made the suggestion. . . . Here is a question of, you might say, divided sovereignty—Federal sovereignty versus State sovereignty, each with its own sphere of responsibility. It was . . . this administration's hope or desire not to have any clash, you might say, but to hope that our good friends in Texas, in the light of their own problems, would do what they felt would be helpful to us in our own overall problem of carrying out the President's wishes of getting more oil to Europe.[19]

The approaches to price were equally revealing. In his State of the Union message to Congress on January 10, 1957, President Eisenhower appealed to the business community to recognize that "national interest must take precedence over the temporary advantages which may be secured by particular groups at the expense of all the people." To hold off inflation, "business in its pricing policy should avoid unnecessary price increases. . . ."[20] The oil price rise that followed this appeal meant an estimated additional annual cost to the consumer of one billion dollars, including a minimum of $85 million to the Armed Forces which purchase over a billion dollars' worth of oil products annually.

Nevertheless, Defense Mobilization Director Flemming explained that "it was not appropriate for me as an official in the executive branch of the Government to comment on the price situation, in view of the fact that the Government is not in that business. . . . The best witnesses . . . obviously are the people who decided to put a price increase into effect."[21]

The Interior Department again concurred. Its representatives had been forewarned of the industry's intentions to raise prices in case of a crisis such as Suez. They even had sat in on oil advisory committee meetings where the likelihood of rising tanker rates and crude prices along with the possibility of government controls on these, in the event of the closing of the canal, had been discussed. Before a House committee, Director Hugh A. Stewart of the Office of Oil and Gas indicated his belief that price increases for producers were long overdue. But since price changes were entirely in the hands of the industry, the Administration's policy precluded his offering any statement as to their causes or justification. "The industry knows exactly why they do certain things and I can only infer. I have no way of knowing what all the factors are. . . . I know about petroleum matters but we confine our efforts to the research and analysis of supply and demand, and very carefully keep out of the question of prices." [22]

Republican Representative Charles A. Wolverton noted that without the guidance of government experts (Director Stewart spent a lifetime in the industry, including some twenty-five years with The Texas Company, from which he was drawing a pension), the Congress would be unable to function in the public interest. It would be forced to rely primarily upon industry data and explanations. "If we are going to do that in this instance, we might just as well repeal and eliminate the ICC and all of the other regulatory bodies and just have industry tell us what ought to be done." To his question, "What source would you suggest that I go to, to seek information that would be helpful from a consumer's viewpoint?" the hearings record the following reply:

Mr. Stewart. May I go off the record, Mr. Chairman?
The Chairman. Yes.
(Discussion off the record.)

On the other side of the Capitol, the questioning of Stewart's superior produced even more frustration.

Senator Kefauver. Isn't it true that the big companies don't want the independents to increase their crude production and that you have done nothing substantially about it, yourself?
Mr. Wormser. I have never heard a company express that thought to me, sir.
. . . Senator Kefauver. Isn't it true that the big companies on your committee fix the international rate for the price of oil on the world market?
Mr. Wormser. I don't know, sir.

. . . Senator Kefauver. What justification do you find for the domestic increase in the price of oil by Humble Oil, followed by many of the others?

Mr. Wormser. I should respectfully suggest that you direct that to the Humble Oil Co.

. . . Senator Kefauver. Might you not even make an effort to protect the American consumer?

Mr. Wormser. Not on prices, sir. We are leaving that severely alone, unless it is specifically directed by Congress.

. . . Senator Kefauver. Do you contemplate asking Congress to do anything on prices?

Mr. Wormser. No, sir.

Senator Kefauver. You mean you are going to sit by and let these companies raise prices?

Mr. Wormser. Operating under a free enterprise economy, sir, I would expect that a free enterprise will take care of it.

. . . Senator Kefauver. Nobody can prevent you from asking these companies to be decent, and hold the prices down. What prevents you from doing so?

Mr. Wormser. Well, I think that is foreign to our responsibility, sir. . . . it would be an interference with the free market.

. . . Senator Kefauver. In the face of the President's general expression of interest and his request, you are going to do nothing to try to keep these prices down?

Mr. Wormser. No, sir.

. . . Senator Kefauver. That is an encouragement for these big companies, because that certainly would be an invitation for other Humble Oil operations which would set up a chain reaction.

Mr. Wormser. We could make an appeal like the President has, but apparently the people of the United States have heard that appeal. . . . We could repeat the President's appeal to the public. I suppose we can do that. I have no objection to that.

. . . Senator Kefauver. Do you have any idea how much additional profits these companies have made by reason of this voluntary agreement?

Mr. Wormser. None whatsoever. . . . We have nothing to do, sir, with the profits of any of the oil companies. . . . These companies are acting at the Government's request. . . .

. . . Senator Kefauver. . . . Suppose they raise the price ten cents a gallon. Would you do anything about that?

Mr. Wormser. Nothing at all.

. . . Senator Kefauver. Fifty cents a gallon?

Mr. Wormser. It is entirely up to them whether they raise it. . . . As a matter of fact, Senator, so far as I am concerned . . . I haven't declared myself for or against a price increase. I am completely neutral, sir.[23]

The new Secretary of the Interior, Fred A. Seaton, was more conscious of his public responsibilities, or at least public relations, than his subordinates had been. He expressed his concern over prices but pointed out that he lacked authority. (Under a revised Defense Production Act the power to control prices had been taken away from the President by the Congress. Even among the congressional critics of the actions of the Administration and the industry in the handling of the oil lift, there was little visible disposition to push legislative action for price controls.) To obtain an agreement from the oilmen to hold prices, he maintained, would flaunt the antitrust safeguards built into the voluntary plan. No immunity was provided for actions on prices. At the same time he admitted he had not made any appeal for cooperation and that he was opposed to price controls. But Mr. Seaton indicated he welcomed a recently launched Justice Department investigation into charges of collusion among the major oil companies to bring about an industry-wide price increase. (A year later, in May 1958, after fifteen months of hearings, a federal grand jury was to indict twenty-nine oil companies, including the giant importers, for having violated the Sherman Act by conspiring in January 1957 to raise and fix crude and gasoline prices. The companies issued the usual disclaimers. Over one hundred oil attorneys began to prepare the defense. "If we lose this," one of them was quoted as saying, "we're well on the road to becoming a public utility." A federal district court in Tulsa subsequently acquitted the defendants. The price increases were held to be rooted in "terrific economic pressures" rather than in any concerted industry action. The government's case, relying heavily on public statements by oil officials and intercompany memos and telephone toll slips, did "not rise above the level of suspicion." The contention developed during the trial that price discussions between a parent and an affiliate constituted conspiracy was also rejected. "If what we did in 1957 was wrong," said the general counsel for one major company, "I frankly don't know how we'll be able to operate.")[24] Meanwhile, the profits of the giant importers for the first quarter of 1957 increased 18 per cent over the comparable period of the previous year with a number of companies reporting the highest quarterly profits in their history.

With oil once more flowing through the Suez Canal and the pipelines, the allowables for domestic production were again cut. By the fall of 1957 Texas wells were operating at a record low of twelve days a month. Domestic producers renewed their assaults upon imports, citing the recent crisis as further illustration of the unreliability and costliness of foreign crude. In face of pressures for strict controls or a tariff, a Cabinet committee ruled that the level of crude imports discouraged home-industry explorations and hence threatened national security. Considerable behind-the-scenes conflict between the respective spokesmen for the domestic and the international producers followed, with the latter resisting legal controls. The President finally called upon the majors to reduce imports, and a Voluntary Oil Import Program was set up within the Interior Department. Its administrator was charged with obtaining from the international companies voluntary compliance with recommended import levels. While some provision was made for newcomers, the level essentially preserved the historic percentages of imports among the majors. Originally exempt from the program, by the end of 1957 the West Coast was also brought into this system of "self-discipline."

Some firms publicly announced their distaste for the program but indicated that a stronger fear of mandatory controls as the alternative would lead them to comply. Not all of them did comply. Tidewater, whose imports were stepped up after a new giant refinery was opened in Delaware—built under the generous tax program and with the expectation of using foreign supplies—viewed its quota as inequitable and tantamount to "economic confiscation." The Sun Oil Company attacked the arrangements as restrictive and in violation of the intent of the antitrust laws. One Texas refiner, frustrated with its allowance and claiming to have exhausted all administrative efforts to obtain relief, filed suit in the federal courts challenging the validity of the entire allocations program. The company had a contract to supply the armed services with jet fuel, but the administrator of the imports regulations, Captain Matthew V. Carson, ruled it was not complying with the program, and hence ineligible to sell to the government.

The Eisenhower Administration reported that the over-all program was a success, and Captain Carson told skeptical independents that crude imports were only one factor in the petroleum industry's problem—"and, at best, a minor one"—citing the decline in consumer demand and the increased use of natural gas.[25] Nevertheless, there was considerable evidence that the restrictions on crude imports were being circumvented by bringing in more semirefined products. Many more refiners clamored for allocations. Domestic producers moved politically for tighter limitations, with the Reciprocal Trade Agreements Act one major congressional target. Early in 1959 the voluntary program was supplanted by a mandatory licensing system. The explanation was "national security." Controls on imports were established, based upon a percentage of the established demand. Every refiner was offered an import quota, whether or not it actually had a record of imports. This was designed to give newer importers a chance to bring in foreign oil. Some immediately traded their quota rights to the large historic importers in exchange for domestic crude, at a profit estimated from $0.50 to $1.00 a barrel. This provoked Representative Charles A. Vanik of Ohio to observe that "free enterprise is indeed a wonderful thing for these refiners when the President creates an asset which they can sell at a handsome profit with no risks involved." [26] More significantly, retaining the quotas on a company rather than a producing-country basis enabled the titans of oil to maintain their cartel patterns. Purchases can be shifted in harmony with prevailing industry needs and attitudes toward individual producer nations rather than any American national policy on energy and imports. The companies have met increased taxes or controls on petroleum production by producing nations such as Venezuela by shifting petroleum purchase to more amenable Middle Eastern areas.

At the same time, many more refining companies are becoming purchasers of imports, including Sun, which had long characterized them as a menace. Independents who have the financial ability and the large oil companies not part of the big seven are flocking to find Canadian, Latin American, African, and other overseas reserves for themselves in the fringe areas not yet staked out. According to Sun's director of foreign operations, the effect of the combination of the rising cost of finding North American reserves, the increased flow of foreign oil into the United States, and the cutback in allowables has been "to put beyond Sun's reach an increasing part of the crude oil it owned underground (heavily in Texas and Louisiana) and to force the company to buy increasing amounts of crude oil to keep its refineries operating." [27] These tend to be wildcat operations with considerable risk that is more than economic, as the leading organization of domestic producers made clear in analyzing these activities: "Governmental policies and laws, and the political and economic climate they provide, are the most important single factor in the future welfare and security of the Western Hemisphere as to petroleum." [28] Thus they too seek the protection of the American flag in dealing with foreign states and with the government of oil.

Meanwhile, the American public remains caught between the conflicting interests within the house of oil. Increasing dependency upon imports means placing increasing power over the world supply and the domestic market in the hands of the giant importing firms. Restrictions on imports subsidize inefficient domestic producers while premising a national policy on the assumption that the cold war will continue indefinitely. They invite retaliation and undermine efforts for greater international trade, ignoring the United States' role as the world's major creditor and that it has been trying to get Europe to lessen its own trade barriers and to integrate its economic policies. They threaten the Good Neighbor Policy, offending countries like Canada and Venezuela which look to their United States sales as a valuable revenue source, while serving as major markets for American goods. The explanation of "national security" also mocks the closely integrated military defense arrangements between Canada and the United States. (Oil entering overland from Canada and Mexico subsequently was exempted from the import restriction plan.) Thus the incongruities of America's program for an adequate oil supply continue. The one certainty is that, in the absence of a defined public policy or even an adequate check, the consumer will continue to pay more under a pricing system largely determined by the industry's private government.

It would be simple to conclude that in the international sphere the oil industry is always the Machiavellian manipulator and the American Government the innocent bystander or agent. Yet ample evidence has been offered thus far to suggest that the alliance between the private government of oil and the public government of the

United States derives in part from an assumption of mutual needs. From the industry's perspective, government sanction for adherence to the world cartel system is essential. For if monopoly is a naughty word and a subversive institution for Americans to accept, the existence of a cartel approaches the unpardonable. Public officials presumably are guided by devotion to the historic premise of antitrust as a way of preserving the competitive character of the economy and the free nature of the social system. But they are not unmindful of the utility of an integrated approach to a fundamental resource. The oil industry offers a ready-made mechanism for national planning that can be extended to international strategy. "National security" provides the uneasy but fortuitous meeting ground for harmonizing oil's imperial commitments and the nation's spiraling world-wide responsibilities.

Some of the New Dealers, not unlike their Republican predecessors, had been attracted by the advantages of an integrated industrial apparatus in seeking to end the chaos of the great depression. The National Industrial Recovery Act, for example, accepted the dominance of the corporation and the trade association in the modern economy. It assumed that these could be made to serve as instruments of public policy. In similar fashion, where Secretary of the Interior Harold L. Ickes chose to cooperate with big oil, it was because he was disturbed by the costs of competition in oil and thought that the responsibility for such national objectives as conservation was more likely to be attained with the cooperation of those who had the effective power. When the country became the arsenal for democracy in World War II, the need for marshaling resources accentuated the convenience of dealing with one integrated industry rather than "thousands" of oilmen. As a condition for contributing to the war mobilization, oil leaders within and outside the government negotiated with public officials to win the assurance of a moratorium from antitrust investigation and litigation. And so the teamwork of industry and government helped to provide the wave of oil upon which, to borrow the rhetoric of World War I, the Allies floated to victory.

There have been occasions when the United States has urged its industry into foreign situations. Military and political leaders have shared the international companies' concern about drainage of domestic reserves, as they have about the machinations of the British in the Middle East. The American industry was moving into an area where traditionally British influence had been paramount. During World War II the State Department's Petroleum attaché in the Near East Division testified that contacts between British-owned oil companies and their government "are so intimate that it is difficult to discuss where the oil companies end and where the Government begins":

> The Government, wherever it has a shadow of influence, uses its power by fair means or underhand to secure markets or concessions for its British owned companies. Every conceivable subterfuge, use of assumed authority over mandates, threat, intimidation, distortion of the laws, or bribery is used to aid their companies in securing oil concessions in weak countries and holding their market against all comers, even British companies that are foreign owned.[29]

The pleading of oilmen for government intervention in Saudi Arabia met a sympathetic response from Mr. Ickes as well as from military officers who backed the requests for loans referred to earlier. In fact, eager to redeploy his energies and talents now that the New Deal was dead, the self-styled curmudgeon enthusiastically seized their arguments as to the vital role of oil. Mr. James Terry Duce of Aramco, for example, had said "if we had found 100,000,000 barrels of oil, we would have been very pleased, but when you begin to find oil in billions of barrels and it looks as though those billions will grow, it becomes not so much a matter of your interest, it becomes a matter of public interest and the national interest. . . ." [30] Ickes pushed this to a conclusion that was subsequently to dissuade the industry from ever again using such language. For as the State Department's Advisor on International Economic Affairs observed, the companies involved "had gone fishing for a cod and had caught a whale" in their Washington journey. If Middle Eastern oil was so basic to American security, Ickes reasoned, why then the United States Government should be directly involved in the management or ownership of the companies. ". . . American private interests have had to compete with the sovereign interests of foreign countries, particularly Great Britain. Any realistic appraisal of the problem of acquiring foreign petroleum reserves for the benefit of the

United States compels the conclusion that American participation must be of a sovereign character compatible with the strength of the competitive forces encountered in any such undertaking." [31] The debates that followed had parallels in 1920 when comparable proposals were made for a United States Oil Corporation.

In July 1943 a Petroleum Reserves Corporation was set up, with Ickes as president and representatives from the major related Cabinet and government offices, to buy or acquire reserves of crude oil outside the United States, including stock in corporations, to transport, store, process, and market and otherwise dispose of such crude and its products, with power to operate refineries, pipelines, and storage tanks outside the United States. The new public corporation sought to buy all or a portion of the stock of the California Arabian Standard Oil Company, following the British and French pattern. This venture met with some State Department disapproval and the full indignation of the two parent oil companies as well as of other industry leaders who attacked this invasion of free enterprise. Protracted negotiations with the California and Texas companies ended in a stalemate, with Ickes concluding that once Rommel had been chased out of North Africa the oil companies "were secure in their concession and more disposed to thumb their nose at us." Colonel Leavell, petroleum attaché of the Near East Division of the State Department who served as joint executive of the Army-Navy Petroleum Board in charge of long-range planning, had this interpretation:

The answer was "No" in effect, "We are under no obligation to our Government, we don't trust you, but if you will invest 150 million dollars in facilities as a guarantee that you will protect us, we will agree not to trade with your enemies and will give you a discount on some future oil." [32]

A proposal for a government-built refinery in the Middle East was also quashed, with the industry constructing one of its own, although it earlier had denied the need. The proposal for a publicly built pipeline, referred to previously, had been pushed by those companies who would gain from it and also presumably operate it. It was rejected. The rest of the industry was highly critical, and the British were fearful of American attempts to take over the Middle East. To the United States Government it meant the companies would maintain a crude oil reserve of one billion barrels, available for government purchase at 25 per cent less than market price. Mr. Ickes insisted that the government corporation was not proposing to compete with private industry: "On the contrary, its purpose is to promote the private oil industry of this nation, and to further the interests of the people of the United States" by helping to offset reserves being drained by the war.

Congressional questioning was sharp.

Senator Edwin Johnson of Colorado. I am somewhat disturbed, in a matter as large as this is . . . why we are approaching it in this back-door method. . . . It seems to me that it is entitled to an open approach, between the powers that are concerned—Britain and Russia and the United States—and the country itself, Arabia, in the regular way and in accordance with the formula as I understand that was laid down in the Atlantic Charter . . . make the world resources available to the world, and here is the first resource that we have, and instead of approaching it on a broad open basis we slip in the back door and we put the heat on Britain by running in ahead of them and building a pipe line, putting them on the spot, and bring them to time, club behind the door, and all that sort of thing, instead of approaching it in the broad, statesmanlike way. I suppose that question ought to be asked the State Department, but since Commodore Carter is the chief advocate of the plan, I would like to submit it to him for his observation.

Commodore Andrew Carter, Petroleum Administrator of the Navy, had been executive officer of the Army-Navy Petroleum Board and later became president of a subsidiary owned by the Texas and California companies. His preliminary study led to the pipeline recommendation.

Commodore Carter. I am only a servant of these departments, Senator, and like any other servant of these departments I can propose and try to find a way to seek solutions, I assure you I don't start to make those effective without making sure of the support I have from those departments. Now, as to your general question, I think the answer is this: The companies approached the Government to help them out. The Government went about helping them out without any idea of working in the shadows from the British at all, because it was quite obvious that nothing could be done in the way of getting a pipe line to the seaboard without British consent. . . .

Senator Johnson. . . . Has the Atlantic Charter and all of its pretty language been forgotten in this particular problem?

Comm. Carter. I think you will find it occurs in all these documents. If it doesn't occur in actual words in some of them, you will find quotations in there paraphrasing the Atlantic Charter right through. . . .

Sen. Johnson. . . . It seems to me that we are working absolutely at cross-purposes to it. We are considering the private investment of some of the companies in the United States. And then I hear you make references every now and then to the fact that we are going to build this pipe line for the American interests and very likely we are going to be called upon to build another pipe line for the British interests— private interests—private American interests and private British interests. Instead of making the resources available to the people of the world, we are turning them over and giving the protection of the flag to private interests.

Comm. Carter. Isn't that tantamount to doing it for the people of the world? After all, those companies don't represent a few individuals such as themselves any more than we in the Navy represent an ownership there. We don't. The Government owns the Navy; the people of the country own the Navy. Similarly the ownership of these companies is scattered among tens of thousands or hundreds of thousands of stockholders, and so far as we are concerned the fact that it happens to be owned by that corporation—one corporation or another—is purely incidental to securing the available resources for this country.

Sen. Johnson. Well, I just don't follow that approach at all. Maybe it is because I don't understand such matters.

Comm. Carter. Well, it is more likely that I don't, sir.[33]

As World War II drew to a close, officials from the government and from some of the international companies broadened their attempts to formulate an international oil policy. A first objective was to stabilize Anglo-American oil relationships and to gain for the United States British recognition of its new role in the Middle East. The ultimate goal was the extension to all countries having an interest in oil of principles affirming the right of equal access of nations to petroleum. The plans also called for the respecting of contracts fair to the economic advancement of the producing countries and the concessionaires. Great emphasis was placed on planning for the efficient and orderly conduct of the petroleum trade based on careful studies of world supply and demand. An International Petroleum Commission was envisioned to handle disputes. Two successive treaties were signed by the two powers, but the first was withdrawn because of industry objections and a revised agreement never received the necessary Senate approval. The agreement was supported by elements in the State and Interior departments, giants like Jersey Standard, and the American Petroleum Institute. Secretary of the Interior Ickes hailed it for opening the door to greater opportunity for American nationals to find oil while consigning to oblivion such restrictive devices as the Red Line Agreement. But there was strong opposition from a number of quarters. To some oilmen this was an invitation to the federal government to share in what were properly the responsibilities of private enterprise. If it first appeared to domestic producers as a kind of international Interstate Oil Compact Commission, it also carried with it the threat of the invasion of states' rights. They speculated whether it would become a new instrument through which the international cartel would regulate the world movement of oil, including United States imports. Industry insistence upon antitrust immunity where the oil companies adopted courses of action recommended by the new commission and approved by their government was also a stumbling block. The Justice Department refused to give such advance sanction. The clause was finally omitted, with the understanding that Secretary Ickes would seek congressional support for the principle. And the suspicion lingered that the agreement was a portent of a grand alliance between the two leading powers with Middle Eastern interests and the world government of oil.

As the United States, through such measures as the "Truman doctrine," has taken over responsibilities traditionally British—paralleling the shift of the center of oil for Europe from the Western Hemisphere to the Middle East—its leaders have shared the concern for keeping Mediterranean trade routes open and shores friendly, whether the base in point be Cyprus, Greece, or Suez. The American Sixth Fleet, complete with guided missiles, nuclear weapons, and jet bombers, rules the Mediterranean. Without any set base, it patrols near Syria, Lebanon, Israel, or North Africa, wherever there may be trouble. The United States is wary of the possibility of Russian expansion in quest of oil and warm-water ports. It fears even more the possibility of internal domination in these areas by Communist or anti-Western forces. The United States resists the notion that the Soviet Union should have a voice in Middle Eastern affairs. Meanwhile, it has built a ring of bases on Russia's southern border that the latter quite easily views as threats to its own security. The United States backs strengthening the armed forces of countries like Saudi Arabia, the object being, in the words of the American ambassador George Wadsworth, "the maintaining of internal security in the country in the sense that the army would be used as an effective armed constabulary . . . to support the throne" and also "to defend the country against any possible aggression from within the area. . . ." Asked in 1957 by a Senate committee examining the proposed "Eisenhower doctrine" for the Middle East whom King Saud felt threatened by, Mr. Wadsworth explained: "Well, you have got the British and the French and the Israelis who pulled a pretty good intervention in Egypt." Mr. Wadsworth also indicated his belief that Aramco "has done a magnificent job of public relations for itself and the United States" and that King Saud is a "good king . . . who has the welfare of his people primarily in mind. . . ." He felt that the much discussed problem of slavery in Saudi Arabia was exaggerated, since it involved African Negroes, was quite paternal, and the slave trade was dying out—this in contradiction to the reports of the British Anti-Slavery Society that slavery is increasing on the Arabian Peninsula, due in large part to the new oil wealth available.[34]

The petroleum industry's foreign policy is also enhanced by the ease with which many American political leaders equate social revolution and nationalization with communism. Indeed, official anxieties at times have provoked some of the leading oilmen to agree privately that while their pipelines and oil routes are vulnerable, the dependence of the producing countries upon the more advanced Western corporations and nations makes the worries of the State Department somewhat exaggerated. But obviously such solicitude generally works in the oilmen's favor and they do nothing to disabuse public servants of these notions which equate public access to oil with private profits from oil.

Appeasement of those Arab leaders who give promise of remaining anti-Soviet and sympathetic to Western oil interests has been a cornerstone of American policy. If the Arabian American Oil Company, troubled over the security of reserves at least as large as those within the United States, caters to all the whims of its feudal hosts —from a 350-mile railroad and a Swiss chef to electric blankets and air conditioning for royal concubine comfort—so does the American Government watching the expensive air base it built at Dhahran. While Dhahran is used as a refueling and loading point for military transports heading for the Far East, King Saud does not allow actual United States militarization. Hence its worth to United States security has been more readily defended by the State Department for protecting oil interests on the Arabian Peninsula than by the Defense Department as a jumping-off spot against the Soviet Union.

Early in 1957 the Arabian despot was ardently courted by the American Government in order to secure a renewal of the base agreement. The United States delegate at the United Nations Economic and Social Council, obviously reluctant to offend Arabian desert chieftains, refused to go along with stronger antislavery conventions backed by most nations. President Eisenhower took the unusual step of greeting King Saud in person at the Washington airport, a courtesy he had extended to no other head of state up to that time. Oil leaders as well as State Department officials met with the king during the negotiations. A formal White House dinner included as guests the top executives of the Arabian American Oil Company, its four parent companies, and related banking interests. Asked why his colleagues received such special consideration in working out these matters of American foreign policy, President Rathbone of Jersey Standard replied, "I presume because they are the ones that have the principal interests." The board of directors of Aramco were hosts at another dinner for King Saud, his delegation, and State Department representatives. Mr. Rathbone explained this was part of protecting the concession: "If he had not been . . . adequately . . . or attractively entertained . . . he would have felt very hurt." [35] Full details of the agreement were never made public. But the United States gained a five-year extension of the right to use the base and, presumably, support of the "Eisenhower doctrine." In return, the activities of the American military mission were to be stepped up and Saudi Arabia was to continue to have the right to purchase military equipment. Throughout the period of the new agreement there were frequent reports that Saudi Arabia, in part prodded by United Arab Republic criticisms, would not renew the agreement in 1962.

Aramco and allied oil groups advised and fought against the United Nations decision to partition Palestine and create Israel. They warned against recognition by the United States, and then, after consultation with Arab leaders, James Terry Duce of Aramco along with other oil leaders recommended to the departments of State and Defense that the United States repudiate its stand. No major company has dared to drill in the new state lest it offend Arab rulers. The refinery at the deep-water port of Haifa, built as one Mediterranean terminus of a vast pipeline from Iraq, has operated at considerably under capacity because of the reluctance of the industry and the Western governments to negotiate with Iraq and with Jordan, whose territory the pipeline crosses, to allow oil to flow to Israel. With a daily capacity of 40,000 barrels, the pipeline has been shut since the Arab invasion of Israel in 1948, and the construction of a larger pipeline running parallel to it was stopped at the Israeli border.

Aramco has accepted the Saudi Arabian stricture that it is not to sell any oil bound for "Jewish destinations." In the summer of 1957, Royal Dutch/Shell and British Petroleum, the largest marketeers in Israel, announced their decision to sell their facilities there "for commercial reasons." This had all the earmarks of a political decision in response to Arab pressures for a tightening of the economic boycott existing since the birth of Israel. Presumably this was done with the knowledge of the British Government, which owns a majority of British Petroleum shares, although Foreign Secretary Selwyn Lloyd insisted that his government's policy was not to interfere with "commercial decisions" of the company.[36]

The development of a strategic major pipeline through Israel to the Mediterranean (paralleling the small one Israel has built from Elath at the north end of the Red Sea to serve the Haifa refinery) to supplement or if necessary by-pass Suez and the other pipelines has not been pushed because of similar oil-industry caution. Nevertheless, Israel feels it can get the necessary Middle East oil, perhaps from Iran or Kuwait, and the French Government and French interests have shown an interest in financing this. Also, since the establishment of the Jewish homeland, major oil companies and tanker fleets have economically quarantined Israeli harbors in response to an Arab League black list that refuses trade with those who deal with Israel. Socony ceased supplying Israel in October 1956, explaining that "we got out of Israel because of the continued and increasing difficulties of doing business simultaneously there and in the Arab countries." [37] To complete the ostracism, the Soviet Union broke its oil-export contract with Israel after the latter's troops entered Egypt in 1956. Thus, Israel has been paying premium prices for Middle Eastern oil (primarily Iranian) that has had to be shipped around the Cape of Good Hope. Its other source for crude has been Venezuela.

From 1958 to 1960 the United States Navy, supported by Aramco warnings, tacitly sanctioned the Arab blockade of Israel and boycott of ships trading with Israel. A cancellation clause in contracts with United States flag ships carrying oil cargoes for the Navy stipulated that tank owners whose ships might be refused accommodations at Arab ports would be responsible for all costs and penalties resulting from the delay. This clause virtually foreclosed bids by tank owners whose ships had traded with Israel. Charter contracts made by the United States Department of Agriculture and by the Commodity Credit Corporation covering surplus foods shipped to the United Arab Republic directly forbid such ships' calling or having called at Israeli ports.

Where Aramco accedes to Saudi Arabian demands that no Jewish personnel work in or deal with the country, the American Government refuses passports and even screens its armed forces and Foreign Service to make sure Saudi Arabia's sovereign "idiosyncrasies," to use Secretary of State Dulles's term, are respected. In 1950 welders being recruited in New York by a subcontractor for Aramco for work on a pipeline found themselves asked about their religious beliefs. A complaint was filed by one applicant, and an investigation was undertaken by the New York State Commission Against Discrimination which subsequently reported:

The investigating commissioner was informed by the Arabian American Oil Company that the Arabian government does not issue visas to persons of the Jewish faith. The company advised that it had an understanding with the Arabian government to screen all prospective employees for work in Arabia before they applied for Arabian visas, for the purpose of excluding persons of the Jewish faith to whom visas will not be granted. The respondent urged the Commission not to take any action which would jeopardize this agreement in view of considerations important to the international interests and security of the United States. . . . The investigating commissioner communicated with the United States Department of State. He was advised by the Political Adviser for the Office of African and Near East Affairs that as a result of the recent conflict between the Arabian countries and Israel, the Arabian governments refuse to grant visas to persons of the Jewish faith for work in any of the Arabian countries. This representative of the Department of State stressed the importance of not having anything interfere with the existing relationship between the Arabian government and the Arabian American Oil Co., explaining that this relationship was the basis for the harmony between this government and the Arabian government and should it be disturbed in any way the international interests of the United States would be seriously affected.

The commission accepted the State Department's reasoning and concluded this was not an unlawful practice. In the summer of 1959 the New York State Supreme Court annulled the commission's findings. The court held that the laws of the state could not be "cast aside to protect the oil profits of Aramco. . . . When Commissioner Carter declares that American interests in the Near East outweigh the abstract vindication of state sovereignty, he makes the commission the vassal of a foreign potentate. . . . The film of oil which blurs the vision of Aramco has apparently affected the commission in this case." [38]

No official change in the status of American Jewish military or civil personnel was announced after the 1957 negotiations with King Saud. A passage in a United States Air Force manual declaring that "individuals of Jewish faith or descent are strictly barred entrance to and transit of Saudi Arabia" had been deleted after congressional pressure prior to Saud's visit. But the actual restrictive practices were continued. American spokesmen explained that while they had mentioned the problem, the king was firm. To avoid any deadlocks practical considerations took precedence over the moral aspects. Mr. Dulles blandly suggested to a press conference that the king's attitude may not have been very receptive because of "the fact that he felt that he had not been given nondiscriminatory treatment himself in the City of New York." [39] This was in reference to Mayor Robert

Wagner's refusal to cooperate with the State Department in extending an official city welcome on the grounds that Saudi Arabia did not allow free Catholic or Protestant worship (chaplains "voluntarily" refrain from wearing clerical garb) and was closed to Jews.

It is clear that hostility to Israel has not been limited to oilmen. In his account of his experiences as a member of the Anglo-American Inquiry on Palestine, Bartley Crum described the "silken curtain" hiding a "sorry and bitter record" of secret doubledealing. ". . . Since September 15, 1938, each time a promise was made to American Jewry regarding Palestine, the State Department promptly sent messages to the Arab rulers discounting it and reassuring them, in effect, that regardless of what was promised publicly to the Jews, nothing would be done to change the situation in Palestine." [40]

Former President Truman recalls that while the United States public policy championed the new social democracy, "the Department of State's specialists on the Near East were, almost without exception, unfriendly to the idea of a Jewish state. . . . Some among them . . . were . . . inclined to be anti-Semitic." [41] There was a prevalent belief that if the Arabs were antagonized, they would go over into the Soviet camp. Mr. Truman's Secretary of Defense, James Forrestal, strongly resented Zionist political pressure in the United States which he felt might result in a denial of access to Middle Eastern oil, without which we could not continue the Marshall Plan, fight a war, or maintain the tempo of our peacetime economy. "American motorcar companies would have to design a four-cylinder motorcar," predicted Forrestal. [42]

Oil has long been a factor in the politics of appeasement, and industry-oriented policies have been justified by political ends. Some State Department men had been reluctant to intervene to prevent the oil shipments and refueling of Axis ships off Latin America and in Spanish ports. Pre-Pearl Harbor oil exports to Spain and Japan were regarded by the Roosevelt Administration as instruments of national policy to forestall further aggression against the East Indies. The American Embassy in Spain developed with Socony, Jersey, the Atlantic Refining Company, and Royal Dutch/Shell a program for maintaining oil imports throughout the war. Mr. Roosevelt is quoted as remarking in a Cabinet meeting that he was willing to buy Spain, to which Secretary of Interior Harold L. Ickes in his diary added, "Apparently the spirit of appeasement will never die." An order from the President six months before Pearl Harbor to Ickes, who was also Petroleum Administrator and had been blocking oil exports to Japan, to clear such shipments through the State Department because of delicate negotiations under way, provided the immediate provocation for a bitter attack on the President. "I have often wondered if I would not be of more help to the people on the outside telling the truth, than on the inside helping to deceive the people." [43]

The Suez coup of 1956 dramatically provided another illustration of the hazards and inconsistencies of American foreign policy. The United States had earlier favored the withdrawal of British strength from the canal area and in general sought to appease President Gamal Abdel Nasser. The Egyptian leader repeatedly declared that the European control of the Suez Canal, like the very existence of Israel, were products of Western imperialism.[44] Inflammatory messages to this effect have been beamed daily over Radio Cairo to the peoples of North Africa and the Middle East, a position backed by the Soviet Union in its quest to establish its sympathies with the aspirations of colonial populations, further Western disunity and gain access to the resources and ports of the Middle East.

The United States was determined to prove that in its new supremacy in this region it was not to be identified with an older colonial tradition. But American policy makers were also aware of Nasser's ambitions for a federation of Arab-speaking Moslem countries from the Atlantic to the Persian Gulf, with Egypt providing the leadership and the financing to come from the billion-dollar annual oil income to Middle Eastern producing countries. It was not the intent of the United States or of the involved oil companies to push too far a unified Arab world, to abdicate the hold over the oil concessions, or to allow any further British-French vacuums to remain unfilled.

The United States had agreed with the United Kingdom and the World Bank to provide a huge loan toward a billion-dollar project for the economic development of the Nile. Seven months later, in July 1956, support for the High Aswan Dam was canceled. The brinkmanship involved in this withdrawal was explained by such factors as Egypt's continued willingness to play off the Soviet Union against the Western powers through new trade and arms agreements, growing doubts as to the financial capacity of Egypt to handle this ambitious economic development program, and Egypt's failure to meet the terms of the original World Bank agreement. It provided the excuse for Nasser's action against the Suez Canal Company.

The United States was determined not to shoot its way through the canal if Egypt was to block the passage of American ships, and it sharply opposed the French-British-Israeli attack upon Egypt that followed. It feared that this would invite the successful entry of Soviet influence in this area and North Africa, with Russia jumping over the northern tier defense of the Baghdad Pact linking Iran, Iraq, Pakistan, Turkey, and Great Britain. This military alliance had been created by the United States, but it then decided to stay out of formal membership lest this political division of the Middle East arouse Arab leaders.

To rush oil to Western Europe to replace the cut-off supplies would be to undercut this delicate juggling and further offend Middle Eastern leaders who identified with Nasser in the struggle. Oilmen repeatedly warned the State Department that such a course would risk all the reserves of the region and perhaps provoke action against American holdings. To abandon Great Britain, France, and the rest of Western Europe completely would be to lose historic allies and customers. And so the diplomatic strategy was to promise oil but to go slow in delivery, first ensuring the end of the conflict and the withdrawal from Egypt of the invading armies. During the critical month of November 1956, the advisory Middle East Emergency Committee (MEEC) responsible for coordinating oil shipments was suspended and American representatives were temporarily withdrawn from participation in joint United States-European efforts. Plans to meet Europe's oil needs worked out during the preceding summer were not implemented until December. Meanwhile, embassy and overseas oil officials advised their home offices that the United States and her oil companies were targets of suspicion and criticism because of this apparent determination by the Eisenhower Administration to punish England and France. In many quarters the charges were made that the oil squeeze was designed not only to restore to Nasser the position he had lost through the military defeat, but also to strengthen the American companies in their rivalry with British oil interests. *The Times* of London commented in late November 1956: "The United States, certainly, could only fear the consequences of an economic crisis in Europe, though such apprehensions seem to have been outweighed until now by a determination to do nothing at the Government level *which could jeopardize American oil extraction in the Middle East*." A Socony Mobil Company memorandum reported that "while most of the industry . . . was strongly urging that MEEC be reactivated, the administration simply refused to. . . ." Another representative warned his company that "the psychological effect of the MEEC not being revitalized can . . . even, in my opinion, lead to panic measures on the part of Governments in control and regulation which the industry may never be completely freed from." [45] When the MEEC was reactivated, the key consideration was one of public relations—to show Europeans that the United States was not disinterested in their fuel plight.

If the oil industry suffered in public relations terms for this passing of the buck, it was paid well for this role. The producers received their price rises and the international companies saw their profits leap in this period. But the prime villains were neither Texas oil barons nor integrated importers. The United States has become the dominant Mediterranean-Middle Eastern power. It now is forced to recognize, however imperfectly, that the old feudal and colonial worlds are dying. Such factors as the presence of oil have set in motion all the currents that mean a change in the social structure and tempo of the Middle East. Masses of people are unwilling to accept themselves, their children, and the physical resources surrounding them primarily as instruments for the well-being of an industrial elite of Western nations. Moral decency, private generosity, and public Point Four programs notwithstanding, the United States has failed to raise its sights high enough in developing a design for coming to terms with the long-run aspirations and needs of the world. Too much of its foreign policy is conducted in terms of security for commercial interests and immediate national advantage in the cold war.

The United States has found it expedient to favor the principle that the canal should be open to all; it cannot bring itself to apply the same criteria to oil—to insist that oil serve the people of the areas where it is found as well as the more advanced nations for whom it means industrial life and profit. Helping Nasser to convert a disastrous military defeat into a diplomatic triumph, the United States found Syria joining Egypt in a new United Arab Republic, with Tapline and the Iraq Petroleum Company pipelines that run through Syria thus coming under the potential control of Egypt. Backing King Saud in his anti-Nasser policies and generally playing up to him as a bulwark of the West's position in the Middle East, the United States saw itself further thwarted by the accession to effective power for several years of his brother, Crown Prince Faisal, who was much more in tune with Arab nationalism and who regarded the Baghdad Pact and similar efforts as Western attempts to divide and rule the Middle East. (King Saud has also been critical of the Baghdad Pact.) Acting as though the world in general and the Arab people in particular share the American obsession over potential Communist military aggression, United States policies have miscalculated the temper of the nationalist forces and assumed that an American-guided Middle East might be acceptable to Arab leaders. Linked with autocrats like King Saud whose interest in using oil royalties for palaces appears to exceed that of bringing the welfare of his people up to minimum standards—his $30 million palace at Riyadh is reported to consume three times the electricity used by the 200,000 inhabitants of the surrounding city—the United States seems uncomprehending of the bitterness this corruption engenders among rising intellectual, merchant, and nationalist groups.

Deploring overt aggression from any nation controlled by international Communism, the United States has furthered an arms race among the Arab nations, equipping Jordan and Saudi Arabia, while Russia has done the same for Syria and Egypt. Meanwhile, King Saud has used his Aramco royalties and advances to support internal unrest in Iraq, Lebanon, and Jordan, to spread anti-British propaganda, and to forestall any Arab-Israeli settlement. Although it has been a leading sponsor of Israel, the only democratic society in the Middle East, the United States has closed its eyes both to King Saud's threat to sacrifice ten million Arab lives to destroy the new state and, until 1956, when the blockade hit American shipping, to Egypt's long-time refusal to allow Israel-bound ships to use the Suez

Canal. In similar fashion, the United States has been reluctant to press Egypt to abandon its blockade of the Straits of Tiran, generally held to be an international waterway, leading from the Red Sea to the Gulf of Aqaba and the Israeli port of Elath—although the United States made a pledge to support "innocent passage" as a condition for Israeli's withdrawal from the Gaza strip and the Gulf of Aqaba region after the Suez fighting. By thus encouraging the belief that Israel is temporary, the United States helps postpone any easing of tension in the Middle East.

In the summer of 1958 a military-led and middle class-dominated coup overthrew a pro-Western, reactionary dictatorship in Iraq. The one Arab country in the Baghdad Pact, this oil-rich country had been a center of British influence in the Middle East and a recipient of considerable American military aid. American Marines landed in Lebanon and British paratroopers descended upon Jordan in an effort to contain the revolt and to bolster the collapsing Western design for the Middle East. The United States explained that its action was taken to protect American lives and prevent the "indirect aggression" of "assassins in plain clothes" seeking to place Lebanon under the domination of Nasser's United Arab Republic. (A *New York Times* dispatch from Beirut reported one "highly experienced military analyst" as guessing that the job of smashing the headquarters of the opposition to the Government "might be done with two light tanks alone.") Meanwhile, the Soviet Union delegate told the United Nations that he detected "an acute smell of oil" underlying the troop movements. And *The New York Times* reported a series of conferences at which President Eisenhower, Secretary of State Dulles, and Foreign Secretary Selwyn Lloyd of Britain had agreed to limit their military action in the Middle East for the time being to Lebanon and Jordan. "Intervention will not be extended to Iraq as long as the revolutionary government in Iraq respects Western oil interests," said the front-page dispatch.[46] This gunboat diplomacy was clearly in line with the State Department's commitment to pipelines and profits.

Once more discounting the bitter seeds of social discontent and Arab nationalism, defenders of these Western actions saw the Iraq revolutionaries as puppets of Moscow and Cairo. Meanwhile, the new government announced a course of neutrality in the struggles between Russia and the Western allies. Nasser was soon a national villain. But there quickly developed evidence of increased internal Communist influence and Soviet technical aid. The new leaders announced that they were not unmindful of the fate of Mossadegh's actions in Iran. They recognized their dependence upon Western markets, pipelines, and capital and hence would respect the properties and concessions of the Iraq Petroleum Company (owned by Jersey, Socony, British Petroleum, Royal Dutch/Shell, Compagnie Française des Pétroles, and the C. S. Gulbenkian estate). But oilmen anticipated increased demands for sharing profits and control. And with the Western diplomats they wondered anxiously where the next Middle Eastern explosion would come. Would it be in the British protectorate of Kuwait? This diminutive desert sheikdom, where the British Petroleum and Gulf companies are partners, virtually floats on oil and is a major supplier of British investment capital as well as crude.

Despite these setbacks, the vacuity and fumbling of American foreign policy and its application to oil still promote the propping up of regimes whose days are numbered and who are prepared to trade their people's physical heritage for dollars and military support. All this takes place with the active participation of oil corporations that seek to integrate the raw material producing countries of the world into the processes of their private government. Late in 1958 the United Nations General Assembly received Soviet-backed resolutions, first proposing that the UN provide aid for nations wishing to develop their own petroleum resources and then one more simply suggesting a study of international cooperation in such development. The Americans immediately responded to the bait of this blunt threat to the international companies and clear provocation to the producing countries of Latin America and the Middle East. "In no time at all the oil lobbyists were swarming around the United Nations," the *St. Louis Post-Dispatch* reported. "There were so many conferences between the oil men and members of the United States delegation that one American diplomat said he told the oil people to 'let us alone so we can protect your interests.'" One oilman, a member of the delegation, "was warned to lie low." Speaking for the United States, Senator Mike Mansfield rose to defend private enterprise and national sovereignty:

If the General Assembly starts with the oil industry today, where shall we stop? Will there be a separate resolution on the steel industry, the flour milling industry, poultry raising, cement manufacturing, automobiles, synthetic fibers or the hula hoop business? [47]

In a setting where we know not where we are going, the quest for oil looms as one clear goal.

10

Oilmen in Government

As the largest producer, the largest source of capital, and the biggest contributor to the global mechanism, we [the United States] must set the pace and assume the responsibility of the majority stockholder in this corporation known as the world. . . . American private enterprise . . . may strike out and save its own position all over the world, or sit by and witness its own funeral. . . . As our country has begun to evolve its overall postwar foreign policy, private enterprise must begin to evolve its foreign and domestic policy, starting with the most important contribution it can make—"men in government."

—"Approach to the Problems in Maintaining and Expanding American Direct Investments Abroad," a talk by Leo D. Welch, treasurer of Standard Oil (New Jersey), Nov. 12, 1946. In 1960 Mr. Welch became chairman.

As industrialism forces the closer integration of all aspects of human affairs, planning for the kinds of direction, choices, and order people may want their society to have becomes imperative. Given the rise of private power systems, leaving things to chance or to the "free play" of the market becomes a cloak for industrial feudalism, however benevolent in the American setting of abundance. In similar fashion, leaving fundamental decisions at the international level to individual national and corporate preference frequently becomes an invitation to further anarchy or imperial rule.

As institutional relationships become more complex and individuals more interdependent, the shifting lines separating what is public from what is private become more difficult to perceive, let alone maintain. The great political struggles involve, first of all, agreement as to what are the issues appropriate for public resolution, the needs urgent for public responsibility, and the forces legitimate for social control. It is such distinctions that provide the balance between the privacy of individual choices and the collectivity of communal purposes at the heart of democratic concern.

"Government," Felix Frankfurter observed in 1930, "is no longer merely to keep the ring, to be a policeman, to secure the observance of elementary decencies. It is now looked upon as one of the energies of civilization. It is being drawn upon for all the great ends of society." [1] Increasingly, the power of the state has been brought into play for leadership in the primary functions of war, welfare, and regulation. The defining of mass social goals portends greater public intervention in relation to private property, power, and plans. And increasingly the public government becomes looked to by all groups for the satisfaction and defense of their private ends. Hence the great clashes over the control and direction of the machinery of government.

Publicly, the oil industry is watchful, critical, contemptuous, and fearful of the capacities and consequences of the exercise of public power. Antitrust actions, like congressional investigations and angry editorials, may never have effectively stopped the growth of monopoly and giantism within the industry. Indeed, in certain respects by defining evil practices antitrust has sanctioned this development. But the successors to the old Standard Oil trust, broken by the courts in 1911, remain conscious of the power of such weapons within the arsenal of the modern state to check, if not control, corporate behavior. Oil messages carry tender references to a happy and mythical past when laissez faire ruled. There is also stern insistence upon preserving what is called, with understandable vagueness, "free enterprise." Accompanying these appeals is an unremitting attack upon the public way as the wrong way of doing things, with the assumption that private efforts invariably mean a higher morality. There is a constant quest of immunity from antitrust legislation. Paralleling this is an equally relentless harassment of public inquiries and of the officials who may dare to pursue them. If power corrupts, why then it is its public aspects that Lord Acton is presumed to have had in mind.

The industry hovers over all public research that might upset its private planning. Every possibility of public competition or of a yardstick for measuring oil's performance, whether in relation to public lands, shale oil, synthetic rubber development, or atomic energy, is studied. The power of taxation, whether a state severance tax or a federal income tax, is viewed as the power to regulate and destroy. Civil servants responsive to a wider public than the interests of oildom are judged threats to the "American way."

Industry leaders have preferred to have the fewest possible dealings with the political processes of government. Some of them are indeed among the last of the industrial pioneers in America. Inheritors of a wagon-and-ox tradition, they "don't want to be regulated by clerks in Washington." But with this romanticism, expressed with genuine feeling by Warwick Downing of Colorado, has come the realization that the meeting of private quests and public needs has permanently catapulted oil into political life. And with this there has been a harsher resistance to the right of public rule. Thus in 1956, W. Alton Jones, chairman of the board of Cities Service, could still describe the New Deal as "the golden era of the professional reformer and the ideological zealot," and the Public Utility Holding Company Act of 1935 as an evil and spiteful product of the latter's destructive genius.[2] In effect, oil's efforts reflect and foster a contempt for democratic premises and processes.

On another level, as has also been discussed earlier, the industry keenly appreciates the worth as an ally of a properly harnessed public government. The protections afforded by the laws of incorporation, the right of patent, and the uses of the courts to hound competitors, federal experimentation and statistical services, geological surveys, tax privileges and subsidies that shift risk taking, access to public lands, the conservation machinery, and diplomatic and military support to maintain a climate conducive for private ventures are all fully, if guardedly, welcomed and promoted. Classroom and popular debates may focus on the virtues and liabilities of big government. To sophisticated industry leaders, the more meaningful question is "whose government?"

From their own immediate experiences, they know that big government is an inevitable consequence of industrialism. In no industry has the corporation gone further in developing the internal controls for operating its complex economic and technical machinery. And it has recognized that the submerging of corporate rivalry through trade associations and more subtle systems of coordination provide one answer to the growing challenge of a publicly determined order. Further to defend its interests and objectives, oil has ranged far beyond the economic boundaries of these organizational activities. It has learned to operate within the entire spectrum of the political processes of the society, reaching out to mold law, the bureaucracies, political machinery, and public opinion.

The industry has understood the need of government for direction. It has also understood that in the absence of public planning and control, day-to-day decisions readily constitute policy. Oil has sought to establish a privately intimate relationship with the administrative processes of government. A first tenet here, expressed in a wartime policy statement by industry representatives serving within the government, requires that "the American petroleum industry should be admitted more fully into the policy councils of the Government of the United States. . . ." [3] The object is sometimes neutralization; the practice is often a marriage of interests; and the consequence too frequently becomes the corrosion or disappearance of distinct and genuine public policy. The story of oilmen in government, then, involves the clash and convergence of two parallel developments of twentieth century America—industrial self-government and positive, popular democracy.

War and the preparation for war have been the catalytic agents in the merger of the public and private governments. The teamwork of the separate corporations during World War I was encouraged by a government anxious to mobilize all its resources. It prepared the groundwork for more permanent structures within and outside the federal government. A National Petroleum War Service Committee had been organized under the formal sponsorship of the then existing Oil Division of the United States Fuel Administration. Its members were major oil-company presidents and it was directed by A. C. Bedford, chairman of the board of Standard Oil (New Jersey). Assured of protection from subsequent antitrust litigation, this committee served as a liaison between the government and the oil corporations, helping to develop and supervise plans for supplying oil necessary for the war. In all these efforts care was taken to maintain the market percentages and power of the key companies. With the fighting over and the wartime agencies about to disband, the oil companies sought ways to continue their joint association outside the governmental frame.

The American Petroleum Institute was a direct outgrowth of this concern. It was founded in 1919, once again under the guidance of Jersey officials. The members of the National Petroleum War Service Committee, the organizers of the API, became the board of directors of the new trade association. Seeking to embrace the entire industry, it was oil's contribution to the general associational movement characteristic of American capitalism at this period.

The American Petroleum Institute was to be a forum for reconciling conflicts within the industry, developing standardized parts and tools, codes of trade practices in production and marketing, and agreements on taxes and overseas exploration. With some of the hazards of competition thus under control, it was hoped that oil could then speak with one voice in Washington and in the countryside, better able to resist government interference and encourage public support for industry positions. Hostility to antitrust action and a desire for general cooperation within the industry were the immediate agenda items. As oil's central problem shifted from a fear of scarcity to a fear of plenty, much of the API's energies soon became focused on the recurring question of balancing supply and demand. During the twenties, the institute took the lead in oil-conservation movements and was instrumental in the setting up of the Federal Oil Conservation Board. API representatives joined forces with public officials to formulate proposals for limiting production. Meanwhile, major oil company executives were accepted as the counselors of diplomats in the international quest for oil.

But it was not until the great depression that the petroleum industry was able once more to gain full entry into the councils of the American Government. By this time the leading American corporations were international organizations skilled in the arts of government. They had acquired an appreciation of the worth in profits and stability of planning on an integrated basis. Some of the New

Dealers were receptive to a planned approach to meet the national economic chaos. They had been influenced earlier by such strains as Thorstein Veblen, Karl Marx, the new nationalism of Herbert Croly as well as by advanced capitalist behavior. Now the depression with its bottomless misery brought sharply into focus their intellectual questioning of the adequacy of the national faith in competition and small business, of the popular and unqualified hostility to bigness and to organization. "Our legislative, administrative and judicial efforts to enforce the principles of the antitrust laws have been a deceitful failure and a continuing public injury for 45 years," Donald R. Richberg, general counsel for the National Recovery Administration, was to proclaim after two years of the Blue Eagle codes:

I say it is a deceitful failure because it has always held out to the American people, to the American consumer, protection from combinations in restraint of trade and combinations to fix artificial prices, and as a matter of fact very little of such protection has ever been given to the consumer, while at the same time there have been put upon necessary cooperation in business, artificial brakes to prevent as a matter of fact the best interests of all concerned, of the producer, labor and the consumer, from being carried forward by cooperative action.[4]

Liberal democracy in 1933 was about to intervene in a range of heretofore private areas, providing a major test of the capacity of government to govern for public ends. In inviting the participation of oilmen and other business leaders, many of the New Dealers also wondered whether they had any choice—if they would be able to guide corporate power if they did not work with it.

The NRA codes were designed to invigorate a sick economy. Faith in the healing qualities of time and of the "free play of a self-regulating market" gave way to government controls over production, wages, working conditions, and prices. The NRA petroleum code was developed under the close supervision of the industry and the American Petroleum Institute. Responsibility for its administration was vested in the Secretary of the Interior, rather than in the National Recovery Administration, and in a Petroleum Administration Board. Working directly with this government body was a Planning and Coordination Committee and a host of subcommittees that reached into the various branches of the industry and regions of the country. These were staffed with industry personnel. The original central committee's membership was the same as the executive committee of oilmen at the Chicago convention that had worked on the code proposals under API leadership. Among the members were the presidents of Socony-Vacuum, Jersey Standard, Indiana Standard, Standard of California, The Texas Company, the API, and a number of independents. There was one substitution. Both Ickes and President Roosevelt agreed that Harry F. Sinclair, a central figure in the Teapot Dome scandal of the twenties, would not be an appropriate choice.

To protect a "public" point of view, there sat with the Planning and Coordination Committee three nonvoting members from the NRA and Mr. Ickes. Two of the three, Michael L. Benedum and James A. Moffett, were long identified with the oil business (and the Democratic party). Moffett had been vice president of Standard Oil (New Jersey) and then occupied a similar position with Standard of California. Donald R. Richberg, the third representative, was later to represent the major oil interests in their political fight against the Mexican expropriation, and his law firm served as Washington counsel for Standard of California. The three played minor roles and their attendance was infrequent. Meanwhile, there was considerable friction between the Petroleum Administration Board and the committee. The authority of the former was often circumvented or undercut by the industry-controlled committees. At one point, the industry pushed in Congress for a separate five-man government committee of oilmen to handle government activities relating to oil —without providing any public control over the industry. Secretary of the Interior Ickes saw this as a plot to by-pass his office and to abdicate all government responsibility. "In my opinion Federal oil control is bound to come and the big oil interests will be well served when the day comes if they should have an ineffective commission of five already in existence." [5]

During the life of the NRA the industry was ruled by an industry committee armed with delegated government authority. The committee's deliberations were closed, and the financing came from the major oil interests. There was less need now to run continually to Washington on each issue of public policy that might affect the industry. Big oil had arrived in government on an official basis. Independents were to complain repeatedly that they were being regulated and judged by their giant competitors who, as government servants, were now gaining vital competitive information, fixing production and refining quotas, and generally implementing trade practices that limited competition.

The NRA codes helped bring some order to a sprawling and distressed industry. But it was a private order. There was little place in what purported to be self-government for any effective representation of workers, consumers, and of broader public considerations. In declaring the NRA unconstitutional, the Supreme Court expressed alarm beyond the fact that trade groups were being endowed with privileges or immunities to cooperate in ending defined unfair trade practices. What was at stake in the codes was a sweeping grant permitting the coercive exercise of the lawmaking power for broad industrial planning by business and for business, without standards prescribed by Congress. "If that conception shall prevail," warned Justice Cardozo in a concurring opinion, "anything that Congress may do within the limits of the commerce clause for the betterment of business may be done by the President upon the recommendation of a trade association by calling it a code. This is delegation running riot." [6] The court seemed primarily concerned with the "unconfined and vagrant" legislative power delegated to the President. But the economic power reality could not be ignored. As the Darrow Board earlier had concluded in its general review for President Roosevelt of the workings of the NRA, "privilege has exerted itself to gather more privilege." [7]

The demise of the NRA did not find the industry unprepared. Harold Ickes had been sympathetic to the need for conservation and to the value of dealing with big responsible corporate units rather than with marginal producers intent on a quick recouping of their investments. (Some of the East Texas oilmen had found it profitable to violate the "hot oil" restrictions. Ickes reported that Vice President Garner, a Texan, advised him to go after them with a club—"We couldn't appeal to the consciences of those oil people because they didn't have any.") [8] But the Secretary was not a friend of unregulated private power. Nor did he interpret the recovery program as an invitation for the government to abdicate its responsibility over natural resources. The oilmen were always fearful of attempts to extend federal control over oil in unwelcomed directions. Antitrust action was still one of the popular rallying points for liberals, and there were those among the New Dealers who strongly, if not consistently, threatened its use. Then too, the specter of a public utility status was always on the horizon. And so oilmen moved away from some of their liberal Democratic associations, preferring again the more pliant powers over production available in the states. But the industry retained the valuable statistical services of the Bureau of Mines and the federal police power prohibiting the interstate and foreign shipment of "hot oil" produced in violation of state production quotas. It intensified its associational efforts through the American Petroleum Institute and many other regional and functional organizations, seeking to perpetuate privately (at one point it unsuccessfully sought Federal Trade Commission approval) the trade practices introduced under the Petroleum Code.

World War II brought the formal and apparently permanent return of the industry to the inner structure of the American Government. This was a global war, and the planes, ships and tanks that dominated it demanded fueling and lubrication at an almost insatiable rate. No nation could martial the production and transportation on the scale demanded—the United States was to provide 6 billion barrels of petroleum before the war ended—and expect the oil supply to be taken care of by chance, by the private choices of individual oil corporations operating in a presumably free market, or by governmental authority diffused among numerous state and federal bureaucracies.

In May 1941 President Roosevelt designated his indefatigable Secretary of the Interior as Petroleum Coordinator for National Defense. (The agency was soon to be called the Office of the Petroleum Coordinator for War and then the Petroleum Administration for War.) Ickes's assignment was to organize for maximum efficiency the development and utilization of petroleum resources and facilities to meet military and civilian needs. Ickes had been watching from "a back-water," it mournfully seemed to him, as the center of national excitement and presidential interest moved away from New Deal reforms and toward the preparedness program. The general public had rarely shown appreciation of his zealous stewardship of the public domain. Now he would have liked to be Secretary of War. But the logistics involved in becoming the "arsenal of democracy" offered a real challenge.

What began as a data-gathering and coordinating office, charged with making recommendations to the industry and to government agencies, was to develop into one of the most important independent wartime agencies, formulating basic petroleum policy and reporting directly to the White House. Responsibility relating to oil had been diffused through thirty federal agencies, ranging from the Maritime Commission, which supervised tanker utilization, and the armed services, which formulated their military requirements, to the Office of Price Administration governing pricing and supplies, and the Office of Production Management, whose Petroleum Unit had been handling such areas as certificates of necessity and materials priorities. An immediate objective of the new agency was to consolidate available knowledge and, wherever possible, all governmental oil activities. As the official history of the Petroleum Administration for War (PAW), a federal document prepared by oilmen in government and financed in part by the industry, explained, "centralized planning and direction were inevitable. . . . Unlimited and undirected competitive activity could not be relied upon to assure the necessary result." [9]

Industry leaders watched these preliminary actions with suspicion. The country was not yet at war. As the president of the American Petroleum Institute put it, Ickes's appointment "was viewed with alarm as the possible beginning of another drive for Federal control." In Ickes's own account of his first meeting with the heads of the oil companies in quest of their participation in the defense planning, he recalled that "it may have been my imagination, but I thought, as I entered the room, that someone quickly but deftly frisked me for concealed weapons. . . ."

After all it was not to be wondered at that the oil men had their fingers crossed when our meeting was called to order. . . . Didn't I look with suspicion on anyone who made a profit? Didn't I believe that Government should rule business with a blacksnake? Wasn't I the "so-and-so" who had tried to take over the oil industry back in 1934? And, finally, hadn't I aspired to be an Oil Czar?

Nor were they reassured by the stern words of his deputy, oilman Ralph K. Davies:

No matter how patriotic and unselfish the component interests and groups within the industry, it is clear that as separate and competing units they cannot act cooperatively, independent of Government direction.

Government and industry here have a common undertaking. Neither one can act effectively by itself. The demand is for teamwork of the highest order.[10]

A first demand in return for the cooperation requested by the government was clearance from antitrust prosecution for all joint advice to be given and actions to be taken by the oil companies in behalf of the national defense. The oilmen also insisted that the government suspend all pending litigation against the industry, including the pipeline rebate case. Assistant Attorney General Thurman W. Arnold reported that "they felt that it was impossible to participate in national defense as long as this suit was hanging over them." This was settled, and "in the confused and hurried situation we thought it was worthwhile to waive" the colossal and probably uncollectable triple damage liability of $2 billion originally involved.[11]

The oilmen received the general assurance that business compliance with public preparedness plans would not be viewed as violations of antitrust laws. Industry groups serving within the federal bureaucracy would be regarded as advisory and responsibility for any actions would be taken by the government after general consultation with the Department of Justice. (As the war progressed, clearance by the War Production Board became sufficient.) The Attorney General promised that Justice Department negotiations concerning current or future antitrust actions would first be checked with the Petroleum Administrator to see whether in his judgment such steps would impede the oil program. As for Ickes, he had come to the conclusion that the oil industry should be "run on the principle of conservation and not directed by a policeman in the form of the Sherman Antitrust Act." He felt that oilmen would accept some federal conservation policy in return for an amendment taking the industry out from under the Sherman Act's jurisdiction. "Moreover, it occurs to me that businessmen generally might be in favor of such a bill . . . because they would regard it as an opening wedge which might result in the amendment or repeal of the antitrust act." [12]

All the Petroleum Administration's work was to be done in closest collaboration with the industry. To this end, the agency was structured along lines paralleling the principal divisions of an integrated oil company. One of Ickes's first moves was to appoint as his deputy Ralph K. Davies who was executive vice president of Standard Oil of California. Under President Roosevelt's order, the full authority possessed by Mr. Ickes could be—and was—delegated to his deputy who took the lead in building the staff. Personnel were recruited chiefly from oil companies, with approximately 75 per cent of the executive and technical staff coming from the industry or closely allied fields. Less than 10 per cent were professional civil servants from elsewhere in the government. For example, H. Chandler Ide, Davies's executive assistant, was brought in from the California company. The chief counsel was J. Howard Marshall, who had been employed by the same company and then became a partner in the firm of its attorneys, Pillsbury, Madison and Sutro. He later was an executive of Ashland Oil and then Signal Oil. S. P. Coleman and Howard W. Page, both from Standard Oil (New Jersey), were the PAW program directors, responsible for integrating long-range plans for meeting the world-wide petroleum requirements of the United States and its Allies. James Terry Duce, active in oil's government relations and vice president of the Arabian American Oil Company, became director of the Foreign Division. The president of Standard-Vacuum, the vast overseas subsidiary jointly controlled by Jersey and Socony, was sent to London as petroleum representative. The oilmen in government generally became full-time public officials, with the differences between their government incomes and their previous salaries taken care of by the private employers.

Fundamental to the entire partnership concept was the creation of an industry committee structure to work with the Petroleum Administration. It was assumed this would mobilize the maximum voluntary support while keeping to a minimum a permanent bureaucracy. At the base of this system were five general district committees, one for each of the regions into which the United States had been divided under the PAW. Each of these districts had a cluster of functional committees, including production, supply, and transportation, refining, distribution, and marketing, and natural gas. There were also numerous subcommittees. The chairmen of the functional committees served on the general committee of the district. Committee members were generally oilmen nominated by the industry. A refining committee, for example, was composed mainly of the heads of refining departments. The official policy viewed them as representing the industry rather than their individual companies or trade associations.

At the national apex of the organization was a Petroleum Industry Council for National Defense, later to be known as the Petroleum Industry War Council (PIWC). This was established some months after the district committees were in operation at the urging of some of the oilmen. They claimed that the unwieldiness of the district setup could be diminished if Ickes could deal directly and centrally with the top oil executives who had the authority within their corporations to get things done quickly. This was to be a representative and responsible industry forum for formulating over-all oil policy, advising the Petroleum Administration, and carrying out any functions assigned to it by the agency. It had a great many subcommittees, including national functional committees. There was also a Foreign Operations Committee, with its own regional and functional subcommittees, to advise the PAW in formulating and administering overseas oil programs. Given the limited staff of the PAW here, many international activities relating to production and distribution were actually carried on by the industry committees that worked with British government and corporate offices.

Again the membership of these national bodies came from the industry. The original nine members of the Foreign Operations Committee were international oil-company executives, and a working relationship was established with British representatives from Anglo-Iranian and Shell. Forty of the originally chosen sixty-six members of the Petroleum Council for National Defense were major oil-company executives and thirteen were oil trade association presidents. Most of them were directors of the American Petroleum Institute, and a third were on the association's executive committee. At one point in the life of the PIWC, thirty-nine had been or were involved in federal antitrust cases, with thirty-six of them having drawn fines. William R. Boyd, Jr., president of the API, was elected chairman of the council, and his staff was also drawn from oil trade associations. By the end of the war, over three thousand oilmen had served on the many industry committees, the majority of them coming from the integrated companies. They received no compensation from the government, and the general staffing and expenses were also provided for by the industry, with the major companies making the greatest contributions. (The East Coast district committee, the largest operation, at one time had a full-time staff of 176 employees.) To avoid legal difficulties in assessing the member companies, industry lawyers had requested the PAW to recommend to the Attorney General the approval of this practice.[13]

An industry advisory system was thus built into the governmental apparatus. At every major point, from the district up to Washington, it paralleled the Petroleum Administration, which in turn was staffed by oilmen temporarily serving as paid government employees. Every policy and administrative decision fell under the scrutiny of the industry. And the PAW had much to give and much to deny to the corporations. It was authorized to regulate the entire petroleum industry from production to usage, although voluntary compliance rather than legal enforcement was its preferred approach. It set production targets. It was the claimant agency for the industry for obtaining and then allocating preference ratings for critical materials for domestic and overseas operations. The PAW took over the review of certificates of necessity for rapid amortization of new plants and equipment. It initiated and administered government financing programs for expanding productive capacity and pipelines. It was the government spokesman for the industry on petroleum pricing recommendations to the Office of Price Administration. It negotiated with the Office of Defense Transportation, the United States Maritime Commission, and the Tanker Control Board regarding tanker car and shipping allocations. Through a range of interagency committees, the PAW had direct access to the chief executives of virtually every key government office, from the Reconstruction Finance Corporation to the State Department, dealing with civilian and military affairs ranging from patent exchanges to manpower. Petroleum attachés, selected from the industry by the Petroleum Administration and employed by the State Department, were assigned to American embassies and missions in London, Paris, Moscow, Cairo, Chungking, Caracas, and elsewhere. Committees of the PIWC worked on foreign supply and European postwar petroleum planning. Another committee was responsible for planning the disposal of government facilities. The PAW sanctioned the limiting of competitive practices that the oil giants themselves privately had long regarded as wasteful. It became the instrument for pushing a conservation program in California favored by the majors and resisted by independent producers who heretofore had been successful in blocking state legislation in this direction. It developed a nation-wide statistics-gathering service on supply and demand. This operation is always at the heart of a private control system and is always a target of trustbusting suspicions. For example, the government's classic 1909 brief against the Standard Oil empire described a secret statistical department. Through it the trust had maintained a national espionage system, complete with private detectives and bribery, for gathering information on the shipments and sales of competitors. The PAW was in a position to ensure that war exigencies and allocations would not upset the historic patterns of markets so carefully worked out in the United States and abroad by the private government of oil.

There was another attraction to the arrangement. Thoughtful business leaders were mindful of the industry's poor public relations, thanks in part to the disclosures of Jersey Standard's tieups with I. G. Farben. Given the temper of prevailing oil criticisms and the subsequent panic occasioned by Pearl Harbor, an alternative to this partnership might well have been to turn petroleum affairs over to a more general war agency or even to the military. Remaining in the background, with the PAW shouldering the official responsibility for the advisory decisions of the PIWC and other oil committees, was shrewd business statesmanship.

Oilmen were also entrenched in Washington wherever there were decisions to be made affecting the industry. For example, Max W. Thornburg, vice president of Bahrein Petroleum Company (owned by The Texas Company and Standard of California), served as petroleum adviser to the State Department. Documents in the possession of the Truman committee, which investigated the national defense program, disclosed that Mr. Thornburg, who was drawing $8,000 from the government and $29,000 from the companies, never lost his concern over the position of the major companies in the Middle East. He worked for the involvement of the United States in Saudi Arabia and for the financial backing of Ibn Saud preparatory to the famous lend-lease arrangements discussed earlier. A letter to Reginald Stoner, a vice president of Standard of California, written in 1941 on the stationery of the State Department, illustrated how Mr. Thornburg kept his private employers well posted:

. . . The approach of large-scale operations in the Near East will—in the reasonably near future—provide ample grounds for the matter of our support to be raised through *purely political channels*—for example, via Kirk in Cairo. [Alexander Kirk was the U.S. Ambassador.] I know that he strongly favors such support, quite apart from oil company interests. Then when Kirk's request hits this Dept.—in the Near East Division which also strongly supports the idea of backing Ibn Saud—it would be passed through various other divisions which have a say in matters of this kind and then start on up the line.

Both Ickes and Davies viewed his activities with distaste, feeling that his major preoccupation was protecting the interests of the integrated companies and maneuvering to get the expropriated oil firms back into Mexico.[14]

Thornburg's successor in the State Department was Charles B. Rayner of Socony-Vacuum. Among those serving on the Foreign Petroleum Operating Board of the Board of Economic Warfare were the presidents of Gulf, Socony, Standard of California, Standard (New Jersey), Texas, and Amerada. B. Brewster Jennings, then senior vice president of Socony, was deputy administrator for tanker operations in the War Shipping Administration. Robert E. Wilson, later to be chairman of the board of Standard (Indiana), headed a number of mobilization activities, including the short-lived Petroleum Unit in the Office of Production Management that was responsible for approving certificates of necessity until the function was transferred to the Petroleum Administration. Oil executives and technicians were generally found in the various petroleum procurement and logistics offices of the military. For example, Rear Admiral Andrew F. Carter, who worked with a number of concerns and then became head of a Caltex shipping subsidiary after his wartime tour of duty, was executive officer of the Army-Navy Petroleum Board of the Joint Chiefs of Staff.

Where there were struggles for competitive advantage among the companies, these apparently carried over into the federal bureaucracy. For example, J. H. Pew of Sun Oil complained to Ickes that the Rubber Reserve Company was "honeycombed with experts who represent Standard Oil of New Jersey and other companies of the opposition." [15] The latter—including Texas, Shell, Standard (Indiana), Continental, Universal Oil Products, and Kellogg—were strenuously advocating that the government adopt their method of making synthetic rubber, while opposing the necessary priorities for the Houdry process in which Sun, Standard of California, Socony, Tidewater, Gulf, and Sinclair had an interest.

The official history of the Petroleum Administration for Defense records that this unique experiment was successful in enlisting the services of a "highly competitive" and "strongly individualistic" industry:

In considering this teamwork, it is frequently difficult to distinguish between the activities of the PAW on the one hand, and the industry on the other. So closely and continuously did they work together, that it is often all but impossible to say where one left off and the other began, or even which one did begin and which one finished.

Petroleum Administrator Ickes told the API in 1945 that each partner had kept faith with the other and together the two had "also kept faith with America." If the industry had been doubtful and offered resistance at points—the *History of the Petroleum Administration for War* does not discuss either doubt or resistance on the part of nonoil officials—"eventually, as the advantages of the partnership became clearly apparent, the viewpoint of the industry became almost unanimously one of enthusiastic and wholehearted endorsement." [16]

The oilmen generally did cooperate, and the PAW was greatly admired in Washington for its efficient organization. The United Nations was supplied with the needed oil. This was recognizable as an astonishing performance, even without the steady stream of self-congratulatory public relations releases from the industry, paid for by the taxpayer in cost-plus contracts, describing their war contributions (along with patriotic pleas to consume less). The record of the PAW earned the commendation from the Army-Navy Petroleum

Board that "at no time did the Services lack for oil" and that "no Government agency and no branch of American industry achieved a prouder war record." [17]

But a democratic society must add other criteria to this evaluation, even in wartime. The oilmen sought and generally received their price for this patriotism, whether it was full consultation prior to any government action or antitrust immunity. They were careful that the mobilization expansion would maintain their existing and postwar controls over every aspect of the industry, from supply and demand to the location of pipelines and the licensing of patents. A Senate staff study noted that membership on the foreign operating committees included individuals and the companies who had participated in the famous "As Is" marketing arrangements initiated in 1928. "In practice the principles of the 'As Is' agreement were recognized in the schedules of distribution and allocation schedules which were worked out for every country in the world." [18]

Frequently, the committees performed essentially administrative and policy-making functions, despite the fiction of their advisory nature. When Secretary of the Interior Oscar Chapman moved to recreate this setup at the time of Korea, the Acting Attorney General wrote him of the concern of the Justice Department over such intermingling of governmental duties with those of the industry advisory committees under the PAW. "It is clear to us that during the operations of the committee system fundamental questions of basic policy were initially resolved by these committees and that resulting government action amounted to no more than giving effect to decisions already made by such committees." [19] (Mr. Chapman was "shocked and surprised" at these criticisms and rejected the proffered warnings.) The PAW and the Petroleum Industry War Council constantly fought for increased delegation of authority from such groups as the War Production Board, with the oilmen aiming for a completely independent agency with full power over oil matters. Meanwhile, the PIWC and Chairman Boyd continued to press for even more broadened antitrust immunity, with final authorization for review resting in the Interior rather than in the Justice Department.

When the rest of the war government wanted to deal with oil questions or with the industry, "proper channels" meant dealing with the committees. When oil people or other citizen groups had problems or complaints relating to petroleum or to the functioning of the PAW, they frequently were referred by the PAW to the appropriate advisory committee. This was a source of frustration to smaller businessmen who often felt discriminated against by the workings of the PAW and by war needs which integrated companies seemed better designed to serve. Those who went to the Justice Department over inequality in treatment were often berated by the advisory committees, who by virtue of their economic and political positions held effective power over their business lives, for this disloyalty to the industry.

Defenders of the decision to bring the industry within the framework of public government insisted that the essentially technical nature of the skills involved, together with the consciences of the individuals and the goldfish-bowl operation of public agencies, kept the oilmen's first loyalty to the national interest. Without doubt, many of the men served intelligently, with dedication and even sacrifice. They resented the stereotype of themselves as creatures of "big oil." Regardless of motives and personal integrity, however, the oilmen came out of a business background with its own rules and standards of conduct. It could never be easy or natural to shed lifetime attitudes and associations. And their futures were with oil, not public service. There remained substantial ground for concern as to whether industry men were protecting corporate profits, the "free enterprise" system, or public interests. Few men were more sensitive to this question than Harold L. Ickes and his aide Ralph K. Davies.

It seemed paradoxical that it was Ickes who accepted and developed this pattern of oilmen in government. No figure in Washington had a more secure reputation as an honest and outspoken public servant. He was fully conscious of the strategic nature of the Interior Department in its guardianship over natural resources and of the pressures and scandals in which it had been involved in the past. An entry in his diary in 1933, his first year as Secretary, describes a first meeting with Harry F. Sinclair in Ickes's office. "I kept wondering whether the ghost of Albert Fall carrying a little black satchel might not emerge from one of the gloomy corners of this office." [20] Fall had been President Harding's Secretary of the Interior. He was sentenced to prison for receiving bribes from Sinclair and from Edward L. Doheny for secretly turning over to them leases on naval reserves at Teapot Dome and Elks Hill. In 1936 Ickes confided in his diary that "an honest and scrupulous man in the oil business is so rare as to rank as a museum piece." [21] He later likened dollar-a-year men serving on the War Production Board to crawling maggots looking out for their private interests.

To those who warned him about business capturing government under cover of the war emergency, Ickes offered the assurance that he had no illusions about oil. But he saw the partnership concept as a risk that had to be balanced against the need for competent men.

Mr. Davies and I both felt that the best way to handle the oil problem was to surround ourselves with men who understood it backwards as well as forwards.

The oil industry today is a highly technical, complex and delicately adjusted affair. . . . We require geologists, geophysicists, and paleontologists in the field; chemists, physicists, and engineers in the refinery; traffic experts, economists, analysts, and highly trained organizers and executives in transportation and distribution. Outside of the personnel of the industry itself there is but little understanding of the finely balanced and intricately interrelated mechanisms of the production, refining, transportation, and marketing of petroleum.

The Secretary further explained that, contrary to some public assumptions about his views, he believed in private enterprise and a minimum of government interference. And he was certain he could never get the "tough hombres" in oil to cooperate—who otherwise "would take the bit in their teeth and run away with it if given any chance"—unless they participated in policy-making.[22] This judgment paralleled Walton Hamilton's definition of the War Production Board "as a House of Delegates from American industry."

Ickes believed that the Interstate Oil Compact, so zealously championed by the oilmen, was window dressing rather than a genuine conservation measure. He resented the clandestine politicking over synthetic rubber and was outraged by the I. G. Farben-Jersey Standard disclosures. But he explained that if the United States did not avail itself of the corporate experts, it would have to do without. He was sympathetic to oil worker union requests for representation on the council. He knew, however, that the industry didn't want labor present, and told the union officials that they would be overwhelmingly outnumbered. Ickes deplored the 27½ per cent depletion allowance as "thoroughly unconscionable," but would not say so publicly lest this put him at cross purposes with the oil interests and make his assignment more difficult. (He hoped it would be stricken from the tax laws, but "if the Administration can't force the item out without me it would not be able to force it out with me.")

My job was to get oil when and where it was needed. . . . After I did that, nothing else mattered. I wasn't changing business habits or building up monopolies. I wasn't even trying to tear down monopolies, because that is not an executive function; it is a duty of Congress. I am not investing in new business enterprises; I am not digging new wells; I am not exploring for oil; I am simply in the position of a coordinator.[23]

At the same time, Ickes prided himself on his managerial talents, his toughness, his ability to deal with men of power, and his dedication to the common good. He insisted that he checked every appointment made to the PAW, and it was his boast that no oil company in the world had a finer technical staff. Throughout the life of the agency he denied that its policies were dominated by the big oil companies. After the war he was to resign from President Truman's Cabinet over the nomination of California oilman Edwin Pauley as Undersecretary of the Navy. It was Pauley who had recommended Ickes to President Roosevelt for the job of Petroleum Administrator. And Ickes in turn had advised the President he had two candidates for the post as his assistant—Pauley and Davies, with strong preference for the latter.

Ralph K. Davies, the central figure in the Petroleum Administration, was generally rated as able and public spirited. He enjoyed the full confidence of his chief.[24] He presided over the regular staff meetings and generally ran the agency. His wartime record and zeal hurt his relations with his own company, which at times balked at carrying out PAW suggestions. But Standard Oil of California continued to pay him $47,500 annually, the difference between his $10,000 government income and his former salary as a vice president. Relations were severed after the war, and Davies became active in a number of other oil operations, including heading the American Independent Oil Company that was to be somewhat of a trouble-maker for the majors at the time of the Iranian settlement. Oilmen more frequently reported their ability to get along with Ickes than with Davies. Joseph Dwyer, assistant to the chairman of the Petroleum Industry War Council, recalled that "Ickes made a wonderful Petroleum Administrator. The only thing we differed on was tidelands. We fought like hell with him up to 1941. But . . . you knew where you stood with him." It was Davies's conviction—and possibly his cross in relation to many of his erstwhile oil brethren —that four years of the PAW proved that "a faithful private servant can become a faithful public servant and a better public servant because he knows the business with which he deals." [25] A California company vice president later summed up the considerable wartime differences that developed between the Deputy Administrator and segments of the industry: "We once had a guy who wanted controls —Ralph Davies. He was socialist-minded." William R. Boyd, Jr., president of the American Petroleum Institute and Chairman of the Petroleum Industry War Council, had a different conclusion in reviewing the record of the PAW: "It was a lucky day for America when the oil industry fell into the hands of its arch-enemy, Harold Ickes." [26]

The war had afforded private and public officials a further glimpse of the benefits—and risks—in operating the industry as "one national oil barrel." Some of the coordinated activities carried within them the seeds of national planning. And it had been seen that oil could not be planned simply within national confines. Under the PAW important governmental beginnings had been made for an extension of this integration into the international oil trade, notably in the working arrangements with the British Government designed to ad-just rivalries over world petroleum development.

This approach represented nothing new to the leaders of the private government of oil. Their industry's history was an experi-ment with techniques for private order. Now war had dramatized the public qualities of this basic commodity and the full value of a coordinated industry. Never again could the American Government be casual or innocent about the functioning of the petroleum in-dustry. The rudiments of planning for war had made visible, if not entirely respectable, the benefits of planning for peace. Given the nature of Soviet-American relations with the indefinite and comprehensive mobilization which kept the United States a global military power, it was accepted by the industry that the pressures for public direction over this resource would grow.

Such planning inherently meant public controls. American business had learned earlier that when government moved to regulate private enterprise, once resistance was ineffective and the inevitable reached, the statesmanlike response was to seek to control or neutralize the process. Now that government was certain to recognize the necessity for permanent intervention, however fragmentary, a similar strategy had to be applied to any new challenge of public planning. From every aspect, as a defense against interference, as a protection against the liberal doctrine of antitrust, and as an aid to maintaining access to government power, the benefits of a partnership in planning were not lost upon the private government of oil. It was not the worth of planning, but rather planning for what, by and responsible to whom, that became the central questions. It was this lesson, learned more aptly by the petroleum industry than by public leaders, that was to govern the former's postwar political behavior.

The Petroleum Administration was liquidated shortly after the end of the war. Most of the emergency controls were abandoned and the industry advisory committees were dissolved. It was recommended that the government maintain a central coordinating agency for its dealings with petroleum, without, of course, any attempt to increase the scope of governmental authority. Out of this there developed the Oil and Gas Division, redesignated in 1955 as the Oil and Gas Office, within the Department of the Interior, which had had many oil responsibilities. Its principal duties have included supervising the Federal Petroleum Board which administers the "hot oil" act, advising the President, the Secretary of the Interior, and other federal offices on oil and gas matters, maintaining liaison with the industry and with such international bodies as NATO and the Organization for European Economic Cooperation, and planning for national emergencies. Ralph Davies served temporarily as its first head. He was soon succeeded by Max W. Ball, a petroleum consultant who had worked for Shell and other companies. In 1949

Hugh A. Stewart took over. Mr. Stewart had spent a lifetime in the business, had been president of the Rocky Mountain Oil and Gas Association, and was on pension from The Texas Company. He was replaced in 1958 by Matthew V. Carson, Jr., a naval officer from Texas who also directed the Voluntary Oil Import Program.

Many oilmen, as well as Ickes and Davies, urged that the government continue the spirit of the partnership concept with the industry established in the Petroleum Industry War Council and other advisory bodies. Cooperation with rather than control over the industry would mean strong support for the new agency. To the oilmen it would provide, in Mr. Davies's words, "their best assurance of continued independence and their best protection against governmental encroachment." [27]

With this understanding, the National Petroleum Council was created, its industry membership serving as an advisory and study body for the Secretary of the Interior. In addition, a Military Petroleum Advisory Board was to advise the Defense and Interior departments on petroleum matters bearing on military planning. Under the Defense Production Act of 1950, a Gas Industry Advisory Council was formed in 1951 to give guidance to the Secretary. Its sixty members usually have been the presidents or top executives of companies engaged in the production, transmission, and distribution of natural gas. A Foreign Petroleum Supply Committee was also established in 1951 to advise on foreign supply problems, with representation from the international companies. With somewhat different origins, a Public Lands Industry Committee was organized in 1954 to act as a go-between for the Interior Department and oil associations and corporations interested in legislative and administrative policies bearing on the leasing of federal lands. Its original membership included the presidents of the Rocky Mountain Oil and Gas and the North Dakota Oil and Gas associations, representatives of the Independent Petroleum Association of America, the Western and the New Mexico Oil and Gas associations, and Warwick Downing for the Interstate Oil Compact Commission. A network of advisory groups was thus built into the structure of the federal government on a permanent basis. Meanwhile, the American Petroleum Institute continued as the central private trade association.

At the first meeting of the National Petroleum Council in 1946,

Interior Secretary Julius A. Krug reassured the oil leaders that there was no intent to increase government power over them and that the Council could do "no greater good to the oil and gas industry than by educating people in the Government in the economies and the problems of the industry." He expressed the hope that "you men will help us with the staffing of our Oil and Gas Division to the end that we will get the kind of people who understand the problems of the industry and who know how to do a good job." [28]

The staff of the Oil and Gas Office has been kept very small and in 1957 operated on a budget of about $500,000. Its director, Hugh A. Stewart, explained that, excluding those administering the Connally "hot oil" act, his office had thirty-three full-time employees, less than half of whom were experienced executive or technical people. (Prior to the Korean war he had a total of six technicians.) Most of them came from the industry.

You may wonder how such a small group can be expected to effectively carry out the assignments. . . .
The secret of our success lies in Government and industry cooperation. . . .
Each year through advisory committees and personal contacts the Federal Government obtains thousands of man hours of invaluable assistance from hundreds of the outstanding leaders and technical experts in this industry. Thus we obtain the distilled knowledge which money could not purchase even though millions of dollars were added to our budget each year.[29]

Every action of the Interior Department—once characterized by Senator Robert M. La Follette, Sr., as the peacetime "sluiceway" for a large part of the corruption to which government is subjected —is closely watched. Discussions and decisions involving oil are quickly transmitted to industry circles and oil newsletters. One former Interior staff member recalled that when in 1949 the Secretary sent an inquiry about inperpetuity leases to the Director of Land Management, the next morning the former received telegrams from Denver, San Francisco, and elsewhere protesting any possible action that might follow. Spokesmen for the involved companies roared with indignation over the "sudden" release of the edited contents of the Federal Trade Commission staff report *The International*

Petroleum Cartel in 1951. They claimed this was a totalitarian tactic since they were given no warning or simultaneous chance to reply. Yet a classified draft of the report had circulated among officials of the State and Interior departments, including oilmen in government, for some time prior to its publication. And it will be recalled that oilmen were participants in the high-level decisions within the government against its publication.

Lines of communication within the Interior Department have always been closely guarded to guarantee oil's direct access to the ear of the Secretary, whether the incumbent has been Ickes, Krug, Oscar L. Chapman, Douglas McKay, or Fred A. Seaton. The oilmen have sought to discourage the creation of any intermediaries in the Secretary's office. This has provoked great resentment among the nucleus of men around the Secretary who have been critical of oil influence or resentful of such attempts to weaken or circumvent their own roles. They see the Secretaries, a strong one like Ickes as well as his much weaker successors, used frequently as fronts who sign the documents, testify before the Congress, and generally act as the chief administrative lobbyist within the federal system for the *de facto* government of oil. "I think our aims are the same," Secretary Chapman told the NPC in 1950 as they were planning for the Korean mobilization. "Our objective, the security of our country, all are the same. Whether you are working in Government or working in your oil interests. . . ."

I don't want to get in a position whereby the Commerce Department has made an allocation to the Interior Department, and then I have to referee the amount of steel for the claiming agents for all of these groups. I am going to put the heat on Commerce, not Interior. . . . I want the full force and effect of this industry to be felt at the right place in Government.[30]

At the second meeting of the National Petroleum Council in 1946, Secretary Krug admitted that some within the government felt that such advisory councils interfered with rather than helped the governmental process determine a public policy for oil. But he assured the assembled guardians that "if I find anyone in this Department sharing that view I will find some way to transfer them to some pleasant spot where maybe that view is more welcome than it is here." [31]

At the time of Korea the National Petroleum Council brought great pressure on Chapman and on the White House to have the recreated Petroleum Administration for Defense set up as an autonomous, vertically integrated body responsible for the full range of the oil industry. They insisted that it report directly to the Secretary, who was also the Administrator, rather than through department channels. Chapman promised the oilmen, who were uneasy over his building of a small staff of his own to ease the anxieties of some regular Interior aides, that not only did he need their suggestions as to the kind of organization that should be formed, but also, "I am going to invite some of you men in to do it." Jubal R. Parten, president of the Woodley Petroleum Company and introduced to the NPC by Mr. Chapman as his chief adviser in the establishment of the new PAD, then took the floor:

. . . I want the oil and gas men in this room to make up their minds that, before they leave Washington, they are going to come up with a concrete suggestion on who that Deputy Administrator is going to be, and after that, of course, the personnel problem will go on to several other levels. . . .

I hope that this council, Mr. Chairman, or if you see fit to delegate the responsibility to the committee on personnel, that that committee take the job seriously and get something done about it before you leave here today, because this organization, whatever you say it should be, in the final analysis, should be set up and set up now.

Hugh Stewart, the Director of the Oil and Gas Division, then spoke for the government of the United States.

Gentlemen, after everyone else has talked as fluently and effectively as you have heard so far today, there is very little left for me to say. I greatly appreciate the fact that the council is giving us advice on the type of organization, that the companies are going to furnish the men and that Mr. Parten and the Secretary will have assistance in selecting or drafting a deputy administrator.

In that connection, since I am more or less in the caliber of a sergeant —I have two corporals and four soldiers in my troop—I can assure you that we will do our level best to take care of the high points, the most urgent points, between now and the time you gentlemen get some reinforcements in here to take over.[32]

The Oil and Gas Division staff and functions, except for the administration of the "hot oil" act, were temporarily transferred to the Petroleum Administration for Defense. An NPC committee of oil executives, chiefly from the giant companies and chaired by W. Alton Jones of Cities Service, met immediately to arrange for the reinforcements requested. It was to supply the Interior Department with a steady stream of temporary personnel, an interesting contrast with other areas of government-business exchanges where the normal peacetime manpower flow tends to be from government to business, and where the level of ability of businessmen in government is often considerably lower. Of the nearly four hundred technicians, executives, and general consultants who served from 1950 to 1954 when the PAD was again abolished and its peacetime personnel and functions returned once more to the Oil and Gas Division, the overwhelming majority were readily identified with oil companies and related occupations.[33]

Bruce K. Brown, president of a Standard (Indiana) affiliate and former chairman of the Military Petroleum Advisory Board, was selected as the Deputy Administrator. The National Petroleum Council had established the principle of rotating in the key PAD posts top-level industry men, who generally served without compensation from the government (WOC). Brown was succeeded by J. Ed Warren, a Texas oil producer and former head of the Independent Petroleum Association of America. Soon after his tour of duty, Warren became vice president in charge of petroleum affairs for the National City Bank of New York. From there he moved into the executive ranks and then the presidency of Cities Service. The last Deputy was Joseph La Fortune, vice chairman of the board of the Warren Petroleum Corporation (the largest independent producer of natural gasoline, which in 1955 was taken over by Gulf), and a former president of the Natural Gasoline Association of America.

Like the PAW, its World War II predecessor, the new Petroleum Administration gained a reputation as one of the most efficient emergency agencies. There were clashes with some of the defense production staff in the Secretary's office and there was resentment over the easement of antitrust liability and over the vigor of Interior Department activities in obtaining controlled materials for the oil industry. A number of the oilmen were viewed as Washington lobbyists for their individual corporations. Deputy Administrator Brown recalled that continuous criticisms by some permanent government employees made it difficult to put the PAD program for accelerated tax amortization into effect and that they "fought it as much as they dared." [34]

The various trade journals, often closely linked to the industry, provide a good insight into the temper of this attitude of government as a private preserve. For example, an editorial in the influential *National Petroleum News* in 1950 labeled government employees as "the inside U.S. Enemy" who hampered mobilization efforts during World War II:

Oil as well as other big industries always will have to be ready to fight smearing attacks from the vicious and even just plain unintelligent bureaucrats and their supporters in Congress. Oil and other industries will be more on trial in any next war than in the last war . . . before a court of critics, if not downright enemies, with "spies" scattered liberally at jobs throughout industry's part of the war effort. . . . As in World War II, regulations for the most part will be drawn by men unfamiliar with a particular business or even any business. Among the volunteers to write these regulations will be the usual lot of unemployed or near-unemployed reformers, people who can easily get away from their present jobs, and others who can use to advantage the thousand or so dollars additional they may get over their present modest pay.

The solution offered was that the American Petroleum Institute, which had been the target of serious antitrust charges in the past, "should take up the task of supervising all personnel that had to do with petroleum supplies no matter in what government service, military or civilian, or in what land." [35]

The suggestion was not as farfetched as it might appear, in view of the relationship the trade association has with government agencies. While the National Petroleum Council does cut across the industry, generally more than half of the hundred-odd members are also directors of the API. In 1958 nearly two-thirds of the API's executive committee were NPC members. Most of the NPC members have been presidents of their companies and many have been registered lobbyists or trade-association officials. A majority of the original membership had been defendants or were convicted in federal antitrust suits.[36] And few, one would guess, have been unemployed or near unemployed. All offices and expenses incurred by the council and its members are paid for by the corporations and individuals involved. Contributions and expenses for the NPC are recognized by the Internal Revenue Bureau as ordinary and necessary business expenses, and hence deductible for federal income tax purposes.

The chairman of the National Petroleum Council has been an oilman rather than a full-time public servant as is customary in other industry advisory bodies serving the government. This dispensation was cleared through the White House. Periodic protests from the Antitrust Division of the Justice Department and compromise proposals for a government co-chairman have evoked the rejoinder from the chairman and the industry that compliance with this practice might mean the dissolution of the council. "If the National Petroleum Council is required to drop its 'industry pilot' and take on a full time government official as its 'scoutmaster,'" warned Bruce K. Brown, "it will be a sorry day for the government, a sorry day for the Council and a sorry day for the petroleum industry."[37] There were protracted negotiations, and the NPC refused to meet for over a year because of this issue. Early in 1959 the council accepted the head of the Oil and Gas Office as co-chairman. Agenda and committee appointments were to be subject to his approval and minutes made available to the federal government.

Walter S. Hallanan, president of the Plymouth Oil Company, has held the post of chairman since the NPC's formation. Plymouth has had offshore leases, and Hallanan served as chairman of the industry's Offshore Lessees Committee during the "tidelands" fight. Mr. Hallanan has also been Republican committeeman from West Virginia and a supporter of Robert Taft, Douglas MacArthur, and Joseph McCarthy. (The latter used a Plymouth plane on some of his speechmaking tours.) Hallanan feels that the maintenance of American business freedom rests more heavily on his industry—"the outstanding symbol" of competitive enterprise—than upon any other. Yet thanks to demagogues, socialists, communists, and others with sinister purpose, he has said, the idea is propagated that the oil industry is an enormous monopoly. Thus it has become a favorite whipping boy in Washington. And oil is a stepchild of the national economy caught by a "double standard of economic morality" that pillories it as a greedy price gouger, as when it seeks to break out of its "captive victim status" in the postwar inflationary spiral. Oil's critics are the "real reactionaries," and a first objective of corporate statesmanship is to fight those who seek government controls over the economy. "America has little to fear from its business giants, who have served the country so well, as compared with the very real and imminent peril that it faces from the giant of government." [38]

At its inception, the council indicated that it would not engage in trade-association activities, and requested antitrust immunity. It received permission from the Justice Department for the advisory and study assignments requested by the Secretary of the Interior, with the understanding that this would not imply the making of policy for the government and that the advisory committee would not become the exclusive channel in the industry for presenting oil views to the government.

NPC studies, made by industry experts, cover the entire range of national petroleum policy as well as many technical questions of common corporate concern. A 1953 *Report of the National Petroleum Council's Committee on the Use of Radio and Radar*, for example, presented the industry's case on this subject to the Interior Department. While the details were technical, it advised that "protection of the petroleum industry's stake in radio demands constant vigilance." The industry is the major industrial user of radio, radar, and television in every stage of operations, from geophysical exploration and offshore drilling to pipeline control. It has been an active claimant before the Federal Communications Commission for channels for its petroleum radio service. It has competed with other groups for private microwave permits. It has fought proposals for banning such private systems and replacing them by common carriers. It remembers that some oil industry communications facilities were closed down by wartime restriction during World War II, and the industry now insists that these are vital to national needs and not to be disturbed, with their control to remain in the hands of the corporations even during national emergencies. (Under civil defense regulations, radio facilities used by fire and police departments, along with those of certain basic utilities, enjoy such rights.) The NPC report recommended to the Secretary of the Interior that all radio matters of industry-wide concern "be left in the capable hands of the American Petroleum Institute's Central Committee on Radio Facilities," and advised all companies using radio to participate in the work of this API committee.[39] Eleven of the thirteen members of the NPC committee, including its chairman (from Shell), were also on the API committee. The chairman of the latter committees (from Humble) was on the NPC committee, and one of the two vice chairmen of the API body (from Standard of California) served in a similar capacity for the NPC advisory group. The secretary of the NPC committee was an attorney who has represented the industry in FCC hearings for new frequency allocations.

Similar patterns have existed in other studies. It will be recalled, for example, how a major Interior Department decision to abandon government support for research on oil from shale derived from an NPC committee report. That committee included the chief executives of the giant corporations and of the API.

A study, *Disaster Planning for the Oil and Gas Industries*, outlined steps for management to consider for continuing plant operations under and after attack. Concern was voiced over the possibility that civil defense authorities might lack an adequate background for appreciating the special character of the oil industry:

It is conceivable that in the immediate post-attack period, the municipal fire equipment might be assigned to fight fires in dwellings or stores while an essential oil or gas facility was being destroyed by fire.

To preclude this, the NPC committee, headed by the chairman of the board of Standard (Indiana), recommended that management encourage appropriate supervisory personnel to take an active part in such organizations at the state and local levels.[40]

The report also warned of "the thousands of intelligent, aggressively organized United States citizens who owe primary loyalty to the international Communist movement." It suggested criteria for plant and personnel security and urged companies to appoint corporate security committees and officers responsible for antiespionage and antisabotage measures. Passing along the advice of the National Industrial Conference Board, it explained that " '. . . even if you don't have a trained saboteur in hire, industrial security can pay off in peacetime. It can help you rid your plants of agitators who create labor unrest, who promote excessive grievances, slowdowns and strikes, and encourage worker antipathy toward management.' "

A companion manual prepared by a task force of the Petroleum Administration for Defense, and published by the NPC in 1955, amplified some of the disaster hazards and considerations. It also spelled out in great detail standards and procedures for conducting loyalty and security investigations of employees. Management was reminded that security clearance determinations must be made "in a manner consistent with traditional American concepts of justice and rights of citizenship." [41] But beliefs, associations, membership in organizations on the Attorney General's list, along with many of the vaguer categories of personal conduct so familiar to the federal loyalty and security programs, were all suggested criteria. And when there was doubt as to a security risk, "the doubt should be resolved in favor of security." Thus, with the blessing of the United States Government, the corporations and their associational arms take on functions and controls over individual citizens characteristic of the national state.

Defenders of the National Petroleum Council insist that it plays no part in politics or legislation in Washington and that it has nothing to do with congressmen or congressional hearings. Yet, as part of its self-assumed guardianship over the Oil and Gas Division, the NPC chairman has testified before a Senate Appropriations Subcommittee in support of funds for this Interior agency. An inter-office memorandum from Mr. Hallanan to the NPC secretary-treasurer, written in 1948, offers a further insight into the zeal with which the council guards its prerogatives:

It has been rumored rather persistently, here in Washington, that the National Resources Security Board [sic] is reaching for full power and control in its preparedness program. It is the impression of some that this agency seeks powers beyond those which were assigned to it by Congress. I have heard considerable criticism as to the philosophies of some of the recommended appointments.

You may have noted that the Armed Services Committee proposes that the President should immediately direct the National Security Resources Board to establish a commission composed of representatives of the major and independent oil men of the Nation, the consuming public and interested agencies of the Government, and instruct it to render a detailed, soundly based report on the Nation's oil problem, its function to be to present to the Congress at the earliest practicable date a fully rounded oil policy adequate to meet the Nation's present and long-range needs.

In another letter I am commenting more fully on this proposal but it occurs to me that it might be helpful, if you deem it advisable, to discuss with Mr. Arthur M. Hill (chairman of the NSRB) and Congressman Dewey Short your views on the petroleum situation.[42]

In the following year Secretary Krug was asked by a House committee for his views on proposed legislation that would establish a Petroleum Policy Council to develop and coordinate national policies on oil, with membership coming from a number of government agencies in addition to the Interior Department. Mr. Krug promptly turned to his industry advisers for their judgment. A committee of leading oilmen was appointed, and the subsequent council report urged the retention of the going partnership between the Oil and Gas Division and the National Petroleum Council. It deplored any further centralization of federal power and responsibility, and suggested that the Secretary recommend to the Congress that the proposed legislation not be enacted. The director of the Oil and Gas Division assured the oilmen that he concurred in the belief that the going relationship between the Interior Department and the NPC be continued. The Oil and Gas Division's functions should be primarily study, explanation, and persuasion.

We would lose effectiveness if we had any authority. We are not authorized to establish Federal policy with respect to oil and gas. We don't want authority to establish policy. All we need and all we want is the right to express our opinions, to offer advice to agencies within the Government, to exchange ideas freely with industry and thereby get voluntary coordination of thinking and activities.[43]

In 1949 the National Petroleum Council prepared for the Secretary of the Interior its version of "A National Oil Policy for the

United States." It made clear the group's interest in furthering private enterprise. The report followed the familiar industry positions in opposing governmental interference with the "free market," whether through synthetics development or natural gas regulation; in favoring a continued depletion allowance and related tax benefits; in insisting that the states should own resources beneath the sea to the outer edge of the continental shelf, and that American nationals should receive diplomatic help in gaining access to world oil supplies. A national oil policy "should operate to strengthen our free institutions by demanding that the issues which periodically arise in an industrial democracy, involving the relations of government and private industry, of state and individual, can be successfully resolved within our existing institutional framework. . . . No government actions specifically affecting the oil industry should be taken without proper regard for the long-term effect and without consultation with the industry." [44]

Comparable patterns have been developed wherever in the federal government there is a responsibility for oil. In the Defense Department, for example, Brigadier General W. W. White, the staff director of the Petroleum Logistics Division in 1954 and 1955, explained that "we build no empires here." General White, a former West Point regular Army-air general who had gone to work for Jersey Standard, was on a two-year tour of reserve active duty. (It is interesting to note that the American Petroleum Institute has encouraged its member companies to sponsor reserve-officer units among their employees. Most of them have been quartermaster outfits. Through the Military Petroleum Supply Agency, now under Navy jurisdiction, the Defense Department contracts for over $1 billion a year in petroleum purchases.) White remained on the pay roll of the Esso Export Corporation (which handled aviation and marine fuel purchases for the parent organization) and received the difference between his military salary and his salary as vice president. His office maintained what he viewed as a "close and cordial" liaison with the API and the oil companies. He pointed to his small government paid staff and observed that by having an industry Military Petroleum Advisory Board, "we in effect get working for us for gratis the companies' total employees and staff."

The Petroleum Logistics Division is a partial successor to the

petroleum committee of the former Munitions Board. It develops
for the Secretary of Defense and the National Security Council
petroleum mobilization and military data and policies, makes judgments for the Office of Defense Mobilization about tax amortization
grants, governs construction materials that may be in short supply,
and handles export controls. The Military Petroleum Advisory Board,
originally established in 1946, had replaced the Petroleum Administration for Defense after the Korean conflict in advising Interior,
Defense, and the Office of Defense Mobilization on top-level military oil and natural gas planning. Supporting it have been a range
of specialized advisory committees with over 250 industry members.
As in the case of the National Petroleum Council, the member
companies have paid the operating costs of the board. Its thirty-two
members, coming from Socony, Jersey, Texas, Standard of California,
Aramco, Sinclair, Gulf, Standard (Indiana), Cities Service, Sun, and
other oil and gas corporations, are nominated by the industry, appointed by the Secretary of the Interior, and cleared for security.
In an interview with the writer, General White refused to discuss
on the grounds of security the disposition of federally held Alaska
oil-reserve lands. Presumably there has been no question as to the
qualifications of the various oilmen who have sat on the board and
whose concern may have been more than academic. Many of their
companies have been quite interested in these lands. The chairman
of the MPAB has been W. W. Keeler, a vice president of Phillips
Oil. Phillips has had a stake in over a million acres in this area.
Former Interior Secretary Chapman has recalled that when Keeler
had been on loan to the Interior Department several years earlier,
he was an unusually persistent claimant for the rights of Phillips.
A former leading oil member of the Petroleum Administration has
described Phillips as a company that "would never do anything or
have any of its brass do anything which did not aid Phillips."

According to former Assistant Secretary of the Interior Felix E.
Wormser, this board "serves also to train industry personnel in the
ways of Government operation and to keep the group advised on
current problems so that an industry staff will be ready at all times
to step into the leading positions of an emergency oil agency, such
as PAW, or PAD. . . ." With little danger of overstatement, Mr.
Wormser was able to report to a Senate appropriations subcommittee

in 1955 that Interior's Oil and Gas Division "has established a most effective relationship with the oil and gas industry" whereby through the National Petroleum Council, Military Petroleum Advisory Board, Foreign Petroleum Supply Committee, and the Gas Industry Advisory Council, "the government is receiving the professional, scientific and economic thinking of the oil and gas industry on deliberations and problems that face us in discharging Federal oil and gas responsibilities." [45]

The Suez crisis of 1956 offered fresh data for an appreciation of how intimate this relationship had become and how dependent the government was upon the industry. The Defense Production Act of 1950 had authorized voluntary agreements among business groups for national defense objectives. These carried immunity from antitrust prosecution, subject to procedural approval by the Justice Department. At the time of the Iranian shutdown in 1951, a "Voluntary Agreement Relating to Foreign Supply of Petroleum to Friendly Foreign Nations" was approved. Under its provisions a Foreign Petroleum Supply Committee was created, dominated by the big five of the American international companies with Stewart P. Coleman, vice president and director of Jersey Standard, as chairman. Working with the Interior Department and the Office of Defense Mobilization—and its British counterpart, the Oil Supply Advisory Committee, headed by Sir William Fraser, chairman of the board of Anglo-Iranian—it replanned market and distribution allocations to compensate for the loss of oil from the rich Iranian fields. This cooperative action was handled with the usual sensitivity to the established relationships among the participating companies. With Iranian oil replaced from other sources, the Attorney General withdrew approval of the voluntary agreement—over the objections of the industry and the PAD. He noted the unusually broad powers the committee had enjoyed, including the gathering of information from competitors, the employment of a nongovernment staff, and the over-all direction of an industry chairman.[46]

Pressures from the industry and the PAD led to a new voluntary agreement in 1953 that provided on a long-run mobilization basis for statistics gathering and emergency planning for potential oil shortages in friendly nations by the Foreign Petroleum Supply Committee. Until August 1955 the "government" director of the voluntary agreement under which the committee functioned was an oil executive who was on leave from his position as managing director of one of the Caltex group, with his compensation coming from this subsidiary of Standard of California and the Texas companies. The director, Franz von Schilling, Jr., had the power to call meetings of the Foreign Petroleum Supply Committee, prepare the agenda, designate other government representatives who might attend, organize studies of petroleum supply and demand, and sit as the government representative at the advisory committee meetings. As the Assistant Attorney General commented, while there was "no indication of any wrongdoing whatever," Mr. Schilling "was put in the unseemly position of policing, directing and reporting on the activities of those very companies on which his immediate livelihood depended." [47]

After repeated criticisms from the Justice Department and the Congress, matched by intense resistance from the industry, provision was made for a full-time government chairman—Hugh A. Stewart, director of the Oil and Gas Office. All individual company statistics were required to be handled by government employees rather than exchanged among the committee members and their industry-appointed and -paid staff. (Forecasts relating to world oil supply and demand so easily become the basis for quota agreements.) The Attorney General reported to the Congress that Interior was gathering a permanent staff of full-time government employees for the new Washington office of the Foreign Petroleum Supply Agreement. "In the meantime, some of the staff formerly employed by the oil company members have been put on the Government payroll as full-time employees." [48]

The oilmen were unhappy over these restrictions on their control over public oil programs, as were their faithful friends in the Interior Department. Secretary Douglas McKay saw these as "emasculating" the defense value of the agreements:

The purpose of the proposal is obviously to convert the work of the committee into a Government operation. That work is of such a technical nature, requiring the skill and knowledge of only those actively engaged in foreign petroleum operations, that it would be practically impossible to acquire and maintain a staff of Government employees who would be qualified to procure and assess the information with the high degree of accuracy required by the Military.[49]

But the oilmen also anticipated the cold war as a permanent feature of national life and they foresaw genuine government planning as the more threatening alternative. Besides, they received an assurance that the government would continue to sanction plans for cooperative action in an emergency, although this apparently was not made clear to the Congress by the Attorney General.

In the summer of 1956 the Suez Canal Company was taken over by Egypt. The Foreign Petroleum Supply Committee met in New York to consider a plan of action to ensure overseas supplies in the event of a Suez blockade. The preliminary draft had been worked out by Mr. Stewart and the counsels of the major international companies who had been rounded up for this task at his suggestion by Stewart P. Coleman of Jersey Standard. The proposal ultimately adopted by the FPSC and approved by the government created a Middle East Emergency Committee to study foreign petroleum requirements and to recommend schedules for meeting these needs.

The new advisory MEEC had generally the same membership of senior oil statesmen from the international companies as its parent body. It included officials from Aramco, Caltex, Creole, Standard-Vacuum, Socony, Standard of California, Standard (New Jersey), Texas, Gulf, Sinclair, Venezuelan Petroleum, Cities Service, Tidewater, Getty, Frontier and American Independent. Three—Aramco, Caltex, and Standard-Vacuum—are jointly owned by other members. Aramco is owned by Jersey, Texas, Socony, and Standard of California; Caltex is owned by Texas and California; and Standard-Vacuum by Jersey and Socony. Creole is Jersey's subsidiary in Venezuela; Venezuelan Petroleum is controlled by Sinclair; and Tidewater is part of the Getty holdings.

Sun Oil, not a target of the world oil cartel charges, but engaged in international operations, was not asked to participate. Several of the smaller members had been added to counter criticisms that independents were being frozen out. M. H. Robineau, president of the Independent Refiners Association of America, had indicated that the interests of his associates were never considered in the planning of the majors on the MEEC. His position was strongly backed by Senator Joseph C. O'Mahoney of Wyoming, a leader in the Senate investigation of the oil lift, who felt that the private enterprise system would be safer with the presence of domestic oilmen on the MEEC. Mr. Robineau's company, Frontier Refining of Wyoming, was added to the advisory committee.

A series of American Independent Oil Company staff memoranda suggested that its officers did not feel their limited production in the Kuwait-Saudi Arabia Neutral Zone warranted full participation. But they were fearful that they might not be able to take care of their customers. "When I talked to Mr. Stewart in Washington about this," American Independent's representative reported to President Ralph K. Davies, "he said he fully appreciated our situation, that this was indeed the reason why I had suggested we become a member of the Middle East Emergency Committee, because as such a member, rather than looking in from the outside, we could perhaps help ourselves as things arose." [50]

This was an emergency, and as later explained, there was no time to create a government staff. The chairman of the new committee was Jersey's Stewart P. Coleman. (Coleman estimated that since the beginning of World War II, he had given between a quarter and a third of his working time to his government posts. These included serving as chairman of the Program Division of the Petroleum Administration for War that was responsible for long-range planning of world-wide petroleum requirements, chairman of the program panel of the Military Petroleum Advisory Board that had a comparable function, and chairman of the Foreign Petroleum Supply Committee.) The chairmen of the various subcommittees along with the staff personnel and the financing came from the industry. The director of the voluntary agreement under which the MEEC functioned and who sat in on all meetings as the full-time Interior employee supervising the agenda, was Ralph S. Fowler, a petroleum consultant who had worked for Aramco from the end of the war until the end of 1954 and had been brought into the government in the summer of 1956. (In 1958 he became Assistant Director of the Oil and Gas Office.) The tanker and supply subcommittees gathered data and prepared plans for the cooperative oil lift. Individual company production and capacity statistics were made available to all the members of the MEEC. In all these activities the MEEC worked closely with the British Oil Supply Advisory Committee (OSAC). This industry committee with representatives from the British international companies had maintained regular liaison with the Foreign Petroleum Supply Committee since 1951. The MEEC later coordinated its efforts with OSAC's successor—the Oil Emergency London Advisory Committee (OELAC)—an industry advisory committee established by the British, Dutch, and French governments and consisting of representatives from British Petroleum, Shell, and Compagnie Française des Pétroles. Once the MEEC was reactivated at the end of November 1956, a new European counterpart group was created to advise on the allocating of oil for Western Europe. This was the Petroleum Industry Emergency Group (OPEG), whose members from the same foreign companies served as "advisers" and agents for the Oil Committee of the seventeen-nation Organization for European Economic Cooperation.[51] It seemed apparent that the MEEC and the member companies were not being bound by the antitrust limitations presumed to govern the parent Foreign Supply Committee. Nor was concern evidenced over the fact that once more the American Government was encouraging the participation of the international companies in practices comparable to those which in the cartel suit charges were viewed as furthering their world-wide control over petroleum.

As seen in the previous chapter, there remains considerable doubt as to the degree of shortage and the success of the MEEC in meeting it. Targets and figures were shifted, at times with the intent to obscure, or as one Socony vice president explained, "sidestep" precise figures on crude oil availability in the United States Gulf area. And as also noted, the American Government was reluctant to allow the MEEC to go ahead with its full plans for supplying Europe until the Suez zone was evacuated by the French and British troops. The individual international oil companies handled the crisis on their own, redeploying considerable oil to Europe prior to receiving the go-ahead signal from President Eisenhower at the end of November for the voluntary implementation of the MEEC plans. The 1957 report of the Senate Subcommittee on Antitrust and Monopoly suggested that, given the industry's own profit incentives to ship oil to its European refineries and customers, "there was no clear showing that cooperative industry action requiring antitrust immunity was needed. . . ."

In a minority dissent, Senator Everett M. Dirksen defended the Eisenhower Administration and exonerated the oil companies. The MEEC operation "was the only logical solution. . . . It worked. The oil lift was a success. Europe's essential oil needs were met without any interference in oil supplies to United States consumers. To say some other plan might have been better is like saying a substitute would have been better after the regular player has just hit a game-winning home run." [52] Chairman Coleman of the MEEC called the Senate report, signed by Democratic Senators Estes Kefauver, Joseph C. O'Mahoney, and Matthew M. Neely, "politically inspired." And President Albert L. Nickerson of Socony deplored the sections on the industry written by the Senate Committee's staff —"people whose capabilities have never been scrutinized by the electorate." [53]

In the absence of careful public planning, adequate governmental supervision, and an over-all national fuel energy policy, a new episode in the recurring Middle East crises of the postwar world had been received with the familiar trained innocence and panic by government officials. Responsibility was quickly delegated to the oil industry. The government leaders involved repeatedly insisted that the Middle East Emergency Committee was voluntary and had no power of compulsion over anyone, not even its own members. Yet once more the private giving of advice and carrying out of "administrative detail" became, both by default and design, public policy making. A price rise, known in advance to the government, was permitted to go uncontested. Imports patterns, allocations, and exchanging of crude oil among the companies to lessen transportation costs, tanker pooling and pipeline rearrangements were handled in a way that guaranteed the international companies greater profits and maintained their marketing practices and relationships to one another. These further weakened the capacity of consumers or independents to challenge the market power of the private world government of oil—all under the friendly protection of federal antitrust immunity and obsequious public officials.

The utility of an integrated rather than a competitive approach had been accepted by the latter. But as one of the staff reports for the Senate investigation of the oil lift concluded, the record leaves an indelible impression that "this was a program conceived by the major oil companies and cast in the mold which fitted their interests." Meanwhile, the United States Government authorities, as explained by the Director of the Oil and Gas Office, had chosen to play the situation by ear.[54]

When in the summer of 1958 the government of Iraq was overthrown and British and American troops entered Lebanon and Jordan, the Secretary of the Interior called to the colors once more the same Foreign Petroleum Supply Committee to prepare the groundwork for a new Middle East Emergency Committee in case production as well as transportation for Europe's oil needs should be threatened this time. It was announced that at least one or two domestic companies would be added to the committee's roster, the chairman would be a full-time government employee, closer liaison would be maintained with other federal agencies, and the disputed provision in the plan for Suez that authorized cooperative action on oil movements *within* the United States would be eliminated. *New York Times* dispatches indicated that "as usual in arrangements of this sort, the antitrust question poses something of an obstacle." Some of the companies were said to be "seeking assurances that they will be immune from antitrust action for any new arrangements into which they might enter." [55] But the changes listed by the Interior Department "are not expected to alter the mode of operation" that prevailed during the Suez emergency. The troublesome problem for a democratic society remained: Who learns what from history?

11

Corporate Statesmanship and Public Policy

The permeability of oil has extended throughout the peacetime machinery of the federal bureaucracy. While both major parties have demonstrated an insensitivity to the consequences for public policy of such penetration, the frank business orientation of the Eisenhower regime allowed this shadow government its most substantial footing. The number of public officials with oil backgrounds or relations has been overwhelming. Such a list could begin with former Secretary of State John Foster Dulles. Until 1949 he was the senior member of Sullivan and Cromwell, the major law firm for the Jersey Standard empire, and involved in many international transactions and in German property cases in the United States. (It should be noted that Covington and Burling, the law firm of his predecessor, Dean Acheson, has also represented Jersey.) Herbert Hoover, Jr., a petroleum engineer and director of Union Oil whose major associations have been with oil, was the State Department's representative in the secret Iranian negotiations. He later became Undersecretary of State and was involved in questions of Middle Eastern policy and represented his Department in many of the top-level Suez arrangements. Winthrop W. Aldrich, head of the Chase Bank, which has long been tied to the Rockefeller and related oil interests, was sent to London in 1953 as United States ambassador. In addition to the general sympathy within the State Department for oil positions, there has also been an interchange of personnel with the industry. For example, William A. Eddy, former educator, OSS chief in North Africa and the first full-time United States resident minister to Saudi

Arabia, became a consultant to the Arabian American Oil Company, handling governmental and public relations. Harold B. Minor, once ambassador to Lebanon, became assistant to James Terry Duce, Aramco's vice president for government relations. Brigadier General Patrick J. Hurley has been an attorney for Sinclair and a special envoy to the Middle East. Henry F. Holland, former Assistant Secretary of State for Inter-American Affairs, has represented oil groups involved in Latin America.

Walter J. Levy, the first chief of the European Cooperation Administration's Petroleum Branch, was a petroleum consultant whose clients included Esso, Caltex, and Shell. He had also been on Averell Harriman's staff when the latter was sent by President Truman to seek a solution to the Iranian dispute. The oil industry has always watched reparations activities carefully. Several oilmen, including Edwin W. Pauley, J. Howard Marshall, and J. R. Parten, served on the Reparations Commission after World War II. James Forrestal, Secretary of the Navy and then first Secretary of Defense, had been head of the investment banking house of Dillon, Reed and Company which helped arrange corporate loans for Middle Eastern oil operations. John L. Sullivan, his successor as Secretary of the Navy, who as Assistant Secretary had handled oil matters for the Navy, has represented Gulf and was active in persuading President Truman against releasing the Federal Trade Commission's oil cartel report. In 1956 E. V. Murphree, president of Esso Research and Engineering and an adviser to the Atomic Energy Commission, was appointed to head the guided-missile program in the Defense Department. He was succeeded by a former research director for Socony Mobil. In 1957 Mr. Eisenhower nominated to the Defense Department, as Assistant Secretary for Research and Engineering, a retired executive on pension from Gulf. A retired vice president of Standard of California who had handled his company's negotiations with the Navy and the Congress over the Elk Hills naval reserve contracts became a special assistant to the Secretary. Military procurement officers frequently are civilians from the oil industry or Army and Navy personnel sent to petroleum indoctrination courses sponsored by several of the giant companies.

Robert B. Anderson, formerly Secretary of the Navy, Deputy Secretary of Defense, and appointed in 1957 Secretary of the Treasury to succeed George M. Humphrey, was a Texan who had been active in oil production. (Humphrey had headed and returned to M. A. Hanna and Company, whose sprawling industrial empire included oil holdings.) Anderson had been manager of the $300 million W. T. Waggoner estate with its extensive oil operations, a member of the National Petroleum Council, and a director of the American Petroleum Institute. He had been seriously considered for the presidency of the latter. As president of the Texas Mid-Continent Oil and Gas Association, he had testified before the Congress against reducing the depletion allowance. He saw this as cutting the ground from under wildcatting:

I think that I know almost every independent oil operator in Texas and a great many in other states of the Union. I know most of those who are engaged in the management of . . . the major companies. They are adventuresome people. . . . They represent to me something in the nature of the folks who were the pioneers of this republic. . . . I do not know why, but the oil industry has come to be thought of as a highly lucrative business.[1]

As Secretary of the Navy he was sympathetic to the opening up of federal lands in Alaska for private development. When Ralph Davies of the American Independent Oil Company went to Washington to protest the exclusiveness of the Iranian settlement and to request participation in the consortium, he was confronted by leading stockholders from his own company, State Department representatives, Secretary of the Treasury George Humphrey, and Robert Anderson.

Wherever there are consultants called in on national policy, the position and power of oil within the business community are sure to be recognized. When, in the face of insistent industry pleading, the decision was made in the closing days of the Truman Administration to drop the criminal indictment against the five American companies involved in the oil cartel case, the final judgment was made through the National Security Council. This supercabinet is the highest agency in the federal structure, operating in secrecy and reporting only to the President. It was designed to assist the President in formulating and integrating policy planning for American military, economic, and international security. Many of its decisions involve oil. Soon after taking office, President Eisenhower appointed seven consultants to the Council. They included the heads of Standard Oil (New Jersey), Monsanto Chemical (which is heavily involved in petrochemicals and now owns Lion Oil), and Pacific Gas and Electric. The latter company, whose president was James B. Black who was also a director of Shell, has ties with Standard of California and has been expanding its natural gas holdings.

In 1954 a special Cabinet Committee on Energy Supplies and Resources Policy was created by the President to evaluate "all factors pertaining to the continued development of energy supplies and resources fuels in the United States, with the aim of strengthening the national defense, providing orderly industrial growth, and assuring supplies for our expanding national economy in any future emergency." [2] The cabinet members were under the chairmanship of Arthur S. Flemming, director of the Office of Defense Mobilization. The research and findings were based on the work of a four-man task force that included Charles J. Potter, president of the Rochester and Pittsburgh Coal Company, and oilman J. Ed Warren, former president of the Independent Petroleum Association of America and then vice president in charge of petroleum affairs for the National City Bank of New York. Mr. Warren, later to become Cities Service president, was responsible for the oil and gas studies. Aiding him were a team of technical consultants, all of whom came from the ranks of the oil and gas industry. The six oil experts included the chief economist of Standard Oil (New Jersey), the chief foreign economist of The Texas Company, the treasurer and director of Humble Oil, the chief economist and assistant to the chairman of the board of Continental Oil, the assistant to the president of the Independent Petroleum Association of America, and a prominent Texas oil attorney who at one time had been employed by Gulf. The gas advisers included the president of the Southern Natural Gas Company, the vice presidents of the Texas Eastern Transmission Corporation and the United Gas Pipe Line Company, and the comptroller of the Columbia Gas Service Systems Corporation.

In 1955 the cabinet members advised the President that "the Federal Government should not control the production, gathering, processing or sale of natural gas prior to its entry into an interstate transmission line." The staff report, prepared by the six oil consultants, warned that the federal regulation on producers selling gas called for by the Phillips decision "would inevitably interfere with petroleum operations and, by reducing incentive, discourage the development of new oil and gas supplies. . . . Accordingly, it is desirable that appropriate legislation be enacted at an early date to remove Federal regulation over gas production and gathering." On the difficult question of oil imports, the cabinet members accepted the industry "unity" position, calling for a balance between imports and the needs of healthy domestic production. They defended tax incentives, including the depletion allowance, for their role in encouraging the development of resources.[3]

A sixty-member Business Advisory Council operating within the Department of Commerce since 1933 has had representatives from such firms as Standard of California, Standard (New Jersey), Texas, Continental and Union. Its executive committee generally constitutes an impressive roster of the captains of industry and finance in the United States. In 1955, for example, the fourteen-member committee included the chairmen of the boards of Jersey Standard, Pacific Gas and Electric, B. F. Goodrich, Libbey-Owens-Ford Glass, and Sears, Roebuck; the presidents of General Electric, Du Pont, and Pittsburgh Consolidated Coal (the nation's largest coal producer, which, under the direction of George M. Humphrey, head of the M. A. Hanna Company, was formed in a merger of a Hanna firm with the Rockefeller-owned Consolidated Coal and the Mellon-owned (Gulf) Pittsburgh Coal companies); and Sidney J. Weinberg, senior partner in the giant investment house of Goldman, Sachs and Company and a director of many leading corporations. In 1956 Eugene Holman, chairman of Jersey Standard, was elected chairman of the Business Advisory Council.

The BAC lacks statutory authority or responsibility. But as described in its bylaws, its primary objectives are:

. . . To submit to the Secretary of Commerce a constructive point of view on matters of public policy affecting the business interests of the country; to respond to requests by the Secretary for advice and assistance in carrying out his administrative responsibilities; and to provide a medium for a better understanding of Government problems by Council membership.[4]

It has made studies on labor policy, foreign trade, corporate size, antitrust, industrial mobilization, strategic materials, atomic energy and taxation. The council's Latin American committee has advised the State Department as well as Commerce, a relationship that a House Judiciary investigation suggested makes possible access to classified materials on foreign policy. Its tax committee has advised the Secretary of the Treasury and has furnished experts on corporate tax law to the Treasury. The council has sponsored semiannual weekend meetings at such vacation resorts as Hot Springs, Virginia, White Sulphur Springs, West Virginia, and Sea Island, Georgia, where leaders of the business community exchange views with government officials and discuss political action in closed sessions. It has given lavish gifts to such public figures as former Secretary of Commerce Charles Sawyer and to Secretary of the Army Robert T. Stevens who had been chairman of the council. The BAC has also been active in recruiting business personnel for government posts. It has made recommendations on those permanent civil servants to be retained, transferred, or dropped.

All council expenses, including the salary of the executive director, have been paid by business. These contributions are tax-exempt. There are no congressional administrative and accounting checks upon the BAC, and, with the support of the Department of Commerce, it has resisted opening its files to legislative investigators. Asked at a press conference in 1955 who paid the bills for a council meeting at White Sulphur Springs that he had attended, Secretary of Commerce Sinclair Weeks replied: "The Government doesn't. I don't know who does. I never paid any attention to the finances." [5] A report of the House of Representatives has concluded that the council, which has selected its own members, "operates more like an exclusive businessman's club with entree into high Government quarters than as a governmental body":

Partaking of both governmental and private characteristics, the BAC is able on the one hand to claim all of the privileges and immunities of the executive departments. On the other hand, unencumbered by the rigid restrictions applicable to Government agencies, BAC is able to cut a wide swath across all areas of Government and business.[6]

The sympathy and support enjoyed by oil cannot be explained simply by the number of its representatives within or advising the government. The engulfing character of oil operations brings a host of related business enterprises and leaders into its orbit. For example, John A. McCone, on the recommendation of Lewis L. Strauss, a utility financier, succeeded the latter as chairman of the Atomic Energy Commission in 1958. McCone had been a partner with the Bechtel interests, active in construction and shipping. (In 1958, S. D. Bechtel, president of the Bechtel Corporation, succeeded Jersey Standard's Eugene Holman as chairman of the BAC.) McCone enterprises have built refineries for Standard of California and operated sizable tanker fleets for Standard of California, Jersey Standard, Union Carbide, Dow Chemical, and others. One of his first acts in office was to appoint an advisory committee on peaceful uses of atomic energy. The eight members included the president of Jersey Standard's chief research organization, a director of Jersey, the former chairman of Standard (Indiana), and the chairman of Pacific Gas and Electric. McCone subsequently arranged for the appointment of Robert E. Wilson, the retired Standard (Indiana) chairman, to the AEC. A successful and conservative Republican, McCone numbered among his close friends the chairman of Union Oil and other oil executives. This identity with which the men of power view one another, along with their frank admiration for the capacity to make deals, to get things done, and for efficiency, bigness, and power, and the frequent sharing of a common social outlook, are also fundamental factors in explaining oil's treatment by other businessmen in government.

This respect and even identity is frequently shared by the military, by career men in government, and by politicians at the policy level. Senate studies of military procurement of jet fuel and other supplies report an "ingrained proclivity" of military contracting officers to lean toward the large manufacturers, even where smaller companies are qualified. When Dwight Eisenhower institutionalized regular stag dinners at the White House to gather information, exchange views, and create a closer bond with national leaders, most of the five hundred guests at his first thirty-eight affairs were from the business and financial worlds. Oil and its satellites were generously represented. Labor Day, 1955, found the President playing golf and bridge with a group of friends who had flown to Denver for the occasion. Among them were the heads of Cities Service, Continental Oil, Coca-Cola, General Electric, Young and Rubicam (advertising), and Frankfort Distilleries. (Frankfort Oil, another Seagram's subsidiary, received a lease for drilling on a federal wildlife refuge in Louisiana, causing a major outcry from conservation groups.) Almost inevitably, there are close associations among American oil, diplomatic, and military representatives stationed abroad, with the social bonds easily spilling over into political relationships. The oilmen are generally attractive, friendly, and intelligent in their governmental dealings. Modestly paid public servants are often flattered by the intimacy with these men whose organizations are at the center of power and by the attention represented in free drinks, Christmas parties, dinners, and other gestures made possible by generous corporate expense accounts. Invitations to speak at conventions, with fees and expenses paid, are welcome opportunities for getting away from Washington, and provide occasions for fraternization. The use of company planes to fly on inspection tours, to plant dedications, or just home is always an attraction. These advantages often give to oilmen the appearance of being relatively free from the organizational harassments that government bureaucrats are wont to bemoan as their peculiar lot.

There are also many inducements, implied or imagined, for responsive handling of oil affairs. It is difficult to believe that an official at the level of a Secretary of Interior could be directly paid off now, as happened in the twenties in the Teapot Dome episode. Then Albert B. Fall had received $100,000 in cash from Edward L. Doheny and $300,000 in Liberty Bonds and cash from Harry F. Sinclair for turning over to their companies naval oil reserve bases. (At the 1920 Republican national convention that nominated Warren G. Harding, a millionaire oilman, prominent in Oklahoma politics, had placed a $500,000 value on the post.) A number of officials, including Attorney General Harry M. Daugherty, who had been Harding's campaign manager, speculated in Sinclair oil stock at the time of the lease deal. After his resignation, Fall served as a consultant for oil interests, including those of Sinclair. Doheny disclosed that, in the best bipartisan tradition, he had employed the services of four former members of Woodrow Wilson's Cabinet—although not in relation to the naval reserves or while they were in office. They were Secretary of the Interior Franklin K. Lane, Secretary of the Treasury William G. McAdoo, Attorney General Thomas W. Gregory, and Secretary of War Lindley M. Garrison. The courts ultimately found the leasing arrangements corrupt and illegal. Fall was fined and convicted for accepting the bribe from Doheny. The oilman, however, was acquitted of charges of conspiring to defraud the government and of bribery. Sinclair ultimately did go to jail in 1929 for contempt of the Senate after he refused to answer questions and for contempt of court after it was discovered he had hired private detectives to trail the jurors. As Senator George W. Norris noted in sorrow and anger, this record of double dealing and double standards "came near demonstrating that under the American system of jurisprudence it was very difficult, if not impossible, to convict one hundred million dollars." [7]

Nevertheless, oil litigation has remained so lucrative as to provide a constant source of temptation, or at least a thought, in the minds of many political figures and government lawyers. Senator Joseph C. O'Mahoney reported that one leading corporate lawyer told him that in his office in one year " 'we distributed $1 million to pay attorneys in the several states to defend one company we operate.' " [8] Rare are the able regulatory officials who cannot report discussions with the regulated interests concerning the greener pastures that could lie ahead if they would behave more cooperatively while in office. "I know of practically no ex-federal official, now a lawyer in Washington, who doesn't have oil or gas clients," observed one prominent officeholder who has dealt with the industry over a lifetime. For example, a former executive director of the Federal Power Commission became the representative of the Texas Gas Transmission Corporation after leaving public office. A former general counsel represented a number of regulated companies before the FPC. An assistant general counsel later represented Tidewater, Atlantic, and other oil firms; another assistant general counsel had Pan American Petroleum Company as one of his clients. Other regulatory officials have become utility consultants while maintaining friendly relations with the FPC.

As technical considerations have become dominant factors in public policy formation, the regulatory agencies have assumed prominent roles in the nation's economic life through their judicial and administrative decision making. It is inevitable that great influence is brought to bear here by private enterprise. Generally this is with far less public attention than would be the case in purely legislative or judicial settings where attempts at direct control over policies and personnel are much more visible and are more likely to encounter defined norms of political ethics, however poorly adhered to.

So long as the agencies and the interests are living in harmony, little publicity is focused upon the doings of the former. But oil—not unlike the utilities, commodity groups, and others—is quick to apply both subtle and direct pressure upon those public servants who assume the public they are primarily responsible to in their handling of oil and gas matters extends beyond the industry. Perhaps the most clear-cut illustration of the exercise of raw power was in the savage assault upon Federal Power Commissioner Leland Olds whose renomination for a third term in 1949 was successfully blocked.

Ostensibly, Olds was rejected and crucified by the Senate because of the "discovery" of radical newspaper writings for the labor press in the twenties. In these writings he had criticized the predatory aspects of capitalism and praised certain social advances in the Soviet Union. John E. Lyle, a congressman from an oil and gas district in Texas whose name was on one bill to exempt natural gas from federal control, was assigned the task of presenting Olds's dangerous background to the Senate committee reviewing his reappointment by President Truman. Listening was a carefully picked committee, chaired by Lyndon Johnson of Texas, who had introduced the witness with a glowing tribute to his war record. Said Lyle:

I am here to oppose Mr. Olds because he has—through a long and prolific career attacked the church; he has attacked our schools; he has ridiculed the symbols of patriotism and loyalty such as the Fourth of July; he has advocated public ownership; he has reserved his applause for Lenin and Lenin's system, and he has found few words of praise for our American system; and, yes, gentlemen, he has seen fit to attack the men who serve as elected representatives in our Government—men such as you. He has characterized you as mere administrative clerks handling administrative details for "an immensely powerful ruling class." [9]

Olds, a religious man, educated in the best traditions of New England Protestant conscience and social work experiences, was quickly and dishonestly branded as a communist.

Despite the fervor of righteous and patriotic indignation that followed, it was clear that the hostility to Olds did not stem from strong (and sometimes out of context) quotations from his articles published in predepression America. Rather was it the zeal and intelligence he had brought to the Federal Power Commission in his ten years of service as a member and chairman. Leland Olds had spent a lifetime developing knowledge about natural resources and utility rate regulation. He was closely identified with the planning for the St. Lawrence Seaway, rural electrification, and many other developments. Olds had gained a national reputation as an eminent and honest defender of consumer rights and the cooperative movements. He was looked to by many state public service commissions for leadership and guidance in detecting inflated utility values and in reducing gas and electric rates. Leland Olds was one of the few public servants who could with ease match the private interests in their technical knowledge. (Any man who knows so much about other peoples' business must be a communist, a utility executive once remarked.) Olds strove to apply this intelligence for goals of economic abundance and political democracy, keeping in active touch with farmers, labor, and other broad-based citizen groups. He thus helped to give to the Federal Power Commission the vitality that so frequently disappears from regulatory agencies as they lose their initial spark and settle down to a comfortable middle age with the interests they are presumed to be supervising.

The immediate crime that evoked the attacks of the gas and oil interests—with his earlier critics, the electric utilities, aiding in the background—was that he had changed his mind on natural gas regulation. Out of FPC experience and research, Olds and two others on the five-man commission, Claude L. Draper and Thomas C. Buchanan, developed the conviction that unless the FPC could regulate the price of gas at the point it was sold to the pipelines for resale in interstate commerce—an interpretation backed by the federal courts—regulation of natural gas pricing at the point where it left the pipeline was futile. It was precisely such opportunity for growth in understanding that had been a vital argument for the establishment of regulatory agencies to support public legislation. And it was such evolution of experience and exercise of discretionary powers that evoked the hostility of the regulated.

Olds's courage in criticizing the Moore-Rizely, Lyle, Kerr, and similar bills that would remove most of industry from jurisdiction of the FPC, leaving consumers dependent upon natural gas at corporate mercy, had put him on trial before the Senate. His case also offered a revealing insight into the nature of much of the anticommunist movement in postwar America. The underlying fear was not of the subversion of the democratic process but rather of the extension of democratic responsibility to areas of private economic power.

The giant oil, gas, and utility interests were careful not to testify. Generally, the attacks came from smaller southwestern oil and gas associations and spokesmen. The immediate question of regulation was scrupulously skirted in most of the debate. Yet the issue was clearly drawn. Oil groups had made explicit their concern that control over natural gas would inevitably be extended to oil production. As Senator Wayne Morse observed, under the banner of free enterprise an industry fraught with great public interest and where competition was often impossible was determined to avoid regulation that really regulated.

One recognized leader in the fight to get a proindustry majority on the commission was Senator Robert S. Kerr, an able and articulate Democrat from Oklahoma and a millionaire oil and gas man. His company, Kerr-McGee, was a close business associate of the Phillips Petroleum Company, a leading producer and the second largest holder of gas reserves in the country. One of the two commissioners friendly to the gas viewpoint was Harrington Wimberly, an Oklahoma publisher and politician whose services as Kerr's campaign manager were rewarded with this appointment in 1945. Wimberly was quoted in a *Fortune* interview as saying: "I don't know whether I'm Senator Kerr's man or whether he's my man. But it is well known that I am for Bob Kerr first, last, and all the time." [10]

Despite a last-minute appeal by President Truman for Democratic senators to show loyalty to their party and interest in the consumer, Olds was denied reappointment. Mr. Truman then failed to maintain the principle of responsible regulation that was at stake. Olds's replacement, former Senator Mon C. Wallgren, was a political choice without experience or particular qualifications in rate regulation. No one in the Senate seemed concerned enough to make this a serious issue. The gas position soon had a strong majority on the commission. By a 4 to 1 vote, the FPC refused to exercise its powers over producer pricing of natural gas in the Phillips case, bringing into effect the essence of the Kerr bill that Mr. Truman had vetoed in 1950. The industry thus gained from the administrative process the exemption from regulation it could not get from the Congress, the federal courts, the President, and public opinion. After his tour of government duty Commissioner Wimberly represented gas clients before the FPC, including the Pacific Northwest Pipeline Corporation and then the El Paso Natural Gas Company. Congressman Lyle later retired to a law practice where he represented oil and gas interests. Part of his income in 1959 came from $29,000 in legal fees from the Panhandle Eastern Pipeline Company. He has used his floor privileges as an ex-member of the House to oppose natural gas regulation. In 1958 he registered as a lobbyist for Shell.

In a manner reminiscent of the Olds case, Federal Trade Commissioner Stephen Spingarn quickly found his character, mental stability, and loyalty publicly questioned after he took a leading part in securing the release of the FTC staff report *The International Petroleum Cartel* in 1952. An *Oil Forum* editorial, widely circulated through the industry's public relations operations, recalled the influence of Alger Hiss in the government, and asked "if there were any communist-inclined officials" in the FTC responsible for the report. It suggested that "it might be well to play safe, and have the FBI investigate every man who participated in its preparation and writing." [11] Industry sources and sympathizers portrayed the FTC, which shares with the Justice Department responsibility for upholding antitrust standards, as a hotbed of radicalism. The men in Congress who encouraged its release and the subsequent cartel suit were denounced as cheap and venal politicians. Spingarn issued indignant disclaimers concerning the insinuations about his motives and patriotism; he also questioned the ethics of the industry in seeking to intimidate an independent commission. This defense was cited by an executive from Hill and Knowlton, the public relations firm employed by the California Texas Oil Company (Caltex, jointly owned by The Texas Company and Standard of California), as evidence of the commissioner's neuroses. "He appears as if he doth protest too much when he refers so much to his loyalty." Little attempt was made to discuss or refute the substance of the carefully documented 378-page report. Nor did the industry appear eager to accept Spingarn's challenge to call for a public hearing to evaluate the data. For, as the Washington public relations representative further explained, "How in the hell do you answer a report which says it is factual and makes no charges?"

The deterioration of the role of the presumably independent regulatory agency proceeded rapidly under the Eisenhower Administration. The concept of a public office as a public trust, however weakly or imperfectly maintained under previous Democratic regimes, found little support. Not that the new leaders were simply and consciously filling black bags. But the vacuum of genuine political direction and the faith in the capacity of businessmen to run the government on sound business lines broke down most safeguards of public responsibility—the promised moral crusade of the Republican party and the unquestioned personal integrity of Dwight Eisenhower notwithstanding.

The corporate supporters of the new Administration knew very well that getting their candidates elected was only the first, and in many respects the easiest, of political objectives. The purpose of politics was to capture control or at least influence substantially the machinery of government toward the victor's private desires and concept of the public good. A major target, little discussed in the election drumbeating, but an urgent consideration in all political planning, was the functioning of the regulatory and licensing agencies. The classic advice in 1892 of corporation counsel Richard Olney to his railroad employer, the Chicago, Burlington and Quincy, was the guiding precept. Olney was about to become Attorney General in President Cleveland's second Administration, and his client wanted him to work from within for the abolition of the Interstate Commerce Commission, the first of the independent federal regulatory agencies, which had been founded in 1887.

My impression would be that looking at the matter from a railroad point of view exclusively it would not be a wise thing to undertake. . . . The attempt would not be likely to succeed; if it did not succeed, and were made on the ground of the inefficiency and uselessness of the Commission, the result would very probably be giving it the power it now lacks. The Commission, as its functions have now been limited by the courts, is, or can be made, of great use to the railroads. It satisfies the popular clamor for a government supervision of railroads, at the same time that that supervision is almost entirely nominal. Further, the older such a commission gets to be, the more inclined it will be found to take the business and railroad view of things. It thus becomes a sort of barrier between the railroad corporations and the people and a sort of protection against hasty and crude legislation hostile to railroad interests. . . . The part of wisdom is not to destroy the Commission, but to utilize it.

Over the years the oil industry had learned to appreciate this wisdom. Its cooperation with the Interstate Commerce Commission provided a classic model for converting federal regulation of pipelines into industry self-government. The Hepburn Act of 1906 had declared pipelines to be common carriers subject to ICC supervision that was to keep the pipelines open to all at reasonable rates. The regulatory authority granted by Congress, dealing largely with rates, was much more limited than was true for railroads, motor carriers, and gas pipelines. American Petroleum Institute pipeline committees, paralleling the structure of the government agency and composed of oil officials, worked closely with ICC staff and became active participants in the entire regulatory process. Company engineers and accountants assigned to ICC offices helped establish the pipeline property valuations basic to rate determination. Meanwhile, the ICC showed little interest in developing the procedures or the independence necessary for effective regulation. Nor did it examine the implications of its partnership with API pipeline committees, despite the antitrust actions against the API and the pipelines in 1940. (An official of The Texas Company who served as chairman of the API pipeline steering committee was also the chairman of the Industry Negotiating Committee for the consent decree.) An investigation by the House of Representatives in 1959 concluded that "in practice the industry itself decides what the ICC will do." The public interest was subordinated to the private interests of the oil companies, and the ICC served "as an instrument for protection against the requirements of the oil pipeline consent decree." [12]

For the oil and gas industry, as for electric power, increasingly the key tribunal has become the Federal Power Commission. In 1953 reappointment was denied to Thomas C. Buchanan, whose term expired and who had been a dissenter in a number of cases where a majority of the FPC chose to move away from its regulatory responsibilities. In his place, President Eisenhower nominated Jerome K. Kuykendall, a lawyer who had represented utilities in rate cases and who had served briefly on the Public Service Commission of the State of Washington. Also selected was Seaborn L. Digby, who was Conservation Commissioner of Louisiana, the second biggest gas-producing state. Digby was an Eisenhower Democrat, for commission membership was supposed to be bipartisan. He had been an attorney for oil interests, including millionaire operator William C. Feazel. Digby was known as a friend of the gas producers, and when he retired from the FPC in 1958 was hailed in the *Oil and Gas Journal* as "one of the firmest advocates of nonregulation." Digby was replaced by John B. Hussey, an attorney whose practice was in oil and gas law and taxation.[13] Hussey had also succeeded Digby as Conservation Commissioner in Louisiana and was considered a staunch defender of producers. He had represented a number of companies, including Sohio and Texas Gas Transmission, while in the Louisiana post. With the approval of Governor Kennon, Hussey also testified in three rate-increase cases before the FPC to indicate his state's opposition to treating gas production as a utility. His appearance had been at the request of three local oil companies (Sun, Union, and Forest) who paid his expenses.

Under Kuykendall's chairmanship, four of the five members of the commission actively supported in congressional testimony and in speeches before the industry bills that would reverse the Supreme Court judgment and would withhold from the Federal Power Commission effective power to supervise the field price of natural gas. They denied that there was a concentration of control over gas reserves that constituted a monopolistic threat warranting a utility status and federal regulation for producers. The majority called for the continuation of free competitive enterprise, restricted only by state conservation considerations. And they further echoed the industry position by insisting that gas prices must be allowed to be at the level of other fuels. "We have heard no demand that the oil production industry should be regulated as a public utility, and do not understand why natural gas production should be so regulated, and oil production should remain unregulated."

The dissents of Commissioner William R. Connole during this

period identified him as the lone defender of the regulation of gas prices and of the national purposes of the Natural Gas Act. Connole's reluctance to allow rate increase without review by the FPC antagonized oil and gas interests. The latter successfully pressured the White House against his reappointment. President Eisenhower subsequently described Connole as too one-sided in favor of consumer interests. "I think I can get a better man, that's all." James C. Hagerty, White House press secretary, further explained that the President believed FPC members "should be representative of all sections of the United States and not one segment of the economy." [14] Morale of publicly dedicated career experts in the agency dropped even further.

After President Eisenhower vetoed one such bill (Harris-Fulbright) in 1956, presumably because of the disclosures involving an intended bribe for the vote of Senator Francis Case of South Dakota, Mr. Kuykendall secretly laid the groundwork for a new bill. His direct instructions from the White House were to maintain the objectives of the rejected bill while harmonizing the interests of the three segments of the industry and filling the requirements stated in the veto message. These included "furthering the long-term interest of consumers in plentiful supplies of gas" and "protecting consumers in their right to fair prices." [15]

Chairman Kuykendall then called in Randall Le Boeuf, Jr., partner in the law firm representing the Consolidated Edison Company of New York, who had been the lobbyist for the distributing companies that had opposed the bill; David Searls, an attorney who worked in behalf of producers; and William Tarver, a former FPC lawyer employed by a pipeline company. "These gentlemen agreed that they would try to put together what they thought would be a good bill, and they did some work on it," explained Mr. Kuykendall. Meanwhile, the head of the Brooklyn Union Gas Company, who had separately organized for a similar purpose some conferences among gas executives from the three portions of the industry, came to the FPC Chairman. "He requested that I defer to him and not have a sort of competing group going. And I acquiesced to that. . . . And so I stepped out of the picture at that time." [16] Kuykendall said he never called the lawyers together again, but kept posted as to where the industry was in its legislative drafting and received from it a statement of principles for a new compromise bill.

At the 1957 hearings on natural gas legislation, Mr. Kuykendall was questioned by Representative Torbert Macdonald of Massachusetts about his responsibility for protecting the consuming public for whom the Federal Power Commission and the Natural Gas Act were created. The commissioner was asked about his reliance on the industry and his failure to consult any consumer group, including the mayors of two hundred large cities that had been actively campaigning for effective regulation. Mr. Kuykendall replied:

In the first place, I knew of no sufficient consumer groups to go to; and I wasn't going to groups. I went to three individuals, and I admonished those individuals that there should be . . . absolute secrecy, because I did not want any rumors started that there might be another gas bill during the last session of Congress.

Furthermore, the pipeline group, and particularly the distributing group, were antagonistic to the producers, and were in, and had the same position as did the consumer, alleged consumer groups, that opposed the bill last time.

That is why I went to Mr. Le Boeuf, who had been the . . . chief spokesman for the opposition to the previous bill. . . .

I got three extremely able men from those 3 segments of the industry, and I believe that among those the consumer interests were adequately represented.[17]

At his renomination hearing in 1957, Kuykendall further defended this action:

It has been insinuated here that I would be unable to protect the public interest or would not do it because I talked with some people in industry, but did not talk with some consumers' groups. I am sure every member of this committee knows that those consumers' groups have a position which they think is right, but they admitted they don't have the technical knowledge, and they are not supposed to have it. They can't have it. They are all in other endeavors. They have a view that a certain law is good for them or is not good for them. They may be right or they may be wrong. Obviously with all the differences of opinion there have been it would be difficult to say precisely who is right and who is wrong. I think the only standards you can go by is what Congress did, as I said.

But it would not have been of any value for me to consult with these groups that Mr. MacDonald says I should have consulted, because I knew very well what their position was. They didn't want any change in the law. They disagreed with the House Commerce Committee. They disagreed with the House of Representatives. They disagreed with the Senate. They disagreed with the Federal Power Commission. They have a perfect right to do that. And they may do that. But there would be no point in talking to those people for the simple reason that they would not contribute anything to drafting a bill because they didn't want a bill.

SENATOR BRICKER: They wanted the Phillips decision of the Supreme Court to become the law of the country.

(John W. Bricker of Ohio was ranking Republican member of the Senate Interstate and Foreign Commerce Committee. His law firm has represented the East Ohio Gas Company, owned by the giant Consolidated Natural Gas Company.)

MR. KUYKENDALL: That is right. They wanted things to stay as they were.[18]

The statement of principles became the basis for a new bill offered by Representative Oren Harris of Arkansas, chairman of the House Interstate and Foreign Commerce Committee. Once again unsavory political factors prevented the gas interests from gaining enough support to have it passed. But during the entire period while they were awaiting congressional action favorable to overriding the Supreme Court's 1954 opinion in the Phillips case, the FPC stalled in carrying out its responsibilities. It reiterated its belief in the difficulty of studying company books to judge the costs of production, when what really seemed at stake was the reluctance of the industry to allow the FPC to do this. Against the dissent of Claude L. Draper, a Republican appointed in 1930, the majority avoided working out a formula for producer rates, preferring to plod along from case to case. It sought to abandon the prudent investment basis for judging prices, setting in its place "market value" criteria that were an invitation to the complete flaunting of consumer safeguards. Thus, through planned administrative inaction, bolstered by the absence of a renewed legislative mandate from advocates of regulation whose energies were absorbed in preventing further damage, many of the hard-earned gains of over a quarter of a century for effective natural gas regulation were emasculated or reversed.

There was also sharp criticism of Mr. Kuykendall's stewardship in electric power and water resource development. Congressional spokesmen from the Pacific Northwest were outraged at the FPC's support of the Idaho Power Company's quest for a license and for accelerated tax amortization for building a series of dams on the Snake River. These were to replace the high Hells Canyon Dam planned by advocates of multipurpose federal development of the Columbia River Basin, of which the Snake River is a part.

Serious question was also raised as to the propriety of Mr. Kuykendall's working with the White House, the Bureau of the Budget, and the Securities and Exchange Commission (another of the supposedly independent regulatory tribunals) to expedite the complex and controversial Dixon-Yates contract. This involved a presidential order to the Atomic Energy Commission to meet growing power needs in the Tennessee Valley area by negotiating with private utilities that would construct an electric generating plant to supply additional electric power to the AEC installations at Oak Ridge, Tennessee, and Paducah, Kentucky. These were the largest single customers of the Tennessee Valley Authority. As the contract finally evolved, the AEC was to act as a broker for the TVA, purchasing private power not for its own national defense purposes but for sale to the TVA for the latter's civilian and industrial customers in the Memphis area. This presumably would replace the power the TVA was furnishing the AEC at Paducah, and thus help meet growing electric energy needs without expanding the TVA. Previous requests by the TVA for additional funds for a steam plant had been repeatedly blocked. The Dixon-Yates arrangements were made against the opposition of a majority of the AEC members and without consultation with the TVA directors. To defenders of the valley authority, it thus seemed as if the Eisenhower Administration's campaign commitment to end "creeping socialism" included as a first step earmarking for destruction the concept of cheap, abundant power and the yardstick concept symbolized by the TVA.

It was subsequently disclosed that Adolphe H. Wenzell, a senior vice president of the First Boston Corporation, a leading investment house dealing in utility issues that was to be involved in the financing of the highly profitable and even risk-proof contract, also served as a consultant to the Bureau of the Budget. There he drafted a plan for getting the federal government out of the power business and worked with government officials, including presidential assistant Sherman Adams, in preparing the Dixon-Yates negotiations. FPC Chairman Kuykendall was charged by Senators Morse, Neuberger, and others with concealing from the public and the Congress the fact that top counsels in his agency had condemned the proposed contract as prejudicial to the interests of the government.[19]

It is a commentary on standards of political morality that these illustrations of private influence upon the federal bureaucracy involving hundreds of millions of dollars and priceless natural resources received little sustained national attention. Similarly, the more dramatic congressional investigation in 1958 of the Federal Communications Commission and its handling of applications for television licenses was headlined for the American people only when Bernard Goldfine and his ubiquitous presents, including vicuña cloth for the President, made their appearance. There seemed little eagerness among congressional leaders, including Oren Harris, chairman of the over-all inquiry that was to look into the behavior of a host of administrative and all the regulatory agencies, to move into such areas as the FPC. And more revealing, in marked contrast to the treatment accorded such genuinely dedicated public servants as Leland Olds, Mr. Kuykendall's renomination won Senate approval.

The Federal Trade Commission also came into sympathetic hands in 1953. President Eisenhower chose as its chairman Edward F. Howrey, a lawyer and lobbyist who had spent a lifetime representing clients brought before the FTC. These included Firestone Tire and Rubber, which was involved in FTC investigations of exclusive tie-up sales with Shell Oil and in quantity discount cases. Howrey assured the Senate committee reviewing his nomination that he would disqualify himself completely in cases where he had been involved. This prompted Senator Warren B. Magnuson to remark, "I am afraid that you might be on a vacation almost permanently down here." [20]

Under Howrey's chairmanship, review and enforcement of antitrust cases declined. Attention was focused more on misleading advertising charges than on major monopoly conditions. Some of the

FTC's legal responsibilities were bargained away at informal conferences with industry groups that had been under its scrutiny. Close ties were developed between the FTC and members of the White House staff, including Sherman Adams. One early action was to eliminate, demote, reassign, or place under close surveillance leading career members in the Bureaus of Antimonopoly and Economics, including those who worked on the oil cartel report. Some of the forty staff dismissals were explained by the new chairman as forced by a congressional reduction in FTC appropriations—a budget cut made with the sanction of Mr. Howrey.[21] Less than three years later he resigned, and his firm was once more representing clients brought before the FTC.

Such conquests at the federal level have not diminished the oil industry's affection for the doctrine of states' rights. Much of this relates to the recognition that it is generally harder to control such figures as a Secretary of the Interior, who, however amenable, is in the national limelight, than a state conservation commissioner who is relatively obscure except to the immediate oil and gas groups concerned. This office is often a center of political interest in producer states. A leading Louisiana oilman contributed heavily to Earl Long's gubernatorial campaign in order to replace a commissioner. In the more sophisticated states you are less likely to see oil that visible in politics. But neither will you see a commissioner who does not identify his state's well-being with that of the oil and gas industry. Veto power is effectively exercised over gubernatorial choices for state geologists and regulatory officers. One can appreciate the virtues of local self-rule when recalling the classic Texas prorationing controversy of 1931. The new East Texas discoveries on dirt farmer holdings were producing at a rate that threatened the pricing of much of the industry. Governor Ross S. Sterling, a former president of Humble Oil (Jersey Standard subsidiary), ordered the state troops under the command of Jacob F. Wolters to close the wells. "Wolters," relates an oil history subsidized by Jersey Standard, "had been called away from his duties as chief counsel for The Texas Company. . . ."[22]

Smaller oilmen feel that they are at a disadvantage when dealing with national regulatory tribunals. This despite the fact that the original advocates of such bodies as the ICC envisioned them as "the poor man's courts." As one Oklahoma independent explained, agencies cast in the mold of the Interstate Commerce Commission, the Federal Communications Commission, or the Federal Power Commission do not afford a forum available to the average producer. His business is not large enough to justify the costs involved in hearings before such an agency. These businessmen often lack any understanding of the administrative procedures and of the rights available to them. "They are fearful to take a position before an administrative agency against one of these major companies because of fear of reprisals." The purchasing companies might no longer take their oil. If an oilman should seek administrative relief, he may be "opposed by a company who has a staff of competent counsel, a staff of competent economic experts, a staff of competent engineers, and he gets his ears whipped down through the inability of those who represent him to properly present his case." [23]

The giants of oil have all these factors built into their operations. Hence they place less reliance on trade association activities, on local politics, and on the role of the conservation commission as their champion. Yet, as seen earlier, however loyal the latter agencies may be to the domestic producer, they are all caught up in the power system of the private government of oil, which extends far beyond their jurisdictions.

Meanwhile, the major corporations and many of their smaller brethren do everything they can to subvert genuine states' rights by using this doctrine as a shield against responsibility to the American people. They exploit resources; they fight severance taxes; they police the regulatory agencies while forestalling the growth of a well paid, professional civil service that could build up the skills, research, and experience needed to deal with oil. They have backed the unequal representation patterns existing in many states. And their general involvement in public affairs has encouraged the image of politics as corrupt, while discouraging the development of responsible political systems and wider citizen participation. States' rights, historically part of the Jeffersonian and Jacksonian design for democracy, have thus too often become distorted to defend precisely what early liberals sought to avoid—the concentrated private economic control of the machinery of government.

The presence within the public bureaucracies of men whose direct origins have been in oil, and the pressures upon those who are supposed to be serving the broadest public, obviously threaten political democracy. Even more disturbing are the consequences of the behavior of those who assume that the public to be served consists of the private interests they most immediately deal with. A citizen's letter of inquiry concerning the functions of the Department of the Interior brought a reply from a responsible official that "the Bureau of Mines is the agency within the Department of the Interior with primary responsibility for and to the petroleum industry." [24] For further reading material, the inquiring citizen was referred to the American Petroleum Institute and the Chase National Bank. When the solicitor of the Interior Department described the National Petroleum Council and the Foreign Petroleum Supply Committee as "altruistic organizations," one's first reaction was to speculate whether this were said tongue-in-cheek. (Apparently it was not.)[25] A cabinet officer defined his role as a protagonist for the petroleum industry. The capacity of the giants of oil to solidify themselves within public machinery prompts smaller industry members to view every decision against them—rightly or wrongly, in cases ranging from pipeline approval to tax benefits—as the predictable products of a rigged system. A congressman (admittedly from Texas) at the hearings on the Suez oil lift said to the president of Jersey Standard that "we had better not keep you too long. You had better get back to your job so that one of the world problems in Washington can be solved with your help." And the chairman of the committee, Oren Harris, concluded several hundred pages of hearings with the observation that "my only criticism does not relate to you, but to the entire industry, that you have not, apparently, thought it an opportunity to tell your story, to get it before the American people in order that they might know the problems of your oil industry, how much it means to the economy of this country, to the health and welfare of all our people." [26]

A question on a staged campaign television program concerning the wisdom of having "big shots" and millionaires in his cabinet brought the following reply from the President of the United States. Citing his appointment of Charles E. Wilson (of "what was good for our country was good for General Motors, and vice versa" fame) to head the Defense Department, with its $40 billion budget, Mr.

Eisenhower declared: "Who would you rather have in charge of that, some failure that never did anything or a successful business man?" [27] A press inquiry about the propriety of having General White serve as director of the Defense Department's Division of Petroleum Logistics while on the Esso pay roll evoked the explanation from the President that White was a Reserve rather than a Regular officer and hence not required to divest himself of his economic interests: "It would be idle to employ as a consultant anyone who didn't know something about the petroleum business. He is bound to come from the petroleum industry." To those who wanted a fuller statement, added Mr. Eisenhower, "I should say, 'Go to see Secretary Wilson.' " [28]

There is a place for pressures on the public bureaucracies, assuming, ideally, that these are open and emanate from a range of sources. There is also need for the specialized intelligence and point of view the men of oil can offer to public policy formation. To reject these functions is to ignore the reality of a social system molded by private property rights and to deny to the various groups the access to government inherent in political democracy. The criteria of representativeness must be broader than a balancing of the demands of segments of the industry. Labor, stockholders, consumers, and the general public all have a stake, only part of which is economic. These influences can serve to prod or check agencies that otherwise might be limited, smug, or arbitrary in their judgments.

Oilmen can rightly resent the blanket charges that they are crude and self-seeking while in government. Individuals have shown character, loyalty, and dedication. Wartime executives and consultants were often highly intelligent and efficient. They tended to come from professional management ranks—often with scientific and technical backgrounds—rather than from the earlier individual entrepreneur tradition. Tough bargainers, they understood the nature of power and its exercise in settings where private objectives had to be tempered by considerations of public reactions. Some, genuinely challenged by the larger problems, developed a broader understanding of public policy needs.

Such factors as individual patriotism and the urgency of the national crisis served as the wartime brakes upon the oilmen in government. What governs their behavior in peacetime service is harder to define. They can be asked to divest themselves completely of their corporate holdings and offices. This still leaves the question of their orientation and perspectives. For the real problem is one of frame of reference rather than of conscious motivation. Where do their choices lie and how are they made when the stake of oil in profits and the going system of private enterprise come into conflict with public considerations? Individuals may be honorable in their private lives and decent in their public lives. Yet "business as usual" has rarely lost its central force, as the war and peacetime record of the "impersonal" corporations and their agents suggests. One needs only to look at the performance of oil in respect to taxes, subsidies, prices, cartels, international concessions, patent rights, and synthetics developments in petroleum and rubber. Advancement and the ability to take one's opportunities are still honored as motivating factors for American life. The business of business is still business. The governmental process offers one more hurdle or channel toward fulfillment of this purpose.

The marriage of private and public governments and purposes, developed in response to the changing conditions of the modern industrial democratic state, may indeed be a triumph for business statesmanship. Such evidence of corporate maturity is a new stage in the public relations of oildom and in the socialization of its internal functioning. This does not dismiss the troublesome observation of A. A. Berle that whereas our ancestors feared that corporations had no conscience, "we are treated to the colder, more modern fear that, perhaps, they do." [29] Simply for a democratic people to share in the celebration over this development of corporate responsibility, where the regulated have become the regulators and the supplicants the tribunes, provides a disturbing measure of political naïveté or indifference. It also suggests the corrosive impact of an acquisitive society upon democratic assumptions. Corporate participation in public policy making cannot be a substitute for public government —unless the American people are prepared to legitimize further the *de facto* government of oil and welcome unabashedly the full-blown emergence of a corporate state.

The public can always get expert advice on petroleum. No industry is more ready to provide this, with or without any built-in advisory or WOC system. And despite industry claims, it is not impossible to attract and develop the technical and economic skills needed within the federal bureaucracy. But to assume that the problems of oil are primarily technical and private, like assuming that the wonders of industrial expansion and American abundance are simply the products of individualism and private enterprise, is the grand misconception that promotes the continued rule of the private government of oil from pine-paneled board headquarters and the more austere public chambers. It also encourages the acceptance of government experts with a trained incapacity for comprehending the wider view of their responsibilities.

Genuine public servants are required, performing within a tradition of public service that will allow them to be effective, and backed by a public that will demand that they be responsible. There is a need for continuity of service. Men like Walter Hallanan of the National Petroleum Council, who has held his chairmanship during the terms of four Interior Secretaries, and Jersey Standard's S. P. Coleman with his numerous posts, have given a continuity to government operations in the face of political and personnel upheavals. But their divided loyalties can never be a substitute for public direction and responsibility. Nor are regulatory bodies likely to recruit effective leadership from politicians whose primary qualifications are "availability."

If industry consultants and advisory groups are needed, they must function within a framework of policies and ethics that is developed publicly and administered clearly. When reviewing the advisory network within Interior, it would be well to recall the warning of Adam Smith whose philosophic exposition of the ideal workings of capitalism in 1776 defenders of contemporary industrial enterprise generally prefer not to quote:

People of the same trade seldom meet together, even for merriment and diversion, but the conversation ends in a conspiracy against the public, or in some contrivance to raise prices. It is impossible indeed to prevent such meetings, by any law which either could be executed, or would be consistent with liberty and justice. But though the law cannot hinder people of the same trade from sometimes assembling together, it ought to do nothing to facilitate such assemblies; much less to render them necessary.[30]

Despite the complaints of most critics of the advisory system, the immediate solution is not in the direction of having government chairmen and government-controlled agenda. Rather is it to keep the identities and functions of the advisory personnel and of the officials with authority separate. An Oil and Gas Office must be more than an instrument of convenience for the industry and a shield from public control. Let the petroleum industry offer its advice, clearly labeled and understood as such. But create the conditions that allow government to govern. Keeping public servants defensive and obsequious will never make them responsible; at best it teaches the wisdom of neutrality. They may have to be just and impartial when dealing with groups that have competing interests. But it is never their function to be neutral to the public welfare.

To continue to frustrate publicly dedicated servants, not simply through poor salaries and limited recognition, but because of lack of public support, is to hasten the demise of responsible, representative government. For too long the image of public officers as corruptible has been accepted as part of the American scene, whether state inspectors checking oil safety conditions in the Rockefeller period, or current regulatory officials in Washington. Yet there is considerable evidence that the standards of day-to-day honesty are surprisingly high, probably far more so than in the private hierarchies of this organizational society. But the general welfare demands more than good character.

Harold Ickes, never the most retiring of men, repeatedly bewailed the fact that he did not receive credit for acts in the public interest. A vigorously prosecuted suit against Standard of California won for the government over $6 million in damages and the revesting of title to a rich section of the naval reserves. Yet this earned little recognition. "If I had stolen $25 I would have been on the front pages of every newspaper in the country." [31] One senses the lonely fate of a champion of public resources after visiting Judge R. V. Bottomly of the Montana Supreme Court. Bottomly was one of the few state attorneys general in the nation to oppose state control of offshore lands. He later fought from the bench industry attempts to exploit his state's public lands. He thus became a major target of the industry and found himself suspect among younger attorneys on the make.

The odds are heavy against conscientious antitrust experts in the

United States Department of Justice maintaining their convictions and morale after they have watched their efforts to carry out the law and the presumed commitments of the Department repeatedly undercut by higher-level political decisions to talk tough publicly to oildom while carrying a light stick. W. B. Watson Snyder, who since the twenties had accumulated a wealth of knowledge that made him the agency's top oil authority, in recent years worked with little assistance in a shared room crowded with papers and briefs. At the time of Snyder's retirement in 1955, Stanley N. Barnes, the Assistant Attorney General in charge of the Antitrust Division, was asked to comment publicly about the accuracy of documents critical of the National Petroleum Council prepared by Snyder. Said Barnes, reluctant to be pinned down, "I think it should be stated that Mr. W. B. W. Snyder was a very enthusiastic antitruster." [32] With no one of comparable experience or stature to succeed him, Snyder left the government earlier than he might have, in large part because of the lack of sustained backing. It was subsequently disclosed that Barnes had purchased $12,000 of Warren Petroleum stock for speculative purposes in November 1955 just after the Justice Department had decided there were no grounds for investigating Warren's merger with Gulf. His chief assistant in the division, Edward A. Foote, had purchased $65,000 worth in his wife's name immediately after the merger announcement. In 1956 Barnes accepted a federal circuit court appointment, and Foote resigned. The stock investments of both were defended by Attorney General Brownell, Jr., as free of any wrongdoing, although subsequent Justice Department rules set stricter limitations governing such behavior.[33]

In the closing hours of the fight over Leland Olds's renomination, Republican Senator George D. Aiken of Vermont summed up what he felt were the real losses and warnings at stake:

Mr. President, it appears that we have met here tonight to put the finishing touches on the career of a public servant who so far as I know has performed his duties in the last 10 years in accordance with the law as laid down by the Congress. . . .

I do not think that Mr. Olds is going to be hurt by those who would crucify him, but I think a great many other folk are going to be. I think the effects of what is being done here tonight will echo down far through the years ahead of us, and will continue to plague those who accuse him much longer than the echoes from Teapot Dome were heard.

Certain public utilities of the country are out to destroy a man for performing his duty. I do not know of anything worse than that. I do not know of anything more detrimental to good government. I do not know of anything to make it more difficult to get men and women to perform the duties of public office. These interests who are devoting every effort to destroy a man, in so doing are doing the most to bring about the very thing they fear the most. Mr. Olds is not going to bring about public ownership of the utilities in this country. If it is brought about, it will be brought about by those who fear it and by the tactics which they employ.[34]

Such pressures are indicative of a social environment where the dominant forces are committed more to private gain than to the general welfare. Neither intelligence, public officials, nor the governmental processes can readily be mustered to serve the highest of human ideals in a setting devoid of genuine public purposes to which people can give of themselves willingly. Where governmental responsibility for oil is badly fragmented, where the public interest is obscured and public support spasmodic, where the men in office disclaim any desire, need, or capacity to make national policy, where the petroleum interests possessing continuity of resources, efforts, and purpose do not want or permit a public policy to be publicly determined, then it seems as if there is *no* Government of the United States.

Needed is a genuine public policy that recognizes that there is a broad national and international interest in oil. This demands public planning for oil, as for other areas of the American society and its international obligations. Without such formulation and implementation of purpose, government can be neither strong enough to do the job of governing nor responsible enough to meet the criteria of political democracy. And from the record of oil alone, there is abundant evidence that the threat to American government stems more from weakness than from any tyrannical use of public power. Government is now the repository of privileges and powers it heretofore had not had or needed the capacity to defend.

Such long-range planning cannot readily come from an Oil and

Gas Office or a Federal Power Commission, especially as now constituted. The former is inadequately designed for such purposes and too closely identified with the industry. The regulatory agency operates in a twilight zone of responsibility. Though claimed by the Congress as an adjunct to its legislative functioning, such commissions lack the kind of direction and open political backing they might receive were they to be frankly recognized as part of the executive branch. To divorce administration and regulation from politics is to cut off these processes from popular review. Yet these agencies also possess an essentially judicial function. It is this aspect of their work that requires independence from the pressures of the regulated interests and the administration in power. As democracy learns to plan on a permanent rather than on a crisis basis, it obviously must develop new techniques and arrangements for the art of governance.

Where, then, can the broad outlines of a national oil program now be thrashed out, developed, and sustained as an integral part of national resource policy and economic life? A democratic citizenry looks elsewhere among the political processes—to debate, to party conflict, and to legislation.

12

Oil and Politics: The Permeability of Oil

"Show me another questionable oil appointment and I'll challenge it," asserted Senator Charles W. Tobey shortly before his death. It was July 1953, and the Eisenhower Administration had been in power for six months. The venerable New Hampshire Republican was being asked if he thought the quick dissipation of the much promised moral crusade through the open political payments being made to the oil industry was comparable to the situation in 1946 and warranted a new inquiry. At that time Tobey had challenged President Truman's nomination of oilman Edwin W. Pauley for Undersecretary of the Navy, intended by Roosevelt and then Truman as a steppingstone to his succeeding James Forrestal as Secretary.

Pauley had headed the Petrol Corporation, a modest-sized firm engaged in the various phases of the industry, and he was also a minor stockholder in Standard of California. He had helped plan the Petroleum Administration for War, had urged Roosevelt and Ickes to take on Ralph Davies as Deputy Administrator, had served overseas as special representative on petroleum supplies for Ickes, and was the United States representative on the Allied Commission on Reparations. The oilman had interests in California "tidelands" production and was active in the political fight for quitclaim legislation. A generous contributor to Democratic causes, he was also a successful money raiser among oil and other corporate interests on the West Coast. (For example, President Collier of Standard of California made a contribution of $1,000 to the Democrats through

341

Pauley. "I am a Republican, and my contributions have always gone the other way, except . . . in 1940," he explained.)[1] Pauley was credited with erasing his party's deficit while serving as secretary, assistant treasurer, and then treasurer of the Democratic National Committee from the end of 1941 to 1945. He had been a leader in the movement to block the renomination of Henry A. Wallace as vice president in 1944, and had actively campaigned for his replacement by Senator Harry S. Truman. Party leaders, including Roosevelt, Truman, and Edward J. Flynn, had been seeking a suitable public appointment for this record of service. To Tobey and others, the post of Secretary of the Navy seemed an obviously inappropriate reward, especially in view of the industry's recurring interest in the Navy's petroleum reserves.

Tobey's well developed moral indignation—later to become a national landmark through the televised Kefauver hearings on organized crime—had been aroused by preliminary disclosures about the machinations of California oil corporations, big and small, in relation to public opinion, politics, and legislation in the state and nation. His object, he had affirmed, was to bring out all the evidence pertaining to "the permeability of oil."[2] Pauley's involvement in the continuing fight between the California majors (supported by Roosevelt, Ickes, the Navy, and other federal offices) and independent producers over the adoption of state "conservation" measures to control production—and the question as to whether financial assistance which the Petrol Corporation had received from Standard of California had a bearing on Pauley's switching sides to favor conservation—provided the points of departure for the inquiry.

Senator Tobey's journey into oil politics led him far beyond any possible original intent to lambaste his Democratic opponents, even though the cast of the Pauley story was predominantly Democratic. Never before in his entire thirty-year political career, Tobey declared, had he been subjected to such intense pressures, all directed against holding the hearings. "This pressure comes from the West and from the East; it represents large capital interests . . . of tremendous influence and importance in the country."[3] Many of the charges and countercharges were never sorted out or pinned down. And despite the readiness with which the Congress generally assigns its own prose to posterity, the hearings were never published. They remain in the storeroom of the Senate Armed Services Committee in the transcript form received from the stenotypist.

The testimony offered insights into the standards of morality of segments of the industry, the legal profession, and politicians. Revealing evidence about the complex interlocking of financial relationships between Standard of California and some of the "independents" was introduced, including the subterfuge employed by the West Coast giant in financing the purchase of Petrol stock and properties through the Signal Oil and Gas Company, the leading West Coast independent. Disturbing charges about sizable sums of money solicited from the industry in return for the consent decree settlement of the Elkins pipeline rate suit in 1941 were aired, although never resolved. (The most repeated Washington version, supported by some observers not usually addicted to unsubstantiated gossip, has been that the Democratic party received $50,000 from each of eighteen oil-company defendants, with the transaction taking place in the Raleigh Hotel in Washington.)

The high stakes in the political battles over "tidelands" were made very apparent. Harold L. Ickes recalled his warning to President Roosevelt against allowing an oilman to become party treasurer, for sooner or later "you are going to have a scandal on your hands." He recounted his version of "the rawest proposition that has ever been made to me"—Pauley's reputed statement in 1944 that he could raise $300,000 for the party from oilmen if the federal government would not press its offshore oil suit designed to establish whether title was with the state of California or the United States.[4] A firm believer in state control of the offshore lands of California, Pauley apparently had explored the issue with everyone he could reach, from Franklin D. Roosevelt on down. Norman Littell, who had been Assistant Attorney General in charge of the Lands Division and chairman of the Interdepartmental Committee (Interior, Justice, Navy, State) appointed by the President in 1939, which recommended that the federal government take legal action in the courts to test title to the lands, described Pauley as a "veritable jack-in-the-box" on the subject who discussed offshore oil with Littell at every occasion. He cited one meeting with Harry J. March, vice president and general counsel of Signal Oil and Gas, who was sharing a hotel suite with Pauley. Littell testified that Pauley prefaced the introduction by saying that while he wouldn't want anything improper done, oil people had contributed to the campaign and "they expected something for their money." [5] Known among some California politicians as "the man with the black bag," March raised money from West Coast oil interests and was actively lobbying for congressional quitclaim legislation rather than for any court determination. March was told the case was already out of Littell's hands and was referred to Solicitor General Biddle, with whom Littell arranged an appointment.

Also portrayed were some of the activities of Welburn Mayock, who had worked as a personal attorney for Pauley as well as for a number of small oil companies and who was brought onto the staff of the National Democratic Committee by Pauley. Mayock's instructions from the California oilman, according to the latter, were to "to be sure that . . . there are no contributions taken that would be embarrassing to the Democratic Committee or in violation of the law." The attorney operated from his party post in behalf of the pending quitclaim legislation. Identifying himself as the committee's general counsel, he made long-distance calls appealing to a number of state attorneys general for their support. "No doubt the toll charges were listed as committee expenses—I didn't give that angle a thought," he admitted to Edward A. Harris of the *St. Louis Post-Dispatch*. "Perhaps it wasn't quite proper, but it didn't occur to me to make a distinction on telephones. I didn't think it would come up." [6] In the course of an investigation of Internal Revenue Service practices several years later, Mr. Mayock offered a frank portrait of "a very close avoidance of the Hatch Act," from which emerged a step-by-step analysis of the intricate political art of raising money and hopes without direct verbal commitments by either recipient or donor. [7]

In 1945, the *St. Louis Post-Dispatch* also traced a Petrol Corporation phone number to the Democratic National Committee headquarters and the desk of William Neal Roach, the party vice chairman. Roach, who had been with the committee since 1928, had joined Pauley's business in 1943 as its representative in connection with government contracts. He returned to the party in 1944. Pauley's successor as treasurer was George Killion, a friend of the oilman who had served in Governor Olson's administration, had participated in the conservation fight, had been a public relations assistant to Ralph Davies in the PAW, and then was recommended by Pauley for the party job. Killion later became president of the American President Lines, controlled by a syndicate formed by Davies and Samuel B. Mosher, president of Signal.

Pauley admitted having introduced William W. Clary, the Assistant Attorney General of California who was a leader in the quitclaim fight while also representing oil interests, to Speaker of the House Samuel Rayburn, to the chairmen of the House and Senate Judiciary committees that were handling quitclaim legislation, and to members of the Senate to discuss offshore oil. "I have done that, and I am sure you have on hundreds, thousands of occasions. I don't think that a man can be in politics. . . ." [8] It was claimed by Ickes and others that Pauley was instrumental in having President Roosevelt, who was worried about holding California in the Democratic fold, instruct his Attorney General to postpone the "tidelands" suit. This was not filed until May 1945, after the election and the President's death. Ickes reported that Pauley even pursued the familiar subject on the special train carrying President Truman and other officials from the interment services for Roosevelt at Hyde Park, reminding Ickes of the earlier position of Interior accepting state ownership. But Truman did go ahead with the court test.

The equally serious interest of the industry in "conservation" also emerged from the hearings. The West Coast majors had campaigned strenuously for production controls and had won the adoption of one such measure (the Sharkey bill) in 1931. But independents, with Pauley as one of their spark plugs, defeated it at a state-wide referendum that followed. The latter group then moved more directly into state politics to gain a sympathetic legislature. Explained Pauley:

We knew that each year we'd have to fight it all over again because most of the members of the Legislature did what the big oil operators told them to do. We had spent half a million dollars beating the measure and didn't want to spend that much each year. It was cheaper to get a new Legislature.[9]

The struggles continued. And then Pauley, who had criticized the NRA codes as a tool of the integrated giants and had been

prosecuted as a "hot-oil" operator, became an advocate of conservation. Intensive pressure tactics by Pauley, vice president Ralph Davies
of Standard of California, Harry March of Signal, President Charles
S. Jones of Richfield, and other oilmen, who jammed the state
legislative chambers during a thirty-four-hour continuous session,
resulted in the passage of a new conservation bill. Governor Culbert
L. Olson signed the (Atkinson) bill, but the charges of a sellout to
Standard Oil intensified. And in 1939 the majors were again thwarted
by an adverse popular referendum, despite their having spent hundreds of thousands of dollars. Their Yes-for-Five Committee deliberately attempted to conceal the fact that Standard of California
was the chief financial source. The sum of $380,000 in contributions
was listed as coming from a title lawyer hired by March of Signal
Oil rather than from the giants themselves. This was an obvious
evasion of the intent of the California corrupt practices safeguards
requiring public disclosures of political donors, although neither
March nor the attorney, Harold Judson of Williamson, Hogan and
Judson, would concede the ethical point.[10] Judson, a friend of
Pauley, was later hired by the United States Justice Department
as Assistant Solicitor General.

Company employees were used on both sides in obtaining and in
blocking petitions. Charges that members of the legislature were
on California Standard's pay roll were made freely. Two legislators,
one of whom became a congressman, received retainers from Pauley's
Petrol Corporation, paid through the latter's advertising firm. According to Tobey, vice president T. S. Petersen of California Standard admitted to him that "we did things that no man should ever
ask a man to do. . . . If we ever entered into a program like that
again, I would resign." [11]

The independents, who opposed conservation as the handmaiden
of the "oil monopoly," also spent considerable sums, with William
Keck of Superior Oil an important contributor. They were accused
of using fraud in obtaining signatures for their petitions and of having resorted to every kind of pressure. They admitted to the hiring
of goon squads, claiming this as self-defense to counter physical
attacks upon their employees and people hired to circulate petitions.
Ickes felt that in opposing the Atkinson bill the independents were
merely defending their right to freeboot without the social restraint

and that they had used "big oil" as a red herring to sidetrack the problem. As for Tobey, after becoming increasingly overwhelmed by this tangled web of organized greed and corruption, he was to conclude that "oil permeates a great deal of our life; it permeates the halls of legislatures; it permeates the Congress." [12]

Pauley vigorously defended his qualifications. Max Truitt, the son-in-law of Democratic Majority Leader Alben W. Barkley, and an active Washington lobbyist whose many clients included Tapline (the Aramco pipeline), served as his counsel. Pauley insisted that he was the victim of vicious and dishonest slugging. He denied knowledge of any pipeline-settlement payoff and of Ickes's charges. "I have never in my life solicited, suggested, or accepted a contingent contribution." Besides, given the federal government's tidelands position, "I don't see at this moment (referring to the 1944 election) that I offered them any great inducement to make a contribution to the Democratic Committee. . . ." [13] Most oil money, he ventured, was then going to the Republicans who may have offered oilmen inducements.

Pauley received the full backing of President Truman, who publicly questioned the accuracy and loyalty of Ickes's charges. Mr. Truman immediately accepted the submitted resignation of his subordinate. Ickes, mindful that "the forces that ruined Secretary Fall will always be playing upon anyone who is Secretary of the Interior," had announced that he could not serve in the same cabinet with the California oilman. And, added Ickes, "I do not have a reputation for dealing recklessly with the truth," and "I don't care to stay in an administration where I am expected to commit perjury for the sake of the party." [14] Truman later explained that, despite Ickes's reputation as a troublemaker and a man difficult to get along with, he was fond of him because he was not a special-interests man. "But when he got too big for his breeches and opposed me openly on my appointment of Pauley, I could not, as President, tolerate that." [15] Thus, one by-product of the Pauley affair, was the end of the public career of the dedicated Bull Moose Republican and self-styled "curmudgeon" who had served as Secretary of the Interior since the beginning of the New Deal.

Some White House aides had originally advised against bringing in Pauley directly. They had suggested instead that he first be given another post for a year, such as the head of the Red Cross, and then be brought in as the ex-Red Cross man instead of ex-oilman. But it was too late. Senator Tobey's predilection for explaining all evil in terms of bad men, whether crude hoodlums, venal business-men, or slick politicians—supported by Ickes's dramatic play upon memories of Teapot Dome—had successfully tuned in to a basic American response. The stigma of "oilman" had become too strong. In the face of further embarrassment to the Administration and certain rejection by the Senate Naval Affairs Committee, Pauley reluctantly requested that his nomination be withdrawn.

There was much to suggest that what Pauley was involved in was not too different from the standard procedures for party fund raising. And while it was quite likely that no direct political rewards were promised in return for contributions or for less than full dedication to the public interest, nevertheless the setting of this giving always suggested the unstated obligation. As Welburn Mayock explained on another occasion, he never made political approaches when seeking special favors from government officials for deserving clients willing to make party contributions. But it was "common knowledge" among all those with whom he dealt that "I was a busy little bee in the campaign." [16] Senator Millard E. Tydings, the conservative Maryland Democrat whose solicitude for Pauley and whose references to Tobey as an inquisitor during the frequent bitter exchanges among the senators caused the New Hampshire Republican to refer to him as the counsel for the defense, made clear his feelings that the whole matter was grossly exaggerated. "All parties go out and get money from any source from which they can get it, all parties." [17]

"Oilmen in politics" has long been a familiar national image, thanks to periodic disclosures concerning the original Rockefeller empire, Teapot Dome, "tidelands," and the Texas millionaires. The activities centering upon each has been the occasion for widespread indignation. But the protest has been short-lived. For each issue has been treated as an isolated phenomenon, somehow deviant from the normal patterns of development of the culture. Thus, the dramatic freewheeling movements in business and politics of a number of contemporary oil producers—coming in a period when corporate policies appear to emerge from cavernous boards and committees untouched by individual judgment or conscience, and when public personalities are both drab and synthetic—make these oilmen easy devils to liberals confronted with the depersonalized power structure of modern America. For example, the vexing question of money in politics has become equated with Texas oil money in politics, a viewpoint encouraged by the rising costs of campaigns, the declining standards of public and private morality, the broad loopholes in our tax laws, and the enlarged egos of some oilmen. A $5,000 contribution by H. L. Hunt in a particular state or $50,000 from H. R. Cullen checkerboarded across the nation—just as oilmen may take up leases in a checkerboard pattern in a promising oil region—wins scare headlines in the liberal and labor press. And deservedly so. But the recorded spending of over $1 million for Averell Harriman's New York gubernatorial victory in 1954 passes without comment, as do the $75,000 required for a single national political television hookup, the minimum expense of $250,000 to run for the Senate in an industrial state such as Illinois, and the estimated minimum outlay by all groups of $180 million in the 1956 national election.

There is distortion, too, in singling out oilmen for their particular preferences and exertions. These are rights that, as individuals, they are entitled to enjoy as freely as farmers, air-line executives, automobile workers, doctors, and Wall Street brokers. There are thousands of oilmen, even if one does gag slightly over the industry's current propaganda about 42,000 "independent" oil companies. Their individual politics, in terms of purpose and party identification, do vary. And the industry has its share of intelligent and even public-spirited persons, despite the notoriety accorded the grasping, the ostentatious, and the primitive. Some oilmen, not unlike other successful businessmen who have moved into the active ranks of the New and Fair deals and the Republican and Democratic parties, enter politics because that is where they now see the excitement and challenge of big stakes. Much of the private satisfaction and public recognition derived from the aggressive efforts and clashes of individual wills, once sought in industry and finance, more and more appear to be attainable in public service. This is not to suggest that the motivations are simply "psychological." Increasingly, the private ends of all individuals and groups are achieved or thwarted through the action or inaction of public government. The larger problem for a political democracy is not that of a few self-seeking individuals, but rather the voice and representation far out of proportion to numbers accorded the economically powerful in the processes of public policy making.

The Pauley hearings barely lifted the curtain on oil. The industry's private machinery of government operates nationally and internationally, frequently with political experience and skill far greater than that possessed by public agencies. Originally, oilmen undoubtedly preferred to be left alone, free to carve out their empires without public interference or partnership. Early political behavior was essentially defensive or supplementary. But as the modern state has taken an increasing interest in the economic consequences of oil operations, business involvement in governmental doings has intensified. Oil has become a participant at every level of public life, from the relationship of the company proration engineer with the state regulatory commission, and the refinery manager with the local chamber of commerce, all the way up to the intimacy of corporate executives with presidents and military planners at home and with diplomats abroad. Often the separate business organizations join together for common political objectives.

Oil increasingly accepts politics as an integral and continuing part of management practices. Uncertainties or dislocations occasioned by faulty public policies can be as threatening to the integrated industry as technical breakdowns. Participation in public debates, party struggles, elections, and legislation thus become components of the industrial process as well as tactics in the furtherance of private power. The oil company must watch and anticipate policy actions by the United States and other governments that might affect oil. It must calculate the impact of its own moves upon public agencies and opinion. Depending upon its degree of direct economic relationship with the consumer and general public, the oil corporation constantly must have an accurate appraisal of the temper of the social environment within which it performs. When to these fairly familiar political factors there are added the internal organizational characteristics of the industry—such as the planning and controls over resources, capital, markets, men, and research, as discussed in an earlier chapter—then the full nature of the oil corporation as a political institution comes sharply into focus.

The men of oil share certain common problems and philosophical approaches. In some phases of production big money can be made suddenly, with individual daring, shrewd bargaining, persistence, and luck. The millionaire wildcatters such as H. L. Hunt, Roy Hugh Cullen, Clint W. Murchison, Sid Richardson, and a host of others have been prototypes of businessmen in other segments of the economy from an earlier period of American history. Their simple image of the boundless opportunity for all who would reach out for it has been reinforced by their own experiences and unchallenged by continuous direct dealings with stockholders, unions, welfare problems, and social responsibility. Interference with profits and regulation by government easily become equated with socialism.

Traditionally, oil producers in Pennsylvania, Texas, Oklahoma, Louisiana, California, and other oil states have exerted considerable influence in elections. Some industry executives speak frankly of their insurance policies, that is, the financial assistance given to all possible victors in primaries, run-offs, and elections. Once Rockefeller, Sr., sent a check to Ohio Republicans with the comment that "our friends do feel that we have not received fair treatment from the Republican Party, but we expect better things in the future." [18] In 1903, when a Standard agent, who was also a member of Congress, was approached by a senator for a loan, he wrote to John D. Archbold, vice president of the company, "Do you want to make the investment?" [19]

In 1957 William A. Dougherty, chief counsel and director of the Consolidated Natural Gas Company, whose $400 million empire includes the East Ohio Gas and the Hope and Peoples Natural Gas companies, gave a $5,000 "loan" to Orville Hodge, Republican state auditor of Illinois, who went to jail in the wake of a scandal involving the embezzlement of a million dollars in state funds. Asked by the Securities and Exchange Commission, which is responsible for enforcing the ban on political gifts by utility holding companies, to explain the payment, Dougherty said he had heard Hodge had a good chance of becoming governor of Illinois. "I thought if I could do him the favor which he had asked me, that I would be in a much better position to get his help" when circumstances requiring such support would arise. Referring to a bill that would have brought one of his client-companies, the Mississippi River Fuel Corporation, under the jurisdiction of the Illinois Commerce Commission, the general counsel explained that since "neither the company nor I wanted that particular legislation passed . . . I thought it would be helpful if I could go to Mr. Hodge and say 'Whom shall I see about working on this bill?' " Planning for "a friendly hearing" seemed to be normal business ethics:

I really was irritated that a lot of this stuff would be gone into . . . with a measly little $5,000 compared with over $1 million that Mr. Hodge had taken out of the state treasury, it seemed to me it was making a mountain out of a molehill.[20]

There are cases where oilmen backed the losing candidate, but immediately after the election graciously repaired the original error by contributing to the deficit drive of the victors.

Recalling his own experiences with the power forces of Texas that finally defeated him as oil considerations gained political ascendancy over traditions of rural protest and depression factors in his district, a state legislator and then New Deal congressman with fifteen years of service made clear his painful conclusion that more than good citizenship is involved in this interest in elections. He described the process whereby an eager candidate is transformed into what he called, in the best Populist tradition, a "common harlot of privilege":

The big boys from the utilities, the banks, the railroads and oil and gas want to contribute to your campaign. They watch you to see if you are okay. Then they'll ask you how you stand on the key issues. If okay, they'll want to contribute. They want your name on the back of their checks.

His record against tax loopholes incurred the wrath of the oil industry and was replaced in 1939 by a congressman who went on to compile a sound oil and gas record. The chastised liberal found an obscure federal legal berth. His successor in Congress was active in steering offshore oil quitclaim legislation through the House. After his retirement, the latter was sought by the American Petroleum Institute to be its official Washington spokesman.

Some oilmen are even more crude in their approach to politics. A regional counsel for one large company summed up its preelection political relations with aspiring officeholders: "You just put good, green folding money in their lily-white hands and be goddamn sure they know why you put it there." [21]

Nevertheless, it is hard to make villains out of these oil producers and their staffs after talking with them in their offices and in the fields. They are generally friendly, rugged, intelligent, and outspoken in their faith in a competitive society. Frequently, they are far more attractive than the modern college-trained corporation executive one increasingly encounters whose pleasant words sound pretested and whose vaunted initiative is repeatedly mocked by the long-distance calls from the regional office in Denver or the home office in Tulsa or New York.

It is now customary to identify oil with the Republican party or the Dixiecrat movement. But oilmen have been active in the Democratic party. During the New Deal they made many cash contributions. In 1936, for example, H. L. Dougherty of the Cities Service Company reported giving $55,000. Walter A. Jones, a Pittsburgh oilman, was also an important contributor in that period. Jacob Blaustein of the American Oil Company (now part of Standard of Indiana) was consistently pro-New Deal. Sid Richardson was friendly with Franklin D. Roosevelt, and his contributions helped maintain a Democratic congress in the 1942 election. In fact the Democrats received sizable oil sums as late as 1944. Postponements of antitrust action until after the 1940 election and of "tidelands" and further antitrust litigation until after the 1944 election were not unrelated to the desire to maintain such generosity. Writing in his diary in 1940 about the determination of the Justice Department to press the huge case pending against the oil industry, Ickes said: "I have come to feel now that I would like to see the suit postponed until at least after elections. Some 3,000 defendants are involved and I can see no good sense in stirring up so many people at this time. . . . The President agreed with my position." [22]

But conservative southern Democrats had found it increasingly difficult to accept the course of the party as it became more and more the party of immigrants, minorities, the Negro, labor, welfare, regulation, and national power. With substantial support from oil, the anti-New Deal elements, which in 1948 were to burst out of the party via the Dixiecrats in a blaze of principle over states' rights, had been preparing a countermovement since 1936. This was long before tidelands or civil rights were made headline issues. The anti-Roosevelt forces in the Texas Democratic convention in 1944 included attorneys from Sinclair, Socony-Vacuum, Humble (Standard of New Jersey), Sun, and other oil and gas companies. These "Texas regulars" had further financial backing from Republicans, including Cullen and other oilmen, who were joined with other big corporate interests for the common and continuing purpose of capturing the "Southern Democracy" and splitting the National Democratic party in order to prevent another Roosevelt victory. Such activities suggest how far the southern states' rights movement, heavily financed by oil and electric power, from its inception has been a creature of the northern financial groups whose colonial empire the South has been.

By 1947 the chairman of the Texas Democratic State Executive Committee could declare: "It may not be a wholesome thing to say, but the oil industry today is in complete control of state politics and state government." [23] And in 1948 prominent oil lawyers who represented the majors as well as the independents had positions of leadership in the Dixiecrats in Alabama, Mississippi, Texas, and Louisiana. In Texas, for example, the first head of the Dixiecrats was Palmer Bradley, a lawyer employed by Standard Oil (New Jersey). In Alabama the leader was Gessner McCorvey, whose clients included Humble, Gulf, and Magnolia. The oil intrigues surrounding the nomination of Mississippi's racist Senator James O. Eastland prompted one veteran Southern political observer to conclude that the state was "still a satellite of Texas." Leander Perez, the political boss of Plaquemines Parish who argued his state's tidelands case in the United States Supreme Court, was the key figure on Louisiana's Democratic Committee seeking to get Truman's name off the Democratic ballot in that state. (Perez's relationships with the oil and sulphur interests operating in his district—with production for 1957 valued at over $200 million—have been the subject of numerous investigations, including one by the Louisiana Crime Commission that ultimately found itself frustrated and then declared unconstitutional for its pains. Companies seeking leases have had to deal with Perez or with land companies that the lawyer controlled or counseled.) Perez joined with others in the nation who had access to oil money in their financing of the Dixiecrats. State control of "tidelands" was a major plank. The Democratic party was sufficiently frightened so that its 1948 platform was silent on the subject. The Republicans favored the "restoration to the states of their historic rights to the tide and submerged lands, tributary waters and streams." Thomas E. Dewey, their presidential candidate, generally avoided taking a public position.

A third party is incapable of gaining control of the machinery of government. The nature of the rules of American political life requires a majority party—and the Dixiecrats carried only four states in 1948. Many Southern Democrats continued to use the disposition of offshore oil lands as an issue for riding to power within their party while rescuing it from the liberal North. Indeed, it was the activities of some of these politicians, including Governor Allan Shivers of Texas, Price Daniel (Texas), Perez, Eastland, Spessard L. Holland (Florida), Strom Thurmond (former governor of South Carolina and states' rights presidential candidate), and Fielding Wright (former governor of Mississippi and Thurmond's running mate), which made the entire "tidelands" issue uncompromisable, long after the major oil interests and the Truman wing of the Democratic party were ready for compromise federal control that would have recognized existing state leases. This latter-day rapprochement accounted for the insistence of ardent states' righters that the real big oil lobby was on the side of federal control and that the essence of the compromise bill introduced by Senator Joseph C. O'Mahoney was drafted by the industry. The behavior of these southern extremists reinforced the image of their movement as primarily an attempt to smash the Democratic party and control the pieces. And it placed upon the shoulders of liberal southerners such as Lister Hill and John Sparkman, who opposed the giveaway, the formidable task of preserving the South for the Democratic party.[24]

Encouraged by such promises as "tidelands," many of the Dixiecrat forces openly moved into the Republican camp. It seemed simple enough for a party so long out of power to buy support with public property, a transaction easily translatable into the well planted mythology about the relation between grass-roots democracy and states' rights.

Oil money was no stranger to the Republican party. The Standard

Oil trust was long a fruitful source for deserving candidates. The company gave $250,000 for McKinley's 1896 campaign against William Jennings Bryan, repeating this contribution in 1900. In 1904, with trustbuster Theodore Roosevelt heading its ticket, the party received a $100,000 "personal" gift from H. H. Rogers of Standard. A succession of millionaire oilmen have controlled the Republican national committeeman seat and much of the party politics in Oklahoma. Oil had backed Warren G. Harding's nomination, in part with eyes on the naval reserves. Harry Sinclair helped pay the Republican party deficit incurred in electing Harding. At one point he made the error of using $185,000 in registered Liberty Bonds obtained from fraudulent corporate transactions that were to be featured in the Teapot Dome exposé. Sinclair, Chairman Robert W. Stewart of Standard (Indiana), and other oil executives had made several million dollars by swindling their stockholders through a dummy corporation handling crude oil at inflated prices. Republican National Chairman Will H. Hays, who was also Postmaster General and once had been an attorney for Sinclair, unsuccessfully tried to conceal the source of the money by having the bonds distributed to prominent Republican contributors who then substituted checks for the troublesome bonds. Hays was later hired as chief lobbyist for the motion picture industry and as the presumed guardian of the nation's morals, reviewing screen presentations. Stewart was ultimately ousted by the Rockefellers in a proxy fight. He received a pension.

The ubiquitous Mr. Cullen of Texas claimed that in 1944 "My family and I probably furnished more money than any other family in the state for the Dewey campaign." [25] The Pew family, which controls Sun Oil, was long a dominant force in Pennsylvania politics. Pew and Rockefeller have given generously in numerous elections over the years. Twelve Pew sources accounted for $216,800 in a listing of Republican contributors for the 1956 federal elections. Fourteen members of the Rockefeller family reported giving $152,-000. The Pews have consistently viewed the New Deal as jeopardizing the fundamentals of the American society.

War hero Dwight D. Eisenhower—sought for the presidency by all political groups, ranging from the Republicans to the Americans for Democratic Action—was studied carefully by the power forces of the economy. Quite early he received assurances of support from the nation's financial centers. Oil also welcomed his candidacy on the Republican ticket, as evidenced by the backing he received from the top officers of Standard of California, Cities Service, Gulf, and the Chase Manhattan Bank, to mention a few. The independent oil millionaires added their endorsements. Cullen reports that he had the general tabbed for some time and that in 1950 he told him that the people of the United States were "sick of politicians. . . . You can be nominated and elected if you refuse to talk politics with anyone. Remain just what you are, a soldier." [26] Sid Richardson visited the general at NATO headquarters in Paris in 1952 and reportedly pledged several million dollars if he would decide to run. Eisenhower's much publicized across-the-seas correspondence with Texas oilman H. Jack Porter that same year revealed his support of state ownership of offshore oil lands: "Federal ownership in this case, as in others, is one that is calculated to bring about steady progress towards centralized ownership and control, a trend which I have bitterly opposed." [27] Coming ten days before the Senate offshore oil vote, this first precampaign pronouncement on any political issue marked the general's formal entry into domestic politics. It also represented a direct bid for the convention support of the states' righters who leaned to Taft or to a third party.

In Louisiana, Texas, and other southern states, major oil company executives and attorneys were prominent in the Republican crusade. The new middle-class professionals and technicians employed by oil were also active, as were many of their wives. Older independent oilmen tended to join in support of Eisenhower while backing the non-Fair Deal Democratic tickets. The Amarillo airport during the Texas Democratic convention was described by a senator from the Southwest as "choked with oil company planes" that had flown in delegates from all over the state. Clint Murchison originally had spent a large sum seeking to build a Democratic party ground swell for Eisenhower. He predicted that as a Republican President the general's "most sanguine hope could be only a bare majority, the implications of which would raise up to haunt him. . . ." But as a Democrat he would have a strong majority in Congress.[28] When this effort failed, he worked for the Republican victory.

Adlai E. Stevenson's forthright stand supporting the Supreme

Court's decisions upholding federal control of offshore oil lands—repeated before Texas audiences in face of bold placards reading "Remember the Alamo and the Tidelands Oil Steal" and numerous clues that this position could lose the state's twenty-four electoral votes for his party—completed the alienation of Texas Governor Allan Shivers and his allies in the South. The latter then announced they could not back their party's candidate. And it further assured oilmen of the wisdom of their choice. It is interesting to recall that vice presidential candidate Richard M. Nixon had predicted Stevenson would make a deal to keep Shivers within the fold. (After his tenure as governor, Shivers became chairman of the board of the Western Pipeline, Inc.) Stevenson did have to be convinced of the case for federal control by his liberal and resource-minded advisers before he came out publicly with his position. His experience as governor and his essentially conservative philosophy had taught him to be wary of the extension of federal jurisdiction. Meanwhile, there was some panic in Republican circles when Eisenhower as candidate publicly admitted that at the time of his original statement on "tidelands" he had not known of the great struggles leading to the Court decisions in favor of federal interest in the offshore lands and that of course "I am one of those who obeys the Supreme Court." But peace of mind returned when he explained that he still was committed to state control and that the Court had upheld the authority of the Congress to confer title to the states. The moral crusade—along with the career of Mr. Nixon—nearly grounded again when it was disclosed that the vice presidential candidate had been the recipient of an $18,000 secret campaign fund, drawn heavily from oilmen, including Herbert Hoover, Jr. This time public relations techniques were employed to save the day. Nixon's famous televised "Checkers" speech reassured the nation of the candidate's dedication to the basic virtues of the home, the family, and the Horatio Alger tradition. Oil money was never mentioned, and soap opera was established as an integral part of the political scene.

Eisenhower's smashing personal victory was quickly followed by a fulsome display of gratitude to its oil supporters. The new Secretary of the Interior, Douglas McKay, told the industry that he had not taken this office to lead a giveaway program of the nation's resources, as charged by his opponents. "All we are doing is giving it back to the people where it belongs." [29] Almost immediately a plan was worked out for the painless killing of the cartel suit against the international companies. The Administration's first major legislative achievement in 1953 was the signing over to the states of portions of the offshore oil lands. This was given top priority in the Senate, despite the imminent expiration of rent controls and the urgency of other broad-based economic measures. Majority Leader Robert Taft kept night and Saturday sessions going to break the attempt of opponents of quitclaim legislation to develop a full debate that might smash through the barrier of an indifferent or oil-oriented press and alert the general public. The curtailment of shale research, the purging of the regulatory agencies, and the general encouragement to giant business amply suggested which people Mr. McKay and his associates had in mind. Small wonder that The Texas Company could soon report to its stockholders and employees that the 1952 election "strongly indicated endorsement of a great deal of what the petroleum industry stands for and believes in." [30]

The various oil interests could all roughly agree on natural resources, taxes, and the menace of regulation and creeping socialism. Yet coming to formal political power could not completely resolve the dilemma of the coalescing oil elements that had helped elect a Republican Administration. Some were unhappy over the new regime's failure to place the whole of the continental shelf in state hands—or at least share the revenues. Many of the independent oilmen, especially the producers of the Southwest, have been essentially isolationist. When the United States joined the United Nations in 1945, Cullen announced that the country was "decaying politically—so fast that it is very doubtful that we can continue as a democracy much longer, unless we retrace our steps. . . ." [31] The Bricker amendment to limit the President's treaty-making powers was a reflection of such fears, and President Eisenhower himself was reported to have voiced annoyance over the financial support given to the movement by Hunt and Cullen.

Caught by reduced allowables, increased imports, and consumer shifts to natural gas, the producers without overseas holdings have resented the reciprocal trade policies defended by the major oil companies and liberal Republicans. They have sponsored congressional drives for import quotas, having the backing of thousands of citi-

zens in oil states who identify their own economic well-being as
dependent upon that of these producers. They also have had the
sympathy of many political leaders. "Failure of oil imports to adjust to demand conditions . . . must be taken as evidence that the
problem cannot be solved without some form of national policy
implemented by Congressional action," Governor Shivers testified,
the ardency of his states' rights passion temporarily subdued.[32] In
California the fight over production controls continued, with independent producers seeing the majors' continued demand for conservation legislation as greasing the skids for accelerated imports
from the Middle East. Meanwhile, the issue remained a hot potato
within both parties as the competing oil interests sought endorsement of their positions. In 1956 the Republican State Committee
avoided taking a stand. A major fight took place in the Democratic
State Central Committee after some of the leaders backed the
majors. At one point, the president of the California Democratic
Council charged that "our whole convention has been taken over
by the oil companies." [33]

Some of the wealthy independent oilmen were disappointed in
President Eisenhower's "acceptance" of the Fair Deal and One
World. The hundreds of thousands of dollars that they have spread
throughout the nation in recent elections is essentially negative in
intent. The roster of generally anti-Eisenhower Republicans supported by oil money included Senators William E. Jenner, Everett
Dirksen, Harry Cain, Karl E. Mundt, Herman Welker, Barry Goldwater, George W. Malone, Zale N. Ecton, and Joseph R. McCarthy.
Special targets in senatorial races have been Margaret Chase Smith,
Dennis Chavez, William Benton, Millard Tydings, William Langer,
Joseph C. O'Mahoney, James E. Murray, Wayne Morse, Paul Douglas, John Carroll, Mike Mansfield, Estes Kefauver, Claude Pepper,
and Frank Graham. In 1954 and 1956, oil money turned up in the
closing days of heated campaigns in the western states and was
used to finance unusually vicious red smears against O'Mahoney in
Wyoming, Murray in Montana, and Carroll in Colorado. With no
thought about the states' rights of the local citizens involved, these
oil barons have preferred to operate in the more sparsely settled states
where it may be easier to swing elections.

According to an uncritical biography of Cullen (who distributed

er's campaign manager as the exploiting of "a very, very big
ot" about Tydings's loyalty and about the report on McCarthy's
ges as a whitewash. Tydings lost. A Senate investigation deplored
tactics of this "despicable, back-street" campaign.[37] But no move
made to deny Butler the seat in the Senate. And the myth was
that anyone who challenged the McCarthy crusade against
munism would be marked for political extinction, with oil
ey providing for the costs of burial. Yet according to Clint
chison, who was not an isolationist or as fanatic as Hunt or
en, this support for McCarthy did not necessarily mean oilmen
cted from the Wisconsin senator help on oil problems in Wash-
on. "Hell, I've got ten men in Congress who are better thought
an McCarthy. I don't need him for influence."[38]

ot all producers behave this way. There are also those like
Parten, president of the Woodley Petroleum Corporation, who
been bluntly anti-McCarthy. "I am for dealing firmly with
ors but not in McCarthy's way—our tradition of civil liberties
ns too much to me to see it sacrificed to catch Communists."[39]
nd J. Howard Marshall, vice president of Signal Oil and Gas,
served on the board of directors of the Fund for the Republic.
aul Getty, who heads an oil empire that includes Tidewater,
is often cited as the richest man in the world, has challenged
standard bugaboos of oilmen. Agreeing that taxes are too high,
as denied they are confiscatory and destructive of initiative. "I
always amused by the businessman whose income has trebled
uadrupled in the last 20 years, and whose stocks are worth ten
s what they were when he bought them, groaning about 'op-
ive taxation.'" Defending organized labor, he sees charges of
munism and racketeering as applying only to a minority of the
ership in the movement. "Free, honest labor unions are our
test guarantees of continuing prosperity and our strongest bul-
against social or economic totalitarianism." He believes that
fear of Russia has been exaggerated. "Communism may be a
at and Russia is powerful, both militarily and industrially. But
ia should be treated as a competitor—not necessarily as an
ny."[40]

me producers, although undoubtedly in the minority, have
ed the more liberal Ralph Yarborough in his political races

at least 100,000 copies of the book), the oilman "assumed a kind
of benevolent protectorate over the political affairs of his state and
country." In 1949 he urged twenty-two senator "friends" to reject
Leland Olds, since the latter "would establish 'social responsibility'
in place of the profit motive. This is conclusive proof that he does
not believe in our form of government. . . ." Cullen later wired
to House Republican Leader Joseph Martin that "we must defeat
these 15 Senators" who did vote for Olds.[34] The Texas oilman
contributed to at least thirty-four election campaigns in twenty-three
states. He and his family were officially reported as spending over
$75,000, but full contributions were estimated by many political
observers to be between $500,000 and $1 million. In 1954 one survey
unearthed $41,000 of reported Cullen contributions.

The 1954 senatorial election in Montana provided one illustration of the techniques used. Cullen sent a letter by way of John T.
Flynn to Arnold Olsen, the state's courageous and ambitious young
Democratic attorney general, saying that he had been advised by
former Senator Burton K. Wheeler that Olsen was interested in
running against the veteran New Dealer James E. Murray in the
primary. Cullen indicated that if Olsen thought he had a chance,
then he would like to help him financially. The would-be benefactor
added that he would like to do this without public disclosure. This
attempt to split the Democratic party failed. But it was cleverly
played, for as state leaders were well aware, Olsen had been sorely
tempted to challenge Murray's hold on the seat. Outside money from
Cullen and other oilmen then proceeded to back the Republican
candidate, Wesley A. D'Ewart, who had been a leading proponent
of natural-resource giveaways during his service in the House of
Representatives. D'Ewart was defeated, but the Eisenhower Administration gave him an appropriate consolation prize—Assistant Secretary of the Interior in charge of conservation.

The extreme right, which regarded the Eisenhower Administration with skepticism and hostility—a view often reciprocated by
the Administration, which wished to guard against any discrediting
of the assiduously cultivated image of enlightened business con-
servatism—has depended heavily upon the fears and finances of
oilmen. Oil producer George W. Armstrong left millions to support
anti-Semitism and white supremacy. Sun Oil money backed the

violently anti-New Deal Liberty League, Sentinels of the Republic, the Associated Farmers, and numerous superpatriotic organizations. In 1934 President Edward G. Seubert of Standard (Indiana) and J. Howard Pew of Sun were leading contributors to the antilabor, anti-TVA, and antigovernment-regulation Crusaders. Pew and Frank Drake of Gulf have been among the financial angels of Spiritual Mobilization, a movement that strongly defends laissez faire and attacks welfare programs. Vance Muse of the Christian Americans Association and the Southern Committee to Uphold the Constitution has received oil support for virulent white supremacist, right-to-work, and other antilabor causes. John H. Kirby, millionaire head of the Kirby Petroleum Company, was chairman of the Southern Committee. Muse was identified with Senator W. Lee "Pappy" O'Daniel and other right-wingers at the Texas Democratic convention in 1944 seeking to force the southern Democratic party away from Roosevelt and the New Deal.[35] That same year, T. H. Barton, chairman of the board of Lion Oil, an integrated company since merged with Monsanto Chemical, ran for the United States Senate from Arkansas. His campaign as a champion of states' rights included the pledge that "Barton opposes unionization of farm labor" and that "the Democratic Party must be kept 'a white man's party.'" Cullen and Hunt have helped finance For America, a political action group that proclaims that "international leadership has captured both parties" and has been pushing the nation into socialism. In 1956 it urged rejection of the major party candidates for president, suggesting instead convention support of such favorite-son contenders as John W. Bricker, James Eastland, William Jenner, and Joseph McCarthy.

In an earlier day the business counterparts of today's independent oilmen had seen Bryan, agrarian unrest, and a stirring labor movement as the roots rather than the symptoms of revolutionary threats to their private worlds. To these contemporary oil producers, labor agitators, intellectuals, and communist conspirators in the State Department have provided equally simple explanations for the mass equalitarian pressures in the strange new world their oil helped make possible but which they cannot always comprehend. H. L. Hunt purchased and distributed thousands of copies of the Jenner Committee's report *Interlocking Subversion in Government Departments*,

which claimed that communist agents had penetrate to guide and pervert basic policies, steal thousands cause the loss of thousands of American lives. A producers hailed the return of Douglas MacArthur States after his recall from Korea by President Trun erally financed the general's Republican presidential 1952 and was indignant at a suggestion that the Pac be offered the number two place on the GOP tick of Lincoln or George Washington as Vice President

Some of them switched to McCarthy in their que at times as much for his brash, gambling, and int instincts as for his limited social orientation. The W gogue, always eager for funds, supporters, and cau sponded, and a mutual courtship ensued. He was ente by a number of Texas millionaires and flown about oil company planes for his speaking engagements. H congressional investigations of subversion received t nancing. Hunt's Facts Forum, which included a na and television program on public affairs, was used t Wisconsin senator's causes and the possibility of Mc(dential timber.

Oil money was sent to eliminate his critics. One tion was in the 1950 contest in Maryland between i lard E. Tydings and John M. Butler. The conservat senator had been chairman of the Senate committee and then rejected the substance of McCarthy's att State Department as a center of communism. Wit from outside the state—including $15,000 from C and H. J. Porter, although this was not reported unt Senate investigation of the election—and direction Lee, a McCarthy friend who had once worked fo Forum and who later was to be rewarded with a seat Communications Commission, the Butler supporte all-out offensive against Tydings. They used such composite photograph, showing Tydings (whom P velt had once tried to have purged from party ranks lawyer-lobbyist's conservatism) and Communist lead together. This faked picture was part of what w

against Allan Shivers in Texas, and also Stevenson against Eisenhower. Then too, "outside oil money pouring into the state for my opponent" has served as a useful bogy or rallying cry in the North and Northwest for candidates desperate for popular support. Conversely, oil money is like honey to many politicians of the Southwest. The "oil interests" can serve as an excellent whipping boy for those posing as crusaders in order to gain the attention and perhaps ultimate support of the companies.

The leadership of the major corporations, unlike the isolationist independents, are international trade-minded. They have substantial overseas reserves and operations. Their serious concern with problems of distribution and marketing makes them sensitive to the attitudes of consumers and the more general public. Sophisticated enough to know you cannot repeal the first half of the twentieth century, and planning for the expansion of their billion-dollar empires through the second half, they generally avoid open attacks on labor unions and welfare legislation. In Louisiana, for example, friends of organized labor have implied that the big companies helped finance the "right to work" law passed in 1954. A major company's chief counsel denied this. "We thought it was an excellent bill, but we were reluctant to take a stand openly. We would lose friends; it was too hot an issue." While generally hostile to unionization, which has not come easily in their refineries, their approach increasingly has been through corporate welfare and paternalism rather than the open and even physical resistance of an earlier period.

While big oil found the natural resources programs and the general orientation of the Eisenhower Administration to its liking, there were reservations. Some executives were disturbed over the Treasury Department's hesitation in taking a forthright stand in favor of 27½ per cent depletion allowance. The legal confusions remaining with regard to offshore boundaries made them uneasy about the intent of the Justice Department. And the President's weakness in using the full power and prestige of his office to defend free trade, along with the general wavering over Middle Eastern policies, led them privately to voice diminished enthusiasm for the nonprofessional leadership of this businessman's Administration. Remaining extremely cautious and public relations-minded, the majors were reluctant to identify publicly with McCarthy and other critics to the right. Some of them feared that the publicity surrounding the senator's frequent jaunts in oil airplanes (notably those of Plymouth and Superior) would lose them congressional support.

Campaign contributions by executives of the major oil companies, as of all corporate interests, are overwhelmingly Republican. A study of the 1952 national elections showed that officials of twenty-two of the largest oil companies contributed $307,705, of which 97 per cent went to Republican candidates and committees. A Senate report covering the 1956 federal elections found that officials of twenty-four of the largest oil companies contributed at least $344,997 to Republican causes. The Democrats received $14,650. The officers and directors of the American Petroleum Institute accounted for $171,750, all to Republicans.[41] These are actually very low amounts in terms of corporate operations and election needs. Of course, by-law corporations are not allowed to contribute directly. Such official figures do little more than suggest the orientation of the oil industry. The statistics are very limited and open to challenge as to accuracy and completeness. They cannot tell about the greater percentage of campaign offerings that are concealed and unreported through cash giving, misleading listings, padded expense accounts, and dummy bonuses for executives, with the understanding that the money is to go for politics. Institutional advertising, "educational" and association activities are often essentially political, as are the quiet loan of corporate facilities and personnel. These reports, with their flabby disclosure requirements, also ignore primary and convention campaigns that are a leading center for oil and general corporate participation, especially in one-party states.

Despite these partisan leanings, the integrated companies have a long view of politics as one of the instruments of business. They appreciate the worth of maintaining good relationships with each of the major parties. They understand what Jay Gould meant in an earlier period when he declared: "In Democratic states I am a Democrat; in Republican states I am a Republican, but I am always for the Erie Railway." In this sense they still function not unlike the original Rockefeller organization, as described by Ida M. Tarbell: "The Standard men as a body have nothing to do with public affairs, except as it is necessary to manipulate them for the 'good of the oil business.' " [42] Taking another leaf from the Rockefeller book, some companies today are reported as making a practice of having vice presidents from both political faiths who can then serve as contact men with their parties. But they much prefer the image of themselves as responsible business statesmen who are prepared to operate within the governmental framework where necessary. Whenever possible, however, their political channel is through the executive and administrative agencies rather than the legislative process—in contrast to the independents and smaller companies.

There has been a cautious but earnest reappraisal of this role. Many of the current executives have risen because of technical and managerial qualities. Competing for the approval of voters in the open goldfish bowl of formal politics seems an uncomfortable and even undignified prospect. Yet there is also within oil circles a recurring feeling of being misunderstood because of their integrated planning and persecuted because of their size. Hence what they feel is their vulnerability in a society whose slogans are still with the "small man." It's been good politics to be antibusiness, bemoaned General Electric in an employee-relations letter to its management.[43] "In England they knight their leading businessmen— over here they indict them," observed Robert E. Wilson, chairman of the board of Standard Oil (Indiana).[44] Speakers before the American Petroleum Institute's annual conventions have insisted that the oilmen must meet these challenges. "Select the most reliable candidate or candidates available and support him openly and actively," former New Deal braintruster Raymond Moley advised them. "Don't listen to the people who tell you that it will hurt your business to take an active part in politics." The alternative was that "you will have no business to lose." [45]

Some executives agree that the time has come for direct and open participation. In an address before the Associated Industries of Georgia, Indiana Standard's Robert E. Wilson criticized businessmen for "lack of courage in leading the fight against both demagoguery and dishonesty in city, state and nation." He called upon them to restore to American public life the high standards of ethical conduct that characterized their economic behavior:

Business and industry leaders, knowing right from wrong and educated regarding the forces of economic law, have a moral responsibility to take the lead in fighting for sound principles and opposing the bad. But how many times have we seen individual businesses and business groups fearing to give public support to sound tax or other economic policies; or refusing to take a firm position against futile and damaging controls for fear of a few transient headlines.

In recent years, we have frequently seen industry caving in before the combined pressures of big labor and big government, even though by so doing management was selling out the customer, the shareholder, the pensioner, and the unrepresented employee.

Many companies have an established policy of avoiding, as if the plague, close contact with local, state, or national "politics." Business leaders of past generations may have had their faults, but I think they, with their rugged individualism, showed more courage on vital issues than do many of our present generation of management. Maybe we have become so obsessed with the desirability of making friends that we are unwilling to make ANY enemies, even of the right kind.[46]

This obligation of the corporation to assume a stewardship of political life, as wealthy predecessors had accepted their economic stewardship, found expression in internal company policies. Frank O. Prior, who became chairman of Standard (Indiana) in 1958, has described his organization's concern with all legislation affecting the national economy and particularly the oil business. "We try to get all our people, all our plant managers, such as refinery managers, all our department heads in all our offices, all our regional managers, and division managers to take a real interest in what is going on and the issue behind any type of legislation that might indirectly or directly affect our business." President T. S. Petersen of Standard Oil of California, one of the more aggressive mammoth corporations in politics, says that as a matter of practical business policy he prods his executives to participate in politics and civic affairs, including making financial contributions. "We don't want anybody around our shop who isn't assuming some kind of responsibility, although, as I say, you can't force people to do that." President A. L. Nickerson of Socony Mobil has explained that as part of his company's continuing political interests it urged employees to write letters to their congressmen, as during the natural gas struggle. But "we made no attempt to find out who did write or who didn't write." [47]

Meanwhile, the United States Chamber of Commerce has been advising all business leaders to enter politics. They are urged to get their employees to vote, encourage management personnel to enter practical politics and give money, discuss political issues in company publications, and permit candidates to tour plants. The Chamber is also pushing the creation of schools for politics for businessmen. General Electric and the Syracuse Manufacturing Association have set up a series of seminars and workshops for middle management officials.

The catalytic most frequently employed to spark as well as defend these actions is the general specter of organized labor's growing political focus. And the most visible symbol is Walter Reuther and the vigor of his United Automobile Workers. The president of the National Association of Manufacturers has warned "that the chief objective of today's labor leadership is not only to extend but to perpetuate its economic and political power. And if they can achieve political dominance they will be able to dictate legislatively what they could not obtain across the bargaining table or justify economically." [48]

In 1958 senior vice president Archie D. Gray of Gulf Oil announced to all employees and shareholders a new company program. He cited a letter written by Ralph W. Gwinn, a strenuous opponent of the welfare state and anti-Eisenhower Republican from New York, in which the congressman explained that restrictions on labor unions were not being adopted because " 'labor—or rather the top officials of organized labor—dominate Congress.' "

"Over 175 members of the House have benefitted from union contributions, free campaign help, radio and TV time, advertising, extensive publicity in the labor press, scores of voluntary workers furnished by the unions, doorbell ringers, telephone brigades and all the rest of it. Business organizations do none of this. Business as such is unorganized politically and therefore impotent.

". . . Union leaders get men elected who agree with them and thereby force government into improper activities. On the other hand, business is not organized politically to restore and maintain the legitimate functions of business.

"But that's not the whole story. Countless smaller groups, organized to get theirs from government, depend on labor's political activity for their success, because union political power is solidly behind every socialist program ever enacted or enlarged by Congress.

"The trouble in Congress is not that we don't know what legislation is needed. The trouble is that we don't have the votes to get it passed. . . ."

"In the opinion of Gulf's management," declared Mr. Gray, "Representative Gwinn's statement is an impelling call to action."

For many years Gulf, together with most other American corporations, has been so busily engaged in business activities that politics has been ignored. But the situation so clearly spelled out by Mr. Gwinn cannot be ignored. Whether we want to be there or not, Gulf and every other American corporation is in politics, up to its ears in politics, and we must either start swimming or drown. Gulf's management would be derelict in its duty to its shareholders and employees alike if it tried to ignore this fact, and did nothing, as Representative Gwinn has put it, "to restore and maintain the legitimate functions of government."

If we are to survive, labor's political power must now be opposed by a matching force, and there is no place in the United States where such a force can be generated except among the corporations that make up American business. Because this is so, Gulf's management has determined that in the future the Corporation will take an increasingly active interest in practical politics. . . .

The company explained that it would study carefully the behavior of all elected public officials as part of its national legislative and information program. But political action by its 161,000 employees, dealers, and shareholders was to begin at the grass roots, Gulf explained in more detail the following year. District managers in marketing, transportation, and production would form "the hard core of the program" and were to be trained by regional political supervisors. "The program will . . . insist that all Gulf personnel involved work with local political leaders and elected representatives" to develop "mutual understanding." Employees were to be encouraged to undertake worth-while civic and political responsibilities —"on a nonpartisan basis." "Since wives are tremendously important in any such program, the Company will also encourage the wives of employees to become active in carrying out the objectives of the program."

The need for financial contributions was also cited, with no mention made of the example set by the Mellon family who control Gulf and who have always been heavy donors. (A Senate report on the 1956 national elections credited the family with a minimum of $100,000 in reported contributions.) Concluded Gulf:

The fact that organized labor has been following a similar line of action is the reason that labor leaders have achieved dominance over our national legislative assembly. If our free competitive institutions are to be preserved from destruction by the unholy combination of predatory gangsterism and crackpot socialism that is thriving under labor's Congressional benevolence, then business has no choice. It must do likewise or throw in the towel.[49]

13

The Oil Lobby

Despite the innocent reluctance displayed by the industry in its political oratory, there has always been a potent "oil lobby." Its functioning dates to the beginning of the modern petroleum industry. In 1866, for example, a federal tax on crude oil was repealed after aroused Pennsylvania producers brought pressure on the House Ways and Means Committee and the Congress, citing hardships to the infant industry. From that time, oil interests knew they could never abandon vigilance in the legislative halls if they were to maintain their defenses against taxation and publicly defined responsibility. Yet they generally have chosen to deny the existence of any such operations. During the 1951 offshore oil fight Senator Tom Connally of Texas insisted that "the only oil lobby involved is opposing state ownership to get cheap federal leases," and that it was forcing the federal government to behave like a common claim jumper.[1] His reference was far from accurate. But it was true that civic virtue was not the only motivating force on the federal control side. Men like former Senator Burton K. Wheeler and former White House adviser Thomas G. Corcoran apparently had their own economic irons in the form of clients with federal claims on offshore oil lands. Two other former senators who lobbied for federal title had shares in a company engaged in nation-wide stock selling based on nothing more than federal applications for offshore leases. And there certainly were those who sincerely felt that title rested with the states and resisted on principle the growth of strong central government. But this did not prove the accuracy of a Senate Interior and Insular Affairs Committee majority report issued in 1953 under the chairmanship of Senator Guy Cordon. This insisted that

372

"nowhere in the long and voluminous record is there a scintilla of evidence even remotely substantiating such a charge" that "those who believe that the States themselves are best qualified to own and manage the lands and resources within their State boundaries are somehow participating in an 'oil grab' as 'stooges' of the oil industry." [2]

The term "oil lobby" is more readily used than defined by critics of the industry. During the tidelands controversy, advocates of the federal position were reluctant to spell out the nature of the lobby and tell who had the heavy investments—let alone mention the entrenchment of oil within the Interior Department. At one heated point, a profederal leader declared that a senatorial colleague of his was only with difficulty holding back from disclosing the contents of a "secret" document that named the oil companies with heavy offshore investments and expectations in the Gulf of Mexico. The document, never cited on the Senate floor, was a publicly advertised brokerage bulletin, available to anyone for the price of a postal card. (The circular listed Kerr-McGee, Cities Service, Pure, Continental, Shell, Phillips, Standard of California, Humble, and Socony.) A civil servant who had dealt with oil for many years explained that such caution was understandable. "Oil goes after individuals down here. Be general, say 'oil lobby.' That's okay. But let a politician or bureaucrat be specific, name names and they'll gun for him." Former Solicitor General Philip B. Perlman, a leading adviser to the defenders of federal control, concurred. When asked why there was no mention of specific oil interests in the strong Senate minority report of 1953 that defined the federal case and in the floor speeches, he cited a casualty list of congressmen who have antagonized oil.

But the fight provided an excellent view of the great pressure ability of the industry in Washington. Deployed in full force were the various echelons of respectable law firms, ex-government and congressional personnel, public relations consultants, former and practicing newsmen also serving as advisers and agents, trade association representatives, sales officers, company vice presidents in charge of governmental relations, company legal counsels and public relations executives, specially mobilized "grass roots" organization spokesmen, and even men of lesser social status who called themselves and registered as lobbyists. Practically every important oil company is generally represented in Washington by men in one or more of these categories, with informal intercompany committees handling such issues as tidelands and imports. The majority do not comply with the limited registration requirements set by the Congress. Standard of California has had a staff ranging from four to thirteen members, "depending," explained Ned Burnham, vice president, "on how much government bothers us." In 1956 President T. S. Petersen described to a Senate committee the California company's approach:

We have a vice president in our company who has the responsibility of handling our legislative affairs. That is his job. It is his work to follow Federal legislation and pretty well legislation that is proposed within the States in which we operate. He has copies of most bills that are pertinent to our own company's operation. They flow in to him. He takes an active interest in them. Obviously the Standard of California can't go out and oppose or put over any measure that it might want to. He has to work with [trade] associations. . . . That Washington office is a service office for our entire corporation. . . . They maintain contact with all the various points here in Washington that this company is concerned with. That is sales to the military, of which there are a great many and amount to a great deal of money, following our contracts with the Department of the Interior who, after all, is the biggest landlord that we deal with. . . . We have a very active contact with the Department of Interior. Mr. Walshe [Woollen H. Walshe] is registered as a lobbyist, and he has opportunity to contact the Members of our Congress here on matters that are of interest to us and to try to explain our viewpoint, where it is appropriate to do so. . . . A small percent of his time is directed to legislative contact here. The big part of his time is employed in the matters of taking care of the contacts here in Washington and Washington has become quite a busy place in the last 15 years for a businessman.[3]

Sidney A. Swensrud, chairman of the board of Gulf, explained that his company did not maintain any regular registered lobbyists. "We have had a permanent representative here in Washington only for the purpose of handling matters with the Government . . . or to follow and report on things of interest. Our representative does not do any contacting with Congress for us." When there have been legislative matters of interest, "and of course, there are frequently," a few of the top officers "sort of handled it in our own way by those of us who might be interested coming down here and testifying before committees, or perhaps going around to visit with some of our Senators or Congressmen and talking the thing over, but we haven't any regular system about it." Under its new political action program, Gulf now has a Washington office headed by its vice president Kermit Roosevelt (formerly of the Central Intelligence Agency). There are individual representatives for legislative, foreign affairs, public relations, and tax matters. The office coordinates all company contacts with the federal bureaucracy and the legislature. "Complete dossiers of all congressmen from the states in which Gulf has an interest will be prepared and parceled out to the regional representatives involved. . . . These dossiers will include not only voting records, but everything that will assist Gulf's people in obtaining a more complete understanding of their elected representatives." [4] Shell Oil has never registered any Washington personnel, H. S. M. Burns, president, reported in 1956, "because we have never lobbied as I understand lobbying." [5] But company executives have worked with some of the trade associations on such matters as natural gas and mineral leasing on Federal lands.

The other companies generally follow similar patterns. Oil lobbying has become a fine art, if not a science. The executive director of the Washington office of the National Association of Manufacturers, in a pamphlet *Know Your Congressman* published in 1944, had this to say about the industry's handling of its appearance in 1939 before the Temporary National Economic Committee which was investigating the concentration of economic power:

For weeks the petroleum group studied the TNEC members and watched their conduct [sic] of witnesses. When the oilmen appeared, they knew the likes and dislikes of each committee member, and they pulled out an organ stop that appealed to everyone on the committee. Even the committee members were high in their praise of what the oil industry had done. And most important of all, it ended the clamor to enact legislation drastically regulating the oil industry.[6]

When a specific issue is at stake, such as the 1953 House of Representatives' investigation of a remarkably coincidental crude oil price rise, informed policy-level officials from the home office testify. But first there is careful briefing by their permanent Washington representatives, who then remain in the background, less likely in this fashion to wear out their welcome. For example, Jersey Standard's public relations firm, Arthur Newmyer and Associates, had five men covering the price hearing. Any criticism of the industry, direct or implied, by a member of Congress is quickly countered with a memorandum from a company in his district pointing out the nature of the "misinformation." Legislators also receive a steady diet of attractively prepared publications on oil supply, taxation, and other problems.

Often the industry prefers to organize "grass roots" pressures. These are planned to appear to emanate spontaneously from jobbers, service-station dealers, customers, and employees. A leading illustration occurred during the majors' opposition to congressional legislation limiting price discrimination by a supplier among his own dealers—a step designed to close an antitrust loophole made possible by a Supreme Court ruling in the "Detroit" case to the effect that offering discounts to select customers to meet competition in good faith did not constitute price discrimination as defined and banned by the Robinson-Patman Act. This "equality of opportunity" measure was backed by most small business groups and the National Congress of Petroleum Retailers, which claims to speak for the majority of service-station operators. While the majors remained relatively silent, a flood of letters and telegrams were sent to Congress by jobbers and dealers protesting the bill and asking to testify. It was disclosed that these were the products of an "educational" campaign, secretly coordinated "on his own" by the head of the marketing division of the American Petroleum Institute, a Shell vice president. These efforts were pushed by field representatives of the giants in 1956 and 1957, who warned dealers and jobbers that the passage of the bill might destroy their businesses. The majors admitted talking to dealers, but denied that the "grass roots" responses were involuntary and came from "captive dealers" holding short-term leases, as charged by one Texas dealers' group. Said Standard of California:

We believe our company has acted entirely within its rights in carrying to our dealers a program of information to point out to them the damaging effects this bad piece of legislation would have on their business and the oil business in general.

It is completely against this company's policies to make any attempt at all to "pressure its dealers" and all our representatives in the field have long-standing instructions to this effect.[7]

Lawyers, both within the corporate structure and on retainer, are an integral part of the oil scene. They handle litigation, develop governmental contacts, and frequently serve as channels for political relationships and party contributions. The prominent law firms may help economic interests gain readier access to the party in power. *Fortune* once noted "the tendency of corporations, following the Truman victory of 1948, to get religion and retain Washington attorneys with Democratic connections."[8] The former New Deal braintruster Thomas G. Corcoran, whose many clients have included the Tennessee Gas Transmission Company, is a leading example of the lawyer whose zeal and political acumen are highly prized and rewarded. Corcoran has been a close political ally of Democratic leader Lyndon Johnson and a key supporter of his presidential aspirations. The former's firm received over $300,000 for legal services and expenses from 1955 through 1959 when the Tennessee Company was seeking rate approvals from the FPC. Corcoran had numerous ex parte discussions with the individual commissioners, a frequent practice in expediting business before the commission, which has been notorious for its cumbersome administrative practices. The law firm of Jacob M. Arvey, Democratic committeeman from Illinois, received a $45,000 retainer from Tennessee Gas over the years 1955 to 1957. The law firm of former New York Governor Thomas E. Dewey had $174,000 of fees received in the period 1957–1958 charged into the rate base of the Natural Gas Pipeline Company of America. The FPC sometimes disallows the inclusion of such legal expenses in corporate rate calculations. Some of the fees to Corcoran and Arvey, for example, were thus not passed along directly to gas customers.

Another former White House assistant, active in Democratic party circles and sometimes mentioned as a possible national chairman, announced: "I'm not a liberal. I have gas clients. I'd have oil, if I could get them." The lawyer-lobbyist firms also provide another link among the power forces of the economy. Sullivan and Cromwell, for example, where John Foster Dulles was long the senior member, has represented the Edison Electric Institute (a major utility association), Jersey Standard, El Paso Natural Gas, Northern Natural Gas, German cartels, and other corporate interests.

The traditional version of the lawyer in Washington often defines his lobbying role as essentially defensive—observing and protesting legislation or administrative and court rulings affecting his employers, or perhaps supporting measures that somehow have gotten into the legislative hopper. But a special study could be made of the growing profession of tax experts who hunt for or create technicalities in the regulations to mask special privilege for clients. At another level, the lawyer works to formulate for public adoption legislative and administrative sanctions that will legitimize economic practices contemplated or already embarked upon by his corporate clients, but which may yet be on the frontier of legality.

Most of the majors rely on their general counsels to follow matters of immediate legislative interest, with other corporate officials, lobbyists, and trade associations acting to implement any decisions reached by the boards of directors. As President A. L. Nickerson of Socony explained:

> We assume that each one of our directors has the obligation of being generally informed of legislation that may be under consideration by the Congress in that director's portfolio or area. However, the primary responsibility for following legislation is in our office of the general counsel. Our general counsel is assisted in carrying out these responsibilities by two legislative representatives. His office will customarily analyze any bill which appears to be of general interest to our company. He will refer that analysis to the one or more directors who may be interested, and together they will decide whether or not there is any action that our company should take with respect to a given bill.[9]

A number of attorneys specialize in watching Interior Department leases on the public domain for the oil companies they serve. Among them have been the former chief counsels for the Geological Survey and the Bureau of Land Management. The late Peter Q. Nyce, an authority on federal leasing, represented a great many major and independent operators on a fee basis. An active although unregistered lobbyist, he enjoyed an unusually intimate relationship with the Senate Interior and Insular Affairs Committee. He sat in on presumably closed hearings, at one hearing was the only nongovernment witness, was allowed to question other witnesses, and even wrote at least two Senate bills on mineral leasing and their accompanying reports. He performed similar services for companion House measures. The lawyer-lobbyist kept at his desk a carefully organized folder tracing the creation of this legislation and his contribution at each stage—presumably for the benefit of paying and prospective clients. Item 30 was a letter from Senator E. V. Robertson of Wyoming, written on the stationery of the Senate Public Lands Committee and dated July 28, 1947. (It was Robertson who had turned over the witnesses to Nyce for questioning.)

DEAR PETE:

Now that the session is over and the Public Lands Program for the current year has been successfully completed, I want to express to you my sincere thanks and deep appreciation for the wise and steady counsel you have given me throughout the months past.

Without the benefit of your training, experience and pleasant personality, I am sure these bills would not have become laws.

I appreciate also your thoughtfulness and expressions in your wires, letters and phone calls as these bills moved through their legislative routine.

Peter Nyce also served as a clearinghouse in raising money from oil clients for deserving legislators who sought his help, including some who publicly have been critics of the "oil lobby." Nyce said, "I made oil companies ante up for various candidates."

The somewhat sinister connotation frequently associated with "lobbying" often troubles lawyers. Former Senator Burton K. Wheeler, once chairman of the Interstate Commerce Committee, who has been registered officially as a lobbyist and practices before such agencies as the Interstate Commerce Commission, accepts the concept as an essential part of the process of democratic participation in government.[10] "However, I never try to influence Congressmen, but rather act as a vehicle through which my clients' views can be expressed to Congress." Clark Clifford, a former White House naval aide and legal counsel to President Truman, has earned handsome retainers representing Standard of California on antitrust matters and in its dealings with the Navy on their joint holdings on the Elk Hills reserve in California. Kerr-McGee and Phillips have also been his clients. Clifford has made clear that "I have not and will not register as a lobbyist for that is not the kind of work we do. We run a law office here, with a background of experience in the general practice of law topped off by an intimate knowledge of how the government operates." [11] Clifford, who takes pride in his role in drafting President Truman's forceful "tidelands" veto message and who also was one of those who advised against the release of the Federal Trade Commission's cartel report, has explained that his office gives policy advice to clients, but did not have and would not use influence in Democratic governmental circles. He also concludes that he never saw any sign of oil influence in the Democratic party during his White House tour of duty and that he did not think oil was a significant factor in American politics.

Although the cocktail party, buttonholing, making the rounds, and testifying are still part of the legislative game, old-fashioned lobbying is increasingly passé at the national level. There is always, however, oil's ability to offer private air transportation to public officials, just as in an earlier period, when the railroads dominated, the pass was standard equipment for a legislator. It would be interesting to have statistics on how many congressmen have availed themselves of this courtesy.

Oil's social "lobby" is also effective. This makes possible the exchange of views at the club, the golf course, the race track, and at dinner parties. One illustration is of the company representative who was sponsored for membership in the highly sought-after Burning Tree Club by the then Senate Majority Leader Robert Taft, was on close terms with the Minority Leader Lyndon Johnson as co-officers of a state society, and was a good friend of Secretary of the Navy Robert B. Anderson. The problem here is not primarily that of conspiracy or design. Rather is it in the nature of oil's vast interests and of the social patterns of the American culture that provide so many informal channels for interchange among people of power throughout the nation.

Lobbying also takes place at the state level. The crude and more obvious practices commonly identified with lobbying are still familiar here. (In early oil days a Standard executive could report to Rockefeller that "I have arranged to kill two bills in Md. legislature at comparatively small expense." The company's political purchases prompted muckraker Henry Demarest Lloyd to conclude that "the Standard has done everything with the Pennsylvania legislature except to refine it.")[12] Oilmen just happen to be passing through the state capitals when the legislatures are in session, stopping off to hold open house at their hotel suites. A roundup of regular Texas lobbyists at work offered by the vigorous *Texas Observer* in 1955 described the meal circuit choices available for hungry legislators. For breakfast, one might patronize the Austin Hotel coffee shop where a Lone Star Gas representative picks up the check; or the East Room of the Austin, where the Texas Independent Producers and Royalty Owners Association plays host. Senators could count on a regular Wednesday meal at the hotel suite of the veteran Phillips lobbyist. Junkets to Mexico and to the Kentucky races and a duck hunt from a Texaco yacht have been accepted by legislators.[13] In addition, active agents represent Texaco, Magnolia, Humble, Stanolind (Indiana Standard), Shell, Transcontinental Gas Pipeline (one of whose lobbyists was formerly chairman of the state House Appropriations Committee), and other oil, gas, and related banking and construction interests. Bribery, tips on oil stock, and good leases are sometimes employed, although difficult to document. (As one southwestern newspaper editor explained, this type of corruption used to be covered, but it takes an active and special staff to run down the names on leases.)

Taxes, leases, royalty payments and well-spacing regulations are generally the major areas of concern. Oil, gas, sulphur, and chemical lobbyists are visible at all sessions of the Louisiana legislature. Leander Perez has shown a repeated capacity to manipulate leasing laws and even the state constitution to maintain his power and wealth in dealing with the absentee corporate representatives and the state government. In Montana, one of the few states that, under the leadership of such men as Judge R. V. Bottomly and Attorney General Arnold Olsen, has managed to hold on to its federal land grants, the oil interests have been trying for many years to get leases on school lands that would continue as long as oil and gas could be produced. They have descended on Helena, hiring an ex-governor and an ex-Supreme Court justice along with leading law firms tied in to the politics of the state. They have lobbied among school organizations. And they have also brought pressure in Washington to revise the state's enabling act to permit the state legislature to lengthen leasing terms. Separate studies could be written on the industry's specific activities in each oil and gas producing state.

On a more systematic basis, the American Petroleum Industries Committee, a branch of the API, has operated in virtually every state capital. Generally there has been a paid executive and a secretarial staff in each office, with the rest of the personnel volunteers. The state committees usually have been chaired and dominated by the majors. Below them have been some three thousand other committees reaching into municipalities and counties so as to be able to mobilize membership for pressure upon city and state governments. Taxes on gasoline have been the avowed focal point, with the parent committee serving as a clearinghouse for research and publicity on tax and regulatory issues. The APIC has resisted every state effort to put petroleum products, notably heating oils, under utility status; it has spoken up whenever marketing regulations have been proposed that threaten the power of the distributors over service stations. And it has advocated before local fire and highway departments heavier truck weight allowances, and before planning commissions it has appealed for more liberal zoning laws for gas stations. Other major concerns have included fighting for an extensive highway building program, while resisting such measures as restrictions against billboards, the diversion of petroleum taxes from highway construction purposes, the closing of new turnpikes to competing gasoline marketers, and federal gasoline taxes.

These bodies presumably serve as "grass roots" arms of the industry. Yet particular state PICs have engaged in the natural gas fight, with the executive officers arranging state meetings to mobilize marketer sentiment for the producer cause, introducing company lobbyists to key government and industry figures in the states, and making contacts with congressional delegations. The level of vigor has varied from state to state. In some areas, information has been circulated about political candidates. The membership is alerted to issues that are in the critical legislative stage, requiring "grass roots" pressure and selective buttonholing by members who are well acquainted with particular public officials.

In Colorado the Oil Industries Committee has had as its registered lobbyist an ex-legislator and Republican floor leader. "I keep close watch on the legislature on oil matters. I make it my business to visit at home each elected state legislator—or perhaps even before he is elected—to get to know him. I want to do this before he comes to Denver where my face is just one of a hundred new ones he'll have to know. If I can get him on a first name calling basis that means a lot. When he comes up to Denver, he'll be lonely, but he'll see a friendly face. I'll help him around, find out what committee he wants, explain about them, and help him get set on the committee if I possibly can." In North Dakota the Committee lobbyist explained: "We are not in politics. But of course we tell members who are their friends and who are not."

The many state, regional, and functional trade associations also play prominent political roles in the state capitals. In Texas, the state division of the Mid-Continent Oil and Gas Association has served in place of the APIC. Its general counsel, Andrew Howsley, a close associate of many politicians, has been described as "the kingpin of the oil lobbyists." In Oklahoma the Mid-Continent fills a similar part. And on the west coast, in California, Oregon, Washington, Nevada, and Arizona, the Western Oil and Gas Association has operated instead of any American Petroleum Industries Committees. Among the other active groups are the Rocky Mountain Oil and Gas Association and the Texas Independent Producers and Royalty Owners Association (TIPRO).

Many of these organizations refer to themselves as spokesmen for the independents and small men of the industry. Actual practices vary considerably. TIPRO bars refiners and integrated companies—"no matter how independent they may be"—and is sharply critical of the international companies. But as one maverick oil editor has noted, "all the 'independent' associations in the oil and gas industry seem to have a way of falling into the hands of the 'big boys' after a few years." Mid-Continent is nominally an independent association. In the words of the president of one of its major state divisions, however, it has been "controlled by the majors. They run it because they finance it largely." Many independents have been on the board of directors, fewer on the executive committee, and by the time you get down to the steering committee, the independents with small assets have been pretty well absent. But the president, a "small" oilman, added: "These big oilmen are fine, broad-minded people—that is why they are big men. If we could just agree on imports, then everything would be fine. I believe the big men will subsidize the views of the little men of the industry." The majors do not let the association discuss imports. "But independents do have a lot of influence." Jake L. Hamon, first independent producer to be chairman of the API, advised a TIPRO audience in 1956 "not to rail at the folk in the big companies . . . because company men are no different from you and me. After all, let us face it, they help us a lot."

They provide the personnel of committees that work on form simplification with the Railroad Commission, on groups that get our compensation rates lowered before the insurance commission, on committees that provide data on tax problems before legislative committees at Austin, not to mention the fact that it is their ad valorum tax experts who fight our battles in every county. At Washington, I don't know how we would get along without the tax men from the big companies who work so tirelessly in defense of our depletion allowance, and our other tax problems. I am also glad that these outfits are big enough to have those research departments, because we are all benefited from results they have obtained.[14]

These groups are generally agreed as to the need for direct political action. Reviewing the unresolved imports and natural gas issues, the president of TIPRO advised his members in 1955 that "it seems to me only fair to tie a few strings to the contributions we make to political organizations and candidates." [15] A keen observer of and participant in southwestern oil activities described how one association's executive director has functioned: A politician running for office may go to see M—— to tell him his tale of woe. He gets sympathy, followed by the statement that the official is sorry but the association has no money and doesn't deal in politics. But he is asked, by the way, where are you staying. A call may come later to his hotel room to have dinner. Joe X, an oilman, happens to join them and the tale of woe is repeated. It is then made clear that of course oil companies don't make political contributions. This may be repeated two or three more times; by then the oilmen know exactly where the eager candidate stands. The evening may be con-

cluded by the oil producer admitting this was a tough situation for
a deserving man—maybe we can help out. "And there it is."

The various associations do not neglect the national scene, and
generally maintain Washington offices. Mid-Continent has been
very active in opposing federal gas controls. Undoubtedly, the most
vigorous oil association lobby is the one supported by the Independent Petroleum Association of America (IPAA). It has headquarters in Tulsa and Washington, but does not operate directly
at the state level. Membership includes small producers as well as
independent integrated oil and gas companies, presumably without
overseas holdings. The IPAA frequently takes the lead on political
issues common to the industry, notably depletion, while charting an
independent's course on the touchy problem of imports. Although
presumably few of its members had or could afford offshore leases
and operations, the IPAA was an important participant in the tidelands fight. Russell B. Brown, its chief Washington representative
for several decades, was known as one of the most effective lobbyists.
Other groups that constitute the "oil and gas lobby" include the
Pennsylvania Grade Crude Oil Association, the Independent
Natural Gas Association, the National Stripper Well Association,
the Committee for Pipe Line Companies, the National Petroleum
Association (representing primarily Eastern refiners), the Western
Petroleum Refiners Association, the Independent Refiners Association of America, the National Oil Jobbers Council (which frequently
grumbles about the depletion allowance and favors imports), a host
of state distributor associations that are usually tied in to the council,
the National Oil Marketers Association (a small group whose counsel, Paul E. Hadlick, has been a sharp critic of most big oil positions), and the American Gas Association, which is primarily a
distributors' group.

The American Petroleum Institute, with main offices in New
York, is the largest and most comprehensive of the associations. It
has representation from all of the oil associations in its councils. Its
membership cuts through the entire industry. But it is clearly dominated by the integrated majors. In the past the API's economic activities came under antitrust fire. And the American Petroleum Industries Committee conducted a federal legislative service that kept

an eye on Washington doings and funneled political reports back to the member companies. The API has preferred, however, to encourage a public image of itself as scholarly and oriented toward technical research. It has prided itself on keeping out of controversy and publicly has acted not unlike an embassy, representing the government of oil to the United States government. For example, it maintained a dignified silence on offshore oil. Yet the API has had a legislative representative in Washington (Joseph Dwyer, the postwar incumbent, had served as special assistant to the API president when the latter headed the Petroleum Industry War Council). The office has sought to keep open channels to the various federal agencies, while advising the industry on legislation and testimony. In its newest phase the American Petroleum Committee has called for a hard-hitting political program. In 1958 it merged the APIC and the Oil Information Committee (OIC), its central public relations arm, into a new Committee on Public Affairs. The intent is that this should become an effective superpolitical group for the entire industry, somewhat along the lines of the original plans of the founders of the API. Meanwhile, the API continues its less publicized ties with the United States government through such agencies as the National Petroleum Council.

While the associations have particular areas of concern and leadership, they frequently team up on wider issues. In the spring of 1956, for example, nineteen independent producers, royalty owners, and drilling-contractor associations banded together to push for imports control. Soon afterward thirty-one Senators—fifteen Republican and sixteen Democrats—were protesting excessive imports to the Office of Defense Mobilization. Some warned that they might not be able to continue their support of reciprocal trade agreements. The API, IPAA, and Mid-Continent have presented joint testimony on natural gas legislation.

Occasionally special groups are formed for single issues. In 1953 a "study group" to consider natural gas regulation legislation was created by the heads of Phillips, Humble, the IPAA, the API, and other industry leaders. After the Supreme Court Phillips decision in the following year, this became the General Gas Committee, with offices in Fort Worth, Texas, and then Washington. It was frankly designed to work for a legislative climate that would allow the exemption of the production and gathering of natural gas from federal regulation. The committee was composed of representatives of most companies, and in 1955 and 1956 listed its income at $118,-625. (This represented only a fraction of the expenses incurred directly by the member companies.) It was chaired by Maston Nixon, president of the Southern Minerals Corporation, a producer of oil and gas owned by Pittsburgh Plate Glass and American Cyanamid. Mr. Nixon was a director of the API and the IPAA, and frequently served in industry activities as a spokesman for smaller producer interests. The General Gas Committee's steering committee was chaired by the head of the Mid-Continent Oil and Gas Association and included top executives from the leading oil and gas producing interests. Its legislative subcommittee was headed by the lobbyists for Mid-Continent and the Independent Petroleum Association of America, with members from the Independent Natural Gas and the Western Oil and Gas Associations and from several companies.

The committee arranged for the organization of data on natural gas for the use of congressional committees and for public and private officials who would testify before them. One team helped governors of states prepare such testimony. The general research was under the direction of John W. Boatwright, an economist on loan from Standard of Indiana. Appropriate portions of Boatwright's own testimony and documentation were actually inserted in this body of hearings by Senator Price Daniel in the midst of or after the testimony of each witness sympathetic to federal control.[16] The General Gas Committee served as a clearinghouse, assuming responsibility for selecting the witnesses to testify on the industry's behalf before congressional committees. An "evidence committee" sought to screen all testimony to unify the industry's presentation. (The vice chairman of this group was Walter S. Hallanan of Plymouth Oil, who was also chairman of the National Petroleum Council. Hallanan also served on the steering committee.) The committee strove to coordinate the direct lobbying of all its members. As Sidney A. Swensrud, chairman of the board of Gulf explained, it sought "to discuss the ways and means of approaching some of the people in Congress, and especially in the Senate, as to who might know some particular Senator, and sort of go over the list and make sure we weren't all trying to see the same Senator.

. . ." [17] The member companies were also urged "to continue your efforts to arouse your employees and others to the dangers of Federal control over the producer of gas; that in any future mailing pieces which you distribute you include a direct request to write Congressmen and Senators to support the Harris bill on similar legislation." [18] Many did so. At least one major company—Standard of Indiana—became so enthusiastic that it paid for nearly one thousand grass-roots telegrams drummed up in Minnesota by sales personnel. The cost was charged to marketing expenses. Some of these telegrams were signed without the consent of the senders, a practice reminiscent of the operations of Cities Service in its all-out war against the Public Utility Holding Company bill in 1935. Plans were also made to secure the cooperation of farmers, ranchers, sheep and goat raisers, the coal, sulphur, and railroad industries, unions in oil, gas, coal, and railroading, chambers of commerce, the National Association of Attorneys General, the Interstate Oil Compact Commission and state government bodies.

One disturbing source of opposition to the gas industry position was the National Institute of Municipal Law Officers (NIMLO), an organization of 985 municipalities who are represented by their chief legal officers. James H. Lee, assistant corporation counsel of Detroit and a key figure in bringing the Phillips case before the Supreme Court, was the leader in the group's demand for natural gas regulation. "It is essential that this pressure be neutralized," Chairman Nixon of the General Gas Committee wrote to President Hines H. Baker of Humble Oil.[19] To this end the committee systematically sought to influence the membership of NIMLO to repudiate their organization's support of the Phillips decision. According to Archie D. Gray, general counsel of Gulf, "we contacted our district sales managers in places like Philadelphia and elsewhere in the State in an effort to have them, if they knew a mayor of some city or town in the State, and who was a member of some of these municipal leagues, contact these mayors and see if he couldn't acquaint them with issues involved in this legislation. Of course, the purpose was to prevent the league, as an organization, from opposing the passage of the Harris-Fulbright bill. This was the purpose of my activities in that State." [20]

In Alabama, where there are many municipally owned gas systems, the industry found that the Alabama Municipal League, an organization of mayors and city officials, was the most effective voice in that state. "So," explained the associate general counsel of the Continental Oil Company, "we undertook to see what, if anything, we could do to neutralize that group." [21] An attorney for Shell reported receiving a $5,000 bonus for similar work. To counter the efforts of the Mayors' Committee on Natural Gas, composed of the mayors of major urban centers who favored gas regulation, a Joint Committee of Consumers and Small Producers of Natural Gas was formed, consisting of a group of mayors under the chairmanship of the former mayor of Indianapolis. This was financed by the gas producers. Chairman Nixon of the General Gas Committee denied that his group's work constituted direct lobbying, although to be on the safe side it did register. (Once, when James H. Lee was testifying before a Senate committee against the Fulbright bill, a Mid-Continent Oil and Gas Association lobbyist proceeded to distribute in the hearing room a mimeographed statement in which the head of the General Gas Committee's steering committee attacked Lee as "unwittingly a victim of Fabian Socialist tactics" who was offering the Congress "statistical baloney.")[22] Once questioned, however, many of the industry executives have been frank to admit this was direct political action, with lobbying as one aspect.

The oil lobby is thus to be found at every level of public government, from the rural county seat where a local representative may be placating a highway commission in relation to complaints about the wear and tear of oil trucks on the roads, and from the Bayonne (New Jersey) Common Council, where in 1880 the Standard company applied extensive pressure to secure a franchise for a pipeline under the streets and in 1957 forced the city fathers to cut expenses and taxes under the threat of closing an older refinery, all the way up to an international agency in Geneva where corporate diplomats are cultivating good will to ensure an appreciation of the place of the industry in long-range energy planning. All of these politicking and pressure activities appear on the generous retainers and pay rolls of the corporations, charged up as business expenses and paid for by the taxpayer and the consumer. The breakdown of taxes on each gallon of gasoline, conspicuously displayed on most service-station pumps as part of the industry's educational program directed against the burdens of big public government, somehow never shows this private taxation for the upkeep of big private government.

Oil does not have to go it alone in its public battles, despite the ample evidence of the abilities in this field. The industry has had staunch political allies in the chambers of commerce—local, state, and national, the National Association of Manufacturers, the Southern States Industrial Council, and other business groups to which they have contributed and on whose boards and committees oilmen are prominent. During the thirties the Liberty League and a whole flock of anti-New Deal organizations received heavy backing from the Mellon (Gulf), Pew (Sun), and Rockefeller families and associates. The extreme right-wing Committee for Constitutional Government has worked closely on oil and gas legislation with men like ex-Senator Ed Moore, millionaire oilman from Oklahoma, and ex-Congressman Samuel B. Pettengil, later an oil company attorney. It sent out millions of pamphlets warning about the reaching out to grab offshore lands by the federal "Octopus on the Potomac." Mining, lumbering, oil equipment, drilling contractor and electric light corporations and trade associations can also be counted on in oil's legislative fights. (In one early "tidelands" bill there was discovered a "joker" clause providing for the return of all navigable waters and natural resources to the states. The effect of this would have been to threaten federal control of hydroelectric development, reclamation, irrigation, flood control, and navigation.) Giant construction contractors, such as George and Herman Brown (of Brown and Root, Inc.) who also have oil-producing properties, are major shareholders in the Texas Eastern Transmission Corporation and do much of their work for petroleum, gas, and chemical companies, are major forces in the general politics of Texas and in the lobbying that engulfs Austin. The railroads, traditional powers in state legislatures, are often to be counted upon as allies because of their oil-land holdings as well as their general business outlook. The Northern Pacific, for example, owns tremendous portions of eastern Montana and western North Dakota. In Louisiana many of the large sugar-cane corporations have oil on their lands.

Oil interests frequently rely upon and are served by special functional groups that focus on single areas. Among these are the American Merchant Marine Institute, the Asphalt Institute, and the Na-

tional Highway Users' Conference—in each of which the major oil
corporations have representatives. The international companies have
backed the pressure organizations favoring reciprocal trade, including
the National Foreign Trade Council, the Committee for Economic
Development, the United States Chamber of Commerce, and the
Venezuelan Chamber of Commerce. Those opposed to imports join
with protectionists in coal and other like-minded industries in such
groups as the American Tariff League, the Foreign Oil Policy Committee (a coalition of coal and oil producers, railroads, labor and
small business interests) and the Nationwide Committee of Industry, Agriculture and Labor on Import-Export Policy.

During the offshore controversy, a special Statewide Tidelands
Committee was formed as an offshoot of the Texas Property De-
fense Association. It drew support and representation from the State
Teachers Association, the Congress of Parents and Teachers, the
State Bar Association, the American Legion, the Veterans of Foreign
Wars, the Texas Water Conservation Association, Soil Conservation
District Supervisors, the Federation of Women's Clubs, the Texas
Press Association, strong patriotic groups, the various chambers of
commerce and many political figures. The committee was organized
with the express purpose of mobilizing sentiment within and beyond
the borders of Texas in favor of state control of offshore oil. In
1951 plans were announced to send representatives "into every state
where we need to develop strength in the United States Senate."
M. K. Weitzel, the committee's secretary who worked with Attorney
General and then Senator Price Daniel, lamented the "unfortunate
factor that this was associated with oil." For the issue was one of
principle in combating "the lying propaganda that is being spewed
out by the federal bureaucrats" and "the incipient socialism we are
approaching." Money from oil companies was not accepted, he explained, "but of course there were people contributing who had oil
properties—especially small, independent operators interested in future development."

The American Bar Association, which views itself as a guardian
of the constitutional heritage, has lent its professional support to
petroleum industry positions. Its stand in favor of state ownership
of offshore oil lands was well publicized. The association has also
supported the adoption of conservation laws that limit production

to consumption demand. Its Mineral Section has selected the lawyers who have written leasing laws for the various states. Less well known is the extent to which the membership of the Mineral Law Section, which frames the Bar Association's positions on such issues, has consisted of oil company lawyers and those on retainers. Some of this work has been underwritten by oil associations. And for twenty-five years the section's secretary was lawyer-lobbyist Peter Q. Nyce.

Buttressing these private forces are the public bureaucracies which, as seen earlier, frequently function as administrative lobbies for policies that are essentially private. Thus, at the federal level, the Secretary of the Interior, his staff, and his industry advisers often appear before other agencies and the Congress as spokesmen for the industry. Interior personnel have lobbied throughout the country for the adoption of prorationing. General E. O. Thompson, of the Texas Railroad Commission, has used his prestige and post as guardian of Texas producer interests to write to all governors to direct the full weight of their offices for the passage of legislation exempting gas producers from federal regulation. The Interstate Oil Compact Commission also plays a legislative role. It has exerted strong pressures on states to adopt proration laws. At one meeting the president of the Ohio Oil Company urged the commission members to "use their persuasive powers and moral support in helping to obtain the legislation needed" among the Rocky Mountain states where such measures were pending.[23] During the fight over Leland Olds, the governor of Kansas wired the Senate that, "as chairman of the Interstate Oil Compact Commission," he opposed Olds's confirmation, fearing his philosophy meant the nationalization of oil and gas.[24] Other chairmen—usually member-state governors— have used IOCC meetings and correspondence to rally coordinated opposition against imports, natural gas regulation, and any investigation of the Compact Commission.

The National Association of Attorneys General (NAAG), organized in 1907 as a clearinghouse on state legal problems, was a leader in the fight for quitclaim legislation. Its Washington representative was Walter R. Johnson, Attorney General of Nebraska, whose special office was responsible for creating and directing state pressures upon congressional delegations. At one point during the offshore oil debate in 1952, Johnson was seated in the Senate chambers at the elbow of Senator Spessard Holland of Florida. The latter, floor leader for the "tidelands bill," had received the consent of his Senate colleagues for according this unusual privilege to a registered lobbyist.[25]

Johnson reported receiving an annual retainer of $18,000 and expenses. Presumably representing the forty-eight state officers on a variety of issues, the NAAG's Washington activities were heavily subsidized from special budgets earmarked by the states most directly involved in the offshore legislation and litigation—California, Louisiana, and Texas. Representatives of the attorneys general of these three states were also active in Washington throughout the controversy and enjoyed generous expense accounts. One assistant attorney general, William W. Clary, who helped in the drafting of quitclaim legislation and who represented a number of companies including Signal Oil and Gas, was paid by both the state of California and the oil industry for his services. Clary's firm, O'Malvoney and Myers, handled titles for the major interests having a stake in offshore oil.

Proponents of federal control were never satisfied with the official explanation of the financing of this NAAG operation. Johnson, in turn, repeatedly denied the oft-made charge that his office was a front for the petroleum industry. A top American Petroleum Institute official agreed that "no oil money backed Johnson, as much as they would have liked to. Oil is too smart for that." Certainly the Attorney General's modest $125-a-month office was very un-oil like in appearance. And he was most sensitive to any suggestion that oil was the issue in the offshore controversy, and always quick to explain that "submerged lands" was the correct focus. Yet the industry was known to have brought great grass-roots pressures on various state attorneys general.

The Washington office closed shortly after the "tidelands" legislative victory in 1953. Johnson later became an attorney for the Flying Tigers, a freight air line whose board chairman, Samuel B. Mosher, was also president of Signal Oil and Gas. This company was the largest independent on the west coast and had sizable holdings in California offshore development. Signal also had intricate and intimate business ties with Standard of California, the leading offshore operator in the Gulf of Mexico.

At least two other publicly employed lobbyists for state ownership lost their jobs shortly after Eisenhower's nomination, so certain was their employer of the passage of the promised quitclaim legislation restoring offshore lands to their "historic" owners. Ex-Senator Sheridan Downey of California had drawn $40,000 a year for his efforts in behalf of the city of Long Beach whose oil properties, valued at several billion dollars, were rented to a combination of oil companies. As a former legislator, Downey enjoyed floor privileges in the Senate. With him went William D. McAdams, a public relations man who previously had worked for the American Medical Association to keep Americans healthy and conservative without "socialized" medicine and for Senator Robert Taft to make him appear less conservative as part of his presidential preparation. McAdams worked to create grass-roots awareness and to push civic organizations such as the Association of Port Authorities and the Council of State Chambers of Commerce to the forefront, rather than allow tidelands to be identified as an oil struggle.

One of the last Downey-McAdams assignments, the New York Times reported, was "to get a plank favoring states' rights on the offshore oil issue written into the Republican platform." With this done and General Eisenhower the chosen candidate, the Long Beach Harbor Commission then exercised its thirty-day cancellation clause to terminate the contracts of the two representatives. At one time McAdams had authored many stirring statements by Senators Nixon, Cain, and others in the battle against creeping socialism. Now he could only comment ruefully with regard to this turn of events which cost him this $25,000-a-year account:

The big corporations and the other fellows who put up money don't feel they need us any more. They figure this is a do-nothing Congress— or that anything it does will be okay for them. They know they've got the votes to put over the tidelands deal. . . .[26]

14

Private Pressure and Political Paralysis

The oil lobby is to be found right within the Congress itself. Twenty-seven per cent of the land area of the United States has oil production or is under lease to the industry. One finds drilling rigs on desolate ranches in Wyoming and in luxurious suburban back yards in Los Angeles, on Texas city garbage dumps and Hollywood movie studio lots, in the bayous of Louisiana, and on the capitol grounds of Oklahoma City. Thirty-two states have oil and gas production. And others live in the expectation of joining these ranks. Soon after oil was discovered in North Dakota in 1951, 70 per cent of the state was under lease. In 1956 the figure for Florida was 52 per cent; for Texas, 49 per cent; for Louisiana, 47 per cent; for Oklahoma, 45 per cent; for Wyoming, 42 per cent; for West Virginia, 40 per cent; for Pennsylvania, 39 per cent; for Colorado, 38 per cent; for Montana, 35 per cent.

Much of the profits go to the giant controlling interests outside the producing regions. And the statistics on education, health, and income suggest that states like Oklahoma, Louisiana, and Texas are far from being paradises for the majority of families. But the wealth created does offer revenue for the state governments, one-eighth royalties for landowners, and jobs and lower taxes for the citizen. There is then created a widely diffused, articulate, and powerful public zealous in the maintenance of this privilege and one with which politicians in oil, as well as nonoil states, must come to terms. Mindful that the gross production tax on the industry accounted for 34 per cent of his state's general revenue fund, the governor of Oklahoma in 1958 pleaded for federal imports control to help his state meet "a crisis against which we are helpless to defend ourselves." [1]

In Louisiana, lease money has been paid to landowners in every one of the state's parishes. Practically every parish has landowners who are receiving oil and gas royalties. The severance tax on oil and gas—fought for by Huey Long—has constituted the state's largest single source of tax revenue. In the fiscal year 1959–1960, this income exceeded $130 million. As early as 1954 Democratic Governor Robert Kennon announced he would again back Eisenhower in 1956, unless the Truman-Stevenson wing lost power within his party. "We're taking in $60 or $70 million in tidelands oil, which we would not have received under the Democrats." [2] He was voicing openly a position echoed by many political leaders, citizens, and educators. In Louisiana, as in Texas and other oil states, public revenues from oil production are usually earmarked for educational purposes. In Texas, nearly half of the state public educational costs are met by petroleum production taxes. Thus, in an official report, Louisiana's Conservation Commissioner John B. Hussey (later of the Federal Power Commission) insisted that "every barrel of foreign oil which supplants Louisiana oil takes money from Louisiana schools." [3] This revenue arrangement frequently allows the industry to sit back in ivory-tower detachment while professional educators and their associations take up the cudgel in Washington to defend the depletion allowance, protest Leland Olds's renomination, and cry that federal control of offshore oil was a diabolic plot against the nation's youth. In Texas the president of the state teachers' association could announce that teachers throughout the state were gathering material on the effects of oil imports on school revenues and were exploring ways to promote the sale of Texas oil. When Robert B. Anderson (later to be Secretary of the Treasury) testified before the House Ways and Means Committee in favor of depletion, he identified himself as an educator—he was chairman of the State Board of Education—rather than as president of the Texas Mid-Continent Oil and Gas Association.

The prevalence and permeability of oil make it almost impossible to find legislators whose positions on petroleum reflect a consistent public concern. Some of the sharpest critics of oil's international machinations, for example, cast avid eyes on the public lands in their states. Some are silent as depletion comes up, for they prefer not to forget their domestic-producer constituents. Nor can the time-honored practice of logrolling be ignored in the maintenance of this political support. Senators from oil states are able to trade their backing of depletion allowance for coal and a host of minerals in return for the preservation of oil's tax subsidy. The history of percentage depletion allowance has been marked by the steady expansion of the list of favored minerals. In 1951 coal received an increase from 5 per cent to 10 per cent, and the list of newcomers included sand, gravel, slate, stone, brick and tile clay, shale, and oyster and clam shells. It would be difficult to conclude that either the threat of scarcity, the imperatives of national defense, or the hazards of exploration were the deciding factors. An attempt by Senator Paul H. Douglas of Illinois to challenge this public generosity earned from Senator Tom Connally of Texas the rebuke that "the Senator from Illinois is greatly concerned about clam shells. He does not have many in his district." [4] Congressional figures frequently apply pressure on the regulatory agencies for favorable pipeline considerations and upon other offices for materials allocations. Senators have interceded with the Interior Department on "hot oil" prosecutions; they have also sought representation in the NRA and the war agencies for representatives of particular companies from their states.

Certainly it is difficult to find a congressman from an oil or gas state who will ever vote "wrong" on oil or gas legislation. The delegations from Kansas, Oklahoma, Arkansas, Texas, and Louisiana voted unanimously in favor of the Harris-Fulbright bill to free gas producers from federal control. Many frankly refer to themselves as oil congressmen, in the same sense that others call themselves cotton- or farm-bloc congressmen. They know what their attitudes on such matters as depletion ought to be. "We oil Congressmen represent our people," explained Tom Steed of Oklahoma. "It is my duty to represent their views. I would be replaced otherwise and would deserve to be." Or, as Dennis Chavez, once the lone southwestern senatorial opponent of the Kerr gas bill, went on record in 1955 when he explained his newer position in favor of the exemption of natural gas production from federal regulation:

Just a few years ago I supported the philosophy that the Federal Government should rigidly control the price of gas at the well. In these intervening years, the State of New Mexico has become the fourth largest producer of natural gas for sale. Since the State of New Mexico is the largest royalty owner of oil in the State, and our public schools and State institutions are largely financed through the revenue derived from the leasing of State lands for oil and gas purposes, it logically follows that the people of New Mexico are direct beneficiaries of the commercial production of this natural resource. In matters such as these, it is not within my province to exercise personal opinion because I am here in Washington to represent New Mexico and to work for her best interest, and it shall always be so.[5]

Nationally, the oil orientation of the Congress has been made simple by the long-time control of the legislative body by southern conservative Democrats whose safe districts at home assure them of seniority and committee chairmanships in Washington. These men generally do not represent a majority of their party or of their constituents. Yet to a great extent the Democratic congressional delegation has become the voice of the Democratic party, with the party tending to stand on its record here rather than on any platform constructed at the conventions. This despite periodic protests from liberals like former Senator Herbert H. Lehman and Mrs. Eleanor Roosevelt. Northern and western industrial centers have been grossly underrepresented in the legislative halls and in the committee chairmanships. In the South and Southwest there are millions of workers, small businessmen, farmers, and consumers—white and Negro—who are not in the oil business, however skillfully a tenuous identity is propagated. As Senator Paul Douglas pointed out during the debates over gas regulation in 1956, New Mexico then had 271 producers and 113,500 consumers of natural gas; Texas had 829 producers and 1,683,400 consumers; Oklahoma had 229 producers and 499,700 consumers; Louisiana had 254 producers and 486,200 consumers; Kansas had 228 producers and 440,900 consumers.[6] Yet when the congressional delegations proclaim their state loyalties on oil issues, they have in mind the oil industry. On natural gas it is the producer and the pipeline, not the consumers, who are the first to be protected.

When national Democratic leaders speak of the imperative for placating the South, it becomes pertinent to ask which South they have in mind. After Stevenson's defeat in 1952, the party line was to be moderate, to keep the southern wing within the fold. The party officially remained relatively quiet on all the resource "give-aways" under the Eisenhower Administration, despite the obvious appeal of the issue and the indignation of some Democrats who had fought valiantly on offshore oil and natural gas against the classic coalition of southern Democrats and conservative Republicans. And in 1956 this interpretation of party harmony garnered for the Democrats a national total of seventy-four electoral votes—from the states of Alabama, Arkansas, Georgia, Mississippi, Missouri, North Carolina, and South Carolina.

Membership on key congressional committees is screened for those who might be hostile to oil's requirements. Under the watchful lieutenantship of Senate Majority Leader Lyndon B. Johnson and Speaker of the House Samuel Rayburn, one test for seats on the powerful Senate Finance Committee and on the House Rules and House Ways and Means Committees has been proper respect for the 27½ per cent depletion allowance. (It is the Ways and Means Committee that initiates revenue legislation and handles tax and tariff matters. The Rules Committee controls the calendar and the precedence of legislation, with the power to pigeonhole.) Paul Douglas, a respected economist and a persistent critic of abuses in tax laws and depletion as well as of governmental waste and congressional pork barrel, was carefully kept off the Senate Finance Committee to which he had aspired and was qualified by intellect and seniority. This was managed through a series of adroit parliamentary maneuvers. At one point in 1955 there were several vacancies, one of which seemed certain to go to the Illinois Democrat. But this was taken by Lyndon Johnson, who later in the same session shifted to another committee. It was not until 1956 and the death of Senator Alben W. Barkley that Douglas was able to breach this stronghold of the bipartisan conservative and pro-big business elite which has served as a watchdog over the Treasury Department, national financial policies, and taxation. "Reliable" men—that is, those representing producer states—dominate the committees dealing with natural resources. Price Daniel, the Texas attorney general who had made "tidelands" his vehicle for capturing a Senate seat in 1952, was quickly placed on the Interior and Insular Affairs Committee by Johnson.

Both Johnson and Rayburn earlier had earned reputations as New Deal liberals. There was a time when the House leader, whose district is not in the center of oil country, had bucked the industry. But his behind-the-scenes parliamentary tactics for the depletion allowance and against gas regulation have reflected his increasing willingness to support oil's expressed needs. In the Kerr bill fight in 1949, Rayburn called for a vote on a Friday afternoon when one-fourth of the House, mostly from neighboring urban centers, had left town. When General Ernest O. Thompson of the Texas Railroad Commission testified in 1957 in the Suez crisis, he had the unusual honor of being formally introduced to the House committee by Speaker Rayburn, who visited the hearing for that purpose. In the audience was Lyndon Johnson.

Johnson had been one of President Roosevelt's young favorites. He reflected the agrarian protest characteristic of a Texas that viewed itself as exploited by the perils of nature and the plots of eastern capital. In 1944, he had attacked the corporate interests, including oil, who had sought to take over the Texas Democratic convention. And in 1946 he voted as a member of the House of Representatives against oil-favored amendments that would further weaken the dying price controls. But a growing industrial economy, the burgeoning power of oil producers, and his own political ambitions moved him away from this position. He developed political ties with some of the oil interests and the contracting firm of Brown and Root. When Johnson assumed his party's floor leadership in 1953, he outlined for the Senate Democratic Conference his guiding principles:

There may be times when I will be in a minority—not just in the Senate but among the Senate Democrats themselves. This I believe is unavoidable and would be unavoidable regardless of any selection that could be made by this conference. No man of integrity can live constantly in the majority.

We have all been sent here by our respective states and we all owe a primary allegiance to our constituents. Since this is a nation made up of states, I have never felt any conflict in loyalty between my State and my Nation. I have represented Texas to the best of my ability in the past. I shall continue to do my utmost to safeguard the interests of my native State in the future and I don't think there is another Senator who will disagree with that thought.[7]

He soon earned a reputation for tactical skill in keeping the factions of the Democratic party in a working coalition, first as the minority opposition and then as the majority party of the Senate. But in the absence of any broad-gauged national program and direction to the record of Johnson and his party during the Eisenhower Administration, one might well have asked, "Harmony for what?" When his party secured a smashing victory in the 1958 congressional elections, Johnson immediately announced that its purpose would be "to be responsible, to be progressive without being radical, to be prudent and conservative without being a mossback, a standpatter." [8]

Johnson negotiated with the State and Defense departments on imports, behaving like an ambassador from his state's industry. He intervened to keep down appropriations that would allow the Justice Department to investigate the Interstate Oil Compact, to help the Federal Power Commission enforce the regulatory functions emphasized by the Supreme Court in the 1954 Phillips decision, and to allow the Navy to drill on its West Coast reserve lands. Johnson sat in on important gas hearings and he was chairman of the subcommittee dealing with the nomination of Leland Olds. He also helped to block any meaningful Senate investigations of lobbying and of campaign expenditures in primary elections. The cover of *The TIPRO Reporter* (Texas Independent Producers and Royalty Owners Association) for October 1954 featured Price Daniel and Lyndon Johnson as "the Senators from and for Texas." Both were hailed as true friends of the oil industry. (Daniel had made his reputation on the "tidelands" issue, but lost the quest for state control of the continental shelf beyond "historic" boundaries. He became a Senate advocate of a higher depletion allowance, perhaps on the assumption that the best defense is a good offense.) Johnson was singled out for his role in the Kerr gas bill and depletion allowance controversies. "Texas independents will be ever grateful for your effective leadership in preserving the depletion allowance," wired TIPRO to Johnson, who replied, "I am here trying to fight the organization's battles every day." [9]

Johnson has been well aware of the possible price for this loyalty.

Like Senator Robert Kerr (a Democrat from Oklahoma and president of the Kerr-McGee Oil Industries), he has been bitter that this identification should be held against him in his ambitions for the Presidency. A courageous fighter on certain issues, Kerr was almost the only political figure who challenged MacArthur when the general was recalled from Korea. Kerr refused to vote on offshore oil roll calls so as to avoid the charge that he was an interested party. His company was one of the largest leaseholders in the Gulf of Mexico. Kerr has insisted that oilmen keep away from politics as much as possible, that they are dumb in relation to legislation, and that "the oil lobby doesn't exist as an active, effective unit." He feels they have often been critical of his record but that he has to "work with sinners who are on Oklahoma's side, although I'd rather work with saints." Kerr is reported to have told a farm audience whose leaders were balking at supporting him for the Presidency because of his oil and gas record that he respected the "right of any American to be against any racket he isn't in on." But his public relations services for the Mid-Continent Oil and Gas Association in the late 1930's and his activities against natural gas regulation are well known, as are his most recent fights against billboard restrictions on federal highways, so bitterly opposed by oil. "Millionaire oilman" and "the Kerr natural gas bill" are tags not easily discarded.

Johnson's problem has been that of commitment rather than of personal holdings. "When I'm investigating military waste . . . I'm a true liberal, a friend of the people," he once declared. "But when I take a position in line with the biggest industry in my state—when I take the position the people of my state want me to take—I'm through in the columns. I'm a reactionary, I'm a scoundrel who has sold out to the interests. . . . Don't think it's not a serious matter for me. I've lost the best chance, maybe the only chance, I have to build up a good reputation and be something more than a Senator." [10]

To some legislators, the moral issue is of a different nature. One veteran Texas representative was musing about conflicting loyalties —a problem that has troubled all thoughtful public servants, whether one reads Plato, Edmund Burke or the *Congressional Record*. He cited depletion as an illustration:

Depletion is a steal, it is robbery. I wonder why the rest of the country stands for it. But nine of eleven of my districts are oil districts, so what can I do. It bothers me. Some day I may vote against it. I've been thinking about it. But of course, if the rest of the country doesn't howl, why should we? But it's outrageous robbery, depleting over and over and over 100%. What will happen to me? Well, the oil companies don't trust me anyways, although I've never done anything against them.

As the periodic debates over the allowance show, oil's influence extends far beyond the leading producing states and the Democratic party. Proposals to lower the percentage are generally quietly side-tracked in committee or impatiently shouted down on the floor—with no vote recorded. This despite party pledges honoring an equitable program. In 1951 a Senate amendment to cut depletion for oil to 15 per cent, offered by Hubert Humphrey of Minnesota, won nine votes, with seventy-one opposed. In 1954 Republican Senator John J. Williams of Delaware proposed a reduction to 15 per cent, and Douglas of Illinois offered an amendment providing for a graduated tax that would help the genuine smaller producers rather than the millionaires and the integrated corporations. They could not get the nineteen votes necessary to order a roll-call vote. The late Matthew M. Neely, a Democrat from West Virginia and a defender of depletion, warned his colleague from Illinois that he was inviting his own defeat on November 2nd. (More than a third of the counties of Illinois had oil or gas production, with the 1953 output valued at $182 million.) Douglas persisted. ". . . I again ask for the yeas and nays. Every man has a right to commit suicide." Only a handful were ready to risk exercising this right by standing up to be counted in an election year. The yeas and nays were not ordered.[11]

Perhaps the most glaring contemporary display of the enfeeblement if not paralysis of the legislative process and of congressional integrity wrought by the presence of oil came in the sequence of events surrounding the vote on the 1956 natural gas bill which sought to exempt producers from federal regulation. There had been intensive lobbying activities—probably more than on any public issue in several decades. There were ominous rumors of campaign contribution payoffs and of political retribution for "wrong" voting. To veteran observers the atmosphere was reminiscent of the Washington scene prior to the passage of the Public Utility Holding Company Act in 1935.

It was a presidential election year and the final congressional lineup on the Harris-Fulbright bill was expected to be close. But the bill's passage was regarded by the coalition of southwestern Democrats and their conservative Republican allies as major legislative business. Lyndon Johnson had taxed the loyalty of liberals by putting the weight of his congressional party leadership behind the measure—despite the opposition of a majority of the Senate Democratic Policy Committee. To the oil and gas industry, this freeing of producers from federal control was the number one political objective. It had worked and waited long—and now victory seemed in sight.

Then, on February 3rd, in the closing days of the debate, Francis Case, a conservative and inconspicuous Republican senator from South Dakota who had served in the Congress for twenty years, rose "to make a difficult speech":

I had not intended to take part in the debate on the pending measure. . . . I know very little about the economics in the collection and distribution of natural gas. I speak, therefore, only because one phase of the matter before us has presented itself to me in an unsought and now unavoidable manner.

Senator Case disclosed that a lawyer had turned over to his election fund in South Dakota an envelope containing twenty-five $100 bills—"the largest single contribution I could remember for any campaign of mine." This was done after the donor had ascertained in Washington and in South Dakota the senator's general sympathies for the Harris-Fulbright bill.

I knew of course that I could have nothing to do with its contents. . . . I knew that if the contribution were listed and reported that a contribution of that size would stick out like a sore thumb among the $5, $10 and $25 run of contributions in any list of mine. . . .

And were I to take advantage of the fact that the contribution was in currency and not report it, I would be the prisoner for the rest of my legislative career of a man whom I had never met, whose restraint, if he wanted a vote some future day, no one was guaranteeing.

And if no exposure ever took place, Mr. President, I come from a state which still cherishes a remark once made by a distinguished predecessor, Hon. William J. Bulow, who once in this Chamber, when he had to oppose a bill many friends wanted, said, "I have to walk with my conscience to the end of my days." . . .

I presume that some people may think the incident might well end at this point. Some one offered us a campaign contribution; handy as it would have been, we decline it. That is that. So what? I am free to vote on the bill as I please. Free to vote for free enterprise. Free to vote against more regulation and red-tape. Free, Mr. President, except for one thing—and that is what this experience reveals as to the nature of the problem before us. . . .

It is idle to pretend . . . that there are not substantial profits in this bill for some person or persons to put up the money to employ the lawyer on that kind of enterprise. Bear in mind that I am not yet a party candidate; I have not been renominated. It is not a matter of establishing a majority in the Senate for a political party—it can only be an interest in what my vote might mean in the immediate future or present.

. . . I have been impressed at times during the debate by many of the arguments advanced for the bill—the encouragement to exploration and development that it would give; the minimizing of Federal regulation; and the avoidance of governmental intrusion into borderline interstate and intrastate cases. . . .

I do not object to the public's paying a fair price for its natural gas, a price that will compensate the producer and the distributor, a price that will, coupled with the existing 27½ per cent depletion allowance, afford abundant encouragement for exploration and development.

The point at which I object, however, Mr. President, is that of doing something so valuable to those interested in natural gas that they advance huge sums of money as a down payment, so to speak, on the profits they expect to harvest.

The other day, the distinguished Senator from Missouri [Mr. Hennings] said on this floor:

"The concentrated money power of the great oil companies, wielded today to influence the decisions of national Government by contributions to both parties in many parts of the United States is a menace to the proper functioning of free government within this country."

Free government . . . requires freedom for those who write the laws. If we pass a law that creates a huge endowment of future profits for holders of gas reserves, we might be mortgaging the issues of the future.

Unrelated legislation could be influenced by the unregulated profits derived from monopoly prices paid by the captive customers at the end of the delivery line. . . .

. . . The creation of a class who can seek to affect the choice of many States' representation in the Congress is a far greater danger to the country than a temporary shortage of gas. The people in the gas and oil business whom I have met are good, decent people. They are convinced that their ideas of good government are sound as any citizen's might be. None of them has ever told me I should vote so and so. But when the passage of a bill becomes so alluring that dollars are advanced to potential candidates even before primaries are held the warning signals go up. . . .[12]

Speaking apologetically, Senator Case asked his colleagues to "pin no halos on me." There was little danger on this score. From that point on, he was to find himself on the defensive. William Fulbright of Arkansas, generally a thoughtful scholar on public issues and who a few years earlier had initiated a valuable inquiry into ethical standards in government, was immediately on his feet. He joined in Case's condemnation of anyone who sought to influence a vote by such means. But he also warned of the possibility that the contributor, not yet identified, might well have been a critic of the bill in a diabolic plot to discredit its intent. In assuming the attitude he had shown, Case "puts within the grasp of any unscrupulous person the power to influence a vote merely by making such an offer," regardless of the worth of the legislation. Fulbright further declared that since, under questioning, Case was not yet prepared to label the offer a bribe, "I cannot understand the charges which have been made." The South Dakotan was "irresponsible" in creating such doubt about the bill. And most serious of all, the timing of the disclosure was "inexcusable."

Senator Ralph E. Flanders of Vermont suggested that his fellow Republican from South Dakota seek "to separate the personal and moral question from the merits of the bill." Mike Monroney of Oklahoma, an advocate of tighter laws governing political morality, deplored the disclosure for feeding the "big-lie" tactics of those who implied "that Senators who support the bill are minions of the oil companies. . . . The corrupt practices pursued in politics should not be allowed to defeat a bill which has been debated freely on its merits." Senator Holland of Florida pleaded with his colleagues "to refrain from questioning the motives of brother Senators."

Case explained that had this incident not occurred, the overwhelmingly favorable mail from his state and his desire to see the state's oil and gas potentials developed would have led him to support the bill. But "I cannot accept the proposition that I can vote for a bill when one of the issues in the bill and one of the main arguments against it is that inordinate profits will be created for some people and that they have a special pecuniary interest in the bill." Meanwhile, Senator Paul Douglas tried to return to the substance of the gas debate, offering further documentation of his contention that the question before the Senate was whether the interests of wealth and power were to run the Government, or whether the Government was to be run in the interests of the great masses of people. But the air was too tense, and a rational discussion of political economy seemed remote. The whole tradition of the Senate as a club appeared to be crumbling.

On the next legislative day, February 6th, Majority Leader Johnson made clear his displeasure over this interruption, and renewed the attack upon Case. The expressed purpose of the Republican from South Dakota in relating the episode, said Johnson, was "to present the predicate for the announcement of how he intends to vote on the legislation pending. . . ." Case "selected . . . those facts which, in his opinion, were sufficient to influence his decision." That was his right. But "the Senate would render itself impotent to conduct its business in orderly fashion if transactions between persons outside the Senate . . . could, when partially reported . . . cause the Senate to set aside indefinitely its order of business."

Mr. President, the Senate of the United States can ill afford to prostrate itself before phantoms. That is what we would be doing if we delayed the vote now at hand. The junior Senator from South Dakota has said that no strings were attached to the sum of money he mentioned in his presentation. Accordingly, his recital of the episode has attached no strings to the Senate's voting. . . .

The Senate would indict itself and return its own conviction in the public eye if independent and honest conclusions were hastily abandoned in fear that expression of these conclusions might be taken as an admission of improper influence. . . . Popular favor, quite as much as the coin of the realm, can lead men into paths of temptation. . . .[13]

Mr. Johnson introduced a resolution, sponsored jointly with Minority Leader William Knowland, calling for a select committee to investigate the incident. Johnson announced that he did not want to see the Senate "start out on a general fishing expedition." But he assured his colleagues that "if there are any other instances, involving any other Senators, and they will rise in their places and call attention to them, I shall be glad to have the episodes they relate included within the scope of the resolution." There were no takers. But as several senators observed off the floor, if everybody who received a contribution from oil interests went before a committee, perhaps half the House and Senate membership would have to appear. Once the resolution was adopted, the leaders arranged for a very safe committee pledged to a speedy and limited investigation. It was chaired by Walter F. George of Georgia. One of its members was Republican H. Styles Bridges of New Hampshire, the only New England senator to support the Kerr bill and a contact man for funds for his party. It was later implied at the hearings that Senator Bridges had dealings with the main lobbyist in question.

Through skillful maneuvering the Senate leadership had successfully by-passed the regular Subcommittee on Privileges and Elections. Johnson explained that "if the matter were referred to any committee whose Members had taken strong positions one way or the other for or against the bill, perhaps that might color their judgment." [14] Thomas C. Hennings, Jr., the chairman of the subcommittee, fitted this portrait. For some time he had been warning of the concentrated money power involved in the gas fight and had sought a broad inquiry into the impact of oil and gas upon legislation and elections. To limit the inquiry to the immediate offer to Case seemed like "storming the citadel with a popgun."

To Hennings, the integrity of the entire Senate and of the democratic process itself was at stake. In competition with the select committee, Hennings made preliminary moves to have his subcommittee investigate the Case incident. But after consultation with Johnson and Knowland, Vice President Richard Nixon, the presiding officer

of the Senate, ruled that the select committee had exclusive jurisdiction. Hennings was then pressured into resigning from his subcommittee, after being challenged on the technicality that there
was a Senate precedent against serving in that role in a year when
the member was up for reelection. (Both George and Carl Hayden
of the four-man select committee were also running that year.) He
acquiesced, Hennings explained, "because of my anxiety that nothing
may impede, impair or delay the inquiry which I started into expenditures to influence legislation." [15]

The special inquiry was anticlimactic and inconclusive. It centered
upon the activities of two obscure lawyers on the pay roll of the
Superior Oil Company. The officers of this producing firm had long
had the reputation for aggressive politicking as well as leasing.
Senator Joseph R. McCarthy, among others, made frequent use of
Superior planes. Its chairman, William M. Keck, was an active
opponent of conservation in California and involved in many political battles. (According to Harold Ickes, the oilman once "even
spoke a kind word for federal regulation, saying that under federal
regulation so much money would not have to be spent on local
officials.")[16]

Elmer Patman, a former chief enforcement officer of the oil and
gas division of the Texas Railroad Commission, had been entrusted
by President Howard B. Keck with a personal campaign contribution fund that he could disburse at his discretion. In the course of
his handling of legal matters in the fifteen to twenty states where
Superior had operations, Patman explained, there were "calls for
donations and contributions to candidates running for office, for
testimonial dinners and for other things" for both political parties.
But, he insisted, "I am a lawyer and not a lobbyist, and never have
been in my life, and not going to start now." [17] For these duties,
he earned $35,000 a year and expenses that ran to about $900 a
month.

One of Patman's actions was to arrange a retainer of $1,000 a
month from Superior for John M. Neff who, beginning in October
1955, was to handle the company's legal work in Nebraska. Earlier,
Neff had worked as a lobbyist in Nebraska to help get conservation machinery adopted. The latter told of spending considerable
time with the state geologist to discuss well spacing and related

matters of concern to producers. Apparently, his only legal work actually performed under the new contract was to determine the attitudes of senators with regard to natural gas legislation and to distribute campaign contributions in behalf of President Keck. Neff also operated in Wyoming, Montana, Iowa, and South Dakota, seeking out the views of the ten senators. As his expense accounts were received by Patman, they were marked for "Natural Gas bill."

The committee was quite sharp in its questioning of Senator Case. He and his decision to vote against the gas bill, rather than the oil interests or the framework within which they operated, were clearly the defendants. At points the committee counsel implied that the money was the excuse rather than the reason for Case's action. The committee concluded that it "had some difficulty in discussing the exact nature of the complaint," especially since Case did not say the offer was a bribe, and the oil agents involved insisted there were no strings attached to their gift. However, "The committee does not intend to cast any reflection upon Senator Case." [18] Neither were there any words of appreciation or understanding of his personal torment and decision in the evasive and oddly written report.

The committee found that the money to Case—who was listed in the "doubtful" column on a printed tally of Senate positions on the bill inadvertently left behind by the lobbyist in one of his calls —was neither a bribe nor an attempt to bribe. But the offer of $2,500 "was for the purpose of influencing the Senator's vote." Although Patman and Neff were on Superior's pay roll, the claim that the cash came from Keck rather than from his company was accepted without any audit. The oil executive was scolded for his "remarkable laxity" in giving his lobbyists such latitude. A searching scrutiny of the origins of the money would have opened the door to an investigation of the prevailing fiction of "personal" campaign contributions by corporate officials. Political workers in South Dakota saw this as a record offering for their sparsely settled state. Keck, however, indicated his feeling that this was essentially a petty amount of money to be talking about—just as some thirty years earlier oil magnate Doheny dismissed the $100,000 cash "loan" turned over to Secretary Fall in a black satchel as "a bagatelle to me." [19] (Superior is rated a favorite stock by investment companies. From 1955

to 1957 it paid no federal corporate income tax. In 1956 it grossed
$90 million and reported a net income of $5 million. In 1957 the
gross was $111 million and the net nearly $19 million. If this case
furthered the declining prestige of the Senate, it seemed to have
only a beneficial impact on the stock of Superior Oil.)

As for the Nebraska lobbyist, the committee observed that he
had "exercised incredibly poor judgment," lobbying in "an inept
fashion" and with "consummate indiscretion." It recommended that
the Justice Department see if any federal statutes had been violated.
It also urged a fuller study and clarification of the lobbying and
corrupt-practices laws. After a grand jury inquiry Patman and Neff
received one-year suspended sentences for failing to register as lobbyists and were fined $2,500 each—an amount which appeared to be
their standard campaign contribution offer. (As Neff had once said
earlier, $2,500 "just seems to stick out everywhere.") Superior was
fined $10,000 for being involved in the failure of the two employees
to register.

Meanwhile, the Senate had not waited for the report. It refused
to recommit the bill. On the same day that it created the select
committee, it raced to approve, by a 53 to 38 vote, the Harris-
Fulbright bill to free natural gas producers from federal control. The
bill was rejected by the President. This veto was arrived at after a
careful discussion among White House political advisers mindful
of the forthcoming presidential election. Mr. Eisenhower assured
the industry that he favored the basic objectives of the bill and
consumers that he was also mindful of their needs. But

since the passage of this bill a body of evidence has accumulated indicating that private persons, apparently representing only a very great
and vital industry, have been seeking to further their own interests by
highly questionable activities. These include efforts I deem to be so
arrogant and so much in defiance of acceptable standards of propriety
as to risk creating doubt among the American people concerning the
integrity of governmental processes.[20]

Until judgments were reached by the Senate investigation and the
Department of Justice, the clouded circumstances made it impossible
to give his approval.

No objection was voiced in the veto message about the windfall of billions of dollars the great oil and gas companies would gain from the law. Nor was mention made of the generous election contributions for the support of "tidelands" and other items not vetoed. In the White House, in the Senate, in the parties and industry circles the failing involved seemed to be more one of manners than of morality. Willie Stark, Robert Penn Warren's fictional prototype of Huey Long, had once caught the distinction quite well. Graft, he held, is "when the fellows do it who don't know which fork to use."

The industry and its legislative supporters were furious at what they felt was Eisenhower's political desertion in the face of public opinion. (Oilmen called this a second betrayal; they had long insisted that President Truman was also slated to approve the Kerr bill in 1949, and the last-minute political calculations of consumer state votes forced a change.) The Senate strategists led by Lyndon Johnson saw the veto as a slap at their decision to ignore Case's warning, and hence an unmistakable insinuation as to the propriety of their own actions in voting for the bill. The move also challenged the conservative Democratic leadership while undercutting liberal Democratic plans to apply the natural-resources "giveaway" label to the Republicans in the election just ahead.

The Senate now had little choice but to authorize a broader investigation of oil and gas influence. Once more there was careful bipartisan maneuvering to keep in safe hands the inquiry into what in many respects was the Senate's own integrity. Much of the politicking centered upon preventing Albert Gore of Tennessee, Hennings's successor to the chairmanship of the Subcommittee on Privileges and Elections, from now following through with the type of investigation Hennings had sought. The solution finally arrived at was to create a new special committee for the broader oil and gas inquiry. Gore was one of the eight senators selected to serve and was slated to lead the group. (A number of his colleagues favoring a genuine investigation accepted the by-passing of the regular subcommittee on this assumption.) But then came a series of skirmishes with Styles Bridges, who was also appointed to the special committee. The powerful Republican, who headed his party's Senate Policy Committee, sought to impose conditions over the rules of procedure and the choice and functioning of the special committee that would have made a forthright investigation impossible. Gore then declined

the chairmanship. The compromise chairman became John L. Mc-
Clellan, a conservative Democrat who generally voted along industry
lines and whose Arkansas law firm has represented a number of oil
interests, including Esso and Carter (both Jersey Standard companies), Tidewater, and Seaboard, partly owned by The Texas Corporation. Bridges became vice chairman. Also on the committee
was Barry Goldwater, a right-wing Republican from Arizona who
admitted receiving an oil contribution as listed from "Keck." Asked
if he would disqualify himself because of this, Goldwater replied:
"Hell no . . . I am not going to get off the committee, and if they
want a fight, let them try to throw me off." He denied that campaign contributions necessarily meant improper influence. "If Mr.
Keck likes the way I vote, he has a perfect right to give money to me.
I have never known Mr. Keck to ask a favor of me. . . . If the CIO
Auto Workers Union likes the way Paul Douglas votes, it has a
right to give money to him." [21]

The committee received an introductory picture of the extent
of industry lobbying. They heard testimony about the activities of
a number of companies and about the General Gas Committee, as
well as about the more extensive public relations operations of the
industry's specially created Natural Gas and Oil Resource Committee which admitted spending nearly $2 million in the gas fight.*
Many oilmen balked at the term "lobbying," and some made clear
their activities were essentially "educational." Despite renewed appeals by Chairman McClellan, no senator volunteered information
on illegal or improper activities to influence legislation. The White
House declined to amplify the President's veto message reference
to arrogant lobbying activities. At one point Senator Clinton P.
Anderson of New Mexico, who had supported the natural gas bill
but was one of the more alert questioners, exclaimed:

It strikes me as a strange situation that the President vetoed the bill
because of the arrogant lobbying, but nobody lobbied, nobody saw anybody lobbying, nobody heard of anybody who lobbied. It was the best
kept secret of the year.[22]

The committee did hear witnesses tell of the lobbying by such
opponents of the Harris-Fulbright bill as the gas distributors' Coun-

* This will be discussed in the next chapter.

cil of Local Gas Companies and the United Automobile, Aircraft and Agricultural Implement Workers. Walter Reuther, the president of the latter union, was one of the first to admit his group was engaged in lobbying. "Our only regret is that we didn't influence enough." [23] The committee castigated a North Dakota editor and a labor radio commentator for glibly charging, without being able to offer substantial documentation, that senators were selling out to "the oil interests" on the Harris-Fulbright bill.

Questioning was never very sustained and the research was limited, although many good leads were available. The committee spent less than half of its allocated budget. Ignored were the full implications of oil's impact in elections and of such uncomfortable matters as the retainer system. McClellan was a judicious chairman, and the committee's report in May 1957 did make a few useful recommendations on tightening controls and disclosure requirements over lobbying registration.[24] It also suggested removing legal limitations on the amounts of money that could be contributed to a presidential campaign, while increasing financial responsibility by the filing of reports. A ceiling of $15,000 in total political contributions by a single individual in a given year was proposed, in place of the current practice of limiting a giver to $5,000 to each of as many candidates or committees as he chooses. The majority refused to include the crucial area of primary elections under these restrictions.

The special committee's efforts were completely and conveniently overshadowed in the press and in politics by a different investigation then taking place and also chaired by Senator McClellan. This was on improper activities in labor and management. Dave Beck and James R. Hoffa, the top officials of the International Brotherhood of Teamsters, were far more attractive objects of congressional wrath. For example, Senator John F. Kennedy of Massachusetts, silent on the lobbying committee, played a vigorous role in the headline inquiry into labor racketeering. An interim report, in March 1958, by the latter committee told of the examination of hundreds of thousands of canceled checks, thousands of pages of ledger sheets and bank statements, staff traveling of 650,000 miles, tracing down thousands of financial transactions, the issuing of 2,740 subpoenas, interviewing in 44 states and the maintenance of offices in 12 cities. This work was done by a staff of 34 assistant counsels and investigators and from 35 to 45 accountants and investigators from the General Accounting Office.[25] One wonders what might have happened if similar zeal and resources had been harnessed for the oil and gas inquiry.

As described in an earlier chapter, the White House in 1957 secretly took the lead in getting industry leaders to work on a new "compromise" bill. Senator Fulbright publicly declared he would not sponsor any new measure in light of the President's weakness. Representative Oren Harris of Arkansas, the co-sponsor of the 1956 bill, was more agreeable. Asked if he thought lobbying would have any adverse effect again, he replied:

I have no scruples about lobbying for this gas bill. Last year it was no different than in many other instances I could cite. If you accepted the theory that was used in vetoing last year's bill, then you could kill *any* bill merely by an uncouth practice.

If I were an oil man, I would make a fighting comeback. I would go to the Congress and let it be known that we're in a business that is honorable and vital. . . . I would promote my cause honestly and fearlessly.[26]

The political tacticians ultimately decided that 1957 was not a propitious year for pushing through the gas bill. While the oilmen chafed at this new postponement, they remained comforted by the continued sympathetic functioning of the Federal Trade Commission and the political pledges for 1958. And despite the dire warnings to the contrary, the expansion of the gas industry continued.

But early in 1958 the table manners of some of its friends once more made natural gas too uncomfortable for public embrace by many congressmen. This time the breach involved the disclosure of a solicitation, aimed at Texas oil and gas men, by Republican National Committeeman H. J. Porter, for a $100 a plate testimonial dinner in honor of House Republican Leader Joseph W. Martin, Jr. Wrote Porter:

Joe Martin . . . has always been a friend of Texas, especially of the oil and gas producing industries. He mustered two-thirds of the Republican votes in the House each time the gas bill passed. . . . As Speaker of the 83rd Congress he led the fight for adoption of tidelands ownership bill.

It will be up to Joe Martin to muster at least 65 percent of the Republican votes in order to pass the gas bill this year. He has to put Republican Members from northern and eastern consuming areas on the spot politically because the bill is not popular due to the distortion of facts by newspaper columnists and others.

The dinner must raise substantial amounts of money for the Republican Party as part of these will go toward the election of Republican Congressmen and Senators.[27]

The Texas Republicans raised an estimated $100,000. But this meant little to the industry in view of the waves of public indignation and political disclaimers that followed. House Democratic Leader Sam Rayburn, who had been scheduled to lead the new legislative drive, deplored the publicity and its consequences. "If Mr. Porter had set out deliberately to kill the bill he could hardly have done a better job." President Eisenhower referred to the appeal as "hopefully . . . an isolated incident" and the Republican National Chairman announced that his committee would not touch the money. Other party leaders, including the chairmen of the Senate and House Republican Campaign Committees, joined in the deploring of the technique. But Senator Andrew F. Shoeppel of Kansas, chairman of the Senate Republican Campaign Committee, quickly added: "We are certainly not going to take the position, however, that any money forwarded to us by the Republican State Finance Committee of Texas will not be accepted." [28]

Once more the interaction between oil and politics highlighted the corrosion of standards of political morality. Once more the expediencies of political commitments and finances challenged the capacity of the United States Congress to function as a genuinely national legislature. As the correlation between campaign contributions and voting behavior has become closer, a clear-cut definition of bribery fades. Throughout the country candidates of different political persuasions have admitted to "running scared" lest they offend oil interests. A liberal senatorial aspirant in the West refused to make oil an issue, although it was basic to the economic future of his state: "I don't want to start up now; I have enough troubles." A vigorous opponent of oil and other corporate interests in state matters, aiming for higher office, was offered financial help by a Texas oil millionaire if he would enter the primaries against the incumbent New Deal senator. He rejected the behind-the-scenes proposal and later explained his refusal to publicize the letter: After all, C—— was doing a decent thing, offering me money. This is the game of politics and I respect his confidences. It is not fair to C——, so we won't publish it. I want to play the game right. This happens all the time.

Speaking invitations at extravagant fees become techniques for aiding the public careers and private exchequers of sympathetic legislators. Most of them are lawyers. With oil litigation so widespread and lucrative, the retainer serves as a time-honored way for buying access, good will—or just silence. It would be valuable for citizens to know how many congressmen either are in the oil business, have leases or stock, or are members of law firms that have oil and gas clients. An earlier generation had learned, thanks to the muckraking disclosures of William Randolph Hearst, that Senator Joseph B. Foraker, a Republican leader from Ohio, was paid generously by the Standard Oil trust for his legal and political services, which included the blocking of legislation in Ohio and Washington. An alert newspaper reader could discover that the sponsors of legislation in 1948 to free gas producers from federal controls were Senator Ed Moore, a millionaire oilman, and Representative Ross Rizley, whose Oklahoma law office has had gas clients that include the giant Cities Service and Panhandle Eastern Pipeline companies. (When a Senate offshore oil inquiry in 1948 was discussing the fact that Assistant Attorney General Clary of California had received part of his income from oil companies, Moore asked, "What is improper about it?")[29] The citizen may be aware of Senator Kerr's activities in behalf of oil and gas. He may also know of the doings of Senator John W. Bricker, whose law firm represented the East Ohio Gas Company as well as the Pennsylvania Railroad. As chairman of the Interstate and Foreign Commerce Committee, Bricker helped the unremitting search for loopholes in the Natural Gas Act of 1938. ("Everyone knows I'm honest, so what's wrong with my being chairman of the committee and receiving money from the law firm?")[30] In 1954 he successfully pushed the Hinshaw bill—without Senate hearings—which exempted from federal control any company buying natural gas at or within a state boundary for consumption within the same state. East Ohio Gas, which in 1950 had lost its claim for such immunity from FPC surveillance in a test case in the United States Supreme Court, was a direct beneficiary. The subsidiary of the great Consolidated Natural Gas Company (once part of the Jersey Standard empire) had claimed it was not interstate since it bought and sold gas—purchased from the pipeline of Hope Natural Gas, also owned by Consolidated, crossing into the state, within the boundaries of Ohio.[31] A veteran Washington figure estimated in 1954 that perhaps 20 per cent of the Congress were so involved. But no one will ever have even an approximation until officials show a willingness and citizens an interest in having the former's private assets a matter of public record.

As always, the funds that loom so large in party planning and for which political workers hunt with such frenzy and receive with such indignity, if not impropriety, are petty items from a corporate perspective. A country that can afford astronomical sums for automobiles, defense, and entertainment and whose subsidies to oil and other private economic activities reach into the billions encourages its politicians to become beggars or sycophants.

The consequences of the continuing anxiety of candidates and parties for minimum funds to conduct campaigns reflect the popular neglect of politics. They also accent the need for a more frontal public approach to financing elections. Broader-based contributions would help to minimize the dependency upon oilmen and other affluent sources whose motives may be honorable but whose effect is at best paternal. The earmarking of public funds for campaign costs and formulation of plans for equal and free access to television should also be examined.

Granted the gas bill was set aside, at least temporarily, just as Edwin Pauley never did receive his appointment. The power of oil has not been limitless, any more than has the paralysis of the legislative process or the benumbing of public sensitivity in relation to oil been total. It is comforting but perilous to conclude, however, that sequences of events, such as involved in the Case episode, have been unique, or that the political activities of the oil and gas industry can be explained away as just those of a pressure group—with the influence it exerts balanced and checked by other groups, or that "somehow" the American political system can contain such activities without inroads upon the essence of political democracy itself. The issue is neither the worth of diversity nor the right of lobbying. Each is inherent in representative government. Nor is the ultimate focus the particular sins of oilmen and oil corporations. These must be weighed against the many genuine industrial achievements of the industry. Nor is the problem simply that of the venality of weak congressmen. The spotlight here belongs more on lawmakers and respectable men with bulging brown brief cases entering the portals of government rather than on lawbreakers and furtive men with little black bags using side entrances of hotels. Government policy on oil has increasingly become indistinguishable from the private policies of oil, with this development carried to new extremes under the Eisenhower Administration which held as principle that government ought to be in the hands of the concerned business community, that is, that part of government which had not already been turned over outright to private control. The resultant corruption has not been of individual men or even of programs for oil, but of the very concept of public policy. Those who most contribute to the political corruption of our times thus foster the popular view of politics as dirty and government as evil. By so doing the people are effectively deterred from understanding and then using politics and government for the formulation of public policies. The fundamental question thus involves the nature of oil as a system of power and the impact upon American institutions and values. It concerns the requirements for responsible government and a democratic society.

There have been numerous investigations of aspects of oil power dating back to the beginnings of the industry. These often have stemmed from what Henry Demarest Lloyd in 1894 described as the "dancing attendance" upon state legislatures, courts, attorneys general, Congress, and the Interstate Commerce Commission which the independent oilman "must add to Thrift, Industry and Sobriety as a condition of survival" in his fights against the original Standard trust.[32] A petition in 1878 by the Petroleum Producers Union to the governor of Pennsylvania during a critical fight against the domination of the railroads, pipelines, and refineries by the Standard monopoly described one such inquiry by the Congress in 1876 as "conducted in a dilatory manner" with "a prominent member of the Standard Oil Company, and not a member of Congress, presiding behind the seat of the chairman":

Vice-President Cassett, of the Pennsylvania Railroad, was the only prominent railway official who appeared in obedience to the subpoenas of the Speaker of the House of Representatives, and he refused to give the committee any information as to the matter under investigation, and the counsel of The Pennsylvania Railroad, ex-Senator Scott, appeared before the committee in justification of his so doing. The financial officer of the Standard Oil Company appeared before the committee, accompanied by a member of Congress—also a member of that Company, and promptly refused to give the committee any information as to the organization, or the names of its members, or its relations with the railroads. The influence and power of the combination was apparent; the committee never reported, never complained of the contempt of its witnesses, and all the evidence and record of its proceedings effectively disappeared.[33]

In 1879 the New York Central's William H. Vanderbilt (to whom has been attributed the classic cry "The public be damned") told the Hepburn Committee in New York that the heads of Standard Oil were very shrewd men. "I don't believe that by any legislative enactment or anything else through any of the states or all of the states, you can keep such men as them down . . . they will be up on top all the time." [34] An Industrial Commission created by the Congress in 1898 to look into trusts was watched closely while Standard executives maintained liaison with key senators to ensure that the solid documentation on the combination movement was followed by timid proposals.

Practically every session of the Congress since the early thirties has seen studies of the economics of oil, ranging from pipeline divorcement to pressures on distribution. The Temporary National Economic Committee hearings brought out a good deal about the industry's economic power, but the over-all conclusions were limited. An industry-wide rise in the prices of oil and gasoline in 1953 provoked considerable public indignation and the beginnings of a useful investigation by the Republican-controlled House Interstate and Foreign Commerce Committee. The industry was polite, cautious, and evasive in the answers—in contrast to earlier times when titans like John D. Archbold and H. H. Rogers were often arrogant, sneering, and evasive. ("I think the anti-trust fever is a craze," a president of two Standard companies wrote Rockefeller in 1888, "which we should meet in a very dignified way and *parry every question* with answers which, while perfectly truthful, are evasive of *bottom* facts.")[35] "These hearings will be put in lavender mothballs," an American Petroleum Institute staff member cryptically observed. "There will never even be a report issued." He was right. But the 1953 hearing room was jammed with oilmen and their lobbyists, lawyers, and public relations experts.

The Suez crisis of 1956 provided another opportunity for a full-scale study. Once again the data was substantial, but there was little disposition or support for following through. Inquiries into money in elections have generally been handled most gingerly, with scant enthusiasm for exploring such specific questions as oil power. As a condition for getting the enacting resolution passed, the extensive inquiries of the House Select Committee on Lobbying Activities in 1950, chaired by Representative Frank Buchanan, never touched oil. Nor did the House Subcommittee on Study of Monopoly Power, chaired by Representative Emanuel Celler. An antitrust investigation in 1955–1956, led by Celler, however, did make a valuable contribution by publishing the minutes of the National Petroleum Council and related materials on oilmen in government.

A hysterical series of hearings by a House Select Committee to Investigate Tax-Exempt Foundations culminated in a report in 1954 that described the existence of an allegedly vast intellectual conspiracy, financed by the Carnegie, Ford, Rockefeller, and similar foundations, to subvert America by promoting empirical research in the social sciences that "ignores moral precepts, principles and established or accepted norms of behavior." The funds were also charged with favoring the "dangerous" cultural-lag approach, collectivism, and internationalism, while inducing the educator "to become an agent for social change." And they were warned to "be very chary of promoting ideas, concepts, and opinions—forming material that runs contrary to what the public currently wishes, approves and likes." The chairman, Representative B. Carroll Reece of Tennessee, refused, however, to include H. L. Hunt's Facts Forum within the purview of his committee.[36] The promising beginnings in 1957 of a thoroughgoing analysis of the workings of the Federal Power Commission and other regulatory agencies by a Subcommittee on Legislative Oversight were sparked by the dramatic public indictments by energetic counsel Bernard Schwartz of the fraternization of administrative officials in the regulatory agencies and presidential aide Sherman Adams in the White House with the regulated. These preliminary disclosures were soon buried in behind-the-scenes intrigue. The counsel found himself the defendant before outraged congressmen. When some of the smoke cleared, Schwartz had been deposed. This climaxed the frustration of Representative Morgan M. Moulder, chairman of the subcommittee. He had already been troubled by the retention of the subpoena power by Oren Harris, chairman of the parent Interstate and Foreign Commerce Committee. And the loyalty of some of the committee staff to the latter underscored the general tone of House leaders that the investigators were to tread lightly. Moulder resigned, and Harris, a frank spokesman for gas producers, formally took over.[37]

No legislative body has ever made an over-all inquiry holding up to public light the full ramifications of the private government of oil. The diffusion of responsibility within the Congress is also a factor. Harold Ickes complained that he, Ralph Davies, or other Petroleum Administration for War officials appeared over one hundred times before some twenty different congressional committees and subcommittees to talk about oil. Investigators always have to cope with the complexity of the subject and the apparent monopoly of knowledge that the industry enjoys. And collectively, oil possesses more experience, as well as direction and backing in dealing with the government, than committee personnel and other public servants have in their dealings with oil. But there are also some men in public office who know the industry well and, if given the chance, would not be awed by oil's studied technique of making technological and economic descriptions incomprehensible.

Congressional hearings on oil frequently have a pathetic quality to them. The few legislators who participate tend to be obsequious, belligerent, or perfunctory, with none of these attitudes too promising for understanding, let alone reasoned action. The congressmen sometimes growl at the corporate witnesses—Why are you so big? Why are your profits so high? Oil was once strenuously self-effacing in its replies, unwilling to admit its power. It would—and still does —talk about the hazards and the wonders of the competitive system. But now more and more the answers tend to be—and with justification—We are big because we have a big job to do. We need profits to plan for the world-wide acquisition of future sources of oil for an expanding economy. And we will grow bigger—we have to. If we don't we won't survive. Nor will the nation, with 70 per cent of its energy now derived from oil and gas. The oilmen then outdo the congressmen in solemn praise of small business and "free enterprise" as the backbone of the American society. And the inquisitors often are lost—in awe and futility—caught by their own platitudes and by complex patterns they are not prepared to dissect, let alone resolve through alternatives.

Too often research is poor or nonexistent, with the legislators lacking the preparation and the time to pursue their familiar elementary questions. This inadequacy, repeatedly experienced by some of oil's leading spokesmen, lends support to the latter's privately voiced but ill-concealed contempt for most elected officials and for what Robert E. Wilson, Indiana Standard's board chairman, once described as "committee after committee, pawing over the same sets of facts and coming up with a chaos of muddled understanding and misunderstanding, mistaken conclusions, and no conclusion at all." [38] To get at the "permeability of oil" congressmen would do well to recall an exchange in 1928 between the painstaking Senator Gerald Nye and the then chairman of Standard of Indiana who had been receiving and putting away "mysterious" Liberty Bonds that featured so prominently in the Teapot Dome scandal. Annoyed by such disclosures, the witness said that all that Nye was proving was that he had a "bigger bump of curiosity than I have." To this, Nye replied, "If we had not had a material bump of curiosity on this committee, we never would have gotten much information." [39]

Also needed is another old-fashioned American trait—a sense of moral indignation rooted in commitment to democratic ideals and needs. For if the experiences of Senators Robert M. La Follette, Thomas J. Walsh, and other investigators into the social consequences of private economic power are any guide, such efforts will be dismissed as "politically inspired." La Follette, a Republican, found his efforts opposed by the leaders of his own party. His office was rifled by a Justice Department agent after he introduced the resolution in favor of an investigation of the Teapot Dome leases. Walsh's life history was closely checked by the Federal Bureau of Investigation in the hope of finding scandalous material to forestall his curiosity about Fall's behavior. In an age of organized euphoria, the discordant "muckraking" of esteemed corporate citizens and the social environment within which they flourish will be deplored as base ingratitude, if not subversion—unless, of course, the press chooses to ignore these approaches entirely.

Most legislative investigations are defensive as well as fragmentary, aiming at the exposure or remedying of a particular abuse. Where legislative policy is explored, as, for example, natural gas regulation, the renewal of the Interstate Oil Compact, the continuation of shale-oil work at Rifle and reciprocal trade, almost invariably the initiative as well as the political organizing drive has come from the industry. It was a major achievement for liberals to fend off the Kerr and related bills. Yet what the Federal Power Commission needs is a clear-cut mandate defining its scope. Court orders, as in the Phillips case, are important, but no substitute for bold legislative planning. Neither major political party has shown the capacity or inclination to fill such policy vacuums. The presumed Republican sympathy for private enterprise is consistently mocked by the party's willing support of the rising corporate "socialist" state. The claim of the Democratic party as to its championship of the common man is repeatedly vitiated by the compromising positions of its congressional standard-bearers on all affairs of oil. The Democratic National Committee ducked on "tidelands" in 1952, despite the courageous position of Adlai Stevenson. And there is no organized public to speak for a broader national interest.

A thorough legislative study of public policy toward oil would be valuable. Its scope would have to range from the very concept of private ownership of subsurface mineral rights and the place of oil in the international energy picture to the assumptions of antitrust and the alternatives available for developing meaningful responsibility and public participation in oil-policy formulation. The direct political influence of oil also requires systematic examination in order that the financial, lobbying, legal, and public relations efforts of the industry's private government may become visible to legislators and citizens. The nature of the Congress may make it impossible for this body to conduct such a study itself. It is conceivable, however, that an independent commission of experts and public servants, divorced from the political qualifications of seniority and interest representation, but responsible to the Congress, might have the necessary freedom and curiosity.

Such studies are always tempting. The intelligently directed use of the subpoena could add substantial documentation, although the oil groups increasingly have developed double sets of files, with one always ready for eager government investigators. The primary need, however, is not for more proof of corruption or irresponsible power. The details about the role of oil in domestic politics or foreign policy at times may be vague. But Americans know more than the trained national innocence implies. A measure of the morale of American democracy is the degree to which the public can still summon indignation over fresh disclosures but rarely show astonishment. There is an unarticulated popular assumption that of course private power and privilege dominate, have an "in" in government, and are "getting theirs." To be effective, "muckraking" must therefore be guided by a political theory and a conception of society.

The nature of petroleum as an integrated national and international force emphasizes the imperative for coordinated, positive policy planning. The diffused system of political responsibility inherent in the American constitutional frame makes such formulation difficult. The power of oil, cutting through political parties whose roots remain essentially local and whose national discipline has been minimal, thus far has made impossible the posing of meaningful alternatives for national policy.

The open activities of oilmen in politics may be legitimate exercises of private rights. And they can be expected to intensify as the demand for placing oil under public review grows. But the manipulation of employees, executives, and corporate resources for corporate political purposes cannot be defended as falling within the purview of democratic citizenship. As one supervisory official of a major oil company, who was required to round up signed telegrams supporting the Harris-Fulbright bill in 1956, privately wrote to Senator Hubert Humphrey, "To me, it is a fraud." He added: "I have thought long and hard before sending this letter. Please use it wisely. My job is in your hands." [40] When, as part of the new political mobilization program of oil and other business interests, the director of the Public Affairs Division of the National Association of Manufacturers calls upon all of business to commit itself "to the principle that all companies as well as individuals must be corporate citizens speaking through corporate leaders," he is heralding a society that bears closer resemblance to Mussolini's Italy than to a democratic America. [41] The oil corporation may be paternal, it may be generous, it may even be wise in its understanding of what constitutes the general welfare. But these considerations do not make it and its leaders politically responsible or representative in relation to employees, stockholders, or the general public.

The raw approach by business to politics may be tempered by public opinions and the changing American scene. But the corporation's primary political objective remains the defense of vast power and privilege. To welcome without question its self-appointed role as a proper model for and guardian of political morality is to provide a disturbing measure of the benumbing of memory, critical judgment—and humor—in contemporary America. Given the permeability in political life and in the administrative state of the modern oil industry and oil considerations, the nation might begin an appraisal of this assumption by recalling from a less highly structured and a less reverent age the pertinent discussions of wardheeler Jawn Cassady and the philosophic saloonkeeper Mr. Dooley. The former was ardent in his defense of the art and virtue of politics:

I niver knew a pollytician to go wrong ontil he'd been contaminated be contact with a business man. . . . What th' business iv this country needs . . . is f'r active young pollyticians to take an inthrest in it an' ilivate it to a higher plane. Me battle cry is: "Honest pollytical methods in th' administhration iv business."

Dooley's skeptical rejoinder was:

It seems to me that the on'y thing to do is to keep pollyticians an' business men apart. They seem to have a bad infloonce on each other. Whiniver I see an aldherman an' a banker walkin' down th' sthreet together I know th' Recordin' Angel will have to ordher another bottle iv ink. [42]

Politics is presumed to be the essential way for the majority of the people to chart and control the direction of their society. And the political party and party responsibility are central tools for guiding the governmental machinery in a coherent and purposeful fashion. They provide a means for holding public policy and rulers accountable primarily to the citizenry rather than to the organized special interests. To allow the cultural focus on getting ahead and individual achievement, along with the cultivated myths of private enterprise and states' rights, to protect the power of oil from public scrutiny and accountability is to frustrate politics, and thus to accept the destruction of democracy. For too long now these have been cloaks for organized greed. They have served to forestall a frontal reexamination of an environment whose tolerance of privilege and rewards for antisocial behavior have corroded opportunities for competition between parties, standards of political morality, and hopes for political responsibility.

15

Public Relations and Private Power

There is a colossal shortage of understanding about the oil industry. . . . We propose to increase that understanding. We propose to do it through a carefully planned series of specific steps that will create a constructive, favorable impression of the oil industry in the public mind. We want the public to like the oil industry.[1]

It was November 1946, and vice president Robert T. Haslam of the Standard Oil Company (New Jersey) was presenting to the twenty-sixth annual meeting of the American Petroleum Institute the postwar public relations program for the industry. This was the product of the extensive deliberations of a seventeen-man API Advisory Subcommittee on Public Relations that were in part based upon the findings of an Opinion Research Corporation study. On the cover of the latter's report had appeared a quotation from Lincoln:

Public sentiment is everything. With public sentiment nothing can fail. Without it, nothing can succeed. Consequently, he who molds public sentiment goes deeper than he who enacts statutes or pronounces decisions. He makes statutes and decisions possible or impossible to be executed.[2]

This was the essence of the advice to the industry. The Republican congressional victory the previous week would not solve all their problems, the oilmen were told.

If this approach catches the spirit of democratic government, it

428

also represents the rationale of modern public relations. Viewed together with oil's entrenched position within government and oil's activities in what is more narrowly viewed as "politics," it provides a key to understanding the political behavior of oil. For public relations is a first line of defense of the organized economic power of the oil industry.

There was nothing new about oil's interest in public relations. It had existed in some forms from the early days of the industry. But there was little need to be defensive in the robber-baron period when predatory business practices were judged to be harmonious with the Constitution, natural law, and human nature. America was expanding and oil was an integral part of that growth. There was no time for democratic or Christian niceties. "Competition is a state of war," the counsels for Standard Oil had argued in their courtroom defense against the federal government's efforts to smash the original trust:

> Price cutting and rebating, collecting information of the trade of competitors, the operation of companies under other names to obviate prejudice or secure an advantage or for whatever reason, are all legal methods of competition whatever moral criticism they may justify. There is no rule of fairness or reasonableness which regulates competition. . . . Those who stand upon an Act [Sherman Antitrust Act of 1890] which encourages competition cannot complain of the extermination which competition involves.[3]

As John D. Rockefeller, Jr., once explained to a Sunday school class, Standard Oil's place illustrated Darwin's survival of the fittest. "The American Beauty rose can be produced in the splendor and fragrance which bring cheer to its beholder only by sacrificing the early buds which grow up around it. This is not an evil tendency in business. It is merely the working-out of a law of nature and a law of God."[4] And as Walter Hallanan, chairman of the National Petroleum Council, echoes, nearly a half-century later: "The experience of those who have engaged in the discovery and development of our oil resources and in their processing and distribution has demonstrated that only the free are strong and that only the strong can be free. There has been no place in this romantic American adventure for the laggards or weaklings."[5]

The rules of the game have been rough. Presumably, the citizen-consumer has always been the gainer. But the mounting organized reaction to monopoly, which found its focus in Rockefeller and was climaxed by the 1911 Standard Oil dissolution decree, together with the uneasy popular awareness that the American dream of equal opportunity for all did not quite square with urban and corporate realities, and also the rise of the mass consumption of petroleum, all served to turn the industry to the business of achieving mass approval for its practices as well as its products. The elder Rockefeller's penchant for secrecy, his confidence that history would judge his achievements wisely, if not kindly, and his disdain for responding to the savage assaults upon the Standard empire by such muckrakers as Henry Demarest Lloyd and Ida M. Tarbell gave way to newer management principles. Early public relations efforts, essentially drumbeating for sales, were adapted to dispelling the image of Rockefeller as a "bad" man. Newspaper stories and magazine portraits of the company and its leaders were now welcomed and even promoted.[6] When in 1914 a grim labor dispute in Ludlow, Colorado, involving several mining companies, including one controlled by the Rockefellers, erupted into raw violence and the slaughter of strikers and their families by state troops, the public outcry forced the absentee owners to reexamine their labor practices and their external relations. Ivy L. Lee was hired to handle publicity. His tactics to make the Rockefellers palatable by emphasizing community deeds and generosity marked the transition between press agentry and modern public relations. The next stages involved modifying the image of the individual oil company as "bad." Measures were taken to remove the curse from the name "Standard" and to make clear that all oil was not "Standard." Gradually all the integrated companies developed public relations programs geared to their individual needs and to industry-wide problems.

The two world wars gave tremendous impetus to the associational and the public relations efforts of the industry. The experiences of both periods demonstrated to oil how positive were the gains when they could openly cooperate rather than compete, with the blessing and indeed often wearing the toga of public government. The American Petroleum Institute was created in 1919 to foster further techniques of industry self-government and gain protection from possible control by public government.

Conversely, both war periods pointed up the possible perils in public regulation and planning for national purposes, since oil was now so basic to the modern economy. In its most sophisticated stage, therefore, the public relations approach has been to assure the nation that the industry and the economic system within which it functions are not "bad," that oil's needs and values are harmonious with those of the American people. From its very inception, the API has worked in this direction, with a formal working public relations group within the institute set up in 1924. Once again there has been a counterpart in American industry's general drive to merchandize the label "free enterprise." This was created to replace such terms as "competitive" and "private enterprise" which seemed so obviously incongruous as descriptions of a highly concentrated industrial bureaucracy whose structure, practices, and aspirations were so remote from the traditional tenets of a capitalist economy.

Once oil recovered from its depression scares of the early thirties, when its leaders even pleaded with the dangerous New Dealers for tight regulation under a government "czar," like much of American enterprise its major spokesmen realized with horror how perilously close they had come to being an accessory to their own socialization. Never again would oil so abdicate. The API redoubled its cooperative endeavors toward corporate self-government. Public relations were intensified, with big government in general and the New Deal in particular prominent targets. Again this had its parallels in the tremendous outlay of money and propaganda by the National Association of Manufacturers, the Liberty League, and similar organizations, all of whom enjoyed oil support.

Oil companies prospered greatly during World War II, and their economic positions seemed solid. There was, however, concern about their postwar relations with government and the public. The Texas Company, which had extensive dealings with Germany, in 1940 removed board chairman Torkild Rieber after the press described some of his courtesies to Nazi representatives in the United States. ("I considered it simply good business.")[7] In the same year the company began its sponsorship of radio broadcasts of the Metropolitan Opera. The disclosures about Jersey Standard's intimacies with I. G. Farben provoked stormy stockholder meetings in 1942 and 1943, and the public reactions rocked the company internally. They posed a public relations problem beyond that of one company, even though much of the press played down the charges. Harold Ickes related how the president of one leading oil company told him that the industry would never be able to get over the scandal. When the story first broke, the executive's wife called him from across the continent to ask him if he could get out of oil and go into some "decent" business. One of Ralph Davies's young daughters wrote her father that her schoolmates had been making remarks about Standard Oil which she thought reflected on him. (Davies was vice president of the separate California company.) But she assured her father that she would always stand by him.

Oil no longer had a formal industry public relations program, its API committee having been disbanded in 1940 because of fear of inviting further antitrust action. A new public relations committee was formed in 1945 under Robert T. Haslam, former general manager of Esso Standard (a Jersey affiliate). Haslam had headed the parent company's public relations defense of its patent tie-ups with I. G. Farben. And so in 1946 the API listened to a report based upon a "scientific" analysis of what the public thought of oil, as gleaned from some ten thousand interviews. "Those Who Know You Well . . . Think Well of You" was the Opinion Research Corporation's theme. "There is no indication of the need for a defensive approach. . . . While the public is willing to accept mistaken ideas about the industry, only small percentages at present have convictions hostile to the industry." [8] There were few public complaints about prices and many compliments about service. But there were three critical areas where the industry lacked support: the widespread impressions that oil holds back new developments, that the companies get together to fix prices, and that the industry is essentially a monopoly with little competition.

This, of course, was due to inadequate information and understanding, primarily on the part of those who did not know the industry, the study explained.

The public's great lack of knowledge and absence of opinion about the oil industry is at once your opportunity and vulnerability. No industry ever had a clearer guide to action. When people have no definite opinion about a subject an opinion vacuum exists which is easily filled by the first plausible idea that comes along. Those minds that now present an opinion vacuum on facts and ideas of major importance to the future welfare of the oil industry can be swayed to either friendly or hostile attitudes *depending on which plausible story they hear first.*

As an illustration the study pointed out that when people were asked how retail gas or oil prices were decided, 56 per cent indicated they did not know, 13 per cent said "they get together" and 31 per cent gave some kind of "competitive" answer. But when asked which of the statements presented came closest to their own idea, 57 per cent chose "the oil companies get together and set prices for their products" while 31 per cent marked "each company sets its own prices to meet competition."

This proved the need to rush in to fill the vacuum by giving the public a few plausible facts about oil. "And if, while convincing them that there are 1) a lot of companies, 2) competing to serve them better, 3) making a lot of products that make life better, 4) treating employees, dealers, and customers fairly, 5) making a moderate profit by dint of good management, you can also demonstrate that your heart is in the right place, the future of free enterprise in the oil business will be as solid as in any business because— Lincoln was right. 'Public sentiment is everything. . . .' " [9]

Here then was the analysis of trained social scientists. How was the challenge to be met? By "Progressive Public Relations for the Progressive Petroleum Industry," Mr. Haslam reported to the API.

The oil industry . . . has never created a long-term characterization by which the public could identify it and approve it. . . . In merchandising products, we try to create one simple impression that can be grasped readily. The same thing has to be done in terms of the industry as a whole!

We recognize the danger of letting the industry be set up in the public mind as essential or basic—attractive as that . . . may seem. In peacetime a characterization like that simply helps keep the industry in the front line for government encroachment. Thirty-six percent of the people who believe in public ownership of the oil industry do so, they say, because they believe the industry is essential. "Essential" industries invite nationalization.

"Oil is ammunition" had offered a strong positive image of the industry during the war. But now the problem was to understand peacetime conditions likely to face the industry and "to be as farsighted in planning our public position as we are in planning sales."

The public relations committee "canvassed and checked and cross-checked dozens of possible characterizations," testing for content value, public acceptance and practical operations.

Out of all this study . . . one characterization emerged with a test score substantially higher than all the rest. It is the characterization embodied in the word PROGRESSIVE. It gave us what we were seeking, a central theme. That . . . *Petroleum is Progressive.*
This is not a slogan. This is a central theme. . . . Here is a true characterization—one we can live with. Here is a friendly characterization that will be more effective than any other in meeting present and future issues.
For example, the progressive character of the industry is its best defense against regulation. A public impressed with that characterization of that industry is likely to think: "Let it alone—there's no need to nationalize a progressive industry."
This progressive characterization can be used to meet many specific issues. For example, it completely offsets the impression that the industry holds back new developments because, obviously, a progressive industry does not hold back. It goes forward. It improves old products. It pioneers with new ones. It is concerned for the welfare of the community in which it operates.
A progressive industry is worthy of fair profits, and the progressive development of the industry requires it to operate at a profit. If the public feels that an industry is progressive, there will be little tendency to think of it as making too much money. . . .
A progressive industry is by nature a competitive industry. . . . This progressive characterization can be projected all down the line. . . .[10]

With some modification, this remained the basic approach of the industry for a decade. Literature, films, pattern speeches, and advertisements all have hammered away at the assumed points of vulnerability. To answer the charges of oligopoly and collusion, for example, the propaganda has been guided by the Opinion Research Corporation finding of a correlation between idea as to number of oil companies and favorable attitude toward oil. On every question the small minority who knew there were over 100 companies in the industry were found to be somewhat more sympathetic than those who thought there were from 11 to 100 companies, and decidedly more friendly than those who assumed there were 10 or less companies. The industry thus reiterates a figure of 42,000 independent competing companies, exclusive of the 200,000 gas-station operators. "When 84 million adults have one fact they will dismiss this charge [of monopoly] against the oil industry." [11] It insists that "prices of oil products are determined by the same economic laws that affect the prices of other commodities." Where 45 per cent of those polled could not name any advances in the manufacture of oil products during the past few years, today the advertisements constantly emphasize new improvements. And as prices have risen since 1946 to become a potential issue, industry ads have focused on how relatively moderate has been the rise, compared to other commodities and how much more the gasoline dollar buys today. For unconvinced ingrates or perhaps the socialist-minded there are also frequent reminders of how much worse things are for the motorist in Russia. Although a 1957 study reported that only 10 per cent of the public favored government ownership of the industry, while 81 per cent opposed such a step, a full-page picture of a shabby Moscow gas station without service or brand identification has been an API favorite.

For a brief while the API's Public Relations Committee relied on the Fred Eldean organization, a professional public relations firm specializing in warding off socialism. Then the program was handled directly by an Oil Industry Information Committee (shortened to Oil Information Committee in 1956) within the API. The big oil companies and the regional oil associations have been well represented on both the board committee and the OIC, with the bulk of the financing coming from the major companies. The OIC operated with about one hundred paid staff people, and its 1956 budget was set at a little over $3 million. Such figures offer only a surface picture of public relations expenditures, since individual oil companies and associations frequently lend their services and personnel for specific chores.

The major tactical need, according to Mr. Haslam's report, was "grass-roots action to merchandise the friendly ideas and impressions we put out. . . ." To this end the OIC had fourteen district offices throughout the country, with New York as headquarters for the editorial, research, and executive personnel. These offices served to guide local public relations efforts while providing literature, speakers, films, and promoting special oil events. OIC preferred to work through local companies or groups, however. If the industry was attacked, one OIC district representative explained, the reply would be made by a local company rather than by the regional office, although OIC might be helping behind the scenes. Pattern speeches "suitable for adaptation by a local oil man" or for use by nonoil industry speakers, with blank spaces for the appropriate community references, were made available. Smaller companies which do not feel they can afford separate public relations departments have been offered ready-made programs prepared by the OIC.

"Oil Progress Week" has been a key annual undertaking. Mayors and governors are asked to issue proclamations recognizing its civic importance. Also involved are such nation-wide publicity efforts as radio and television shows, testimonial dinners with the Secretary of the Interior and comparable officials as guest speakers, oil-derived clothing fashion shows, oil fairs, between-halves programs at high-school football games, and "Oilman for a Day" programs. With the national office providing basic guidance, this promotion brings into play one of OIC's proudest instruments—the 40,000 oil people who serve as volunteers on more than 5,000 local committees. In 1955 the target was "the recruitment and indoctrination . . . of a fully-staffed, functioning committee in every community of 5,000 or more persons." [12] These people, mainly gas-station operators, jobbers, and employees, theoretically serve as ideal campaigners for the industry, since they tend to be identified in their communities as honest, hard-working "independent" businessmen whom the citizen sees as competing for his patronage and their livelihood through courtesy and service. (An opinion study for the OIC in 1953 indicated that 89 per cent of the public viewed local retail gasoline prices as roughly uniform and 77 per cent assumed these were set by the companies rather than by the dealers; yet over half apparently accepted the image of the latter as "independent businessmen.")[13] "Meet a man *we* work for!" proclaims an Esso advertisement introducing the friendly, competent service-station dealer. "Chances are you thought it was the other way around. But this man doesn't work for us. In fact, the shoe is on the other foot." [14] Meanwhile upon his shoulders, the dealer is repeatedly told, rests the burden of protecting the entire oil industry from the threats of government ownership or control:

> As a *progressive* oil man, you know that no one part of the oil industry can prosper unless the industry *as a whole* is free to serve the public in its own way—free from unnecessary restraints and regulations. . . . If misconceptions are allowed to persist, eventually they will threaten the very existence of the oil industry, and the jobs of oil men and women everywhere. And there is another, even greater, threat hidden in these mistaken ideas. If it were possible to undermine public confidence in the oil and other businesses, it would be possible to destroy the public's belief in the American competitive enterprise system itself.[15]

The volunteers are expected to reach local churches, clubs, mass media, and schools and to draw attention to oil in every way possible. Periodic "meet the press" projects entail bringing to every newspaper and radio station a fact book about oil while getting better acquainted with the editors, reporters and broadcasters. At the end of 1954 OIC reported that 85 per cent of all daily newspapers, 78 per cent of all radio stations, 90 per cent of all TV stations, and 38 per cent of all weekly newspapers in the OIC districts were personally contacted by oilmen. The immediate target was to reach every daily and weekly newspaper editor and every radio and TV station program manager in the country.

The OIC's 1953 report to the API cited among its accomplishments the following:

> Specially prepared editorials and articles dealing with the oil industry were placed in many national magazines in 1953. These included The Saturday Evening Post, Time, Newsweek, Pathfinder, Popular Mechanics, Popular Science and Business Week. Numerous news and feature stories were placed in the daily press. Wire and photo services . . . carried syndicated stories. Many ran special Oil Progress Week stories.[16]

The 1954 report told of continued article assistance and promotion. "Instances of misinformation in a few articles were answered again with facts, in friendly and personal meetings with editors. Arrangements were made in some cases to review future articles for accuracy before their appearance. Book publishers, too, were aided by manuscript reviews. . . ." Special distribution to government officials, writers, editors, and economists was made of two oil studies, *Price Making and Price Behavior in the Petroleum Industry* (Yale University Press) by Ralph Cassady, Jr., and *The Growth of Integrated Oil Companies* (Harvard University Graduate School of Business) by John G. McLean and Robert W. Haigh. (Cassady, Director of the Bureau of Research at the University of California, Los Angeles, has hailed the industry's competitive qualities in a full-page advertisement sponsored by the API and appearing in such magazines as *Newsweek, U.S. News & World Report,* and *Time.* McLean, a former Harvard faculty member, is vice president of Continental Oil.) "Above all," concluded the OIC report, "throughout the range of our special editorial services, there was a strengthened feeling of cooperation among editors and writers who, without being subjected to the all too familiar pressures of the 'planted' story, appreciate OIIC's informative aid." [17]

Schools have become a major target. Company employees have been urged to participate in Parent-Teacher Association activities and develop good relations with principals and school superintendents. The OIC has prepared a series of "textbooklets" and film strips dealing with science, social studies, economics, and conservation. A study, "What Makes This Nation Go," describes in fairly enlightened although certainly loaded fashion, the evolution of the "truly competitive" oil industry and its place in the economy.[18] While no author credit is indicated, the pamphlet was written by economist Robert L. Heilbroner, author of the popular *The Worldly Philosophers.* In 1955 the OIC reported that oil programs had been introduced into some 5,000 high schools and that 1,650,000 texts had been distributed in the current school year. In 1957 it claimed that 12,000 schools were participating. "We just don't dump texts or send them out," explained the API man in charge of the school program. "We work through grass roots. We want to reach high school kids; that's the way to get the whole country thinking our way eventually." They speak of ultimately reaching every single high school student and then the grade schools. The local committeemen play host to or visit the school boards, principals, and teachers to gain formal acceptance. As one local news story reported: "Representatives of the oil industry, high school principals and science teachers will meet at the Westchester Country Club next Thursday to consider advisability of incorporating studies of petroleum production and distribution into the schools' curricula." [19]

Some districts have special "meet the teacher weeks"; others sponsor banquets. Teachers' colleges, summer workshops, and school conventions are increasingly covered, with one inducement being attractive films and other visual aids to bring "realism" into the classroom of the harried schoolmarm. A Texaco report on the use in an Arkansas school of an Aramco film *Desert Venture* on Saudi Arabia records the excited reactions of the children: "Oil companies had a hard time drilling in all that heat and sand and flies. They worked three years before they struck a good oil well." "I am a country boy and I think it was wonderful how oil companies brought that water so people could grow their crops." A girl was thrilled that the homes built by the company "were air-conditioned and so pretty inside and the people living in them looked happy." Beamed teacher: "At first I was afraid some parts might be a little difficult for third-graders to understand. But you can see they are retaining an amazing amount of facts." [20]

Farmers and women are regarded as specialized audiences, with speakers, films, exhibits, and advertisements aimed at their organizations, publications, and fairs. Oil executives frequently have explored ways for the more intensive involvement of their employees. P. C. Spencer, chairman of Sinclair, has called for the men who direct oil companies to "make it plain to all employees that they believe in the OIIC program and want to support it wholeheartedly." [21] OIC officials have worked "to convince oil companies that each should appoint an employee to be responsible for distribution of OIIC materials within the company." [22] Women employees in the Desk and Derrick Clubs are viewed as excellent workers in oil's grass-roots crusade. This organization frankly views itself, in the words of a past president, "as a public relations segment of the petroleum industry." [23] Some 80 per cent of their time and program are required to be educational about oil. Industry leaders generally address their meetings, not infrequently exhorting political participation on oil matters. One local president explained: "If we are educated, we will bring the oil industry's message to the public." When asked if D and D have sessions on such topics as depletion allowances, the answer was yes. Asked if all sides are heard, including the critics of depletion, the reply was that speakers came from the industry. ". . . We can't get someone outside industry who is qualified."

The Boys Scouts of America are also courted. When the Scouts were engaged in a "geology month" project in October 1957, the API helped prepare a geology kit for each of the 68,000 troop units. Oil Information Committee volunteers were urged to make the most of a tie-in with Oil Progress Week, which also fell in October, by offering talks, displays, and films to the youngsters. In many districts such aid has been supplemented by special tours and field trips. On the West Coast some Boy Scouts have benefited from a geology counselor at their summer camp, his salary contributed by a number of oil companies.

Even the Cub Scouts, ages eight to eleven, have been recruited, with oil perhaps expected to join God and country as objects of duty of the nation's youth. April 1954 was observed as oil month, with a million Cub Scouts busily engaged in putting together and coloring 100,000 cutout kits showing the importance of oil in American life. With each kit a booklet telling the story of the competitive oil industry was thoughtfully included for the den mothers to read to the Cubs at each pack meeting. The real value of all this, explained OIC's director, Admiral H. B. Miller, was not so much the youngsters playing with the cutouts as it was their showing all this material to their parents.

The range of possibilities are apparently limitless and the results rewarding, OIC literature advises jobbers, urging their participation in this public relations:

As part of an educational program arranged by a Kansas oilmen's club, fifty-two selected Boy Scouts made a tour through every type of oil facility in the area. A police escort accompanied the caravan and guides at each installation explained what their guests saw. The boys were conducted through drilling and producing facilities, a refinery, a pipe line terminal, a bulk plant and a service station.

"Before they left the service station," a host jobber explains, "all hands tore into hot dogs, ice cream and soda pop. Finally, 52 tired and thoroughly stuffed young gentlemen were delivered to their respective doorsteps—much the wiser, and far more friendly to the oil industry as a result of their experience."

Adds the API: "See what participation in the OIIC program can do, Mr. Jobber?" [24]

Thus, the API strives to fill the opinion vacuum, generally careful to avoid specific references to controversies such as "tidelands." "No one, to our knowledge has worked more diligently or intelligently than OIIC," Dr. Claude Robinson, president of the Opinion Research Corporation told the API eight years after his original report. "It is our professional judgment that OIIC has written and is writing a significant chapter in the art of public persuasion." [25]

The regional and other associations are also very much involved in this total effort and with less subtlety as to political objective. The Rocky Mountain Oil and Gas Association, for example, offers this explanation of its activities:

Our goal is understanding; our media is "grass roots" public relations; our results are evidenced in the several legislatures of the Rocky Mountain area. . . .

By "grass roots" public relations we mean contacting not only the legislators, the various governmental commissions and boards; but, also the non-oil and gas businessmen and women. In small homogeneous groups such as Lions, Rotary, Kiwanis, Civitans, United Commercial Travelers, Parent Teacher Associations, Chambers of Commerce and many others—we reach a heterogeneous public with the story of oil and gas industry.[26]

The major integrated companies have their own public relations programs. "We want people to like us and the free economy of which we are a part," explains a public relations manual of Standard (Indiana). Then the public will buy our products and "take Standard's side on controversial issues." [27] Increasingly sensitive to charges that their refining operations contribute to water and air pollution, oil companies have become active participants in research to find and remove possible causes of this pollution. (Oil producers have resisted enactment of federal laws and enforcement of state laws to abate stream pollution caused in drilling.)

When the oil industry raced to explore the continental shelf beneath the waters of the Gulf of Mexico, it encountered the hostility of fishing communities fearful that the detonations involved in the seismic tests portended the destruction of their oyster beds and their shrimp-breeding grounds as well as of their way of life. The oil companies denied that these operations would threaten native livelihoods, and painted glowing pictures of the new economy. Meanwhile, as later described by the API, they "quietly set about correcting the error at the source." To get at this "misinformed public opinion," they sponsored local conservation agents "who could speak the patois of the coastal residents." They also hired some of the more prominent fishermen to staff geophysical boat crews:

> In this way the conscientious objectors were given an on-the-spot view of—and an intimate insight into—what was taking place. Then, as new ambassadors, these former objectors reaffirmed the truth to their kinfolk and their friends, and eventually a healthier atmosphere of cooperation pervaded the area.[28]

Standard (New Jersey) also sponsored the production of a fine film, *Louisiana Story* by Robert Flaherty, to reassure the outside world of the corporation's sensitivity to the beauties of the bayous and of the natives' emergent appreciation for the strange new setting of derricks and drillers.

One basic public relations tactic is to establish a local character to corporate behavior. A manual of Standard (Indiana) advises its managerial personnel:

> Personal contacts are of great importance. It is expected that refinery management and the community relations representative will have a wide personal acquaintance with publishers, editors, reporters and other executives of publications and radio and television stations in the refinery area. The community relations representative is to correlate his personal contacts with those of refinery management and develop good working relationships with editorial writers, city editors, reporters, columnists— "the working press." . . . Refinery management is responsible for encouraging executives and other employees to take part in civic affairs.

. . . Local management determines which are the leading local groups and encourages representation in them.[29]

These generally include youth groups, fund-raising drives, church activities, boards of education, boards of regents, library boards, planning commissions, boards of trade and toastmasters, advertising, fraternal, and social clubs. "Social clubs . . . include athletic, city, and county clubs where individual memberships enable employees to develop associations and friendships that benefit the company." In the case of company-assigned memberships, "employees who accept appointments to civic or charitable committees should do so with the understanding that the company wants them to become leaders and to earn reputations for getting things done."

Local plant managers are told what kinds of company contributions are permissible and which are to be refused. After many pages of careful detail, including how to write a letter to accompany a contribution, the manual warns that "managers should avoid giving any impression that decisions regarding local contributions are made at the General Office."

The large oil firms generally have separate public relations departments with staffs of fifteen to twenty-five headed by top-echelon executives. Their work is an integral management function. Many have separate school and college divisions. In addition, numerous executives throughout the organization serve in essentially public relations capacities. The companies often also employ outside public relations firms on a retainer basis.

Standard (New Jersey) maintains the most extensive and sophisticated of oil public relations programs. Memories of Rockefeller's sharp dealings, the 1914 Ludlow massacres and even "business as usual" with Nazi Germany presumably are dim. And certainly they are overshadowed by the community-mindedness of the third-generation Rockefellers and recent executives like Frank W. Abrams. Yet the organization remains vigilant, with public relations an essential part of all activities. In 1955 the parent company had about 35 people in strictly functional public relations posts; affiliates employed about 380 more. Some 40 Jersey companies had organized public relations departments. The holding company conducts regular courses for their public relations officers.

Arthur G. Newmyer and Associates serves as Standard's public relations consultant in Washington. It works with the Earl Newsom organization in New York, which was hired after the I. G. Farben stories broke and which later aided Jersey in setting up its own public relations department. These counsels were credited with ending much of the official hostility to the company occasioned by the wartime disclosures. Newmyer, which has also represented Ford, American Locomotive, and Atlas Powder, is careful to make clear it is neither lobbyist nor 5 per center. This is a "low-pressure approach to Washington," and the firm keeps away from pending legislation, explained James M. Newmyer. Standard is viewed as too complex for lobbyists who at best would quickly wear out their welcome. Nor is this role putting "sweet-smelling honey" over the actions of our client, he added. Rather do they help the oil company establish policy by seeking to create better relations between government and business, getting company officials better acquainted with their counterparts in government, reporting on Washington events and on the tone of government officials, advising congressmen as to who in Standard might best speak for the company on specific issues, advising company executives how to testify, promoting executive appearances before such groups as the National Press Club, and generally working to create a climate of "mutual confidence."

Harmony is not always the end. When the Federal Trade Commission oil cartel report was released, Hill and Knowlton, the public relations firm for Caltex (the California-Texas Oil Company, owned jointly by The Texas Company and Standard Oil of California) launched an attack upon the document. The substance of the analysis was evaded. Instead, a brochure, *As U.S. Editors View the Oil Charges,* containing reprints of critical editorials describing the report's release as "political" and threatening to natural security were sent to foreign and American newspapers and government officials. The loyalty of Commissioner Stephen Spingarn and other FTC personnel was questioned.

More frequently, however, the public relations firm seeks to keep the integrated oil companies out of controversy or from being publicly identified with extreme positions. Specially created organizations or groups such as the United States Chamber of Commerce, which circulated radio scripts for "grass roots" consumption, were relied on for public relations during the "tidelands" fight. Gulf, Standard (Indiana), Socony-Vacuum, Texaco, Sun, and others have contributed to such "free enterprise" propaganda vehicles as the American Enterprise Association and the Foundation for Economic Education, with the Sun Oil Company probably the most willing to be so identified publicly.

Independent producers without concern for consumer good will can have fewer inhibitions. H. R. Cullen has distributed hundreds of thousands of copies of *The Road Ahead*, John T. Flynn's attack upon the welfare state. From 1951 to 1956, when he withdrew support, H. L. Hunt openly sponsored "Facts Forum." This "All-American" team, as it was called, was his tax-favored, "non-partisan, educational" effort to restore to American hearts and minds the spirit that once made the country "the land of the free and the home of the brave." This meant fighting welfare measures, communism, and internationalism, while supporting McCarthy and his type of patriotism. For according to Hunt, the battle line in the coming struggle for American and world rule is between the left—"the mistaken," who range from Communist and Fifth Amendment witnesses to New Dealers—and the right—"the constructionists" who would defend opportunity and enterprise. There is no place for the "wholly indefinite and uncertain Middle-of-the-Road thinking" (such as an Eisenhower might offer) which is "the stronghold of entrenched apathy, capable of saving nothing" because of its flabby convictions.[30] The apparatus for this crusade included a number of programs on some three hundred radio and television stations (often granted free "public service" time worth an estimated $3 million to $5 million a year), periodic literature, free circulating libraries of books and films, and neighborhood discussion groups. One unusual creation was cash awards for letters to the editors sent by "Facts Forum" followers to their local newspapers. The Texas oilman exhorted businessmen to take responsibility for molding public opinion. Such activity might not only save freedom, he suggested, but at the same time have a dollar-and-cents value. Placing patriotic messages in advertisements would add patronage and profits from appreciative freedom-loving customers.

Oil public relations can be mobilized for immediate short-run issues as well. And when the stakes are high enough, the fundamental distinction between the primitives and the sophisticates fades, as does the mythical line between politics and public relations. The story of the defeat in Colorado in 1952 of a constitutional amendment authorizing a severance tax on petroleum, the familiar tax device in most producing states, provides a clear illustration of what lies behind the façade.

There had been considerable feeling in the state that the oil industry, which produced $70 million worth of crude oil in 1951, was not paying its fair share of taxes. Repeatedly frustrated by the lobbying of the industry and the resultant failure of the legislature to act on any severance-tax proposals, civic groups mustered more than 40,000 signatures to initiate an amendment on the ballot to allow the voters to decide directly. The Oil Severance Tax Committee was a genuine grass-roots movement, sparked by women's volunteer groups, PTA, teachers, school districts, and Farmers Union, Grange, and union members. A week before the election the prediction, backed by polls, was that amendment Number 4, providing for a 5 per cent severance tax to be earmarked for school purposes, would win easily.

The industry, however, had not been idle. After considerable discussion, Colorado Oil and Gas Industries, Inc., was formed to fight the amendment. This had been created, according to the then president of the Rocky Mountain Oil and Gas Association, "under the guidance of a special committee of our Executive Committee." Originally it was to be called the Colorado Natural Resources Development Council, but there was some feeling, explained one spokesman, that to conceal the interest of the oil and gas industry was dishonest. The president of the new group, Charles D. Edmonson, was also chairman of the Rocky Mountain Oil and Gas Association's legislative committee for Colorado. William "Scotty" Jack, executive vice president of the association, who in 1954 was Democratic candidate for governor of Wyoming, was assigned the direction of the campaign. Some of the literature of Colorado Oil and Gas Industries described it, in very fine print, as "a group of small independent oil men banded together for the purpose of fighting excessive, discriminatory, taxation." The modest identification was understandable since the chief finances were generally assumed to have come from the California Company, the largest producer in the state and a subsidiary of Standard Oil of California. As one veteran observer explained, the Rocky Mountain Oil and Gas Association does not have too much money, except as the majors pour it in when they want something done.

Edward M. Hunter and Company was hired to handle the publicity. Former newsman Hunter was a backer of Taft in 1952, and when hired was also publicity director of the GOP state central committee. "I am an advertising man, not a public relations man. I will help in a public relations campaign, however," declared Hunter.

The first step was a public-opinion study. In January 1952 Research Services, Inc., completed a field study of public awareness and voter inclination relating to oil in general and the severance tax:

At the present time a majority of the voters of Colorado approve a severance tax on oil. Severance tax proponents favor the tax because they think it is a good revenue raiser, the oil industry can afford the tax and under their present thinking *it will not hurt them personally.* . . . Those who disapprove of the levy oppose it on the grounds that taxes are high enough already, the oil industry is taxed enough now, and the tax might *discourage the development of the oil industry in Colorado.* . . . There is every reason to believe that an oil severance tax measure, if placed before the voters *today,* would pass by a large majority. . . . However, it is apparent that over-all attitudes are not *solidly structured* at this time, being based both on lack of information and misinformation. Thus, they are considered flexible and . . . susceptible to certain reforms. . . . Those who have heard of the tax are more inclined to favor its passage. In other words, it appears that pro-severance propaganda has, thus far, had some effect on developing attitudes contrary to oil interests. . . . However, this survey was taken before any real concerted action by the oil industry, and consequently, might be expected to produce this negative finding.[31]

With the weightings to the various answers as a guide, a high-powered program was launched, designed to reach every industry, interest group, and club in the state. Special focus was placed on gaining the support of allied industries such as utilities and transportation. A speakers' bureau was established, and civic groups throughout the state were solicited as to their desire for a speaker whose "presentation will be factual, non-political and informative." [32]

The campaign plan even had provision for "G-2, intelligence" to handle "political" matters. Subsidiary organizations were set up in each of the state's four congressional districts. Card files were created on the leaders and opinion makers of each community, with notations being made as to occupation, employer, voting preference, position, and degree of interest in the campaign, whom they influenced, who influenced them, lodge membership and public activity, and whether they had any personal economic interest in oil.

Public relations specialists from oil companies were loaned to the campaign, and the Colorado Petroleum Industries Committee, the OIC local office, and the women employees in the Desk and Derrick Clubs also participated. Groups like the Colorado Mining Association and the Colorado Motor Carriers helped in the mailing of literature.

In the closing weeks, letters were sent to employees of the oil companies in the Colorado Oil and Gas Industries:

The proposed severance tax, Amendment No. 4 on the November 4th ballot, is a threat to your future and the future of the entire Colorado oil and gas industry. With your full support, we can defeat this unnecessary and unreasonable tax. Remember, you have a personal stake in this ballot.

The letters then told employees how to contact their neighbors, each employee being asked to get ten voters to pledge a "No" vote:

Ask them to vote no on Amendment No. 4. If they indicate they will vote No, fill out one of the enclosed pledge cards. Do not ask them to sign the card. You Fill It Out. Sign your name and the name of your company on the bottom two lines. Return pledge cards and any unused literature to the Desk and Derrick Club representative in your organization. . . .[33]

A progress report announced that "considerable success is anticipated from this activity." [34]

Meanwhile, the state was subjected to a steady barrage of billboards, posters, leaflets, stickers, newspaper advertisements, radio programs, animated TV cartoons, and hundreds of spot announcements, all of which increased in intensity as the election drew near.

Every Denver bus had a foot-high black-and-yellow cardboard sign stretched above the front bumper, urging citizens to vote NO. Special pamphlets were addressed to the mining, agricultural, school, business, labor, and white-collar segments of the state. Workers in the field were advised: "Please watch all the newspapers in your immediate vicinity for any letters from readers, particularly if such letters are in support of the severance tax. We believe that each such letter should be individually answered and preferably by someone locally. However, the Denver office will go to any pains and take the necessary amount of time to make the individual replies, either under the signature of someone in your area or, if you prefer, by Charles D. Edmonson, president of the Colorado Oil and Gas Industries, Inc." [35]

The theme was always the same. "Vote No." "Pericolo." "Peligro." "Danger." "You may be next!" In big ads the farmer was warned that "It Could Happen . . . a severance tax on agricultural products." "5%—wheat and sugar beets could be next!"

The severance tax is a spreading form of taxation. All natural resources are the logical prey of this insidious form of taxation . . . a tax on the yield of the land . . . a tax on the production made possible by the toil and investment of an individual or group. A severance tax on other natural resources nearly always spreads to a severance tax on agricultural products. . . . Protect Colorado's Agricultural Products and Natural Resources from Discriminatory Taxation. . . .

As a further thought, another ad reminded that "Every Farmer is a Potential Oilman." Ranchers were similarly prodded.

In the mining and lumbering areas on the western slope, advertisements and leaflets appeared showing closed mine doors. "It Could Happen to You! This is a ghost mine. It could be the fate of many mines if the severance method of taxation is ever initiated in our state. The proposed oil and gas severance tax is the FIRST STEP in a program to load ADDITIONAL taxes on *all* natural resources." Main street was told that if the mines would be forced to shut down, then "payrolls would dwindle . . . employment would drop. . . ."

Oil workers, farmers, and taxpayers were advised that "oil operators may cap their wells in Colorado" and send their drilling crews elsewhere. "You may be next." Parents and educators were informed that oil and education go "forward together," and that "higher oil and gas taxes" would mean "less money for schools" since some school funds were derived from state lands on which the schools owned all the mineral rights, and also, earmarking severance tax money for schools might just mean that the legislature would cut regular school appropriations. Taxpayers were told that this would create "another tax-devouring bureau" with "boondoggling jobs." The general irritation with Colorado's many earmarked taxes was also played up as further handcuffing of pressed legislators. (But no mention was made of the industry's nation-wide campaign to earmark gasoline taxes for roads and thus promote greater sales and profits.) Mindful of the opinion survey warning that "the public pictures the oil industry as a 'wealthy' enterprise," the plea was made not to hamper an industry trying to get on a firm footing. Meanwhile, with little publicity the industry continued to sink wells in the state (the Independent Petroleum Association of America estimated the total value at the wells of crude oil produced in Colorado through 1952 at more than $400 million).

Perhaps most cynical of all the tactics was the repeatedly published prediction that Colorado's potentially great industry, the production of oil from shale, "will be stopped dead in its tracks if you allow the proposed oil and gas severance tax to become part of our state constitution." Shale deposits on the western slope could yield an estimated 1.5 trillion barrels of oil. But blocking its development and the experiments at the government's plant at Rifle has been the oil industry which fears what this would do to its control over prices and markets if it is produced and marketed at competitive prices beyond the pale of oil's private government.

All these appeals were in keeping with the findings of the first and then a second opinion study that noted that most of those who gave wrong answers as to what a severance tax was "believed a severance tax applied only to the 'oil industry' and did not indicate in any way that a severance tax could be applied to any natural resource." [36]

As late as October 23rd, a Denver Post poll showed that 63 per cent of the voters planned to vote for the tax and 21 per cent against, as opposed to 59 per cent for in April and 61 per cent in September.[37]

But significantly, the second industry survey, submitted before the election, found that "voters have become more confused about the issue."

The confusion came to a climax with announcements by Governor Dan Thornton, and then, in the very closing days of the campaign, by the state board of education, that they opposed a severance tax that was earmarked and whose source was an amendment rather than legislation. The action of the board was released to the press through Colorado Gas and Oil Industries, Inc. This unusual arrangement was worked out by a board member, who was also an independent oil operator, and oil lobbyist Marion Strain. Immediately, the board's position was featured in all the oil propaganda. On November 4th the tax was decisively defeated.

Thus ended what an editorial writer for the *Denver Post* called "one of the most misleading campaigns to which Colorado voters have ever been submitted." Proponents of the tax indicated that the belated announcement by the school board was the decisive factor, and some saw the direct influence of oil in the action of several of its members. Estimates as to what oil spent vary from $250,000 to $500,000, although the representative of the Colorado Petroleum Industries Committee of the API thought this was greatly exaggerated. Ed Hunter refused to say, explaining to the author that he was ethically bound not to discuss finances. The question of Mrs. James Railey, who headed the tax movement from her home on contributions of about $3,000, remained: "Can money buy everything?"

The *Denver Post* was subject to great pressure. One staff writer reported that the president of the California Company tried to get his job after he had written critically of the company and also that the *Post* advertising manager had asked him to go easy on Continental Oil while they were placing advertisements. But the paper was steadfast in its support of the tax, a welcome contrast to the position of its predecessor owners whose silence had been directly bought in Teapot Dome days. A few days before the election, the *Post* had to remind the industry editorially of the distinction between a free and a kept press. The president of the Rocky Mountain Oil and Gas Association had complained in a speech that "You'll find page after page of lucrative advertising opposing the severance

tax in the Denver *Post* and on the next page there will be an editorial advocating the adoption of the severance tax. The *Post* is
biting the hand that feeds it." [38]

But oil brought primarily a postponement. For the legislature
subsequently acknowledged the basic public sentiment by adopting
a moderate nonearmarked severance tax on a graduated basis, the
latter provision softening the opposition of smaller independent producers. The industry continued to expand. But undaunted, the
companies paid the taxes under protest and challenged the law as
discriminatory and unconstitutional in a series of court actions.

Reviewing his campaign two years later, Hunter concluded that
people do not believe newspapers, for they are too dishonest and
sensational. "They believe our advertisements. You can have your
editorials against me. I'll have the ads and influential people. . . ."
As for his opponents—teachers and preachers were always the worst
ones with whom to deal. "They get emotional in political fights and
indulge in recriminations. . . . I don't lie. It's bad business in advertising. Sooner or later it catches up with you."

Hunter's work on oil provided Governor Thornton, at odds with
the advertising man, with a plausible reason for forcing his resignation as publicity director of the GOP state central committee in the
fall of 1952. "I did not want to be identified in any way with a man
tied up with the oil interests or any other lobby." [39] But in the 1954
election Hunter played a prominent role in the last-minute attacks
of the Republicans against Democratic senatorial candidate John
Carroll. These attacks suggested that Carroll, who was defeated, was
part of a "Communist-coddling clique." The campaign was financed
by out-of-state oil money.

The most recent and full-blown application of public relations
has centered around the regulation of natural gas. In the Phillips
decision of June 1954, the Supreme Court had ruled that Federal
Power Commission responsibilities under the Natural Gas Act of
1938 includes the control over prices charged by producers selling
gas in interstate commerce. An FPC sympathetic to the industry
has been reluctant to accept the role. But producers have sought a
legislative as well as an administrative overruling of the court, one
that would fence off their operations from any future controls. For
like most of the special interests who made hay under the warmth

of the Eisenhower Administration's dedication to business, oil and gas assumed that Republican rule was likely to be relatively short and that the President's majority was a personal rather than a party triumph. They knew that the Democratic party congressional leadership was on their side and that men like Lyndon Johnson could be counted upon to keep down FPC appropriations while forestalling legislative pressures for effective regulation. But they also remembered that it was a Democratic President, sensitive to the political consequences of the growing national dependence upon gas, who had vetoed industry-favored bills. And many congressmen, irrespective of party affiliations, feared to support them openly because of the potential wrath of urban consumers.

Plans were thus drawn to employ all the talent, experience, and resources of the industry to develop a grass-roots base for legislation exempting producers from regulation. In October 1954 a special Natural Gas and Oil Resources Committee (NGORC) was created to inform the public about the gas industry and the need to prevent "the cancer of Federal bureau control." On the advice of industry lawyers, it was to be kept separate from the lobbying activities of the General Gas Committee, which was organized almost simultaneously and with similar corporate backing. For the NGORC's function was "long-range education." Headquarters were established in New York, with fifteen regional districts and subsidiary committees in each state bearing the name of the individual state to suggest a local character to the structure. Nearly every state chairman was from a major oil company. Baird H. Markham, former director of the American Petroleum Industries Committee, the API's legislative arm, was hired as the executive officer. The firm of Hill and Knowlton, with long experience in representing the Iron and Steel Institute, Republic Steel, Procter and Gamble, the National Association of Manufacturers, and electric utilities, was retained as public relations counsel. It was active at all levels of planning and at one point had seventeen full-time and fifteen to twenty part-time staff working on this account. The firm received $400,000 in fees for its services.

The inevitable survey by the Opinion Research Corporation helped to set the direction of the campaign. A study of the attitudes of "thought leaders"—businessmen, clergy, editors, engineers, doctors, lawyers, teachers and other professionals—concluded that the new committee faced "a formidable task" in building support against regulation of producers' prices, for 56 per cent of those questioned favored such restraints. There would not be too much gain in appealing to the 17 per cent interviewed whom the study classified as "socialist." (A "socialist" was one who responded positively to three or four of the following four questions: "Do you think it is the responsibility of the federal government to see that everyone who is willing and able to work has a job? If times get hard and prices go down, do you think the government should try to prevent wage rates from falling . . . ? The wealth of the nation is becoming more and more concentrated in the hands of the wealthiest 10 per cent of the families. Do you agree or disagree? Both the government and banks now make loans to business. In the years ahead, would you like to see the government take over more of the lending to business, or do less of it?") But middle-of-the-roaders and free enterprise, those who tended to be against such positions, could be influenced by exposure to the proper reasons.[40]

Hill and Knowlton then outlined basic principles for an integrated public relations and advertising effort. It too emphasized to its clients the difficulty of putting the case across since it "is necessarily involved and does not lend itself to glib generalization—as does, for example, the pro-regulation case." [41] The public relations firm warned that "superficial observers" would tend to accept the Supreme Court ruling; that the proposed legislation could easily be interpreted as another giveaway being sneaked through by the interests; and that a large segment of the population was automatically suspicious of anything advocated by big companies or Texas millionaires. But apparently Hill and Knowlton had faith that the right approach, backed by money and organization, could turn the tide.

The ORC study had suggested that the key to molding opinion was in that many of those who favored regulation thought most producers were large, noncompetitive companies, essentially of a public utility nature. These misinformed people assumed prices paid to producers were a considerable factor in retail gas pricing and that regulation would protect consumers. Only a few knew that future supplies were in jeopardy because producers' prices "were now regulated" by the FPC. "The only way they [the public] can learn the truth of the matter is through us," declared L. F. McCollum, a former Jersey Standard executive and the president of Continental Oil, who became chairman of the NGORC. "We have the facts. Properly informed, the American people will be on our side." [42]

The battle for truth and justice was to be fought in the name of the five thousand to eight thousand (industry literature wavered) independent natural gas producers who had a stake in exemption from regulation. Their "keen competition" assured abundant low-cost fuel and served as a better regulator than the federal government, without curtailing risk capital for exploration. Hill and Knowlton advised that the campaign had to be impressive enough to gain widespread attention, "but not so flamboyant as to make it appear to be backed by limitless resources." To further a grass-roots appearance, it recommended that "there should be a conscious effort to play down the New York headquarters."

The complexity of the problem and the substantial producer arguments were to be brought out by making it clear that there was more to the case than could appear in a single advertisement. "This can be achieved by having each ad invite readers to send for a booklet. (Thereby, incidentally, meeting the advertising criterion of inviting the reader to 'do something.')" To combat the sneak giveaway charges, "the program should stress that the public is being invited and urged to examine the issue carefully. This means making repeated use of such phrases as 'The American public is entitled to know the facts' or 'You have a right and an obligation to learn. . . .' "

Hill and Knowlton also warned that care should be taken "to avoid seeming to square off against the entire Supreme Court of the United States." If necessary, the gas men could refer to the 5 to 3 majority interpretation in the Phillips case. But "where we can we should avoid specifically mentioning the Court in ads." The public relations experts also suggested that labels like "socialism" and "bureaucracy" not be overworked and that the program "should avoid seeming to threaten or scare. . . . This means it is far better to emphasize that free competition is the best way to assure abundance than to say or imply 'we will cut off the supply unless . . .' " [43]

Advertisements in over a thousand newspapers soon blanketed consumer regions. Some of these specifically referred to the Harris bill, despite the Natural Gas and Oil Resources Committee's disclaimer as to political activity. Editors were cultivated by oil executives, while their offices received news releases, feature stories, background material, and suggested editorials to enable the press "to comment constructively." [44] On the advice of Hill and Knowlton, free-lance writers were stimulated to develop stories sympathetic to the gas industry. There were hundreds of radio and television broadcasts. A film produced by the Ethyl Corporation was shown widely. All the mass media were monitored to check against "misinformation." Basic information kits were distributed to farmers, businessmen, and other special publics. Leaflets were prepared for insertion with customer bills, stockholder dividends, royalty owner checks, and employee pay checks.

Local oilmen, often armed with manuscripts prepared in the Empire State Building, spoke to civic organizations. Housewives were important audiences. "Our job," explained McCollum, "is to let Mrs. America know what Federal regulations of field gas prices will mean to her—not in technical or legal terms, but in terms of her own every day experiences of cooking, cleaning, washing, and keeping warm." [45] Only pennies per month were at stake for each home, the industry pleaded, ignoring the warning from proponents of genuine regulation that exempting the big producers would cost consumers hundreds of millions of dollars annually. But as a Shell female staff member in charge of woman's programs explained in a public relations guidebook, the gas men were not to fear being sentimental or using emotional appeals, for women like that.

With thirty-five "independent" producers providing over 70 per cent of all the gas sold to the interstate pipelines, and twenty-two of these producers being major oil companies—the term "independent" implying only their separation from pipeline companies—it was clear why the giants of oil and gas spearheaded this campaign. Twenty-six of these corporations contributed better than 80 per cent of the nearly $2 million received by the NGORC between October 1954 and March 1956. Eight of them, led by Humble (Jersey), accounted for over half of the total amount. The $2 million did not include the expenses of the individual corporations who participated. An estimated three thousand oil employees assisted in the campaign, with some companies assigning district personnel to work with the NGORC. A number of employees were on direct loan. Presumably all of these costs were deducted as business costs, just as many of the companies treated their contributions as tax-deductible expenses for long-range education rather than as nondeductible politicking costs. The latter approach subsequently was disallowed by the Internal Revenue Service.

Jobbers and dealers were frequently called upon to participate. Asked if the nature of the dealer's relationship with the huge supplying companies didn't imply coercion, the president of Hill and Knowlton doubted that the oil company exercised that much power and ventured that he "can't imagine his not wanting to help an oil company in a fight like this." [46]

Some companies held briefing sessions for their employees. Others sent letters to supervisory personnel, often following models worked out by the national committee. Standard (Indiana) provided all its Illinois employees with a point-by-point refutation of a speech by Senator Paul Douglas. But, the company's president explained, in order to adhere to the NGORC's definition as an educational rather than a legislative force, "whenever we felt that discussion of the Harris-Fulbright bill would be more effective, our people carried on their discussions as Standard Oil Co. representatives or in their personal capacities, and in no way acted for the NGORC. At no time did Standard Oil Co. feel inhibited about referring to the bill." [47]

Virtually every company's stockholders' report and employees magazine discussed the gas issue. The March 1955 *Beacon*, a monthly "published by and for the employees of the Ohio Oil Company and its subsidiaries," called for "a pen-and-ink path to our representatives in Washington. . . ."

Further, each of us has become an educator. Since we are so enthusiastic toward bringing amendment to the Gas Case, we want to tell our neighbors and friends (especially those who are not in the petroleum industry) about it.[48]

K. S. Adams, chairman of Phillips, wrote company employees that "each of you as employees and most of you also as natural gas consumers have a personal stake in removing federal regulation":

You will be expected to know more about this case than others because Phillips was a principal party in the court case which imposed regulation. Because of this, you will have a greater opportunity than most oil industry employees to assist personally, in conversations and correspondence with your neighbors and other influential people, in this important public information task. I am sure you will carry out your share in a typical Phillips manner.[49]

At every point the industry and its paid defenders called this a fight to save the American way of life from socialism. But tears for the "little man" and "free enterprise" notwithstanding, they have rejected compromise legislation that would exempt the small, genuinely independent and competitive gas producer from regulation. Keeping bureaucrats from Mrs. America's kitchen range has been the public appeal. Keeping Mr. and Mrs. America from exercising any control over the power of the industry is the private purpose. And public relations has been the technique for getting the poorly organized consumer to support—or at least not oppose—a cause inimical to his own welfare.

It would be simple to conclude from these vast and varied public relations efforts on a note affirming the essential villainy of the oil industry. Oil's determination to push the worth of its principles as well as its products is understandable. The problem for society is the existence of such systems of private power, backed by billions of dollars, with the capacity to distort government and politics at every point of contact. There is danger, however, in taking every claim of public relations people at face value since their presumed anonymity is likely to be outweighed by a passion for self-justification. For example, the effectiveness, let alone willingness, of the local gasoline dealer in talking about the virtues of the competitive oil industry when his customers drive in for a tankful of gas during Oil Progress Week sounds more impressive in a Rockefeller Center office than in a New England filling station. Harried dealers are often quite skeptical about such talk in general and also about the kind of competition in which they find themselves. Those who support Oil Progress Week tend to do it more in terms of sales than ideology. Just as they are not always enthusiastic about the many free services their suppliers advertise and they are expected to offer the consumer, similarly their "voluntary" public relations efforts are often more the product of pressure than of commitment. Jobbers have been more openly critical. One former president of the Tennessee Oil Men's Association has claimed that many of his associates feel the OIC has been "a subsidized mouthpiece for the major oil companies. So far as the jobber is concerned, they tear down with bad marketing practices whatever good will they build up through OIIC." [50] And there is considerable evidence, some from studies made for the OIC by Columbia University's Bureau of Applied Social Research, that the American public has not been affected by the obvious publicity devices and may not even be listening.[51] Even the meaningfulness of the much discussed propaganda network of the primitives must be reassessed when one notes, for example, that in Hunt's Facts Forum public-opinion polls, 86 per cent of the respondents answered affirmatively to the intriguingly worded question, "Should we let the Chinese fight the Reds?" 83 per cent to "Are Communists in the U.S. conniving to promote juvenile delinquency?" and 71 per cent to "Are both parties being influenced by Communists?" [52]

Nor have industry leaders themselves been completely ensnared by all their own propaganda. As businessmen they have not been convinced of the return from a twelve-year investment (1947–1958) of $29 million in the immediate OIC budget—and of many times this amount in corporate budgets. This despite the impressive statistics on pamphlets distributed and the continuing series of Opinion Research Corporation studies which usually have claimed an improving climate of opinion for oil since 1946 when the postwar programs were launched. As technicians and even as management experts, the oilmen are often skeptical about the endless "scientific" questionaires and the voluminous reports on variations in the public pulse which so delight their hired scholars. They are suspicious of, if not hostile to, the public relations men without oil backgrounds who manipulate words and a phantom public rather than things and tangible customers.

The oilmen speculate that perhaps they have been fighting the wrong battle in their quest for popular approval. Apparently the American people have accepted the efficiency of the industry, its research for improved products and even, in many respects, its size. "People recognize and approve the tremendous material contributions of the oil industry, and of all big business, to human comfort and well-being," an OIC self-study suggested.[53]

Yet the oilmen also note that a large majority of the American people still assume, most of them disapprovingly, that the industry is controlled by one or a few companies. The oilmen express unhappiness that their critics should maintain that it is profits that motivate the private government of oil and that the general public should retain a fear about "a possible misuse of the great power that resides in the oil industry" in its international grip over this natural resource. For such "misconceptions" provide the setting for a demand for governmental restraints upon oil's corporate practices, privileges, and power. They open the door to recurring political attacks upon their reputations, their industry, and their legislative goals, to the stubborn although limited congressional questioning of the depletion allowance and other tax benefits, to the frustration of natural gas legislation, to the attempts to have the Justice Department and the Federal Trade Commission restrain corporate growth, to the continuation of the generally New Dealish tone to domestic political expectations, and to the lack of public appreciation for giant oil's difficulties with the restive nationalist movements in foreign producing areas.

Left-wing agitators are responsible for planting the notion of a monolithic industry and the solution of a public utility status for oil and gas, President Frank M. Porter of the American Petroleum Institute has warned in his repeated appeals for industry unity. The citizen who advocates such control has been poisoned into believing "that his troubles do not spring from any fault of his own, not from his ineptitude, and apathy, but from a social system that he thinks is stacked against him. Refusing to climb the rungs of the ladder of success by his own efforts, he denounces society for failing to provide him with an elevator." Oil's detractors have been "in a lynching mood. Their aim is the complete nationalization of oil and all its workings." If the claim is accepted that oil should be regulated because it is a natural resource and a monopoly, then all the nation's basic industries would suffer a similar fate. "Either the oil industry stays free or one by one the lights of private enterprise will go out and the darkness of authoritarian government will settle over our land." [54]

At the 1958 API meeting, coming after the liberal sweep of congressional elections, this theme prevailed. Political considerations took a clear precedence over technological and economic discussions. "You are misunderstood, you are taken advantage of," Lyle C. Wilson, general manager of United Press International in Washington, advised the assembled oilmen. This was because of poor public relations that allowed the opinion to prevail in Washington that the oil industry "gets something for nothing and wants more." This jealous view has been fostered by "the Left Wing of American politics," which "plays harder than you fellows are likely to fight" and "is going to move in on you." President Porter agreed that "the outlook is as gloomy today as it has ever been in my 42 years of association with the petroleum industry."

I am even beginning to wonder if we are entering a new Ice Age for all private enterprise, with ours chosen as the first industry to get the big freeze. But I do not believe we are doomed unless we doom ourselves with inactivity. A warm response now from industry people can melt the ice and change the hostile climate that presses in on us. But it must be a *very* warm response.[55]

The giant of oil had been "tongue-tied" and "pussyfooting," the leaders agreed. "We're too bloody modest," declared H. S. M. Burns, president of Shell and 1958 API chairman.[56] The time was long overdue for oil to flex its political muscles in an all-out public relations drive under the direct control of the industry heads. The Oil Information Committee ("our fire-prevention unit," explained Burns) and the American Petroleum Industries Committee ("the fire-fighting unit," handling governmental relations) were merged into a Committee on Public Affairs. Membership on the committee was drawn principally from the major companies, with a Socony executive as chairman. A paid permanent staff was established in New York and Washington. The old field offices of the APIC and OIC were merged and recreated on a state basis, with the names of the units varying from state to state to suggest an autonomous character.
The mandate of the Committee on Public Affairs was:

1. To stimulate the timely discussion of information concerning the petroleum industry so that public opinion and decisions relating to it will be founded in fact.

2. To develop a climate of opinion in which a privately-managed and competitive petroleum industry can best serve the American people and strengthen the national economy.

3. To encourage acceptance by all those engaged in the petroleum industry of their responsibility to assist government at all levels in matters of public interest affecting the industry and its customers.

The old theme, "oil is progressive" was replaced by the insistence that oil is a good citizen. With the tendency toward bigness "bound to become increasingly apparent in the next few years," B. Brewster Jennings, chairman of the board of Socony, has suggested, the urgency for the business community is to understand "how deep-seated is the American public's fear of great concentrations of power" and to "reduce the public's fear of business power to a realistic level." [57] If it was no longer necessary to defend oil's achievements primarily in material terms, it was disastrous to explain the economics of the modern industry largely in terms of traditional economic theory, reasoned an OIC planning group. By so doing, oil "has in effect been conceding unnecessarily an advantage to the critics of large industry who still use traditional economic theory as the basis for much of their criticism." [58] Instead of centering its public relations around such classical capitalist themes as "competition, the profit motive, the individual businessman, private ownership, etc.," which had long been proclaimed as providing the best of possible economic environments, now oil must demonstrate the inadequacies of these premises and replace them "by concepts more congruent with the startlingly new and dynamic capitalism, typified by large enterprise, that has evolved in the United States." The new capitalism, it must be shown, is not dominated by predatory barons engaged in organized plunder. Governing the integrated corporations are a trained, salaried managerial class dedicated to production and harmonizing the needs of the stockholder, the employee, the consumer, the general public, and the enterprise itself. All references to the profit motive must make clear that profits are rooted, not in unbridled greed, but in fairness and concern for future growth.

The overriding imperative was to drive home a contemporary recognition that "the social responsibilities and economic activities of large corporations are so inextricably intermingled as to amount to the same thing." [59] As Richard Rollins of Atlantic Refining, retiring chairman of the OIC, told the API in 1956 in discussing preliminary plans for the new drive:

Our program will be geared to placing new emphasis on the ethical, moral, and social contributions. We shall endeavor to show that oil men share and treasure the identical desires and aspirations common to every American and that we have a social responsibility.[60]

Transforming deeply ingrained images of an institution would require a long-range public relations effort, the OIC study concluded. But, given the right information, in the end the public would understand that "oil is responsible."

Regardless of motives, it is difficult to challenge the contributions of many of oil's services and leaders, the free distribution of 180 million road maps annually, the support of little theaters, hospitals, museums, and universities, the Folger Shakespeare Library in Washington, the radio sponsoring of Toscanini concerts and the Metropolitan Opera, the dramatic rescue by Jersey of TV's "The Play of the Week" when the program needed a sponsor, and the bold benefactions of the Rockefellers in health, research, and education estimated to range from $400 million to $2 billion. Certainly it was hard for the director of Montana's state historical museum to question oil's generosity. He once asked the industry for $7,500 to help fix up an oil room, and received $13,900 with the advice to "do what you want with it"—a sharp contrast with his two-year struggle with Anaconda for funds for a mining frontier room.

As the early Rockefeller grants to the University of Chicago ("The good Lord gave me my money and how could I withhold it from the University . . . ?") and comparable histories of other institutions have shown, oilmen and companies have long been interested in the nation's colleges and universities. Petroleum-oriented research has been a familiar part of the graduate school scene, as have corporate fellowships in science, engineering, and business administration. Individual oil producers have been patrons of favorite universities. Perhaps the most dramatic illustration were H. R. Cullen's gifts of over $30 million to the University of Houston where he had served as chairman of the Board of Regents. "Houston is proud to have been the place where the touch of the hand of Cullen's

[sic] has been permitted to fall by Almighty God," intoned the city's mayor on one occasion.[61]

But since 1953, meeting the financial problems of higher education at the undergraduate level has become a central proving ground for business commitment to "responsibility." There is no secret as to the immediate motives and appeals. A landmark speech in 1947 by Frank W. Abrams, chairman of the board of Standard Oil (New Jersey), provided a key. The occasion was a meeting inaugurating the "Crisis in Education" campaign of the Advertising Council, and his subject was "The Stake of Business in American Education." Abrams asked the assembled business leaders to imagine themselves in a situation in which they had been "called in to direct the reorganization of an old-established enterprise—American Education, Inc." They quickly see lagging production, declining quality, serious personnel problems, obsolete plant, and a product that "is often out-of-date." What was the stake of businessmen in all this?

We have something more than the normal interest of the good citizen who wants to see the world in which we live a better world for men of all faiths.

First, consider our direct selfish interest in people considered as markets. Markets are people. There is impressive evidence to show that the earning power, and therefore the purchasing power, of people tends to be geared to their level of education. . . .

Individual income or earning power is not the only factor that influences the expansion of markets. Education sharpens the desire of the individual for commodities such as books, newspapers, automobiles, better houses, and even the kind of food he eats. Statistical studies show a definite correlation between educational level, earning power, and the consumption of all commodities.

All of which means that the more high school and college graduates there are in this country, the higher standard of living all of us enjoy, and that is simply another way of saying the more prosperous customers American business and industry have.

Markets are one side of the coin. But obviously there is another. If education increases income, it also increases productivity. We may say, then, that business depends upon education not only to provide more profitable markets but to provide more productive manpower.[62]

Thus did higher learning in America serve the ends of a business society dedicated to the acquisition of more and more.

This speech had been worked out by the public relations firm that had been hired to dispel the image occasioned by the exposure of Jersey's ties with I. G. Farben. As Abrams later explained, "the Earl Newsom Company who helped prepare the text did such a convincing job that I found myself the first convert to my message. It gave me a worth-while objective to carry on in business retirement." [63] He then became chairman of the executive committee of the Council for Financial Aid to Education. This organization has been involved in stimulating corporate support and includes among its directors the heads of some of the nation's leading businesses and a number of college presidents.

In his original speech Abrams suggested another level of concern that business had in education—the attitudes of the citizenry and the relation of an informed electorate to a healthy climate for private enterprise. "People with information are inclined to more moderate opinions, whereas those without information are apt to be extremists." This has been spelled out with varying degrees of subtlety by oil and other businessmen active in this movement. In a commencement address at Drury College, Springfield, Missouri, K. S. Adams, chairman of the Phillips Petroleum Company, called upon centers of higher learning to face up to the growing threat to freedom in the modern world:

> Your question naturally is, "How do we go about meeting it. Teaching must be practical. Freedom is a broad and often intangible concept. Shall we talk about freedom of speech, of religion, of assembly, of the right to choose those who govern? Just what facet of freedom should we present to our young people?"
> The answer lies in where the opponents of freedom are striking their hardest blows—our free, competitive enterprise system.

Mr. Adams saw the antifreedom forces infiltrating labor and government, beating the drum for programs that would require higher taxes upon business, pressing for federal regulation over the natural gas and other industries, and seeking to prejudice teachers against businessmen. The real objective is nationalization. These forces know that "once they have control of the people's tools of production and pocketbooks through ownership of their business, it will be no trouble at all to control their words, their worship, their votes, their very lives":

So to meet the challenge of teaching freedom, it is imperative that our young people understand the free enterprise system as thoroughly as the multiplication tables. Recent opinion surveys of some of our nation's students show that this is not being achieved. . . .

We believe and have been proved correct by the millions of bathtubs, refrigerators, automobiles, telephones, and other evidences of our progress, that only when the spirit of man is free will he produce effectively. And we believe, and history has proved us correct, that only when the entire field of production is privately owned and operated will the spirit of man be free.[64]

Many executives deny there are strings attached or intended as part of their giving. But their general social outlook almost naturally leads them to assume free enterprise is an integral part of the American way and hence deserving of educational support. As Mr. Abrams later noted, "Many business leaders today are convinced that what happens to American education will eventually happen to America —and that means to American business." [65] If the corporation did not support education, then the federal government would. This would mean increased taxes upon business, without business exercising control over the purposes. And the youth of America would quickly come to accept the beneficence of a welfare superstate. This attitude was encouraged by a New Jersey Superior Court ruling in 1953 that rejected a stockholders' challenge as an unlawful exercise of management powers a corporate gift to Princeton University. Wrote Judge Alfred A. Stein:

The proofs before me are abundant that Princeton emphasizes by precept and indoctrination the principles which are very vital to the preservation of our own democratic system of business and government, particularly vital at this time when alien ideologies seek to impose themselves upon our habits and our dreams for the future. I cannot conceive of any greater benefit to corporations in this country than to build, and continue to build, respect for and adherence to a system of free enterprise and democratic government, the serious impairment of either of which may well spell the destruction of all corporate enterprise. Nothing that aids or promotes the growth and service of the American university or college in respect of the matters here discussed can possibly be anything short of direct benefit to every corporation in the land.[66]

Business leaders are not unmindful of the financial exigencies and the growing demands by a wider public seeking access to universities that college administrators and trustees must face. The latter govern giant educational plants and share managerial responsibilities and often outlooks with their industrial counterparts. Their public utterances and private manner frequently reflect the desire to assure potential donors of the soundness of their educational institutions as going concerns and their essential loyalty to the established order. As president of Columbia University, Dwight Eisenhower may have been somewhat unsophisticated when he solicited Texas oil millionaire H. R. Cullen in the following words: "Of course, as I have told you I hope to interest you also in Columbia University. . . . One of the basic reasons for the existence of such a national institution is to prepare our young people for effective citizenship in a free country. Columbia stands for free competitive enterprise." [67] But the temptation is great even for professional educators to underplay the possible risk to the highest commitment of academic life to free inquiry. It was a statement by Princeton in the court case just cited that reasoned that the survival of private education is "essential to the continuance of our free enterprise system of society in which corporations have flourished and attained the wealth, might, power and influence on all our lives they possess."

Spurred on by such responses, as well as by an administered price economy that enables such costs to be built into consumer prices and by federal revenue policies that permit business deductions of up to 5 per cent of net income for such gifts—thus making the corporations an arbiter of the use of what otherwise would be public money—business has intensified its activities in this direction. A study by the Council for Financial Aid to Education indicated that in 1956 "corporate investments in education," to use their happy phrase, by 275 firms with combined net incomes before taxes of $11 billion was nearly $29 million. This represented 34 per cent of their total contributions of $84 million, or a trebling of education's share of corporate gifts in eight years. A minute amount in corporate terms, this was a substantial sum in the national total of university budgets, although for many institutions the share was so small as to offer the taste rather than the substance of opulence. A rising percentage—37.5 per cent in 1956—was given with no restrictions on its use. There was also evidence of a growing willingness to support liberal arts as well as scientific and technical studies. Fifteen petroleum (and coal) companies were cited as contributing on the average two-tenths of one per cent of their net income before taxes, with nine oil companies—the largest number in any industrial category—giving $100,000 or more.[68]

In keeping with its economic position, Jersey Standard has been prominent in this movement to win the confidence of educators, intellectuals, and the public. Top-flight films have been produced. Affiliates have sponsored painting contests and provided extensive photography services. There have been conferences on corporate practices where professors have been given access to operations and then asked for criticisms. Consultant fees have also been paid to individual professors. Several executives have served on the boards of trustees of universities. In 1951 Standard announced a plan to hire ten or more college teachers for a year, paying their regular salaries and giving them definite assignments. It was expected that social scientists would predominate. "We feel that there has long been a need for a bridge between the campus and industry. What we are doing we hope is a modest start toward bridging it. . . . We shall try to choose people for whom we can do the most good and who can do the most good for us." [69]

As part of its recognition of the pressures upon higher education, in December 1954 Standard gave a gift of $450,000 to 138 private colleges. No school was to receive more than $5,000. In addition, the company and several of its affiliates gave $135,000 to the National Fund for Medical Education and the United Negro College Fund. This brought their gifts to American education to a million dollars for the year. In the following year the parent company and a group of affiliates created the Esso Education Fund to coordinate their giving programs. In honor of the company's seventy-fifth anniversary, the company announced in 1957 a $1.5 million grant for a three-year program to promote better teaching in the sciences and engineering through summer institutes and grants to teachers and schools. From 1955–1960 the Esso Foundation distributed nearly $8 million, often in unrestricted grants, to some 400 institutions in fulfilling Jersey's role as a "corporate citizen." "Our two bits' worth

. . . isn't going to solve the problem," explained Standard's board chairman, Eugene Holman. "But it may help a bit—we hope even stimulate others." [70]

In addition to a sizable graduate fellowship program for research in chemistry, geology, and related subjects, Shell has been active in promoting the study of science in the high schools and colleges. Merit fellowships for further study are offered high-school teachers of mathematics and science. Shell's plant management throughout the country is encouraged to cooperate with educators, promote lectures and supervised tours and offer employment to teachers. The Shell Companies Foundation, established in 1953, gave over $500,000 to higher education in 1957. A number of companies, including Gulf, Phillips, and Ohio Oil, give scholarships to children of employees. In addition to the usual grants, Gulf also has an alumnus gift-matching program to stimulate degree-holding employees to contribute to their alma maters. The company has also hired approximately fifteen college teachers each summer as consultants to help assist academic salary levels and increase professional competence. Gulf reported that it contributed almost $750,000 to educational institutions in 1958. Socony Mobil gave nearly $700,000 in 1956 to colleges and universities. In the previous year Socony established a chair in chemical engineering at Cornell University to be filled by a professor with considerable industrial experience and good contacts with industry. "We believe the new chair . . . will be unique not only because of the emphasis on undergraduate teaching," explained Deane W. Malott, president of Cornell, "but also because of the provision for filling it with a chemical engineer who will share strong practical experience with his students. The provisions for the teacher's continuing consultation with industry should enhance the possibilities of this interesting venture in engineering education." [71]

Standard (Indiana) has long concentrated extensively on young people in all its public relations efforts. Its Standard Oil Foundation pays special attention to farm youth in the 4-H clubs and the Future Farmers of America and to Junior Achievement, a national youth organization that helps teenagers to understand and even embark on small corporations. This is a good investment, the midwestern giant explains to its employees in a booklet discussing why it sponsors youth and educational activities: "Business success depends on their future buying power, on their ability and willingness to work, and on the kind of government they support." [72] Standard has prepared petroleum display kits and charts for use in the grade schools. It has distributed a monthly newsreel, "The News Magazine of the Screen," for students in the schools in its territory. In 1957, it channeled $700,000 to higher education.

Standard of California also is involved in relatively extensive educational efforts. Since 1928 it has sponsored radio music programs for school listening. In 1958 it began to cosponsor a nation-wide television program to provide college credit in physics for high-school science teachers. Science Fairs, Business-Education Days, motion pictures, seminars on company operations for college professors, scholarships and research grants are also part of the more than a million-dollar annual outlay. All this, the company assures its stockholders, is sound—"being within the bounds of economic business operations," and practical—"the program is a two-way street with benefits both going out and coming in." One direct gain is the creating of "a responsive climate in which the Company may more effectively conduct its business." [73]

Texaco gives about $500,000 a year to higher education, primarily in scholarships. These scholarships are administered by the colleges and based on their own choice of candidates and standards, with the oil company stipulating that the course of study chosen by the recipient must be one that could eventually lead to employment in the petroleum industry. "All that Texaco asks in return is for him, as a highly trained and educated individual, to take his place in the free enterprise system which helped prepare him for his role in life." [74]

A glimpse into the nature of that role in the organizational world was furnished by an employment guidance pamphlet, *So You Want a Better Job*, prepared by Socony. This offered earnest advice to college students on such matters as the rewards accorded workers who shouldered responsibility, the importance of not calling the boss "Jack," the pitfalls of drink, and the virtues of honesty. A paragraph on "Personal Viewpoint" was of particular interest:

Personal views can cause a lot of trouble. Remember then to keep them always conservative. The "isms" are out. Business being what it is, it naturally looks with disfavor on the wild-eyed radical or even the moderate pink. On the other hand, I think you will find very few organizations who will attempt to dictate the political party of their employees.[75]

Between 1947 and 1954 some 300,000 copies of this guide to organizational green pastures had been distributed to potential executives through college placement offices, apparently without question by any college administrators or faculty. Then this ode to conformity drew comment from a student writing in *The Daily Princetonian*. This was followed by a public criticism by Norman Thomas that resulted in an apology from Socony's director of industrial relations. The latter stated that while it was surprising to encounter such "misinterpretation" of the intent of Socony—"the management of this company would be the last to suggest or want any curtailment of free expression"—the first two sentences, when taken out of context, "do sound awful." [76]

In the interests of good public relations, a revised edition was immediately prepared. Familiarity with the boss and excessive drinking were still frowned upon; honesty and hard work still heralded. The only change was the offending paragraph on "Personal Viewpoint," which now read:

You may have strong views about a lot of things, including religion, politics, economics, business affairs. That's fine. The world needs different viewpoints; blind conformity means stagnation. You won't get far unless you think for yourself. But personal views, if advanced with vehemence, bitterness or ridicule can complicate your relationships with your fellow workers. Good relationships may share with energy and ability as aids to winning promotion. Furthermore, there is a time and place for everything. Ask yourself whether you would pay a man to debate during working hours on matters far removed from the work in hand.[77]

Yet with due respect for the decency of Socony's management and its personal commitment to the values of a free society, these verbal alterations failed to conceal the harsh reality that Socony was closer to the truth the first time. Sensitive public relations cannot change the fact that the corporate way of life as we now know it does not place the highest premium on individuality and that the corporation more readily bestows its sovereign favors of security and advance-

ment upon those who fit its mold and offer their highest loyalty to
the goals of the team.

Oil has a right to be heard. And aid to higher education is a
responsible approach, however much one may quail at the assumption that the search for knowledge should ultimately reveal private
enterprise as the highest creation of man and however much one
may deplore the support of education in so rich a society by the
back door of corporate generosity. But when viewed in the context
of the full range of oil's courtship of the American people, from
broad advertising to political persuasion, this concern for education
emerges as one more tactic for dealing with public reactions, for
reinforcing public acceptance of private power and privilege.

According to Edward L. Bernays, the "dean" of public relations
practitioners, public relations "is the attempt, by information, persuasion, and adjustment, to engineer public support for an activity,
cause, movement, or institution." [78] John W. Hill, chairman of the
board of Hill and Knowlton, calls public relations "an outgrowth
of our free society, in which the ideal of an enlightened and rational
public opinion is brought even closer as understanding increases between groups and individuals." [79] One appreciates the need for
establishing genuine communications in a complex society where
access to the public ear is so difficult. There are honest and legitimate uses of public relations as informational tools. Yet these advertising and public relations campaigns of the petroleum industry,
along with those of its corporate brethren, pose problems that strike
at the essence of democratic performance and survival. They represent a one-way communications bridge to close the gap between the
masses of people and those who control the great collective organizations in a society whose assumptions are that the rulers should be
accountable to public opinion through continuing discussion.

The vast productive capacity of the American economy forces the
continued discovery for new wants. "Customers must be created in
as great a quantity as products are mass-produced," said Robert E.
Kenyon, Jr., publisher of the marketing weekly *Printer's Ink* as he
projected a $25 billion national advertising bill for 1965. "Advertising
is the mechanized process by which prospects are created for countless products, converted into customers and kept as steady customers.
Advertising is to marketing what the machine is to manufacturing." [80]

Market research, increasingly predicated on the assumption that it is emotional rather than critical reactions that motivate much of human behavior, is employed to interpret, heighten, and reassure the desire to buy and consume. To influence people "to behave as advertising wanted them to behave," advises Ernest Dichter, president of the Institute for Motivational Research, which numbers oil companies among its clients, it is necessary to stop and study the basic psychological mechanisms at work, including "the forms of resistance, appeals, and subtle motivations which interfere with the smooth and intelligent functioning of human behavior. . . . The moment the public acts critically a good portion of the sales effectiveness has been destroyed." [81]

With conscious borrowing from the techniques for the selling of goods and services, there has developed the auxiliary industry of engineering mass acceptance of corporate causes. Just as the object of advertising is to minimize random action on the part of the consumer, so is the ultimate goal of public relations to condition the habits and the opinions of people so that they will respond in channeled patterns, while maintaining the illusion that their choices are free. The consequence is the integration of the individual as consumer and citizen into the corporate process.

There remains considerable room for skepticism as to the "scientific" nature of these efforts. This despite the impressive claims, psychological jargon, academic credentials, and retainers of many public relations men. But the massiveness and pervasiveness of oil propaganda, the variety of techniques, and the great wealth and organization behind these tactics in themselves raise questions as to the opportunity of the American people to hear the full facts and alternative positions relating to public oil policy. One API staff member estimated oil's nonmarketing public relations expenditures for 1954 at $50 million. But it is almost impossible to arrive at conclusive figures; it is far easier to estimate the cost of how oil brings its messages to the public than the cost of preparing what the industry says.

In all this it is impossible to discount the frequently deceptive or dishonest character to these public relations efforts. One wonders as to the full nature of "public relations" when one encounters a public relations firm keeping full dossiers on the attitudes and behavior of regulatory officials, when at least one major firm maintains a security officer, when a public relations man is credited with directing the campaign to block the renomination of Leland Olds, when another leads the "big doubt" assault upon Senator Tydings in Maryland, when one reads congressional testimony describing state legislators on the pay roll of a firm doing public relations work for an oil company (one of these legislators is now a congressman), when charges are encountered that attacks upon Standard of California were paid for by Standard to help push public support of a "conservation" measure, when a state director of public relations for a leading oil company sanctions the sending of fake telegrams to Congress, and when a public relations firm paid by oil guides anti-Israel propaganda in the United States. The creation of oil "front groups," the planting of half-truths as news, the creation and spreading of false concepts, such as the reputed threat of federal control of offshore oil to the inland waterways of individual states, and the substitution of slogans for facts, as seen in the repeated usage of "tidelands" to include underwater lands extending far out into the continental shelf, are equally disturbing illustrations of the contempt for public intelligence. They reflect a cynical willingness to manipulate people upon the payment of a fee, to invade the privacy of the subconscious, and to develop acceptance without understanding—all for the ends of the private government of oil.

The deliberate manipulation of the historic symbols of the culture, such as "grass roots," "states' rights," and "private enterprise" is a further industry tactic for obscuring its power. Oil uses the image of the small independent producer for sympathy as its mining counterparts have used the picture of the lone sourdough with his pickax, the utilities have used "widows and orphans," and the giant agricultural industries have used the sturdy family farmer. A capitalist, explains an official of Standard Oil of Ohio in a company magazine, is "the man who sits next to you at the ball park, the girl in the Easter parade, the boy racing by on a bike. A capitalist is Mr. or Mrs. or Miss Doakes who owns one or more shares of stock in one or another of America's companies or commercial enterprises." [82] The news program "Your Esso Reporter," which is handled by one agency, is heard several times daily over fifty different radio stations from Maine to Louisiana, reports Jersey Standard's *The Lamp*. "Of course, his voice has a twang in Maine and a drawl in Louisiana, for every Esso Reporter is a local newscaster." [83]

In its shift to "corporate responsibility," the petroleum industry claims to be presenting a conservative (but progressive) philosophy for contemporary America. What emerges more clearly, however, are essentially slick homilies and crudely disguised public bribes to protect narrow economic interests. The appeals are frequently irrational and frankly tuned in to popular fears. While the primitives tend to play by ear, the more sophisticated branches of the industry employ motivational research psychologists to determine exactly what it is the people fear and how their anxieties can be manipulated to evoke the desired attitudes toward oil and free enterprise.

The job of oilmen as "statesmen and architects of a free world," Mrs. Oveta Culp Hobby, co-publisher of the *Houston Post* and Secretary of Health, Education, and Welfare, told the API right after the 1952 Eisenhower victory, was to use the great battery of modern mass communications

to increase everywhere the number of informed and thinking men and women, and make them active partners with you in your great undertaking; by facts and figures to teach them that great industries are not the natural enemies of the little man, but the defenders of his liberty and the actual creators of those things which he cherishes in his present way of life. . . . The biggest part of the job before you is to create a receptive atmosphere, a climate where people are ready and willing to believe you. . . . Sincerity and warmth, respect and understanding of the other man's feelings and attitudes, may be as important as the facts themselves. If what you say and what you do causes people to want to understand you, to want to cooperate with you, to feel that you are on their team and they are on your team, then your task will be much easier. Once you have overcome the emotional blocks, you will have no difficulty of convincing people with your facts.[84]

Said a public relations staff man in summarizing the Colorado severance tax campaign, "We got the people so they just automatically voted 'No.' "

The cumulative effect of the endless and sugar-coated repetition of a "few plausible facts" contributes to the benumbing of independent critical judgment in a society whose ultimate faith is in the ability of people, given the fullest facts, to reason and make intelligent decisions. It dissuades people from facing up to basic questions about the power structure of American society and the requirements for effective political democracy. Thus the ultimate consequence of this use of fear as a political weapon is to discount genuine public opinion as a social force, to disparage the processes of democratic government, and to discourage the citizen from using them to achieve a responsible society.

The public relations efforts are enhanced by the all too frequent absence of sustained critical public opinion or organizational positions to counter any of the points advanced by oil. The essential abdication, if not complicity, of much of the press is an important factor here. The mass media have become concentrated big business. As such they often display as their first loyalty an identity with other controllers of property rather than a militant commitment to the ideals and obligations of free and responsible inquiry. Radio and television have developed primarily as instruments for selling sponsored products rather than as creative tools for elevating public debate through truthful, comprehensive, and interpretative accounts of public issues.

The day when newspapers in the United States were financially indebted to oil companies seems past, although one occasionally encounters such charges. As a history of Jersey Standard records, "as early as 1898 Standard Oil began to change its relations with newspapers. Instead of making loans, as had been done for a few journals, Archbold and his associates began to make contracts for advertising and news insertions with a large number of editors." [85] Today it is an oversimplification to say advertising influences what the media present. Yet one cannot help speculating about the correlation between their behavior and the almost daily blanketing of the press with gasoline and institutional ads. The Jersey corporation alone reported that its affiliates spent $45 million in 1959 for marketing advertising. Presumably most of the nation's newspapers did not profit directly the way some Texas papers did in a "Remember the Tidelands" crusade by selling to local sponsors full-page mats prepared by the Texas Statewide Tidelands Committee and distributed with the help of the Texas Press Association. Nor are the writers and editors beyond the oil-producing regions so directly susceptible to the role of oil in the community power structure. But oil news is generally considered to be technical. Flattered by the attention of the industry, dependent upon oilmen for information, and sensitive to the business identification of their employers, oil reporters tend to toe the mark. There is rarely any genuinely critical appraisal. Newsmen in producing areas say that on occasions they have been offered fees to write feature stories on the romance of oil for industry publications. Some newsmen have served on the side as paid public relations consultants for oil companies.

A few papers, such as the *St. Louis Post-Dispatch*, the *New York Post*, *The Washington Post*, and the *Madison Capital Times*, along with more local papers such as Ronnie Dugger's *Texas Observer* and Harry Billings's *The People's Voice* (Montana), columnists like the late Thomas L. Stokes and cartoonists Herblock and Fitzpatrick, have taken seriously Joseph Pulitzer's half-century-old advice to "always oppose privileged classes and public plunderers." But it is difficult to justify either as responsible or free such items as the playing down of the Truman Committee's findings about the relation of Jersey Standard and I. G. Farben; the respectful silence during the 1952 campaign about Richard Nixon's secret fund, in good part from California oilmen; the widespread treatment of Senator Wayne Morse's filibuster against the offshore oil bill in 1953 as a sports event, while virtually ignoring its very relevant contents; the Associated Press story in 1953 claiming that the offshore debate was "blocking consideration of other important legislation" when in fact, as the *St. Louis Post-Dispatch* forced the AP to admit, no basic legislation was being held up; the failure of so many papers to carry roll-call summaries on "tidelands" and other key votes; the playing down of the forced resignation of Republican National Committee Chairman C. Wesley Roberts in the opening months of the Eisenhower crusade because of disclosures about his lobbying and public relations activities for such clients as the Cities Service Gas Company; and the general willingness to run press releases as news.

The growth of "government by handout" is also a factor here. In many respects the press has become an instrument of national policy, and given the role of such groups as oil within the formal federal framework, an appendage of the power forces of the society.

One wonders as to the spontaneity with which so many American papers denounced the highly complex oil cartel report prepared by the Federal Trade Commission. One also wonders how the public can hold its leaders accountable when top-level agencies such as the National Security Council and the Central Intelligence Agency (CIA) and critical issues such as the role of the United States in the Iranian revolution, the tax benefits to oildom, and the disposal of Alaskan naval reserves are cloaked from review by the public and often the Congress—but not from oildom—by the convenient rubber-stamp curtain of "national security." As James Reston, chief of the Washington Bureau of the *New York Times*, testified in 1955:

The news of the CIA and its operatives all over the world often confronts us with the most embarrassment that any reporter can be confronted with, the dilemma as to whether he is going to tell the truth or whether he is going to mislead the American people by putting out something put out by the Government which he knows not to be true.[86]

Public relations reinforces a climate sympathetic to the continued power of the private government of oil. But this effort has not created the vacuum of community-oriented goals. Modern America would blanch at the frank approach to character training that John D. Rockefeller, Sr., received from his father. "I cheat my boys every time I get a chance. . . . I trade with the boys and skin 'em, and I just beat 'em every time I can. I want to make 'em sharp." [87] But shrewd dealing and getting something for nothing have long been accepted ingredients for success. When a millionaire oil operator running for public office in Louisiana in 1939 was criticized for "seeing his opportunities" and making a killing on leases on state-owned lands, he answered: "I had vision; I had the courage to speculate, and I am entitled to credit for that success." [88]

Louis Roussel, another millionaire oilman, has recalled his envy of the free-spending, hellraising seismographic crews in Louisiana to whom he had been bootlegging whisky when he was seventeen: "I nagged at them to tell me how to get into their racket."

"Hell, son," the superintendent said, "don't mess around with dynamite. Just get yourself an oil well, and you can buy and sell us, the whole damn town of Thibodaux, and every bootlegger on the bayou."

A few years later Roussel received his chance.

> I could speak French—or the Cajun patois that passes for it along the Louisiana bayous—and one day I went along with a lease promoter to act as interpreter. Through me he talked a farmer into selling the oil rights to his land for one dollar an acre. Two days later he resold each one of these acres for $55.
>
> Don't get the idea that the farmer got bilked out of any money. In the first place, I could have talked to him six months without convincing him there was a chance oil was underneath his land. In the second, the farmer would have been unable to get the $55 price because he had neither the time, the contacts or the knowledge of where to go to get it. That takes experience, and, as I was to learn the hard way, it takes plenty of time.
>
> But $54 profit on each acre! [89]

In 1957 Senator Dennis Chavez of New Mexico, long a critic of out-of-state oil interests who repeatedly had sought to unseat him because of his earlier natural gas voting record, told his state's Oil and Gas Association that he now welcomed their contributions in developing New Mexico's fast-growing gas industry. He no longer was bitter over an estimated $200,000 placed by oil in support of one opponent, Sinclair attorney Patrick J. Hurley:

> I am not here to scold you. . . . You are a great bunch of people, and I like you and admire you. Maybe I envy many of you, too. . . . We are all capitalists at heart. Each wants to make money, big money. There is nothing wrong with this. I certainly wish I could do it.

But he advised his state's benefactors that their big problem was to improve their public relations. They should go easy on the Cadillacs, the big tips, the big talk. And the election money could better be spent by educating the consumer about the industry. "It has never been easy to marshal the poor behind the rich in any battle." [90]

Oil has chanted the litanies about "free enterprise" that Main Street wants to hear and believe. The American farmer, often a speculator, does envision himself as a potential oilman. And viewing the natural resources of the nation as legitimate and unlimited private plunder did not originate with oil. It has been an integral if not too flattering part of the American record in the opening up of all national resources, including the soil. The entire petroleum process, starting with the concept of private ownership of subsurface mineral rights, has given millions of people dreams of one-eighth royalties. Stock and lease advertisements constantly hammer away at this expectation of boodle. "I can see two groups of people," writes one dealer:

> One group, composed of some rather disconsolate individuals—looking somewhat "sour" and resentful—seem to be lamenting, "We never have a chance. Opportunity is dead. There are no new frontiers to explore in America."
>
> But the other group is refreshingly different. They are smiling happily, and—they seem to be stuffing large bundles of "FOLDING MONEY" into their pockets. . . .

The latter, of course, had invested in low-priced wildcat leases. A few years ago these venturesome spirits were (presumably like the prospective customers) "a somewhat seedy lot." But now they were "in the chips . . . driving around in high-powered Cadillacs." *"Land to which you can obtain a lease on the oil rights today for $10 or less per acre may 'tomorrow' prove salable for $1,000 to $5,000 or more per acre,"* announces another broker. "Remember— Sid Richardson parlayed just four lonesome $10 bills into a billion and a quarter dollar fortune—by getting a *West Texas lease*—that turned out to be lucky." "Buy your lease in the area where the big, successful operators are buying . . . sandwiched right in between leases held by two huge major oil companies," urges the president of the Bonanza Lease Company of Fort Worth. "When you play where they play you are getting the advantage of their costly secret information, even though you do not know the details of that information." Corporate stock splitting and employee stock-purchasing plans have been developed by major oil companies to broaden their base of popular support. A soap company advertises an oil well as first prize in a jingle contest—"Have money flowing in for years." A children's game is called "Be a Texas Millionaire."

Educators in oil and gas regions frequently display an unscholarly eagerness to support the political concerns of their petroleum patrons. A number of Texas college presidents and professors played prominent "front" roles in the assault upon Leland Olds during the hearing over his reappointment in 1949. One president voiced horror that a man "unfriendly to corporations and to corporate interests" should serve on the FPC.[91] School of business and economics professors have appeared in paid testimonials and have become involved in an interchange between university and oil management circles, each enjoying the prestige contributed by such association. With a few notable exceptions, practically every book on oil is subsidized by the industry. And there is a growing list of historians, economists, sociologists, and psychologists writing company studies and histories. Many are drawing funds directly from the industry. Others simply share the new "revisionist" approach to economic history that now concludes that the early muckraking of corporate development and power was essentially "feminine." Teacher associations, not unmindful of the considerable appropriations derived from oil, have openly propagandized and lobbied on oil matters.

Many universities have major oil holdings, investments, and even gasoline stations. Not surprisingly, petroleum common stocks are the largest of industrial holdings in university-endowment portfolios, with Jersey Standard probably the most popular. The University of Texas has several thousand oil and gas wells. In 1956 its oil-derived permanent fund exceeded $250 million. That year, a crusading student editor of the *Daily Texan*, taking the precepts of journalism seriously, editorialized against natural gas legislation freeing producers from control and generally showed skepticism as to the sanctity of oil. The University of Texas Board of Regents, all appointed by Governor Allan Shivers, quickly moved to censure the student. Explained one oil operator-regent:

> We feel the *Daily Texan* is going out of bounds to discuss the Fulbright Harris natural gas bill when 66 percent of Texas tax money comes from oil and gas. . . . We're just trying to hold Willie [William W. Morris, the editor] to a college yell.[92]

That oil literature and polls are so extensively and uncritically used in nonoil state schools is again more of a commentary on the ethical judgment and reward system of the education profession than on the acquisitive instincts of the industry. In 1953 the Opinion Research Corporation reported to the OIC that most educators approved of their texts: "Only a few feel the booklets are biased, and even some of these say they approve of the bias." An eastern high school principal was quoted as saying: "These booklets look okay to me. I don't see any company name on them. We sure don't want to advertise any one company." A director of curriculum in a midwestern city explained that the use of any company advertising was prohibited. But "we do approve of Institute or Associational material." [93] Kenneth G. Oberholtzer, Denver's superintendent of schools and past president of the American Association of School Administrators, complimented the industry for the school program. "You have struck oil in a new territory . . ." [94]

The Opinion Research Corporation advised, however, that despite this attitude, "few of them are naïve enough to believe that the petroleum industry is spending the amount of money . . . for completely unselfish reasons. Most of them recognize that this is a public relations effort, so there is no point in denying that the booklets are designed to teach people the facts about the oil industry in the hope that it will raise their appraisal of it. Obviously, however, there is no need to raise this point unless the teacher does."

The current material expectations from oil of so many in the American society and the organized application of mass persuasion techniques combine to develop acceptance for the values of bigness, money, and power, while obscuring the full nature and impact of the private government of oil. Meanwhile, the latter prepares to meet any threat from popular judgment and from the formal political framework designed to restrain and prevent unbridled power. Oil moves to integrate human behavior for its corporate ends and to widen its controls over the social environment within which it functions. As this collectivization continues, one wonders which groups and which leaders will retain the will and the capacity to raise the larger points about the proper climate for a responsible and democratic society.

16

Private Power and Democratic Directions

"Tidelands," Suez, natural gas, Iran, depletion, Saudi Arabia, conservation, imports, shale, Venezuela, antitrust—oil is in the headlines almost daily. Each of these issues is approached by the American people on a crisis basis, with the operative myth that they are separate economic or political considerations. Yet the story of oil underscores the imperative for facing up in coherent fashion to the realities of modern industrial life.

While no industry can match it in size and scope, the essential patterns of internal organization and of relationships with the larger community are in no sense developments unique to oil. The benefits to the nation's level of living and security from the many technological advances are impressive—as are the productive and distributive efficiencies of the integrated enterprises that dominate the economy. It is easy to recognize the inadequacies of the classic liberal warnings against the curse of bigness. One must give pause, however, before celebrating the emergence of the new corporate society.

Protests about the behavior of oil date back to the industry's beginnings. From the producer resentment over prices charged by Pennsylvania teamsters and then the flagrant discrimination in Rockefeller's usage of the railroad rebate and drawback to the current appeals of dealers and jobbers for protection against distributor domination, the giants of oil have been blamed for destroying small business. The vivid portrait of Standard Oil by Ida M. Tarbell and Henry D. Lloyd created a public image that has persisted for over half a century. To a nation whose roots and faith in family farming and independent business as ways of life were increasingly shaken by the trend of modern capitalism, the oil trust dramatized the menace of concentrated economic power. Oil's public relations is still geared largely to meeting these charges.

The performance of the private government that controls this basic energy resource has implications far beyond the familiar issue of "monopoly" and its effects upon small business, competition, and even the consumer. Out of habit of language the American oil industry is called private. But there is little that is private about its impact. At stake are questions that go to the heart of American social structure and to the premises of United States international conduct. They relate to power and purpose. They strike at the liberal faith in progress and at the belief that man has the capacity to be the architect of his fate. They force a redefinition of traditional democratic assumptions about the nature of freedom, the rights of property, the uses of government, the avenues for social change, the participation of the citizenry, the potentials of "human nature."

Given the reality of the politics of oil, what meaning can be given to political democracy? Do technological developments inevitably demand an integration of all human activity? Does such ordering force the concentration of power—whether private or public, national or international? Can such power be held accountable? Can a system of diffused political power as now constituted stand up to the private organizations in the various areas of American life? Can this system be adapted to facilitate the planning and the controls that may be needed? How far could antitrust and other remedies for irresponsible monopoly power be strengthened to keep alive genuine competition? Or have we passed the point of no return? What are the most efficient, productively and socially, forms of organization for serving the consumer and larger public needs? Which of the personal freedoms and choices that liberal society has cherished can be maintained in a setting of big technology? How can this society develop the purposes, the machinery, the public service, the intelligence, the organized public, and the general climate to sustain the ideal of representative government?

Questions about private power and public purposes seem out of order in a culture where things are always getting better—where intelligence, freedom, the profit incentive, and the generosity of nature have combined to create such remarkable well-being. Yet it is perilous to continue to ignore or discount the grave disabilities accumulated along with this material growth. The nation has been living on the fat of its heritage and wealth that has allowed an unparalleled margin for error and waste. Moral smugness has fostered an attitude of superiority and fear, rather than understanding, toward the multiple revolutions convulsing much of the world. This insensitivity places the United States on the brink of war wherever people are on the march against want and tyranny. At home ignorance and mass absorption in personal advancement have resulted in complacency toward fundamental antidemocratic developments.

The central consideration emerging from the analysis of the politics of oil is the incompatibility of a socially irresponsible system of power with the goal of a truly democratic society. A corrosion of democratic principles and practices pervades wherever the interests of private oil and public policy meet. The attractions of privilege and power derived from the control of oil invite pressures, from small as well as big business, that mock the ideals of responsible government, a just society, and a peaceful world.

There is an impelling need to understand the new industrialism and the mass society it has brought, and to experiment boldly to create an environment within which democratic values and institutions can flourish—or at least have a chance. The modern industrial setting consists of planned, rational systems of order. Designed to minimize chance and instability, they embrace widening areas of human behavior and institutional functioning. As seen in the case of oil, however, this planning is primarily private and for the ends of efficient profit making. There are areas of public planning in the United States. Generally, these are focused on warmaking and on servicing private enterprise, although there are significant but fragmentary welfare programs aimed at putting a floor under the economy.

But the collectivization of the economic process has also had a profound effect on the general quality of the culture and on the conditions and choices for purposeful living available to the individual. Out of competitive, acquisitive behavior have emerged corporate empires in the major industrial sectors of the economy.

Anonymous managerial elites rule vast physical plants and inter-changeable human cogs. These new centers of power take upon themselves the role of guardians of the "American way," from edu-cation to foreign policy. With the development of "corporate citizen-ship," individual citizens progressively appear to accept themselves as ciphers, well fed but politically impotent. A new kind of personality becomes the model, one whose guiding rule is, in the words of for-mer General Electric vice president T. K. Quinn, "Don't stick your neck out." The broadened expectation of rewards and the pyramided structure of power thus combine to challenge the essence of liberal democracy and its requirement of a wide diffusion of social power among citizens confident in their responsibilities and capacities. These consequences, whether recognized or unrecognized, are un-critically accepted as peripheral by-products of the new economy.

The further temptation, carefully cultivated by the opinion-molding apparatus of the power forces of the society, is resignation to "the march of technology" as inevitably including in its wake the concen-tration of power in corporate hands in the United States and the dehumanization of man. The blessings of bigness and integration are measured in degrees of comfort. Physical mobility is confused with a more satisfying personal freedom.

Even if one is prepared to accept corporate paternalism as a way of life, there is ample evidence that what is good for such industries as oil is not necessarily good for all. Dealings with the Nazi state and I. G. Farben, the withholding of research data, the choking off of full competition from synthetic fuels, the ruthless crushing of small businesses, the organized opposition to public welfare measures in such areas as education, health, and social security, the gutting of tax programs, the perversion of foreign policy, and interfering in the affairs of other countries are but a few contemporary illustrations of the limits of oil's perspective.

The case for public planning is strengthened by the recognition that the industrial process now operative is a product of man's in-telligence. The political, the legal, and the social framework sup-porting and guiding these technological developments have also been constructed by men. The central point here is that men have choices, that there is the potential to create an environment that will en-courage life-affirming values and responsible institutions. The odds may be against effective action for attaining such goals. One cannot ignore the massive nature of the new society and the pervasive feeling it engenders that the main directions of this apparently impersonally guided juggernaut are not reversible. Nor can one minimize the entrenched positions of power groups, such as those that control oil, as measured against the inadequacies of popular awareness and political tools for responsible government. Nor is there any guarantee that people want to rise above their daily concerns to maintain the human spirit, to close the awesome gaps between knowledge and power, and to rule intelligently. A machine culture requires discipline and hierarchy. Harnessed for warmaking, the productive system becomes increasingly enmeshed with the military apparatus. An emerging garrison state distributes its rewards widely throughout the economy. The leadership and alliance of specialists in production and violence are accepted as a necessary price for national security. Surrender of individual rights inherent in the liberal-humanist tradition, and perhaps the annihilation of the human personality, as we idealize it, may be inevitable.

It is in the nature of men to hope and to aspire. The alternatives now visible emphasize mass manipulation, organized greed, and total destruction. People of heart should not have to accept these tendencies without understanding their cause and without opportunity for resistance.

It is understandably overwhelming to contemplate reversing the trend toward bigness in oil. From the standpoint of economic efficiency, certainly much of the production process and the competitive heritage of the industry has been wasteful. There are genuine advantages in integration. The fundamental mischief occasioned by accepting subsurface minerals as private property—a view not held in many countries—is too far along in the United States to rescind. But property rights, like property responsibilities, are neither absolute nor unchanging. It does not follow that the nation's policies should credit the industry with creating this resource. The oilmen did not put petroleum into the ground. They are not responsible for the major technological advances that foster the need for petroleum. There is no defense for the continued abuse of resources, by either irresponsible producers or consumers. Nor is there justification for maintaining incongruous public policies. The United States espouses the ideal of competitive enterprise and continues a range of anti-trust actions. At the same time it furthers the concentration of economic power and the conditions of privilege through war contracts and subsidies, favored access to the governmental machinery, and such discriminatory tax programs as the depletion allowance. Neither the economic bullying resulting from the sheer size of the oil giants nor their political aggressiveness can be accepted as unavoidable aspects of the industrial process, if the American people hope to achieve a responsible government and a social democracy.

It is folly to allow the development of energy resources—the mainspring of modern civilization—to be determined by choices and conflicts rooted in the power-profit motives of a few. The public will rarely be served by assuming that genuine policy can emerge from the almost exclusive participation of private and presumably competitive claimants. With much of the cream skimmed off the nation's natural physical wealth, the struggles over who shall control and develop these resources and for what ends are intensifying. The record of oil shows the difficulty of finding any group who can speak for the consumer and for long-run public interests. It is equally foolish to rely upon state governments in the United States to provide the necessary policies for holding accountable a world-wide system of power. State governments are inadequate for the task, and frequently they serve as agents for the private exploitative interests within their borders. In such a setting, the federal government must play a key role, not as a neutral or as the judge, but as champion of the public welfare.

What is required is public planning, not just of oil, but of all energy resources. Needed is an integrated national policy to replace the current legally archaic, administratively irresponsible and politically contradictory approach to oil and other resources. Long-range plans must be formulated for the related use and conservation of all energy resources—coal, oil, gas, hydroelectric power, atomic and solar energy. These plans must be predicated on the assumptions of an expanding economy and of a world heavily dependent upon the stability of the United States. Such planning would offer the opportunity to guide the profound physical and social changes occasioned by the accelerated pace of technological innovation. Within the United States there will be a doubling of energy consumption in the next two decades. For other areas of the world the percentage increase will be even more startling as people strive to catch up with the more developed nations—or even just cling to their present inadequate levels. The world must reckon with a population explosion that may increase the human race from 2.8 billion in 1959 to 3.8 billion in 1975 and 6 billion by the year 2000. Given such elementary facts, planning is neither visionary nor radical.

Oil and gas are increasingly expensive resources. Reserves are not unlimited. The nation should not allow similar patterns to be repeated. Shale should be publicly developed, or at least kept as a lever for use by the United States in dealing with the oil industry. Experiments to obtain oil from coal should be given high priority. Public and offshore lands should be treated as national treasures rather than as private booty. Reserves should be controlled, and where necessary, used for yardstick operations that would give the public a meaningful check over oil operations. Nuclear energy, basically developed as a public industry with at least $18 billion of taxpayer money directly invested, should be a major focus of public planning. Cooperatives, small atomic plants, and other organizational and technical arrangements that might promise abundance without concentration of power should be encouraged. The verdict is not conclusive that technology must by definition result in centralization.

The establishment of a research agency, perhaps similar to the former National Resources Committee, could provide a modest but invaluable beginning. This would have to be not just another private advisory body built into the government, but rather a genuinely public-oriented agency staffed by men of the highest intelligence, expertise, and public commitment. Long-range plans would then offer meaningful criteria for judging the worth of conservation, tax, and other programs in terms of conditions of optimum economic and social performance. The agency could present a fresh approach to the recurring and somewhat fraudulent debate over imports, perhaps reexamining the feasibility of "stockpiling" domestic oil fields for emergency use, while drawing more freely upon overseas sources and compensating domestic producers openly for their discoveries and deferred profits. Planning would focus on necessary directions for public and private research. It could provide a timetable, based on community needs rather than on corporate profits, for the intro-

duction of new energy sources. Planning would also offer clear guide-
posts as to what kinds and degrees of political tools and controls
are needed for the most fruitful organization of the resources of the
society. Here the possibility of further regulation, including placing
oil in the category of a public utility, needs careful study. Such
formulations might offer to oilmen incentive and guidelines for re-
appraising their prevailing practices in terms of defined standards of
the public weal.

There is no magic in public controls—any more than national
planning guarantees the good society. But a sense of purpose is a
first step in challenging the power of the private government of oil.
Regulation for public ends, measured against broadly determined
criteria of public policy, can help create responsibility to the citizenry
in the exercise of power by the giant private and public organizations
that now rule. Such classic liberal devices as antitrust may still play
a meaningful role in putting a brake upon undesirable giantism, in
keeping energy resources competitive with one another, in blocking
the stranglehold over patents, pipelines, and dealers, and generally
in limiting the use of raw economic power to create monopoly in
the name of technology. One doesn't know how effective this might
be, for antitrust has never been given consistent support. Many
scholars believe that much can be done. But unless placed within
a broader social policy, antitrust is a negative approach. It is no
substitute for coherent economic planning.

To some contemporary liberals, fear of the new corporate be-
hemoths is obsessive. They waste little time with the pretense that
the American economic machinery follows the precepts of Adam
Smith. Checks upon unbridled economic power, argues David E.
Lilienthal, now come from the evolution of standards of public
control, from a heightened sense of responsibility by business leaders,
and from the competition among corporate and industrial clusters.
The former head of the Tennessee Valley Authority and the Atomic
Energy Commission, the two largest and most daring public enterprises in American history, concludes that corporate economic power
"has been so watered down that it is hardly recognizable as 'economic
power.'" Thus, "bigness can become an expression of the heroic
size of man himself as he comes to a new-found greatness." [1] To this
view, conservative economist Sumner H. Slichter has added the

reassurance that "the argument that bigness threatens our political liberties is without foundation. If there is any one handicap that bigness possesses, it is lack of political influence." [2]

Economist John K. Galbraith agrees that the acid test of responsibility is resolved, not through the marketplace, but through countervailing power systems, both public and private.[3] Entire industries now compete with one another, as aluminum with steel and air lines with railroads. Huge purchasing chains restrain producers. The A.&P. becomes an agent for the consumer. Organized labor represents the counterpoise to organized business. A strong government moves to throw its weight wherever one organized element of the society threatens to dominate. The Wagner Act supported the right of collective bargaining and helped unions develop an effective counterbalance to management. Agricultural legislation strengthens the bargaining power of the farmer squeezed between the giant producers who sell to him and the giant processors who buy from him. The competition of individuals is replaced by the competition of groups. Other observers see the counterparts of the checks and balances of the market in the political contests among competing and presumably equal pressure groups. These groups align and realign on issues, presumably with no one element dominating. The abuses of irresponsible economic power are minimized. Liberalism remains a viable concept, adapted in pluralistic form to modern industrial conditions.

This is an intelligent explanation for certain developments since the New Deal. It also offers comfort to those troubled by the organizational revolution. Unfortunately, "countervailing power" does not account for the continued concentration of economic power and political privilege. "Countervailing power" ignores the extent to which presumably competing blocs may share a common interest detrimental to the public welfare. Applied to oil—and Galbraith admits its limited relevance here—the theory ignores the structural and policy relationships among the basic energy industries as now constituted. Then, too, oil's capacity to take advantage of scientific research, to move into petrochemicals, shale, and synthetic fuels, and its growing interest in atomic energy, emphasize the extent to which bigness begets bigness. It foretells the direction of the "new competition" if the choices are left to oil.

Labor's demands have restrained management practices, gained respect and security for the worker, and contributed to a sharing of wealth. Its efforts have been primarily in terms of its own survival and for improvement of the immediate conditions of its members. In many respects labor has functioned as a conservative force, notwithstanding the social idealism it has offered at points in the nation's development. Its greatest successes have been in the most concentrated areas of the economy. There are notable exceptions, as in the building trades and trucking. But few would argue that the results here have been simply a public good. And organized labor's political power to shape general public actions is far less effective than its critics would have the nation believe.

In oil, unionization thus far has had limited success. The major union—the Oil, Chemical and Atomic Workers International—is a respected and responsible organization. Its focus is on wages and working conditions as it seeks to gain a foothold in the industry. On some political and economic issues it tends to identify with the industry. (In 1918 the first convention of the oil workers' union called for nationalization of the industry.) Most of the industry's working force remains unorganized or in independent and company unions. Building a unified movement is difficult. In the past the companies openly fought unions. They did not hesitate to employ violence. After the Ludlow massacre in 1914, Standard Oil shifted its own tactics and began to develop company unions as part of its industrial and public relations. This model was copied by many other firms. Today the oil companies are very paternal. Wages, pensions, and fringe benefits are relatively high, and profit-sharing is widespread. Plants are scattered and bargaining generally is local rather than company or industry-wide. Oil probably has the highest investment per employee of any industry. Automation creates fewer production jobs while increasing the more difficult-to-organize technical and white collar positions. There was a 50 per cent increase in the latter category during the period 1947–1956, while the number of production workers remained almost constant.

The image of government as a countervailing force fails to meet the empirical test of how legislative policy is made and how government regulation actually works. It underestimates the extent to which interests such as oil act as the guardians and captors of presumably public agencies while encouraging popular contempt for the uses of politics and government. To recognize the capacity to distort representative government inherent in the power of petroleum is not to deny the theoretical power of politics as an instrument for social change and control. But the translation of this potential into the actual remains an unresolved challenge. At its core this challenge asks whether political democracy can function in a collectivized industrial society.

Democrats need not—and dare not—run scared from the concept of public planning and from the controls inherent in such an approach. Controls must certainly be handled with responsibility and concern for safeguarding the individual's rights of due process and other civil liberties. The issue is not controls versus no controls. It is rather the irresponsible rule of private systems of order as opposed to the responsible rule of public and private ones. This is a highly centralized, organized, and hence controlled society—with much of the ordering privately or narrowly focused. Controls can be coercions imposed on the freedom of men. The giant organizations we now know do indeed invite the regimentation and suffocation of the individual spirit. Modern business civilization, with its anarchy of irresponsible giants and the elevation of a small industrial-political elite, shows little promise of maintaining an open society of free men. To allow such private power to rule in the name of individual liberty or national security is to thwart political democracy. For democracy is a way of governance, and big government is a necessary reaction to big technology, big business, and big money. Government is to be used rather than simply feared. Its purpose is to expand the range of genuine choices available to the citizenry. Tools of governance developed within a constitutional frame hopefully will support such choices.

The petroleum industry may be betting that the American people do not give a damn about private power and public policy so long as they can speed sixty miles an hour on a no-stop thruway in a two-toned sedan filled with high-test gasoline reinforced by the latest secret additive. They may be right. But all the industry's political efforts show that they know what is obscure or obscured for so much of the public. They recognize and fear the potential power of informed public opinion and action inspired by tough-minded and imaginative leadership. And they are taking no chances. Proposals for inquiry, for regulation, or for genuine public participation in the formulation of oil policy are repeatedly attacked. "That's socialism in the raw," commented one API representative in response to former Congressman John Heselton's modest suggestions along such lines. If oil comes under more government scrutiny, its efforts to capture the machinery of public government will increase. The industry's deliberate manipulation of the historic symbols of the culture—"grass roots," "states' rights," "private enterprise"—will weave a tighter web around the public mind. Perhaps too late, the American people may awaken to the full impact of organized economic power upon their political institutions.

To be paralyzed by such bogy terms as "socialism" is to admit the inevitability of corporate rule. Loyalty to such concepts as "private enterprise" has less and less meaning, given the character of industrialism and modern organization. If energy resources in the United States are to remain in private hands, the justification must not be the "principle" of private property. Highest public needs cannot be confused with maximum profits and controls for existing corporate systems. Where private investments can serve as tools to enrich rather than to impoverish creative living and community responsibility, they should be retained and encouraged. Where they do not, the argument for clinging to such tools is unconvincing. It means abdicating an exciting chance to develop a new society.

The nation must constantly ask where it wants to go, which values it wants to preserve and strengthen—and then look at the going institutions to see what is usable and relevant. There is much that needs to be studied and appraised. The American people are understandably committed to enjoying and expanding abundance. If they can also insist that they want to expand the channels for discussion and dissent, keep a creative spirit alive, encourage a responsible press, build a school system that honors free inquiry, minimize governmental secrecy, strengthen party debate and responsibility, and strive to further a tradition of public service, then there is a much less realistic base to the sloganized fears of public planning. The centralization of irresponsible political power is a genuine threat. There is ample evidence, however, that the deepest assault upon the tenets of a free society has not come from government in the

United States. The assault has come rather from the vacuums of public purpose and responsibility and from the organized power of private collectives over the lives of citizens.

The integrated character of the petroleum industry demands national policy. So also does the international range of oil force a coherent foreign policy and ultimately an international approach. The sovereign character of the nation state can no more be considered the ultimate in human organization than can private ownership of natural resources. The challenge is to introduce broader standards than those of corporate profits and national advantage.

Oil has been a critical point of great-power rivalry and international conflict. There is growing urgency to work out a world plan that will promote its use for the greater benefit of all mankind, while establishing a scientific balance between such demands and the productivity of nature. The United States must strive to match its overseas good will and humanitarianism with intelligence, direction, and leadership, with diplomacy preceding rather than following the petroleum dollar. Who gains if economic aid to emerging industrial countries reverts to the international oil companies in payment for inflated oil prices?

In relation to Latin America there is the need for the United States to identify with the social revolutions that spell the ultimate doom of feudal-militaristic dictatorships. Treating these awakening nations as equals rather than as raw-material-producing colonies, and respecting their planned economies and nationalization programs as perhaps inevitable developments in their quest for improvement, may make good business sense too. United States-Cuban relations illustrate how difficult these adjustments can be, given such provocations as the abusive demagoguery of Fidel Castro, the seizure of the oil refineries and other American property, and the growing alliance with the Soviet bloc. But economic and military sanctions that are rooted in the acceptance of the cold war as the governing condition of foreign policy and that equate American security with oil and other corporate interests help to push the Castro regime into willing Communist arms. Such acts misinterpret the temper of the social revolutions yet to come in much of Latin America. And they lend support to one view that holds that the patterns of control within the United States make it impossible for the country to throw its great resources on the side of most of mankind in their revolutionary struggles.

In the Middle East, Russia and the United States could back a settlement that would provide for the development of oil resources in a manner beneficial to the region and to the rest of the world. Neither great power will long gain by viewing these vast reserves and the people who reside in these areas as objects of exploitation or as pawns in the cold war. Trying to keep the Arab world divided and offering aid in exchange for bases, military partnerships, and political loyalty are cynical, shortsighted approaches. In the long pull, such manipulation feeds the flames of Arab nationalism and the hatred toward the ruling groups who have been willing to barter their people's resources in return for maintenance of their own private power and privilege. It would be folly to slide into a nuclear war over oil. Yet the danger is always real, as the record of Soviet intrigue and Anglo-American gunboat diplomacy indicate. It is in the interest of both great powers to support the neutralization of the Middle East, removing it from the stakes of the cold war. This step would be in keeping with the desires of the people of the area and would in itself lessen the chances of war. Political accommodation between the United States and the Soviet Union is not likely to come on ideological terms. But reduction of conflicts over substantive issues such as petroleum can pave the way for a more peaceful world.

The international corporations and the individual states have limited perspectives in their approaches to oil. The oilmen speak strongly of their heavy investments in producing areas. What they often mean is their anticipation of fabulous profits. The peoples of oil-producing countries are now demanding the right to control resources within their borders. Local Arab rulers also have interests limited by particular national aspirations. Neither the Western corporations nor the newer Soviet competition in the Middle East nor the emerging Arab states are capable of handling petroleum in the interests of both producer and consumer nations. One step toward a world approach would be the placing of oil and all energy resources under international authority, with the United Nations serving as the parent body. In more immediate terms, there should be created an international agency empowered to study and devise ways to ensure that all the regions of the world capable of producing oil can do so without being doomed to remain one-crop dependencies of the more advanced nations. Development funds and technical skills could be made available to producing nations. Equal access to all buyers and shippers must be guaranteed, as must the steady flow of petroleum at fair prices. Prices and production of oil need regulation and stability, as the industry well knows. But the criteria must be world needs and genuine conservation considerations.

In the Middle East a United Nations Development Authority with representation from all the interested nations and corporations should assume responsibility for production planning and for the construction of new pipelines. Huge incomes are now derived from the sale of crude oil. The Middle Eastern nations receive annually a billion dollars in royalties and potential future revenues are estimated to total $100 billion. This should be used for the fullest social reform and economic development of the region. The American contribution to a full-scale aid program requires not charity or surplus disposal, but a concerted mobilization of the nation's under-employed industrial capacity. It is in the self-interest of the more advanced nations to close the growing gap in levels of economic attainment between them and the underdeveloped areas. For these disparities increasingly replace the cold war as the crucial factor of world tension.

The American heritage has been individualistic. Its patterns are now collective and its problems organizational. Its economic code has been "Get yours." Big oil represents "getting yours" in its most developed form. Where the nation has been alarmed, it has inveighed against the successes of the oil industry. What is required is a reexamination of the code itself and of the preponderant national concern with production, efficiency, and pecuniary incentives.

The United States' historic fears of concentrated public power and the monolithic state are preeminently justified by the repeated experiences of men with government as coercive and irresponsible tyranny. They have been translated in America into political institutions premised on the broad diffusion of public power. The problem now is how to deal with a concentrated private international government of oil. It suggests the need for an approach to politics that develops a structure of private initiative and government power that can be both creative and responsible. It requires a recognition of the totalitarian potentials of a highly industrialized community. It calls for the search for a social framework within which the individual spirit and community values can thrive, where the culture respects and supports health, education, intellectual freedom, meaningful work, and high creative levels as primary human needs. A new theory of positive, responsible government needs to be worked out by those who wish to preserve what is the best in the liberal tradition and are still ready to believe that the condition of man is not hopeless, however difficult the immediate tasks ahead may be.

Oil and other resources, along with modern techniques of organization, can be instruments for helping men to live in peace, which requires international political order and responsibility; with plenty, which demands individual opportunity along with world economic cooperation and integration based on science and technology as the servants rather than the masters; and with dignity, which presumes a general cultural environment distinguished by respect for the privacy of human beings and by values that offer people goals beyond survival, comfort, or acquisitiveness.

The challenge is to harness imagination, intelligence, will, and political tools for guiding the mass society that has emerged. If such ends are to be within the realm of the attainable rather than the illusory, then, to borrow Gunnar Myrdal's phrase, "The world cannot be run as a company town." Whether the "owner" be an individual, a corporation, a class, a nation, or a cartel, we must reexamine the premises we live by and the institutions we live with. The importance and the record of oil make this resource a useful starting point.

Notes

CHAPTER 1: *Introduction* (Pages 1–10)

1. For a cogent essay which views power in this positive fashion, see Robert S. Lynd, "Power in American Society As Resource and Problem," in Arthur Kornhauser, ed., *Problems of Power in American Democracy* (Detroit, Wayne State University Press, 1957).

2. J. Frederic Dewhurst and Associates, *America's Needs and Resources: A New Survey* (New York, The Twentieth Century Fund, 1955), p. 754. This, together with W. S. Woytinsky and E. S. Woytinsky, *World Population and Production* (New York, The Twentieth Century Fund, 1953), and *Resources For Freedom*, the five-volume Report of the President's Material Policy Commission (Washington, United States Government Printing Office, 1952), offers useful data on resource capacities and needs.

3. Harrison Brown, *The Challenge of Man's Future* (New York, Viking, 1954), p. 161. An exciting and sobering analysis of some of the questions raised by resources and technological patterns.

4. Adlai E. Stevenson, "My Faith in Democratic Capitalism," *Fortune*, October 1955. In *Posthistoric Man* (Chapel Hill, University of North Carolina, 1950), a provocative interpretation of the consequences of man's uses of intelligence and organization, the architect Roderick Seidenberg argues that "order demands order" and organization "demands further organization."

5. Paul H. Giddens, *Standard Oil Company* (Indiana): *Oil Pioneer of the Middle West* (New York, Appleton-Century-Crofts, 1955), p. 711.

6. "New Horizons in Foreign Oil," *The Lamp*, Standard Oil Company (New Jersey), Summer 1956, p. 5.

CHAPTER 2: *A Portrait in Oil* (Pages 11–33)

Most of the material of this chapter comes from extensive interviewing by the writer in North Dakota and from the local press and state and

499

corporate documents. Individual interviews by the writer generally will not be footnoted in the book.

1. *Congressional Record*, 83rd Congress, 2nd Session, Aug. 16, 1954, pp. 14644–14645.

CHAPTER 3: *The Private Government of Oil* (Pages 34–64)

1. "Petroleum and Natural Gas," preprint from *Mineral Facts and Problems*, Bulletin 556, Bureau of Mines, United States Department of the Interior (Washington, United States Government Printing Office, 1955), pp. 12, 17.

2. *Naval Reactor Program and Shipping Project*, Hearings before Subcommittee of the Joint Committee on Atomic Energy, U.S. Congress, 85th Congress, 1st Session (Washington, 1957), pp. 2–6, 16, 22.

3. The figures in this section are based upon various government, corporation, and industry publications and the following Chase Manhattan Bank Petroleum Department reports: Frederick G. Coqueron, *Annual Financial Analysis of the Petroleum Industry 1956* (New York, 1957); Joseph E. Pogue and Kenneth E. Hill, *Future Growth and Financial Requirements of the World Petroleum Industry* (New York, 1957); Frederick G. Coqueron and Joseph E. Pogue, *Investment Patterns in the World Petroleum Industry* (New York, 1956); Frederick G. Coqueron, *Annual Analysis of the Petroleum Industry 1959* (New York, 1960).

See also *The Oil Producing Industry in Your State, 1958*, Independent Petroleum Association of America (Tulsa), a helpful source for state production information; *Facts About Oil*, American Petroleum Institute (New York, 1954, 1957); *Business and Economic Conditions*, First National City Bank Monthly Letter (New York, April 1957); *The Exchange*, New York Stock Exchange (New York, November 1954).

4. These figures are compiled from the annual reports to stockholders of the various companies discussed. The Texas Company quotation is from its *Report for the Six Months Ending June 30, 1955* (New York, 1955). For an overview of corporate size, see "The Fortune Directory," annual listings of the 500 largest United States industrial corporations, *Fortune*, July 1955–1960.

5. Jersey Standard annual reports and also reports of annual stockholder meetings. The quotation is from *The Lamp*, Standard Oil Company (New Jersey), 75th Anniversary Issue, 1957, p. 69.

6. *New York Times*, Dec. 17, 1956; also *News Summary No. 50*, U.S. Federal Trade Commission (Washington, Dec. 19, 1956).

7. Mimeographed report prepared by Donald P. McHugh, co-counsel, Subcommittee on Antitrust and Monopoly, Committee on the Judiciary, U.S. Senate, 85th Congress, 1st Session, for its hearings on *Emergency Oil Lift Program and Related Oil Problems* (Washington, 1957), p. 33.

8. See *Oil and Gas Journal,* March 25 and April 8, 1957.

9. *Emergency Oil Lift Program and Related Oil Problems,* Joint Hearings before Subcommittees of the Committee on the Judiciary and Committee on Interior and Insular Affairs, U.S. Senate, 85th Congress, 1st Session (Washington, 1957), Part 1, p. 458, testimony of M. H. Robineau. Hereafter this shall be cited as Senate *Emergency Oil Lift* hearings.

10. Senate *Emergency Oil Lift* hearings, Part 1, p. 792.

11. *Ibid.,* Part 1, pp. 790, 828–829 and Part 2, pp. 1085–1086.

12. *Ibid.,* Part 1, pp. 791 and 799.

13. *Ibid.,* Part 2, pp. 1383, 1385, 1389–1390, testimony of Reid Brazell, president of Leonard Refineries.

14. *Ibid.,* Part 1, p. 285 ff., testimony of Rear Admiral O. P. Lattu; also, *New York Times,* Aug. 9, 1957.

15. *Gasoline Price War in New Jersey,* Hearings before a Subcommittee of the Select Committee on Small Business, U.S. Senate, 84th Congress (Washington, 1956), Part 3, p. 403. Document in testimony of Herbert Willetts, vice president, Socony Mobil Oil Co.

16. *A Statement of Service Station Dealer Policy,* Esso Standard Oil Co., 1956.

17. *Distribution Problems,* Hearings before Subcommittee No. 5 of the Select Committee on Small Business, U.S. House of Representatives, 84th Congress, 1st Session (Washington, 1955), p. 801, testimony of Leland F. Johnson.

18. *WOC's and Government Advisory Group,* Hearings before Antitrust Subcommittee of the Committee on the Judiciary, U.S. House of Representatives, 84th Congress, 1st Session (Washington, 1955), Part III, p. 2225.

19. Walter S. Hallanan, president, Plymouth Oil Company and chairman, National Petroleum Council, in Leonard M. Fanning, editor, *Our Oil Resources* (New York, McGraw-Hill, 1950), p. 3. This is a useful volume for industry positions on national oil policy.

20. *The Sohioan,* Standard Oil Company of Ohio, February 1958, p. 3.

21. *An Introduction to Standard Oil Company (New Jersey),* Standard Oil Company (New Jersey), 1954, p. 20.

22. *The Sohioan, op. cit.,* p. 4.

23. *Stockholder Reports*, Standard Oil Company (New Jersey), 1942, 1943 (the Gerard statement is on p. 21), 1952, 1957.

24. Reese H. Taylor, "Wanted: Integrated Oil Men," speech before the American Petroleum Institute, San Francisco, Nov. 15, 1955.

25. *The Coordination of Motive, Men and Money in Industrial Research*, a survey of organization and business practices conducted by the Department on Organization of the Standard Oil Company of California, 1946.

26. Robert E. Wilson "Incentives for Research," speech before the Engineers' Club of St. Louis, Mo., April 18, 1946.

27. "Research and Development Costs in American Industry, 1956, *Reviews of Data on Research and Development*, National Science Foundation (Washington, May 1958).

28. E. D. Reeves, "Management of Industrial Research," speech before Fourth Annual Conference on Industrial Research, Arden House, Harriman, New York, reprinted by Standard Oil Development Company, June 1953.

29. *Automation and Technological Change*, Hearings before the Subcommittee on Economic Stabilization of the Joint Committee on the Economic Report, U.S. Congress, 84th Congress, 1st Session (Washington, 1955), p. 613; see also pp. 34 and 489.

30. *Synthetic Liquid Fuels*, Hearings before a Subcommittee of the Committee on Public Lands and Surveys, U.S. Senate, 78th Congress, 1st Session (Washington, 1943), p. 90.

31. *United States v. Atlantic Refining Co., Et Al.*, Civil Action No. 14060, District of Columbia, December 1941. See also *Consent Decree Program of the Department of Justice*, Report of the Antitrust Subcommittee of the Committee on the Judiciary, U.S. House of Representatives, 86th Congress, 1st Session (Washington, 1959), pp. 121ff.

32. *Concentration in American Industry*, Report of the Subcommittee on Antitrust and Monopoly to the Committee on the Judiciary, U.S. Senate, 85th Congress, 1st Session (Washington, 1957), for interesting breakdowns in petroleum and other industries.

33. *Ethyl Gasoline Corporation of America v. United States*, 309 U.S. 436 (1940); see also, *United States v. American Petroleum Institute*, Civil Action No. 8524, District of Columbia, 1940. See, for example, *Rubber*, Part 11 of *Investigation of the National Defense Program*, Hearings before a Special Committee Investigating the National Defense Program, U.S. Senate, 77th Congress, 1st Session (Washington, 1942), *passim*.

A separate volume could be written on the tangled history of the

Universal Oil Products Company which has been a research center and licensing agency for basic petroleum refining processes. After many years of cracking patent litigation, this company came under the control of Standard of California, Standard (Indiana), Standard (New Jersey), Texas, and Shell under what became known as the "Peace of 1931." With certain patents running out and the possibility of antitrust difficulties imminent, the decision was made in 1944 to turn over the stock of the oil-company owners to the American Chemical Society. Profits were to be used for petroleum research, and the Guaranty Trust Company of New York was to act as trustee responsible for the management. The Society's Petroleum Research Fund received very little money for the first ten years, but Universal's research facilities became increasingly important to refiners. In 1956 a financial recommendation was made to dispose of the stock. This made independent refiners fearful that Universal would fall into the hands of a giant oil or chemical company that would then cut them off from the fruits of expensive techniques and research. By court agreement, the Guaranty Trust Company promised a public sale of the stock, with ownership to be dispersed and the program for refiners continued.

34. *The Service Station Operator*, E. I. duPont de Nemours and Co. (Wilmington, 1955 and 1956), 2nd Report, pp. 8–9; 5th Report, p. 11.

35. These quotations on the New Jersey price war are from *Gasoline Price War in New Jersey, op. cit.*, in the order in which they are used, Part 3 (1956), p. 234; Part 1 (1955), pp. 34, 49, 39; Part 2 (1955), pp. 122–123, 129–130, 125, 79.

36. *A Statement of Service Station Dealer Policy, op. cit.*; also *Business Week*, May 25, 1957.

37. *Gasoline Price War in New Jersey, op. cit.*, Part 1, p. 48.

38. *API Directory 1955*, American Petroleum Institute (New York).

39. H. A. Inness Brown, "Pump Island Calling Supplier" in *American Petroleum Institute Quarterly*, Summer 1957, pp. 20–23.

40. *Second Report to the President of the United States*, National Recovery Review Board (Washington, 1934), mimeographed, p. 51.

41. *United States v. American Petroleum Institute, Et Al., op. cit.*, mimeographed, pp. 29ff., 43.

42. Donald M. Nelson, *Arsenal of Democracy: The Story of American War Production* (New York, Harcourt, Brace, 1946), p. 99.

43. *United States v. Standard Oil Company of California, Et Al.*, Civil Action No. 11584–C (U.S. District Court for Southern District of California), May 1950. Also, Final Judgment, June 19, 1959. In 1961 the Department of Justice dropped its complaint against Texaco, the

seventh defendant (*New York Times*, March 9, 1961). *United States v. Standard Oil Company (New Jersey), Esso Standard Oil Company* and *Standard Oil Company (Kentucky)*, Civil Action No. 3722 (U.S. District Court for the Western District of Kentucky), Dec. 2, 1958.

44. H. S. M. Burns, "Industrial Fission," a paper presented at general session of 35th annual meeting of API, San Francisco, California, November 17, 1955.

45. Notes of conversations of W. O. Inglis with Rockefeller, quoted in Allan Nevins' *John D. Rockefeller: The Heroic Age of American Enterprise* (New York, Charles Scribner's Sons, 1940), I, 622.

CHAPTER 4: *Toward World Government* (Pages 65–79)

1. See, for example: *Peaceful Uses of Atomic Energy*, Report of the Panel on the Impact of the Peaceful Uses of Atomic Energy, Joint Committee on Atomic Energy, U.S. Congress, 84th Congress, 2d Session (Washington, 1956), Vol. 2, estimates of Wallace E. Pratt, pp. 89ff.; *Petroleum Survey*, Preliminary Report of the Committee on Interstate and Foreign Commerce, U.S. House of Representatives, 85th Congress, 1st Session (Washington, 1957), pp. 9–12; Eugene Ayres and Charles A. Scarlott, *Energy Sources—The Wealth of the World* (New York, McGraw Hill, 1952); Harrison Brown, James Bonner, and John Weir, *The Next Hundred Years* (New York, Viking, 1957), pp. 95–102 and *passim; Oil and Gas Journal*, Dec. 31, 1956, pp. 105–106; July 29, 1957, pp. 167–168; Dec. 29, 1958; Dec. 28, 1959; Coqueron and Pogue, *Investment Patterns in the World Petroleum Industry* (New York, 1956), pp. 49–55; Pogue and Hill, *Future Growth . . . of the World Petroleum Industry* (New York, 1957), *passim*.

2. For an account of the conversion from coal to oil, the role of Lord Fisher as the chief advocate, and of Churchill as First Lord of the Admiralty, see Winston Churchill, *The World Crisis* (New York, Scribner's, 1931), especially Book I.

3. *Economic Development in the Middle East 1954–1955*, Supplement to World Economic Survey, 1955, United Nations, Department of Economic and Social Affairs (New York, 1956), pp. 56–57. *Investment Patterns in the World Petroleum Industry, op. cit.*, pp. 21ff.

4. *The Price of Oil in Western Europe*, Economic Commission for Europe, United Nations Economic and Social Council (Geneva, 1955), p. 15; *Petroleum Arrangements with Saudi Arabia*, Part 41, Investigation of the National Defense Program, Hearings before a Special Committee

Investigating the National Defense Program, U.S. Senate, 80th Congress, 1st Session (Washington, 1948), pp. 24978–24981, 25008–25010, 25022; Senate *Emergency Oil Lift* hearings, Part 2, testimony of F. A. Davies, James Terry Duce, and Douglas Erskine of Arabian American Oil Company, pp. 1391ff.

5. *The International Petroleum Cartel*, Staff Report to the Federal Trade Commission, released through Subcommittee on Monopoly of Select Committee on Small Business, U.S. Senate, 83d Congress, 2d Session (Washington, 1952), pp. 47–112.

For text of "red line" agreement, see *Current Antitrust Problems*, Hearings before Antitrust Subcommittee (Subcommittee No. 5) of the Committee on the Judiciary, U.S. House of Representatives, 84th Congress, 1st Session (Washington, 1955), Part 2, pp. 1004–1054. See also *United States of America v. Standard Oil Company (New Jersey), Et Al.*, Civil Action No. 86–27, District of Columbia, April 1953.

6. Senate *Emergency Oil Lift* hearings, Part 2, p. 1535. Many affiliates of the giants are "paper" companies, maintained for legal or fiscal reasons.

7. *The International Petroleum Cartel, op. cit.*, p. 200; see also pp. 197–274.

8. *Ibid.*, pp. 101, 104.

9. *United States of America v. Standard Oil Company (New Jersey), Et Al., op. cit.*

10. Amended Answer of Defendant The Texas Company, *United States of America v. Standard Oil Company (New Jersey), Et Al.*, Civil Action No. 86–27, pp. 2, 14.

11. Answer of Defendant Socony-Vacuum Oil Co., reprinted in *Current Antitrust Problems, op. cit.*, Part 2, pp. 839–902.

12. Answer of Defendant Gulf Oil Corporation, *United States of America v. Standard Oil Company (New Jersey), Et Al.*, Civil Action No. 86–27.

13. *The International Petroleum Cartel, op. cit.*, p. 307.

14. *Current Antitrust Problems, op. cit.*, Part 2, pp. 822–823, 826.

15. "What Price Oil," *The Economist*, Feb. 26, 1955, pp. 739–740.

16. A. A. Berle, Jr., *The 20th Century Capitalist Revolution* (New York, Harcourt, Brace, 1954), p. 157.

CHAPTER 5: *Private Planning and Public Resources* (Pages 80–131)

1. L. F. McCollum, address at annual meeting of American Petroleum Institute, Nov. 11, 1948.

2. *Oil and Gas Leases*, Report of a Subcommittee of the Committee on Interior and Insular Affairs, U.S. Senate, 84th Congress, 2d Session (Washington, 1957), p. 7. See also the hearings of this subcommittee held in 1956, *Investigation of Observance or Nonobservance of Acreage Limitations of the Mineral Leasing Act*.

There have been many public hearings and documents relating to each of the resources discussed in this chapter. To keep these notes from becoming overwhelming, generally there will be cited only those documents from which quotations or unusually pertinent data not otherwise available have been taken.

3. *Wildlife Refuge Disposal Policy*, Hearings before the Committee on Merchant Marine and Fisheries, U.S. House of Representatives, 84th Congress, 2d Session (Washington, 1956). See also, *Preservation of National Wildlife Refuges*, a report by this committee, 1956.

4. *National Petroleum News*, Dec. 29, 1920. See also Josephus Daniels, *The Wilson Era* (Chapel Hill, University of North Carolina, 1946), pp. 246–248.

5. Editorial, *Oil and Gas Journal*, May 14, 1956. *A National Oil Policy for the United States*, a report of the National Petroleum Council (Washington, 1949), pp. 20–21.

6. *Naval Petroleum Reserves*, Hearings before the Committee on Armed Services, U.S. House of Representatives, 83d Congress, 1st Session (Washington, 1953), p. 255.

7. *Congressional Record*, 67th Congress, 2d Session, Vol. 62, April 28, 1922, quoted in Belle Case La Follette and Fola La Follette, *Robert M. La Follette* (New York, Macmillan, 1953), II, 1049.

8. For a beautiful picture of the continental shelf, see Rachel L. Carson, *The Sea Around Us* (New York, Oxford, 1950).

9. *The Secret Diary of Harold L. Ickes*, three volumes (New York, Simon & Schuster, 1953, 1954), May 2, 1937. Hereafter this will be cited as *Ickes Diary*.

10. *Congressional Record*, 83d Congress, 1st Session, April 2, 1953, pp. A1905–1906.

11. For the texts of the court opinions, see *Submerged Lands Act*, Report of the Committee on Interior and Insular Affairs, U.S. Senate, 83d Congress, 1st Session (Washington, 1953). The quotation appears on p. 37. This is a useful brief summary volume offering the arguments for state control and a number of key documents. *Minority Views*, printed separately as Part 2, is a concise statement of the case for federal control.

12. *Ibid.*, p. 46.

13. Senator Wayne L. Morse in *Congressional Record*, 83d Congress, 1st Session, April 25, 1953, p. 3973.

14. Address by Hall Hammond, Attorney General of Maryland and chairman of Submerged Lands Committee of the National Association of Attorneys General, before American Association of Port Authorities, New York, October 26, 1951.

15. *New Orleans Item*, Nov. 12, 1949.

16. *New York Times*, May 24, 1953.

17. *Ibid.*, April 20, 1953.

18. *Submerged Lands Act, op. cit.*, p. 8.

19. *State of Arkansas v. Douglas McKay, Secretary of the Interior, Et Al.*, Civil Action No. 3109–53, District of Columbia, 1953.

20. *New York Times*, March 16, 1954; Dec. 7, 10 and 28, 1957; June 1, 1960.

21. *Oil and Gas Journal*, Oct. 11, 1954.

22. *Annual Report 1954*, Tide Water Associated Oil Company, p. 5.

23. *Petroleum World and Oil*, May 26, 1955, p. 30. See also, *Bulletin*, Standard Oil Company of California, July 1957.

24. *Policy Declaration on Natural Resources 1954*, Chamber of Commerce of the United States, Washington, p. 20.

25. *Petroleum World and Oil*, May 23, 1957; *Oil and Gas Journal*, Feb. 17, 1958; *1958 Annual Report, Union Oil Company of California*, pp. 11–12.

26. The Millikan testimony is in *Interior Department and Related Agencies Appropriations for 1956*, Hearings before a Subcommittee of the Committee on Appropriations, U.S. Senate, 84th Congress, 1st Session (Washington, 1955), p. 506.

27. The Shivers statement is in *Accessibility of Strategic and Critical Materials to the United States in Time of War and for Our Expanding Economy*, Report of the Minerals, Materials and Fuels Economic Subcommittee of the Committee on Interior and Insular Affairs, 83d Congress, 2d Session (Washington, 1954), p. 380.

28. *Secretary of the Interior-Designate Douglas McKay*, Hearings before the Committee on Interior and Insular Affairs, U.S. Senate, 83d Congress, 1st Session (Washington, 1953), p. 9.

29. *Survey Report, Bureau of Mines*, U.S. Department of the Interior, May 20, 1954, p. 23.

30. *Report of the National Petroleum Council's Committee on Shale Oil Policy*, National Petroleum Council (Washington, Jan. 25, 1955).

31. For statements of Bureau of Mines findings, see *Synthetic Liquid Fuels*, Annual Report of the Secretary of the Interior, for 1955, Part 2,

"Oil From Oil Shale" (Washington, 1956); also, earlier annual reports, as required under the Synthetic Liquid Fuels Act of 1944.

It is generally believed that crude petroleum can be produced from the abundant tar sands found in Alberta, Canada, and in Utah. Once the industry decides this supply will not upset the balance, it can be expected to be utilized. For Americans who think their country is the only one susceptible to the controls of the private timetable of oil, a study of Canadian tar sands is enlightening. This pattern was suggested to the writer by R. C. Fitzsimmons of Edmonton, Alberta, who had bitter firsthand experience in trying to develop tar sands. See R. C. Fitzsimmons, *The Truth About Alberta Tar Sands* (Edmonton, 1953).

32. Carl Bosch, president of I. G. Farben, quoted in testimony of Heinrich Kronstein, U.S. Department of Justice, *Patents*, Hearings before the Committee on Patents, United States Senate, 77th Congress, 2d Session (Washington, 1942), Part 3, p. 1319.

33. Badische, Anilin und Soda-Fabrik, a major unit of I. G. Farben, which produced nitrogen and nitrate of soda. Quoted in Wendell Berge, *Cartels, Challenge to a Free World* (Washington, Public Affairs Press, 1946), pp. 210–211.

34. *Investigation of the National Defense Program*, Hearings before a Special Committee Investigating the National Defense Program, U.S. Senate, 77th Congress, 1st Session (Washington, 1942), Part 11, *Rubber*, pp. 4590–4591; also p. 4312. See this volume for the key documents of these agreements.

35. *Elimination of German Resources for War*, Hearings before a Subcommittee of the Committee on Military Affairs, U.S. Senate, 79th Congress, 2d Session (Washington, 1946), Part 10, *I. G. Farben Exhibits*, p. 1299. These hearings are extremely valuable for understanding these corporate operations and their relationship to the Nazi state.

36. *Ibid.*, Part 7, *I. G. Farben Material Submitted by the War Department*, December 1945, pp. 989–990.

37. *Utilization of Farm Crops*, Hearings before a Subcommittee of the Committee on Agriculture and Forestry, U.S. Senate, 77th Congress, 2d Session (Washington, 1942), Part 4, *Industrial Alcohol and Synthetic Rubber*, pp. 1198–1199; also, in Part 3, p. 1068.

38. *Investigation of the National Defense Program, op. cit.*, Part 11, pp. 4360, 4361, 4363; also 4342–4344, 4824–4826, 4819–4823, 4888–4904.

39. *Ibid.*, pp. 4499–4516. Quotation is on p. 4500.

40. *Ibid.*, pp. 4768, 4830ff.

41. *Elimination of German Resources for War, op. cit.*, Part 10, pp. 1305–1306.

42. Letter of Clarence A. Davis, Under Secretary of the Interior, *Harper's*, August 1956.

43. See, for example, *Synthetic Liquid Fuels*, Annual Report of the Secretary of the Interior for 1955 (Washington, 1956), Part 1, *Oil from Coal*; also earlier annual reports. See also *Synthetic Liquid Fuels*, Hearings before a Subcommittee of the Committee on Public Lands and Surveys, U.S. Senate, 78th Congress, 1st Session (Washington, 1943). A rich source of data on coal, shale, etc. For a write-up on Karrick, his process, and his difficulties with the industry and the government, see *The Christian Science Monitor*, March 20, 1950.

In the summer of 1957, Standard of California began to sell in the Rocky Mountain area a gasoline made from uintaite, a solid hydrocarbon ore found in Utah and Colorado and known commercially as Gilsonite. The refinery, owned by Barber Oil and California Standard, is described as the nation's first venture in producing for the market gasoline from a raw material other than crude oil. See *Wall Street Journal*, Aug. 2, 1957, and *Business Week*, Aug. 10, 1957.

44. *Investigation of the National Defense Program, op. cit.*, Part 11, pp. 4600–4601; also, 4313–4314, 4597–4598. The "full marriage" expression, used by a top official, appears on p. 4582.

45. *Ibid.*, pp. 4599–4600; also pp. 4314 and 4629.

46. *The Annual Meeting—A Stenographic Report*, Standard Oil Company (New Jersey), June 2, 1942 (New York, June 10, 1942), pp. 17–18. The minutes of Jersey's stockholder meetings during this period make fascinating reading.

47. *Investigation of the National Defense Program, op. cit.*, Part 11, pp. 4583–4584.

48. *Ibid.*, pp. 4311, 4340–4341, 4584–4587, 4719, 4810–4811; also, *Patents, op. cit.*, Part 7, pp. 3410, 4135–4136. For Howard's version of this entire affair, see Frank A. Howard, *Buna Rubber* (New York, D. Van Nostrand, 1947).

49. Donald M. Nelson, *Arsenal of Democracy, op. cit.*, p. 139.

50. *Investigation of the National Defense Program, op. cit.*, Part 11, pp. 4603–4605; also, pp. 4608, 4315–4316, 4720, 4731–4733, 4812.

51. *Investigation of the National Defense Program*, Additional Report of the Special Committee Investigating the National Defense Program, U.S. Senate, 77th Congress, 2d Session (Washington, 1942), Report No. 480, Part 7, *Rubber*, p. 35.

On the patent pool, see *Investigation of the National Defense Program, op. cit.,* Part 11, p. 4720; also, *Utilization of Farm Crops, op. cit.,* Part 7 (78th Congress, 1st Session), pp. 2023ff, 2048ff; and in Part 8, pp. 2434ff.

52. *Investigation of the National Defense Program, op. cit.,* Part 11, pp. 4630–4631; also 4318, 4393. See note 33 of Chapter 3.

53. *Ibid.,* pp. 4560–4561.

54. *Utilization of Farm Crops, op. cit.,* Part 3, pp. 1059–1060 (Mr. Farish); p. 912 (Senator Gillette).

55. *Ibid.,* p. 1044.

56. See, for example, *Congressional Record,* March 28, 1957, pp. 4058–4060.

57. *Program for Disposal to Private Industry of Government-Owned Rubber-Producing Facilities,* Reconstruction Finance Corporation (Washington, 1953), pp. 3–4.

58. *New York Times,* April 15, 1953.

59. *Adverse Report on Disapproval of Proposed Sale of Government-Owned Rubber-Producing Facilities,* with Minority Views; Report No. 117, Committee on Banking and Currency, U.S. Senate, 84th Congress, 1st Session (Washington, 1955).

For a separate report on the Shell purchases, see Report No. 118. See also, *Disposal of Rubber Plants,* Hearings before the Committee on Banking and Currency, U.S. Senate, 83d Congress, 1st Session (Washington, 1953); *Investigation of the Preparedness Program,* First Report of the Preparedness Subcommittee of the Committee on Armed Services, U.S. Senate, 81st Congress, 2d Session (Washington, 1950), Document No. 230.

60. *Resources for Freedom, op. cit.,* Vol. 3, *The Outlook for Energy Sources,* p. 16.

61. For a summary account, see *Investigation of Concentration of Economic Power,* Temporary National Economic Committee, U.S. Senate, 76th Congress, 3d Session (Washington, 1940), Monograph No. 36, *Reports of the Federal Trade Commission on Natural Gas and Natural Gas Pipe Lines in U.S.A.,* pp. 3–222.

There have been experiments with shipping natural gas in liquified form by tanker from the U.S. to Great Britain. See *Business Week,* March 22, 1958; *The Economist,* Feb. 21, 1959.

62. When defending higher gas rates, Phillips says that, owing to the greater quantities of gas found in the deeper drilling that characterizes current operations, in effect producers are now searching primarily for gas, rather than regarding gas as incidental in the search for oil. *Opening*

Statement by H. K. Hudson, attorney for Phillips, before Federal Power Commission in Docket No. G-1148, Feb. 10, 1957, mimeographed. See, for example, pp. 4, 18. See also Lyon F. Terry and John G. Winger, *Future Growth of the Natural Gas Industry* (New York, Chase Manhattan Bank, 1957).

63. For Olds's explanation as to the evolution of his thinking, see *Natural Gas Act Amendments*, Hearings before Subcommittee of the Committee on Interstate and Foreign Commerce, U.S. House of Representatives, 81st Congress, 1st Session (Washington, 1949), pp. 195–279. There are a number of important documents for understanding this issue in this volume. See also, Leland Olds, *Regulation of Field Prices of Natural Gas in the Public Interest* (Washington, Energy Research Associates, 1955), mimeographed.

64. *Interstate Natural Gas Co. v. Federal Power Commission*, 331 U.S. 682. *Phillips Petroleum Co. v. State of Wisconsin, City of Detroit*, etc., 347 U.S. 672. See also James R. Durfee, "Wisconsin and the Phillips Case" in *Public Utilities Fortnightly*, Jan. 20, 1955, p. 75; *Amendments to the Natural Gas Act*, Hearings before the Committee on Interstate and Foreign Commerce, U.S. Senate, 84th Congress, 1st Session (Washington, 1955). Durfee's testimony begins on p. 459. The entire volume offers a good picture of the range of interests and arguments involved in the regulation of natural gas producers.

65. *Amendments to the Natural Gas Act*, Hearings before the Committee on Interstate and Foreign Commerce, U.S. House of Representatives, 80th Congress, 1st Session (Washington, 1947), pp. 145, 156; also, p. 153.

The leading industry expert in recent hearings has been John W. Boatwright of Standard Oil (Indiana). See, for example, *Natural Gas Act*, Hearings before the Committee on Interstate and Foreign Commerce, U.S. House of Representatives, 84th Congress, 1st Session (Washington, 1955), pp. 299ff.

66. Testimony of Senator Fulbright in *Amendments to the Natural Gas Act*, Senate hearings, 1955, *op. cit.*, pp. 10–51.

67. *Congressional Record*, 84th Congress, 2d Session, Jan. 20, 1956, p. 853; Jan. 23, 1956, pp. 882–917; and Jan. 24, 1956, pp. 966–1022. Also, reprint of article by Douglas in *Congressional Record*, Jan. 12, 1956, pp. A252–A255.

68. *Natural Gas Act*, House hearings, 1955, *op. cit.*, pp. 24, 26.

The right of states to put a floor under these prices was denied by a Supreme Court order in 1958, reaffirming earlier rulings (*New York Times*, Jan. 21, 1958).

69. *Natural Gas, A Brief Review,* Natural Gas and Oil Resources Committee, New York, p. 11.

70. *Resources for Freedom, op. cit.,* Vol. 3, p. 21.

71. *Direct Sales by Producers of Natural Gas to Reporting Interstate Natural Gas Pipeline Companies—1955,* Federal Power Commission. Also, *Congressional Record,* Feb. 3, 1956, p. 1677; Feb. 6, 1956, pp. 1831–1835.

72. For Senator Case's speech, see *Congressional Record,* Feb. 3, 1956, pp. 1691–1694. Mr. Porter's remarks were in the American Petroleum Institute *Quarterly,* Spring 1956, p. 5.

73. *Congressional Record,* 85th Congress, 1st Session, Jan. 16, 1957, p. 556.

74. *New York Times,* April 18, 1957.

75. *Ibid.,* March 31, 1957.

76. *Wall Street Journal,* June 10, 1957; *New York Times,* June 20, 1957.

77. *New York Times,* Dec. 9, 1958.

78. *The Independent Petroleum Company,* Hearings before a Special Committee Investigating Petroleum Resources, U.S. Senate, 79th Congress, 2d Session (Washington, 1946), p. 423.

79. *Amendments to the Natural Gas Act,* House hearings, 1947, *op. cit.,* p. 59 and *Amendments to the Natural Gas Act,* Senate hearings, 1955, *op. cit.,* p. 52.

80. *Our Sun,* Spring 1956, p. 9; *Texaco Topics,* Dec. 1954; *Philnews* (Phillips Oil), January 1955. Gov. Shivers, "What Conservation Means to the Nation's Security Under State Administration," *Interstate Oil Compact Quarterly Bulletin,* Vol. XIII, Nos. 3 and 4, December 1954, p. 8. Walter S. Hallanan in *Oil and Gas Journal,* Jan. 31, 1955, p. 114.

81. *Amendments to the Natural Gas Act,* House hearings, 1947, *op. cit.,* p. 154.

82. Leland Olds, *Natural Gas Act Amendments,* House hearings, 1949, *op. cit.,* p. 222.

CHAPTER 6: *The Uses of Public Government* (Pages 132–150)

1. Ida M. Tarbell, *The History of the Standard Oil Company* (New York, McClure, Phillips, 1904), Vol. One, p. 115.

2. *Petroleum: The Story of an American Industry,* American Petroleum Institute, 1949, p. 100.

3. *Investigation of Concentration of Economic Power*, Hearings before the Temporary National Economic Committee, Congress of the United States, 76th Congress, 2nd Session (Washington, 1940), Part 17, *Petroleum Industry*, pp. 9784–9785, 9952.

4. Speech before the annual meeting of the Independent Petroleum Association of America, Dallas, Oct. 29, 1957.

5. William L. Horner, *A Survey of Unitized Oil Field Conservation Projects as of December 31, 1956*, 1957, a report filed with Engineering Committee of the Interstate Oil Compact Commission.

6. *Petroleum Code Hearing*, Transcript of Proceedings, National Industrial Recovery Administration, July 24 to Aug. 3, 1933, Release No. 96, Section 301, pp. 3001, 3003; Section 302, p. 3033; Section 305, p. 3062; Section 702, p. 7021.

7. *Ibid.*, Section 302, p. 3019, statement by Jack Blalock of Texas, leader of the Independent Petroleum Association Opposed to Monopoly.

8. *Ickes Diary*, Sept. 21, 1933.

9. California, the major source of supply for the Pacific Coast area, is the leading nonmember among oil states. Over 90 per cent of the region's energy is derived from oil and gas. California has had a prorationing system based upon voluntary agreements among the integrated oil companies—Standard of California, Shell, Texaco, Tidewater, Union, General (a Socony Mobil subsidiary) and Richfield—who have dominated the region through direct control of about half of California's crude production and over 90 per cent of the refining. The Conservation Committee of California Oil Producers, rooted in a voluntary statistics-gathering association formed in 1930, has been charged in federal antitrust suits with curtailing the production and stabilizing the prices of majors and independent producers through an elaborate quota system reaching every well under the guise of conservation. Until very recently this organization had no legal status, but the threat inherent in the suit forced the companies to receive approval from the state legislature. Markets and competition have been controlled as if the large companies "were a single concern with a single management." (*United States v. Standard Oil Company of California, Et Al., op. cit.*) Attempts to push "conservation" laws that would put state power behind unitization efforts have provoked bitter political controversies over the years. Many independent producers charge that where conservation once had been a rationalization for dealing with oversupply, today, when production is less than consumer needs, the objective is a market demand system backed by the state and dominated by the integrated companies which

would make room for the latter's imports. As further evidence some oilmen point to the blocking by the majors of a projected pipeline that would bring crude oil from West Texas fields to Los Angeles.

10. Speech before the annual meeting of the Independent Petroleum Association of America, Tulsa, Oct. 25, 1954.

11. *Ibid.*

12. Testimony of President W. K. Whiteford, Senate *Emergency Oil Lift* hearings, *op. cit.*, Part 2, p. 1260.

13. For a useful but uncritical account of the career of Thompson and his relation to Texas oil, see James A. Clark, *Three Stars for the Colonel* (New York, Random House, 1954).

14. Speech before Houston chapter, American Institute of Mining, Metallurgical, and Petroleum Engineers, Jan. 15, 1957, reprinted in *Compact Comments*, Interstate Oil Compact Commission, February 1957. Also, *Oil and Gas Journal*, Jan. 21, 1957, p. 74.

15. Senate *Emergency Oil Lift* hearings, *op. cit.*, Part 1, p. 764. 75th *Annual Meeting*, Report of Standard Oil Company (New Jersey), May 22, 1957, p. 31.

16. *Petroleum Survey*, Hearings before the Committee on Interstate and Foreign Commerce, U.S. House of Representatives, 85th Congress, 1st Session (Washington, 1957), p. 219.

17. *Development of Mineral Resources of the Public Lands of the United States*, Hearings before a Subcommittee of the Committee on Public Lands and Surveys, U.S. Senate, 77th Congress, 2nd Session (Washington, 1942), Part 3, p. 1123.

18. *Compact Comments, op. cit.*

19. *Oil for Today and Tomorrow*, Interstate Oil Compact Commission, Oklahoma City, 1953, p. 67.

20. Eugene V. Rostow, *A National Policy for the Oil Industry* (New Haven, Yale, 1948), p. 27. This is a very useful study and one of the few books on oil policy not subsidized by the industry.

21. Frank M. Porter, president, American Petroleum Institute, in Harold Fleming, *Oil Prices and Competition*, American Petroleum Institute, 1953, p. iii.

22. *Departments of State, Justice, The Judiciary, and Related Agencies Appropriations, 1957*, Hearings before the Subcommittee of the Committee on Appropriations, U.S. Senate, 84th Congress, 2nd Session (Washington, 1956), pp. 71–72.

23. *Report of the Attorney General*, pursuant to Section 2 of the Joint Resolution of July 28, 1955, consenting to an Interstate Compact to Conserve Oil and Gas, Washington, 1956.

24. *Second Report of the Attorney General,* 1957, pp. 18–19, 26, 30, 46, 49.

25. *Oil Supply and Distribution Problems,* A Final Report of the Special Committee to Study Problems of American Small Business, U.S. Senate, Report No. 25, 81st Congress, 1st Session (Washington, 1949), p. 13.

"There is a mechanism controlling the production of crude oil to market demand (or below) that operates as smoothly and effectively as the finest watch. During the year and a half the committee has been investigating the oil industry, there has never been a real over-all shortage of petroleum. Price increases on crude oil have been frequent and substantial, going from $1.25 per barrel at the end of 1945 to $2.65 per barrel in the spring of 1947, with several companies posting $3 per barrel as this report is written. At the time the consumers were feeling the greatest pinch in January and February 1947, there were 220 million barrels of crude oil in storage, mainly controlled by the larger units, which could have been distributed among independent refiners who were running under capacity. But the controlled economy existing in the oil industry needs an absolute balance of supply and demand, because it does not contemplate drawing on stocks. When the Bureau of Mines, through their monthly forecasts of demand, underestimated the demand by close to 2 percent for each of the years 1946 and 1947, the spot shortages followed as night the day. The mechanism was wound too tight. Independent refiners could not take more oil out of their own wells because of State proration laws, and the integrated companies would not allow them to take their crude oil except by a processing or tied-in sales agreement. Those cut off of supply by independent refiners, or by integrated units desiring to favor one customer over another, were suffering, and in turn their consumer accounts were without oil. A truly competitive system, based only on real conservation practices, could not possibly have held the flow of oil so close to market demand."

CHAPTER 7: *The Privilege of Power* (Pages 151–181)

1. *Congressional Record,* 82nd Congress, 1st Session, Sept. 20, 1951, pp. 11725–11726.

2. *Congressional Record,* 85th Congress, 1st Session, March 27, 1957, pp. 3987–3988.

3. Speech before Independent Petroleum Association of America, Denver, May 4, 1954.

4. *American Petroleum Institute Quarterly,* Winter 1952–1953.

5. Arthur A. Smith in *Federal Tax Policy for Economic Growth and Stability,* U.S. Congress, Joint Committee on the Economic Report (Washington, 1955), p. 488.

6. *Congressional Record,* 82nd Congress, 1st Session, Sept. 20, 1951, p. 11724; 85th Congress, 1st Session, March 27, 1957, p. 3978. Also, *Federal Tax Policy for Economic Growth and Stability, op. cit.,* pp. 888ff.

7. W. Earl Turner, *Statutory Percentage Depletion,* Texas Independent Producers and Royalty Owners Association, Austin, 1955, p. 45.

8. *Revenue Revision of 1950,* Hearings before the Committee on Ways and Means, U.S. House of Representatives, 81st Congress, 2nd Session (Washington, 1950), I, 189.

9. *Congressional Record,* 82nd Congress, 1st Session, Sept. 20, 1951, p. 11730. Also, *Resources for Freedom,* report of the President's Materials Policy Commission (Washington, 1952), V, 12–15.

10. Richard Austin Smith, "The Fifty-Million-Dollar Man," *Fortune,* November 1957. Getty explained that if he sold his holdings, he would hope to get several billion dollars. "But remember, a billion dollars isn't worth what it used to be" (*New York Times,* Oct. 28, 1957).

11. Reprinted in *Revenue Revision of 1950, op. cit.,* pp. 2–7.

12. *Nomination of Robert B. Anderson, Secretary of the Treasury— Designate,* Hearing before the Committee on Finance, U.S. Senate, 85th Congress, 1st Session (Washington, 1957), pp. 12–14. Also, *Oil and Gas Journal,* March 25, 1957.

13. *New York Times,* May 23, 1957.

14. Letter from Dan Throop Smith, Deputy to the Secretary, to Harry F. Byrd, Chairman, Senate Committee on Finance, May 6, 1958.

15. *Congressional Record,* 85th Congress, 1st Session, March 27, 1957, p. 3975.

16. *Revenue Revision of 1950, op. cit.,* pp. 56 and 181. Also, *General Revenue Revision,* Hearings before the Committee on Ways and Means, U.S. House of Representatives (Washington, 1953), Part 3, pp. 1981ff.

17. The quotation is from *Certificates of Necessity and Government Plant Expansion Loans,* Fifth Intermediate Report of the Committee on Expenditures in the Executive Departments, U.S. House of Representatives, 82nd Congress, 1st Session (Washington, 1951), p. 1 and *passim.*

Figures cited are taken from *Certificates of Necessity,* releases of the Office of Defense Mobilization, Executive Office of the President (Washington, 1954–1957). Among the oil recipients a few weeks later was

The Texas Company, petroleum storage facilities, $1,190,500 and $82,000 certified, with 30 per cent and 25 per cent allowed, and refining facilities, $1,693,000, $5,433,500, $3,740,500, $550,000, and $4,359,000, with 65 to 100 per cent of these amounts allowed. Standard Oil Company (Indiana) received 65 per cent and 45 per cent for refining facilities certified at $4,385,000 and $911,000. Socony-Vacuum Oil Company was allowed 65 per cent for a natural gasoline plant certified at $1,744,-000.

Among the numerous other certificates issued since the end of the Korean War, to cite only a few, have been 65 per cent and 45 per cent of Sinclair Refining Company facilities certified at $8,200,000 and $4,100,000; Esso Standard Oil Company, refining facilities at Linden, New Jersey, certified at $11,671,000 and $3,243,600, with 55 per cent and 45 per cent allowed; Humble Oil and Refining Company, refining facilities at Baytown, Texas, certified at $28,000, $356,500, $770,500, and $3,393,500, with 50 to 65 per cent allowed; the Ethyl Corporation, research and development, $1,100,000 at 40 per cent; Gulf Oil Corporation, petroleum refining facilities at Port Arthur, $7,711,300 and $21,-333,500, at 45 per cent and 55 per cent; Southwestern Oil and Refining Company, petroleum refining facilities at Corpus Christi, $495,000 and $1,650,000, 45 per cent and 65 per cent allowed; the much advertised Tide Water Associated Oil Company crude oil refinery at Delaware City, Delaware, $42,670,000 and $57,400,000, 40 per cent and 65 per cent allowed; Southern Pacific Pipe Lines, petroleum pipelines, certified at $3,232,000 and $25,918,000, 40 per cent and 25 per cent allowed; Sun Oil Company, research and development facilities, $962,000, at 40 per cent; Pure Oil Company, petroleum refining, $897,300 and $4,535,000, at 45 per cent and 65 per cent; Cities Service Oil Company, refining facilities, $2,069,000, $4,500,000 and $2,345,000, at 45 per cent, 65 per cent and 100 per cent; Shell Oil Company, refining facilities, $10,550,000 and $3,450,000, at 65 per cent and 45 per cent. In a two-week period in 1956, certificates of necessity received by the Phillips Petroleum Company totaled approximately $49 million for oil-refining and alkylate facilities, with the percentage allowed ranging from 15 per cent on a $30,000 portion of a project to 100 per cent on a $14 million construction.

18. *Inquiry into the Policies, Procedure and Program Involving Granting of Certificates of Necessity and Defense Loans,* Hearings before a Subcommittee of the Committee on Expenditures in the Executive Departments, U.S. House of Representatives, 82nd Congress, 1st Session (Washington, 1951), pp. 30–32.

19. *Investigation of the National Defense Program,* Additional Report of the Special Committee Investigating the National Defense Program, 80th Congress, 2nd Session, Report No. 440, Part 2, *Renegotiation,* pp. 233–234.

20. Testimony of Russell B. Brown, *Development of Mineral Resources of the Public Lands of the United States,* Hearings before a Subcommittee of the Committee on Public Lands and Surveys, U.S. Senate, 77th Congress, 2nd Session (Washington, 1942), pp. 1387–1388.

21. *A Report of 5-Year Amortization of Emergency Defense Facilities Under Section 168 of the Internal Revenue Code of 1954,* staff report of the Joint Committee on Internal Revenue Taxation, U.S. Congress (Washington, 1956); also, *Rapid Amortization of Emergency Facilities,* Hearings before the Committee on Finance, U.S. Senate, 85th Congress, 1st Session (Washington, 1957).

22. *Certificates of Necessity and Government Plant Expansion Loans, op. cit.,* p. 2.

23. *Petroleum Survey,* Hearings, H.R., 85th Congress, 1st Session (Washington, 1957), p. 361.

24. *National Petroleum News,* July 21, 1954.

25. *Sources of Supply of Oil and Other Petroleum Products for the West Coast of the United States for Military and Other Requirements,* Hearings before the Subcommittee for Special Investigations of the Committee on Armed Services, U.S. House of Representatives, 84th Congress, 1st Session (Washington, 1955). See also Senate *Emergency Oil Lift* hearings, *op. cit.,* Part 2, pp. 1541ff., and Part 3, pp. 2000–2006.

26. Minutes of NPC meeting of September 29, 1953, reprinted in *WOC's and Government Advisory Groups,* Hearing before Antitrust Subcommittee of the Committee on the Judiciary, U.S. House of Representatives, 84th Congress, 2nd Session (Washington, 1956), Part IV, pp. 2639–2646.

27. *A Report of 5-Year Amortization of Emergency Defense Facilities, op. cit.,* p. 6.

28. *Report of the Attorney General of the United States,* Prepared Pursuant to Section 708(e) of the Defense Production Act of 1950, As Amended (Washington, 1956), pp. 2, 10–19. See also *Economic Concentration and World War II,* Report of the Smaller War Plants Corporation to the Special Committee to Study Problems of American Small Business, U.S. Senate, 79th Congress, 2nd Session (Washington, 1946), pp. 169–170.

29. *Ickes Diary,* Aug. 10, 1940.

30. *Ship Transfers to Foreign Flag*, Hearings before the Merchant Marine and Fisheries Subcommittee of the Committee on Interstate and Foreign Commerce, U.S. Senate, 85th Congress, 1st Session (Washington, 1957), *passim*.

31. *New York Times*, April 6, 1958.

32. "The Fifth Arm of the United States," March 17, 1958, mimeographed statement distributed by American Merchant Marine Institute.

33. *New York Herald Tribune*, March 29, 1958, and *New York Times*, March 29, 1958.

34. "Putting the Clock Back in Shipping," March 17, 1958, mimeographed statement distributed by American Merchant Marine Institute. See also "European Propaganda Against United States-Controlled Ships Under Liberian and Panamanian Flags," Jan. 28, 1958. Also, *New York Times*, April 3, 13, 1958.

35. *The President's Proposal on the Middle East*, Hearings before the Committee on Foreign Relations and the Committee on Armed Services, U.S. Senate, 85th Congress, 1st Session (Washington, 1957), Part III, p. 639.

36. *Oil, Key to Progress and Security*, American Petroleum Institute, 1951.

37. *Oil and Gas Journal*, Nov. 1, 1954.

CHAPTER 8: *The Blending of Public and Private Abroad*

(Pages 182–229)

1. *Newsletter* No. 6637, for issue of Dec. 21, 1953, quoted with permission of Time, Inc.

2. *The Lamp*, Standard Oil Company (New Jersey), Summer 1956, p. 4.

3. *New York Times*, March 7, 1957; Nov. 9, 1959; May 8, 1960. Also, *Wall Street Journal*, April 24, 1959; Oct. 18, 1960; and *Oil and Gas Journal*, May 18, 1959.

4. Senate *Emergency Oil Lift* hearings, *op. cit.*, Part 2, p. 1247.

5. "Joint Oil Producing Ventures in the Middle East—Their Status under United States Antitrust Laws," a statement by Standard Oil Co. (New Jersey) to the Attorney General's National Committee to Study the Antitrust Laws, reprinted in *Current Antitrust Problems*, Hearings before the Antitrust Subcommittee of the Committee on the Judiciary, U.S. House of Representatives, 84th Congress, 1st Session (Washington, 1955), Part II, p. 828.

6. Senate *Emergency Oil Lift* hearings, *op. cit.*, Part 4, pp. 2379–2382.

7. *A National Oil Policy for the United States*, a report of the National Petroleum Council, 1949, p. 16.

8. Augustus C. Long, before the New York Chamber of Commerce, *New York Times*, June 7, 1957.

9. "United States Foreign Petroleum Policy," State Department paper, Feb. 10, 1944, submitted for *Investigation of the National Defense Program*, Additional Report of the Special Committee Investigating the National Defense Program, U.S. Senate, 78th Congress, 2nd Session (Washington, 1944), Report No. 10, Part 15, *Report of Subcommittee Concerning Investigations Overseas*, p. 578.

10. *Ibid.*, p. 575.

11. *Ibid.*, p. 576.

12. *Ibid.*, p. 573.

13. Quoted in Howard F. Cline, *The United States and Mexico* (Cambridge, Harvard, 1953), p. 155.

14. Statement to press, June 12, 1925, reprinted in Ernest Gruening, *Mexico and Its Heritage* (New York, Century, 1928), p. 601.

15. *Nomination of Edwin W. Pauley for Appointment as Under Secretary of the Navy*, Committee on Naval Affairs, U.S. Senate, 79th Congress, 2nd Session (Washington, 1946), original transcript, Vol. 12, pp. 1974–1988.

16. *A National Oil Policy for the United States*, *op. cit.*, p. 18.

17. *Bulletin*, Standard Oil Company of California, October 1956. For comparable statements, see Augustus Long, chairman of the board of Texaco, "The Sanctity of Contracts," in *Texaco Star*, Winter 1956–1957; also, Howard W. Page, director, Jersey Standard, "What the Middle East Means to Us," in *The Lamp*, Winter 1956; also, F. A. Davies, chairman of board of Aramco, testifying at Senate *Emergency Oil Lift* hearings, *op. cit.*, Part 2, p. 1462.

18. *New York Times*, Oct. 28, 1955. The story from the United Nations begins: "The United States has begun a drive to scuttle a section of the proposed Covenant of Human Rights that poses a threat to its business interests abroad."

19. *New York Times*, Jan. 6, 1958, and *New York Post*, Aug. 14, 1957.

20. *Investigation of the National Defense Program*, *op. cit.*, 80th Congress, 2nd Session (Washington, 1948), Report No. 440, Part 5, *Navy Purchases of Middle East Oil*, p. 317.

21. *Investigation of the National Defense Program*, Hearings before a Special Committee Investigating the National Defense Program, U.S.

Senate, 80th Congress, 1st Session (Washington, 1948), Part 41, *Petroleum Arrangements with Saudi Arabia*, pp. 24756–24757.

22. *Ibid.*, pp. 25216–25217, 25446.

23. *Ibid.*, pp. 24723–24724.

24. Letter of Russell C. Harrington, Commissioner of Internal Revenue, U.S. Treasury Department, to Senator John J. Williams, March 11, 1957, reprinted in *Congressional Record*, 85th Congress, 1st Session, July 23, 1957, pp. 11232–11233.

25. *Hearings Before Special Committee to Investigate Petroleum Resources*, U.S. Senate, Executive Session, 78th Congress, 2nd Session (Washington, 1944), Vol. 4, pp. 494–496.

26. *United States Aid Operations in Iran*, Hearings before a Subcommittee of the Committee on Government Operations, U.S. House of Representatives, 84th Congress, 2nd Session (Washington, 1956). Also *First Report*, 85th Congress, 1st Session (Washington, 1957).

27. Benjamin Shwadran, *The Middle East, Oil and the Great Powers* (New York, Praeger, 1955), p. 145.

28. *New York Times*, July 10, 1953.

29. *United States Aid Operations in Iran*, Hearings, *op. cit.*, p. 954. See also Richard and Gladys Harkness, "The Mysterious Doings of the CIA," *Saturday Evening Post*, Nov. 6, 1954.

30. *The Mutual Security Act of 1954*, Hearings before the Committee on Foreign Affairs, U.S. House of Representatives, 83rd Congress, 2nd Session (Washington, 1954), pp. 503, 569–570.

31. *United States Aid Operations in Iran*, Hearings and Report, *op. cit.*, *passim*.

32. *Current Antitrust Problems*, Hearings, *op. cit.*, Part I, pp. 268–269 and *passim*; Part II, pp. 1555–1572. These volumes contain many documents and official statements bearing on the Iranian situation.

33. *The President's Proposal on the Middle East*, *op. cit.*, Part II, p. 625.

34. *New York Times*, Aug. 6, 1954; also *New York Journal of Commerce*, Aug. 9, 1954.

35. *Current Antitrust Problems*, *op. cit.*, Part II, p. 1559.

36. Letter from Eugene Holman, president, July 9, 1952, reprinted in *Monopoly and Cartels*, Hearings before a Subcommittee of the Select Committee on Small Business, U.S. Senate, 82nd Congress, 2nd Session (Washington, 1952), Part I, pp. 137–138.

37. *Current Antitrust Problems*, *op. cit.*, Part II, p. 827. See also *Report of the Attorney General's National Committee to Study the Antitrust Laws* (Washington, 1955), pp. 92–109.

38. *Congressional Record*, 82nd Congress, 2nd Session, Aug. 18, 1952, pp. A5180–A5184.

39. *New York Times*, Jan. 13, 1953.

40. *Current Antitrust Problems, op. cit.*, Part II, p. 742.

41. *Attorney General's Conference Re: International Oil Cartel*, U.S. Department of Justice, Washington, April 14, 1953, p. 6.

42. *Ibid.*, pp. 5, 8, 9, 13, 14.

43. *New York Times*, June 29, 1958; also, various releases of the Investment Guaranties Staff of the International Cooperation Administration. See E. Groen, "The Significance of the Marshall Plan for the Petroleum Industry in Europe," in *The Third World Petroleum Congress*, a report to the Select Committees on Small Business, U.S. Senate and House of Representatives, 82nd Congress, 2nd Session (Washington, 1952), pp. 37–73.

44. *Monopoly and Cartels*, Hearings, *op. cit.*, p. 143.

45. *The International Petroleum Cartel, op. cit.*, pp. 366–367.

46. *Monopoly and Cartels*, Hearings, *op. cit.*, p. 145.

47. "ECA's attempt to eliminate price discrimination within the Mediterranean area was met with strong reaction by the oil companies and the trade press. Immediately upon advice of the new ECA regulations, Caltex publicly announced that it would not supply petroleum products under ECA financing 'at substantial arbitrary reductions below the lowest competitive prices which the new ECA regulations would impose.' Although no similar announcements were made by the other American companies, no petroleum products, with one exception, have been supplied under ECA or MSA financing from the Middle East to participating countries in the Mediterranean since the effective date of the new price limitations. The single exception referred to above was in the winter of 1951 when the city of Athens was faced with an imminent cut off of electric power supply due to the inability to procure fuel oil for nondollar payment. It then became necessary for MSA to grant a waiver, on a temporary 6-month basis, and Caltex supplied at the United States Gulf price plus freight from the Persian Gulf."— "Statement of the Mutual Security Administration Concerning Its Relations with International Oil Companies with Respect to Petroleum Prices," Aug. 15, 1952, in *Monopoly and Cartels*, Hearings, *op. cit.*, p. 149.

48. *New York Times*, Aug. 23, 1952.

In a series of amended complaints in 1956, the government shifted the basis of its claims to the period from the outbreak of the Korean War to the end of 1952 when there could be no dispute that the government's lowest competitive price regulation was operative. Damages totaling $225 million were sought. A sweeping district court opinion in the summer of 1957 dismissed the complaint against the Caltex group (Texas, Standard of California, and their common affiliates). In a legalistic analysis that skirted most of the economic realities governing the industry, the judge held that the prices were the lowest competitively available; that there was no basis for the comparison with cheaper Western Hemisphere exports, and that internal transactions could not be considered sales. Socal and Texas were not in a legal sense engaged in joint ventures, in the use of subsidiaries for wrongdoing or subterfuge, in the sharing of profits and losses or in the exchange of basic information concerning their areas of competition:

"All Socal and Texas did, in effect, was to agree that it would be to their mutual advantage not to compete in certain markets. Texas relinquished its marketing superiority in return for Middle Eastern crude oil; Socal gave up some of its crude to acquire necessary marketing outlets. They agreed to cooperate in supplying certain areas with crude oil and refined products, but an agreement falls far short of a joint venture."

The judgment of the ECA, which was neither a procuring nor a purchasing agent, was a guide for the buyers and "there is no corresponding admonition that sellers should not charge more." No fraud was involved and the ECA had accepted these prices. At one point the opinion suggested that in the government's case "the defendants are . . . reduced to the status of non-profit organizations." The government had not proved its case, and it remained to be seen whether it would go ahead with companion suits against Jersey and Socony. In 1959, the U.S. Court of Appeals upheld the district court's dismissal of the suit.

See Opinion of Judge Thomas F. Murphy, *United States v. Standard Oil Company of California, The Texas Company, Bahrein Petroleum Company, Ltd., California-Texas Oil Company, Ltd., Caltex Oceanic Ltd., and Mid-East Crude Sales Company.* Civil Action No. 78–152 (U.S. District Court, Southern District of New York), July 17, 1957.

49. *Investigation of the National Defense Program,* Hearings, *op. cit.,* Part 41, pp. 24923 and 25364.

50. *Investigation of the National Defense Program,* Report No. 440, Part 5, *op. cit.,* p. 338.

51. Senate *Emergency Oil Lift* hearings, *op. cit.,* Part 2, pp. 1430–1431, 1437.

52. *Ibid.,* p. 1469. Testimony of F. A. Davies. See also *1956 Report of Operations to the Saudi Arab Government,* Arabian American Oil Com-

pany, 1957. Also, *Congressional Record*, 85th Congress, 1st Session, March 27, 1957, pp. 3981–3982, and *The International Petroleum Cartel, op. cit.*, p. 128.

53. Statement of G. M. Neville, assistant counsel, in *Petroleum, the Antitrust Laws and Government Policies*, Report of Subcommittee on Antitrust and Monopoly of Committee on the Judiciary, U.S. Senate, 85th Congress, 1st Session (Washington, 1957), pp. 34–41.

54. Senate *Emergency Oil Lift* hearings, *op. cit.*, Part 2, p. 1473.

55. Letter to *Washington Post*, May 2, 1957. Also, Aramco press release, April 22, 1957.

56. Letter from R. L. Keyes, president, Arabian American Oil Company to Rep. Charles A. Vanik, Feb. 20, 1957, in *Congressional Record*, 85th Congress, 1st Session, March 14, 1957, p. A2079. Also, Senate *Emergency Oil Lift* hearings, *op. cit.*, Part 2, p. 1434.

57. Testimony of George F. James, *General Revenue Revision*, Hearings before the Committee on Ways and Means, U.S. House of Representatives, 83rd Congress, 1st Session (Washington, 1953), Part 2, p. 1449.

58. Senate *Emergency Oil Lift* hearings, *op. cit.*, Part 2, p. 1436.

59. Press conference, *New York Times*, April 18, 1957.

60. G. M. Neville, in *Petroleum, the Antitrust Laws and Government Policies, op. cit.*, pp. 37–38.

CHAPTER 9: *Private Profits and National Security* (Pages 230–266)

1. Eugene Holman, "Building Prosperity Through World Trade," speech before annual meeting of the National Foreign Trade Council, November 1953, reprinted as advertisement in *Atlantic Monthly*, February 1954.

2. *There's No Security in Foreign Oil*, Independent Petroleum Association of America, no date.

3. Testimony of W. A. Delaney, Jr., Senate *Emergency Oil Lift* hearings, *op. cit.*, Part 2, p. 898.

4. *The TIPRO Reporter*, Texas Independent Producers and Royalty Owners Association, June 1956, p. 27.

5. *There's No Security in Foreign Oil, op. cit.*

6. A. E. Hermann, president of TIPRO, quoted in *Information Service*, TIPRO, Aug. 13, 1956.

7. Senate *Emergency Oil Lift* hearings, *op. cit.*, Part 1, p. 524.

8. *Oil and Gas Journal*, Nov. 7, 1955.

9. H. S. M. Burns, "Industrial Fission," a paper presented at general session of 35th annual meeting of API, San Francisco, Calif., Nov. 17, 1955.

10. Russell B. Brown, quoted in *Oil and Gas Journal*, Feb. 14, 1955.

11. *The TIPRO Reporter*, June 1956, p. 10.

12. *The TIPRO Reporter*, November–December 1954, p. 7.

13. *Resources for Freedom*, Report of President's Materials Policy Commission, Vol. I, *Foundations for Growth and Security*, p. 79.

14. *Defense Essentiality and Foreign Economic Policy, Case Study: Watch Industry and Precision Skills*, Report of the Joint Economic Committee, Report No. 2629, 84th Congress, 2nd Session (Washington, 1956), p. 2.

15. Notes of A. C. Ingraham, Aug. 15, 1956, in Senate *Emergency Oil Lift* hearings, *op. cit.*, Part 2, p. 1461, and Part 4, pp. 2386–2387.

According to Ingraham, at a later point Secretary Dulles "asked if there were any questions and Stewart Coleman, of Jersey [Standard], asked about oil concessions in South America—expressing the view that nationalization meant violation of contracts. Secretary Dulles gave the view that he did not think that these assets were impressed with international interests and that we could not object if shareholders received fair compensation. It might be considered morally wrong, but a Nation still has the power to nationalize."

16. Text of hearing reprinted in Senate *Emergency Oil Lift* hearings, *op. cit.*, Part 3, pp. 1712–1713.

17. Frank M. Porter at press conference, Feb. 18, 1957, quoted in *Petroleum World and Oil*, Feb. 21, 1957.

18. Senate *Emergency Oil Lift* hearings, *op. cit.*, Part 1, pp. 39, 63, 79.

19. *Petroleum Survey*, H.R. 85th Congress, 1st Session, pp. 138–139. The portion of Mr. Wormser's testimony beginning "Here is a question" was taken from the Senate *Emergency Oil Lift* hearings, *op. cit.*, Part 1, p. 137.

20. *New York Times*, Jan. 11, 1957.

21. Senate *Emergency Oil Lift* hearings, *op. cit.*, Part 1, pp. 44–45.

22. *Petroleum Survey*, *op. cit.*, pp. 75, 77.

23. Senate *Emergency Oil Lift* hearings, *op. cit.*, Part 1, pp. 89–96.

24. *United States v. Arkansas Fuel Oil Corporation, Et Al.*, Criminal No. 3450 (United States District Court for the Eastern District of Virginia), May 29, 1958. The trial was shifted to Tulsa at the request of the defendants. See *Wall Street Journal*, Feb. 1, 1960, and *New York Times*, Feb. 14, 1960.

25. Statement before twelfth annual meeting, TIPRO, San Antonio, May 12, 1958.

26. *Congressional Record*, 86th Congress, 1st Session, April 7, 1959, p. 4906.

27. Ted C. Stauffer, quoted in *Wall Street Journal*, Feb. 12, 1958.

28. *Petroleum in the Western Hemisphere*, Report of the Western Hemisphere Oil Study Committee of the Independent Petroleum Association of America, 1952, p. 17.

29. Testimony of Col. John Holland Leavell, *Hearings before Special Committee to Investigate Petroleum Resources*, *op. cit.*, Vol. 1, p. 145.

30. *Ibid.*, Vol. 4, pp. 455–456.

31. Herbert Feis, *Seen From E. A., Three International Episodes* (New York, Alfred A. Knopf, 1947), p. 129. Also, *Investigation of the National Defense Program*, Hearings, *op. cit.*, Part 41, p. 25237.

32. *Hearings Before Special Committee to Investigate Petroleum Resources*, *op. cit.*, Vol. 1, p. 32.

33. *Ibid.*, Vol. 3, pp. 326–330; also, press release, dated February 6, 1944, following p. 361.

34. *The President's Proposal on the Middle East*, *op. cit.*, Part II, pp. 644, 647, 658, 669, 671; also *Wall Street Journal*, April 10, 1956.

35. Senate *Emergency Oil Lift* hearings, *op. cit.*, Part 2, pp. 1245, 1249; also, *New York Times*, Jan. 31, 1957.

36. *New York Times*, July 30, 1957.

37. Senate *Emergency Oil Lift* hearings, *op. cit.*, p. 1519.

38. *1950 Report of Progress*, New York State Commission Against Discrimination, pp. 47–48. Also, *New York Times*, July 16, 17, 1959.

Aramco's counsel told the commission that the company also avoided employing Jews in any of its *American* operations in order to avoid offending the Arabian Government. To get around the state law against discrimination, Aramco had asked all applicants to fill out Saudi Arabian visa applications, which require a statement of religion.

In supporting Aramco's position, William M. Rountree, the State Department's Assistant Secretary for Near East and South Asian Affairs, had written the commission: "Any finding by the commission which would compel Aramco to employ persons of the Jewish faith in Saudi Arabia would hardly be made effective in view of the known attitude of the Saudi government. Efforts by Aramco to implement such a finding would most certainly prejudice the company's operations in that country and would probably adversely affect the United States' interests there as well" (*New York Times*, May 19, 1959).

39. See, for example, *New York Times*, Oct. 9, 1956; April 24, 1957;

New York Post, Feb. 11, 1957. Also, *The Dahran Airfield*, American Jewish Congress (New York, 1957).

40. Bartley C. Crum, *Behind the Silken Curtain* (New York, Simon and Schuster, 1947), pp. 36–37.

41. Harry S. Truman *Memoirs* (New York, Doubleday, 1956), Vol. 2, *Years of Trial and Hope*, pp. 162, 164.

42. *The Forrestal Diaries*, edited by Walter Millis (New York, Viking, 1951), pp. 323–324, 356–369.

43. *Ickes Diary*, June 22, 1941, and March 22, 1942.

44. See Gamal Abdel Nasser, *Egypt's Liberation (The Philosophy of the Revolution)* (Washington, Public Affairs Press, 1955).

45. Senate *Emergency Oil Lift* hearings, *op. cit.*, Part 4, pp. 2401, 2410, 2834.

46. *New York Times*, July 16, 18, 22, 1958.

47. *St. Louis Post-Dispatch*, Dec. 5, 9, 1958.

CHAPTER 10: *Oilmen in Government* (Pages 267–309)

1. Felix Frankfurter, *The Public and Its Government* (New Haven, Yale University Press, 1930), p. 24.

2. W. Alton Jones, "The Cities Service Story," *Service*, Cities Service, January 1956, p. 21. The Public Utility Holding Company Act required the empire founded by H. L. Doherty to divest itself of its investments in public utilities.

3. "A Foreign Oil Policy for the United States," reprinted in *The Independent Petroleum Company*, Hearings before a Special Committee Investigating Petroleum Resources, U.S. Senate, 79th Congress, 2nd Session (Washington, 1946), p. 433.

4. *Investigation of the National Recovery Administration*, Hearings before the Committee on Finance, U.S. Senate, 74th Congress, 1st Session (Washington, 1935), Part 1, p. 9.

5. *Ickes Diary*, Aug. 10, 1935. See also Donald Richberg, *My Hero* (New York, Putnam, 1954), memoirs.

6. *Schecter Poultry Corporation v. United States*, 295 U.S. 495 (1935). See also *Panama Refining Company v. Ryan*, 293 U.S. 388 (1935).

7. *Third Report to the President of the United States*, National Recovery Review Board (Washington, 1935), mimeographed, p. 35.

See also René de Visme Williamson, *The Politics of Planning in the Oil Industry Under the Code* (New York, Harper, 1936); William J.

Kemnitzer, *Rebirth of Monopoly* (New York, Harper, 1938); and "National Petroleum Council," document prepared by W. B. W. Snyder, Antitrust Division, U.S. Dept. of Justice, Dec. 8, 1950, reprinted in *WOC's and Government Advisory Groups, op. cit.,* Part III, pp. 2220–2226.

8. *Ickes Diary,* Jan. 23, 1934.

9. John W. Frey and H. Chandler Ide, *A History of the Petroleum Administration for War* (Washington, 1946), p. 16.

10. *Ibid.,* pp. 12–13, 56. Also, Harold L. Ickes, *Fightin' Oil* (New York, Alfred A. Knopf, 1943), p. 71.

11. *Utilization of Farm Crops, Industrial Alcohol and Synthetic Rubber,* Hearings before a Subcommittee of the Committee on Agriculture and Forestry, U.S. Senate, 77th Congress, 2nd Session (Washington, 1942), Part 1, p. 295. See also *A History of the Petroleum Administration for War, op. cit.,* pp. 382–383.

12. *Ickes Diary,* April 12, 1941.

13. Ickes and Davies anticipated the election of Boyd, whom they regarded as an exponent of the point of view of the big companies. But Ickes reported that he and Davies thought it better to keep their hands off.

The Justice Department has been critical of the practice of having full-time trade association representatives serve on industry advisory committees. See *WOC's and Government Advisory Groups, op. cit.,* Part I, pp. 591–592; Part III, pp. 2235–2236; Part IV, pp. 2335–2338.

For a full listing of PAW personnel and committees, see *A History of the Petroleum Administration for War, op. cit.,* pp. 301–349, 353.

14. *Investigation of the National Defense Program, op. cit.,* Hearings, Part 41, *Petroleum Arrangements with Saudi Arabia,* pp. 25444–25445, also, pp. 24587, 24921, 25239–25240, 25209–25215, 25265.

See also *Investigation of the National Defense Program, op. cit.,* Report No. 440, Part 5, *Navy Purchases of Middle East Oil,* pp. 340–342; and *Nomination of Edwin W. Pauley for Appointment as Under Secretary of the Navy, op. cit.,* Vol. 2, pp. 235–237.

15. *Ickes Diary,* July 26, 1942.

16. *A History of the Petroleum Administration for War, op. cit.,* pp. 2, 55–56, 65.

17. *Ibid.,* p. 288.

18. *Petroleum, the Antitrust Laws and Government Policies, op. cit.,* pp. 18–19.

19. *WOC's and Government Advisory Groups, op. cit.,* Part IV, pp. 2324–2339.

20. *Ickes Diary*, Aug. 21, 1933.

21. *Ibid.*, July 21, 1936. Ickes was referring to Alfred M. Landon, Governor of Kansas and Republican nominee for President, who had been in the oil business. ". . . Someone will run him, and if it isn't the big interests, I will be very much surprised."

22. Ickes, *Fightin' Oil*, pp. 79–80 and p. viii. Also, *Ickes Diary*, June 22, 1941.

23. *Ickes Diary*, April 5 and 19, June 7 and 14, Aug. 8, 1942.

24. ". . . In all my years of contact with business leaders . . . I have never encountered greater loyalty or more unselfish devotion to a job, or more intelligent cooperation, than I have found in . . . Ralph K. Davies" (Ickes, *Fightin' Oil*, p. 74).

25. *Wartime Petroleum Policy Under the Petroleum Administration for War*, Hearings before Special Committee to Investigate Petroleum Resources, U.S. Senate, 79th Congress, 2nd Session (Washington, 1946), p. 251.

26. Boyd, quoted in *Petroleum War Organization*, Natural Resources Department, U.S. Chamber of Commerce (Washington, 1943), p. 3.

27. *A History of the Petroleum Administration for War, op. cit.*, p. 297.

28. Minutes of National Petroleum Council, June 21, 1946, reprinted in *WOC's and Government Advisory Groups, op. cit.*, Part IV, pp. 2299–3000. See also remarks of Davies, pp. 2292–2298.

29. Address by Hugh A. Stewart before Independent Oil Producers and Landowners Association, Tri-State, Inc., Mount Vernon, Ill., June 21, 1957.

30. Minutes of NPC, Sept. 28, 1950, reprinted in *WOC's and Government Advisory Groups, op. cit.*, Part IV, p. 2540.

31. *Ibid.*, Minutes, Sept. 26, 1946, p. 2312.

32. *Ibid.*, Minutes, Sept. 28, 1950, pp. 2541–2542, 2545.

33. For a list of these "reinforcements," see *ibid.*, pp. 2547–2580.

34. *National Petroleum News*, July 21, 1954, p. 19.

35. *Ibid.*, Aug. 30, 1950, p. 22.

36. *WOC's and Government Advisory Groups, op. cit.*, Part IV, pp. 2268–2289.

37. Quoted in *National Petroleum News*, April 1956.

38. *Petroleum Survey, op. cit.*, p. 388. Also, Leonard M. Fanning, editor, *Our Oil Resources, op. cit.*, p. 5.

39. Pp. 5 and 6. In December 1960 the Federal Communications Commission announced the easing of its restrictive licensing policies

in relation to private microwave systems (*New York Times*, Dec. 25, 1960).

40. National Petroleum Council, 1955, pp. 7, 13–15.

41. *Security Principles for the Petroleum and Gas Industries*, National Petroleum Council, 1955, pp. 23–25. For a discussion of some of the implications of such corporate activity, see A. A. Berle, Jr., *The 20th Century Capitalist Revolution, op. cit.*, Chap. III.

42. May 19, 1948.

43. Hugh A. Stewart, Minutes of NPC, Oct. 25, 1949, reprinted in *WOC's and Government Advisory Groups, op. cit.*, Part IV, p. 2528.

44. *A National Oil Policy for the United States*, 1949, pp. 3, 5.

45. Address before Independent Petroleum Association of America, Tulsa, Oct. 25, 1954. Also, testimony in *Interior Department and Related Agency Appropriations for 1956*, Hearings before a Subcommittee of the Committee on Appropriations, U.S. Senate, 84th Congress, 1st Session (Washington, 1955), p. 74. The Military Petroleum Advisory Board suspended its functioning beginning in February 1958 because of the fear of some of the companies as to antitrust implications.

46. *Report of the Attorney General of the United States*, prepared pursuant to Section 708(e) of the Defense Production Act of 1950, as amended (Washington, 1955), pp. B10–B11.

47. *WOC's and Government Advisory Groups, op. cit.*, Part I, p. 548.

48. *Report of the Attorney General of the United States, op. cit.* (Washington, 1956), p. 23.

49. Letter to Attorney General Herbert Brownell, Jr., January 26, 1956, reprinted in Senate *Emergency Oil Lift* hearings, *op. cit.*, Part 3, p. 1991.

50. Senate *Emergency Oil Lift* hearings, *op. cit.*, Part 4, p. 2546.

51. *Europe's Need for Oil*, Organization for European Economic Cooperation (Paris, 1958), *passim*. Also, *Report to the Secretary of the Interior from the Director of the Voluntary Agreement Relating to Foreign Petroleum Supply, As Amended, May 8, 1956* (Washington, 1957).

52. *Petroleum, the Antitrust Laws and Government Policies, op. cit.*, pp. 4, 94–96.

53. *New York Times*, Aug. 27, 1957; *Petroleum World and Oil*, July 4, 1957.

54. *Petroleum, the Antitrust Laws and Government Policies, op. cit.*, p. 51. Also, *New York Times*, Feb. 2, 1957.

55. *New York Times*, July 19 and 31, 1958. Also, remarks by Secretary of the Interior Seaton at meeting of Foreign Petroleum Supply Committee (Washington, July 23, 1958).

CHAPTER 11: *Corporate Statesmanship and Public Policy*
(Pages 310–340)

1. *Revenue Revision of 1950*, Hearings before the Committee on Ways and Means, U.S. House of Representatives, 81st Congress, 2nd Session (Washington, 1950), pp. 822 and 825.

2. Press release, Office of Defense Mobilization, Sept. 20, 1954, reprinted in *WOC's and Government Advisory Groups, op. cit.*, Part III, pp. 1334–1335. See also pp. 1324ff; 1497–1499. And *Congressional Record*, 84th Congress, 2nd Session, Feb. 3, 1956, pp. 1698–1700.

3. "Report on Energy Supplies and Resources Policy," reprinted in *WOC's and Government Advisory Groups, op. cit.*, Part III, pp. 1337–1340. "Oil and Gas Report," prepared by staff consultants, pp. 1516–1561.

4. Reprinted in *WOC's and Government Advisory Groups, op. cit.*, Part II, p. 968.

5. Press conference, Aug. 11, 1955, in *Interim Report on the Business Advisory Council for the Department of Commerce*, Antitrust Subcommittee of the Committee on the Judiciary, U.S. House of Representatives, 84th Congress, 1st Session (Washington, 1955), p. 14.

6. *Ibid.*, pp. 29–30.

7. *Fighting Liberal*, the autobiography of George W. Norris (New York, Macmillan, 1946), p. 233. See also M. R. Werner, *Privileged Characters* (New York, McBride, 1935), Chap. II, and M. R. Werner and John Starr, *Teapot Dome* (New York, Viking, 1959).

8. *Congressional Record*, 85th Congress, 1st Session (Washington, 1957), p. 1170.

9. *Reappointment of Leland Olds to Federal Power Commission*, Hearings before a Subcommittee of the Committee on Interstate and Foreign Commerce, U.S. Senate, 81st Congress, 1st Session (Washington, 1949), p. 29.

For an account of the rejection of Olds, see Joseph P. Harris, *The Advice and Consent of the Senate* (Berkeley, University of California, 1953), Chap. XI.

10. John Osborne, "Natural Gas and the Authoritarian 'Liberals,'" *Fortune*, May 1952, p. 190.

11. Editorial, September 1952, reprinted in *As U.S. Editors View the Oil Charges*, compiled by Hill and Knowlton, Inc., for California-Texas Oil Company, Ltd. (New York, 1952), p. 17.

12. Olney is quoted in Matthew Josephson, *The Politicos, 1865–1896* (New York, Harcourt, Brace, 1938), p. 526.

The quotations relating to pipeline regulation are from *Consent Decree Program of the Department of Justice,* Report of the Antitrust Subcommittee of the Committee on the Judiciary, U.S. House of Representatives, 86th Congress, 1st Session (Washington, 1959), pp. 300–301. See also Hearings, Part I, *Oil Pipelines,* Vol. I and II, 1957, for rich documentation.

13. *Oil and Gas Journal,* May 19, 1958. *Miscellaneous Nominations* (John B. Hussey to FPC), Hearings before the Committee on Interstate and Foreign Commerce, U.S. Senate, 85th Congress, 1st and 2nd Sessions (Washington, 1958), pp. 194–221.

14. *Amendments to the Natural Gas Act,* Hearings before the Committee on Interstate and Foreign Commerce, U.S. Senate, 84th Congress, 1st Session (Washington, 1955), p. 1170. Also, *New York Times,* April 28, May 13, May 17, 1960.

15. Message from the President, Feb. 17, 1956, reprinted in *Nomination of Jerome K. Kuykendall to Federal Power Commission,* Hearings before the Committee on Interstate and Foreign Commerce, U.S. Senate, 85th Congress, 1st Session (Washington, 1957), p. 187. See entire volume for Kuykendall's attitude and role.

16. *Natural Gas Act (Regulation of Producers' Prices),* Hearings before the Committee on Interstate and Foreign Commerce, U.S. House of Representatives, 85th Congress, 1st Session (Washington, 1957), p. 127. For Le Boeuf's account, see pp. 733–839.

17. *Ibid.,* p. 129.

18. *Nomination of Jerome K. Kuykendall to Federal Power Commission, op. cit.,* p. 197.

19. *The Organization and Procedures of the Federal Regulatory Commissions and Agencies and Their Effect on Small Business,* Hearings before Subcommittee No. 1 of Select Committee on Small Business, U.S. House of Representatives, 84th Congress, 1st Session (Washington, 1956), Part II, *Federal Power Commission.* Also, *Report* (House Report No. 2967, 84th Congress, 2nd Session).

See also *Report on the November 13, 1954, Waiver Action by the Joint Committee on Atomic Energy—83rd Congress, 2nd Session— Utility Contract Between Atomic Energy Commission and the Mississippi Valley Generating Co.,* Joint Committee on Atomic Energy, 84th Congress, 1st Session (Washington, 1955). See p. 23 for further sources.

Disclosures about the contract made the Eisenhower Administration increasingly uncomfortable. When the City of Memphis announced its preference for building a municipal plant rather than using the private power supplied by Dixon-Yates, this provided the Administration the excuse to cancel the contract. In the course of the suit, the Justice Department adopted many of the criticisms made earlier against the contract. For example, see *New York Times*, July 13, 1956.

20. *Nomination of Edward F. Howrey to Federal Trade Commission*, Hearings before the Committee on Interstate and Foreign Commerce, U.S. Senate, 83rd Congress, 1st Session (Washington, 1953), pp. 13–14.

21. *The Organization and Procedures of the Federal Regulatory Commissions and Agencies and Their Effect on Small Business, op. cit.*, Part I, *Federal Trade Commission*. Also, *New York Times*, Sept. 3, 1953.

22. Carl Coke Rister, *Oil! Titan of the Southwest* (Norman, University of Oklahoma, 1949), p. 320.

23. Testimony of W. A. Delaney, Jr., Senate *Emergency Oil Lift* hearings, *op. cit.*, Part 2, pp. 885–886, 906.

24. Letter to the author, July 21, 1954.

25. Speech by J. Ruel Armstrong before the Section of Mineral Law, American Bar Association convention, Philadelphia, Aug. 24, 1955.

26. Representative Bruce Alger to M. J. Rathbone, *Petroleum Survey, op. cit.*, p. 359. The Harris quotation is on p. 381.

27. *New York Times*, Oct. 13, 1956.

28. Press conference, *ibid.*, Aug. 5, 1955.

29. A. A. Berle, Jr., *The 20th Century Capitalist Revolution, op. cit.*, p. 184.

30. Adam Smith, *An Inquiry into the Nature and Causes of the Wealth of Nations*, 1776 (New York, Random House, 1937), p. 128.

31. *Ickes Diary*, Nov. 19, 1939; Feb. 4, 1940.

32. *WOC's and Government Advisory Groups, op. cit.*, Part III, p. 2219.

33. *New York Times*, Jan. 12, 14, 1957; March 30, 1957.

34. *Congressional Record*, 81st Congress, 1st Session, Oct. 12, 1949, p. 14377.

CHAPTER 12: *Oil and Politics: The Permeability of Oil*
(Pages 341–371)

1. *Nomination of Edwin W. Pauley for Appointment as Under Secretary of the Navy, op. cit.*, Vol. 8, p. 1368.

2. *Ibid.*, Vol. 6, p. 941.

3. *Ibid.*, Vol. 1, p. 32.

4. *Ibid.*, Vol. 12, p. 2037; Vol. 4, pp. 689–691.

5. *Ibid.*, Vol. 2, pp. 289ff. As part of the picture of the permeability

of oil, it should be noted that Littell later had as his clients claimants for federal offshore oil leases.

6. *Ibid.*, Vol. 3, pp. 409–410. Also, *St. Louis Post-Dispatch*, Nov. 14 and 15, 1945.

7. *Internal Revenue Investigation*, Hearings before a Subcommittee of the Committee on Ways and Means, U.S. House of Representatives, 83rd Congress, 1st Session (Washington, 1953), Part D, p. 1440.

8. *Nomination of Edwin W. Pauley*, Vol. 1, pp. 39ff.; Vol. 3, p. 521.

9. *St. Louis Post-Dispatch*, Oct. 18, 1945.

10. *Nomination of Edwin W. Pauley*, Vol. 6, pp. 1088–1091; Vol. 7, pp. 1131–1137.

11. *Ibid.*, Vol. 11, p. 1785.

12. *Ibid.*, Vol. 6, p. 941.

13. *Ibid.*, Vol. 14, p. 2267; also, Vol. 3, pp. 411–412.

14. Letter of resignation and press conference, *New York Times*, Feb. 14, 1946.

15. Harry S. Truman *Memoirs, op. cit.*, Vol. 1, *Year of Decisions*, 1955, pp. 554–555.

16. Ickes recalled that Mayock "ran a very active law business, a procurement business, from the Democratic National Headquarters until I protested both to the National Chairman and to the President, and he was packed back to California from whence he should never have been brought" (*Nomination of Edwin W. Pauley*, Vol. 12, p. 2025).

But Mr. Mayock's talents were not to be denied. In 1948 the tax lawyer was serving as a volunteer legal counsel and money raiser for the National Committee. In one case he turned over $30,000 of a $65,000 cash fee received from a businessman for a favorable tax ruling by the Treasury Department to the committee. Mayock said he assumed the businessman was "trying to purchase my services as a political figure rather than my skill as a lawyer." Mayock offered no intimation to Secretary of the Treasury Snyder that tied in to the ruling was a campaign contribution. "The contact was political, yes, but I didn't and never did call up and say, 'I am on the national committee; I want to see you right now, and throw everybody out while I get in.' I have never done that in my life, and I have never made a political approach." But it was "common knowledge" that "I was a busy little bee in the campaign." Mayock said that the $30,000 he turned over to the committee was rejected because no donors were listed and the Hatch Act prohibited individual contributions of more than $5,000—a law that made politics "difficult, dangerous and complex, . . . and practically impossible to carry on the functions of the democracy in a proper manner. . . ." And so, feeling that his party, "for which I had the highest regard and loyalty," was in battle, Mayock adopted the "Devil's ethics" to work out what he described as "a very close avoidance of the Hatch Act." This involved distributing the money to individuals who would then funnel it back to the National Committee (*Internal Revenue Investigation, op. cit.*, pp. 1411–1458).

17. *Nomination of Edwin W. Pauley*, Vol. 3, p. 405.

18. Ralph W. Hidy and Muriel E. Hidy, *Pioneering in Big Business 1882–1911*, History of Standard Oil Company (New Jersey) (New York, Harper, 1955), p. 213.

19. Allan Nevins, *John D. Rockefeller: The Heroic Age of American Enterprise* (New York, Scribner's, 1940), Vol. 2, p. 507.

20. *Official Report of Proceedings Before the Securities and Exchange Commission in the Matter of William A. Dougherty*, Securities and Exchange Commission, Docket Section, Docket No. 4–90, Washington, July 9, 1957, pp. 7–11, 18. Also, *In the Matter of Union Electric Company*, Docket No. V–124, March 5, 1957, pp. 60ff.

21. Reported by a veteran Southwestern newsman who has covered oil activities.

22. *Ickes Diary*, Sept. 28, 1940.

23. R. W. Calvert, quoted by Hart Stilwell in the latter's chapter on Texas in Robert S. Allen, editor, *Our Sovereign State* (New York, Vanguard, 1949), p. 315.

24. John U. Barr, a Southern industrialist, an executive of the Southern States Industrial Council, a leader of the right-to-work movement, active in the fight to challenge FDR by proposing the nomination of conservative Senator Harry Byrd (Virginia) at the 1944 convention, and a leader in the Dixiecrat walkout of 1948, has insisted to the writer that "our aim was not to destroy but to preserve the Democratic Party."

25. Letter to President Truman, quoted in Ed Kilman and Theon Wright, *Hugh Roy Cullen: A Story of American Opportunity* (New York, Prentice-Hall, 1954), p. 234.

26. *Ibid.*, p. 287.

27. Letter, dated March 23, 1952, quoted in *Dallas News*, April 7, 1952.

28. Memorandum by Murchison that Sid Richardson took along on his 1952 visit to Eisenhower in Paris, quoted in series of articles by Edward T. Folliard, *Washington Post*, Feb. 17, 1954.

29. Address before National Petroleum Council, minutes for Sept. 29, 1953, reprinted in *WOC's and Government Advisory Groups, op. cit.*, Part IV, p. 2639.

30. *The Texaco Star*, The Texas Company, Spring 1953.

31. *Hugh Roy Cullen, op. cit.*, p. 234.

32. *Stockpile and Accessibility of Strategic and Critical Materials to the United States in Time of War*, Hearings before the Special Subcommittee on Minerals, Materials and Fuel Economics of the Committee on Interior and Insular Affairs, U.S. Senate, 83rd Congress, 1st and 2nd Sessions (Washington, 1954), Part 6, p. 205.

33. *New York Times*, Sept. 3, 1956.

34. *Hugh Roy Cullen, op. cit.*, p. 270. Cullen died in 1957.

35. See *Investigation of Lobbying Activities*, Hearings before a Special Committee to Investigate Lobbying Activities, U.S. Senate, 74th Congress, 2nd Session (Washington, 1936), Parts 5 and 6.

36. *Washington Post*, Feb. 15, 1954.

37. *Maryland Senatorial Election of 1950*, Hearings before the Subcommittee on Privileges and Elections of the Committee on Rules and Administration, U.S. Senate, 82nd Congress, 1st Session (Washington, 1951), pp. 272, 276. Also, Report No. 647, p. 6.

38. Quoted in *New York Post*, July 7, 1953.

39. Charles J. V. Murphy, "Texas Business and McCarthy," *Fortune*, May 1954. Parten has since become a director of The Pure Oil Co. and Marshall has become president of the Union Texas Natural Gas Co.

40. J. Paul Getty, "You Can Make a Million," *True*, June 1958.

41. *1956 Presidential and Senatorial Campaign Contributions and Practices*, Hearings before the Subcommittee on Privileges and Elections of the Committee on Rules and Administration, U.S. Senate, 84th Congress, 2nd Session (Washington, 1956), Part 1, pp. 4–5. Also, Report, *1956 General Election Campaigns*, 85th Congress, 1st Session, pp. 13, 77–78, 87.

Alexander Heard, *The Costs of Democracy* (Chapel Hill, University of North Carolina, 1960), offers a thorough picture of the problem of money in elections.

42. Ida M. Tarbell, *The History of the Standard Oil Company, op. cit.*, Vol. 2, p. 290.

43. *Employee Relations News Letter*, May 28, 1956.

44. Robert E. Wilson, "Business Ethics in Mid-Century," address before annual meeting of the Associated Industries of Georgia, Atlanta, Oct. 16, 1953.

45. *API Quarterly*, Summer 1954.

46. Robert E. Wilson, *op. cit.*

47. *Oil and Gas Lobby Investigation*, Hearings before the Special Committee to Investigate Political Activities, Lobbying, and Campaign

Contributions, U.S. Senate, 84th Congress, 2nd Session (Washington, 1956), pp. 397, 420–421, 464–465.

48. Cola G. Parker, March 19, 1956, quoted in *Organized Labor's Program to* ORGANIZE *the Legislative Halls*, National Association of Manufacturers, 1956.

49. Letter to employees and shareholders, Sept. 9, 1958. Also, "A Political Program for Gulf Oil Corporation," adopted June 1959.

CHAPTER 13: *The Oil Lobby* (Pages 372–394)

1. *Washington Post*, July 25, 1951.

2. *Submerged Lands Act*, Report of Committee on Interior and Insular Affairs, U.S. Senate, 83rd Congress, 1st Session (Washington, 1953), Report No. 133, p. 8. Part 2 contains the minority positions and is an excellent presentation of the case for federal control.

3. *Oil and Gas Lobby Investigation, op. cit.*, p. 459.

4. *Ibid.*, pp. 470–471. Also, "A Political Program for Gulf Oil Corporation," June 1959.

5. *Ibid.*, p. 433.

6. Walter Chamblin, *Know Your Congressman*, National Association of Manufacturers, 1944.

7. Statement by Standard of California, Jan. 31, 1957, in letter from Woollen H. Walshe, the company's Washington representative, to Representative Wright Patman. *Congressional Record*, 85th Congress, 1st Session, Feb. 5, 1957, p. 1403. See also *Congressional Record*, Jan. 28, 1957, pp. 930–933, and Jan. 29, 1957, pp. 1102–1103.

8. "Lawyers and Lobbyists," *Fortune*, February 1952, p. 142. The fees of attorneys who have represented gas interests before the FPC, cited in this paragraph of the text, can be found in FPC materials and testimony in *Ex Parte Communications and Other Problems*, Hearings before a Subcommittee of the Committee on Interstate and Foreign Commerce, U.S. House of Representatives, 86th Congress, 2nd Session (Washington, 1960). See also *Independent Regulatory Commissions*, Staff Report to the Special Subcommittee on Legislative Oversight of the Committee on Interstate and Foreign Commerce, U.S. House of Representatives, 86th Congress, 2nd Session (Washington, 1960), and the report of the same subcommittee, *Independent Regulatory Commissions* (Washington, 1961).

9. *Oil and Gas Lobby Investigation, op. cit.*, p. 416.

10. *Congressional Quarterly Weekly Report*, Vol. XI, No. 21, week ending May 22, 1953, pp. 660–662.

11. "Lawyers and Lobbyists," *op. cit.*, p. 144. An interview with the author of this book was terminated when Clifford departed for a visit with then Secretary of the Navy Robert B. Anderson to discuss California naval reserves.

12. Ralph W. Hidy and Muriel E. Hidy, *Pioneering in Big Business, op. cit.*, p. 213. See Henry Demarest Lloyd, *Wealth Against Commonwealth* (New York, Harper, 1894).

13. Ronnie Dugger, "Austin Lobbyists at Work," *The Texas Observer*, May 23, 1955. Dugger is the editor of this vigorous independent weekly.

14. The maverick oil editor was Henry Hough, *Rocky Mountain Oil Reporter*, November 1953. The Hamon speech was reprinted in *The TIPRO Reporter*, March–April, 1956.

15. A. P. King, Jr., *The TIPRO Reporter*, June 1955, p. 23.

16. See *Amendments to the Natural Gas Act* hearings (1955), *op. cit., passim.*

17. *Oil and Gas Lobby Investigation, op. cit.*, p. 478. This volume of hearings offers considerable data on the background and functioning of the General Gas Committee.

18. *Ibid.*, p. 543.

19. *Ibid.*, p. 543.

20. *Ibid.*, p. 483.

21. *Ibid.*, p. 490.

22. Statement by R. F. Windfohr, release date May 19, 1955.

23. J. C. Donnell, II, *Oil and Gas Journal*, Sept. 20, 1954.

24. Telegram from Governor Frank Carlson, *Reappointment of Leland Olds to Federal Power Commission, op. cit.*, p. 10.

25. *Congressional Record*, 82nd Congress, 2nd Session, March 25, 1952, p. 2860. See also *Congressional Record*, March 26, 1952, pp. 2922–2932.

26. *New York Times*, Dec. 18, 1952; also, *New York Post*, April 19, 1953.

CHAPTER 14: *Private Pressure and Political Paralysis*
(Pages 395–427)

1. *New York Times*, March 22, 1958.

2. *Ibid.*, Nov. 27, 1954.

3. *Oil and Gas*, Department of Conservation, State of Louisiana, Biennial Report, 1952–1953.

4. *Congressional Record*, 82nd Congress, 1st Session, Sept. 28, 1951, pp. 12335–12336.

5. *Amendments to the Natural Gas Act, op. cit.*, Hearings (1955), p. 1823.

6. *Congressional Record*, 84th Congress, 2nd Session, Jan. 12, 1956, pp. 378–379.

7. Statement by Lyndon B. Johnson at the Senate Democratic Conference, Jan. 2, 1953.

8. *New York Times*, Nov. 20, 1958.

9. *The TIPRO Reporter*, August 1954 and September–October, 1954.

10. John Osborne, "Natural Gas and the Authoritarian 'Liberals,' " *Fortune*, May 1942.

11. *Congressional Record*, 83rd Congress, 2nd Session, June 30, 1954, p. 8864. In 1957 Douglas and Williams could muster only seven votes, including their own. But in 1958 the critics of depletion found their position considerably strengthened, with two depletion-cut amendments losing 26–63 and 31–58. *Congressional Record*, 85th Congress, 2nd Session, Aug. 11, 1958, p. 15558.

12. *Congressional Record*, 84th Congress, 2nd Session, Feb. 3, 1956, pp. 1691ff.

13. *Ibid.*, Feb. 6, 1956, pp. 1765ff.

14. *Ibid.*, p. 1769.

15. *Ibid.*, pp. 1773–1775 and *New York Times*, Feb. 14, 1956.

16. *Ickes Diary*, March 13, 1941.

17. *Hearings Relative to Senate Resolution 205*, Hearings before the Select Committee for Contribution Investigation, U.S. Senate, 84th Congress, 2nd Session (Washington, 1956), pp. 150–153. Patman once authored a congressional report critical of the world oil cartel. See *The Third World Petroleum Congress*, report to Select Committees on Small Business, U.S. Senate and House of Representatives, 82nd Congress, 2nd Session (Washington, 1952).

18. *Report of the Select Committee for Contribution Investigation*, Report No. 1724, 1956, p. 3.

19. Edward L. Doheny, Jan. 24, 1924, before Senate committee investigating Teapot Dome, quoted in Josephine O'Keane, *Thomas J. Walsh: A Senator from Montana* (Francestown, New Hampshire, Marshall Jones Company, 1955), p. 3. See also Samuel Hopkins Adams, *Incredible Era: The Life and Times of Warren Gamaliel Harding* (Boston, Houghton Mifflin, 1939), p. 349.

20. *New York Times*, Feb. 18, 1956.

21. *Ibid.*, March 6, 1956; also *Congressional Record*, 84th Congress,

2nd Session, Feb. 6, 1956, p. 1801, and New York Post, March 5, 1956.

22. Oil and Gas Lobby Investigation, op. cit., p. 172.

23. Ibid., p. 258.

24. Final Report of the Special Committee to Investigate Political Activities, Lobbying, and Campaign Contributions, U.S. Senate, 85th Congress, 1st Session (Washington, 1957), Report No. 395.

25. Interim Report of the Select Committee on Improper Activities in the Labor or Management Field, U.S. Senate, 85th Congress, 2nd Session (Washington, 1958), Report No. 1417, p. 2.

26. Oil and Gas Journal, May 6, 1957, pp. 78–80.

27. Washington Post and Times Herald, Feb. 11, 1958.

28. New York Times, Feb. 12, 13 and 27, 1958; Washington Post and Times Herald, Feb. 13, 1958.

The Texas Republican Executive Committee subsequently gave Porter a unanimous vote of confidence and announced it would keep the $100,-000 political fund he raised in Texas for state political purposes. The Martin dinner was defended as "a legitimate and well-established fund raising approach for which no apology is needed" (Washington Post and Times Herald, March 4, 1958).

29. Title to Submerged Lands Beneath Tidal and Navigable Waters, Joint Hearings before the Committees on the Judiciary, U.S. Congress, 80th Congress, 2nd Session (Washington, 1948), p. 1580.

30. Washington Daily News, Oct. 9, 1953.

31. On Dec. 1, 1958, the FPC announced a total of 119 companies had been exempted fully or partially from regulation under the Natural Gas Act since the enactment of the Hinshaw amendment in 1954. Release No. 10,172.

32. Wealth Against Commonwealth (New York, Harper, 1894), p. 242.

33. Reprinted in Ida M. Tarbell, The History of the Standard Oil Company, op. cit., I, 386.

34. Ibid., II, 388.

35. Allan Nevins, John D. Rockefeller, op. cit., II, 42–44; also, Ralph W. Hidy and Muriel E. Hidy, Pioneering in Big Business, op. cit., p. 214.

36. Tax Exempt Foundations, Report of the Special Committee to Investigate Tax-Exempt Foundations and Comparable Organizations, U.S. House of Representatives, 83rd Congress, 2nd Session (Washington, 1954), House Report No. 2681, pp. 18, 20, 60, 422–423. A minority statement by Representatives Wayne L. Hays and Gracie Pfost repudiated both the "cynical" conduct of the hearings and the "misleading"

tone of the report as placing an "ugly stain" on the record of the House of Representatives itself.

37. *Investigation of Regulatory Commissions and Agencies,* Hearings before a Subcommittee of the Committee on Interstate and Foreign Commerce, U.S. House of Representatives, 85th Congress, 2nd Session (Washington, 1958). Also, *Independent Regulatory Commissions,* House Report No. 2711, 1959. For an account by the former chief counsel, see Bernard Schwartz, *The Professor and the Commissions* (New York, Alfred A. Knopf, 1959).

38. Speech before American Petroleum Institute, Nov. 10, 1948.

39. Quoted in M. R. Werner, *Privileged Characters, op. cit.,* p. 40.

40. *Congressional Record,* 84th Congress, 2nd Session, Jan. 31, 1956, p. 1448.

41. Carl Biemiller, *NAM News,* Sept. 19, 1958.

42. "Business and Political Honesty," Finley Peter Dunne, *Dissertations,* 1906, reprinted in *Mr. Dooley: Now and Forever* (Stanford, Academic Reprints, 1954), pp. 260–266.

CHAPTER 15: *Public Relations and Private Power* (Pages 428–482)

1. Robert T. Haslam, "Progressive Public Relations for the Progressive Petroleum Industry," Nov. 26, 1946.

2. *Those Who Know You Well . . . Think Well of You,* a report by Opinion Research Corporation, Princeton, 1946.

3. Quoted in Frank A. Fetter, *The Masquerade of Monopoly* (New York, Harcourt, Brace, 1931), pp. 29–30.

4. Quoted in William J. Ghent, *Our Benevolent Feudalism* (New York, Macmillan, 1902), p. 29.

5. Walter S. Hallanan, "The Role of Private Enterprise in the Development of Oil Resources," in Leonard M. Fanning, *Our Oil Resources, op. cit.,* p. 1.

6. See Joseph I. C. Clarke, *My Life and Memories* (New York, Dodd, Mead, 1926), Chaps. XXXVII–XXXVIII. Clarke was hired to handle publicity for Standard. Also, Allan Nevins, *John D. Rockefeller, op. cit.,* II, especially Chaps. XLIV–XLVI.

7. *New York Times,* Aug. 2 and 13, 1940. An official history of The Texas Company, written by Pulitzer Prize-winner Marquis James, simply records without explanation that Rieber resigned after western Europe was overrun by the Nazis. *The Texaco Story,* The Texas Company, 1953, p. 70.

One of the key Hitler representatives was Gerhard Westrick who circulated among business leaders to urge upon them the value of working for peaceful relations between the United States and Germany.

8. *Those Who Know You Well . . . Think Well of You, op. cit.*, p. 35.

9. *Ibid.*, pp. 20, 30–31.

10. Robert T. Haslam, *op. cit.*

11. *Those Who Know You Well . . . Think Well of You, op. cit.*, pp. 18, 22–23, 26.

12. *The OIIC Reports to the API*, American Petroleum Institute, 1954, p. 15.

13. *The Public Appraises the Oil Industry*, National Survey 1953, for the OIIC, Opinion Research Corporation, Princeton, 1953. Also, National Survey 1957, published in 1958.

14. Advertisement, *New York Times*, Nov. 9, 1956.

15. *Oil's Way of Winning Friends*, Oil Industry Information Committee, 1954, pp. 3 and 5.

16. *7 Steps Forward*, OIIC Report to the American Petroleum Institute, 1953, p. 7.

17. *The OIIC Reports to the API*, *op. cit.*, p. 13.

18. *What Makes This Nation Go*, American Petroleum Institute, 1954.

19. *Yonkers Herald-Statesman*, May 1, 1953.

20. "Learning Can Be Fun with Films," *Texaco Topics*, The Texas Company, October 1956.

21. *New York Journal of Commerce*, Nov. 10, 1952.

22. *API Quarterly*, American Petroleum Institute, Winter 1954–1955, p. 47.

23. Mrs. Lee Wilson Hoover, address before Second Annual Convention, Association of Desk and Derrick Clubs of North America, Denver, Sept. 11, 1953.

24. *Mister Jobber*, American Petroleum Institute, no date.

25. *Oil and Gas Journal*, Nov. 15, 1954, p. 149.

26. *1954 Directory*, Rocky Mountain Oil and Gas Association, pp. 61–62.

27. *Refinery Public Relations Manual*, prepared by Public Relations Department, Standard Oil (Indiana).

28. Garrie N. Hall, "The Challenge Offshore," *API Quarterly*, Spring 1958.

29. *Refinery Public Relations Manual, op. cit.*

30. H. L. Hunt, "Add Patriotism to Ads," *Facts Forum News*, Dallas, March 1955.

31. *Colorado Oil Industry Survey*, Research Services, Inc., January 1952.

32. Form letter from Colorado Oil and Gas Industries, Sept. 17, 1952.

33. Letter dated Oct. 20, 1952.

34. *Progress Report*, Colorado Oil and Gas Industries, Oct. 6, 1952.

35. *Bulletin*, Colorado Oil and Gas Industries, no date.

36. *Colorado Oil Industry Survey*, No. 2, Research Services, Inc., October 1952, pp. 2, 14.

37. *Denver Post*, Oct. 23, 1952.

38. *Ibid.*, Nov. 1, 1952.

39. *Ibid.*, Sept. 26, 1952.

40. *Thought Leaders' Views on Regulation of Natural Gas Producers*, an opinion survey for the Natural Gas and Oil Resources Committee, Opinion Research Corporation, Princeton, 1955, p. 3.

41. *Basic Principles for Advertising Program*, Hill and Knowlton, Dec. 29, 1954, p. 1.

42. L. F. McCollum, "The Effect on the American Consumer of Federal Regulation of Natural Gas," address before Independent Petroleum Association of America, Tulsa, Oct. 26, 1954.

43. *Basic Principles for Advertising Program*, *op. cit.*, pp. 3–5.

44. *Preliminary Outline of Public Relations Program Recommendations for the Natural Gas and Oil Resources Committee*, Hill and Knowlton, 1954, p. 10.

45. L. F. McCollum, *op. cit.*

46. Testimony of Bert C. Goss, *Oil and Gas Lobby Investigation*, *op. cit.*, p. 171.

47. Testimony of Frank O. Prior, in *ibid.*, p. 393.

48. "A Look at the Gas Case," *The Beacon*, Ohio Oil Company, March 1955, p. 2.

49. K. S. Adams, "As I See It," *Philnews*, Phillips Petroleum Company, November 1954, p. 3.

50. E. J. Connable, *National Petroleum News*, January 1955.

51. *An Evaluation of Oil Progress Week*, 1952; also, 1953.

52. *Facts Forum News Release*, Dallas, Dec. 6, 1954; Feb. 10, 1955; March 10, 1955.

53. "How to Take the Sin Out of Size," from a staff study of the Oil Industry Information Committee of the API, *Public Relations Journal*, November 1956.

54. Frank M. Porter, address before Independent Petroleum Association of America, Los Angeles, reprinted in *Oil and Gas Journal*, May 7, 1956.

55. Annual Meeting, American Petroleum Institute, Nov. 10, 1958.

56. *Oil and Gas Journal,* Nov. 18, 1957.

57. "The Other Side of Freedom: Responsibility," *API Quarterly,* Winter 1956–1957. "I don't think this fear will ever be completely removed," Jennings continued, "and I don't think it should be. It is a healthy, indeed necessary, condition of democracy that a people be wary about allowing power to concentrate too much in any organization, group, government unit, or individual."

58. "How to Take the Sin Out of Size," *op. cit.*

59. *Ibid.*

60. *Oil and Gas Journal,* Nov. 19, 1956.

61. *St. Louis Post-Dispatch,* Dec. 26, 1954. See also *New York Times,* Nov. 21, 1953, and July 5, 1957.

62. Frank W. Abrams, "The Stake of Business in American Education," Standard Oil Company (New Jersey), 1947.

63. Frank W. Abrams, "Who Is to Pay for Our Colleges?" *API Quarterly,* Autumn 1957. Mr. Abrams served on the Board of Trustees of Syracuse University since 1947 and in 1960 he became chairman.

64. K. S. Adams, "Education's Challenge," Commencement Address, Drury College, Springfield, Mo., May 30, 1955.

65. "Who Is to Pay for Our Colleges?" *op. cit.*

66. *The A. P. Smith Manufacturing Company, Plaintiff v. Ruth F. Barlow, Et Al., Defendants,* Superior Court of New Jersey, Chancery Division, decided May 19, 1953, *Report of Cases,* Newark, Vol. XXVI, 1953, pp. 106–125.

67. Quoted in Ed Kilman and Theon Wright, *Hugh Roy Cullen, op. cit.,* p. 279.

68. *The Trend Is Up,* Council for Financial Aid to Education, New York, August 1958.

69. *New York Times,* May 18, 1951.

70. *The Wall Street Journal,* Feb. 19, 1958. Also, *Financial Support to Education,* 1954; *Esso Education Foundation,* 1956; and *A Program to Advance the Teaching of Science and Engineering,* 1957, reports by Standard Oil Company (New Jersey). Also, *The Lamp,* Fall 1960.

71. *Public Relations Journal,* September 1955, p. 24.

72. *Youth and Educational Activities,* Employees' Pocket Manual, Standard Oil Company (Indiana), Chicago, 1954.

73. *A Report to Stockholders,* 3rd Quarter of 1958, Standard Oil Company of California, December 1958.

74. "Giving for the Sake of Learning," *Texaco Topics,* November 1957, p. 4.

75. Paul W. Boynton, *So You Want a Better Job*, Socony-Vacuum Oil Company, New York, 1947, p. 16. Mr. Boynton was Supervisor of Employment.

76. Letter from C. F. Beatty, director in charge of Industrial Relations, to Norman Thomas, Dec. 10, 1954. Also, Norman Thomas, letter to the editor, *Washington Post*, Dec. 21, 1954.

77. *So You Want a Better Job, op. cit.*, revised edition, 1955.

78. Edward L. Bernays, editor, *The Engineering of Consent* (Norman, Oklahoma, University of Oklahoma, 1955), pp. 3–4.

79. John W. Hill, *Corporate Public Relations, Arm of Modern Management* (New York, Harper, 1958), p. ix.

80. Robert E. Kenyon, Jr., "Advertising and the Marketing Concept," address before 28th Annual Boston Conference on Distribution, Oct. 23, 1956. *New York Times* version of his remarks was slightly different: "Advertising must mass-produce customers as factories mass-produce products in a growing economy" (Oct. 24, 1956).

81. Ernest Dichter, address before Association of National Advertisers, Hot Springs, Va., *New York Times*, March 18, 1953; also, "A Credo for Modern Research and Advertising," address before the Advertising Federation of America, Miami Beach, June 11, 1957.

82. "Keeping Up With 30,000 Capitalists," *The Sohioan*, February 1954, p. 2.

83. "News on the Air," *The Lamp*, March 1954.

84. Oveta Culp Hobby, "A Search for Understanding," address before American Petroleum Institute, Chicago, Nov. 13, 1952.

85. Ralph W. Hidy and Muriel E. Hidy, *Pioneering in Big Business, op. cit.*, pp. 660–661.

86. *Availability of Information from Federal Departments and Agencies*, Hearings before a Subcommittee of the Committee on Government Operations, U.S. House of Representatives, 84th Congress, 1st Session (Washington, 1956), Part 1, *Panel Discussion with Editors et al.*, p. 27.

87. Allan Nevins, *John D. Rockefeller, op. cit.*, I, 93.

88. Harvey J. Peltier, candidate for lieutenant governor, quoted in *New Orleans Item-Tribune*, Nov. 27, 1939. See also Nov. 8, 1939.

89. Louis Roussel, "How I Made a Million," *Stag*, September 1955.

90. Dennis Chavez, address before New Mexico Oil and Gas Association, Santa Fe, Nov. 26, 1957.

91. *Renomination of Leland Olds to Federal Power Commission, op. cit.*, pp. 234–236; also, pp. 10, 291.

92. *The Texas Observer*, Feb. 15 and 22, 1956. See also William W. Morris, "Mississippi Rebel on a Texas Campus," *The Nation*, March 24, 1956.

93. *Teachers' Appraisals of the Petroleum School Series Booklets*, an opinion survey for the OIIC, Opinion Research Corporation, Princeton, 1953, pp. iv, B-6, B-7.

94. *Highlights, Rocky Mountain District*, OIIC, Denver, Spring 1954. Oberholtzer's enthusiasm has been featured in a full-page API advertisement. See *National Petroleum News*, August 1956.

CHAPTER 16: *Private Power and Democratic Directions*

(Pages 483–498)

1. David E. Lilienthal, *Big Business: A New Era* (New York, Harper, 1952), pp. 26, 204.

2. *New York Times*, July 28, 1955.

3. John K. Galbraith, *American Capitalism: The Concept of Countervailing Power* (Boston, Houghton Mifflin, 1952).

Index